Families as They Really Are

Second Edition

Recent Sociology Titles from W. W. Norton

To learn more about Norton Sociology, please visit wwnorton.com/soc.

Families as They Really Are

Second Edition

EDITED BY

BARBARA J. RISMAN
University of Illinois at Chicago

VIRGINIA E. RUTTER
Framingham State University

WITH CONTRIBUTIONS BY
AMY BRAINER

W. W. Norton & Company ■ New York ■ London

W. W. NORTON & COMPANY has been independent since its founding in 1923, when William Warder Norton and Mary D. Herter Norton first published lectures delivered at the People's Institute, the adult education division of New York City's Cooper Union. The firm soon expanded its program beyond the Institute, publishing books by celebrated academics from America and abroad. By midcentury, the two major pillars of Norton's publishing program—trade books and college texts—were firmly established. In the 1950s, the Norton family transferred control of the company to its employees, and today—with a staff of four hundred and a comparable number of trade, college, and professional titles published each year—W. W. Norton & Company stands as the largest and oldest publishing house owned wholly by its employees.

Editor: Sasha Levitt
Associate Editor: Nicole Sawa
Editorial Assistants: Thea Goodrich and Mary Williams
Project Editor: Sujin Hong
Marketing Manager: Julia Hall
Production Manager: Vanessa Nuttry
Design Director: Hope Miller Goodell
Permissions Manager: Megan Jackson
Composition: Jouve
Manufacturing: Maple Press

Library of Congress Cataloging-in-Publication Data

Families as they really are / edited by Barbara J. Risman, Virginia Rutter. — 2nd edition.
    pages cm
  Includes bibliographical references and index.
  ISBN 978-0-393-93767-1 (pbk. : alk. paper)
  1. Families—United States—History.   I. Risman, Barbara J., 1956-   II. Rutter, Virginia.
  HQ535.F354 2015
  306.850973—dc23   2014045917

W. W. Norton & Company, Inc., 500 Fifth Avenue, New York, NY 10110-0017
WWNORTON.COM

W. W. Norton & Company Ltd., 15 Carlisle Street, London W1D 3BS

7 8 9 0

Contents

Part Three: The Diversity of American Families Today

Part Four: Intimacy in the Twenty-First Century

Part Five: Marriage and Divorce: Does Policy Matter?

Part Six: A Generational Dance: How Parents and Kids Relate

Part Seven: Unequal Lives: Families across Economic and Citizenship Divides

Conclusion

PART ONE

How We Know What We Know about Families

1

Springing Forward from the Past

An Introduction

Barbara J. Risman and Virginia E. Rutter

This anthology is written primarily by members of the Council on Contemporary Families (CCF), an interdisciplinary community of experts who study and work with families. Our organizational mission is to provide accurate information about how families really are to the public at large. Most but not all of us are university faculty. What we all share is a commitment to using research and clinical expertise to enhance the national conversation about what contemporary families need and how these needs can best be met. The Council is nonpartisan and our members support a wide variety of social policies, but we all strongly believe that social science should be used for the public good and that research should be used to support the diversity of families, since families of all kinds provide people with their most intimate relationships.

One of the Council's unique contributions is to provide journalists with accurate information about today's families. We act as a referral system to find the best experts for journalists when they research a story. We also publish Briefing Papers and Symposiums to highlight what should be getting coverage, what you should be learning about in the newspapers but are not. In some of these briefs and symposiums, we identify the most important new studies just coming out. In others, we integrate findings that have begun to accumulate to provide strong empirical evidence about important issues facing families today. We provide this same information to policy makers at the local and national level. Our members write op-ed for news outlets. With this anthology, we bring our contributions to students as well.

Every chapter in this book is a new contribution to the research and theory about families. We have included most of the chapters from the earlier edition, but added new and exciting research on diverse American families. The chapters aren't reprints; you won't find them anywhere else. As a unique feature of this book, we incorporate CCF Briefing Papers (including briefs, fact sheets, and symposiums) along with the news coverage that was based on them. These special studies were released by CCF for the public. They concisely summarize the latest research findings for a general audience, to help people make informed decisions about issues that matter to them. Most were widely covered by news media. We show you not only the newest work of the leading scholars in the field, but also how their work contributes to the coverage and understanding of families that you, your friends, and your family read about in newspapers and magazines.

This is a perfect example of how academic and clinical experts make a difference outside the ivory tower. It shows you why intellectual work, studying and writing about people, matters. Our goal is to bring cutting-edge research and clinical expertise to all Americans so that people understand their own lives and the lives of those around them more fully. We provide information that could lead to better social policy, built more on a clear and fair reading of the evidence than on passion and stereotypes.

The book is divided into thematic parts that include original chapters, reports from CCF, and news coverage of the work you are studying. We've also created a teaching guide where instructors can find questions for discussion and other materials to accompany the book.

Part One includes this overview of our book and chapters about how we know what we know about families. These essays are designed to challenge you to be skeptical of all research, including the studies provided in this book. These essays were originally presented at the CCF Tenth Anniversary Symposium in a session on how to assess contemporary knowledge about families. Andrew Cherlin tackles the paradox of twenty-first-century science, articulating both the reality that all science is a cultural product (as the categories scientists choose reflect their worldviews, including values), while at the same time noting that empirical research does indeed help explain what's happening around us and in our own lives. Cherlin concludes that all readers must critically assess scientific claims in light of the biases a researcher might bring to the table. Philip Cowan clarifies an error often made when interpreting social science—the confusion of correlation with causation. He cautions all readers to question *why* something happens and not simply to presume that because two social trends begin simultaneously, one has caused the other. Linda Burton discusses the kind of information we can only learn from longitudinal ethnography, explaining how we need to go beyond survey data to uncover the full story of people's lives and relationships. Burton shows how research based on interviews and observations provides essential evidence for social policy. Part One ends with a CCF Brief by Anthony Mancini and George A. Bonanno on "The Trouble with Averages," which is further discussed in Stephanie Coontz's *New York Times* article "When Numbers Mislead." The CCF Brief and Coontz's article give you examples of how to be cautious, skeptical, smart readers of research.

In **Part Two**, "How We Got Here," several leading historians and social scientists provide compelling evidence that what we think of as the *traditional* family has changed over the course of history. Stephanie Coontz provides a sweeping overview of the dramatic changes in how families operate, and she discusses who is even considered kin from the earliest moments of history. Steven Mintz follows a similar strategy, but he focuses specifically on the fate of American children in the last three centuries. Mintz provides convincing evidence that while some parts of childhood might be harder today, many of America's children are better off now than ever before. Mintz's chapter on childhood is followed by his short essay that appeared in the national press; his focus is on the relevance today for lessons from history. This part of the book includes a CCF Brief by historian Susan Matt. She looks to the past to illustrate common myths about homesickness among young people—especially as they go to college today. Donna Franklin's research suggests that professional-class African American couples pioneered modern marriage. African Americans were the first in the United States to accept that women could have both serious intellectual lives and careers while also being wives and mothers. Franklin argues that while white women were forced to choose between marriage and career into the twentieth century, college-educated African American women and their husbands were inventing the contemporary marriage of equals. Brian Powell and his colleagues provide a historical perspective on how quickly Americans' definitions of family have changed, from excluding same-sex couples to including them. We then provide a clip of how this research was covered in the news. We end Part Two with a chapter by Kerry Ann Rockquemore and Loren Henderson, who take us on a historical ride from the days when interracial marriage was illegal up to the civil rights era. They conclude with information about today's interracial couples and their children. Interracial couples are also highlighted in a CCF Brief by Kimberlyn Fong, who gives us an overview of trends in interracial marriage upon the fiftieth anniversary of the 1964 Civil Rights Act.

Part Three of the book is the longest, because when we talk about the "Diversity of American Families Today," there is quite a lot to say. We begin with a chapter that addresses the time-honored question for students and scholars of families: "What is family?" Here, Karen Struening shows how the legal system often lags behind the reality of how people live their lives. She provides concrete examples about same-sex marriage and technology-assisted reproduction showing how the law seems to be in flux, with state decisions at odds with each other and often with the federal courts as well. Following Struening is a chapter by Amy Blackstone and Amy Greenleaf that highlights how childfree couples make their relationships into families, including an interesting account of how they incorporate their pets as family members. A CCF Fact Sheet and a blog highlight how single people fit into our mostly coupled world. In their chapter, Pamela J. Smock and Wendy D. Manning write about the "cohabitation revolution" in the United States. The authors trace the change from cohabitation being seen as "living in sin" to being seen as simply a stage of courtship. They show how quickly change can happen: one generation's sin is the next one's transition to marriage. On this same topic, Arielle Kuperberg offers more new research in a CCF Brief. Kuperberg tells us that in the past, people thought that cohabitation made divorce more likely. But her research demonstrates that cohabitation doesn't cause divorce and probably never did. The expert commentaries in the brief show that issues like the age a romance begins and a person's level of education play a bigger role in the vulnerability of relationships than does cohabitation itself.

From cohabitation, we turn to sibling relationships with Amy Brainer's chapter about relationships between straight young people and their lesbian, gay, or bisexual brothers and sisters. From siblings, we go to the issue of interracial marriage with a CCF Symposium on interracial marriage. Stanford law professor Ralph Richard Banks introduces a provocative proposal regarding interracial marriage among African American women. Numerous black, feminist, and sexuality scholars then rebut Banks's arguments. In this symposium, you can see how Banks's proposal for African American women was covered in the news, too. In another take on interracial relationships, Jennifer Lee reviews data on interracial marriage and the meaning of multiraciality for *Sociological Images*. Jenny Davis's column for *Cyborgology* analyzes racist patterns of behavior among online daters. In a series of chapters on diverse families, we cover common types of families as well as newer variations. One very common family type in today's world is one in which both parents work for pay. Shannon N. Davis and Brittany Owen offer a look at how couples organized their families before, during, and after the Great Recession. They show us how, without public policies like a funded family and medical leave act, middle- and working-class families face daily challenges in keeping life together. We next provide several articles addressing research on gay men and lesbians. Robert-Jay Green's chapter traces how gay couples have changed from outlaws (not too long ago gay sex was outlawed in some states) to in-laws as gay marriage becomes ever more accepted, and now legitimate by federal law, if not yet in all states. Mignon R. Moore writes about

African American lesbian relationships and how these women negotiate equality with one another.

In **Part Four**, we focus on physical intimacy—that is, sex. We begin with a chapter by Pepper Schwartz in which she writes that, despite all the sexual imagery in our society, we are still deeply afraid of sex. Schwartz identifies several social policies that result from this fear. For example, the federal government has supported abstinence education, even when more than half of all teenagers in high school are having sex. Schwartz concludes by examining why we are so afraid of something so natural. Adina Nack's chapter provides one answer. Nack suggests it is because of the STD epidemic among youth today. Nack explains the high rates of those with a variety of STDs and how people in relationships—including new relationships—navigate discussions of sexually transmitted disease status. A CCF Fact Sheet that she wrote provides key information on sexual health. Finally, Nack focuses on a contested realm—HPV vaccinations—in a column for *Ms.* magazine where she discusses how boys get left out through sexist and homophobic attitudes toward the HPV vaccine. The last chapter in Part Four is an article by Elizabeth A. Armstrong, Paula England, and Alison C.K. Fogarty. Armstrong and her colleagues suggest that college students are not afraid of sex, because hooking up (or casual sex outside of relationships) appears to be common on today's campuses. These authors look at the kinds of sexual pleasure older adolescents and young adults experience before marriage. In a world where college students are more likely to hook up than to date, what does that mean for sexuality? Does this new form of sex indicate gender equality? Are orgasm rates equal for men and women in hookups? Armstrong and her colleagues show us that for women, orgasm rates seem to increase when there is greater familiarity with sexual partners, but this result is less true for men. The authors suggest that the gender revolution has yet to reach its full flowering in the distribution of sexual pleasure, at least in casual heterosexual sex. Following Armstrong's chapter, Rachel Allison tells the story of her research with Barbara Risman on commuter students, those mostly from working-class backgrounds, who do *not* tend to participate in the college hookup scene. We also include a debate, covered in news media, about research on whether really egalitarian marriages are less erotically charged than more male-dominated ones.

In **Part Five**, we focus on marriage and divorce, and whether social policies or therapeutic interventions can, or should, try to influence people to marry or to stay married. Orit Avishai, Melanie Heath, and Jennifer Randles's chapter on political efforts to promote marriage, known as "the marriage movement," describes how marriage promotion has been implemented—and the limits of that implementation for achieving goals such as economic or family stability. A CCF Brief by Kristi Williams zeroes in on how limited marriage promotion has been for poverty reduction. You can read how Williams's work was covered as a journalist asks and answers the question of why marriage might not be the answer for low-income moms. The topic of single moms leads directly to a concern with divorce, because some—though certainly not all—women become single mothers after divorce. Virginia Rutter provides a methodological critique of the studies purporting to show that divorce hurts everyone, sharing her personal life history to illustrate the argument. Philip Cohen's *Family Inequality* column on his research concerning the impact of the Great Recession on divorce rates notes, as Rutter did, how media can be misleading when reporting on divorce rates. It is clearly the case that children growing up in divorced and remarried households face some unique challenges. Marilyn Coleman and Lawrence Ganong debunk the many myths surrounding stepfamilies. What helps stepfamilies succeed? Being realistic and recognizing the diversity of stepfamilies. What harms stepfamilies? The myths that propose one size fits all or that assume the worst. The last chapter in Part Five, by Philip A. Cowan and Carolyn Pape Cowan, tries to reframe the debate about what's good for children. The authors go from focusing on whether the children's parents are married to how well those parents work together to care for their kids. Wrapping up Part Five, Philip Cohen's CCF Brief on antipoverty programs in the United States over the past fifty years identifies what has helped—and what has failed.

In **Part Six** we focus on intergenerational issues between parents and children. We begin with a chapter on parenting adult children. In it, Joshua Coleman offers another view of parenting, one that we often ignore. He reminds us that parenting doesn't end when children graduate high school, college, or even marry. Intergenerational relationships and parenting are lifetime concerns. Following Joshua Coleman's chapter is a news article that includes an interview with him and offers advice about what parents should know before their college grads move back home. Next is a CCF Brief by Elizabeth Gregory on older mothers. She demonstrates yet another way that family timing isn't the same for everyone. Her finding that older mothers having babies is a trend made the news, as you can see in the story that follows her chapter. In another chapter on parent-child relationships, Lorena Garcia writes about how Latina mothers tell their daughters about their family responsibilities. But families are not always all from the same racial or ethnic group, and Pamela Anne Quiroz's chapter addresses the complicated lives of those who adopt transnationally. Quiroz's chapter focuses on those she labels as *neoethnics*, "people whose identities have literally been recreated through the act of adoption." How parents attempt to raise children from other cultures is at the core of this chapter. The next chapter also focuses on how parents raise children who are different from themselves, in this case, children born intersex. Georgiann Davis's interviews with people active in the intersex community draw attention to how the medical world leads new parents to transform children with intersex traits into the sexual binary—you are either male or female—instead of treating intersex traits as normal and part of the natural variation of bodies. In a column for the *Advocate*, Davis zeroes in on another group that fails to normalize intersex traits when she calls out Fox News for treating intersex as a punch line. From families with intersex children, we move to a passionately written chapter based both on research and personal experience. In the chapter titled "The Power of Queer: How 'Guy Moms' Challenge Heteronormative Assumptions about Mothering and Family," Raine Dozier examines the challenges—from institutions as well as other people—faced by parents who do not fit into familiar sexual binaries. Along the way, Dozier, like Davis, shows readers how beliefs about what is *natural* are just another social construction. A column by Ashir Leah KaneRisman for *Offbeat Bride* gives a first-person account of gender bending in the face of planning a wedding. The issue of diversity of families is made plain in the final piece in Part Six, where Lisa Wade updates *Sociological Images* with class and race demographics of LGBT families.

In **Part Seven**, we focus on how families must navigate inequality across economic classes and because of their immigration status. Two chapters help us answer the question, what do we know about immigrant families as they really are? Etiony Aldarondo and Edward Ameen review the research on contemporary immigrants and show how immigrant families struggle to become part of the American mosaic without losing their own cultural heritage. Andrew Cherlin's *Washington Post* editorial reminds readers that no matter who marries or why, gay or straight, from the middle of the country or some other country, one thing is for sure—there is no picture-perfect, typical American family anymore. Next is a chapter on gender and immigration. Pallavi Banerjee focuses on the effect of immigrant visas that are designated for "dependent" spouses, presuming they are women who do not want or need to work. In this chapter, Banerjee looks at what happens when men hold those visas and their wives are the migrant labor breadwinners. In a column for *Ms.* magazine, Banerjee shows that our visa policy requires the wives (and sometimes husbands) of immigrants to remain economic dependents, which weakens rather than strengthens the families involved.

We move from a focus on immigrants to the problems faced by those who struggle economically. These chapters on economic inequality suggest that perhaps the most important issues to consider when we worry about tomorrow's families are poverty and the impact of unequal beginnings on future possibilities. These chapters include a focus on how children growing up in households with few economic resources struggle to even imagine their place in the American dream. Frank Furstenberg shows how social class sets the parameters for the daily life experience of today's children. Annette Lareau describes how parents from different social classes hold different child-rearing philosophies, with the consequence that children from the middle class are brought up with strategies that enable them to develop the skills and attitudes valued for good jobs in twenty-first-century America. Kevin Roy and Natasha Cabrera focus attention on low-income families by tracing the kinds of involvement of fathers in such families. They offer a model of father involvement that moves far beyond the notion of fathers simply as income providers. A *Sociological Images* blog post from Lisa Wade affirms Roy and Cabrera's observations, highlighting the similarities among fathers from different races. We end Part Seven with a chapter on how mass incarceration has severely affected the opportunities for a great number of families. In their chapter, Bryan L. Sykes and Becky Pettit explain how imprisoning so many parents hurts not only them, but their spouses, children, and neighbors. In a *Girl w/ Pen!* column about mass incarceration, Virginia Rutter writes about the extent to which men in the United States are ever incarcerated (one in eight).

Part Eight is devoted to understanding how the changes in women's and men's lives have changed families. Only a few generations ago, a child born with a penis would have had an entirely different future than one born with a vagina. The penis-holder would have been expected to learn a trade or get an education, earn a living, and spend most of his time supporting his family. His contributions to child rearing primarily would have been his paycheck. The vagina-holder would have been expected to find a husband (who would support her economically, if possible) and spend most of her time and attention on kin keeping, raising children, caring for aging parents, and supporting her man. Although space limits do not allow us to fully discuss why we have seen a gender revolution, we offer just a few possibilities. Surely women's ability to control if and when to have a baby, by effective birth control and access to abortion, has allowed us to think about and plan for roles beyond the family. And the feminist movement helped to point out the inequity of limiting women's lives to the family when they were educated and capable of challenges beyond the domestic. The simple assumption that a penis-holder and a vagina-holder should necessarily have different life opportunities seems vaguely quaint now, but it was taken for granted as the natural order of things not very long ago. Clearly, the gender revolution has had an impact on families. If women are not primarily focused on creating and managing the domestic sphere, what will happen to the children, home-cooked meals, and the warmth of the hearth? If women are expecting men to treat them as equals and not as helpmates, will marriage thrive, or wither away? And what about sex? Has equality come to that part of men and women's lives? The chapters in this section address these important issues.

The first chapter addresses what has changed—and what has not—among today's tween-agers. Barbara J. Risman and Elizabeth Seale's chapter asks how far the gender revolution has come for today's children. They report that girls have benefited much from the feminist-inspired changes of the twentieth century, but that boys seem sadly stuck with gender expectations that keep them tightly constrained within narrow stereotypes of masculinity. Girls still worry very much about how they look, but not too much about acting feminine. Boys who don't act very much like all the other boys live in fear of being viciously teased. Kathleen Gerson's research focuses on twenty- and thirty-somethings as they talk about their goals for balancing work and family. Young adults today are children of the gender revolution. Their baby boom parents were the first to move into uncharted territory, with feminist mothers, frequent parental divorces, and blended families. Gerson finds that today's young adults, both women and men, want to balance work that matters with time left for investing in their relationships and often in parenting. But she also finds that if they have trouble with such a balancing act, men and women have starkly different fallback plans. A CCF Fact Sheet by Jonathan Bearak and Paula England demonstrates a historic reversal that highlights the changing context of women's options: Higher education, unlike in the past, makes marriage *more* likely for women. News coverage, which follows the Fact Sheet, highlights the new timing—women seek education now *before* they marry. From young adults' views of marriage, we move to whether marriage has or has not changed. Oriel Sullivan provides quantitative evidence that men's contribution to the household, or what used to be called "women's work," has increased over the last few decades. Kristen Myers and Ilana Demantas look inside couples where men's traditional breadwinning doesn't occur and describes how couples navigate men's caregiving. These chapters suggest that trends are in the right direction—but the pace of change is slow. The CCF Symposium on equal pay documents the combination of positive changes and some of the remaining inequality in pay gaps between men and women. It specifies how the size of the gender pay gap varies by race and ethnicity. Stephanie Coontz's *Sunday Times of London* column "Yes, I've Folded Up My Masculine Mystique, Honey" puts the symposium's research in context. Finally, Philip N. Cohen's assessment of concerns about a gender revolution gone too far is answered in "Still a Man's World."

This anthology owes much to all the members of the Council on Contemporary Families who have contributed to it. This second edition has changed significantly, as the research on families has moved forward, and concern for an ever more diverse set of American families grows. The co-authors want to thank Amy Brainer, who was lead editorial assistant on this edition and is also a contributor. We owe a huge debt to Stephanie Coontz for her extremely helpful editorial work on many of the original chapters and unending support for this project. Thanks also go to our original editor at Norton, Karl Bakeman, who conceived the idea for this anthology to begin with, and encouraged us to move forward with a second edition. We also want to thank Sasha Levitt, our current editor, who has been exceedingly supportive, encouraging, and responsive—and has helped us through a challenging year of editing. Barbara would like to dedicate this book to her husband, Randall Liss, who is living proof that statistical regularities do not explain individual lives. His nurturing and homemaking have made this project—and the rest of Barbara's complicated professional life—possible. Barbara also dedicates this book to her daughter, Ashir Leah KaneRisman and her daughter's wife, Caitlin Cotter, with the hope that wherever they decide to make their home, their family will be accepted and valued. Virginia dedicates this book to her mother, Joanna Pittman Fox, who died while the book was being edited. To the end, she taught Virginia about family diversity by her example.

The Council on Contemporary Families was created over a decade ago because our founding members saw the press misinterpreting good science—sometimes naively, and sometimes because they had been misinformed by ideological right-wing think tanks. The Council is dedicated to providing good scientific research and clinical expertise to the public and policy makers alike. We invite you to read the chapters, briefs, and articles in this anthology with the critical lenses provided by Cherlin, Cowan, and Burton in their chapters on evaluating research. Science is always in the act of becoming, and this book is offered in the spirit of contributing the best information we have now to the body of knowledge available to us all. All the authors have contributed their time and effort to this volume, and all proceeds will help CCF in its mission to diffuse the best new knowledge we have on families, with the firm belief that knowledge is power.

2

One Thousand and Forty-Nine Reasons Why It's Hard to Know When a Fact Is a Fact

Andrew J. Cherlin

W hen is a fact a fact? If you are a postmodernist, the answer is clear: never. Postmodern critics of standard social science argue that the conclusions we draw are not, and cannot be, genuinely objective. Rather, they say, our findings are contaminated in several ways. First, the questions we ask and the point of view we take often reflect our values, whether those are an enthusiasm for feminist or civil-rights-inspired activism or a belief in the importance of marriage and premarital chastity. Even the categories and labels we use often reflect values-based assumptions.

Here is an example from my field, family demography: In 1941, Paul Glick, the Bureau of the Census demographer who virtually created the field, wrote a pioneering article entitled "Types of Families: An Analysis of Census Data.[1] Glick divided American families into three groups: (1) normal families, a category that consisted of all two-parent families; (2) other male-headed families; and (3) other female-headed families. The implication, of course, was that all single-parent families were abnormal.

Or consider contemporary debates over immigration, which may be shaped by whether one uses the term *illegal alien* or *undocumented immigrant*. The first conjures up an image of a law-breaking invader from outer space; the second conveys an image of a striving newcomer who merely lacks the right papers.

Recognizing that most researchers draw upon particular values when they choose what categories to use and what questions to ask does not mean that all data are suspect or that all interpretations of data are equally valid. But it does drive home the importance of treating so-called facts critically and of questioning their origins and purposes. When we read facts, we should ask ourselves a few key questions: Who produced this fact? Was it a person or an organization that promotes a particular point of view? What was the purpose of making this fact known? What do we know about the relationship of this fact to other facts or trends?

Consider familyfacts.org, a website operated by the Heritage Foundation. It publicizes findings from social scientific research on family life. On its home page, familyfacts.org presents itself as a neutral clearinghouse for family research: "The Heritage Foundation's familyfacts.org catalogs social science findings on the family, society and religion gleaned from peer-reviewed journals, books and government surveys. Serving policy makers, journalists, scholars and the general public, familyfacts.org makes social science research easily accessible to the non-specialist."

In 2008, this site featured a "top ten" list of findings about how children in different kinds of families fare in school. According to each finding, children living with two parents were doing better than children living with one parent or with stepparents. Here are two of the findings: "Kindergartners in intact families have higher average reading scores than peers in stepfamilies or cohabiting families" and "First-graders whose mothers were married when they were born are less likely to engage in disruptive behavior with peers and teachers than those whose mothers were single or cohabiting." In fact, virtually all of the thousands of findings on the site support the view that marriage is best for children and that religion improves family outcomes.

These findings are not falsified. They are taken from reputable studies published in well-regarded journals such as the *Journal of Marriage and Family* and, by and large, are described accurately. A naive user might think that this is all social scientists know. But the facts reported on this site have been selected to support a particular conclusion, while facts that modify, complicate, or challenge that conclusion are not reported.

For example, the site quotes a 1998 article that I co-wrote about a study showing that children whose parents had divorced had a higher risk of emotional problems in adulthood.[2] Yet that same article also showed that some of the emotional problems had been visible in childhood before the parents even divorced, but this additional finding was not mentioned. Nor does the site mention a 1991 article that I co-wrote that also suggested that some of the problems experienced by children from divorced families might have occurred even had the parents stayed together.[3] This is not a fact that familyfacts.org thinks you need to know.

Which findings are included and which are excluded make sense if one knows that the Heritage Foundation, a conservative think tank, promotes the values of institutions such as "traditional" marriage and religion. This is not to say that one should disregard the findings on familyfacts.org; in fact, much evidence does suggest that growing up with two parents is beneficial to children. But the informed reader will know that it is necessary to go elsewhere to see whether the kinds of findings that are cataloged at familyfacts.org tell the whole story.

Conservatives are not the only ones who use facts in ways that reflect their values. In the 1980s, when homelessness was first being recognized as a social problem, many news stories included the information that 2 to 3 million Americans were homeless. Soon this figure became an accepted fact. Yet it subsequently came to light that this fact had been provided by a leading advocate for the homeless, Mitch Snyder, who basically made a guess. He said in a television interview:

> Everybody demanded it. Everybody said we want a number. . . . We got on the phone, we made a lot of calls, we talked to a lot of people, and we said, "Okay, here are some numbers."[4]

Snyder was just doing what advocates usually do: providing the largest credible estimate of how many people are affected by the problem they want to alleviate or by the disease they would like to cure or by the injustice they want to remedy. In counting the homeless, as in estimating the number of women who have been raped or who experience eating disorders, advocates often take the most expansive definition of the problem and adjust for underreporting. But such estimates are especially susceptible to manipulation for dramatic effect.

More recently, we have heard much in debates over same-sex partnerships about the 1,049 federal benefits and rights that marriage supposedly confers on husbands and wives. This number appeared in the late 1990s and was soon cited everywhere as a fact about the legal benefits of marriage. In 1999, advocates of same-sex marriage, while welcoming the Vermont legislation that created the nation's first civil unions, noted that state-level recognition of gay unions would not provide the partners with the federal benefits of marriage. Hanna Rosin reported in the *Washington Post*:

> The plaintiffs in the Vermont case documented a long list of benefits granted to married couples but denied to gay ones. The 300 state and 1,049 federal laws cover such matters as the right to pay taxes jointly, and social security benefits.[5]

Ever since, reputable newspapers around the country and politicians on both sides of the political spectrum have accepted this claim as fact, derived from a federal study conducted by the General Accounting Office. The precision of this fact—not 1,048 or 1,050 but exactly 1,049—gave it such verisimilitude that no one challenged it. And its magnitude suggested an overwhelming bias in favor of marriage, making it an attractive "fact" that could be used by proponents of same-sex marriage, just as the people who constructed the Heritage website were attracted to only some of the "facts" reported by family researchers on divorce. But in hindsight, its precision and size are the very factors that should have suggested caution in using this fact.

The source of this "fact" was indeed a federal study, but the study did not establish what these and many other news reports have since claimed. In 1996, when Congress enacted the Defense of Marriage Act, Representative Henry Hyde requested that the General Accounting Office identify all federal laws that involved benefits, rights, and privileges that depend on being married. As the GAO staff discussed this request with Hyde's staff, they agreed to broaden the scope of the study to include "all those laws in the United States Code in which marital status is a factor, even though some of those laws may not directly create benefits, rights, or privileges."[6] In other words, the GAO counted all laws that involved marriage, including those that *penalized* married couples.

One of the 1,049 laws, for example, is a statute that limits the amount of certain crop support payments that one person can receive. For this purpose, a married couple is considered to be one person. But an unmarried couple can apparently escape this restriction and each receives the maximum amount. Another law mandates that a candidate may not spend more than $50,000 of his or her own money, or the money of his or her immediate family, on a political campaign and still be eligible for federal funding; but there's nothing to prevent the candidate's unmarried partner from kicking in additional funds.

Many of the so-called benefits of marriage, furthermore, are trivial. It is true that one law discriminates against cohabiting couples by making it a federal crime to try to influence United States officials by threatening to kill their spouses, whereas it seems not to be a federal crime to threaten to kill their cohabiting partners. But this "benefit" of marriage applies to very few couples.

It did not take weeks of research in dusty government archives to get to the bottom of this; rather, I found the information on the Internet in less than an hour. That so many people had quoted the number without checking it shows how easily a "fact" can become part of the dialogue about social and political issues.

What happens to a fact of this kind is that it becomes a symbol of the issue in dispute. Clearly, marriage does provide some important federal benefits. Only married couples can file their federal tax returns jointly; and only married people can continue to receive part of their partner's Social Security benefits after the partner dies. But the figure of 1,049 benefits became a dramatic, and at first glance convincing, stand-in for the general privilege of being married in American society. It was this general privilege that really was the point of the debate.

This was the reasoning of the Massachusetts Supreme Court in ruling that restricting marriage to heterosexuals was unacceptable even if same-sex partners were given the same legal status. Marriage, the judges wrote, is more than a collection of benefits; rather, it is a "status that is specially recognized in society." Denying same-sex couples that special status, the justices argued would create a "stigma of exclusion."[7]

Debating the abstract notion of social status is, however, more difficult than debating legal benefits. Advocates therefore focused on the 1,049 benefits as a way of building support for their more general position. Many debates over social and political issues revolve around symbols such as this one, and it is in the interest of each side to define the symbol in the largest or the smallest terms possible to bolster their case.

Whether everyone knows where the supposed facts come from, as is the case with the findings displayed on the familyfacts.org website, or whether no one seems to know, as with the apocryphal 1,049 benefits, the careful user of facts will not take them at face value. At the least, the user must examine (or uncover) the source and determine its position on the issues. Even your most trusted friends probably care about the social and political issues they discuss, which makes it difficult for them to be truly balanced in the facts they tell you about. And as a rule, no organization that takes sides in a public debate will provide facts that should be considered fully objective and balanced. To be sure, some organizations may be more transparent and balanced, and others more opaque and one-sided, in their use of facts. But even the fairest will have made choices about what questions to ask, what counts as good research, and on what basis one draws conclusions. Unless you understand where the source is coming from, it's hard to evaluate the information it provides. And that's a fact.

Notes

1.   Glick (1941).
2.   Cherlin, Chase-Lansdale, and McRae (1998).
3.   Cherlin et al. (1991).
4.   Snyder in Jencks (1994).
5.   Rosin (1999).
6.   U.S. General Accounting Office (1997).
7.   Goodrich v. Department of Public Health (2003).

3

When Is a Relationship between Facts a Causal One?

Philip A. Cowan

After checking the accuracy of facts, as Cherlin's paper urges us to do, the next step is to examine critically the way people interpret the relationship of one fact to another. It is a fact, for example, that substantial numbers of children are growing up in single-parent families. Or, more precisely, it is a fact that many children are growing up in households that do not contain two parents who are married to each other. Some of these families have only one parent in the home, while others may have two parents who are cohabiting. It is also a fact that, in general, children and couples in nonmarried families are not faring as well as those in married families. Members of such families have less income and lower levels of physical and mental health, and the children have more emotional problems and behavior problems.[1] It is tempting to conclude from these facts that living in a single-parent household is the *cause* of these difficulties.

But when we look at all people who live in single-parent households, we find a larger number of people with preexisting financial, health, or emotional disadvantages than we find in the married-couple population. It may be these characteristics of the adults in the family, rather than single parenthood per se, that make them less likely to get or stay married and more likely to raise children who exhibit behavior problems. If so, it would be inaccurate to say that divorce or unwed behavior *causes* problems in children. In many cases, the problems seen in children raised by these individuals might develop even if the parents were able—or were forced—to stay together.

The problem of overstating causal conclusions from correlational data is not the sole property of the political left or political right. Both sides are too quick to draw support from social science research when the correlations support their cherished conclusions. Supporters of the political right tend to select studies that show correlations between divorce and negative outcomes for children. Supporters of the political left tend to select studies that show correlations between poverty and negative outcomes for children. The point here is not that these claims are wrong, but that most studies do not provide evidence for the causal assertions and policy conclusions that are made on both sides of the political spectrum.

We need to make a slight digression here. It is always legitimate and possible to make policy arguments on moral or value grounds. That is, if one's values lead to the conclusion that cohabitation is a sin, and that having children compounds that sin, it is part of the bedrock of democracy that one can argue strongly on moral grounds that laws should be made to prevent cohabitation and foster marriage. What we're concerned with here are cases in which reporters or politicians buttress their arguments with conclusions drawn from social science research. The key is for us to be explicit about when we are making arguments from a values perspective and when we are arguing based on social science research.

BASIC PROBLEMS IN THE INTERPRETATION OF RESEARCH FACTS

1. Causal facts always imply a direction of effects—the cause, A, comes before the effect, B. But statements based on statistical correlations can *never* tell us about the direction of effects. For example, it is a fact that there is a correlation between being married and having better-functioning lives and between non-marriage and financial or emotional difficulties. But we do not know whether marriage produces the partners' better functioning or whether better-functioning partners tend to marry. That is, selection effects that guide who gets married may influence the results.

2. An important corollary of point 1 is that when two social trends vary together, it is not possible to conclude that one causes the other. Increases in the proportion of mothers of young children in the workforce occurred in the mid-twentieth century around the same time that the divorce rate went up. On the basis of these two facts alone we cannot point to women's working as a cause of the increase in divorce. Why not? First, we don't know from these two statistics whether the divorces occurred more often in the families of women who went to work. And second, we do not know whether these two trends are associated with other factors that may plausibly have caused the increase in divorce.

3. Reasoning backwards about causality produces backward thinking. Most newspaper and magazine articles on family issues rely on research that starts

with outcomes of interest right now and look backwards for potential explanations, because that's what most research does. For example, investigators take two groups of couples, one in which there are high levels of domestic violence, and another in which there has never been any domestic violence. They look at their histories, and find that the couples with domestic violence are much more likely to have been abused by their parents than the harmonious couples. Does this demonstrate that early abuse is a cause of domestic violence? No. What's missing from the picture is information from studies that follow families forward. These studies usually find that even if some of the abused children grow up to form violent relationships with a spouse, the majority of children who experience early abuse do not wind up in violent relationships. That is, you can't generalize with any degree of certainty from looking backwards that abused children are highly likely to establish distressing relationships.

In this example, even if early abuse were found to be a cause of domestic violence, we might try to change each partner's understanding of the past through psychotherapy, but we could not reverse the early abuse. Other examples, though, seem to suggest that if we can identify the cause, a quick fix is possible. We know, for example, that there is a correlation between cohabitation and higher rates of domestic violence, but it would be dangerous to conclude that a causal relation exists and recommend that cohabiters should marry. Rather than their failure to marry producing domestic violence, it may have been their stormy relationship that led them not to marry in the first place. If this were the case, a policy that created incentives to marry could result in creating more harm to both the couple and their children.

4. Correlations can result from a third variable that produces the association between them. It is a fact that children whose parents are divorced, or who live with a single parent who never married, tend to have more emotional, behavioral, and academic difficulties than children whose parents are married. It is possible, though, that some of the negative effects of divorce and single parenthood come from the fact that these households have lower incomes, and that the consequences of low income in terms of reduced resources are responsible, at least in part, for children's difficulties.

5. Many studies of families focus on family status and not on family processes or relationship quality. Most studies of marriage and divorce, especially in sociology and social welfare, attempt to link couple status (married, cohabiting, divorced, single) with child and family outcomes. For example, in Waite and Gallagher's "The Case for Marriage," almost all the studies they cite contrast married couples with cohabiting couples or single adults. In each chapter, they present evidence that the strongest positive findings occur for *happily married* couples. But in the policy summary at the end of the book,

the authors revert to the argument that "married is better," ignoring the issue of quality altogether.

What the advocates for marriage ignore or dismiss are the hundreds of studies showing that high unresolved marital conflict erodes couple relationships and affects children negatively.[2] Unless we are talking about "good" marriages, getting couples to marry will not provide a solution to social problems of poverty and less effective child rearing.

The Importance of Systematic Studies that Include Randomized Clinical Trials with Control Groups

Every day, the popular press, TV, government websites, and self-help books make new claims that a particular program proposed for families, or one already in operation, is effective. What is surprising is that most of these programs have no systematic evaluations at all. In order to assert that individuals, couples, and families are better off *because* of a program than they were before, what do we need?

First, we need to be able to determine that whoever is providing the information does not have an interest in consciously or unconsciously skewing the results. For example, if the intervention staff is providing the data, it is easy to see how they might be motivated or self-deluded to make higher ratings of the participants on the post-intervention assessments. When program evaluations include data from outside observers, as well as from therapists and clients, the inclusion of multiple perspectives makes statements about improvement more credible.

Second, even with a study that contains the most objective, unbiased assessments of outcome, a control group is still needed. You can't simply claim that the program is a success if the participants show positive changes. What if the average participant in a job-training program has a statistically significantly higher income a year after the program ends? How can we rule out the possibility that these results come from an economic boom in which most families have higher incomes a year later? That is, the fact of increased income does not support a causal interpretation about the impact of the intervention until we know what happens to a comparable *untreated* group.

Similarly, what if a group of children becomes less aggressive with their peers after their parents take a class on managing children's aggression? Again, we need to know whether children whose parents did not take such a class also became less aggressive as they grew older or whether we can show that the declines in aggression are associated with parents' more effective parenting strategies.

We know that it is not always possible to do controlled experiments. To test the hypothesis that married parents provide a better environment for children's development, we cannot assign some single parents to the "get married" group and others to the "remain single" controls. In this case, there are responsible ways of gathering data to rule out alternative hypotheses so that we can come to a more informed decision about the impact of marriage on children's adaptation. One method is to measure a number of variables that could possibly influence A and B groups differently and "subtract them" from the outcome to see if any effect of the intervention remains. This method is only as powerful as the resourcefulness of the investigator in thinking about what else outside of the intervention could have created the results. A second, more powerful method is to conduct a longitudinal study (e.g., before and after divorce) and determine whether, on the average, any change in the children can be identified from before to after their parents' divorce.

CONCLUSIONS

Both the political left and the political right have jumped to conclusions in the debate about marriage, based on the erroneous assumption that correlations support causal inferences. From the right we hear: "Married families do better; let's get those single moms married or make it harder for couples to divorce." From the left we hear: "Unmarried mothers are poor, and poor families have difficulty; let's give them money and jobs."

What we need to remember is that explanations of how two facts are connected can seem simple, but they are often exceedingly complex. At the same time that women started to work outside the home in greater numbers than they had following World War II, the incidence of divorce increased sharply. This correlation cannot be interpreted to mean that working women destroy marital life. Unpacking the causal connection requires very thoughtful systematic research, accompanied by interventions, if possible, that test hypotheses about the direction of effects. I am aware that this kind of rigorous exploration takes time, and that policy decisions must often be made in the absence of scientific proof that the proposed action will have the desired effects. What I want to convey to social service providers and policy makers is that causality is extremely difficult to nail down. We must all read accounts of research with a critical eye. The kind of complexity hidden within a "simple" correlation cannot be communicated or understood in simple sound bites.

NOTES

1. Waite and Gallagher (2000).
2. Cowan and Cowan (2002); Cummings and Davies (1994); Emery (1999); Gottman and Notarius (2002).

4

Uncovering Hidden Facts that Matter in Interpreting Individuals' Behaviors

An Ethnographic Lens

Linda M. Burton

As a social scientist who has conducted ethnographic research on low-income families for over two decades, I would argue that longitudinal ethnography moves us closer than most data collection methods to uncovering hidden facts that shape individuals' behaviors. Ethnographic research is a method of gathering data about individuals' thoughts, behaviors, and experiences in the context of their everyday lives. In ethnography, researchers engage systematically with those they are studying, participating in multiple domains of their lives and asking in-depth questions about the information they are learning.

Ethnographic research differs from surveys of human behaviors in several important ways. While surveys typically ask an individual a series of questions with fixed-option responses, usually at one point in time, ethnographers record *over time* both what individuals say about their own behaviors and what they actually do. In the process, ethnographers build trusting relationships with those they study by listening without judgment and keeping promises of confidentiality. Ethnographers are typically able to uncover hidden data about respondents through long engagement with them and by *being there* when research participants are ready to reveal previously concealed information, on their own terms. In settings in which those studied are concerned about revealing too much of themselves, it is not until a long-term comfortable relationship has been established that research participants will share information that exposes potentially disparaging knowledge about them or important others in their social worlds.

In addition to uncovering hidden information, ethnography can also offer a check against exaggeration of such information. In the course of observing participants and doing informal yet in-depth questioning, ethnographers are able to gather many perspectives on the issue in question—and, hence, they can provide reliability checks on statements made by informants. Occasions can arise in which ethnographers experience contradictions between what people tell them and what ethnographers actually observe them doing or hear reported from others. By being there over time and participating in the social world being studied, ethnographers gain opportunities to uncover new, contradictory, and verifiable forms of data as they occur.

As a result, ethnographers' assessments of respondents usually go well beyond the "public face" and socially appropriate façades individuals tend to put on their responses to general questions. They also typically uncover patterns of behavior or experiences that informants are either ashamed to admit or that they may not even initially regard as relevant to helping ethnographers understand and interpret their lives. Such was the case in the Three-City Study ethnography of economically disadvantaged families in Boston, Chicago, and San Antonio.[1] This multiyear team ethnography was designed to examine the impact of welfare reform in the lives of low-income African American, Latino, Hispanic, and non-Hispanic white families and revealed, beyond the ethnographers' initial estimates, that domestic violence and sexual abuse were far more central to understanding low-income women's day-to-day life experiences and vulnerability than most researchers had recognized.

More than two-thirds of the mothers who participated in the ethnography (N5256) eventually disclosed that they had been sexually abused or had experienced domestic violence as children and/or as adults. Yet in most cases, it took more than six months of in-depth interviews with and participant observations of respondents for this information to come out, and in almost 20 percent of the cases, the information emerged only after ten to twenty-four months of ethnographer's "being there" with the mothers and their families. Three patterns of disclosing sexual abuse and domestic violence were identified in the ethnographic data: trigger topics disclosure, crisis or recent event disclosure, and ethnographer-prompted disclosure.

The *trigger topics* disclosure pattern occurred when mothers unexpectedly revealed sexual abuse and domestic violence histories to ethnographers when they were asked about topics such as health, intimate relationships, transportation, work history, and intergenerational caregiving. Seventy-one percent of disclosures conformed to this trigger topics pattern. For example, during an interview about her general health, a thirty-seven-year-old African American mother of three commented that "my pregnancy with Dante was hard because

I was sick." The ethnographer neutrally asked for more information: "You were sick?"

> Yeah, he had been sleeping around and gave me gonorrhea. I'm still embarrassed talking about it. Sometimes I didn't want to sleep with him but he'd rape me. I told him I was gonna call the police and he said, "Go ahead. Ain't nobody gonna arrest me for wanting to be with my woman."

A different informant revealed experiences with abuse when the ethnographer asked how she had met her husband. Liza stated that this was a "funny story" and noted that she had met her husband just after ending a relationship with a man who had broken her nose. Yet another example of such unprompted disclosure was one that occurred during the twenty-third visit to the home of Delilah, a forty-year-old European American divorcée and mother of four children. The ethnographer was conducting a follow-up interview concerning Delilah's past and current work experiences, because Delilah had failed to mention particulars about her work history over the previous two years of interviews. At this point, Delilah finally told the ethnographer that she had once worked at a bank as a switchboard operator, but quit when her former husband physically injured her. Delilah stated: "I went to work with a black eye. People at the bank noticed. When it happened a second time, I felt embarrassed coming to work, so I quit like cold turkey."

The second most common pattern of disclosure, accounting for almost 20 percent of the reports, was the *crisis* or *recent event* disclosure pattern. This pattern occurred when the ethnographer unexpectedly "walked in" on a domestic violence situation when she was visiting the participant, or when the participant experienced a sexual abuse or domestic violence episode a few days or weeks prior to the ethnographer's regularly scheduled visit. In both instances, the abuse situation was "fresh" in the minds of mothers, and they chose to discuss it with their ethnographers in great detail. In most of these cases, the ethnographers had suspected abuse (as indicated in ethnographers' field notes and in discussions with their supervisors and team members), but they hadn't felt that they could directly ask the participant about it. For example, Janine, the ethnographer for Patrice, a twenty-eight-year-old European mother of two, describes the circumstances that led to Patrice's crisis-prompted disclosure:

> I arrived at Patrice's house 10 minutes before the interview only to find the streets covered with cops, patrol cars, and an ambulance. . . . Patrice was on the porch screaming, her face bloody and cut. The kids were running around everywhere screaming and crying. . . . I feared that my worst suspicions about the prevalence of

domestic violence in Patrice's life were about to be confirmed. . . . When I visited Patrice three weeks later, the flood gates opened without me asking. I listened as she told me everything about the incident and about other incidents of physical and sexual abuse that she had experienced since childhood.

The third pattern, *ethnographer-prompted* disclosure, occurred when ethnographers directly asked mothers about their past and current experiences with sexual abuse or domestic violence. Ethnographers usually asked direct but open-ended questions about these topics in an interview if they noticed a behavioral reaction from mothers when discussing their intimate relationships with their partners. Only 10 percent of all disclosures came from such prompts.

It is also important to note that only 12 percent of the mothers who revealed sexual abuse and domestic violence experiences to the ethnographers did so during visits or participant observations that occurred in the first three months of their involvement in the study. Twenty-nine percent disclosed sexual abuse and domestic violence experiences after four to six months of visits with the ethnographers, 40 percent after seven to nine months of visits, and 19 percent after ten to twenty-four months of visits.

The prolonged wait before most informants revealed their history of sexual abuse and/or domestic violence reveals the importance of ethnographers' investing enough time and participation in the mothers' lives to reach "turning points" in their relationships. A turning point is the moment when participants trust ethnographers enough to share intimate, sensitive, and sometimes highly painful information. That such revelations often occurred almost accidentally or unintentionally suggests that ethnographic studies may capture much more of the actual incidence of violence in poor women's lives than official police reports or surveys, thus uncovering vital yet hidden facts that matter for accurately interpreting individuals' behaviors.

NOTE

1. A detailed description of the Three-City Study and a series of reports are available at www.jhu.edu/~welfare.

CCF Brief

THE TROUBLE WITH AVERAGES: THE IMPACT OF MAJOR LIFE EVENTS AND ACUTE STRESS MAY NOT BE WHAT YOU THINK

Anthony D. Mancini and George A. Bonanno | May 2013

Life changes, sometimes for happy reasons and sometimes for sad ones. Marriage is assumed to be a happy occasion, and divorce a very difficult one. Losing a loved one is thought to be almost unbearable. Other stressful events, such as military deployment, are considered to pose a substantial risk of post-traumatic stress disorder. Are these beliefs accurate? What is the impact of these events on our well-being and functioning, both in the short and the long term?

This is a critical question. Traditionally, researchers have answered it by examining the *average* response to these events. When we are trying to characterize a population, the average is usually the most appropriate way of doing so. Many phenomena assume a so-called normal or bell-shaped distribution. Under such circumstances, the average provides an accurate summary because it is the value most characteristic of the most people, and other values are distributed symmetrically on either side of it.

Sometimes Averages Are *NOT* an Accurate Summary of the Whole

However, in a number of circumstances the average is not characteristic of the whole. For example, when you have different populations grouped together (a "mixture distribution"), the average is not an accurate summary of the whole. Consider height, for example. If we want to characterize height meaningfully, we would describe the average height of men and the average height of women, not the average height of human beings.

Another example is a distribution that is skewed in one direction. A well-known example is household income. Most of the population is grouped on the lower end of the income distribution, while a small proportion of extremely wealthy individuals stretches and distorts the distribution. As a result, the average is artificially inflated and is not representative of the whole.

A third example comes into play when we study changes in people's life satisfaction and well-being across time, particularly following major life events and acute stress. Although people's well-being is generally stable (often called a "setpoint"), it can fluctuate considerably following major life events and acute stress. And the nature of this fluctuation can vary dramatically from person to person. Because of that variability, the average may not represent the way most people respond to these events.

Following loss, for example, most people report a modest, short-lived increase in distress that subsides within a few months. However, some people report substantial and long-lasting distress symptoms while others experience moderately elevated distress that gradually resolves. When we take the average of these patterns, it appears that grief tends to persist. However, this pattern actually characterizes only a minority of grievers. Most people get back to normal within a few months. In this case, the average response distorts our understanding of the variety of people's actual responses.

Along with other colleagues, we have explored these effects in a series of studies examining bereavement, divorce, marriage, childbirth, military deployment, traumatic injury, and other stressors. We find that, in many instances, the average response to these transitions is representative of only a small subset of people. Indeed, the degree of variability in people's responses is startling.

For example, we examined the effects of marriage, divorce, and bereavement on life satisfaction up to four years after the event. Unlike much previous research, our study followed a large representative sample of more than 16,000 people, assessing them yearly with questions about life events and overall life satisfaction. This design allowed us to assess how people were doing both four years before and four years after a significant life event, a crucial factor. We were startled to discover how tremendously diverse people's reactions to these seemingly universal stressors actually were. In each case, people's response tended to cluster into three or four distinct and very different groupings, each of which differed from the overall average.

Does Getting Married Make People Happier?

Almost 80 percent of the people we studied reported high subjective well-being in the years both *before and after* the marriage. But they saw no significant change as a result of marrying. However, the remaining individuals showed markedly different reactions to marriage. Almost 10 percent showed decreasing well-being in the years before the marriage, followed by gradually increasing well-being afterward. Another 6 percent demonstrated a sharp *decrease* in well-being after the marriage. And the smallest group (5.2 percent) experienced a sharp *increase* in well-being in the years leading up to marriage and then sustained that well-being afterward.

These findings suggest that, on balance, the effects of marriage are modest and relatively short lived and that the greatest benefit is enjoyed by only a small subset of people. But this small subset affects the average response, creating a false portrait of the effect of marriage on life satisfaction. Indeed, a basic problem with those who promote marriage as the path to happiness—or with any research that ignores inter-individual variability—is that they paint with too broad a brush.

How Much Do Divorce and Bereavement Reduce Well-Being?

The effect of divorce on life satisfaction showed even more variety. The pattern we would likely anticipate—a decline in life satisfaction following the divorce—was shown by just 19 percent of the participants. Almost 72 percent of the people whose marriages dissolved showed relatively high levels of life satisfaction before the divorce and experienced essentially no change after it. Perhaps most surprisingly, we found a small but significant proportion of people, almost 10 percent, who showed substantial *increases* in well-being afterward. These findings provide a more balanced perspective on claims about the long-term negative effects of divorce, at least for adults.

There were more surprises still when we examined people's reactions to losing a spouse. The conventional pattern of grieving—a sharp dip and a gradual return to pre-loss levels of life satisfaction—was apparent in only about 20 percent of the bereaved and was equally prevalent for men and women. Most grievers (59 percent) showed a remarkable degree of resilience, reporting stable levels of life satisfaction both before and after the loss. Contrary to the notion that older adults are especially vulnerable to loneliness and depression after bereavement, the members of the sample most likely to report stable levels of well-being were, in fact, the oldest.

Another group, almost 15 percent, had very low levels of life satisfaction before the loss. People in this group experienced a slight worsening and then a return to pre-loss levels but essentially maintained their already low levels of life satisfaction. In other words, the low life satisfaction of this group was not a consequence of the loss but instead a continuation of chronic low life satisfaction.

Finally, about 5 percent of grievers *improved* following the loss, a pattern that has now been demonstrated in a number of other studies. It is not clear why this group improved, but it is possible they were involved in caregiving for a chronically ill spouse or were locked into a bad marriage. The key point here is that these anomalous patterns and varied reactions are completely obscured when we rely on average responses.

Military Deployment and Distressed Soldiers

When we studied military deployment, we again found divergent reaction patterns among a large representative sample of over 6,000 persons deployed to Iraq or Afghanistan. Contrary to the widespread assumption that post-traumatic stress disorder (PTSD) is rife among returning military personnel, more than 80 percent of these soldiers displayed normal levels of functioning before and after deployment, and only about 7 percent showed substantially elevated symptoms of PTSD.

These results should reassure people who hesitate to hire returning veterans, but they offer no support for cutting back treatment programs for veterans. In fact, our findings suggest that more attention should be paid to evaluating soldiers' well-being and providing treatment when needed *before* as well as after deployment. This is because we found a small group of individuals who showed elevated distress both before and after deployment. Their difficulties might have been attributed to a deployment-related PTSD if we hadn't been able to demonstrate that their functioning was already impaired *before* the deployment. Interestingly, among the factors that distinguished this group was a greater likelihood of heavy drinking and smoking, suggesting preexisting and maladaptive efforts to cope with stress.

Why This Variability Matters

Our research has confirmed—in study after study—that people respond in surprisingly diverse ways to a wide variety of life events and acute stressors. The reasons for these diverse patterns of response are not entirely clear. Evidence suggests that a wide variety of factors are at play, including personality dimensions, social and environmental supports, and genetic vulnerabilities. Indeed, it appears that some people are inherently more reactive both to acute stress and to positive events, thriving more than others in response to beneficent experiences and supportive environments but struggling more when faced with significant adversity or a hostile environment. Whatever the explanation, when we rely on averages, we often invent a normative reaction that does not exist.

Our Research Has Real-Life Consequences

Reliance on average responses has led to the cultural assumption that most people experience considerable distress following loss and traumatic events and that everyone can benefit from professional intervention. After 9/11, for example, counselors and therapists descended on New York City to provide early interventions, particularly to emergency service workers, assuming that they were at high risk of developing PTSD. In fact, most people—even those who experience high levels of exposure to acute stress—recover without professional help.

And we now know that many early interventions are actually harmful and can impede natural processes of recovery. For example, critical incident stress debriefing was once a widely used technique immediately following a traumatic event. But it actually resulted in increased distress three years later among survivors of motor vehicle accidents who received this treatment, compared to survivors who received no treatment. Meta-analyses have confirmed these findings, and it is now considered a harmful psychological treatment.

The same principle applies to grief therapy, which has also been assumed to be helpful for anyone who suffers a loss. On the contrary, grief therapy benefits only people with persistent and elevated distress following a loss. Like early interventions for traumatic events, this treatment may even harm people with normative grief reactions.

Adopting a more nuanced understanding of life events and acute stress complicates the conventional wisdom that divorce always results in misery, interpersonal loss in long-term distress, or military deployment in high rates of post-traumatic stress disorder. Discovering anomalous reactions, such as increased happiness following divorce or long-term reductions in satisfaction following marriage, undermines the idea that we can develop one-size-fits-all social policies or therapeutic tools. The next step is to better understand why people display such different response patterns.

In the News

WHEN NUMBERS MISLEAD

New York Times, May 25, 2013

Stephanie Coontz

It's always seductive to know where one stands in relation to the average. As an overly confident college freshman, the first time I received a below-average score on an exam was a needed wake-up call. Today, I find it encouraging to read that I exercise more than the average woman my age.

Averages are useful because many traits, behaviors and outcomes are distributed in a bell-shaped curve, with most results clustered around the middle and a much smaller group of outliers at the high and low ends. Knowing the average number of births in an area can help builders decide how many bedrooms are likely to be needed in new houses, and alert policy makers to a brewing fertility crisis.

But averages can be misleading when a distribution is heavily skewed at one end, with a small number of unrepresentative outliers pulling the average in their direction. In 2011, for example, the average income of the 7,878 households in Steubenville, Ohio, was $46,341. But if just two people, Warren Buffett and Oprah Winfrey, relocated to that city, the average household income in Steubenville would rise 62 percent overnight, to $75,263 per household.

Outliers can also pull an average down, leading social scientists to overstate the risks of particular events.

Most children of divorced parents turn out to be as well adjusted as children of married parents, but the much smaller number who lead very troubled lives can lower the average outcome for the whole group, producing exaggerated estimates of the impact of divorce.

Things get even messier in cases in which people have very different responses to life events. In these cases, the "average" response often does not in any way match the "typical" experience. There may even be three or four distinct "typical" experiences. This problem is more common than many researchers have previously realized, according to a paper to be released this week by the Council on Contemporary Families, where I am the director of research and public education.

On average, people's reactions to stressful events like divorce or bereavement indicate a sharp and long-lasting decline in personal well-being, followed by a slow and gradual recovery. And on average, married individuals report themselves happier than single or divorced ones. But in this new paper, "The Trouble with Averages," psychologists Anthony Mancini and George Bonanno show that treating the average response as if it was the normal or typical outcome can lead to bad social policy and inappropriate therapeutic responses.

In the case of loss, the average is skewed by a relatively small percentage of people who exhibit substantial, persistent distress. Most people actually experience "a modest, short-lived increase in distress that subsides within a few months." When Mancini, Bonanno, and colleagues studied people's reaction to the loss of a spouse, they found that only 20 percent of the bereaved went through the "conventional" pattern of grieving—a sharp dip in well-being followed by a gradual return to previous levels of satisfaction. Almost 60 percent did not experience persistent sadness.

When we assume that "normal" people need "time to heal," or discourage individuals from making any decisions until a year or more after a loss, as some grief counselors do, we may be giving inappropriate advice. Such advice can cause people who feel ready to move on to wonder if they are hardhearted.

Almost 15 percent of the bereaved individuals that the researchers studied reported persistently low levels of life satisfaction after their loss. But because they measured people's well-being four years before as well as after the loss, the researchers were able to show that this was not caused by the bereavement. Rather, it was part of a chronic pattern of low life satisfaction that long preceded the loss.

Surprisingly, about 5 percent of the sample reported higher life satisfaction after their loss. They might have been in a stressful caregiving role or trapped in an unhappy marriage. Treating them as if they ought to be depressed could just make them feel guilty.

Does the fact that on average married people are happier mean that we should promote marriage?

The vast majority of people that Mancini, Bonanno, and colleagues studied—almost 80 percent—already reported high levels of well-being before getting married, with no significant increase afterward. More often, marriage seems to be a reward for having a high level of well-being than a route to attaining it.

A small group—5 percent—experienced increasing well-being in the years before the marriage, then sustained that afterward. But 6 percent demonstrated a sharp decrease in well-being in the years following their marriage.

Only 10 percent found that getting married cured their unhappiness. These individuals had experienced decreasing well-being in the years before their marriage but became happier afterward.

The beneficial effect of marriage for this small group supports an earlier study by the sociologists Adrianne Frech and Kristi Williams showing that the average association of marriage with improved mental health is largely driven by the comparatively small number of individuals who are seriously depressed before getting married.

When the sociologists Sheela Kennedy and Frank Furstenberg studied marriage and divorce, they found that for people who had been in the highest-quality marriages, divorce produced very large and persistent decreases in overall happiness. But for people who had been in the lowest-quality marriages, divorce was associated with an increase in happiness. And the majority of divorced people were resilient. They did not experience large declines in happiness, and their depression levels did not differ significantly from those of people who remained in marriages of a similar quality.

Most people would agree that single motherhood is stressful. Yet consider the startling finding by Kristi Williams, Sharon Sassler and their coauthors that young, single, black and Hispanic mothers who married after their child's birth had worse midlife health than those who hadn't married by the age of 40.

I am not advocating that we give up on averages. Used cautiously, they help to analyze patterns and formulate policies. But given the variety of circumstances that exist in the messy real world, we ought to think twice before doling out one-size-fits-all advice to individuals on the basis of averages. ▰

PART TWO

How We
Got Here

5

The Evolution of American Families

Stephanie Coontz

What is a family? An Internet search of dictionaries yielded the following definitions: "parents and children, whether living together or not"; "any group of persons closely related by blood"; "a group of persons who form a household under one head"; and "the basic unit of society consisting of two or more adults joined by marriage and cooperating in the care and rearing of their children." But of course these definitions refer to very different residential and relational arrangements, and through most of history, few people would have accepted the idea that more than one of these definitions could count as a family.[1]

From the early Middle Ages to the eighteenth century, the European nobility generally used the term *family* not to refer to married parents and their children but rather to the larger kinship group from which they derived their claims to privilege and property. By contrast, most middle-class Europeans and North Americans defined family on the basis of common residence under the authority of a household head rather than on blood relatedness, a definition that included boarders or servants as family members. Samuel Pepys began his famous seventeenth-century English diary with the words: "I lived in Axe Yard, having my wife, and servant Jane, and no more in family than us three." In 1820, the publisher Everard Peck and his wife, childless newlyweds, established a new household in Rochester, New York, and wrote home: "We collected our family together which consists of seven persons and we think ourselves pleasantly situated."

Not until the mid-nineteenth century did the word *family* commonly come to refer just to a married couple with their co-resident children, excluding household residents or more distant kin. This more limited definition spread widely during the 1800s, and by the end of that century, the restriction of the word to the immediate, co-residential family was so prevalent that the adjective *extended* had to be added when people referred to kin beyond the household.

In some societies, even the simple biological definition of family can get complicated. When a woman of the Toda people of southern India gets married, she marries all her husband's brothers, even those not yet born. Each child she bears is assigned an individual father, but the assignment is based on social rather than biological criteria. Among some African and Native American groups, a woman could traditionally become a "female husband" by taking a wife. The children the wife brought to the marriage or bore by various lovers were considered part of the family of the female husband, who was entitled to their labor and loyalty and from whom they derived their status and roles.

In kinship societies that trace descent exclusively through the maternal or paternal line, rather than through both parents, children are considered part of the family of only one spouse, and spouses themselves often do not count as family. In ancient China, it was said that "you have only one family, but you can always get another wife." In the late seventeenth century, some European writers also used the word *family* to refer exclusively to a man's offspring rather than his spouse, as in the phrase "his family and wife."

In some societies, a child's biological relation to a parent is only recognized when the parents are in a socially sanctioned marriage. The Lakher of Southeast Asia view a child as linked to his or her mother solely through the mother's relationship to the father. If the parents divorce, the mother is no longer considered to have any relationship to her children. She could, theoretically, even marry her son, since the group's incest taboos would not be considered applicable.

Through much of European history, a child born outside an approved marriage was a *filius nulius*—literally a child of no one, with a claim on no one. Not until 1968 did the United States Supreme Court rule that children born out of wedlock had the right to collect debts owed to their parents, sue for the wrongful death of a parent, and inherit family holdings.

By contrast, the indigenous societies of northeastern North America seldom distinguished between "legitimate" and "illegitimate" children. When a Jesuit missionary told a Montagnais-Naskapi Indian living in what is now Canada that he should keep tighter control over his wife in order to ensure that the children she bore were "his," the man replied: "You French people love only your own children; but we love all the children of our tribe."

In one society, the Mosuo or Na of China, family arrangements do not include marriage at all. In this society, brothers and sisters form the central family unit. Brothers and sisters do not have sex together—indeed, the incest taboo is so strong that it even prohibits siblings from having intense emotional discussions. But the children that the women bear by lovers who usually only visit them at night are raised by the sibling group, not the biological parents.

The eminent anthropologist J. P. Murdock once defined the family as a social unit that shares common residence, economic cooperation, and reproduction. But among the Yoruba of Africa, the family is not a unit of production or consumption, as husbands and wives do not even share a common budget. Men of the Gururumba people of New Guinea sleep in separate houses and work separate plots of land from their wives. In the southern colonies of early America, the families of indentured servants were broken up, with husbands, wives, and even very young children living in different households for many years at a time.

Prohibitions against incest among family members are nearly universal. But the definition of what family relations are close enough to constitute incest varies considerably. In traditional Islamic societies, marriage between the children of two sisters is considered a form of incest. So is marriage between two people who shared the same milk as infants, even if it was from a wet nurse not related to either of them. Marriage between the children of two brothers, however, is a favored pattern. Among the aristocracy in ancient Egypt, brother-sister marriages, especially between half-brothers and sisters, were common. The medieval church in Europe, by contrast, prohibited marriage between cousins up to seven degrees removed.

The historical and cross-cultural diversity of family life extends also to the emotional meanings attached to families and the psychological dynamics within them. For example, what is now considered healthy parent-child bonding in our society (see Coleman in Chapter 24 of this volume) may be viewed as selfishness, narcissism, or pathological isolation by cultures that stress child exchange and fostering as ways of cementing social ties. In Polynesia, eastern Oceania, the Caribbean, and the West Indies (and also in sixteenth-century Europe and colonial America) offering your child to friends, neighbors, or other kin for adoption or prolonged co-residence was not considered abandonment but was rather a mark of parental responsibility, ensuring that the child developed access to support systems and social knowledge beyond what the immediate family could provide.

Modern Americans often focus on the need for strong mother-daughter and father-son identification. But in matrilineal societies, where descent is traced through the female line, a man usually has much closer ties with his nephews than with his sons. Among the Trobriand Islanders, where a child's biological father is considered merely a "relation by marriage," the strongest legal and emotional bonds are between children and their maternal uncle. Among the patrilineal Cheyenne, by contrast, at least after the rise of the fur trade with Europeans made women's traditional work of tanning hides more onerous, mother-daughter relations were expected to be tense or even hostile, and girls tended to establish their closest relationships with paternal aunts.

These examples show that there is no universal definition of family that fits the reality of all cultural groups and historical periods. Yet almost all societies use the term to endow certain sexual relations and biological connections (or fictive biological connections) with special privileges and obligations. Within the same society, groups with different positions in the rank or class structure may have to organize their reproduction, caregiving, and interpersonal obligations in distinctive ways, and therefore several different family arrangements may coexist in the same culture. But the family that is codified as "normal" in law and ideology tends to represent the interests and ideals of the dominant members of society. Often, however, that ideal family coexists with, or even depends upon, a very different set of family arrangements among members of less powerful social groups.

FAMILY SYSTEMS OF EARLY AMERICA

In sixteenth- and seventeenth-century America, three very different systems of social and personal reproduction were practiced respectively by Native American kinship societies, the conquering Europeans, and the Africans brought as captives by the Europeans. At the time of European exploration of the New World, North American native societies used family ties to organize nearly all the political, military, and economic transactions that in Europe were becoming regulated by the state. Kinship rules and marital alliances regulated an individual's place in the overall social network, establishing who owed what to whom in terms of producing and sharing resources and conducting interpersonal relationships.[2]

When society is organized through a state system, sharp distinctions are made between family duties and civil duties, domestic functions and political ones. But prior to sustained contact with Europeans, North American indigenous peoples had few institutions organized on any basis other than kinship. Some groups, such as the Cherokee, had a special governing body for times of war (and the influence of such groups grew once Native Americans engaged in regular conflicts with settlers), but most of the time village elders, representing different kin groups, made decisions. The indigenous peoples of North America, unlike some groups in South America, had no institutionalized courts, police, army, or agencies to tax or coerce labor. Kin obligations organized not just the production and distribution of goods but also the negotiation of conflicts and the administration of justice. Murder, for example, was an offense not against the state but against the kin group, and it was therefore the responsibility and right of kin to punish the perpetrator.

The nuclear family did not own productive property, such as land or animals, and could not, therefore, sell such resources or lose them to debt. Subsistence tools and their products were made and owned by individuals rather than families. Hunting and gathering grounds and other resources were either available to all or were controlled by the larger kin group, and even there, property rights were not absolute. Indians had no concept that land could be permanently sold and access to it monopolized, although they gladly accepted gifts in exchange for the right to use land. This led to many misunderstandings and much hostility between settlers and natives, who were astonished when Europeans they had allowed to settle somewhere then fenced off traditional hunting grounds.

The nuclear family's lack of private property meant that Indian families had less economic autonomy than European households vis-à-vis other families. On the other hand, the lack of a state gave Indian families more political autonomy, because people were not bound to follow a leader for any longer than they cared to do so.

The European families that came to North America were products of a developing market economy and international mercantile system. The way they organized production, exchange, land ownership, and social control put Europeans on a collision course with Indian patterns of existence. Europeans also operated within the framework of a centralized state apparatus whose claims to political authority and whose notion of territorial boundaries and national interests had no counterpart among Native Americans.[3] Colonial families had far more extensive property and inheritance rights than Indian families, but they were also subject to stringent controls by state and church institutions. Wealthy colonial families had much more limited obligations to share surpluses than Native Americans, so right from the beginning there were substantial differences in wealth and resources among colonial families and among the indigenous peoples.[4]

Yet we cannot understand colonial families if we project back onto them modern notions of individualism and nuclear family self-sufficiency. Colonial society was based on a system of agrarian household production, sustained by a patriarchal political and ideological structure that greatly constrained the individual freedom of action of individual households. The property-owning nuclear family was the basis of the social hierarchy, but poor people tended to be brought into propertied households as apprentices, servants, or temporary lodgers. Colonial authorities tried to ensure that everyone was a member of a family. The man or woman outside a family hierarchy was a threat to the social order. A household head exerted authority over all household members, and little distinction was made between a biological child and an unrelated household member of about the same age.

The colonists' insistence that people be members of families and accept the authority of the household head might suggest that the family was the most important institution of colonial society. Yet we need to distinguish between the importance of families as an institution in colonial life and the importance of the individual family. The biological family was less sacrosanct, and less sentimentalized, than it would become in the nineteenth century. Colonial society demanded membership in a *properly ordered* family and subordinated actual blood or marital family ties to that end.

The lower classes often lived, either together or separately, in the households of their employers. A child might be removed from his or her biological family and placed in another family if his or her parents were deemed unworthy by authorities. Many families voluntarily sent their children to live in another household at a relatively young age to work as a servant or apprentice or simply to develop wider social connections. At home, the nuclear family did not retreat into an oasis of privacy. Parents and children ate—and often slept in the same room—with other household members, whether they were related or not.

Marriage, too, was much less sentimentalized than it became in the nineteenth century. Men often married because they needed someone to help them on the farm or in their business, or because a woman came with a handsome dowry. Women married for similar economic and social reasons. It was hoped that love would develop (in moderation) after marriage, but prior to the late eighteenth century, love was not supposed to be the primary motive for marriage, and children were expected to be guided by their parents' wishes in their matches.

Contact with the European colonists was devastating to the Native American family system. Having no domestic animals such as pigs, chickens, or cattle, the Indians had no acquired immunities to the diseases associated with such animals. Massive epidemics sometimes killed more than half a group's members, decimating kin networks and tearing apart the social fabric of life. Many Indian groups were either exterminated or driven onto marginal land that did not support traditional methods of social organization and subsistence. Even where native societies successfully defended themselves, armed conflict with the settlers elevated the role of young males at the expense of elders and women. Traders, colonial political officials, and Christian missionaries deliberately undermined the authority of extended kinship and community groups.

But Indian collective traditions were surprisingly resilient, and European Americans spent the entire nineteenth century trying to extinguish them. They passed laws requiring Indians to hold property as individuals or nuclear families rather than as larger kinship groups. They tried to impose European gender roles on the organization of work and social life. And Indian children were often forced into boarding schools where teachers tried to wipe out all the cultural traditions the children had learned from their elders.

The Africans who were captured and taken to the New World to serve the white settlers also came from kinship-based societies, although some of those societies had more complex political institutions and larger status differences than were found among the indigenous people of North America. The family arrangements of African slaves and their descendants varied depending on whether they lived in great cotton or tobacco plantations utilizing gang labor, small backwoods farms where one or two slaves lived and worked under a master's close supervision, colonial villages where there were just a few personal slaves or servants, or the free black settlements that gradually emerged in some areas. But in all these settings, Africans had to deal with their involuntary relocation to America, the loss of their languages, the brutality of slavery, and the gradual hardening of racial attitudes over the first two centuries of colonization.[5]

Gender imbalance on large plantations and small farms meant that many slaves remained single, and married couples often could not reside together. Slave families were constantly broken up by routine sales; as punishment for misbehavior; and when owners died, paid off debts, or reallocated their labor force between often far-flung properties. So slave families were not usually nuclear, nor were slave households organized around long-term monogamous married couples. Within the constraints of the slave trade and the plantation system, slaves adapted African cultural traditions to their new realities, using child-centered rather than marriage-centered family systems, adoptive and fictive kin ties, ritual co-parenting or godparenting, and complex naming patterns designed to maintain or recreate extended kin.

Slave families were shaped by the strategies they had to develop to accommodate as well as to resist their masters' world. But slave-owning families were also changed by the experience of slavery. Anxieties about racial/sexual hierarchies created high levels of sexual hypocrisy among Southern planters. Fears that blacks and poor whites might make common cause fostered pervasive patterns of violence against other whites as well as against slaves. And attempts to legitimize the "honor" of slave society in the face of growing Northern antislavery sentiment led to elaborate displays of patriarchy and deference, both in family life and in the community at large.

THE RISE OF THE DOMESTIC FAMILY IDEAL

During the second half of the eighteenth century, especially in the northern colonies, economic, political, and religious forces began to undermine the patriarchal and hierarchical social order that had prevailed in the seventeenth century.

The power of elders to dictate to the young, and of elites to control the daily life of the lower classes, weakened. But economic dependence and social inequality increased as many farmers fell into debt and lost their farms while some merchants and manufacturers became very wealthy.

From about the 1820s, the spread of a market economy led to the gradual separation of home and work, market production and household production.[6] This created new tensions between family activities and "economic" activities. Households could no longer get by as they had traditionally, mostly consuming things they made, grew, or bartered in the community. Diaries of the day increasingly complain about the need to earn cash. But in the era before cheap mass production, families could not yet rely on ready-made purchased goods even when they could raise a cash income. Even in middle-class homes, an immense amount of labor was required to make purchased goods usable. Families no longer had to spin their own cotton and grind their own grain, but someone still had to sew factory-produced cloth into clothes and painstakingly sift store-bought flour to rid it of impurities.

Many families responded by reorganizing their division of labor by age and gender. Men (and children, too, in working-class families) began to specialize in paid work outside the home. Unmarried women also started to work outside the home to bring in cash by doing women's traditional work in factories or as household help, or filling the multiplying jobs in teaching. (Among the impoverished lower classes in the growing cities, some women also turned to prostitution.)

But wives, who had once played a vital role in producing for the household and marketing their surpluses, and who had often delegated housework and child care to servants or older children, now began to devote the bulk of their attention to housework, sewing, and child rearing. Once referred to as yoke-mates and meet-helps, wives increasingly were seen as being responsible for the family comfort rather than co-producers of the family's subsistence.

As a market economy supplanted self-sufficient farms and household businesses, middle-class sons were less likely to inherit the family farm or assume their father's occupation. So parents had to prepare their male children for new kinds of employment in the wage economy, and their daughters for a new form of domestic life. The middle classes began to keep their children at home longer and concentrate their resources on fewer children, often subsidizing their children's schooling or work training rather than utilizing their labor to augment family finances. While in the past, children had started work in the family farm or business at an early age, or had been sent out to work in other people's homes, they were now seen as little innocents who needed to be protected within the family circle. A new middle-class ideal of parenting placed mothers at the emotional center of family life and gave them the task of inculcating in their children ideals of sexual restraint, temperance, family solidarity, conservative business habits, diligence, prolonged education, and delayed marriage. This became the new "norm" for family life as popularized in the advice books and novels that proliferated in the early nineteenth century.

Yet middle-class white mothers were able to focus on child rearing and "ladylike" domestic tasks only because they could rely on a pool of individuals who had no option but to engage in paid labor outside their own homes. The extension of childhood for the middle class required the foreshortening of childhood and the denial of private family life for the slaves who provided cotton to the new textile mills, the working-class women and children who worked long hours in factories or tenement workshops to produce store-bought cloth, and the immigrant or African American mothers and daughters who left their own homes to clean and do the laundry for their middle-class mistresses.[7] (We see a similar pattern today; many egalitarian dual-earner families depend on the low-paid housework and child-care services of women who do what used to be the middle-class wife's domestic tasks but whose wages offer them no opportunity to achieve the economic and personal independence that the middle-class woman gains from her paid labor.)

For all the sexual prudery of nineteenth-century middle-class families, their urgent need for fertility restriction so that resources could be concentrated on fewer children led to interesting contradictions. By the time of the Civil War, the typical client of an abortionist in mid-nineteenth-century America was not a desperate unwed woman, but a respectable middle-class wife. By the end of the nineteenth century, there was a backlash in the form of laws criminalizing abortion and prohibiting the dissemination of contraceptive information or devices, but also a growing movement to defy those laws and extend women's access to birth control.[8]

As Americans adapted family life to the demands of an industrializing society during the nineteenth century, American families took on many of the characteristics associated with "the modern family." They became smaller, with fewer children. They focused more tightly around the nuclear core, putting greater distance between blood relatives and servants or boarders. Parents became more emotionally involved in child rearing and for a longer period. Marriage came to be seen as primarily about love, although the law continued to support men's legal and economic authority in the home. The distinction between home and work, both physically and conceptually, sharpened.

Average trends, however, obscure tremendous differences among and within the rapidly changing ethnic groups and classes of the industrializing United States. New professions opened up for middle-class and skilled workers, and during the Gilded Age, some entrepreneurs made vast fortunes, but job insecurity became more pronounced for laborers. More than 10 million immigrants arrived from Europe between 1830 and 1882, and each wave successively filled the lowest rungs of the industrial job ladder. Their distinctive cultural and class traditions interacted with the ways they developed to cope with the particular occupations they entered, and the housing conditions and social prejudices they met, to create new variations in family life and gender relations.

After the Civil War, African Americans who moved North found it hard to get a foothold on those rungs at all, and they were relegated to unskilled laboring jobs and segregated sections of the city, compelling new family adaptations. In the South, African American families eked out a tenuous living as sharecroppers, domestics, or agricultural wage workers. After the end of Radical Reconstruction, they also had to cope with an upsurge of mob violence and the passage of Jim Crow laws designed to restore white supremacy.

The result was that at the same time as the new ideal of the domestic middle-class family became enshrined in the dominant culture, diversity in family life actually increased. Middle-class children were now exempted from the farmwork or household tasks that all children traditionally had done. But working-class youth streamed out of the home into mines and mills, where they faced a much longer and more dangerous workday than in the past. Class differences in family arrangements, home furnishings, consumption patterns, and household organization *widened* in the second half of the nineteenth century.

There was also much more variation in the life course of individuals than would be seen through most of the twentieth century. There were greater differences among young people in the nineteenth century in the age at which they left school and home, married and set up households than among their counterparts in the first seventy years of the twentieth century. There was also more mixing of age groups than we see today, with less segregation of youth into specialized grades at school.

Although there has been a long-term trend toward restriction of household membership to the nuclear family, this was slowed down between 1870 and 1890 as some groups saw an increase in temporary co-residence with other kin, while others took in boarders or lodgers. On average, birthrates fell by nearly 40 percent between 1855 and 1915, but the fertility of some unskilled and semiskilled workers actually *rose* during this period.

The changes that helped produce more "modern" family forms, then, started at different times in different classes, meant different things to families occupying different positions in the industrial order, and did not proceed in a straight line. Family "modernization" was not the result of some general, steady evolution of "the" family, as early family sociologists suggested, but was the outcome of *diverging* and *contradictory* responses that occurred in different areas and classes at various times.

Michael Katz, Michael Doucet, and Mark Stern list five major changes in family organization that accompanied industrialization: (1) the separation of home and work, (2) the reduction of household membership to its nuclear core, (3) the fall in marital fertility, (4) the more extended residence of children in their parents' home, and (5) the lengthened time that husbands and wives lived together after their children left home. "The first two began among the working class and among the wage-earning segment of the business class (clerks and kindred workers). The third started among the business class, particularly among its least affluent, most specialized, and most mobile sectors. The fourth began at about the same time in both the working and business class, though the children of the former usually went to work and the latter to school."[9]

The fifth change—the longer period that husband and wives live together after the children are gone—did not occur until the twentieth century, and represented a reversal of nineteenth-century trends. So did a sixth major change that created more convergence among families over the course of the twentieth century: the reintegration of women into productive work, especially the entry of mothers into paid work outside the home.

The Regulation of Marriage

Another change in family life that did not proceed in a linear way involved the state's regulation of marriage. From the time of the American Revolution until after the Civil War, American authorities did not inquire too closely as to whether a couple had taken out a valid license. If a couple acted as if they were married, they were treated as such. Until the 1860s, state Supreme Courts routinely ruled that cohabitation, especially if accompanied by a couple's acceptance in their local community, was sufficient evidence of a valid marriage. In consequence, informal marriage and self-divorce were quite common in this era, and interracial marriage was more frequent in the first three-quarters of the nineteenth century compared to the 1880s to the 1930s, when the government began to exert stricter control over who could marry and who could not.[10]

The United States began to invalidate common-law and informal marriages in the late nineteenth century as part of a broader attempt to exert more government control over private behavior. By the 1920s, thirty-eight states had laws prohibiting whites from marrying blacks, mulattoes, Japanese, Chinese, Indians, Mongolians, Malays, or Filipinos. Twelve states forbade marriage to a "drunk" or a "mental defective."[11]

After the 1920s, however, this restrictive trend began to be reversed, and the right to marry was gradually extended to almost all heterosexuals over a certain age. In the civil rights era of the 1960s, this was to culminate in Supreme Court rulings that invalidated laws against interracial marriage and overturned the right of prison officials or employers to prohibit inmates or workers from marrying.

THE FAMILY CONSUMER ECONOMY

Around the beginning of the twentieth century, a national system of mass production and mass communication replaced the decentralized production of goods and culture that had prevailed until the 1890s. Some huge new trends—the standardization of economic production, the development of schooling into the teenage years, the abolition of child labor, the spread of a national radio and film industry (and later television), and the growth of a consumer economy—created new similarities and new differences in people's experience of family life.

By the 1920s, for the first time, a slight majority of children came to live in families where the father was the breadwinner, the mother did not have paid employment outside the home, and the children were in school rather than at work. Numerous immigrant families, however, continued to pull their children out of school to go to work. African American families kept their children in school longer than almost all immigrant groups, but their wives were much more likely than either native-born or immigrant women to work outside the home.

The early twentieth century saw a breakdown of the nineteenth-century system of sexual segregation. Single women entered new occupations and exercised new social freedoms. Women finally won the right to vote. An autonomous and increasingly sexualized youth culture emerged, as youth from many different class backgrounds interacted in high schools and middle-class youth adopted the new institution of "dating" pioneered by working-class youth and a newly visible African American urban culture. Dating replaced the nineteenth-century middle-class courting system of "calling," where the girl and her family invited a young man to call and the couple socialized on the porch or in the living room under the watchful eyes of parents. By contrast, dating took place away from home, and since the male typically paid for a date, the initiative shifted to him. Young people—especially girls—gained more independence from parental oversight, but girls also incurred more responsibility for preventing their dates from going "too far."[12]

There was a profound change at this time in the dominant ideological portrayal of family life. In the nineteenth century, ties to siblings, parents, and close same-sex friends had been as emotionally intense as the ties between spouses.

Women often called their husbands "Mr. so-and-so," but wrote passionately in their diaries about their pet names and physically affectionate interactions with female friends. Men and women alike had waxed as sentimental about their love for siblings and parents as they did for their intended marital partner.

Now, however, the center of emotional life shifted to the husband-wife bond and to the immediate nuclear family. Young adults were encouraged to cut "the silver cord" that bound them to their mother. The same-sex "crushes" that had been viewed indulgently in the late nineteenth century came to be seen as threats to the primacy of heterosexual love ties.

The growing emphasis on companionship and mutual sexual satisfaction in marriage brought new intimacy to married life. But it also encouraged premarital sexual experimentation. For the first time, a majority of the boys who had sex before marriage did so with girls they had dated rather than with prostitutes. And it is not surprising that the higher standards for marriage also created an unwillingness to settle for what used to be considered adequate relationships. "Great expectations," as historian Elaine Tyler May points out, could also generate great disappointments.[13] The divorce rate more than tripled in the 1920s.

All these changes created a sense of panic about "the future of the family" that was every bit as intense as the family values debates of the 1980s and 1990s. Commentators in the 1920s hearkened back to the "good old days," bemoaning the sexual revolution, the fragility of nuclear family ties, women's "selfish" use of contraception, decline of respect for elders, the loss of extended kin ties, and the threat of the "Emancipated Woman." "Is Marriage on the Skids?" asked one magazine article of the day. Another asked despairingly, "What Is the Family Still Good For?"

The challenges of the Great Depression and World War II in the 1930s and 1940s put these concerns on the back burner. But disturbing family changes continued. During the Depression, divorce rates fell, but so did marriage rates. Desertion and domestic violence rose sharply. Economic stress often led to punitive parenting that left children with scars still visible to researchers decades later. Birthrates plummeted. Many wives had to go to work to make ends meet, but disapproval of working wives increased, with many observers complaining that they were stealing jobs from unemployed men.

World War II stimulated a marriage boom, as couples rushed to wed before the men shipped off to war. Wives who worked in the war industries while the men were away garnered social approval—as long as they were willing to quit their jobs when the men came home. But by the end of the war, most women workers in the war industry were telling pollsters they did not want to quit their jobs. Rates of unwed motherhood soared during the war, and by 1947 one in every three marriages was ending in divorce.

So as the war ended, the fears about family life that had troubled observers during the Roaring Twenties reemerged. But several factors soon combined to assuage those fears. Couples who had postponed having children because of the war now rushed to have them. The enormous deferred consumption of the war years, as well as the sense that people's family lives had been put on hold, led to a huge demand for new houses and other consumer goods. This was reinforced by a concerted campaign by businesses, advertisers, therapists, the new profession of marriage counselors, and the mass media to convince people that they could find happiness through nuclear-family consumerism.

There was a renewed emphasis on female domesticity in the postwar years. Women were told that they could help the veterans readjust to civilian life by giving up the independent decision making they had engaged in while the men were gone. They were urged to forgo the challenges of the work world and seek fulfillment in domestic chores. Politicians rewrote the tax code to favor male breadwinner families over dual-earner families, explicitly to discourage wives from working. Psychiatrists—who had largely replaced ministers as the source of advice for families—claimed that any woman who desired anything other than marriage, motherhood, and domesticity was deeply neurotic.[14]

The home-centered life was supported by an unprecedented postwar economic boom. Family wage jobs became more plentiful for blue-collar workers, especially when the Eisenhower administration embarked on a massive highway-building project. And the government handed out unprecedented subsidies for family formation, home ownership, and higher education. Forty percent of the young men starting families at the end of World War II were eligible for veterans' benefits, which were much more generous than they are today. The government encouraged banks to accept lower down payments and offer longer payment terms to young men, and veterans could sometimes put down just one dollar to sign a mortgage on a new home. The National Defense Education Act subsidized individuals who majored in fields such as engineering that were considered vital to national security.

Such government subsidies, combined with high rates of unionization, rapid economic expansion, and an explosion of housing construction and financing options, gave young families a tremendous economic jump start, created predictable paths out of poverty, and led to unprecedented increases in real wages. White male workers had a degree of job security that is increasingly elusive in the modern economy. Between 1947 and 1973, real wages rose, on average, by 81 percent, and the gap between the rich and poor declined significantly. The income of the bottom 80 percent of the population grew faster than the income of the richest 1 percent, with the most rapid gains of all made by the poorest 20 percent of the population.

The result was a boom in family life, so that by the early 1950s it appeared that the threat of women's emancipation and family instability had been turned back. For the first time in sixty years, the age of marriage and parenthood fell, the proportion of marriages ending in divorce dropped, and the birthrate soared. The percentage of women remaining single reached a hundred-year low. The proportion of children who were raised by a breadwinner father and a homemaker mother and who stayed in school until graduation from high school reached an all-time high. Although more women attended college than before the war, they graduated at much lower rates than men, and more and more opted to get an MRS degree rather than a BA degree. And the powerful new medium of television broadcast nightly pictures of suburban families where homemaker moms had dinner on the table every night and raised healthy children who never talked back or got into any trouble that couldn't be solved by a fatherly lecture.

We now know, of course, that the experience of many families with problems such as battering, alcoholism, and incest was swept under the rug in the 1950s. So was the rampant discrimination against African Americans and Hispanics, women, elders, gay men, lesbians, political dissidents, religious minorities, and the handicapped. Despite rising real wages, 30 percent of American children lived in poverty during the fifties—a higher figure than today. African American married-couple families had a poverty rate of nearly 50 percent. Institutionalized racism was the law in the South, and in the North there was daily violence in the cities against African Americans who attempted to move into white neighborhoods or use public parks and swim areas.

Meanwhile, underneath the surface stability of the era, the temporary triumph of nuclear-family domesticity was already being eroded. The expansion of the service and retail sections of the economy required new workers, and employers were especially eager to hire women, who were seen as less likely to join unions and were thought to be easier to move in and out of the labor market than men. But because the average age of marriage had fallen to about twenty years old, there were not enough single women to fill the demand for workers, so employers began to make changes in hiring practices to recruit married women.

Despite the dominance of full-time homemakers on TV sitcoms, the employment of women soared in the 1950s, quickly topping its wartime peak. And the fastest-growing segment of this female labor force was married women with school-age children. Indeed, economists later found that the labor force participation of wives played a central role in the spread of upward mobility and the reduction of poverty during the 1950s, and it paved the way for new work aspirations among the daughters of these women.

At the dawn of the 1960s, a national poll of American housewives found that although most declared that they were happier in their marriages than their own parents were, 90 percent of them also said that they did not want their daughters to follow in their footsteps. Instead, they hoped their daughters would postpone marriage longer and get more education and work experience.[15]

As early as 1957, the divorce rate had started to climb once more. And during the 1960s, the age of marriage also began to rise, especially as more women postponed marriage for education. As the "baby boom generation" grew up, there was a huge increase in the percentage of singles in the population, accelerating the acceptance of premarital sex that had begun to spread as early as the 1920s. The women's liberation movement helped expose the complex varieties of family experience that lay beneath the Ozzie and Harriet images of the time.[16] By the end of the 1960s, family diversity had begun to accelerate and had become more visible.

For the most part, middle-class wives and mothers entered the labor force in the 1950s and 1960s in response to new opportunities, but as the prolonged postwar expansion of real wages and social benefits came to an end in the 1970s, ever more wives and mothers of all social classes and racial-ethnic groups soon found that paid work had become a matter of economic necessity. By 1973, real wages were falling, especially for young families. Housing inflation made it less possible for a single breadwinner to afford a home. By the late 1970s, cuts in government services had gutted the antipoverty programs that in 1970 had brought child poverty to an all-time low (a low not equaled since). Still, despite these threats to families, the success of the women's movement in combating hiring and pay discrimination gave many women more economic independence than they had previously enjoyed.

The combination of expanding social freedoms for women and youth and contracting economic opportunities for blue-collar men made the 1970s and 1980s a time of turmoil. Real wages fell for workers without a college degree, and economic inequality increased, making it harder to form and maintain families. Old marital norms came into conflict with new family work patterns, leading to tensions between husbands and wives over housework. From a different angle, new social freedoms encouraged more people to feel free to leave a marriage they deemed unsatisfactory. Divorce rates reached an all-time high in 1979–1980, and it was women who initiated most divorces. As courts began to protect the rights of children born out of wedlock, fewer women felt compelled to enter a shotgun marriage if they became pregnant.[17]

Women's workforce participation continued to mount. In 1950, only a quarter of all wives were in the paid labor force, and just 16 percent of all children had mothers who worked outside the home. By 1991, nearly two-thirds of all married women with children were in the labor force. Fifty-nine percent of children, including a majority of preschoolers, had mothers who worked outside the home.

Meanwhile, new waves of immigrants began to arrive, the majority now coming from Asia, Latin America, and the Caribbean, rather than from Europe, as had been true in the early twentieth century when the United States had experienced its previous high point of immigration. By the 1990s, racial and ethnic diversity had reached historic highs, creating a new acceptance of family diversity and intermarriage but also fanning new racial and ethnic tensions, especially as growing socioeconomic inequality threatened the American assumption that each generation would live better than its parents.[18]

In the past fifteen years, some of the trends that undermined family stability in the late twentieth century have leveled off or decreased. Divorce rates have come down since their peak in 1979–1980, especially for college-educated couples. When divorce does occur, fewer couples engage in prolonged, bitter battles, and fewer men lose contact with their children. Teen birthrates have dropped sharply. Although the entry of women into the workforce in the 1970s initially resulted in a small decline in the amount of time that mothers spent with their children, the continued expansion of time that women spend in paid labor has since been accompanied by an increase in time with children. Mothers in both two-earner and one-earner families now spend more time with their children than they did in 1960, and fathers have also dramatically increased their time with their children.[19]

But family diversification continues apace. There has been a dramatic increase in the number of couples who live together outside marriage. Gay and lesbian couples are permanently out of the closet and seek the same legal rights as heterosexual couples. While teen births have gone down, more unwed women in their twenties and thirties are having children. And, as described in other articles in this volume, family arrangements and values continue to differ by social class, religion, race, and ethnicity.

The lessons from history are both positive and negative. American families have always been in flux, and many different family arrangements and values have worked for various groups at different times. We should not assume that recent changes in family forms and practices are inevitably destructive (see Rutter in Chapter 21 of this volume). But it is also true that families have always been fragile, vulnerable to economic stress, and needful of practical and emotional support from beyond the nuclear family. And new opportunities for individuals and families to succeed have also brought new ways for them to fail.

Still, it would be a terrible mistake to delude people into believing that if we could only restore the family values and forms of the past we would not have to confront the sweeping changes America is experiencing in gender and age relations, racial and ethnic patterns, the distribution of jobs and income, and even our experience of time and space. There are many historical precedents of families and communities successfully reorganizing themselves in response to social change. But these examples should inspire us to construct *new* family values and social-support institutions rather than trying to recreate some (largely mythical) "traditional" family of the past.

NOTES

1. For the following section of this article, see Stephanie Coontz, *The Social Origins of Private Life: A History of American Families, 1600–1900* (New York: W. W. Norton, 1988); Barrie Thorne and Marilyn Yalom, *Rethinking the Family: Some Feminist Questions* (Boston: Northeastern University Press, 1992); Stephanie Coontz, *Marriage, A History: How Love Conquered Marriage* (New York: Penguin Books, 2006); K. Ishwaran, *Family and Marriage: Cross-Cultural Perspectives* (Toronto: Thompson Educational Publishing, 1992); Bron B. Ingoldsby and Suzanna D. Smith, *Families in Global and Multicultural Perspective*, 2nd ed. (Thousand Oaks, CA: Sage Publications, 2006); Cai Hua, *A Society Without Fathers or Husbands: The Na of China* (Cambridge, MA: MIT Press, 2001).

2. On Native American families, see Coontz, *The Social Origins of Private Life* (1988); Ward Stavig, "'Living in Offense of Our Lord': Indigenous Sexual Values and Marital Life in the Colonial Crucible," *Hispanic American Historical Review* 75 (1995): 597–622; Cynthia Kennedy, *Braided Relations, Entwined Lives: The Women of Charleston's Urban Slave Society* (Bloomington: Indiana University Press, 2005); Susan Lobo, *Native American Voices: A Reader* (New York: Longman, 1998); David Wallace Adams, *Education for Extinction: American Indians and the Boarding School Experience, 1875–1928* (Lawrence: University Press of Kansas, 1988); Virginia Bergman Peters, *Women of the Earth Lodges: Tribal Life on the Plains* (New Haven, CT: Archon Books, 1995).

3. On European family history, see Coontz, *Marriage, A History* (2006); Beatrice Gottlieb, *The Family in the Western World from the Black Death to the Industrial Age* (New York: Oxford University Press, 1993); Andre Burguiere et al., *A History of the Family* (Cambridge, MA: Belknap Press, 1996); Wally Seccombe, *A Millennium of Family Change* (London: Verso, 1992); Rosemary O'Day, *The Family and Family Relationships, 1500–1900* (London: Palgrave Macmillan, 1994).

4. On colonial families, see Coontz, *The Social Origins of Private Life* (1988); Steven Mintz and Susan Kellogg, *Domestic Revolutions: A Social History of American Family Life* (New York: Free Press, 1988).

5. On African American families in slavery and freedom, see Brenda E. Stevenson, *Life in Black and White: Family and Community in the Slave South* (New York: Oxford University Press, 1996); Leith Mullings, *On Our Own Terms: Race, Class, and Gender in the Lives of African-American Women* (New York: Routledge, 1997); Stephanie McCurry, *Masters of Small Worlds: Yeoman Households, Gender Relations, and the Political Culture of the Antebellum South Carolina Low Country* (Athens: University of Georgia Press, 1995); Jennifer Ritterhouse, *Growing Up Jim Crow: How Black and White Southern Children Learned Race* (Chapel Hill: University of North Carolina Press, 2006); David

Barry Gaspar and Darlene Clark Hine, *More Than Chattel: Black Women and Slavery in the Americas* (Bloomington: Indiana University Press, 1996); Tia Miles, *Ties That Bind: The Story of an Afro-Cherokee Family in Slavery and Freedom* (Berkeley: University of California Press, 2005); Harriette Pipes McAdoo, *Black Families*, 4th ed. (Thousand Oaks, CA: Sage Publications, 2007).

6. On the mutual interaction and transformation of the economy and of family life in both the middle and working classes, see Coontz, *The Social Origins of Private Life* (1988); Mary P. Ryan, *Cradle of the Middle Class: The Family in Oneida County, New York, 1790–1865* (New York: Cambridge University Press, 1983); Jeanne Boydston, *Home and Work: Housework, Wages, and the Ideology of Labor in the Early Republic* (New York: Oxford University Press, 1990).

7. On the interactions and mutual dependencies of families of different classes and racial-ethnic identities, see Stephanie Coontz, Maya Parson, and Gabrielle Raley, *American Families: A Multicultural Reader* (New York: Routledge, 2008); Theresa L. Amott and Julie A. Matthaei, *Race, Gender, and Work: A Multicultural Economic History of Women in the United States* (Boston: South End Press, 1991); Vicki Ruiz and Ellen DuBois, *Unequal Sisters: A Multicultural Reader in U.S. Women's History*, 3rd ed. (New York: Routledge, 2000).

8. John D'Emilio and Estelle B. Freedman, *Intimate Matters: A History of Sexuality in America*, 2nd ed. (Chicago: University of Chicago Press, 1997).

9. Michael B. Katz, Michael J. Doucet, and Mark J. Stern, *The Social Organization of Early Industrial Capitalism* (Cambridge, MA: Harvard University Press, 1982), p. 347.

10. Clare A. Lyons, *Sex among the Rabble: An Intimate History of Gender and Power in the Age of Revolution* (Chapel Hill: University of North Carolina Press, 2006); Nancy Cott, *Public Vows: A History of Marriage and the Nation* (Cambridge, MA: Harvard University Press, 2000); Aaron Gullickson, "Black/White Interracial Marriage Trends, 1850–2000," *Journal of Family History* 31, no. 3 (2006): 1–24.

11. Rachel Moran, *Interracial Intimacy: The Regulation of Race and Romance* (Chicago: University of Chicago Press, 2001); Peter Wallenstein, *Tell the Court I Love My Wife: Race, Marriage, and Law—An American History* (New York: Palgrave Macmillan, 2002).

12. On the new trends in family life and gender relations between 1900 and the end of World War II, see Beth L. Bailey, *From Front Porch to Back Seat: Courtship in Twentieth-Century America* (Baltimore: Johns Hopkins University Press, 1989) and Coontz, *Marriage, A History* (2006).

13. Elaine Tyler May, *Great Expectations: Marriage and Divorce in Post-Victorian America* (Chicago: University of Chicago Press, 1980).

14. On postwar families, see Elaine Tyler May, *Homeward Bound: American Families in the Cold War Era* (New York: Basic Books, 1988); Jessica Weiss, *To Have and to Hold: Marriage, the Baby Boom, and Social Change* (Chicago: University of Chicago Press, 2000); Stephanie Coontz, *The Way We Never Were: American Families and the Nostalgia Trap* (New York: Basic Books, 2000).

15. George Gallup and Evan Hill, "The American Woman," *The Saturday Evening Post* (December 22–29, 1962), pp. 16–26.

16. Ruth Rosen, *The World Split Open: How the Women's Movement Changed America* (New York: Penguin Books, 2000).

17. For a detailed exploration of these complicated economic and social trends in two American families, see Judith Stacey, *Brave New Families: Stories of Domestic Upheaval in Late Twentieth-Century America* (New York: Basic Books, 1990).

18. On the recent history of immigration and other sources of cultural, religious and economic family diversity, see Barbara C. Aswad and Barbara Bilge, *Family and Gender among American Muslims: Issues Facing Middle-Eastern Immigrants and Their Descendants* (Philadelphia: Temple University Press, 1996); Donna Gabaccia and Vicki L. Ruiz, *American Dreaming, Global Realities: Rethinking U.S. Immigration History* (Chicago: University of Chicago Press, 2006); Bill Ong Hing, *Making and Remaking Asian America through Immigration Policy, 1850–1990* (Stanford, CA: Stanford University Press, 1993); Jennifer S. Hirsch, *A Courtship after Marriage: Sexuality and Love in Mexican Transnational Communities* (Berkeley: University of California Press, 2003); Juanita Tamayo Lott, *Common Destiny: Filipino American Generations* (Lanham, MD: Rowman & Littlefield, 2006); Mario Maffi, *Gateway to the Promised Lands: Ethnic Cultures on New York's Lower East Side* (New York: New York University Press, 1995); Mae M. Ngai, *Impossible Subjects: Illegal Aliens and the Making of Modern America* (Princeton, NJ: Princeton University Press, 2004); Mae Paomay Tung, *Chinese Americans and Their Immigrant Parents: Conflict, Identity, and Values* (Binghamton, NY: Haworth Press, 2000); Diane C. Vecchio, *Merchants, Midwives, and Laboring Women: Italian Migrants in Urban America* (Champaign: University of Illinois Press, 2006); Bernard P. Wong, *The Chinese in Silicon Valley: Globalization, Social Networks, and Ethnic Identity* (Lanham, MD: Rowman & Littlefield, 2006); Lillian B. Rubin, *Families on the Fault Line* (New York: HarperCollins, 1994); Arlene S. Skolnick and Jerome H. Skolnick, *Family in Transition*, 12th ed. (Boston: Allyn & Bacon, 2003); Maxime Baca Zinn, D. Stanley Eitzen, and Barbara Wells, *Diversity in Families*, 8th ed. (Boston: Allyn & Bacon, 2008).

19. Suzanne M. Bianchi, John P. Robinson, and Melissa A. Milkie, *Changing Rhythms of Family Life* (New York: Russell Sage Foundation, 2006).

6

American Childhood as a Social and Cultural Construct

Steven Mintz

N ot an unchanging, biologically determined stage of life, childhood is a social and cultural construct that varies by region, class, and historical era. Over the past four centuries, every aspect of childhood, including methods of child rearing; the nature of children's play; the duration of schooling; the participation of young people in work; and the demarcation points between childhood, adolescence, and adulthood have shifted significantly. This history provides an essential perspective on the questions of whether children's well-being has declined in recent years, whether children are growing up faster than in the past, and whether the United States is a particularly child-friendly country.

Today, Americans have a firm, although somewhat contradictory, conception of childhood. On the one hand, childhood is romanticized as a time of carefree innocence, when children should play freely, untouched by the cares of the adult world. But at the same time, many middle-class mothers and fathers engage in intensive parenting designed to stimulate their children's development. They buy them educational toys, involve them in a host of organized enrichment activities, and intensively read and talk to their children, in hopes of cultivating their talents and skills. Schools, too, now place greater emphasis on early academic achievement, and marketers are targeting children with an intensity previously reserved for adult consumers. Some observers fear that our society is taking the playfulness out of childhood.[1]

Childhood is not some unchanging, biologically determined stage of life. The whole concept of childhood is a social and cultural construct that varies by region, class, and historical era.[2] Over the past four centuries, almost all aspects of childhood—including children's relationships with their parents and peers, their proportion in the population, and their paths toward adulthood—have changed dramatically. Societal views about methods of child rearing, the nature of children's play, the ideal duration of schooling, the participation of young people in work, and the demarcation points between childhood, adolescence, and adulthood have shifted significantly. In this article, I trace the changing concepts of childhood from early colonial America until today. I conclude by comparing the status of today's children with the status of those from the past.

Two centuries ago, the experience of youth was very different from what it is today. Segregation by age was far less prevalent, and chronological age played a smaller role in determining status. Adults were also far less likely to sentimentalize children as special creatures who were more innocent and vulnerable than adults.

Language itself illustrates how perceptions of childhood differed from those today. Two hundred years ago, the words used to describe stages of childhood were far less precise than those we now use. *Infancy* referred not to the first months after birth, but to the whole period when children were dependent on their mother, typically until the age of five or six. The words *childhood* and *youth* could refer to someone as young as five or as old as the early twenties.

In that era, Americans did not have a category for "adolescent" or "teenager." The vagueness of the broader term *youth* reflected how fluidly the stages of life were viewed in that era. Chronological age mattered less than physical strength, size, and maturity. Young people were not automatically granted full adult status upon reaching a certain societally agreed upon age. They became full adults only when they married and set up their own farm or entered a full-time trade or profession. In some cases that might be as early as the mid- or late teens, but usually it did not occur until the late twenties or even the early thirties.[3]

Although there were important regional differences in children's experiences, depending on the prevalence or paucity of slavery and indentured servitude in a given area, most seventeenth-century American colonists regarded children as "adults-in-training." It was recognized that children differed from adults in their mental, moral, and physical capabilities, and the colonists distinguished between childhood, an intermediate stage they called youth, and adulthood. But in colonial America, a parent's duty was to hurry the child toward adult status. Infants, being unable to stand or speak, were thought to lack two essential attributes of full humanity, and infancy was therefore regarded as a state of deficiency to be rushed through as quickly as possible. Parents discouraged infants from crawling, and placed them in "walking stools" to get them on their feet. Rods were affixed along the spines of very young children to encourage adult posture.

The goal was to get children speaking, reading, reasoning, and contributing to their family's economic well-being as quickly as possible. A key element in this process was early involvement in work, either within the parental home or outside as a servant or apprentice. Before the mid-eighteenth century, most adults exhibited surprisingly little interest in their children's very first years of life. Children's play was commonly dismissed as trivial and insignificant. In that era, adults rarely looked back on their childhood with nostalgia or fondness.

During the eighteenth century, a shift in parental attitudes took place. Fewer parents expected children to act as miniature adults, to bow or doff their hats in their parents' presence, or to stand during meals. Instead of addressing parents as "sir" and "madam," children began calling them "papa" and "mama."

By the end of the eighteenth century, furniture specifically designed for children was being widely produced. Painted in pastel colors and decorated with pictures of animals or figures from nursery rhymes, the new furniture reflected a growing popular notion of childhood as a time of innocence and playfulness.

Parents began to regard children not as incomplete adults but as innocent, malleable, and fragile creatures who needed to be sheltered from contamination. Childhood came to be seen not simply as a prelude to adulthood but as a separate stage of life that required special care and institutions to protect it.

By the early nineteenth century, mothers in the rapidly expanding middle class in the Northeastern states were embracing an amalgam of child-rearing ideas. From Jean-Jacques Rousseau and the Romantic poets, middle-class parents acquired the idea that childhood was a special stage of life, intimately connected with nature, and purer and morally superior to adulthood. From the philosopher John Locke, they took the notion that children were highly malleable creatures and that a republican form of government required parents to instill a capacity for self-government in their offspring. From evangelical Protestants, the middle class adopted the idea that parents must implant proper moral character in children and insulate them from the corruptions of the adult world.

Behind these developments was a growing belief that childhood should be devoted to education and building character as well as play. Middle-class children were no longer sent out to work at an early age, but parents began to believe that their children's play should foster their moral growth. Because parents in the emerging middle class could not automatically transfer their societal status to their children through bequests of family lands, transmission of craft skills, or selection of a marriage partner, they adopted new strategies to give their children a boost by limiting the number of their offspring through birth control and prolonging the transition to adulthood through intensive maternal nurturing and extended schooling.

Over time, the concept of childhood became divided into much more precise, uniform, and prescriptive stages. Adults began to hold much more rigid views about what was appropriate at each stage. By the mid-nineteenth century, informal patterns of child rearing were being supplanted by more structured forms. Schools began to follow prescribed grade-specific curricula. Adult-sponsored and adult-organized activities began replacing activities that young people organized informally on their own.

The dramatic reduction in the birthrate over the past two centuries also altered the concept of childhood. In the mid-nineteenth century, children made up fully one-half of the population. By 1900 their proportion had declined to one-third of the population. As parents had fewer children and had them over a shorter time span, families became more clearly divided into distinct generations, and parents had the opportunity to lavish more time, attention, and resources on each child.

Yet until the early twentieth century, there was still a high degree of diversity in the experience of childhood, based on social class, gender, and race, and accentuated by the rapid and uneven expansion of industrial capitalism. The children of the urban middle class, prosperous commercial farmers, and southern planters enjoyed increasingly long childhoods and were free from major household or work responsibilities until their late teens or twenties. But the offspring of urban workers, frontier farmers, and blacks, both slave and free, had briefer childhoods and became involved in work inside or outside the home before they reached their teens.

Urban working-class children often contributed to the family economy through scavenging and collecting coal, wood, and other items that could be used at home or sold, or by taking part in the street trades, selling gum, peanuts, newspapers, and the like. In industrial towns, young people under the age of fifteen contributed on average about 20 percent of their family's income. In mining areas, boys as young as ten began working in the pits as breakers, separating coal from slate and wood, and then graduated into full-fledged miners in their mid- or late teens.

On farms, children as young as five might pull weeds or keep birds and cattle away from crops. By the age of eight, many were tending the livestock, and as they grew older they milked cows, churned butter, fed chickens, collected eggs, hauled water, scrubbed laundry, and harvested crops. A blurring of gender duties among children and youth was especially common on frontier farms.

Schooling in the nineteenth century varied as widely as did work routines. In the rural North, the Midwest, and the Far West, most mid- and late-nineteenth-century students attended one-room schools for three to six months a year. But city children spent nine months a year attending age-graded classes, taught by professional teachers. In rural and urban areas, girls generally received more schooling than boys.[4]

As the nineteenth century drew to an end, middle-class parents were starting to embrace the idea that child rearing should be scientific. Through the Child Study movement, teachers and mothers, under the direction of psychologists, identified a series of stages of child development, culminating in the "discovery"—more accurately the invention—of adolescence, a period marked by emotional and psychological turmoil tied to the biological changes associated with puberty. Within the middle class, acceptance of the concept of scientific parenting was reflected in young people's remaining longer within the parental home and spending longer periods in formal schooling.

The attempt to apply scientific principles to the care of children produced new kinds of child-rearing manuals, now written by doctors and psychologists rather than ministers, as had previously been the case. The most influential manual was Dr. Luther Emmett Holt's *The Care and Feeding of Children*, first published in 1894. In an era when a well-adjusted adult was viewed as a creature of habit and self-control, Holt stressed the importance of imposing regular habits on infants by rigidly scheduling a child's feeding, bathing, sleeping, and bowel movements. He also advised mothers to guard vigilantly against germs and to avoid undue stimulation of infants—for example, by kissing their babies. Holt also advised parents to ignore their baby's crying and to break such habits as thumb sucking.[5]

At about the same time, self-described "child-savers" launched a concerted campaign to universalize the middle-class model of childhood, in which childhood was defined as a period during which young people should be insulated from the stresses and corrupting influences of the adult world and free from adult-like responsibilities. Trying to universalize the modern ideal of a sheltered childhood without regard to a child's class, ethnicity, gender, and race was a highly uneven process and to this day has never encompassed all American children.

But by the early twentieth century, the middle-class conception of "modern childhood" had generally been accepted as the societal norm, although progress was slow and bitterly resisted. Child labor was not finally outlawed until the 1930s, and not until the 1950s did high school attendance become a universal experience.

During the 1920s and 1930s, the field of child psychology exerted a growing influence on middle-class parenting. It provided a new language to describe children's emotional problems. Concepts like sibling rivalry, inferiority complexes, phobias, maladjustment, and Oedipus complexes gained wide acceptance. Child psychology also offered new insights into the effects of different styles of parenting, such as demanding and permissive forms. It categorized the stages and milestones of children's development and the characteristics of children at particular ages. This was when, for example, the phrase "terrible twos" was coined.

The growing prosperity of the 1920s made the late-nineteenth-century emphasis on rigid self-control and regularity seem outmoded. The new model for a well-adjusted adult was a more easygoing figure who was capable of enjoying leisure. There was a reaction against the mechanistic and behaviorist notion that children's behavior should and could be molded by scientific control. Popular dispensers of advice now advocated a more relaxed approach to child rearing, emphasizing the importance of meeting the emotional needs of babies. The title of a 1936 book by pediatrician C. Anderson Aldrich—*Babies Are Human Beings*—summed up the new attitude.[6]

The stresses and uncertainties of the Great Depression of the 1930s and World War II made parents much more anxious about child rearing. In the postwar era, many psychologists asserted that faulty mothering was the cause of lasting psychological problems in children. Leading psychologists such as Theodore Lidz, Irving Bieber, and Erik Erikson linked schizophrenia, homosexuality, and identity diffusion to mothers who displaced their frustrations and their needs for independence onto their children.

Many psychologists worried that boys, being raised almost exclusively by women, might fail to develop an appropriate sex-role identity. In retrospect, these fears reflected the fact that mothers were playing a much more exclusive role in raising their children than ever before in American history.[7]

By the 1950s, developments were already under way that would bring down the curtain on "modern childhood" and replace it with something we might call "postmodern childhood." Postmodern childhood is a product of radical changes in society that led in the space of just over thirty years to the breakdown of dominant norms regarding the family, gender expectations, age, and even reproduction (see Coontz in Chapter 5 of this volume).

Children today grow up under different circumstances than their immediate predecessors. They are more likely to experience their parents' divorce. They are more likely to have a working mother and to spend significant amounts of time unsupervised by adults. They are more likely to grow up without siblings. They are more likely to hold a job during high school.

Age norms once considered "natural" have been thrown into question. Even the bedrock biological process of sexual maturation has accelerated. Adolescent girls today, for example, enter puberty at an earlier age and are much more likely to have sexual relations during their mid-teens than their peers did a half century ago.[8]

While society still assumes that the young are fundamentally different from adults—that they should spend their first eighteen years in the parental home and should devote their time to education in age-graded schools—it is also clear that basic aspects of the ideal of a protected childhood, in which the young are kept isolated from adult realities, have broken down.[9] Postmodern children are independent consumers and participate in a separate, semiautonomous youth culture. Adults quite rightly assume that even preadolescents know a great deal about the realities of the adult world.

Since the early 1970s, a variety of factors have contributed to a surge in the scope and intensity of parental anxieties about child rearing. As parents had fewer children, they invested more emotional energy in each child. Greater professional expertise about children, coupled with a proliferation of research and advocacy organizations, media outlets, and government agencies responsible for children's health and safety, made parents more aware of threats to children's well-being. Many middle-class parents responded by trying to protect their children from every imaginable harm by baby-proofing their homes, using car seats, requiring bicycle helmets, and the like—things unknown a generation earlier.

Middle-class parents also worried that their offspring might underperform compared to peers and looked for ways to maximize their children's physical, social, and intellectual development. The goal of postwar parents had been to raise normal children who fit in. Middle-class parents now try to give their child a competitive advantage, a trend spurred by fears of downward mobility and anxiety that parents may not be able to pass on their status and social class to their children (see Coleman in Chapter 24 of this volume).

Today we no longer see early childhood as a stage to be rushed through. Early childhood is viewed as the formative stage for later life. Society believes that children's experiences during the first two or three years of life mold their personality, lay the foundation for future cognitive and psychological development, and leave a lasting imprint on their emotional life. We also assume that children's development proceeds through a series of physical, psychological, social, and cognitive stages. It is accepted that even very young children have a capacity to learn, that play serves valuable developmental functions, and that growing up requires children to separate emotionally and psychologically from their parents.

There are, however, significant class differences in contemporary parenting practices, as sociologist Annette Lareau has shown (see the CCF Brief at the end of Chapter 31 of this volume). Working-class and poor mothers and fathers are much more likely to believe that child development occurs naturally and spontaneously. Unlike their middle-class counterparts, many working-class parents reject the notion that successful child rearing requires parents to actively stimulate their children's development by organizing their leisure activities, chauffeuring them to lessons, or supervising their homework.

Lareau has shown that middle-class parents spend more time in conversation with their children, read to them more often, employ a larger vocabulary, and are more likely to try to reason with their children rather than simply enforce rules. Middle-class parents are also more likely to place their children in adult-supervised enrichment activities, while children in working-class and poor families spend more time in free, unstructured play and are more likely to socialize with extended family.[10]

Although the middle-class ideal of child rearing has become the societal norm, social class remains a primary determinant of children's well-being.[11] In recent years, social conservatives have argued that family structure is a primary source of inequality in children's well-being, while political liberals tend to focus on ethnicity, race, and gender. But the most powerful predictor of children's welfare is, in fact, social and economic class. Economic distress contributes to family instability, inadequate health care, high degrees of mobility, and elevated levels of stress and depression.

As in the nineteenth century, social class significantly differentiates contemporary American childhoods. There is a vast difference between the highly pressured, hyperorganized, fast-track childhoods of affluent children and the very different kind of stressed childhoods experienced by the one-third of all children who live in poverty at some point before the age of eighteen.

In many affluent families, the boundaries between parental work and family life have blurred. Parents often try to cope by tightly organizing their children's lives. But most affluent children are unsupervised by their parents for large portions of the day and have their own television and computer, which gives them unmediated access to information. Many affluent families swing back and forth between parental distance from children caused by work pressures and parental indulgence as fathers and mothers try to compensate for parenting too little.

Meanwhile, one-sixth of all children live in poverty at any given time, including 36 percent of black children and 34 percent of Hispanic children. Children who live in poverty generally experience limited adult supervision, inferior schooling, and a lack of easy access to productive diversions and activities.

How does the status of children today compare with the past? Are children better off or worse off? This question has been of importance to every generation.

One of this country's oldest convictions is a belief in the decline of the younger generation. For more than three centuries, American adults have worried that children are growing ever more disobedient and disrespectful. In 1657, a Puritan minister, Ezekiel Rogers, lamented: "I find the greatest trouble and grief about the rising generation. . . . Much ado I have with my own family . . . the young breed doth much afflict me."[12]

But wistfulness about a golden age of childhood is invariably misleading. There has never been a golden age of childhood, when the overwhelming majority of American children have been well cared for and had idyllic lives. Nostalgia typically represents a yearning not for the past as it really was but rather for a whitewashed fantasy about the past.

In 1820, children constituted about half of the workers in the early factories. As recently as the 1940s, fewer than half of all high school students graduated. More than half a century ago, Alfred Kinsey's studies found rates of sexual abuse similar to those reported today. His interviews indicated that 12 percent of pre-adolescent girls had been the victims of exhibitionists and that 9 percent of girls had had their genitals fondled.

We also forget that the introduction of every new form of entertainment over the past century has been accompanied by dire warnings about its impact on children. The anxiety over video games and the Internet are only the latest in a long line of supposed threats to children that included television, movies, radio, and comic books.[13]

The danger of nostalgia is that it creates unrealistic expectations, guilt, and anger.[14] If we cling to a fantasy that once upon a time childhood and youth were years of carefree adventure, we have to ignore the fact that for most children in the past, growing up was anything but easy. Disease, death of a parent, family disruption, and early entry into the world of work were integral parts of family life. The notion of a long childhood, devoted to education and free from adult-like responsibilities, is a very recent invention, a product of the past century and a half, and one that only became a reality for a majority of children after World War II.

Another problem with nostalgia about childhood in the past is that it assumes that the family home was traditionally a haven and bastion of stability in an ever-changing world. Throughout American history, however, family stability has been the exception, not the norm. As late as the beginning of the twentieth century, fully one-third of all American children spent at least part of their childhood in a single-parent home, and as recently as 1940, one child in ten did not live with either parent—compared to one in twenty-five today.[15]

There have been genuine gains achieved in children's lives, such as the outlawing of child labor, the expansion of schooling, the growing awareness about the evils of child abuse. But the history of childhood has not been a story of steady, linear progress.

Each generation of children has had to wrestle with the specific social, political, and economic constraints of its own historical period. In our own time, the young have had to struggle with high rates of family instability, a growing disconnection from adults, and the expectation that all children should pursue the same academic path at the same pace, even as the attainment of full adulthood recedes ever further into the future.

Profound class differences in children's experience persist and have even grown in salience over the past thirty years. Poor children grow up in an "ecology of poverty," characterized by substandard housing, inadequate schooling, deficient health care, unstable living arrangements, and limited access to decent child care. Many poor children are exposed to violence and have parents who suffer from depression stemming from erratic incomes and demanding work hours. In recent years, the gap between poor and working-class and affluent children in rates of attending four-year colleges has widened.[16]

Even for children of the middle class and the stably employed working class, American society is not as child-friendly as we might hope. Literary critic Daniel Kline persuasively suggests that contemporary American society subjects the young to three forms of psychological violence that we tend to ignore. First is the violence of expectations, in which children are pushed beyond their social, physical, and academic capabilities, largely as an expression of their parents' needs. Then there is the violence of labeling normal childish behavior (for example, childhood exuberance or interest in sex) as pathological. Third is the violence of representation, in which children and adolescents are exploited by advertisers, marketers, purveyors of popular culture, and politicians, who exploit parental anxieties as well as young peoples' desire to be stylish, independent, and defiant, and eroticize teenage and preadolescent girls.[17]

I believe there is a fourth form of psychological abuse: seeing children as objects to be shaped and molded for their own good. Contemporary American society is much more controlling of young people in an institutional and ideological sense than its predecessors. And as the baby-boom generation ages, American society has become increasingly adult-oriented, with fewer "free" spaces for the young, a society in which youth are primarily valued as service workers and consumers.

For more than three centuries, despite massive evidence to the contrary, America has considered itself to be an especially child-centered society. Yet in no other advanced country do so many young people grow up in poverty or without health care, nor does any other Western society provide so few resources for child care or restrict paid parental leave so stringently.

This paradox is not new. Since the early nineteenth century, the United States has developed a host of institutions specifically aimed at the young: the common school, the Sunday school, the orphanage, the house of refuge, the reformatory, the children's hospital, the juvenile court, and a wide variety of youth organizations. All were envisioned as caring, developmental, and educational institutions that would serve children's interests. In practice, however, they frequently end up being primarily custodial and disciplinary.

Many of the reforms that were supposed to help children were adopted in part because they served the needs, interests, and convenience of adults. The abolition of child labor removed competition from an overcrowded labor market. Separating children by age-based grades not only made it easier to handle children within schools, it also divided the young into convenient market segments.

The most important lesson that grows out of understanding the history of childhood is the simplest. While many fear that American society has changed too much, the sad fact is that it has changed too little. Americans have failed to adapt social institutions to new realities, to the fact that the young mature more rapidly than they did in the past, that most mothers of preschoolers now participate in the paid workforce, and that a near majority of children will spend substantial parts of their childhood in a single-parent, cohabitating-parent, or stepparent household.

As we navigate a new century of childhood, we need to pose new questions. How can we provide better care for the young, especially the one-sixth who are growing up in poverty? How can we better connect the worlds of adults and the young? How can we give the young more ways to demonstrate their growing competence and maturity? How can we tame a violence-laced, sex-saturated popular culture without undercutting a commitment to freedom and a respect for the free-floating world of fantasy?

Notes

1. Annette Lareau, *Unequal Childhoods: Class, Race, and Family Life* (Berkeley: University of California Press, 2003).

2. Colin Heywood, *A History of Childhood: Children and Childhood in the West from Medieval to Modern Times* (Cambridge, UK: Polity Press, 2001); Joseph Illick, *American Childhood* (Philadelphia: University of Pennsylvania Press, 2002); James A. Schultz, *The Knowledge of Childhood in the German Middle Ages, 1100–1350* (Philadelphia: University of Pennsylvania Press, 1995), p. 11.

3. Howard P. Chudacoff, *How Old Are You? Age Consciousness in American Society* (Princeton: Princeton University Press, 1989); Joseph F. Kett, *Rites of Passage: Adolescence in America* (New York: Basic, 1977).

4. Priscilla Clement, *Growing Pains: Children in the Industrial Age, 1850–1890* (New York: Twayne, 1997); David Nasaw, *Children in the City: At Work and at Play* (Garden City, NY: Anchor Press/Doubleday, 1985); Christine Stansell, *City of Women: Sex and Class in New York, 1789–1860* (New York: Knopf, 1986).

5. Ann Hulbert, *Raising America: Experts, Parents, and a Century of Advice about Children* (New York: Knopf, 2003); Julia Grant, *Raising Baby by the Book: The Education of American Mothers* (New Haven, CT: Yale University Press, 1998).

6. Kathleen W. Jones, *Taming the Troublesome Child* (Cambridge, MA: Harvard University Press, 1999).

7. Steven Mintz and Susan Kellogg, *Domestic Revolutions: A Social History of American Family Life* (New York: Free Press, 1988), p. 189.

8. On changes in the onset of sexual maturation, see Marcia E. Herman-Giddens et al., "Secondary Sexual Characteristics and Menses in Young Girls Seen in Office Practice: A Study from the Pediatric Research in Office Settings Network," *Pediatrics* 9, no. 4 (April 1997): 505–12. In 1890, the average age of menarche in the United States was estimated to be 14.8 years; by the 1990s, the average age had fallen to 12.5 (12.1 for African American girls and 12.8 for girls of northern European ancestry). According to the study, which tracked 17,000 girls to find out when they hit different markers of puberty, 15 percent of white girls and 48 percent of African American girls showed signs of breast development or pubic hair by age eight. For conflicting views on whether the age of menarche has fallen, see Lisa Belkin, "The Making of an 8-Year-Old Woman," *New York Times*, December 24, 2000; Gina Kolata, "Doubters Fault Theory Finding Earlier Puberty, " *New York Times*," February 20, 2001; Gina Kolata, "2 Endocrinology Groups Raise Doubt on Earlier Onset of Girls' Puberty," *New York Times*, March 3, 2001.

9. Stephen Robertson, "The Disappearance of Childhood," http://teaching.arts.usyd.edu .au/ history/2044/.

10. Lareau, *Unequal Childhoods* (2003).

11. David I. Macleod, *The Age of the Child: Children in America, 1890–1912* (New York: Twayne, 1998).

12. Rogers quoted in James Axtell, *The School Upon a Hill: Education and Society in Colonial New England* (New Haven, CT: Yale University Press, 1974), p. 28.

13. Hard as it is to believe, in 1951 a leading television critic decried the quality of children's television. Jack Gould, radio and TV critic for the *New York Times* from the late 1940s to 1972, complained that there was "nothing on science, seldom anything on the country's cultural heritage, no introduction to fine books, scant emphasis on the people of other lands, and little concern over hobbies and other things for children to do themselves besides watch television." *Chicago Sun Times*, August 9, 1998, p. 35.

14. Phil Scraton, ed., *"Childhood" in "Crisis"?* (London: University College of London Press, 1997), pp. 161, 164.

15. Richard Weissbourd, *The Vulnerable Child: What Really Hurts America's Children and What We Can Do about It* (Reading, MA: Addison-Wesley, 1996), p. 48.

16. Ibid.

17. Daniel T. Kline, "Holding Therapy," March 7, 1998, History-Child-Family Listserv (history-child-family@mailbase.ac.uk).

In the News

A "GOLDEN AGE" OF CHILDHOOD?

Christian Science Monitor, April 28, 2005

Steven Mintz

Many of America's 78 million baby boomers may feel a bit older when they realize that this year marks the 50th anniversary of Play-Doh, the fried-chicken TV dinner, and the air-powered Burp gun. The LEGO "system of play"—28 sets and 8 vehicles—was launched in 1955. And it's the year McDonald's Corp. was founded.

Today, we look back nostalgically to the 1950s as a time of a more innocent childhood. Life was safer as well as simpler then, we sigh. We worry that modern mass culture has undermined the influence of parents, and that aggressive advertising is distorting children's diet, their body image, and their attitude toward material possessions.

But by placing '50s culture on such a lofty pedestal, we fail to appreciate the huge advances that have made childhood, in many ways, a safer and more sheltered time today. What's more, such attitudes overlook the fact that much of what troubles parents today dated from that era.

For instance, the modern commercialization of childhood is in fact a direct outcome of forces that were set in motion during the 1950s. The first baby-boomer fad—the Davy Crockett coonskin cap, introduced in 1955—revealed the huge commercial potential of marketing directly to children. With products like Matchbox cars (launched in England in 1953), Trix cereal (1954), "Mad" (which changed from a comic book into a magazine in 1955), and Barbie (1959), marketers discovered that it was possible to target kids as consumers, separate and apart from their parents.

Television provided the ideal medium for reaching child consumers. ABC introduced one of the first children's television shows, "Disneyland," in 1954, and "The Mickey Mouse Club" the next year. "Disneyland" was the forerunner of modern infomercials: a program-length advertisement for Walt Disney's about-to-open theme park. Shows like "Captain Kangaroo," which debuted on CBS in 1955, contributed to the emergence of an insular world of childhood wholly separate from that of adults.

Today, we look back to the 1950s as a safer, more orderly time for raising children. But that's not how it seemed to many parents then. At the end of the decade, the infant and child mortality rate was four times as high as it is today—the scourge of polio had claimed the lives of 3,000 children annually until the Salk vaccine was developed in 1955.

Two-thirds of black children and more than a fifth of their white counterparts lived in poverty as recently as 1955. By contrast, 34 percent of African American children and 14 percent of white children lived in poverty as of 2003. And even though the Supreme Court ruled school segregation unconstitutional in 1954, by 1960 just 1 percent of black children in the South attended integrated schools. Meanwhile, nearly a million children with disabilities were denied public schooling as uneducable. And 40 percent of kids dropped out of school before graduating high school.

Happy sitcom reruns to the contrary, the parents of 50 years ago were not insulated from fears about youth violence and children's poor academic achievement. In 1955, several Congressional hearings investigated the link between television and children's violence, while others warned of the corrupting effects of comic books. In 1955 alone, Congress considered nearly 200 bills aimed at combating what was seen as an epidemic of juvenile delinquency. Rudolph Flesch's 1955 bestseller, "Why Johnny Can't Read," announced that "3,500 years of civilization" were being lost due to bad schools and incompetent teachers. (This prompted publisher Houghton Mifflin to ask Theodor Geisel, aka Dr. Seuss, to write and illustrate an easy-read that would become "The Cat in the Hat.") The anxieties that obsess parents today— children's safety, morals, and international competitiveness—took root in the seemingly tranquil 1950s.

Nor were 1950s children protected from sexual and physical abuse or exploitation. In 1955, Vladimir Nabokov published "Lolita," with its shocking depiction of a middle-aged man's "affair" with a 12-year-old girl. The book broke a taboo on that subject in what may well have been the first high-profile commercialization of the eroticization of pre- and pubescent girls that is now standard commercial fare.

Certainly parents face new challenges today, as they grapple with expanding work pressures, changing family forms, and an accelerating commercialization of private life. But romanticizing the 1950s as the supposed golden age of American childhood ignores the fact that many of today's problems actually took root then and obscures real gains made in child welfare since then. Who knows whether 50 years from now, this may be the platinum age of childhood? ▄

CCF Brief

HOMESICK KIDS AND HELICOPTER PARENTS: ARE TODAY'S YOUNG ADULTS TOO EMOTIONALLY DEPENDENT ON PARENTS?

Susan Matt | September 2011

As colleges across the country begin the new school year, we hear a chorus of warnings about a generation of young adults unable or unwilling to "leave the nest." Phrases are bandied about: "failure to launch," "the Peter Pan syndrome," "boomerang kids" who can't seem to leave home and establish an independent life. Undergirding these warnings is a fear that the younger generation is growing soft, losing the pioneer independence and rugged individualism that once built this nation.

But a glance at the past suggests it may not be the behavior of youths that has changed so much as the response by adults. Only over the past ninety years did American culture come to define young adults' continued reliance on parental guidance and their longing to return home as a sign of psychological maladjustment.

These days, in an effort to help students develop more individual self-reliance, some colleges have developed "Parting Ceremonies," designed to establish a decisive separation from their parents. At Morehouse College, the ceremony ends with the incoming freshmen marching through the campus gates, which then swing closed, shutting all parents outside. Other educational institutions have created formal "hit the road" departure rituals designed to hustle parents off campus and encourage students to start organizing their own lives. College counseling centers advise students to limit the time they spend thinking of home or talking with family and to combat unproductive feelings of homesickness by getting involved in new activities and making new friends.

Yet to the consternation of many, it is hard to break young people of their desire to "call home"—or actually return there. A recent study found that college students at Middlebury and University of Michigan were in touch with their parents an average of 13 times each week. One *New York Times* columnist lamented that this "alarmingly frequent" contact "significantly reduces independence." Others have described the cell phone as "the world's longest umbilical cord," inhibiting the ability of young people to stand on their own two feet.

According to social media expert Sherry Turkle, director of MIT's Initiative on Technology and Self, many young people today grow up "with the idea that they don't have to separate from their parents," a process that twentieth-century psychologists saw as an essential part of maturation. "Something has become the norm that was [once] considered pathological."

A look back at the history of homesickness, however, suggests that earlier generations had just as difficult a time leaving home as do modern Americans. But in the nineteenth century, homesickness was not seen as a symptom of poor adjustment or psychological imbalance. It was considered a serious medical condition that might strike any person who was separated from home and family. According to physicians of the era, symptoms of acute homesickness, then called nostalgia, included loss of appetite, "mental dejection," "irregular action of the bowels," hysterical weeping, "throbbing of the temporal arteries," "incontinence," "cerebral derangement," and sometimes even death. Since love of home and mother were considered signs of a virtuous character, no shame was attached to being diagnosed with this potentially fatal condition. The only known cure was to send the sufferer home.

Of course, this was not always possible. For example, soldiers who went off to war could not be sent home when they came down with a bout of nostalgia. So military officials often prohibited army bands from playing "Home, Sweet Home," for fear it might touch off an epidemic of homesickness in the ranks. Despite such precautions, during the Civil War, doctors diagnosed 5,000 Union soldiers with serious clinical cases of nostalgia and determined that 74 men had died from it.

Perhaps it is true that many young Americans today are too dependent on their parents. But a look back at the history of homesickness suggests that, long before e-mail and the cell phone, earlier generations also had a hard time leaving home and parents behind. Then, however, instead of blaming parents for not sufficiently preparing their children for independence, traditional American culture encouraged such interdependence between the generations.

7

African Americans and the Birth of the Modern Marriage

Donna L. Franklin

A long tradition of dual-career partnerships has defined most marriages among African American professionals at least since the late nineteenth century. This model, which is relatively new for whites, has been overlooked by many family historians and social scientists. This chapter will explore two fundamental questions related to these revolutionary marriages: why marriage conventions differed for professional whites and blacks, and how distinct cultural values regarding women emerged in the African American community.

We can trace the roots of dual-career marriages in the black professional community to the late nineteenth and early twentieth centuries. In an era when very few married white women worked outside the home, married black females were combining care for their families with employment responsibilities.

As industrial capitalism developed, with its low wages, obstacles to upward mobility, and poor working conditions, marriage became an attractive alternative to working for many white women. At the same time, in the culture as a whole a new ideal took hold—the image of women as fragile, delicate, and economically dependent, needing to be sheltered and supported.

The different conventions regarding work and marriage in the white and black communities were reflected in a letter that the leading women's suffragist, Susan B. Anthony, wrote to her black friend and fellow activist, Ida B. Wells-Barnett, in 1890. Anthony had never married and doubted that women could combine marriage with a career. She lamented that Wells-Barnett's activism was suffering since she married and began having children:

Women like you who have a special call for work should never marry. I know of no one in all this country better fitted to do the work you had in hand. Since you've gotten married, agitation practically seems to have ceased. Besides, you're trying to help in the formation of this league and your baby needs your attention at home. You're distracted over the thought that he's not being looked after as he would be if you were there, and that makes for divided duty.

When Ida B. Wells moved to Chicago and married Ferdinand Barnett, she was thirty-two and her antilynching campaign was in full swing. Their marriage was a union of two black professionals. He was a prominent Chicago attorney and founder and publisher of the *Conservator*, Chicago's first black newspaper. Barnett never expected Wells to stay home and be a housewife after their marriage. He employed household help, and he personally did most of the cooking for the family. Their temperaments complemented each other. Their daughter, Alfreda Duster, remembered that her "father was a very mild mannered man; he was not aggressive . . . or outspoken like my mother."[1] With the support of her husband, Ida B. Wells-Barnett remained a force to be reckoned with both inside and outside the home.

But even with such a supportive husband, Wells struggled with the conflicting demands of activism and her maternal role. She had her first child during an election year and was asked to campaign throughout Illinois for the Women's State Central Committee, a Republican political organization. She agreed on the condition that a nurse be provided to help with her six-month-old son. Wells-Barnett recalled, "I honestly believe that I am the only woman in the United States who ever traveled throughout the country with a nursing baby to make political speeches."

A year later she was pregnant again. By then her husband had been appointed assistant state's attorney. She resigned from the presidency of the Ida B. Wells Club and announced that she was retiring from public life to devote more time to her family. The "retirement" lasted five months.

Black women seemed to have an easier time juggling the role of activist with the role of mother and wife. This was reflected in the dramatic differences in the marital status of white and black women activists at the end of the nineteenth century. Historian Linda Gordon found that 85 percent of black women activists were married, compared to only 34 percent of white women activists.

Another factor in the difference between marriage rates for black and white women activists is that the pool of marriageable males was much smaller for white women during this historical period. More Americans were killed during the Civil War than during any other war the nation has fought. Hundreds of thousands of husbands, fathers, sons, and lovers were killed, and many more were disabled, resulting in a generation of white women who had limited prospects for marriage. In a culture in which women were defined by their relationship to men, many white women would for the first time be forced to discover their independence from men.[2] Black women did not suffer the same deficit of marriageable men because although black men rushed to enlist in the Union army when they were finally allowed to join, they suffered far fewer casualties because they were rarely allowed to actually bear arms.[3]

Yet, although barely one-third of the white activists had married, Gordon reports that "the white women, with few exceptions, tended to view married women's economic dependence on men as desirable and their employment as a misfortune." Anna Julia Cooper, the fourth black woman to receive a doctorate, offered an alternative perspective. She married and was widowed at an early age and advised black women to seek egalitarian marriages. Cooper also believed that all married women should earn a livelihood because it "renders women less dependent on the marriage relationship for physical support (which, by the way, does not always accompany it)."

In Cooper's opinion, the question was not "How shall I so cramp, stunt, simplify, and nullify myself as to make me eligible to the honor of being swallowed up by some little man? But the problem rests with the man as to how he can so develop . . . to reach the ideal of a generation of women who demand the noblest, grandest, and best achievement of which he is capable."[4]

In general, black female activists were viewed more favorably within their own community than were their white counterparts because they were seen as fighting for the greater good of all black people and did not pose a threat to the political objectives of black men. Slavery, having rendered black men and women equally powerless, had leveled the gender "playing field" within the black community. In contrast, much of white women's activism, such as the fight for female suffrage, posed a direct challenge to the privileges of white men and patriarchy.

When historian Stephanie J. Shaw examined the lives of professional black women from the 1870s through the 1950s, she found that 74 percent were married at least once in their lifetime. In addition to being more likely than their white activist counterparts to be married, 51 percent of them had professional husbands. Among the more affluent black women who emerged as leaders, marriage to prominent black men often gave them a distinct advantage in that it gave them greater access to the network of powerful black men. Shaw notes that many of the women in her study had been socialized in such a way that "the model of womanhood held before [them] was one of achievement in *both* the public and private spheres. Parents cast domesticity as a complement rather than a contradiction to success in public arenas."

Ida B. Wells made a similar point when speaking about balancing mother-hood with her activism. Although she did not have the "longing for children that so many women have," she was glad that she had them nonetheless, adding that not having children robbed women "of one of the most glorious advantages in the development of their own womanhood."[5]

The lives of white activists Alice Freeman Palmer and Antoinette Louisa Brown Blackwell are indicative of a different convention. In 1881, twenty-six-year-old Alice Freeman became president of Wellesley College, the first female to head a nationally known institution of higher education. During her tenure as president, she met George Palmer, a Harvard professor, and in 1887, upon announcing her engagement to him, she resigned as Wellesley's president.

Antoinette Louisa Brown Blackwell, a women's rights activist and social reformer, was the first American woman to become an ordained minister. She married Samuel Charles Blackwell, an abolitionist businessman. After her marriage, even though she had a sympathetic husband, she struggled to combine marriage and her "intellectual work." They had seven children, two of whom died in infancy. While she was raising her children, Brown Blackwell for the most part gave up public speaking. She continued, however, to study; and as her children got older, she wrote and published many books on science and philosophy. Although she was more in favor of marriage than Susan B. Anthony, she had doubts about a woman's ability to juggle marriage, a family, and a career. She advocated part-time work for married women, with their husbands helping out with child care and housework.[6]

FREE AT LAST

The defeat of the Confederacy in the Civil War and the abolition of slavery brought profound changes to black family life, altering the economic, social, and legal arrangements within which the former slaves lived. Freed slaves began creating communities, establishing networks of institutions, churches, schools, and mutual aid societies. When they were slaves, blacks had established secret churches and families, and after emancipation these institutions provided an important sense of community. With their newfound freedom, black men and women shared a common dream of living as free people.

The freed slaves particularly welcomed the opportunity to marry, a right that had been denied to them. In 1850, escaped slave Henry Bibb had written that "there are no class of people in the United States who so highly appreciate the legality of marriage as those persons who have been held and treated as property." When laws were passed requiring marriages among former slaves to be registered, some whites were "astonished by the eagerness with which former slaves legalized their marriage bonds."[7]

THE CLUB WOMEN'S MOVEMENT

The efforts of Ida B. Wells-Barnett to build a broad campaign against lynching by lecturing to groups in the United States and internationally, despite her increasing family responsibilities, had the side effect of fostering the growth of black women's clubs.

In response to a letter from an Englishwoman who had become interested in the issue of lynching after hearing Wells-Barnett give a speech in Britain,[8] John W. Jacks, president of the Missouri Press Association, published an open letter asserting that:

> Out of some 200 [Negroes] in this vicinity it is doubtful if there are a dozen virtuous women or that number who are not daily thieving from white people. To illustrate how they regard virtue in a woman, one of them, a negro woman, who asked who a certain negro woman who had lately moved into the neighborhood was. She turned up her nose and said, "The negroes will have nothing to do with "dat nigger," she won't let any man except her husband sleep with her, and we don't 'sociate with her."[9]

Josephine St. Pierre Ruffin, editor of *The Woman's Era*, the first American magazine owned and managed by black women, widely circulated Jacks's letter to prominent black women around the country, and the ensuing indignation led to organizing the first national conference to discuss black women's social concerns. In July 1895, a hundred women from ten states convened to formulate plans for a national federation of black women.

The following year, Ruffin, who was president of the Women's Club of Boston, called the first Conference of Negro Women, which launched the National Association of Colored Women (NACW) under the motto "lifting as we climb."

These club women, primarily northerners, were reformers and activists who subscribed to the class values of Victorian America. The NACW's goal was to uplift poor women by emphasizing respectable behavior and introducing alternate images of black females. Ruffin saw it as "fitting" for the women of the race to take the lead in the movement, while recognizing "the necessity of the sympathy of our husbands, brothers, and fathers." She emphasized that the movement "is led and directed by women for the good of women and men, for the benefit of all humanity."

The club women's movement enabled black women to take a leadership role in their communities and to participate with black men in "uplifting" the race. African American Studies professor Paula Giddings notes that at a time when patriarchal notions of men's roles were dominant, "there was a greater acceptance among black men of women in activist roles than there was in the broader society."[10]

A BLACK WOMAN'S ERA

Although black women faced many challenges, the emergence of black female leaders and the conscious efforts to improve the education of black women bore significant fruit around the turn of the century. Novelist Frances Harper, whose writings focused on the political struggles of African American people, characterized this period as a "woman's era." Chicago activist Fannie Barrier Williams declared that although "the colored man and the colored woman started even, the achievements of black women during this period eclipsed black men."[11]

From 1890 to 1910, the number of professional black women increased by 219 percent, compared to a 51 percent rise for black men. In 1890, about 25 percent of all black professionals were women. By 1910, that number had risen to 43 percent. The growing achievement of women was reflected in the fact that in 1910 female graduates outnumbered male graduates by two to one at Dunbar High School, the leading black high school in Washington, DC.[12]

In her study of black women's education, Jeanne Noble argued that black women had higher levels of educational achievement than men because the

> social system of the Negro rewarded the enterprising, clever, ambitious woman. Later, when attitudes that challenged the women's right to college education emerged, missionaries and earlier college founders were able to overcome these attitudes partly because of the need for teachers to educate the masses of ignorant Negroes.[13]

The perceived limitations in job opportunities for black men also contributed to the disparity between male and female academic achievement. Benjamin Mays, who received a PhD from the University of Chicago and became president of Morehouse College, faced great opposition to his education from his father, who believed the only occupations for black men were preaching and farming.

Two additional factors encouraged black women's academic achievements. The first was the high probability that even married black women would need to find employment outside the home. In addition, many black women sought to avoid the degradation of domestic service, seen as a continuation of the oppression they had experienced during slavery.

The growth in black women's quest for education during this period can be seen in the enrollment trends at the thirteen schools of higher education run by the Baptist Home Mission. In 1880, male enrollment in these schools was twice as high as female enrollment. But by 1892, female students outnumbered males nearly three to two, and 120 of the 202 teachers were women. Most of the female students specialized in teacher training.

Not only were black women going to school in increasing numbers, they were also providing leadership by founding new schools specifically to train black women. Lucy C. Laney, Nannie Helen Burroughs, Charlotte Hawkins Brown, and Mary McLeod Bethune all founded training institutions.

In addition, black women actively challenged the authority of black men. Charlotte Hawkins Brown, for example, declared that her own work and writings were just as important as those of Booker T. Washington. Nannie Burroughs defied the male-dominated leadership so forcibly that she nearly lost church financial support for the National Training School for Women. Burroughs also canceled a speech before the National Christian Mission when administrators insisted on censoring her remarks.

THE COMMITMENT TO MARRIAGE

When studying black middle- and upper-income women in Illinois at the turn of the century, the historian Shirley Carlson found that

> the black community did not regard intelligence and femininity as conflicting values, as the larger society did. That society often expressed the fear that intelligent women would develop masculine characteristics. . . . Blacks seemed to have no such trepidations, or at least they were willing to have their women take these risks.[14]

Many prominent black women were married to professional black men. In addition to Wells and Barnett, there were figures like Shirley Graham DuBois, an author, composer, playwright, and activist, who was married to W. E. B. DuBois, a scholar, visionary, activist, and author. Teacher and social worker Sadie Grey Mays was the wife of Benjamin Mays, mentor to Martin Luther King Jr., and president of Morehouse College. Eslanda Goode Robeson was a writer and social anthropologist, and was business manager for her husband Paul Robeson, the athlete, lawyer, author, activist, actor, and singer.

Margaret Murray Washington was president of the National Federation of Afro-American Women and was the wife of Booker T. Washington, president of Tuskegee Institute. Lugenia Hope Burns had a distinguished career as a social work reformer and was married to John Hope, the first black president of Atlanta

University. Josephine Wilson Bruce, the first African American principal of a Cleveland public school, was married to the first African American to serve a full term in the United States Senate, Blanche K. Bruce.

Josephine St. Pierre Ruffin, the editor and publisher of *The Women's Era*, was married to George L. Ruffin, a member of the Boston City Council and Boston's first black judge. Madam C. J. Walker, owner of a beauty products company, was the first self-made female millionaire (black or white) and was married to a newspaperman, Charles J. Walker. Mary Terrell was a distinguished educator, suffragette, and civil rights activist, whose husband, Robert Terrell, was a Harvard graduate and principal of the M Street High School and the first African American judge on the DC Municipal Court.

In that era, prominent black women tended to have experienced greater upward mobility than their white counterparts. About 90 percent of the black women who were classified as middle to upper class had been born into working-class families, compared to 35 percent of white women. The difference arose in part because blacks had been emancipated for only a relatively short time, and higher education was the vehicle for social mobility for African Americans. Surveys conducted during that period found that black women were going to college for two primary reasons: to train for a vocation and to prepare for marriage and family life.[15]

Many educated black males were also enthusiastic about marriage and family life with an educated woman. Lugenia Burns and John Hope were both University of Chicago graduate students during their courtship. John, eager to marry and start a family, proposed after Lugenia received her degree. But she had been looking forward to a life of service and declined John's first proposal. Lugenia had four other men also vying for her hand in marriage. But John had an advantage over her other suitors because of his commitment to marital equality. He wrote her a letter saying that when they marry "neither of us [is] to be the servant, yet both of us gladly serve each other in love and patience."[16]

In writing about these marriages, Dr. Marion Cuthbert described them as a "deference of comradeship" by the men to their wives.[17] Anna Julia Cooper described the wives as having a "partnership with husbands on a plane of intellectual equality."[18]

CHANGES IN AFRICAN AMERICAN MARRIAGE

The strong tradition of black women's education and professional employment that began during the club women's movement continued through the twentieth century. Jessie Bernard documented the higher levels of professional achievement found among black women, noting that in 1960 black women constituted 60.8 percent of black professionals, while white women constituted only 37.2 percent of the white professional class.[19]

One reason for the lower professional involvement of white women was the persistence of the nineteenth-century ethos that a woman's place was in the home. When Adlai Stevenson addressed the graduating class of Smith College (ironically the alma mater of both Gloria Steinem and Betty Friedan) in 1955, he told the students that their role in life was to "restore valid, meaningful purpose to life in your home."[20]

Three decades after Jessie Bernard's study of black and white females in the professions, Andrew Hacker found that black women made up 65.1 percent of black professionals, a rise of less than 5 percent, while white women had increased 15 points to 52.6 percent of white professionals.[21] The women's movement had been a catalyst for white women to move into the professional arena. An analysis conducted since Hacker's has found that despite gains in educational attainment and occupational status between 1975 and 2000, the median earnings of white women grew by 32 percent while the median earnings of black women grew by only 22 percent. In addition, although the proportion of black women with college degrees increased, a racial gap in education has endured. In 2007, a study found that 19 percent of black women 25 and older had college degrees compared with over 30 percent of white and non-Hispanic women.[22] This gap is even wider between white and black men.

In the three decades between the Bernard and Hacker studies, the black community has undergone what demographers describe as a "marriage squeeze," where a decrease in the availability of eligible partners leads to lower marriage rates, especially among women.

Using the College and Beyond (C&B) database, which contains the records of more than 80,000 undergraduate students who matriculated at twenty-eight academically selective colleges and universities in 1951, 1976, and 1989, we can compare the marriage and divorce patterns of black and white college-educated men and women. The "marriage squeeze" is reflected in the marriage rates of black graduates of these academically selective institutions roughly twenty years after they entered these schools. Blacks in the database were less likely to be married and more likely to be divorced or separated than their white counterparts. Whereas 77 percent of white women were married, 51 percent of black women were. For male graduates, these figures were 79 percent and 61 percent, respectively. Some 14 percent of the black women were divorced or separated, compared to 6 percent of the white female graduates. For males, the differences in divorce and separation rates were miniscule: 6 percent for black men and 5 percent for white men. Of the four groups, black women had by far the highest rates of marital breakups.[23]

Although the marriage squeeze and/or the mate availability perspectives were first used to explain trends among blacks in lower economic strata, it also affects higher educated black women in that fewer black men with equivalent education are available for them to marry. Social scientists and policy analysts have not paid enough attention to the challenges faced by professional black women in this regard.

For African American women, the marriage squeeze has been exacerbated by the marriage of some of the most eligible black men to either white or Hispanic women. The C&B database didn't indicate the race of a graduate's spouse, but there is reason to believe that many of the black male graduates are not married to black women. In the three decades since the *Loving v. Virginia* decision was declared unconstitutional, ending all race-based legal restrictions on marriage, mixed couples tripled from 2 percent to 6 percent of all marriages. Black/white interracial married couples have increased from 51,000 in 1960 to 363,000 in 2000, a sevenfold increase. Most of these marriages were of professional black men to white or Hispanic women. In view of this, it is not surprising that well-educated black women have fewer marriage options than their black male counterparts.

Black women are also more likely to be married to men who earn less money than they do. Data from the C&B studies show that white married women's *household* incomes were higher than those of black married female graduates, even though the *personal* incomes of the black women were 6 percent higher. This is because the husbands of white women graduates made substantially more money than the husbands of the black women. In fact, black women graduates also earned considerably *more* money than their husbands—exactly the opposite of the pattern for the white women graduates. This was because many of the black women graduates were married to men with less education than they had.

My analysis of the data indicates that the black women graduates, on average, contributed 63 percent of the household income, while white women graduates earned 40 percent of the total household income. Not surprisingly, the income of both black and white male graduates was substantially higher than it was for female graduates. What is more interesting is that the white and black male graduates, on average, earned 78 and 75 percent of the household income respectively.[24] This suggests that the male graduates may have entered more traditional marriages, in terms of gender, than either the white or black female graduates.

In classic exchange theory, traditional marriage has been described as an exchange of a male's economic resources for a female's social and domestic services. As American couples make the transition from more traditional to modern marriages, these marital exchanges are changing, which can be a source of tension and conflict. A wealth of research suggests that when couples get married, they bring with them a mixture of the "good things" and "bad things" from earlier generations, making the transition from traditional to modern marriages a challenging one. On the whole, both black and white male graduates, with substantially higher incomes than those of their wives, are in more traditional marriages than female graduates. This may help explain their lower divorce rates and the fact that differences between the divorce rates of black and white males were infinitesimal.

The tensions and pressures in college-educated professional black women's marriages, however, are reflected in their much higher rates of divorce and separation. As noted earlier, household income for white women graduates was higher than for black women even though their own earnings were, on average, 6 percent lower than those of the black women and considerably lower than their husbands' earnings. This seems to indicate that white women graduates may "downsize" their careers as they perform more family functions than their husbands, who focus on increasing their incomes. Black women had less opportunity or pressure to downsize their careers.

Some black wives may harbor anger and resentment that they earn more than their husbands, and some husbands may be resentful that they do not earn enough money to have wives who can downsize their careers, and that anger may be displaced or misdirected at spouses. This may help explain the higher divorce and separation rates of African American female graduates.

Bart Landry analyzed data from the National Survey of Families and Households (NSFH), which was first conducted in 1987–1988, and he found that black husbands contributed somewhat more to household chores than white husbands. According to Landry, black husbands spent on average 22.2 hours on household tasks, whereas white husbands spent 18.4 hours.[25] Other studies have supported Landry's findings and suggest that the greater involvement of black husbands in household chores may be one way of compensating for their smaller incomes relative to their wives.

The late C. Wright Mills, in *The Sociological Imagination*, distinguished between an individual's personal troubles, such as being unable to find a job or being involved in a divorce, and public issues, such as patterns of widespread joblessness or high rates of marital disruption. Mills argued that the "sociological imagination" allows us to see the interconnection between an individual's troubles and broader patterns in society.[26]

Marriage in the African American community is a case in point. The historical analysis of black marriage over the past 100 years demonstrates that African Americans were in the vanguard of creating the modern egalitarian marriage. Marriage has both public and private domains, and the evolution of the institution is determined both by the individual emotions, cultural ideals, practices that couples bring to their unions, and by the values and constraints of any given historical moment. African Americans have helped shape modern marriage, and now they must adapt to economic circumstances where wives are not only equal partners, but often outearn their husbands. The complex reality that couples must pave new paths but also feel pressure to adapt to current conditions must be addressed as we create public policy to support marriage as an institution.

Notes

1. Wells and Duster (1970), p. 101.
2. Gordon (1991), p. 583.
3. Wells and Duster (1970), p. 244.
4. Cooper in Loewenberg and Bogin (1976), p. 325.
5. Wells and Duster (1970), p. 251.
6. Harris (1978).
7. Foner (1988), p. 84.
8. See Giddings (2008).
9. Jacks in Moses (1978), p. 115.
10. Giddings (1985), p. 59.
11. Williams (1904), p. 544.
12. Higginbotham (1993), p. 41.
13. Noble (1956), p. 45.
14. Carlson (1992), p. 24.
15. Higginbotham (1993), p. 24.
16. Hope in Rouse (1989), p. 23–24.
17. Cuthbert (1936), p. 48.
18. Cooper in Carby (1987), p. 100.
19. Bernard (1966), p. 68–70.
20. Stevenson in Mintz and Kellogg (1988), p. 181.
21. Hacker (1992), p. 120.
22. Bowen and Bok (1998), pp. 175–176.
23. Bowen and Bok (1998), p. 175–176.
24. Bowen and Bok (1998), p. 176–178.
25. Landry (2000), p. 158–159.
26. Mills (1959).

8

Changing Counts, Counting Change

*Americans' Movement toward a More Inclusive
Definition of Family*

Brian Powell, Catherine Bolzendahl, Claudia Geist,
and Lala Carr Steelman[1]

This chapter invites students to think about the meaning and definition of family—more specifically, which living arrangements count and do not count as family. We focus on Americans' responses to interviews (from 2003 and 2006) that were the empirical basis of our book *Counted Out: Same-Sex Relations and Americans' Definitions of Family*, as well to a third wave of interviews collected in 2010. These data point to:

1. Large differences in how Americans see certain living arrangements—nearly everyone sees a husband and wife with children as family, and very few (less than 10 percent) see housemates as family.

2. A great deal of disagreement about whether gay and lesbian couples (both with and without children) count as family.

3. Three broad groups of Americans: exclusionists, moderates, and inclusionists. In discussing these groups, we point to some themes that emerged in our interviews and key words that were emphasized by each group.

4. A huge change in these views in a very short period of time—an increasing number of Americans are counting same-sex couples in their definition of family. This change parallels the movement toward greater approval of same-sex marriage. The factors behind these changes—among these, generational

changes and increased contact with lesbians, gay men, and their families—suggest that Americans will continue to move toward a more inclusive vision of family.

The term *family* is ubiquitous. We hear of family values, family meals, family vacations, family-friendly policies, family hour on television, family visitation hours at hospitals, and pro-family advocacy groups, among others. Although it might be assumed that everyone understands what *family* implies, there is no universally accepted definition of what it is. Despite its common usage, the definition of family—and in particular, which living arrangements count as family and which ones are counted out—continues to be questioned and debated. Does a couple have to be married to be counted as a family? Is the presence of children a requirement for being counted as family? Do gay and lesbian couples count? Do housemates count?

The answers to these questions are important. Americans now have a diversity of living arrangements—more so than ever before. Whether these living arrangements are seen as family can have direct consequences for people's lives. Families enjoy many rights and privileges—ranging from family discounts to inheritance rights—that are not provided to others. Imagine, for example, finding out your partner whom you have been living with for over a decade was seriously hurt in a car accident but you were not allowed to visit him or her in the hospital because you were not counted as a family member. Imagine that after spending forty years together and building a life with a partner, you find that all your joint possessions were taken away upon your partner's death because the two of you were not seen as a family. Imagine being informed that your child was going to be removed from a school because the school officials did not consider you and your partner to be a family. Knowing where we all stand in our definitions of family tells us who is seen as deserving of the rights and privileges of family. Understanding how our definitions have changed also provides insight into how law, culture, and society may be shifting overall.

For over a decade, we have been studying Americans' definitions of family and have focused on a simple question: What living arrangements do Americans count *in* their definition of family and what living arrangements are counted *out* of the definition of family? To answer this question, we conducted interviews in 2003, 2006, and 2010 with more than two thousand Americans.[2] More specifically, we asked:

> People these days have differing opinions of what counts as a family. Next, I will read you a number of living arrangements and I will ask you whether you personally think this arrangement counts as family.

Many different living arrangements could fall under the category of family. For this project, we asked about eleven of these arrangements:

- A husband and a wife living together with one or more of their children

- A man and a woman living together as an unmarried couple with one or more of their children

- A man living alone with one or more of his children

- A woman living alone with one of more of her children

- Two women living together as a couple with one or more of their children

- Two men living together as a couple with one or more of their children

- A husband and a wife living together with no children

- A man and a woman living together as an unmarried couple who have no children

- Two people living together as housemates who are not living as a couple and have no children

- Two women living together as a couple who have no children

- Two men living together as a couple who have no children

These living arrangements vary along three key dimensions: whether they are married, cohabiting, or single; whether they are a couple; and whether they have children.

WHICH LIVING ARRANGEMENTS COUNT AS FAMILY?

Figure 8.1 displays the percentage of Americans in the 2010 survey who viewed each living arrangement as a family. Looking at these responses, we see a great deal of agreement about some living arrangements, but a great deal of disagreement about others. Regarding agreement, everyone (100 percent) counted a husband, a wife, and their children as a family. Closely following were a single mother and her children (96 percent), a single father and his children (95 percent), and a married heterosexual couple without children (92 percent).

There also was a great deal of agreement regarding housemates, but in this case nearly everyone (90 percent) agreed that housemates did not count as a family. This was even true among young adults—including college-aged adults who recently may have lived with housemates and presumably should be most open regarding this living arrangement. In fact, the group most likely to say that housemates count as family ironically consisted of people from the other side of the spectrum: adults over the age of sixty-four. Their greater receptiveness

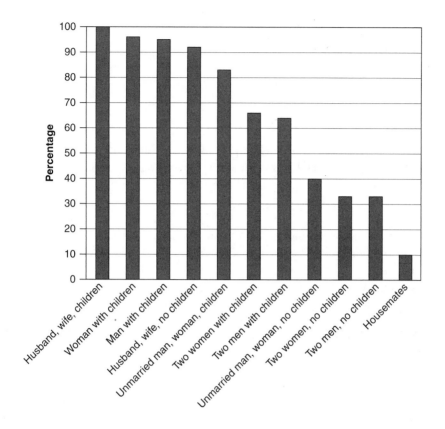

Figure 8.1 | Which Living Arrangements Count as Family?

Source: *Constructing the Family Survey* (Powell 2010).

to what some refer to as "chosen family" may be due to their recognition of the increasing number of people from their generation who share living facilities with non-relatives and the decreasing number who live nearby their extended kin.[3] In this regard, the oldest participants in our survey were the most expansive; however, they were not as expansive in their views of other living arrangements, as we discuss later in this chapter.

In contrast to their shared agreement that married heterosexual couples (with or without children) and single-parent households counted as family and house-mates did not, Americans varied considerably in their views regarding unmarried heterosexual couples and especially same-sex couples. Regarding a man and woman living together as an unmarried couple, approximately five-sixths of Americans (83 percent) conferred family status to this couple if it had children, but only two-fifths (40 percent) counted this couple as a family if it was childless. The numbers for same-sex couples are even lower: almost two-thirds defined a lesbian couple (66 percent) or a gay male couple (64 percent) with children as a family, while only one-third (33 percent) counted either couple as a family if it was childless.

PATTERNS IN FAMILY DEFINITIONS

These percentages provide just one picture—a very broad one—of how Americans define family. But there is a different way of looking at Americans' responses: by examining how these responses cluster together.[4] The people we interviewed fell into three categories:

- *Exclusionists*: Exclusionists take the most restrictive definition of family of the three groups. They believe in the most "traditional" definition of family, or what the Canadian sociologist Dorothy Smith called the Standard North American Family—which strongly emphasizes heterosexual, married households, and, in particular, those that include children and those in which women and men assume traditional gender roles.[5] Exclusionists may accept other family forms, but only under certain conditions. For example, exclusionists may count single-parent households as family, but do so only because they are giving these households, in the words of one person we interviewed, "the benefit of the doubt" by assuming that the single parenthood was involuntary (for example, being a widow or widower). Exclusionists are divided about the inclusion of cohabiting heterosexual couples as family, but unequivocally exclude same-sex couples with or without children in their definition of family.

- *Inclusionists*: At the other end of the continuum, inclusionists embrace a very broad, all-encompassing definition of family that includes each living arrangement (other than roommates) as family—as long as the living arrangement feels like and functions like a family. This group makes little or no distinction between households with and without children, between married and unmarried households, and—in sharp contrast to exclusionists—between same-sex and heterosexual households.

- *Moderates*: Moderates are positioned between exclusionists and inclusionists. If exclusionists are closed and inclusionists are open in their definitions of family, the best word for moderates is *ajar*. That is, they are partially open to a more expansive definition of family, especially if, as we discuss later, the people in the household show some signal of commitment to each other.

These signals can include marriage or the presence of children. For moderates, married couples and all living arrangements that involve children—including same-sex couples with children—count as family.

HOW AMERICANS TALK ABOUT FAMILY

To better understand exclusionists, moderates, and inclusionists, we asked people to explain why they counted certain living arrangements but not others as family and to describe what they thought determined whether a living arrangement is a family. Exclusionists, moderates, and inclusionists relied on starkly different frameworks and emphasized different words in their explanations. To summarize these differences, Figure 8.2 identifies some of the most frequently used words in the interviews in 2010. As you can see, comments regarding the Bible—for example, "it's the rules, the Bible," "what the Bible tells me," and "the Bible is very specific about it"—as well as religion and God were most frequently brought up by exclusionists. In fact, nearly four-fifths (79 percent) of all references to the word *Bible* were made by exclusionists; to this group, the definition of family is firmly rooted in religious tradition and the Bible. The remaining one-fifth (21 percent) were made by moderates. Conspicuously absent were inclusionists—none of whom explicitly referred to the Bible.

Exclusionists also were much more likely to discuss family in gender-specific terms—for example, "husband and wife," "a biblical reference to a man and a woman," and "a relationship between a man and a woman." These comments often were accompanied by a discussion of legal institutions, especially marriage. To exclusionists, the legal status of marriage was fundamental to the definition of family—for example, "it's a legal relationship. You need to make it legal when living together," "as long as they're a legally constituted couple, they're a family: legally married, it's husband and wife," and "it's a legal, lawful relationship." In other words, exclusionists were most likely to focus on the structure of family—a structure that was sanctioned by the law or religion.

If exclusionists emphasized structure, inclusionists emphasized function. That is, inclusionists focused on how families act and what families actually do. To inclusionists, if a living arrangement acted like a family and felt like a family, it was a family.

In many ways, inclusionists were the most romantic of the three groups. Their frequent discussions of love signaled their romantic view of families—for example, "people who love each other, that's all," "a group of people that was together and love each other are a family," and "it's two souls together who love

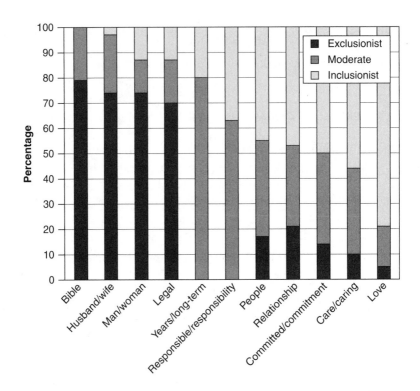

Figure 8.2 | Words Frequently Used by Exclusionists, Moderates, or Inclusionists

Source: *Constructing the Family Survey* (Powell 2010).

each other and have a commitment to each other." Approximately four-fifths (79 percent) of the references to love were made by inclusionists, in contrast to the very few mentions of this word (5 percent) by exclusionists. To inclusionists, it did not matter if the living arrangement was man/woman, two women, or two men as long as they're "living together, sharing love, and sharing their lives with one another." In fact, because most inclusionists did not distinguish between heterosexual and same-sex couples, they were much more likely than exclusionists to refer to *relationships* or *people* (as opposed to gender-specific or legal terms like *husband* and *wife*), for example:

> People living together are the unit, no matter what their marital status and what their sexual preference is. If they're living together with same goals, to me, that constitutes a family.

Not only were inclusionists the most romantic; they also were the most pragmatic. For example, they were more likely—in fact, over five times more likely—than exclusionists to mention the word *care* (or the phrase "taking care of"), often at the same time that they referred to *love* or *commitment*:

> people committed to one another wanting the best for each other with a mutual love and respect. They take care of each other and make sure their needs are met, everyone's needs are met.

Moderates also often used *commitment*, but in a different way than that used by inclusionists. Inclusionists started with the assumption that if a couple defined itself as a family, it automatically should be seen as committed and as a family. Moderates required a more clear-cut signal that the couple was committed. This signal could be in the form of marriage or parenthood. But the reason these were signals is that both suggested a permanent relationship—or at least a relationship that was hard to dissolve. As one respondent explained:

> A family is a group of people who have responsibility for each other and who you cannot get away from. For example, maybe two people live together, even have a relationship. But they can leave anytime, you know. But with children, they will carry these things for life.

The absence of marriage for most same-sex couples was problematic for our survey purposes. Same-sex marriage was illegal in every state during our first set of interviews in 2003 and was legal in very few states (Iowa, Massachusetts, New Hampshire, and Vermont, along with Washington, DC) during our third wave of interviews in 2010. This situation made it difficult for moderates to see a same-sex couple without children as sufficiently committed to be a family, as seen in the following comments:

> Oh, God! Okay to me, it's like people that are planning on being together for a long period of time. Like being together forever. I've heard of best friends moving in together, and they're kind of like family. So, to me, it's two people that are going to be committed to each other for the long haul, not just . . . I don't know. No, I mean, I'm not saying that two men and two women can't be in it for the long haul, but there's nothing binding them together.

At the time of the writing of this essay, same-sex marriage was legalized in seventeen states and Washington, DC, and the prohibition against same-sex marriage was being challenged in several other states. The increasing number of states that permit same-sex marriage means that gay and lesbian couples will have more opportunities to "be in it for the long haul"—as the moderate above described it—because there's something (that is, marriage) binding them together.

Regardless of the current status of same-sex marriage, moderates also were willing to look for other markers of commitment. Among these was the duration of the relationship—in particular, the presence of a long-term relationship, regardless of marital status or parenthood:

> I think it's a long-term couple, whether you're a man and woman, woman and woman, or man and man. Whether you have children or not. If you're a long-term couple, I think that's a family.

The frequent references to relationship length led us to ask a series of supplementary questions that spoke to this issue. Recall that moderates considered a same-sex couple a family only if the couple had children. We decided to provide additional information about childless same-sex couples. We asked whether moderates (as well as inclusionists and exclusionists) considered a childless same-sex couple a family "from the moment they move in together" and, if not then, "if they have lived together as a couple for ten years." This information dramatically changed moderates' views. Almost three-fifths (58 percent) now counted a childless same-sex couple as a family if the couple had lived together for a decade. In other words, time together is such a compelling indicator of commitment that it can push many moderates toward a more inclusive vision of family.

Evidence of responsibility, we found, was another proxy for commitment. This responsibility could be emotional, personal, or financial, or some combination of these:

> My definition of a family? I guess one or more people that live together under one roof with or without children where there is some semblance of responsibility toward each other. More than just monetarily but also romantically. . . . If they have a mutual dependence on each other.

When we asked more detailed questions, we discovered that moderates' willingness to take into account other indicators of commitment beyond parenthood and marriage also provided an opening for moderates to move further away from the views of exclusionists and closer to those of inclusionists. We suspect that the more moderates become aware of people in other living arrangements who are committed to each other and who are responsible for each other, the more receptive they will become to a more inclusive definition of family.

CHANGES IN FAMILY DEFINITIONS OVER TIME

Social scientists who study public opinion are documenting slow—often blazingly slow—changes in social attitudes. It is rare for public views to change dramatically in a short period of time. Views regarding the definition of family are an important exception, as can be seen in Figure 8.3. In 2003, almost half (45 percent) of Americans were exclusionists. Far more Americans were exclusionists than either moderates (29 percent) or inclusionists (25 percent).[6] In a short period of time, however, the number of exclusionists decreased while the number of both moderates and inclusionists increased. By 2010, the country was evenly divided among exclusionists (34 percent), moderates (34 percent), and inclusionists (33 percent). To put it another way, in 2003, approximately half of all Americans counted at least some type of same-sex couple (for example, a lesbian couple with children) as a family; but by 2010, two-thirds of Americans were willing to do so. This is one of the most remarkable, rapid changes in public opinion that we have seen.

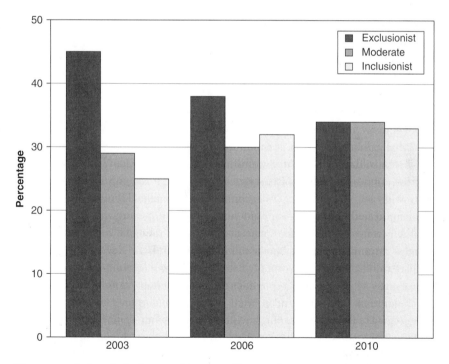

Figure 8.3 | Family Definition Clusters: Changes between 2003, 2006, and 2010

Source: *Constructing the Family Survey* (Powell 2003, 2006, 2010).

These changes also mirror changing attitudes toward same-sex marriage. Nearly every exclusionist staunchly opposed same-sex marriage, while nearly every inclusionist favored it. Moderates fell in between—at least half were in favor of same-sex marriage. Given the decrease in the number of exclusionists and corresponding increase in the number of inclusionists and moderates since 2003, it is not surprising that support for same-sex marriage increased so much in such a short period of time. In 2003, approximately three-fifths of the Americans we interviewed opposed same-sex marriage. Americans' views on this topic shifted so quickly that by 2010, the tide had turned and more Americans were in favor of same-sex marriage than opposed it. Today, virtually all national polls confirm that a clear majority of Americans believe that same-sex couples should have the legal right to marry.

What accounts for this remarkable turnabout in Americans' views? Several factors come into play. Among these is "cohort replacement"—younger generations who grew up in different times becoming the older generations. Earlier we noted that the oldest participants in our survey were the most likely to include housemates in their definition of family. But they also were the most likely to be exclusionist and the least likely to count any type of same-sex couples in their definition of family. The conservative views of adults over the age of sixty-four were a mirror image of the more liberal views of adults under the age of thirty, who were the most likely to be inclusionist. It is true that sometimes people become more conservative as they age. But with cohort replacement, change is not about aging. Instead, we observed that the shift to more inclusionists and fewer exclusionists is about generations—members of the younger generation are likely to continue to hold their inclusionist views as they age. This means that as the younger generation replaces the older one, the number of inclusionists and moderates will rise and the number of exclusionists will decline while the support for same-sex marriage will continue to increase—even if no one changes his or her mind about these topics.

But people, even members of the oldest generations, are changing their minds—or, as some commentators call it, evolving. This evolution is due at least in part to Americans' increased contact with—or increased recognition that they know—gay men and lesbians and same-sex couples. For decades, social psychologists have posited and confirmed that increased intergroup contact can reduce prejudice toward and discrimination against minority group members.[7] This insight applies to attitudes about sexuality and views regarding who counts as a family. From our interviews, we find that a growing number of Americans realize that some of their relatives, friends, co-workers, and neighbors are gay or lesbian. Our interviews also show that Americans who know someone who is gay or lesbian—and especially Americans who are close to someone who is gay or lesbian—are much more inclusive in their definitions of family. Interestingly, even "knowing" a gay or lesbian fictional character from a television show (for example, *Glee* or *Modern Family*) or an openly gay media or public figure (for example, Anderson Cooper or Ellen DeGeneres) can trigger similarly favorable reactions to those elicited by direct interpersonal contact. In other words, contact—both real and mediated—is a driving force behind Americans' greater openness toward a broad range of family forms.

These factors, along with others (for example, the rising number of people who see sexuality as an unchangeable orientation instead of a choice), give us great confidence in predicting that Americans will continue to move toward a more inclusive definition of family that recognizes families as they really are: people who love each other, who care for each other, and who are committed to and are responsible for each other. We see a day in the near future when same-sex households will gain the acceptance that other families receive and when same-sex couples will no longer be counted out.

NOTES

1. The authors thank the many graduate and undergraduate students who served on the research team that conducted these interviews. Special thanks are owed to Oren Pizmomy-Levy and Christina Ek, who offered valuable feedback on this manuscript.

2. More information about the project and a more detailed discussion of the patterns can be found in Powell, Bolzendahl, Geist, and Steelman (2010).

3. For a discussion of the various conceptualizations of chosen family, see Weston (1997).

4. We used a method called Latent Statistical Analysis that allowed us to identify the way people's views clustered together. For more information regarding latent class analysis, see McCutcheon (1987).

5. A more detailed description and critique of the Standard North American Family can be found in Smith (1993).

6. Some percentages in Figure 8.3 do not add to 100 because of rounding errors: 45.3 percent of Americans were exclusionists, but this number was rounded to its closest whole number (45 percent).

7. For a discussion of the contact hypothesis, which was introduced by psychologist Gordon Allport (1954), see Pettigrew and Tropp (2006).

In Other Words

FAFSA FORM WILL NOW RECOGNIZE COLLEGE STUDENTS' SAME-SEX PARENTS

ThinkProgress, April 29, 2013

Crosby Burns

Today the U.S. Department of Education announced a small but significant change to the FAFSA, the Free Application for Federal Student Aid, that will make the application a more fair, effective, and efficient tool for students seeking financial aid to finance their college education.

The FAFSA currently uses the terms "mother/stepmother" and "father/stepfather" when requesting information about an applicant's parents. Applicants with same-sex parents then must either arbitrarily designate one parent as "mother" and the other as "father," or omit one parent from the form entirely. In other words, the current FAFSA puts these applicants in a lose-lose scenario forcing them to complete and submit an application that is inaccurate and not reflective of their family structure.

Today's proposal will help change that. For the 2014–2015 FAFSA, the Department will amend the terms "Mother/Stepmother" and "Father/Stepfather" to instead read "Parent 1" and "Parent 2." This change also means that for the first time the Department will collect same-sex parents' financial information in the same way that it does for different-sex parents. In addition to accurately reflecting LGBT families, these changes will capture the economic situation of these families so that students applying for aid can access financial aid based on their true financial need—without any bearing on their parents' sexual orientation.

This change mimics similar changes made at other federal agencies. In 2011, for example, the State Department initiated reforms to give passport forms a more gender-neutral parental designation. Doing so required minimal changes to federal forms while significantly enhancing the accuracy, fairness, effectiveness, and efficiency of government operations.

At its core, this much-needed change achieves two important policy objectives.

First, this change guarantees that all families are treated fairly and equally in the higher education financial aid process. Without accurate language to describe their families, students with same-sex parents are likely to see their application delayed due to often unavoidable inaccuracies. Some may not even submit an application at all due to the complexity and confusion caused by the FAFSA's use of gendered language. What results is inequitable access to financial aid for students with same-sex parents. This change significantly levels the playing field for these applicants.

Second, this change advances the efficiency and effectiveness of delivering aid based on need, and not allowing irrelevant factors such as sexual orientation to factor into the application process. Financial aid should be allocated based solely on financial need. Allowing other factors to enter the process results in the imprudent use of taxpayer dollars. The proposed change from the Department would be a significant step forward toward enhancing the efficient use of federal funds.

What's more, these proposed changes are likely to have a ripple effect throughout the college financial aid system. Many private organizations, non-profits, and local and state government serve as significant sources of financial aid for potential college students. Because many of these entities model their application for higher education financial aid after the FAFSA, the proposed changes will likely have a trickle-down effect such that the entire process becomes more fair for these students.

Still, anti-gay adoption laws and the Defense of Marriage Act (DOMA) continue to present a number of problems for students with same-sex parents. Nevertheless, today's announcement is a huge step forward for LGBT equality in higher education, one that other agencies should also implement so that all families are treated equally under the law. ■

9

Interracial Families in Post–Civil Rights America

Kerry Ann Rockquemore and Loren Henderson

In the four decades since the U.S. Supreme Court declared laws prohibiting interracial marriage unconstitutional, the number of interracial families in America has rapidly increased. But interracial families continue to face unique external pressures and internal relational dynamics due to the persistence of racism in America. While formal structural barriers have been reduced, interracial dating on campuses has increased, and attitudes toward acceptance of interracial marriage have improved, interracial couplings continue to be the rare exception (and not the rule) when it comes to new marriages. This chapter explores why interracial families continue to be so uncommon in the United States, and it describes the challenges interracial families face in dealing with individual and institutional racism, responding to the disapproval of family members, and raising mixed-race children in what is still not a "color-blind" world.

June 12, 2007, marked the fortieth anniversary of the historic Supreme Court decision (*Loving v. Virginia*) that struck down state laws prohibiting interracial marriage. Reporters celebrated the fourfold increase in interracial marriage rates since 1970 and the corresponding decline in opposition to interracial marriage in opinion polls. The concurrent rise of political superstar Barack Obama and a proliferation of multiracial celebrities, athletes, and writers have further focused national attention on interracial families and reframed their mixed-race offspring from "tragic mulattoes" to "Generation E.A.: Ethnically Ambiguous."[1] Indeed, the message repeatedly put forward in the media and in popular discourse is that in post–civil rights America, love, marriage, and child rearing are all color-blind.

Less well reported is that interracial marriages represent a tiny sliver of all marriages in the United States. In 1970, less than 1 percent of marriages were interracial, and by 2005 that number increased to 7.5 percent of all marriages. Stated differently, over 92 percent of all marriages today are between people of the same race. Interestingly, of the 7.5 percent of marriages that are interracial, marriages between blacks and whites remain the least likely combination. While it is true that more young people today are dating and living with someone of a different race, those interracial relationships are far less likely than same-race relationships to lead to marriage.[2] Many argue that race is declining in significance, but the fact that interracial marriages continue to hover in the single digits—and are least likely between blacks and whites—suggests that the color-blind rhetoric may be ahead of reality.

The disconnection between Americans' attitudes toward interracial marriage and their behavior illustrates the awkward historical moment that we currently inhabit. On the one hand, in the four decades since the U.S. Supreme Court declared laws prohibiting interracial marriage unconstitutional, the number of interracial families in the United States has rapidly increased, interracial dating on college campuses has become more common, and attitudes toward interracial marriage have improved.[3] On the other hand, interracial families continue to report unique external pressures due to the persistence of racism and negotiations over the classification of their mixed-race children. As a result, interracial couplings continue to be the rare exception (and certainly not the rule) when it comes to marriage in the United States.

At a deeper level, the discrepancy between attitudes and behavior mirrors the changing nature of race relations in the United States. Several decades after the passage of civil rights legislation, structurally rooted racial inequalities continue to persist in our social institutions, ranging from public schools to health care to the criminal justice system. Yet, despite these racial inequalities, Americans increasingly believe that race is declining in significance, and many have adopted a "color-blind" ideology in which racism and discrimination are viewed as relics of the past, inequalities are understood to be class-based (as opposed to race-based), and where institutions and individuals are assumed to act in race-neutral ways. This simultaneous denial of racial inequalities and widespread desire to move "beyond race" stand in stark contrast to the persistence of race as a determining factor in life chances, opportunities, and mate selection.[4]

In this chapter, we examine the disconnection between beliefs and behavior by exploring the distinctive challenges that interracial families face in a simultaneously "color-blind" and racialized world. We focus specifically on interracial relationships between blacks and whites because they are the two groups that have the greatest social distance, their coupling carries the greatest social stigma, and the relative rarity of intermarriage between the two groups best illustrates the influence that structural patterns hold over our seemingly individual decisions about whom we have sex with, date, and marry.[5] We also explore the challenges associated with raising mixed-race children and how those challenges have changed over time. Our central goal is to make visible the invisible racial structures to better understand why interracial families continue to be so uncommon in the United States in spite of the widespread perception that we live in a post-racial and "color-blind" society.

THE HISTORY OF BLACK/WHITE COUPLING

Interracial relationships, marriages, and children are of great interest to family researchers because they exist outside the "normal" patterns of mate selection. In other words, when individuals date and marry across the color line, they are defying long-standing patterns of racial endogamy (i.e., marrying someone within your own racial group). The historical norm in American families has been to date, marry, and have children with someone of the same race. As a result, when people partner cross-racially, it not only seems "different" or "unusual," but depending on the time period, it may also have been unimaginable, illegal, nonconsensual, and/or dangerous. Every historical moment has its own specific racial stratification system at work. That system not only outlines the rules of behavior between races but also shapes how we understand our own race, the relative position of racial groups, and our individual expectations about the race of our sexual, dating, and marital partners.

Throughout U.S. history, black sexuality and marriage have been the subject of legal, cultural, and political regulation because of the flawed beliefs that (1) black people are fundamentally and biologically *different* from whites, and that (2) blacks are intellectually, culturally, and genetically *inferior* to whites.[6] During various historical periods, racial stratification systems (grounded in beliefs of white superiority) have supported elaborate mechanisms of separation and necessitated endogamy so that blacks and whites were not only expected, but *required* to create families within their own racial groups. Social norms and laws prohibiting interracial marriage emerged to support racial stratification systems (such as slavery or segregation) so that interracial sex and marriage were institutionally restricted through the legal system and individually regulated through interpersonal violence, rape, and intimidation.[7]

As a system of stratification, slavery relied upon ideas of racial difference and black inferiority to rationalize the domination and exploitation of Africans in America. As slaves, blacks were considered subhuman property of their slave owners. In order to control slaves and maintain white supremacy, interracial coupling was strictly prohibited, and the one-drop rule was used to determine who was "black."[8] Miscegenation (or racial mixing) was strictly regulated so that "black blood" would not taint the purity of the white race. In spite of formal prohibitions against miscegenation, however, black female slaves were regularly sexually assaulted and raped by white slave owners. Because of the one-drop rule and the slave system, their mixed-race children were considered black, became part of the slave population, and were counted as the property of their biological fathers. In contrast, white women were protected from the specter of black male sexuality because while a mixed-race child in the slave quarters may have been socially tolerated and considered a financial asset, a mixed-race child born to a white woman directly threatened the purity of the white race and the logic of the slave system. Because of this unequal sense of threat, the mere hint of sexual contact between black men and white women was punishable by public beating, castration, and/or death.

After the Civil War, slavery was replaced by a new system of racial stratification: segregation. While the system changed, the core beliefs of racial difference and black inferiority stayed the same. Blacks were no longer slaves, but they were still believed to be biologically *different* from whites, and intellectually *inferior* to whites. Segregation required the formalization of antimiscegenation laws and explicit legal definitions of who belonged in the category "black." In this historical context, the norm of racial endogamy, firmly rooted in the ideology of white supremacy, was a powerful mechanism shaping an individual's mate selection options. Blacks and whites were legally and socially prohibited from cross-racial contact, and blacks were terrorized by widespread lynchings and brutal violence. Blacks and whites were "separate but equal" in law, and separate and grossly unequal in reality. Interracial marriages were illegal, mixed-race children were considered black, and any form of cross-racial coupling was the ultimate cultural taboo.

The civil rights movement challenged the ideology of white supremacy, institutional inequalities, and individual racism. Activists and intellectuals fought fiercely against the social system of segregation and the ideological belief in black inferiority that it rested upon. In the process, progressives denounced the institutional policies and procedures that inhibited black people's mobility, and they sought to alter black individuals' self-perceptions so that they would value blackness. In this historical period of social change, formal prohibitions against interracial marriage were targeted, and in 1967, the Supreme Court ruled that all state-level antimiscegenation laws were unconstitutional. But while legal and institutional victories had been won, interracial marriages remained rare in the landscape of American families.[9]

When we consider the link between racial stratification systems, racial ideology, and the history of interracial sex and marriage between blacks and whites, we can better understand the stigma attached to interracial marriage and how that stigma is connected to a fundamentally flawed set of beliefs about race (as a biological category) and racial groups (as both different and unequal to one another). The ideas of racial difference and white superiority were historically constructed by the dominant group to support existing racial stratification systems and shaped what is considered a "normal" American family by determining whether (or not) individuals could marry cross-racially. In addition, the elaborate rules of racial categorization that were designed to keep people apart also mandated that mixed-race children were "black" (and black only) irrespective of their mixed ancestry and physical appearance. Because the one-drop rule and the norm of racial endogamy have been uniquely constructed and enforced for blacks and because they are inseparable from the history of slavery and segregation, they allow a particularly clear illustration of the link between structure and mate selection. Throughout American history, black sexuality and marriage have been the subject of legal, cultural, and political control and regulation, shaping what we typically consider an individual choice. While the *Loving v. Virginia* decision terminated state laws against interracial marriage, the norm of racial endogamy and lingering biological notions of race resulted in a social landscape where blacks and whites were expected to marry within their own racial groups.

In post–civil rights America, the legal barriers against interracial marriages no longer exist and attitudes toward interracial dating and marriage have steadily improved in opinion polls. Given the widespread contention that Americans are "color-blind" and that racism is a relic of the past, we would expect that interracial couples would face few interpersonal or institutional obstacles. But researchers have repeatedly documented the myriad ways that interracial couples face covert discrimination and overt racism from family members, friends, and strangers in public places. Additionally, interracial families continue to face subtle institutional and structural forces that marginalize their existence and diminish their quality of life. Below we explain the common external pressures that interracial families face, describe the coping strategies used in the context of such marriages, explore how such couples raise their mixed-race children, and consider what the totality of their lived experiences tell us about the changing nature of race relations in the United States.

EXTERNAL PRESSURES: BORDER PATROLLING IN BLACK AND WHITE

While attitudes toward interracial relationships in national opinion surveys continue to trend in the positive direction of acceptance (for both blacks and whites), the story is a bit more complicated on the ground. Sociologist Erica Childs found that blacks and whites tend to lean in opposite directions in terms of differentiating their *general attitudes* about interracial relationships from their assessment of *specific family members* who are interracially married.[10] Blacks tend to disapprove of interracial relationships generally, but they are tolerant and make exceptions for their family and friends. By contrast, whites tend to express approval of interracial relationships generally, but they disapprove of those relationships for their immediate family or friends.

Heather Dalmage argues that the discrepancy between the attitudes of blacks and whites lies in differential conceptions of same-race relationships. For blacks, marrying within one's racial group is perceived as strengthening the black family and supporting unification in a group struggling for survival and liberation. By contrast, whites tend to support same-race relationships, but they do so unreflectively.[11] These differential views of race and marriage affect how individuals interpret and construct the consequences of interracial coupling. Irrespective of race, class, or gender, those within interracial relationships find themselves regularly faced with insulting questions and forced to legitimize their relationships as loving and consensual in ways that mono-racial couples never consider. These daily experiences, and the harsh realities that interracial couples face, create unique stressors that put additional strains on such relationships and may explain the higher divorce rate among interracial marriages and may also contribute to the decision of many interracial couples to cohabitate instead of marry.[12]

Both black and white partners in interracial relationships commonly report experiencing a particular form of racial hostility that Heather Dalmage describes as border patrolling.[13] Dalmage details various behaviors and attitudes expressed by white family members, friends, peers, and strangers that communicate a consistent and clear message: same-race dating and marriage are "normal," and interracial coupling is "different" and "problematic." When individuals date or marry cross-racially, previously unarticulated boundaries between blacks and whites break out into the open, shifting the way that they are perceived by others, changing their relationships with friends and family, and making them the targets of hostility by strangers. Border patrolling occurs for both black and white partners, although the way it manifests is differentiated by race and gender.

White women who marry black men describe being verbally harassed, socially ostracized, and/or excommunicated from family and friendship networks. As a result, some feel they have been recategorized as inherently "flawed" or "polluted" by other whites, and they describe themselves as "no longer white" or "symbolically black" because of the wholesale rejection and ostracism they experience in their social network. One of Erica Childs's white respondents (named

Kayla) described the response of her white family and friends when she started dating a black man:

> I lost every friend I had. My friends stopped calling me, whenever I would ask them to do something they would be busy, and my ex-boyfriend said I had lost it and was dating someone black to embarrass him.[14]

Kayla experienced a common type of resistance to interracial dating: rejection by her friends and shaming by her former white boyfriend. Her friends' rejection of her because she is dating a black man lies in their (conscious or unconscious) belief that same-race dating is "normal" and that dating a black man is deviant behavior because blacks are *different* from whites. Kayla's ex-boyfriend goes a step beyond ignoring her by openly stating his belief that she was dating someone black to embarrass him. This further illustrates his assumption that blacks are not just different, but *inferior to* whites (i.e., he's embarrassed because she's done something wrong by dating a black man, and that reflects negatively on him).

While white women who date interracially face resistance, marriage is considered a far more serious border crossing because of the implicit long-term commitment and prospect of raising mixed-race children. Interracially married white women, particularly those with mixed-race children, experience more intense and consistent forms of border patrolling, in response to which they may need to protect themselves and their children from overtly racist insults, haggle over how their children will be racially categorized, or deal with nuanced slights, glares, and inappropriate questions that people ask in order to make sense of their family.[15]

White male partners in interracial marriages also experience border patrolling, but it is distinctly different in form and content from that experienced by interracially married white women and is tied to the historical legacy of interracial intimacy. Unlike white women who report being policed and/or openly harassed (by both blacks and whites), white men who are partnered with black women describe resistance to their interracial coupling as expressions of curiosity, confusion, or concern. They are less likely to experience direct and open hostility from whites, but they do report experiencing it from black men. For example, Warren (one of Amy Steinbugler's white male respondents) described the way black men responded to his interracial relationship:

> They'd be like, "Whoa, sister what are you doing with this guy?" I mean it has never—on occasion once or twice was it black women. At least not outspoken, it wasn't white people. The most outspoken were black men who did not like the fact that you could—a white man could have one of their black sisters. They definitely did not like that. It wouldn't be a problem for a black man, if a brother has a white woman. That's cool. The other way it doesn't work.[16]

Black spouses in interracial marriages also experience border patrolling, but it differs from that experienced by their white partners. While all border patrolling rests on the assumption that interracial relationships are "deviant," "disruptive," and "wrong," black partners describe the disapproving responses they receive from other blacks as attacks on their racial identity, group loyalty, and self-worth as a black person.[17] Black partners report negative character judgments, ostracism, speculation about their authenticity as black, and accusations that they are suffering from internalized racism. Often, black partners feel forced to legitimize their relationship to family and friends as a loving partnership, as opposed to a wholesale rejection of members of their own racial group. Daily negotiations over how to present an interracial relationship as loving and healthy can be challenging for many couples, particularly at the outset of their relationship.

The border patrolling that black women and men experience in response to their choice of a white marital partner not only differs in content from that experienced by whites, but it is also distinctly gendered. Black men in interracial relationships may be perceived as "weak," a "sell-out," or disconnected from the black community, and they may face the verbal attacks of other blacks who perceive their coupling as "treachery," "betrayal," and a weakening of the black family. They must also continually negotiate public space and expend energy calculating their safety when accompanying their white partner. While all black men must negotiate public space around police, security guards, and others holding negative stereotypical views, being a black man and coded as having a sexual relationship with a white woman provides an additional layer of vulnerability to harassment.

Like interracially married black men, black women face social consequences such as being seen as a sell-out or "wanting to be white." But black women may also be viewed by those in the black community as "disloyal" for "giving their bodies" to white men, and this is particularly problematic because of the history of exploitative sexual relations between white men and black women. Family members sometimes suspect and fear that black women in interracial relationships will be exposed to racist verbal abuse when arguing with their partners, or explicit racism by their partner's family members. Black women also report being accused of social climbing or attempting to raise their social or economic status by marrying a white male.

Looking Behind the Stereotype of the "Angry Black Woman"

Using survey data, researchers have found that black women hold the least favorable attitudes toward interracial relationships. Qualitative interview studies of black male/white female couples often feature narrative descriptions of mistreatment, hostility, and/or experiences of such couples being openly and publicly challenged about their relationships by black women. Indeed, the "angry black woman" is a persistent image in discussions of interracial intimacy.[18] But few researchers go further to ask why this pattern might exist, what relationship it has to historical trends, and what factors fuel the lack of support for interracial coupling that is expressed by black women.

Notably, researcher Erica Childs interviewed black women to better understand their perspective. She concluded that their responses to interracial relationships are shaped by both white supremacy and structural inequalities that influence who black women perceive they can and should marry.[19] Specifically, black women feel limited by Eurocentric standards of beauty that prize blond hair, blue eyes, and white skin, thereby reducing black women's attractiveness to both black and white partners.[20] As a result, some black women see interracial dating as black men's internalization of racism in which they devalue and reject black women as beautiful and/or preferable partners. Such feelings are compounded by a unique demographic reality: the limited pool of marriageable black men due to disproportionately high incarceration rates, drug abuse, homicide, and unemployment.[21] The cumulative effect of these factors is a large pool of single black women competing for a small number of marriageable black men and feeling their value as potential mates weighed against a white beauty standard. As a result, black women often describe feeling "put down," "left out," and/or "disrespected" by black men who choose to date white women. As Childs's respondent described:

> As a black woman, it is difficult enough to have to deal with whites who [act] as if [black] is inferior, but it is even harder to have your own men act like white is better and systematically choose white women over you; it is hard not to get angry because it feels as if no one values your worth as a woman.[22]

COPING STRATEGIES: FROM COLOR BLINDNESS TO RACIAL LITERACY

The emotionally charged and hostile reactions toward interracial relationships can be painful for those who are interracially married, even if it's clear how differing social locations, histories, and beliefs shape those responses. The problem faced by many interracial families is that unlike the invisible forces of institutional racism (such as differential incarceration rates), interracial coupling is highly visible and easily targeted. Through social sanctions, isolation, and disapproval, interracial dating is far easier to target and resist than any of the structural factors that influence mate selection.

Facing the daily realities of border patrolling, individual partners within inter-racial families are forced to develop coping strategies that range from denial to resistance. Coping strategies tend to evolve from an individual's racial world-view. The sheer act of marrying cross-racially challenges racial borders, and yet some individuals rely on color-blind discourse to interpret the responses of others to their relationship. For them, daily negotiations involve patterns of systematic denial of racist actions against their relationship, particularly when they come from close friends and family. White partners who have been socialized not to talk about race often want to avoid conflict in order to protect their family and friends from being characterized as racist. When explicitly racist incidents occur, they work to forget, ignore, reconstruct, cover up, and deny the problematic actions of their loved ones. This denial can lead to complications within their marital relationships, because the black partner may feel as if the white partner is not defending him or her while the white partner may feel torn between his or her family and partner. The white partner may also feel ashamed and confused when parents who profess to be "color-blind"—and have raised them to treat everyone equally—suddenly resist their relationship with someone of a different race.[23]

Alternatively, some whites are personally transformed by their intimate rela-tionships with a black partner and cope in ways that are similar to those of blacks who have been racially socialized to recognize and resist racism and racial inequalities. Interracially married whites may never have thought about being white, and/or they may have been blind to discrimination prior to their relation-ship. But once coupled with a black partner, these same individuals describe being forced to contend with the ambiguities, contradictions, and racism that are triggered by their relationship. Being exposed to the everyday experiences of racism faced by their black partners and/or their mixed-race children can be a transformative and painful process for white partners.[24] If they were previously shielded from the negative effects of racism, they may be forced to rethink their previous understanding of race relations, confront white privilege, and reexam-ine their own beliefs about race as well as those of their immediate family and friends. In other words, experiencing negative sanctions for partnering with a person of color can transform interracial intimacy into a micro-level politi-cal site that leads some (not all) white partners to shift their stance from one of *color blindness* to *racial cognizance* or *racial literacy*.[25] France Winddance Twine and Amy Steinbugler describe racial literacy as a set of everyday analytic prac-tices that include

(1) a recognition of the symbolic and material value of Whiteness; (2) the defini-tion of *racism* as a current social problem rather than a historical legacy; (3) an

understanding that racial identities are *learned* and an outcome of social practices; (4) the possession of racial grammar and a vocabulary that facilitates a discussion of race, racism, and antiracism; (5) the ability to translate (interpret) racial codes and racialized practices; and (6) an analysis of the ways that racism is mediated by class inequalities, gender hierarchies, and heteronormativity.[26]

This rethinking of race, racism, and racial identity helps white partners to cultivate a critical analysis to understand how larger sociopolitical and historical forces shape the different types of resistance to their interracial relationship that they experience from whites and blacks.

In terms of coping with external pressure and border patrolling, racial literacy leads individuals to reorganize their social networks and reorient their behaviors. For example, Glenn was an interracially married, white male respondent of Twine and Steinbugler. He described how the development of racial literacy increased his awareness of "everyday racism" and racial practices using the following example:

> Now having spent time with [my wife], I realize that I am a bit [racist] in terms of . . . preconceptions and ideas that you have [about black people]. . . . There were jokes about the length of a black man's penis. . . . My attitude then was, "Well, I'd quite like somebody to make a joke about . . . how big mine was." And [my wife] sort of explained to me . . . , and once it had been explained to me, I thought, "You're right." I used to tell jokes like that, but I've avoided those now. . . . As soon as somebody starts to tell a joke that's got any mention of the race of whatever the person, I tend to frown. And then afterwards I dissect the joke.[27]

Glenn's wife helped him to understand how the common social practice of joking about black men's penises was degrading to black people. Glenn's new understanding about racism and how it is reproduced in the everyday practice of joke telling has altered his behavior. Instead of telling these jokes, he now resists their telling and has the mental tools to deconstruct them to the joke teller. His emergent racial literacy enables such daily acts of resistance to the racism and border patrolling that he experiences as a white man married to a black woman.

WHAT ABOUT THE CHILDREN?

One of the most common concerns that interracial couples face is "what about the children?" Implicit in this question is the idea that mixed-race children will be social misfits ("neither fish nor fowl") who will be rejected by both blacks and whites and will be plagued by various pathologies, including depression, identity confusion, and double rejection. In addition to issues of psychological adjustment and racial identity development, "what about the children?" is also a literal question in terms of how mixed-race children will be racially socialized by their parents, as well as classified by the state, institutional bureaucracies, and on various government forms. These "tragic mulatto" stereotypes are not surprising given that throughout American history, racial group membership has been understood as mutually exclusive so that individuals can belong to one (and only one) race. The one-drop rule mandated that mixed-race children be categorized as black and develop a black identity. Only recently have multiracial groups and parents of mixed-race children begun to question and push back against the one-drop rule and the logic underlying it.

While it is true that raising mixed-race children presents particular challenges for parents, the stereotypes of identity confusion are not supported by recent research. Instead, mixed-race adolescents and young adults are creating identities that reflect their particular social context. For example, Kerry Ann Rockquemore and David Brunsma studied mixed-race college students (with one black and one white parent) and found that individuals chose between five different racial identities.[28] Some mixed-race students identified exclusively with the race of one of their parents, self-identifying as "black" (or less commonly as "white"). Others blended the ancestry of both their parents to create a hybrid identity as "biracial," "multiracial," or "mixed." Others shifted between several different identities ("black," "white," and/or "biracial"), depending on where they were and whom they were interacting with in any given environment. Still others refused any racial categorization whatsoever and instead identified themselves as "human."[29] In this way, they were neither constrained by the one-drop rule nor disallowed from the development of an identity that reflects their ancestry, physical appearance, and childhood socialization.

The second important and consistently documented fact about mixed-race children is that, in addition to *variation* in how they racially self-identify, their racial identity may change over their lifetime. This differs from conceptualizations of single-race identity because identity development for mixed-race individuals neither occurs in a predictable linear fashion nor has a single endpoint. Numerous researchers have documented how racial identity is dynamic and changing as their mixed-race respondents move through their lives, shifting and changing as they are linked to social, material, cultural, economic, and institutional forces.[30] For example, Steven Hitlin, Scott Brown, and Glen Elder demonstrate how mixed-race adolescents follow various "pathways of racial self-identification" over time and are four times more likely to switch their racial identity than to consistently report the same identification over time.[31] While change occurs, it varies between diversifying, consolidating, or maintaining "multiracial" self-identification.

Certainly, mixed-race children and adolescents face situations in which they are literally forced into self-designating as a member of just one racial group (for example, on government forms, applications, and school admission forms). Yet, even describing their racial identity as a "choice" obfuscates the reality that such choices are constrained by physical appearance, the broader context and history of American race relations, and institutional mandates of identification. Raising healthy mixed-race children and navigating the reality of race and racism in their children's lives creates an additional layer of complexity that is utterly unique to interracial families.

FAMILIES AS THEY REALLY ARE: RACIALLY HOMOGENEOUS

Considering families *as they really are* involves asking critical questions about why dominant patterns in marriages exist, what historical factors underlie those dominant patterns, and what prevents those dominant patterns from changing. In this chapter, we have asked why interracial marriages remain the rare exception in the United States, what happens to individuals who dare to break out of the dominant pattern of marrying someone of the same race, and why racial patterns of endogamy for blacks and whites have been so very slow to change. In that process, it's clear that the seemingly individual decision about whom you find attractive, desire sexually, hook up with, date, live with, marry, divorce, and/or have children with are all "choices" that are fundamentally shaped by race relations and racial ideology in your particular historical moment. In the United States, our rhetoric and thinking may encourage a color-blind worldview, but those who cross the color line experience border patrolling that works against— and fundamentally contradicts—the color-blind ideas that racism is a relic of the past and that race no longer matters in our intimate relationships.

The discrepancy between color-blind beliefs and the reality of resistance to interracial marriages helps us to better understand the slow pace of change in interracial intimacy. When we consider the history of separation and social distance between blacks and whites, as well as the deep well of ideological beliefs about the differences between groups, it is unsurprising that interracial families today continue to face hostility, ostracism, and concern over the fate of their children. And yet, ironically, it is the children of interracial unions who may just force a reconciliation of color-blind attitudes and racist behavior by openly challenging the logic of white supremacy, recognizing the social construction of racial groups, and pushing our country into a new and honest dialogue about the reality of race in America.

NOTES

1. The phrase "Generation E.A." was used by Ruth La Ferla (2003) to describe the trend in advertising to use multiracial and ethnically ambiguous models because racial ambiguity is "chic" among young adults.

2. Simmons and O'Connell (2003) provide an overview of married and cohabitating couples using census data. Qian (1997) documents the differential rates of out-marriage for blacks, Asians, and Native Americans. For an overview of interracial marriage patterns in the United States, see Rosenfeld (2007).

3. Between 1958 and 1997, white approval of intermarriage with blacks rose from 4 percent to 67 percent. Approval rates are even higher among blacks; 87 percent of blacks reported approval of intermarriage in 1997 (Schuman, Steeh, Bobo, and Kryson, 1997).

4. Oliver and Shapiro's *Black Wealth/White Wealth* (1997) provides an overview of persistent institutional and economic inequalities between blacks and whites. Eduardo Bonilla-Silva (2001, 2003) describes the ideology of color blindness that underlies the Latin Americanization of race relations in the United States.

5. We focus explicitly on heterosexual couples in this chapter due to the dearth of empirical research on same-sex interracial couples. Steinbugler (2005) is a notable exception.

6. See Tukufu Zuberi, *Thicker Than Blood* (2001), as well as Omi and Winant (1994) for a macro-structural analysis of race, racial categories, and racism.

7. See Randall Kennedy's *Interracial Intimacies* (2003) for an historical analysis of interracial sex and coupling.

8. The "one-drop rule" mandates that anyone with one drop of "black blood" is a member of the black race. The idea is that "black blood" taints the purity of whiteness; therefore, even "one drop" deprives a person of any claim to whiteness. For an overview of the history of the one-drop rule, see F. James Davis, *Who Is Black?* (1991).

9. See Root (2001).

10. See Childs (2005b).

11. See Dalmage (2000).

12. Cohabitation can be seen as qualitatively different from legal marriage in terms of structure and interaction. Given that cohabitating couples may be seen as less stable, this may increase the perception that interracial couples are not as committed to their relationships as are same-race couples (Bratter and Eschbach, 2006).

13. See Dalmage (2000).

14. See Childs (2005b), p. 60.

15. See Dalmage (2000).

16. Steinbugler (2005), p. 433.

17. See Dalmage (2000).

18. See Todd et al. (1992) and McNamara, Tempenis, and Walton (1999).

19. See Childs (2005a).

20. See Russell, Wilson, and Hall (1993).

21. Patricia Hill Collins (2004) critically examines how European notions of femininity and beauty combine with new forms of racism to disadvantage black women.

22. Childs (2005a), p. 554.

23. See Childs (2005b).

24. Some of the most powerful illustrations of the transformative power of interracial relationships appear in memoirs such as Jane Lazarre's *Beyond the Whiteness of Whiteness* (1996) and Maureen Reddy's *Crossing the Color Line* (1994).

25. Frankenberg (1993) describes the discrimination and intolerance that white women in interracial couples experience secondhand as "rebound racism." Her analysis suggests that intimate relationships between whites and blacks shift white women's perspective on race relations and racism. She uses the term *racial cognizance* to describe a more advanced stage of understanding that whites evolve into as part of their development in interracial relationships.

26. See Twine and Steinbugler (2006), p. 344.

27. The excerpt is drawn from Twine and Steinbugler (2006), p. 354.

28. Rockquemore and Brunsma (2001).

29. This variation in racial identity has been replicated using various methodologies and data sets; for example, see Renn (2004) and Harris and Sim (2002).

30. See Renn (2004) and Wallace (2001).

31. See Hitlin, Brown, and Elder (2006).

CCF Brief

CHANGES IN INTERRACIAL MARRIAGE

Kimberlyn Fong | February 2014

In the past fifty years, there has been a true revolution in American attitudes toward interracial marriage. In the years when the Civil Rights Act was being debated, only 4 percent of Americans said they approved of marriages between white and blacks. Today 77 percent of the public approves, an all-time high.

During slavery and Reconstruction, interracial marriage between whites and free blacks, while less common than today, was not as rare as might be expected. In fact, actual rates of intermarriage were higher in the mid-nineteenth century than they were in the mid-twentieth. After emancipation freed African American slaves in 1863, intermarriage rates declined, in part because the larger size of the black population made it easier for blacks to find black marriage partners of the opposite sex, in part because of new laws forbidding "miscegenation" and intensified vigilante action by whites trying to reimpose racial boundaries.

Between 1913 and 1964, more than half the states in the country had antimiscegenation laws prohibiting intermarriage not just between whites and blacks, but also between white and Asians or Native Americans. Some prohibited African Americans from marrying anyone other than another black person. In the postwar period, many states repealed these laws; but in 1967, three years after passage of the Civil Rights Act, sixteen states still retained and enforced antimiscegenation laws.

As late as 1980, less than 7 percent of new marriages in the United States were between spouses of a different race or ethnicity from one another. By 2010, that had more than doubled, to 15 percent.

Today, among the four major racial and ethnic groups in the United States, Asians and Hispanics have the highest level of intermarriage rates. Interestingly, however, recent increases in Latino immigration have enlarged the pool of Hispanic partners and actually led to a decline in intermarriage between Hispanics and other groups. Between 1990 and 2000, intermarriage among all young couples with at least one Hispanic partner decreased from 33 percent to 23 percent.

Nevertheless, of approximately 275,500 new interracial or interethnic marriages in 2010, white/Hispanic couples were the most common, accounting for more than four in ten (43 percent). Fourteen percent of new marriages were between whites and Asians, making these the second most common interracial marriage. White/black couples were the least common, at 12 percent.

There are interesting gender differences in interracial marriage, and these have changed over time. From 1850 until 1920, unions between black men and white women were more common than those between white men and black women. Between 1940 and 1960, by contrast, the numbers of white men who married black women and of black men who married white women were almost equal. After 1960, however, the sex ratio turned in favor of black men and white female unions again, reaching a high of 80 percent in 1980. Today, black men are twice as likely to marry interracially as black women are. Among Asians, the gender pattern runs the other way. About 36 percent of Asian female newlyweds married outside their race, compared with just 17 percent of Asian male newlyweds.

As intermarriage has become more common, public opinion has become more accepting. As late as 1986, nearly three in ten Americans (28 percent) said marriage between people of different races was not acceptable for anyone, while an additional 37 percent said that it might be acceptable for others, but not for themselves. Today 63 percent of Americans say it "would be fine" with them if a member of their own family were to marry someone outside their own racial or ethnic group.

And this acceptance is not just an abstract value. A 1997 Gallup national survey of people ages thirteen to nineteen found that 64 percent of black, Hispanic, or Asian teens who had ever dated and who attended schools with students of more than one race reported dating someone who was white. On the other hand, daters from different races are still less likely to end up tying the knot than same-race daters. The odds of going from dating to living together or getting married are one in four for same-race daters and about one in five for interracial daters. Nevertheless, these trends suggest that interracial marriages will continue to become more common in the United States, and they will be much more acceptable than they were fifty years ago.

PART THREE

The Diversity of American Families Today

10

Families "In Law" and Families "In Practice"

Does the Law Recognize Families as They Really Are?

Karen Struening[1]

Since its inception, the United States, following English common law, has used the principles of marriage and biology to define who is a parent. However, as this book shows, today's families take many different forms, including same-sex families, families formed through the use of new fertility technologies, adoption, different-sex cohabitants and their children, single mothers, extended kin and children, stepfamilies, and married couples with their own biological children. The purpose of this chapter is to ask the question: Is the law doing an adequate job of recognizing families as they really are? My answer is that we are in a time of significant change and just how well the law is doing is difficult to determine. The number of states that allow same-sex marriage is increasing at a rapid rate. This is an important recognition of new family forms on the part of the state. However, many families do not receive state recognition, and this places the relationships that adults have created with their children at risk. If the law is to adequately protect families as they really are, it must be able to move beyond the principles of marriage and biology. This chapter will show that in some cases, the law has expanded beyond these principles to affirm new forms of family. However, at the same time, executive branch policy, courts, and popular ballots have reaffirmed the different-sex, marriage-based, biological conception of family. Through an examination of same-sex parenthood and family formation using new fertility technologies, this chapter will explore how far the law has gone in recognizing "families in practice."

As the chapters in this book make clear, contemporary families in the United States take many different forms. This raises the question, has the law been able to keep pace with the families that individuals living in the United States are creating? Before we get to this question, we may want to ask, why is legal recognition important to families? In this chapter, I make the assumption that the purpose of family law, in the words of political theorist Mary Shanley, is to "create conditions under which people are best able to make deep commitments of emotional and material support to one another."[2] The law cannot facilitate and protect unilateral and mutual dependencies unless it recognizes and protects new family forms.[3] But when new family forms emerge, judges and legislators do not always resolve disputes equitably or protect the welfare and interests of children and parents. In addition to the stigma and discrimination they face, new family forms do not easily fit into old legal categories. As a consequence, the law does not always recognize families as they really are.

Since its inception, family law in the United States has used marriage and biology to define the family. The traditional model of family, as constructed by law, has been a married, different-sex couple with their own biological children. Until recently, the legal basis of motherhood was the biological connection between gestational mother and child. In contrast, fatherhood was based on marriage to the gestational mother.[4] The emergence of new family forms, including but not limited to families headed by same-sex couples and families formed through the use of new fertility technologies and surrogacy contracts, has undermined the biological and marital bases of family law.

During the last year, the U.S. public has witnessed a rapid expansion of the marital rights of same-sex couples. Indeed, change in this area is so rapid that by the time this book goes to print, the information provided here may well be outdated. As of November 15, 2014, thirty-three states and the District of Columbia permit the marriage of same-sex couples.[5] The Supreme Court put California back on the list of states recognizing same-sex marriage in a ruling that denied legal standing to the proponents of Proposition Eight, a referendum that banned same-sex marriage in California. The Court's ruling in *Hollingsworth v. Perry* said that the federal district court's decision to strike down Proposition Eight must stand because the state of California was not willing to appeal the lower court's decision.[6]

The decision made by the Supreme Court in *United States v. Windsor* is driving marriage equality rulings in federal courts across the country. The Defense of Marriage Act (DOMA) was passed by Congress and signed into law by President Clinton in 1996. DOMA prevented married same-sex couples from receiving federal benefits enjoyed by married different-sex couples. The Court decided that couples who marry in states that recognize same-sex marriage cannot be treated differently than their heterosexual peers by the federal government. Married same-sex couples will now be able to access key immigration, tax, and Social Security benefits denied to them under the federal DOMA.[7] However, as Justice Scalia predicted at the time, the impact of *Windsor* went far beyond striking down a part of DOMA.[8] The forceful moral language used by Justice Kennedy, who wrote the majority decision, spurred a flurry of lower-court decisions. These rulings were allowed to stand by the Supreme Court on October 6, 2014, when the Court refused to weigh in on the issue of marriage equality.[9] The question now is when the Supreme Court will choose to take a same-sex marriage case. This prospect has been made more likely since the federal appeals court for the 6th Circuit ruled to uphold bans on same-sex marriage by overturning lower-court rulings in cases from Kentucky, Michigan, Ohio, and Tennessee.[10] When federal courts of appeals disagree, it is the responsibility of the Supreme Court to resolve the issue.

The *Windsor* decision and stronger public support for same-sex marriage have brought about a tremendous change in family law.[11] Many more couples will now be able to marry and access the right to adoption and second-parent adoption. This is an amazing victory for all people who support the legal recognition of diverse families. However, there is an irony in the expansion of marital rights to same-sex couples. It reinforces the legal tool of marriage at a time when fewer heterosexual couples are marrying. What is really necessary in this time of family diversity is to find ways to recognize and protect families without relying either on biology or marriage.

As nontraditional families have struggled to gain parenting rights in the courts, judges have been forced to consider the question, who qualifies as a parent? Faced with this challenge, some judges have responded by reforming and stretching legal principles to recognize families that do not fit the traditional model. However, at the same time that some courts and state legislators have made rulings and written statutes recognizing new family forms, other judges, state, and federal legislatures, the American public through the use of ballot measures, and the executive branch have acted to reassert the heterosexual model with its reliance on marriage and biology. Although it is very likely that more states will join the thirty-five that now allow same-sex marriage, there remain many states, including those in the 6th Circuit, that have maintained their bans. Additionally, the Obama administration has continued the Bush administration's Healthy Marriage Initiative, which encourages low-income couples to form "healthy" marriages. The Healthy Marriage Initiative provides money to state agencies, universities, and nonprofits that offer marriage education programs to low-income couples who are receiving public benefits or who are involved in the child welfare system.[12] Finally, conservative family values advocates and court opinions rejecting same-sex marriage have relied on theories of marriage rooted in gender difference and biology.[13]

This conflict between accepting and rejecting new family forms indicates that judges, legislators, and the executive branch, as well as the American public, are ambivalent about moving beyond the traditional definition of family.[14] Unfortunately, failing to recognize families as they really are makes it difficult for the law to facilitate and protect relationships of mutual and unilateral dependency. When the law does not recognize families as they really are, children suffer in many different ways. Children may be denied economic support, health insurance, an inheritance, or Social Security death and disability benefits. Perhaps most devastating, if their parents separate, and the court does not recognize their nonbiological parent as a parent, children may lose contact with someone who planned their birth, looked forward to their arrival, and cared for them since the day they were born.

A Note on Family Law

The United States has two parallel court systems: one at the federal level and the other at the state level. Family law, which includes areas such as marriage, divorce, parentage, child custody, child support, and the regulation of parent-child relationships, is primarily a matter of state law. This means that it is largely written by state legislatures and interpreted and applied by state courts. Consequently, family law differs from state to state. This means that new family forms exist in an unpredictable environment and are highly vulnerable to legislative and judicial decisions. Additionally, securing parentage recognition is often a costly and lengthy process.

While family law is a state matter, the Supreme Court has built a constitutional framework for judicial decisions regarding the family. Under the due process clause of the Fourteenth Amendment, the Supreme Court has affirmed parental autonomy in regard to the raising of children,[15] the right to marry,[16] the right to marry the person of one's choice without regard to race,[17] the right to live in an extended family,[18] the right to use birth control,[19] the right to end a pregnancy,[20] and the right to engage in private same-sex sexual conduct.[21] The Court also has invoked the equal protection clause of the Fourteenth Amendment to prohibit the differential treatment of children born to unmarried parents[22] and has protected the right of unmarried fathers to the custody of their children.[23] These rulings have limited the ability of the state to arbitrarily interfere with the choices individuals make about their intimate associations and increased, to some extent, the range of family forms that are considered legitimate. By ruling that states must treat individuals born within and outside of marriage equally and by protecting an unmarried father's rights to his biological children, the Court decreased the power of marital status to determine how rights and benefits are distributed. And by recognizing a right of privacy that includes both the right to use birth control and the right to terminate a pregnancy (subject to an increasing amount of regulation in some states), the Court made marriage more of a choice and less of a necessity. Additionally, in recognizing a right to privacy, the Court paved the way for the decriminalization of sex outside of marriage for heterosexuals, which in turn lessoned the stigma attached to birth outside of marriage and cohabitation.[24]

BIOLOGY AND MARRIAGE DEFINE THE FAMILY IN LAW

As noted above, until recently the legal definition of family has been based on marriage and biology. In practice this has meant that the law privileged the marital relationship, drawing a sharp boundary around the married couple and their children. Until the development of new family forms, such as families headed by a lesbian couple or the increased use of fertility technologies and surrogacy contracts, legal motherhood was defined almost exclusively by biology: a woman was considered a child's legal mother if she gave birth to that child. In contrast to biologically based motherhood, the legal definition of fatherhood was founded on marital status.[25] What mattered for men was not whether they were the biological father of a child, but whether they were married to the child's mother. If they were, men incurred all the responsibilities of fatherhood; if they were not, they incurred none. This definition of legal fatherhood served two purposes: (1) it protected a married man and his estate from the consequences of his out-of-wedlock sexual activity, and (2) it gave children conceived through a wife's adulterous affair the opportunity to be considered legitimate and to inherit from the husband of their mother. The consequences of basing paternity on marriage were dire for unmarried women and their children. Before the nineteenth century, a child born to an unmarried mother did not belong to the family of either his biological father or his biological mother.[26]

Along with having no responsibilities, unwed fathers also had no rights. This changed in 1972 in a Supreme Court decision called *Stanley v. Illinois*, in which the Supreme Court ruled under the equal protection clause that unwed fathers could not be treated differently than unwed mothers.[27] Upon the death of their mother, Stanley's children, whom he had lived with and cared for, were placed in foster care. The state of Illinois considered Stanley a legal stranger to his children with no custodial rights. The Supreme Court struck down the Illinois law and reunited Stanley with his children. As paternity tests have become reliable and cohabitation and nonmarital birth have increased, federal and state laws have affirmed both the rights and responsibilities of unmarried fathers. The federal Family Support Act[28] requires states to identify the biological fathers of children born to women on public assistance in order to recoup public dollars spent on the mother and her children. The Uniform Parentage Act, first promulgated in 1973 by the National Conference of Commissioners on Uniform State Laws and revised in 2000 and 2002, outlines how an unmarried father can establish a legal connection with his child.[29] It includes signing a paternity registry, signing the child's birth certificate, or residing with the child and holding the child out to the world as his own. While the presumption of fatherhood is rebuttable, it establishes the right to parenthood in the absence of a legal challenge.

Despite the strengthening of rights for unwed, biological fathers, a 1989 Supreme Court case reaffirmed the traditional doctrine of marital presumption. The case of *Michael H. v. Gerald D.* involves a woman, who, while married to Gerald D., had an affair with Michael H., and lived with him and their biological child intermittently before reuniting with her husband.[30] The Supreme Court held that neither Michael H., who had lived with and held his biological child out to the world as his own, nor his daughter through her legal guardian, had standing to petition the court for visitation rights. In this case, the Court allowed marital presumption to trump an established relationship between a biological father and his child. However, this decision is destined to be eroded as more and more biological fathers fight for their rights. As noted by family law expert David Meyer, in a growing number of states, unmarried men are being allowed to use DNA testing to prove paternity despite the objections of the biological mother's husband.[31]

The legal primacy of the marital model also can be seen when marriages dissolve or families take forms other than two married (different-sex) parents with biological children. For example, until recently, the law held that adoption could occur only if the biological mother gave up all legal rights to her child. This rule grew out of a heterosexual adoption scenario in which a couple with fertility problems sought out a woman who wanted to give her baby up for adoption. In these cases, the mother was required to sign away her parentage rights. According to David Meyer, "In myriad ways, the law often reflected an assumption that adoptive parents were second-best 'stand-ins' in circumstances where the 'real'— i.e., biological—parents were simply unavailable." Meyer explains that every effort was made to simulate a biological family, including "matching" the child's ethnic and religious background to that of her adoptive parents.[32]

A similar example can be seen in the case of children who have been taken by the state from their biological mothers because of abuse or neglect. According to the 1997 Adoption and Safe Families Act (ASFA),[33] terminating the rights of the biological mother and placing the child up for adoption with nonrelatives is preferable to allowing children to live indefinitely in kinship care with a grandmother or aunt.[34] Kinship care allows children to retain relationships both with their mother and with their extended family and does not require that the biological mother's rights be terminated. It breaks with the traditional model by allowing a child to have more than one maternal figure in his or her life and by locating parental authority in someone who is neither the biological nor adoptive parent of the child. According to ASFA, it is preferable to sever all of a child's existing caretaking bonds in order to reconstitute the exclusivity of the marriage-based family.

Family privacy and parental autonomy are positive values because they protect the parent-child bond from arbitrary action on the part of the state and other third parties. But some legal theorists have suggested that the exclusivity of parental rights goes too far and is based on the idea that children are little more than their parents' possessions. Supreme Court Justice John Paul Stevens expressed this view in a dissent to a 2000 case, *Trowel v. Granville*, that drew a bright line around a mother and her children (the father was deceased) and denied visitation rights to grandparents: "At a minimum, our prior cases recognizing that children are, generally speaking, constitutionally protected actors, require that this Court reject any suggestion that when it comes to parental rights, children are so much chattel."[35] Stevens's point was that parental autonomy and the privacy of the parent-child bond should not be used to separate children from adults with whom they have developed significant relationships. This point becomes particularly salient during a period in which emerging forms of relationship have not yet received legal recognition. Judges, particularly those who adhere to the marriage and biology model, may not believe that individuals who are actually functioning as parents in children's lives fit the legal definition of parent. As a result, they will not act to protect the relationship between a child and her nonbiological, nonmarital parent.

COURTS CONFRONT LESBIAN CO-PARENTS

The recognition of marriage equality in more and more states has transformed the parenting rights of same-sex couples. Couples who choose to marry in states that recognize same-sex marriage should not find it difficult for the nonbiological parent to adopt the child of his or her partner. Nor should married couples find it difficult to jointly adopt a child from an adoption agency. However, not all same-sex couples want to marry, and until same-sex marriage becomes a national right, parenting status remains uncertain for many lesbian and gay parents. According to recent estimates, between 2 and 2.8 million children are being raised by lesbian, gay, bisexual, or transgender (LGBT) parents. In addition, an increasing number of gay and lesbian couples and individuals are adopting children from adoption agencies. Eight percent of same-sex couples reported raising an adopted child in 2000; by 2009, 19 percent reported doing so.[36] Second-parent adoption remains one of the best ways for LGBT co-parents to secure parenting rights for both parents. It allows the nonbiological parent to adopt her child without severing the rights of the biological parent. In cases where one individual in the relationship has adopted a child (many adoption agencies will not allow lesbian or gay couples to jointly adopt), second-parent adoption also can be used. According to a 2014 report, second-parent adoption is available in twenty-four states and the District of Columbia, while eight states have laws or court decisions that explicitly ban this practice.[37] In the remaining states, it is not clear whether a judge will approve a second-parent adoption if the couple is unmarried or the state does not allow same-sex marriage.

Many lesbian couples use donor insemination to have children. In the early nineties, as the dissolution of lesbian relationships reached the courts, most judges considered the nonbiological mother to be a legal stranger to the child she had co-parented and dismissed the nonbiological mother's claim to visitation or custody rights.[38] If these mothers had been unmarried heterosexual fathers, simply living with their children and holding them out to the world as their own would have sufficed to earn them presumptive parenthood. But because family law regarding mothers asserted that (1) biology determines maternity, (2) a child can have only one mother, and (3) the legal parent is given exclusive rights to her child, the courts did not initially recognize the parental status of nonbiological mothers.

In the mid '90s, some courts on both coasts and in the mid Atlantic and Great Lakes regions began to recognize the visitation and custodial petitions of nonbiological mothers. To receive visitation or custodial rights, a petitioner must go through a two-step process. First, the court must grant the petitioner legal standing or recognize her as someone who has a legitimate claim to visitation or custodial rights. Second, the court must determine whether visitation or shared custody is in the best interest of the child. Heterosexual stepparents have been granted standing to petition for visitation under the legal principle of de facto parentage (the court recognizes that an individual is playing a parent-like role in a child's life) and parenthood by estoppel (the court recognizes that the biological parent through word or deed has given her partner the expectation that she will enjoy the rights and the duties of a parent).[39]

In several cases, these principles were extended to lesbian co-parenting cases. For example, a New Jersey review court, while affirming the biological mother's contention that as the legal mother she has a constitutionally protected right to the "care, custody and nurture of her child," went on to argue that

> at the heart of the psychological parent cases is a recognition that children have a strong interest in maintaining the ties that connect them to adults who love and provide for them. That interest, for constitutional reasons as well as social purposes, lies in the emotional bonds that develop between family members as a result of shared daily life.[40]

Summarizing a Wisconsin ruling[41] that had established a test for when a third party qualifies as a psychological parent, the court stated:

> The legal parent must consent to and foster the relationship between the third party and the child; the third party must have lived with the child; the third party must perform parental functions for the child to a significant degree; and most important, a parent-child bond must be forged.[42]

The first factor shows that the legal parent and her partner intended to create a family together. The second shows that the co-parent was a part of the child's daily life, and the third that she performed routine acts of care. The fourth requires expert testimony on the strength of the parent-child bond that emerged out of these daily acts of care.

The New Jersey court went on to state that a person who is determined to be a psychological parent "stands in parity" with the legal parent in regards to visitation or custody rights. However, once the court assessed the best interests of the child, it concluded that greater weight should be given to the legal/biological parent's claim. While the New Jersey court took significant steps toward the view that biology is not the sole determinant of parenthood, in the end biology was allowed to be the decisive factor. The court reasoned that children have a stronger interest in maintaining their connection with their biological parent than with their nonbiological parent, because only the former can satisfy the child's desire for knowledge of her or his biological roots. In general, most de facto parent cases have awarded visitation rights but stopped short of awarding joint custody or transferring legal custody from the biological mother to the psychological or de facto parent.

Courts also have recognized parenthood by estoppel in cases where it can be shown through a contract, verbal agreement, and/or the conduct of the parties, that the couple intended to raise a child or children jointly as co-parents. In the case of *Elisa B. v. Superior Court*, the court concluded that Elisa, who had been the primary earner in a same-sex-headed family, owed child support.[43] After the relationship between Elisa and Emily dissolved, Elisa, the nonbiological parent, denied that she was the legal parent of her ex-partner's biological children. The court reasoned that by planning and carrying out the pregnancy and childbirth with her partner, and by caring for and financially supporting their children, Elisa created certain expectations on her partner's part, which in turn determined the actions that Emily took. Emily would not have sought out artificial insemination and become pregnant if Elisa had not made certain commitments to her. Importantly, the court ruled in *Elisa B.* and its sister case, *Kristine H. v. Lisa R.*, that a child can have two mothers.[44] Although Elisa and Emily had never registered as domestic partners, the court pointed to the fact that California had recently enacted registered domestic partnership legislation that gave same-sex couples the same parenting rights as married different-sex couples.

At present, if a couple is unmarried and lives in a state that does not allow marriage, the optimal legal mechanism for protecting the parenting rights of non biological parents is second-parent adoption. Second-parent adoption allows the nonbiological parent to adopt the child or children of the biological mother without forcing the biological mother to give up her parenting rights. If a gay man adopts a child as an individual, the co-parent of his child also can use second parent adoption to obtain legal parentage. As mentioned above, currently almost half of all states plus the District of Columbia explicitly permit second-parent adoption. Second-parent adoption is advocated by family lawyers because states are required by the Full Faith and Credit Act to recognize the court decisions of other states. In contrast, states are not compelled to recognize out-of-state marriages. This is because marriage laws are created by statute, and states are not compelled to recognize the statutes of their fellow states, but they are required to recognize out-of-state court judgments.[45] Consequently, a child born to a married same-sex couple who has not pursued adoption will be legally considered to have two parents in one state, but not in another.

Nancy Polikoff, a leader in the area of LGBT family law, argues that lesbian donor insemination presents both practical and equal protection problems because it requires the nonbiological mother to adopt her own child.[46] Second-parent adoption is a costly and lengthy process that does not guarantee that the child has a relationship with both of her parents from the day she is born. It normally requires a home visit and a background check on the nonbiological mother. In contrast, the father in a cohabitating couple that uses donor insemination is presumed to be the father of his partner's child as long as he consents to the donor insemination process in writing or holds the child out to be his own after the child is born. No court intervention is required. Polikoff points out that current law creates a new form of illegitimacy or second-class status among families headed by lesbian couples.[47] Those who have married or entered into a domestic partnership or civil union are considered under the law to be the parents of any children born during the duration of the marriage, domestic partnership, or civil union. However, same-sex couples that cannot (because of where they live) or have not (because of their value preferences) married or joined in a recognized relationship must go through an expensive adoption process. The children of unwed lesbian co-parents are illegitimate in the sense that only the biological mother is recognized without a court order and from the birth of her child.

To remedy the differential treatment of lesbian co-parents using donor insemination, Polikoff calls for the "enactment of a gender-neutral and marital status-neutral statute assigning parentage based on consent to the insemination with the intent to parent."[48] She points to the District of Columbia (DC), which has created parenting legislation with lesbian couples using donor insemination in mind. DC's statute treats an unwed, nonbiological lesbian co-parent as if she were a nonbiological, unwed father. The lesbian co-parent is able to establish parenting rights if she consents to the donor insemination of her partner with the intent of being a parent. Consent is indicated in one of two ways: the first is by authorizing the donor insemination by signature. The second is by living with the child and holding the child out to the world as her own. If the nonbiological mother signs consent to donor insemination with the intent to parent form, the DC statute allows both parents' names to be placed on the child's birth certificate. Thus the child has two parents from birth, whether they have married or entered into a civil union or domestic partnership.

Many of the children living in households headed by same-sex couples are not adequately protected by laws that fail to recognize their relationships with loving parents. However, the cases and statutes described above show that the law has the conceptual resources to recognize new family forms. Whether it is the doctrine of de facto parenthood or the consent to inseminate with the intent of parenting, parenthood can be based on principles other than marriage and biology. As we examine issues associated with new fertility technologies, we will find that they too move beyond a biological conception of parenthood.

COURTS CONFRONT ASSISTED CONCEPTION

The use of fertility technologies and surrogacy arrangements demonstrates the appeal of the biologically based family while at the same time upending it. Until recently, family law has been built around the assumption that families are created through "natural," meaning unassisted, procreation and that children are genetically related to both of their parents. This model of family assumes that sexual intercourse, the provision of genetic material, the conception of the child-to-be, and birth are all one seamless process involving one man and one woman. Fertility technologies and surrogacy arrangements disrupt this assumption. Assisted conception allows for genetic contributions to come from individuals who will never have a social or legal relationship to the children their genes helped to create. In addition, while procreation requires gametes from both a man and a woman, cases involving fertility technologies and surrogacy arrangements show us that conception cannot be understood solely as a biological process: it also has a social dimension. Biology and marriage are not the only factors that lead to parentage. It is the decision to bring a child into the world and the act of caring for him or her that make someone a parent.

Before the development of donor insemination in the 1940s, couples who lacked the ability to procreate "naturally" had only one alternative to childlessness: adoption.[49] Today, 30,000 children are born through donor insemination each year.[50] For some couples, assisted conception is attractive because it allows for at least one individual to have a biological connection to the resulting child. In addition, it allows heterosexual couples to create the illusion that they are a "normal" family with biological children. An essentially unregulated practice in the United States, donor insemination is available to single women, lesbian couples, and unmarried heterosexual couples. When used by single women and lesbian couples, donor insemination no longer functions to support the illusion that all families are composed of two different-sex parents and their own biological children. Instead, it opens up the jarring prospect that procreation is a social as well as a biological phenomenon that can be separated from the different-sex couple. Consider that most states deny parenting rights to anonymous sperm donors.[51] This means that children born to lesbian couples with the use of sperm donors (provided the donor was unknown to the recipient and the procedure was carried out by a doctor) do not have legal fathers. As discussed above, some states will recognize the nonbiological mother while others will not.

In vitro fertilization (IVF) requires eggs to be fertilized in a test tube, before becoming implanted in the gestational mother's womb. First successfully attempted in 1978, today IVF leads to the birth of 58,000 or 1 percent of the babies born in the United States each year.[52] The market in genetic material that makes artificial insemination and in vitro fertilization possible is largely unregulated. When a heterosexual couple uses this procedure, access to another woman's eggs allows the gestational mother to give birth to a child who is genetically related to her male partner. Under such circumstances, a couple may feel that both partners have contributed to the birth of the child. Lesbian couples, with the assistance of a sperm donor, can do the same if one partner donates her egg to the other, who then bears the resulting child. Gay male couples also can take part in the biological process of birth, by fertilizing a donated egg with a mixture of their sperm and arranging for the services of a gestational surrogate.

Traditional and gestational surrogacy contracts refer to an agreement between a woman and a couple (or an individual) in which the woman agrees to bear a child that she then turns over to the commissioning couple. In traditional surrogacy, sperm from the man in the commissioning couple is used to fertilize the egg of the gestational mother. However, for reasons revealed below, 95 percent of surrogacy arrangements are gestational contracts, which means the egg of the woman who will bear the child is not used. Statute and case law on surrogacy contracts vary significantly across the United States, and most states refuse to recognize surrogacy contracts.[53] Currently, New York and Michigan make initiating a surrogacy contract punishable by a fine. In contrast, California and Connecticut have guidelines for surrogacy agreements and recognize them. In addition, even in states where statutes are restrictive, actual practice may be more permissive. According to the Society for Assisted Reproductive Technologies, 1,100 children are born through surrogacy arrangements each year, although family lawyers call that a conservative estimate.[54] Unlike in IVF, which partially or fully separates gestation from genetic material, surrogacy may separate the decision to bring a child into the world and become a parent from the biology of genetic material and gestation. Although most gestational surrogacy arrangements involve genetic material from the commissioning couple, in some cases a biological relationship between intended parents and child is entirely lacking.

In a famous case of traditional surrogacy that reached a New Jersey court in 1986, Mary Beth Whitehead, who had agreed in exchange for a fee to bear a child using her own egg and sperm belonging to the husband of the commissioning couple (Elizabeth and William Stern), refused to relinquish the child.[55] The trial court ruled in favor of upholding the surrogacy contract and would have terminated Whitehead's parenting rights, but the Supreme Court of New Jersey reversed the lower court's decision, declared the contract invalid, and ruled that Whitehead was the child's legal mother and that William Stern was the child's legal father. It gave custody to William Stern and his wife, who was now prohibited from adopting her husband's child, and gave Whitehead visitation rights. This arrangement was based, in part, on a biological theory of parenting rights. Although it had voided the surrogacy contract, the court nonetheless did not think of Mr. Stern as a mere sperm donor with legally weak grounds to claim parentage. He was given full parenting rights, and his wife was declared a legal stranger to her husband's child. Even though it was the Sterns who decided to have a child, planned for its birth, and initiated the pregnancy, Ms. Whitehead best fit the biologically based legal definition of a mother: she had contributed her genetic material, carried the fetus to term, and given birth to the child. Like Elizabeth Stern, Whitehead's husband, William, was considered a legal stranger to the child.

To avoid the fate of the Sterns, most commissioning couples now combine in vitro fertilization, using the wife's egg or a donated egg, with surrogacy arrangements. While gestational surrogacy is more complicated and expensive than artificially inseminating the woman contracted to carry out the pregnancy, it has been successfully used in California to protect commissioning couples from parenthood claims brought by surrogate mothers. In *Johnson v. Calvert*, the court faced a disputed surrogacy case in which one woman, the wife in the commissioning couple, provided genetic material and another, the surrogate, provided gestational capacity. Because the biological bases of motherhood were perfectly split, the court adopted an intent-based theory of parentage.[56] This means the court looked at conception, pregnancy, and birth not simply as biological processes but as activities emanating from a deliberate intention to have a child. The court emphasized that it was the commissioning couple who had sought and initiated the birth of the child. Its decision gave exclusive parenting rights to the commissioning couple, whose actions, the court reasoned, had actually caused the child to be born.

The court's decision in *Johnson* is significant because it recognizes that parenting rights can rest on nonbiological as well as biological factors. In *Johnson*, the court granted custody to a woman who claimed parentage based on both intention and genetic material; but in another case, *In re marriage of Buzzanca*, California awarded custody to a commissioning mother who had no genetic connection to the child.[57] The intent to have a child is essential to creating a pre-birth investment in the baby yet to be born. Although historically this pre-birth investment has been entwined with contributing genetic material, undergoing pregnancy, and giving birth to a child, surrogacy arrangements allow for nonbiological pre-birth investments. Decisions such as *Johnson* and *In re marriage of Buzzanca* demonstrate the ability of courts to conceptualize parenthood as the product of the intention to have a child and not solely as the product of a "natural" biological process.

Like the families of co-parenting lesbian and gay male couples, various kinds of families created through assisted conception have required courts to rethink how the law approaches parentage. Same-sex and different-sex couples using fertility technologies have pushed courts to consider how much weight should be given to biology and how much weight should be given to social factors such as intention. However, a reverse trend is also evident: some judges and policy makers are acting to reassert the married, different-sex, biological conception of family.

ATTEMPTS TO REASSERT THE MARRIAGE AND BIOLOGY MODEL

Public opinion is often divided about the direction of family law and policy. People are ambivalent about divorce rates, nonmarital childbearing by heterosexual couples or single mothers, surrogacy contracts, and gay and lesbian families.[58] During the 1970s, a backlash began against the women's and LGBT movements that eventually morphed into the 1980s crusade for traditional family values and the 1990s marriage movement. The leaders of these successive movements have all argued that the development of new family forms constitutes a national crisis and is the cause of numerous social ills.[59]

At times conservative leaders have been partially successful in enlisting policy makers, as well as broad swaths of the American public, to their side. Family values supporters argue that (1) marriage is the foundation of the family and (2) the marital relationship is rooted in biological (gender) difference.[60] For example, here is how the Council on Family Law describes its preferred definition of marriage:

> It fosters and maintains connections between children and their natural parents.
> It sustains a complex form of social interdependency between men and women. It
> supports an integrated form of parenthood, uniting the biological (or adoptive),
> gestational, and social roles that parents play.[61]

The Council on Family Law stops short of condemning different-sex couples who adopt, but it rejects families headed by same-sex couples and families that separate intention from genetic material or gestation. Advocates of this position claim that when the law recognizes nonmarital and nonbiological (with the exception of different-sex adoption) forms of family, it undermines the marriage and biology model by indicating that the state has no clear preference for it. Alternatively, when the state establishes benefits and rights exclusively for different-sex couples who are married, and makes it difficult or risky to create new family forms, it actively discourages those new family forms. As believers in the power of law to channel individuals into state-preferred behavior patterns, family values advocates actively oppose efforts to facilitate adult and parent-child relationships that are not rooted in different-sex marriage and biological difference.

The marriage and biological model is largely accepted by some court decisions opposed to marriage equality. In *Hernandez v. Robles*,[62] the Court of Appeals (New York's Supreme Court) was asked to determine if New York's practice of limiting marriage to different-sex couples was constitutional (the New York State Assembly approved same-sex marriage eleven years later in 2011). According to the court, the purpose of marriage is to channel natural procreators into a state-sponsored union. Therefore, the state acts within its mandate to provide for the public health—and, in particular, the welfare of children—when it offers potential procreators incentives to marry (for example, benefits that cannot be obtained by unmarried couples). The odd part of New York's argument is that only unmediated, "natural" sexual intercourse qualifies as procreation. The court found a significant legal difference between assisted and unassisted procreation. Same-sex couples are legitimately excluded from the state's bargain with potential procreators because they require fertility technologies and surrogacy arrangements to have children.

Writing about same-sex couples, the court explains: "These couples can become parents by adoption, or by artificial insemination or other technological marvels, but they do not become parents as a result of accident or impulse."[63] The difference between unassisted and assisted conception is held to be relevant by the court because different-sex couples are in danger of reproducing spontaneously without forming stable and committed relationships; same-sex couples, who must visit fertility clinics together and negotiate contracts with surrogates, are not. While this may sound like a strange sort of backhanded compliment—same-sex couples are responsible procreators, different-sex couples are not—it suggests, especially given the use of the phrase "other technological marvels," that individuals who require assistance to procreate are not meant to have children.

The majority opinion's emphasis on the natural and biological is taken even further by the concurring opinion. Justifying the limitation of marriage to different-sex couples, Justice Graffeo explains: "The binary nature of marriage—its inclusion of one man and one woman—reflects the biological fact that human procreation cannot be accomplished without the genetic contribution of both a male and a female."[64] According to Justice Graffeo, marriage—clearly a legal, social, intentional practice—is the mere reflection of a biological process.

Of course, the technological marvels that the majority opinion refers to have become quite common. While procreation continues to require the genetic contribution of one man and one woman, the intention to have a child together may be formed and carried out by two women or two men. In addition, court decisions such as *Johnson* and *In re marriage of Buzzanca*, in which the court resolved surrogacy disputes by awarding sole custody of the child to the commissioning couple, understand procreation as a social as well as a biological phenomenon. It is difficult to see how the right to marry can be exclusively linked to unassisted procreation when fertility technologies have effectively severed the intention to procreate from both the provision of genetic material and sexual intercourse.

Moreover, the idea that marriage and family are based on "natural procreation" is another way of saying that only different-sex couples can form "real" families. Such statements reveal animus toward LGBT families and refuse to treat their caring relationships with the dignity they deserve. As mentioned at the beginning of this chapter, marriage and family are about unilateral (parent and child) and mutual (adult and adult) caring relationships. Acts of care, not simply shared genetic material, are necessary to produce loving bonds between parents and children.

The reassertion of different-sex marriage also can be seen in the federal government's adoption of the goals of the marriage movement.[65] In 2002, under the banner of the Healthy Marriage Initiative, the Bush administration began to develop programs designed to promote marriage by increasing marriage rates among low-income couples. The U.S. Department of Health and Human Services, through one of its agencies, the Administration for Families and Children, offered grants to state agencies, universities, and nonprofits to create marriage education programs for young unmarried couples with a child or children and married couples.[66] The idea behind marriage education is to encourage the marriage of unmarried couples with children and strengthen the marriages of already married couples. In 2006, as part the Deficit Reduction Act of 2005, Congress reauthorized the Personal Responsibility and Work Opportunity Reconciliation Act (PRWORA) and appropriated $150 million a year for marriage promotion and the Responsible Fatherhood Initiative, with the stipulation that not more than $50 million could be spent on fatherhood programs each year.[67]

So far, the Healthy Marriage Initiative has not been able to meet its primary goal. According to a program evaluation funded by the government, young couples who volunteer for marriage skills training are no more likely to marry or stay married than couples in control groups. However, married couples do see a slight increase in marital happiness after they have participated in marriage education.[68] President Obama has continued the Healthy Marriage Initiative but has shifted the amount of money spent on marriage education ($75 million) and responsible fatherhood programs ($75 million).[69]

Advocates of these programs point out that many low-income couples cannot afford marriage therapy and that adding soft skills to programs that also offer job training and other hard skills is beneficial for low-income couples who face multiple life stressors. However, supporters of individual liberty respond that government should not bring its power to bear on what is a deeply personal choice. A pluralistic society should not privilege one family form above all others, and it should not place pressure to make value-based choices on specific racial or economic groups whose dependence on government agencies places their voluntary consent to participate in marriage programs in doubt.[70]

Attempts to strengthen the marital and biological bases of the family are bound to disadvantage emerging family forms. Privileging one family form above all others, whether because it is headed by a different-sex married couple or because its children were conceived without "technological marvels," fails to protect the materially and emotionally interdependent associations we call families. Government has an essential role to play in supporting families by supplementing family resources and providing help in times of family dissolution and crisis. It is failing to perform that role if it does not recognize and reinforce the bonds between all well-functioning parents and their children. The time for comprehensive relationship and parentage legislation has arrived in the United States. As this article shows, we can move beyond marriage and biology as the basis of the family.

THE FUTURE OF FAMILY LAW

Historically, family law has exercised a channeling, or if you prefer, disciplinary function. By this I mean that the law has been used to mold families so that they meet the needs of the state and reflect the majority's morality. In more recent years, as family forms have diversified and greater weight has been given to individual liberty and gender equality, family law has begun to accommodate the choices individuals make in regard to forming families. As a result, it has done a better job recognizing and protecting families as they really are.

At the same time, opposition to recognizing families as they really are has not evaporated. Proponents of the marriage movement and potential candidates for the 2016 election such as Ted Cruz believe that recognizing nontraditional family forms will increase the number of parents who are unable to provide their children with stable homes.[71] This belief is based on the assumption that different-sex marriage and biology are the foundations of the family and that alternative ways of thinking about the family are deeply flawed. However, judges who have had to grapple with rendering judgments about real families show us that this belief is groundless. In many of the cases discussed above, judges were able to articulate criteria that allow us to define parenthood without relying on marriage or biology. They looked instead at other factors such as daily acts of care on the part of a nonbiological parent, parent-child bonding, agreements between same-sex partners, and the intent of an infertile different-sex couple to bring a child into the world.

As this chapter suggests, family law varies in its ability to protect nontraditional families from state to state and even from one jurisdiction to another. But this does not mean that the law lacks conceptual resources for arriving at new ways of defining family. If it is to realize its purpose of facilitating deep commitments of emotional and material support, the law must move beyond a purely marital and biological conception of family.

Notes

1. I would like to thank Derek Wikstrom for his excellent work as research assistant on this book chapter. Additionally, I would like to thank my colleague, Richard B. Bernstein, for his advice and assistance.
2. Shanley (2001), p. 7. On the various functions that family law serves and how they sometimes conflict, see McClain (2007).
3. Martha Fineman has written powerfully about how dependencies structure families and the relationships among families, civil society, and the state in *The Autonomy Myth: A Theory of Dependency* (New York: The New Press, 2004).
4. The legal presumption that the child of a man's wife was his did not begin to change until the 1980s, when reliable paternity tests became available. See Carbone (2005).
5. As of December 15, 2014, the following states recognize same-sex marriage: AK, AZ, CA, CO, CT, DE, HI, IA, ID, IL, IN, KS, MA, MD, ME, MN, MT, NC, NH, NJ, NM, NV, NY, OK, OR, PA, RI, SC, UT, VA, VT, WA, WI, WV, WY, and the District of Columbia and St. Louis, Missouri. See Freedom to Marry. Retrieved on November 15, 2014, at http://www.freedomtomarry.org/states/.
6. Liptak (2013).
7. *Ibid.*
8. Richard Gonzales, "Flood of Gay Marriage Cases Releasing Stream of Federal Rulings," National Public Radio, February 15, 2014.
9. Liptak (2014).
10. Adam Polaski, "6th Circuit Court Breaks from Unanimous Appellate Rulings, Upholds Discrimination." Freedom to Marry, November 6, 2014. Retrieved on November 15, 2014, at http://www.freedomtomarry.org/blog/entry/6th-circuit-appeals-court-breaks -from-unanimous-appellate-rulings-upholds-d.
11. According to the Pew Research Center, as of February 23, 2014, 55 percent of the population support same-sex marriage. See Pew Research Center. Retrieved on November 15, 2014, at http://www.pewresearch.org/data-trend/domestic-issues /attitudes-on-gay-marriage/.
12. Office of Family Assistance, Agency for Children and Families, *About the Healthy Family Initiative*, Department of Health and Human Services, Washington, DC. Retrieved on June 12, 2013, at http://www.acf.hhs.gov/programs/ofa/programs /healthy-marriage/about.
13. The Family Law Council (2005).
14. According to *New York Times* blogger Nate Silver, an average of eight national polls conducted in 2013 shows that 51 percent of the public supports same-sex marriage. Moreover, it is likely that support will increase incrementally at a steady rate. See Silver (2013).
15. *Meyer v. Nebraska*, 262 U.S. 390 (1923); *Pierce v. Society of Sisters*, 268 U.S. 510 (1925); *Prince v. Massachusetts*, 321 U.S. 158 (1944).

16. *Zablocki v. Redhail*, 434 U.S. 374 (1978). This decision struck down a Wisconsin law prohibiting individuals who owed child support from marrying and declared the right to marry to be a fundamental right.

17. *Loving v. Virginia*, 388 U.S. 1 (1967). This decision was based on both the Equal Protection clause and the Due Process clause of the Fourteenth Amendment.

18. *Moore v. East Cleveland*, 431 U.S. 494 (1977).

19. *Griswold v. Connecticut*, 381 U.S. 479 (1965); *Eisenstadt v. Baird*, 405 U.S. 438 (1972).

20. *Roe v. Wade*, 410 U.S. 113 (1973); *Planned Parenthood v. Casey*, 505 U.S. 833 (1992).

21. *Lawrence v. Texas*, 539 U.S. 558 (2003).

22. *Levy v. Louisiana*, 391 U.S. 68 (1968). This decision declared that under the Equal Protection clause, so-called illegitimate children had to be treated the same as legitimate children in wrongful death suits.

23. *Stanley v. Illinois*, 405 U.S. 645 (1972).

24. Grossman (2012).

25. *Ibid.*, p. 693.

26. *Ibid.*

27. *Stanley v. Illinois*, 405 U.S. 645 (1972).

28. Pub. L. 100-485 (1988).

29. Uniform Law Commissioners, NCCUSL, *Summary of the Uniform Parentage Act* (Revised 2002). Retrieved on June 20, 2010, at www.nccusl.org/nccusl/uniformact_summaries/uniformacts-s-upa.asp.

30. *Michael H. v. Gerald D.*, 491 U.S. 110 (1989).

31. Meyer (2006), p. 139.

32. *Ibid.*, p. 131.

33. Pub. L. 105-89 (1997).

34. My thanks to Kathryn Krase for explaining the problems with adoption policy to me. For more on how adoption policy can undermine kinship care, see Dorothy E. Roberts, "Kinship Care and the Price of State Care for Children," 76 *Chi-Kent. L. Rev.* 1619 (2001).

35. *Troxel v. Granville*, 530 U.S. 57 (2000) (Justice John Paul Stevens, dissenting).

36. Travernise (2011), p. 11.

37. According to the Human Rights Campaign, the states that recognize same-sex, second-parent adoption are California, Colorado, Connecticut, Delaware, District of Columbia, Hawaii, Idaho, Illinois, Indiana, Iowa, Maine, Maryland, Massachusetts, Minnesota, Montana, Nevada, New Hampshire, New Jersey, New Mexico, New York, Oregon, Pennsylvania, Rhode Island, Vermont, and Washington. See Human Rights Campaign, "Parenting Law: Second Parent of Stepparent Adoption." Retrieved on November 15, 2014, at http://hrc-assets.s3-website-us-east-1.amazonaws.com//files/assets/resources/second_parent_adoption_6-10-2014.pdf.

38. *Alison D. v. Virginia M.*, 572 N.E. 2d 27 (N.Y. 1991); *Nancy S. v. Michele G.*, 279 Cal. Rptr. 212 (Ct. App. 1991). But in 1991 in Washington, DC, a lesbian couple was able to secure the joint adoption of their children. See *In re Adoption of Minor T.*, 17 *Fam. L. Rptr.* 1523 (D.C. Super Ct. 1991).

39. Polikoff (1990).

40. *V.C. v. M.J.B.*, 748 A.2d 539, 550 (N.J. 2000).

41. *In re Custody of H.S. H.-K.*, 533 N.W. 2d 419 (Wis. 1995).

42. *V.C. v. M.J.B.*, 748 A.2d 539, 551 (N.J. 2000).
43. *Elisa B. v. Superior Court*, 117 P. 3d 660 (Cal. 2005); *Kristine H. v. Lisa R.*, 117 P.3d 690 (Cal. 2005).
44. Polikoff (2009), p. 220.
45. Movement Advancement Project (2011), p. 35.
46. Polikoff (2009), p. 206.
47. *Ibid.*, p. 226.
48. *Ibid.*, p. 265.
49. According to Polikoff, "Adoption was unknown at common law and therefore in the United States it required statutory authorization. The first adoption statute was not enacted until 1851 in Massachusetts. Well into the twentieth century, adoption was a second-class legal status that did not create a parent-child relationship for all purposes" (citations removed). Polikoff (2009), p. 214.
50. Movement Advancement Project (2011), p. 34.
51. Wadlington and O'Brien (2007), p. 113; 116 *Harv. L. Rev.* 2052 (May 2003), p. 2067.
52. Russell (2010).
53. Hinson and McBrien (2013).
54. Zernike (2012), p. 22.
55. *In the Matter of Baby M*, 537 A.2d 1227 (N.J. 1988).
56. *Johnson v. Calvert* 5 Cal. 4th 84 (1993).
57. *In re marriage of Buzzanca*, 61 Cal. App. 4th 1410 (Cal. App. 1998).
58. As noted in footnote 10, a slight majority of Americans appear to approve of same-sex marriage.
59. The Family Law Council (2005). For a critique of the family values movement, see Struening (2002).
60. For more on marriage and gender difference, see McClain (2007).
61. The Family Law Council (2005), p. 20.
62. *Hernandez v. Robles*, 855 N.E. 2d 1 (N.Y. 2000).
63. *Ibid.*, p. 7.
64. *Ibid.*, p. 15 (Justice Graffeo, concurring).
65. For a detailed analysis of the Marriage Movement, see McClain (2006).
66. Administration for Children and Families Archives (2013).
67. See Struening (2007), p. 244.
68. Hsueh et al. (2011).
69. Administration for Children and Families (2013).
70. See Struening (2007), p. 254.
71. The Family Law Council (2005).

11

Childfree Families

Amy Blackstone and Amy Greenleaf

"Family is your supportive community. It's the people you feel a sense of responsibility to that you don't simply give up on and you don't simply throw away."

— Bill, a married man in his late thirties

"Family is comfort. It is a feeling of belonging."

— Brittany, a married woman in her late forties

"Family is my partnership with Emily."

— Bruce, a married man in his thirties

"Family is the idea of people bonding together and taking care of each other and becoming a unit."

— Kim, a married woman in her forties

"Family is me and Tim and our little kids [nods toward pet dogs lounging on the floor]."

— Mandy, a married woman in her thirties

W/hat does family mean to you? For many people, family includes parents
and children. But not every adult, as is the case for those quoted on the
previous page, chooses to have kids of his or her own. What do we call the bonds
and household arrangements created by people who don't have children? Are
adults without kids also without family? How do we know what counts as family
and what does not?

It would be easy to say that family can be whatever we want it to be, and in
many ways, that is true. But leaving the definition at that does not help us understand what families are, why they matter, and what purpose they serve. This
chapter considers how adults without children "do" family. Just as gender scholars note that gender is something that is accomplished through our interactions
with others,[1] family too is something we create, something we *do* rather than
something we simply *have* or *are*.[2] By examining families in this way, we shift our
focus from simply defining family to understanding how the notion of family is
constructed, changed, and maintained.[3]

Families help societies meet many of the needs of their members.[4] In particular, families serve several functions, including providing emotional and sexual
companionship for members, facilitating economic provision for members, providing a home to members, and facilitating biological and social reproduction.[5]
These functions, however, are grounded in the presumption that all families
include children. In a previous publication, the first author presented findings
from prior research to examine how childfree families might fulfill similar functions as families that include children.[6] Here, we extend that work by presenting findings from interviews with 45 childfree adults (31 women, 14 men) to
understand how the childfree "do" family. We use the term *childfree* to refer to
individuals who have made the explicit and intentional choice not to have or rear
children. Two of the functions in particular, companionship and reproduction,
are relevant because they reveal how childfree families are both similar to and
different from families that include children.

EMOTIONAL AND SEXUAL COMPANIONSHIP FOR MEMBERS

A key function of families is to serve as a source of emotional support and sexual intimacy for members.[7] Just as families with children provide intimacy and
companionship for members, so too do childfree families. In fact, some research
shows that childfree families may offer greater emotional rewards to their adult
members than do families with children. Several studies have found that marital
satisfaction among nonparents is much higher than that of parents.[8] These studies also show that parents experience depression more often than nonparents and

that they are generally less happy than nonparents, suggesting that emotional well-being for adult members may be a unique strength of childfree families. When asked why they do not want children, one of the most common responses is that the childfree prefer to focus their time and energy on nurturing their relationship with their partner.[9]

In our interviews with childfree adults, the freedom to nurture sexual companionship with their partner came up as one reason these individuals prefer not to form households that include children. Janet, a woman in her thirties who lives with her male partner, shared: "One my favorite things [about my childfree life] is my healthy sex life. One thing I've seen with people who have kids is how horrible their sex life is. I don't want to lose that [with my partner]." Jan, a married woman in her forties, shared that not having to worry about getting pregnant and enjoying her sexual freedom enhanced her sense of sexual connection with her partner, Fred, noting that the pressure to have children "is simply a way to control women's sexuality."

Others described their perception that the emotional intimacy they felt with their partners differed from those of their friends who have kids. In reflecting on how his life might differ if he and his wife had kids, Jack, a man in his early forties, stated:

> Everything would be different! (Laughing) So much different. I guess we could go on for a while but our marriage is very independent. We're very fluid and with a child, you need to have built-in routines and times and stuff like that. We're very flexible with everything that we do.

Jack's wife, Kim, nodded throughout Jack's remarks, adding that their current arrangement, in which they are both independent but also a couple, makes their relationship strong.

Mandy and Tim, a married couple in their late thirties, suggested that not having kids enabled them to take the time to nurture their relationship in ways that would not be possible if they had kids. Mandy said, "Last year, we went on vacation for seventeen days. That's a long time to be hauling kids around. It would never have been possible with kids because of the nature of it." Both Tim and Mandy went on to reminisce about that trip along with others they have taken together, saying the trips were essential to their connection as a couple. They said their travels helped them understand each other, know one another's quirks, and enjoy each other's company.

Robin and Joel, a married couple in their late thirties, felt similarly. When asked what they most appreciate about being childfree, Robin said it was being able to spend time with Joel. Joel said, "The freedom, the ability to do anything with each other spontaneously. . . . It's mostly the freedom of our schedule. Being with each other and being able to do as we wish together." Robin and Joel went on to recount some of their favorite spontaneous outings—movies, lunches out, road trips—all activities that they felt brought them closer together as a couple and that they said would not have been possible had they chosen to have kids.

The notion that they are closer to each other than couples who are parents came up in nearly all the interviews with childfree adults who were in long-term relationships. This is one area where childfree families felt they *differed* from parent/child families. Yet some things were not different. An area where the childfree said they have something in common with parents is in the nurturing roles they play for dependent others in their household. Nurturing is one way of attaining the emotional intimacy humans need. In the case of the childfree, such nurturing was directed at pets. While most interviewees noted that pets and children are vastly different beings with vastly different needs, some spoke of their pets *as* their children; others did not call their pets children, but did note and appreciate the bond they share with their pets. These childfree families fulfill the need for emotional intimacy not just through their relationships with significant other humans but also through their relationships with their pets.

As noted in Mandy's description of family provided at the outset of this chapter, some childfree include their pets in their definitions of family, suggesting that these nonhuman companions play an exceedingly important role in their lives. In describing the role that her pets play in her family, Nicole said simply, "Pets have always been members of the family." Others used similar language to describe their pets—some going so far, as noted above, as to describe their pets as their children. Most acknowledged that caring for pets and caring for children differ dramatically at the same time that they emphasized the importance of their pets to their own emotional fulfillment. As Tanya said, "My ex-husband and I both view our cats as our children. He refers to them as 'the boys.' And for me, my cats really are a big part of my life."

For Tanya, a woman in her forties who had recently divorced her husband of ten years, the post-divorce arrangement around her pet cats obliged her to maintain a relationship with her ex-husband in much the same way children serve as a compulsory link between divorced parents. She shared that her ex-husband "still has contact with me because of the cats." Tanya went on to say,

> Honestly, our whole divorce went very smoothly except for the cats. The only thing that we ever argued about as we went through the process was the cats. I got to keep the cats but he wanted to still have the keys to the house and come visit them when I'm not here. I had interesting conversations with people about, you know, should we be doing this and there are many people who firmly believe no way he shouldn't

have access to your cats, they're not children so he shouldn't and then there are a couple of people who have gone through divorce situations, guys especially, who've said to me I wasn't able to see my children the way I wanted to and he certainly should be able to see the cats because he treats them as his children.

In the end, Tanya and her ex came up with an arrangement that worked for them, where he would visit only at times that she told him she would not be at home. But she did note that they may not have contact at all any more if it weren't for their "shared custody" of the cats.

In sum, childfree families serve to meet the emotional and sexual companionship needs of their members in ways that are both similar to and different from families with kids. Childfree couples note that they may have more time, energy, and financial resources available to dedicate to nurturing their partnerships than do parents. At the same time, they speculate that in at least some ways, their emotional and other connections to their pets may resemble parents' connections to their children. In other words, while the couple relationship is central to childfree families, other beings also play a role in facilitating their emotional well-being and providing companionship.

BIOLOGICAL AND SOCIAL REPRODUCTION

Another way that families help meet the needs of societies is through reproduction. Biological reproduction is perhaps the first thing that comes to mind when people think about the purpose of families. Clearly, childfree families do not participate in this aspect of reproduction. But producing more humans is only one aspect of bringing new members into a culture. When a new person enters our culture, someone must engage in "various kinds of work—mental, manual, and emotional—aimed at providing the historically and socially, as well as biologically, defined care necessary to maintain existing life and to reproduce the next generation."[10] Social reproduction includes all the roles, actions, and responsibilities needed to help individuals become participating and contributing members of society. As childfree individuals note, this role is not limited to those who participate in biological reproduction.

One myth of the childfree is that they do not like children.[11] The reality is that many childfree not only like children, but children play significant roles in their lives. As Jack put it, "There are a lot of kids in our lives. Just look at our fridge. [Nods to refrigerator covered in artwork by nieces, nephews, and the children of their friends.]" The childfree I have interviewed include people engaged in professional roles that place them in the position of helping to rear the next generation. Others, like Tanya and Allison, worked as babysitters and nannies when they were younger and enjoyed the experience. Tanya described becoming "quite attached" to the children she cared for. Allison noted, "I have really enjoyed being around kids my whole life." Bob, a man in his thirties who was engaged to his female partner, noted, "When I go over to people's houses who have kids, I like playing with the kids. I enjoy it. In fact, it's often easier to hang out with some people's kids than with the parents." In other words, for most child-free people, the choice not to have kids is not about a dislike of children. Many of them are involved in the lives of the children they know.

Notably, over 25 percent of the childfree in our sample have relationships with children because of their professional connections to them. The sample includes therapists, social workers, counselors, pediatricians, elementary and high school teachers, and others with education degrees seeking work in the field. Kate, a young woman in her twenties with an education degree, summed up what was echoed in several of the interviews when she said, "I am able to relate to kids in a certain way. I have the ability to be really patient and I want to make sure that children have access to advocacy and to adults who aren't parents."

Indeed, one of the strongest themes to emerge from the analysis of our interviews was that participants emphasized how their status as childfree enabled them to have unique and important relationships with children *because* they are childfree. As Kim said when she described her relationship with the daughter of one of her close friends, "I get to be her playmate." Kim noted that her friend's child sees her as a peer; a much different role than the child's parents play. Participants' friendships with children came up frequently in the interviews. Kim, married to Jack, who is quoted earlier in this section, went on to say, "We're good with little kids. We try to invite the kids [of our friends] over and we all have this sort of joke that our house is called summer camp."

Jack followed up on what Kim shared:

> As the couple without kids, we have more of an ability to play with kids than other couples. When we come to [friends'] houses [who have kids], we actually really do that role with their kids, like an aunt and uncle thing. We just get in there and hang out. It's really funny because the kids see us as a bigger, older friend. We have a lot of really good relationships with a bunch of kids because we have the time to do that. I have two nephews who I see a lot and I mean we can really focus on them. There's a lot of attention we can give them.

Aside from their unique friendships with children, participants also described how not having kids themselves made them more available to take on special responsibilities for the kids in their lives, such as through legal guardianship or as godparents. Tanya described the relationship she and her ex-husband shared with their nephew:

> My ex-husband and I had an opportunity with his nephew, who is college-aged, to take him in. He comes from a family where there's a lot of mental illness and the parents have not, cannot, achieve much in life. So when our nephew was struggling in college, he got kicked out and we took him in. He lived with us for five or six months because we wanted to help care for him. We wanted to provide someone who had so much potential with the opportunity to see a different way of living. . . . I think it really did make a difference for our nephew. . . . We took him to different places; we took him to wonderful restaurants, to concerts, to New York City and gallery openings. . . . We introduced him to our friends and it was just a world so far from what he had grown up with.

Allison and her husband, a couple in their mid-thirties, believe they are in a unique position to offer their nine-year-old niece a broader view of the world than she may receive without their involvement:

> We really, really, really enjoy spending time with our niece. Last Christmas we suggested to have her come stay with us for a few days, for long weekends especially in the summers. She's always so sad when we leave her house to go home and we thought it would be nice for the parents but mostly really a nice change of environment for our niece. I just feel like I get some of her issues [including OCD and anxiety] on a different level than her mom and grandma do. I just feel like it would be good for her to maybe have a connection with someone else who sees her in a different way than the people who interact with her on a regular basis.

Jan and Fred, a married couple in their forties, also described significant relationships with nieces, nephews, and their friends' kids. Noting that some of their friends had questioned their choice to marry given their choice not to have kids, Jan shared her emphatic disagreement with the notion that the purpose of marriage was to produce children: "The idea that the whole purpose in life is to create babies is pretty ugly. The expectation that every woman is gonna have children is a way of controlling women's bodies, it's a lack of control over reproduction." While childfree families control their own reproduction by opting not to reproduce in a biological sense, they do contribute in significant ways to the social reproduction function of families. As the adage goes, it takes a village to raise a child. Childfree families are one example of where and how that happens.

WHAT IS FAMILY? EXPANDING THE BOUNDARIES

Childfree families fulfill nearly all the same functional purposes as families that include children. They also help us think differently about why individuals form bonds with others, what roles families serve in our lives, and the diversity of ways that individuals "do" family. This chapter has demonstrated that the child-free form bonds with others that help to meet their human need for emotional and sexual companionship and our cultural need for producing new members of society who have been socialized according to our cultural values and norms.

Today, 20 percent of women in the United States do not have children, a number that has increased steadily and doubled since the 1970s.[12] Thanks to the efforts of the feminist movement in increasing opportunities for women and to the increasing availability of reliable methods of birth control, more and more adults are creating families of their choosing. Examining the lives of the child-free reveals that these individuals form bonds to create family in much the same way that parents do. At the same time, the childfree demonstrate that having children is not a prerequisite to forming families that fulfill emotional needs and that support social reproduction in our society.

NOTES

1. West and Zimmerman (1987).
2. Oswald, Blume, and Marks (2005).
3. Oswald, Blume, and Marks (2005); Gubrium and Holstein (1990); Oswald and Sutter (2004).
4. Knox (2011).
5. Blackstone (2014); Bogenschneider (2006); Henslin (2010); Horwitz (2005); Kramer (2011).
6. Blackstone (2014).
7. Kramer (2011).
8. Angeles (2010); Burman and de Anda (1986); Hansen (2012); Somers (1993); Twenge, Campbell, and Foster (2003); Zagura (2012).
9. DeOllos and Kapinus (2002); Houseknecht (1987); Tomczak (2012); Veevers (1980).
10. Laslett and Brenner (1989).
11. Blackstone (2013).
12. Dye (2008); Osborne (2003).

CCF Facts

AGING ALONE IN AMERICA

Eric Klinenberg, Stacy Torres, and Elena Portacolone | May 2013

In 2020, there will be more Americans over age sixty-five than under age fifteen. By 2030 the number of people over sixty-five will double, while the number of those over eighty will nearly triple.

It's not just the number of elders in America that is unprecedented: There has also been a revolution in how and where the elderly live. One hundred years ago, 70 percent of American widows and widowers moved in with their families. Today nearly the same proportion of widows and widowers live alone. As late as 1950, only 10 percent of all Americans over age sixty-five lived alone. Today, by contrast, a full third of all older Americans live alone, a figure that rises to 40 percent for those eighty-five and older. The practice is likely to accelerate with the graying of the baby boom generation, whose first members turned sixty-five in 2011.

This is not a bad news story about the younger generation refusing to take in their aging parents. In fact, a recent Pew Research Center survey found that more of the younger generation than the elder generation believes that young people have an obligation to take in their aging parents. Older Americans typically prefer to remain in their own homes, a trend gerontologists call "aging in place." A 2005 AARP survey of 1,005 adults fifty and older found that 89 percent wanted to age in place. Indeed, those who age alone often say that their sense of dignity and integrity depends on their capacity to maintain their own home. If bad health or economic insecurity forced them to move in with family or, worse, a nursing home, they say, this would be a devastating loss of face as well as privacy.

Before Social Security, most widowed or unmarried elders had to move in with relatives or go to "rest homes" because they simply could not afford otherwise. In the 1950s, 35 percent of older people lived in poverty. The poverty rate for older people had fallen to 15 percent by the 1970s and has hovered between 10 and 12.5 percent since the 1980s, a trend that has correlated with rising levels of independent living among widowed and divorced elders.

The preference for solo living seems to be an international trend, even in cultures that have traditionally valued multigenerational households. In Seoul, Korea, the number of elders living alone has soared by more than 129 percent since 2000. A 2010 survey found that more elderly Koreans (30.4 percent) would rather live in nursing homes than move in with their children (21.5 percent).

Living alone does not equal social isolation. Life course transitions such as retirement provide people with more free time to socialize, and social participation and volunteering actually increase with age. Contrary to stereotype, older people who live alone are *more* likely than their married counterparts to spend time with friends and neighbors.

Elders today maintain their physical capabilities longer than ever, and the cognitive and physiological declines that people experience as they grow older are often overstated. Disability rates have been falling. And a 2009 Pew Research Center survey found that the percentage of young and middle-aged adults who expected to experience problems associated with old age such as memory loss, serious illness, or lack of sexual activity was much higher than the percentage of older adults who reported actually dealing with these issues.

Still, living alone poses real challenges to elders. Deteriorating mental or physical health may limit a person's ability to participate in social interactions outside the home. Having no children, or living far away from them, especially increases the risk of social isolation.

Living alone is a financial strain for elders who must meet maintenance expenses, property taxes—and often mortgage payments as well—on a fixed income. This is a particular problem for the 20 percent of older Americans who have no other source of income. Medicare does not reimburse long-term visits of home care aides. Nor does it cover hearing aids, dental care and dentures, eye glasses, or routine foot care. An individual who has less than $2,000 in savings can have a public home care aide provided by the government, but anyone with more than this has to spend down all their assets (with the exception of their home, their car, and $2,000 in the bank) to become eligible for such assistance.

Aging alone is especially difficult for renters. Only 7 percent of Americans between the ages of sixty-two and eighty-two receive rental subsidies. In Los Angeles, rental costs account for more than half of the expenses faced by the average older renter who lives alone. No wonder that, according to research by the UCLA Center for Health Policy Research, 70 percent of older renters living alone in California struggle to make ends meet.

The vulnerabilities of older Americans differ by gender, race, and ethnicity. Women are more likely to age alone: 37 percent of American women sixty-five and older live alone, compared to 19 percent of men the same age. Almost half (47 percent) of women seventy-five and older live alone. While 43 percent of men aged ninety and older are married, only 6 percent of same-aged women are. Black women become widows in greater numbers and at younger ages because on average black men die earlier than white men.

Elderly women have some advantages when it comes to living alone. Women are better at cultivating and maintaining social ties, and as a consequence they are less likely to be socially isolated. A 2007 study funded by the Economic and Social Research Council found that women over sixty who lived alone expressed more happiness with their lives than married women of the same age.

But women are also more vulnerable to poverty than men. In 2009, the overall poverty rate for women over sixty-five was 10.7 percent, compared to 6.6 percent for older men. And poverty rates for older women of color are particularly high. Thirty-eight percent of black women and 41 percent of Hispanic women who live alone are poor.

Race, ethnicity, and gender interact with aging in complicated ways. Older men living alone have lower poverty rates than their female counterparts but face greater difficulties maintaining social networks. For example, widowers typically lose contact with the social circles that their wives maintained. Older white men are better off economically than older black and Hispanic men, but white, widowed, older men face the greatest risk of suicide. The suicide rate for white men over the age of eighty is six times the overall suicide rate and three times higher than that of same-aged African American men.

The desire to age in place shows no sign of subsiding. Rising rates of lifelong singlehood and divorce will only further the trend of going solo: While divorce rates have fallen for younger Americans over the past 30 years, the divorce rate for people over sixty-five has doubled since 1990.

Are we ready to accommodate the needs of future Americans aging alone? Not really. Although the private sector has ample capacity to provide long-term home caregivers, meal deliveries, and other such services for affluent elders who go solo, the monthly checks from Social Security and the Supplemental Security Income program come nowhere near covering such expenses for those without substantial other sources of income. Today these economically vulnerable Americans represent the majority of those aging alone. As the numbers of older solo dwellers increase, providing more care and support for those who choose or are obliged to live alone will become a major policy challenge.

In the News

LONELINESS AND RACE IN THE TWILIGHT YEARS

DCentric, May 1, 2012

. Elahe Izadi

The quality of life for the elderly varies by race, and a new report from the Council on Contemporary Families sheds light on how loneliness affects seniors.

The report, by the nonprofit, non-partisan group based at University of Miami, found that elderly women are more likely to live alone and face higher poverty rates than men. But poverty is even higher for black and Hispanic women. Elderly black women are more likely to be widows because black men don't live as long as white men. The average white man lives seven years longer than the average black man.

Older white men are better off financially than any other elderly group, but suicide is most prevalent for the widowed among them, according to the report. The suicide rate for white men over 80 is six times the overall average in the U.S., and three times the rate for black men of the same age.

Blacks and Latinos have a tougher time financially during retirement than whites for a number of reasons. For instance, poverty is more prevalent among elderly people of color, who are less likely to have workplace retirement plans than whites.

The elderly population in D.C. is majority black, but whites 75 and older in the city are more likely to live alone, according to census estimates:

	Total house-holds with someone 75+	One-person, 75+ households	Percentage of one-person, 75+ households
Black	17,337	7,979	46%
White	7,590	4,549	60%
Hispanic	859	373	43%

Source: 2010 U.S. Census Bureau estimates.

Some other takeaways from the report: women over 60 who live alone are happier than married women of the same age, and older, solitary men have more trouble maintaining social networks than women living alone. ▬

12

New Couples, New Families

The Cohabitation Revolution in the United States

Pamela J. Smock and Wendy D. Manning

L iving in sin, playing house, shacking up, living together, cohabitation—what was a rare phenomenon just three decades ago has now become a typical experience in many people's lives. In 2002, over 60 percent of women ages twenty-five to thirty-nine had cohabited at least once.[1] Just seven years earlier, this percentage was roughly 48 percent.[2] A change of this magnitude in such a short time is striking. Indeed, cohabitation has become an integral part of the courtship process, and even adolescents are expressing an interest in cohabiting at some point in the future.[3]

This chapter explores the "cohabitation revolution," a phenomenon that is changing the way Americans date, enter marriage, and form families. We address a series of questions: Who cohabits? Why? Does cohabitation usually lead to marriage among heterosexual couples? What are cohabiting relationships like? How often are children a part of cohabiting households? Do cohabiting couples divide household chores more equally than married couples?

We summarize social science knowledge about these questions, focusing on heterosexual cohabitation. We review research done by others and interweave findings from in-depth interviews we have done with over 350 young adults to find out how people today are thinking about, and experiencing, cohabiting relationships. These men and women are from diverse racial and ethnic back-grounds, and they represent a range of social classes (from the near-poor to the middle class).

WHO COHABITS?

Currently, over 7.8 million households in the United States are headed by a cohabiting couple[4]; indeed, cohabiting has become increasingly common in all demographic groups. Consider the following: Cohabitation, rather than marriage, has become the most common way co-residential romantic relationships are now being formed. Among couples who began such relationships between 1997 and 2001, 68 percent of them began by cohabiting, and just 32 percent began by marrying.

Further, the percentage of marriages that start as cohabitations continues to climb. About forty years ago (1965–1974) only 10 percent of marriages were preceded by cohabitation. About half (57 percent) of first marriages between 1990 and 1994 were preceded by cohabitation, increasing to roughly two-thirds for those marrying recently.[5]

The flip side is that the percentage of marriages begun *without* first living together has dropped from 43 percent to one-third between 1990 and the late 2000s. That is, marrying "directly," without living together first, has become the rarer phenomenon.

There are some differences in the characteristics of people who are more or less likely to live together. First, education matters. The most highly educated are somewhat less likely to cohabit. Recent national data show that 45 percent of nineteen- to forty-four-year-old women who are college graduates have cohabited, compared with 64 percent of women who have not completed high school.[6] These differences in educational attainment correspond with the relative educational advantage that married couples enjoy compared to heterosexual cohabiting couples. In 2012, 35 percent of husbands and 34 percent of wives were college graduates compared to 19 percent and 22 percent of cohabiting men and women.[7]

Closely related to this finding, cohabiting couples tend to have lower incomes than married couples. In the year 2012, approximately 37 percent of married men had earnings over $50,000, compared to 21 percent of cohabiting men. Just 13 percent of married men had earnings of $100,000 or more, compared to only 4 percent of cohabiting men. Also, cohabitors' levels of unemployment are more than twice as high as those of married men and women, and cohabiting families with children also experience higher poverty rates than married families with children.[8]

These educational and income differences are consistent with a large number of studies that show that being well-off financially and having high levels of education increase the chances of marriage both for people who are living together and those who are not.[9] Scholars refer to this pattern as selection—that is, marriage tends to be "selective" of those with better economic prospects and more financial security.[10]

In our own conversations with cohabiting young adults, we find that many (about 70 percent) believe their money situation must be solid before they will feel ready for marriage.[11] We asked cohabitors what needs to be "in place" for them to decide to marry, because many report that they would like to marry. The following excerpts from our interviews are illustrative:

> I don't really know 'cause the love is there uh . . . trust is there. Everything's there except money.
>
> > (Black male, recently unemployed, age 29)

> I: OK. What would have had to [have] been in place for you to have gotten married?
> R: Money.
> I: OK. Tell me a little bit about what that means.
> R: Money means um . . . stability. I don't want to struggle. . . . and income-wise we were still both struggling.
>
> > (Black female store supervisor and college student, age 36)

> Ah. School was not finished, but I never really considered that an impediment, but the financial situation certainly was one.
>
> > (White male information systems manager, age 33)

> I: What are the kinds of things that needed to be in place for you to get married?
> R: Um, we wanted one of our educations to be done at least. Basically just trying to get caught up on some bills . . . and be able to afford a wedding.
>
> > (White male assistant production supervisor, age 27)

A third factor that seems to distinguish people who decide to live together versus those who do not can loosely be understood under the rubric of "traditional" versus "liberal." Cohabitation tends to be less common among those who hold strong religious convictions against cohabitation, who are more conservative, and who are less supportive of equality between men and women.[12] These traditional people, particularly those who consider cohabitation to be inconsistent with their religious beliefs, constitute a subgroup that is more likely to marry directly, without living together first.

It should be noted that there are few racial-ethnic differences in "who cohabits." Blacks, non-Hispanic whites, foreign-born, and U.S.-born Hispanics have similar chances of cohabiting. Further, the fraction of those who have ever cohabited has increased for all groups.[13]

All in all, cohabitation is becoming much more common in the United States. It is important to underscore that any existing differences are only tendencies that, arguably, may narrow in future years as cohabitation becomes even more popular. We might do well to reframe the question used by much past research on "who cohabits?" Rather, we might ask, "Who does not cohabit?"

Why Move In Together?

For heterosexual couples who have the option to marry, an important question has sparked much speculation: Why are people living together? Why not just get married?

Our interviews suggest that young adults perceive cohabitation to be an obvious and sensible thing to do. They articulate several motives for living together.

One motive is a combination of wanting to spend more time together and more pragmatic considerations such as logistics. That is, if a couple is *already* spending several nights together, why not just move in together? As one man told us: "I was going to be there more, we might as well live together . . . instead of driving to see each other all the time." Indeed, we have found that, for many couples, the "decision" to cohabit is not really a decision at all. It is a gradual process as couples spend more and more nights together and just "end up" having moved in; they often cannot even state the date their cohabitation began. We term this phenomenon a "slide" into cohabitation.[14] As twenty-three-year-old Daniela told us, her boyfriend just never went home:

> He had come over, and we had talked and we had, he had spent the night and then from then on he had stayed the night, so basically he ended up staying there, he just never went home, he just honestly never went home. I guess he had just got out of a relationship, the person he was living with before, he was staying with an uncle and then once we met, it was like love at first sight or whatever and um, he never went home, he stayed with me.

Similarly, Steve, a computer consultant, recounted:

> She stayed at my house more and more from spending the night once to not going home to her parents' house for a week at a time and then you know . . . so there was no official starting date. I did take note when the frilly fufu soaps showed up in my bathroom that she'd probably moved in at that point.

A second motive for cohabitation concerns finances. Most of our interviewees talked about how living together allows couples to save money by pooling resources and sharing in a variety of expenses, such as rent, gas, electricity, and groceries. Again and again, we heard statements like these: "Most people do it because of the bills." "Why are we paying for two apartments? Let's move in," or "Two's cheaper than one," or "I mean we spent the majority of our time together, but yet we were both paying at two separate places and it just made more sense for us to live together."

Third, young adults perceive cohabitation as an important way to evaluate compatibility for marriage; this theme was highly dominant in our interviews. It's a way of learning about one another, finding out about the other person's habits (and deciding if you can tolerate them), and figuring out whether the relationship is strong or can become strong. As one woman put it, cohabitation allows "partners to work through issues or habits before marriage."

Fear of divorce is very much intertwined with the motive of checking compatibility. The young adults we interviewed were quite sensitive to high divorce rates, often mentioning that one out of two marriages ends in divorce, and high proportions of them had experienced the divorces of their parents or close friends or relatives. They expressed concerns about not rushing into marriage, believing it essential to do everything possible to learn enough about the other person and the relationship to avoid divorce. For them, moving in together just makes sense and reduces the risk of eventual divorce; they think that not living together first would be foolish.

What Are Cohabiting Relationships Like?

Cohabiting relationships are not all the same. Scientists have studied various dimensions of cohabiting relationships; we focus on several that have received the most attention. Specifically, they vary in the relationship quality and stability (e.g., whether the couple breaks up or marries), the presence of children, and the division of unpaid household labor.

Relationship Quality and Stability

Studies of cohabiting couples suggest that, overall, they experience slightly lower relationship quality and levels of commitment than do married couples.[15] But the "overall" here is very important. Many cohabiting couples, especially those with plans to marry, are just as satisfied and committed to their relationships as married couples.[16] They also enjoy relationship quality on par with that of married couples.

What are the chances that such a couple will go on to marry rather than ending their relationship or continuing to cohabit? Information gathered about cohabitations begun between 1997 and 2001 tells us that about one-half got married. Within five years of the start of a cohabiting relationship, 49 percent headed to the altar, 37 percent broke up, and about 14 percent continued to cohabit.[17] These breakup rates are higher than those for married couples; only about 20 percent of marriages dissolve within five years.[18] When thinking about these numbers, it is important to keep in mind that while most cohabiting couples want or expect to marry, not all of them hold such intentions. One-quarter of cohabiting women living with a boyfriend explicitly stated that they did *not* expect to marry him.[19]

A commonly asked question is whether marriages preceded by cohabitation last as long as marriages begun without living together first. Many people believe that living together first makes a couple much more likely to divorce, despite what our interviewees believed about living together as a way to protect a relationship from divorce. Scientists studying this issue reach different conclusions, depending on the information they use, how old that information is, and the factors they consider. But generally the conclusion was that couples who lived together first had somewhat higher odds of divorce.[20]

However, new studies using recent data are finding that marriages begun by cohabitation are *not* more prone to divorce than those that begin without living together. As more and more couples live together before going to the altar, it makes sense that cohabitation would not make marriages more divorce-prone.[21] In other words, cohabitation has become the normative step toward marriage.

Children and Cohabiting Families

The popular image of cohabitation as revolving solely around two romantically involved people increasingly distorts reality. Many cohabiting relationships include children—about 40 percent of the relationships.[22] About half of these children are born to the cohabiting couple. The rest of the children find themselves in cohabiting families because their biological parent enters a cohabiting relationship.[23]

Scholars agree that cohabitation is increasingly becoming a context for childbearing and child rearing; it is estimated that about 40–50 percent of children born in the early 1990s will spend time in a cohabiting-parent family. It is well-known that a substantial proportion of children in the United States are born outside of marriage (40 percent). Less well-known is that most of these children, about 60 percent, are being born to couples who are living together. Broken down into broad racial and ethnic categories, this translates into about 61 percent of births for non-Hispanic white and Hispanic women, and 30 percent among African American women.[24] Notably, these births are not all occurring among the young and never-married. Roughly 20 percent of births after marital separation or divorce are occurring in cohabiting unions.[25]

Trends over time can give us clues about possible futures. The percentage of children born in cohabiting unions doubled between 1980–1984 and 1990–1994. Further, the share of births to cohabiting mothers increased substantially more during this time period than did the share to single mothers not living with a partner. It is also noteworthy that children born to cohabiting couples are less likely to be reported as "unplanned" than those born to single women.[26] *Unplanned* means that a mother states that she didn't want a(nother) baby or that the pregnancy came too soon. Overall, the percentage of women stating their child was planned is 54 percent for cohabiting women compared with 39 percent for single women.[27]

Certainly, "planning" measures have been criticized. This is because they ask a woman to reflect on what took place after her baby has already been born, likely coloring her response in a favorable direction and underestimating the percentage deemed as unplanned. But these numbers are useful in that they indicate a gap between single and cohabiting women: the latter are substantially more likely to state that the birth was planned. This lends credence to the idea that cohabitation is increasingly considered an appropriate family context for childbearing and parenting.

As noted earlier, children may also experience living in a cohabiting family, full-time or part-time, depending on custody arrangements, if their biological mother or father starts living with her or his romantic partner. This family can be considered a type of stepfamily. In fact, if we include cohabitation in addition to marriage, approximately half of all stepfamilies in the United States are now formed through cohabitation rather than through marriage.[28]

THE DIVISION OF HOUSEHOLD LABOR

Who does the everyday chores in cohabiting households? Such labor, often also termed domestic labor, includes unpaid activities such as cleaning, cooking, laundry, child care, shopping, paying bills, and many other kinds of work necessary to keep the lives of individuals and families running.

Research on married couples is clear on this point. While husbands have increased the amount of time they spend taking care of children and, to some extent, doing housework, wives still do the bulk of this labor.[29] Even counting what we might think of as "men's tasks" (yard work, taking out the garbage, household repairs, car maintenance) and despite the massive number of wives who have paid employment, most marriages are still characterized by gender inequality in the amount of household labor performed.[30]

Research on cohabiting couples also suggests a gender divide, despite such couples holding more egalitarian gender attitudes than married couples. One study reports that cohabiting men do the same amount of household labor per week as married men (nineteen and eighteen hours, respectively), while cohabiting women perform thirty-one hours of household labor per week compared to thirty-seven hours for married women.[31]

Another study tracked *changes* in men's and women's housework hours as they entered and exited cohabiting and marital unions.[32] The key finding is telling: Men substantially reduce their housework time when they enter *either* marriage or cohabitation, whereas women increase theirs under the same circumstances. As the author of the study concludes:

> the results show that entry into cohabitation induces changes in housework behavior that are no less gender-typical than does entry into marriage . . . the fact of entry into a coresidential union is of greater consequence for housework time than the form of that union.[33]

These findings echo what we learned in our interviews. Cohabiting young adults described their domestic lives in a way that suggests a relatively traditional division of labor. Cohabiting women appear to do most of the cleaning, cooking, and daily household tasks, while cohabiting men tend to focus on the traditionally male tasks described earlier. While there are exceptions, this generalization holds for most of the cohabitors we interviewed.

THE COHABITATION REVOLUTION: CONCLUDING THOUGHTS

> Workers in family agencies sometimes meet the couple or family which exists without benefit of marriage. No one knows how many such families there are in the general population, but those which come to light when their problems bring them to our agencies for assistance suggest that the average city contains a considerable number of them.[34]

What a long way we've come since social scientist Raymond Stevens wrote the above words nearly 75 years ago about cases of unmarried couples coming to the attention of urban social service agencies. From today's vantage point, it is clear that cohabitation has evolved to dramatically alter the ways that people form romantic relationships, live in them, parent, and marry. For most adults marrying for the first time, cohabitation comes first; for divorced adults, cohabitation before remarriage is even more commonplace.[35]

We would argue that cohabitation is indeed a "revolution." It is broad-based, affecting nearly all population subgroups, which suggests that state and religious structures are not dictating the parameters of adult relationships. At the same time, we would also call attention to the point that, in many ways, such as the presence of children and the division of household labor, cohabiting families are not all that different from married-couple families. Inequality in household labor, for example, mirrors what we have known for years about inequality in marriage, demonstrating how even dramatic change can coexist with continuity.

The cohabitation revolution is not, in our view, a transitory blip. While the pace of growth in cohabiting households appears to have slowed during the 1990s,[36] it is still growing. It has become the typical path to marriage and remarriage, and most young to middle-aged adults have cohabited at one time or another.

The cohabitation revolution serves as an example of how an initially novel idea or solution about how to "do" relationships has diffused within a culture and then taken on a life of its own. We would argue that high levels of cohabitation will be sustained, and further accelerated, in this way. An important aspect of this process is that new generations of young adults are coming of age within a social milieu (e.g., society, media, parents, relatives, neighbors, siblings, peers) in which large proportions of people have experienced and accept cohabitation. Moreover, increasing numbers of children will be coming of age having been born into a cohabiting family. Such patterns will reinforce the idea of cohabitation as a regular and quite predictable feature of family life, even as it adds flux and new complexities to our lives.

In the end, we are reminded of comments made by some of the young adults we interviewed. To paraphrase them, but preserving their essence: "That's really interesting. Why would you want to ask about cohabitation?? It's, well, it's just so normal!"

Notes

Some research discussed in this chapter was made possible from grants from the National Institutes of Health, Eunice Kennedy Shriver National Institute of Child Health and Human Development (R01 HD040910 and R03 HD039835) to the first and second authors, and to the Population Studies Center, University of Michigan and the Center for Family and Demographic Research, Bowling Green State University (R24 HD41028 and R24 HD050959).

1. See U.S. Department of Health and Human Services (2005).
2. See Bumpass and Lu (2000).
3. See Manning, Longmore, and Giordano (2007).
4. See U.S. Census Bureau (2012).
5. See Bumpass and Lu (2000); Bumpass and Sweet (1989); Copen, Daniels, Vespa, and Mosher (2012); Kennedy and Bumpass (2007); Manning (2010).
6. See Kennedy and Bumpass (2007).

7. See Fields and Casper (2001); U.S. Census Bureau (2012, Table FG3); U.S. Census Bureau (2012, Table UC3).
8. See Fields and Casper (2001); Manning and Brown (2006); U.S. Census Bureau (2012, Table FG3); U.S. Census Bureau (2012, Table UC3).
9. See Smock, Manning, and Porter (2005) for a review of such studies.
10. See Smock and Manning (2004) for further discussion of the selection issue and its implications for debates about family policy.
11. See Smock, Manning, and Porter (2005).
12. See Clarkberg, Stolzenberg, and Waite (1995); Lye and Waldron (1997); Thornton, Axinn, and Hill (1992).
13. See Kennedy and Bumpass (2007).
14. See Manning and Smock (2005).
15. See Nock (1995).
16. See Brown and Booth (1996).
17. See Kennedy and Bumpass (2007).
18. See Bumpass and Sweet (1989).
19. See Manning and Smock (2002).
20. See Smock (2000).
21. See Copen, Daniels, Vespa, and Mosher (2012); Manning and Cohen (2012).
22. See Fields and Casper (2001).
23. See Acs and Nelson (2002).
24. See Bumpass and Lu (2000); Kennedy and Bumpass (2007); Lichter (2012); Manlove, Ryan, Wildsmith, and Franzetta (2012).
25. See Brown (2000).
26. Manning (2001); Musick (2002).
27. See Musick (2002).
28. See Bumpass, Raley, and Sweet (1995).
29. See Sullivan in Chapter 36 of this volume.
30. See Smock and Noonan (2005).
31. See South and Spitze (1994).
32. See Gupta (1999).
33. *Ibid.*, p. 710.
34. See Stevens (1940).
35. There is even some evidence that cohabitation may be *replacing* remarriage for adults who are middle-aged or older.
36. See Casper and Bianchi (2002).

CCF Brief

DOES PREMARITAL COHABITATION RAISE YOUR RISK OF DIVORCE?

Arielle Kuperberg | March 2014

In the last fifty years, the percentage of men and women who cohabit before marriage—"living in sin," as it was still called in the 1960s—has increased by almost 900 percent. Today 70 percent of women aged thirty to thirty-four have cohabited with a male partner, and two-thirds of new marriages take place between couples who have already lived together for an average of thirty-one months.

These trends are troubling to some because nearly a dozen studies from the 1970s into the early 2000s showed that men and women who lived together before marriage were far more likely to divorce than couples who moved directly from dating to marriage. In fact, on average, researchers found that couples who cohabited before marriage had a 33 percent higher chance of divorcing than couples who moved in together after the wedding ceremony. In light of those findings, some commentators have argued that reducing the stigma attached to living together outside marriage has been a mistake, leading many young couples to make decisions that put their future marriage at risk.

In the last two years, newer research has suggested that the risk associated with premarital cohabitation may be receding. Sociologists Wendy Manning and Jessica Cohen found that for marriages formed since the mid-1990s, living together before marriage did not raise the risk of divorce. In fact, for a minority of women with higher than average risks of divorce—women with a premarital birth, women raised in single or stepparent families, or women who had had more than the median number of sex partners—living together while engaged was actually more protective against divorce than moving directly into marriage.

My research, featured in the April 2014 issue of the *Journal of Marriage and Family*, suggests studies have consistently overstated the risk of premarital cohabitation, and continue to do so even for marriages formed since the mid-1990s. This is because they have been comparing couples by their age at marriage rather than by their age when they moved in together. On average, cohabitors move in together and start trying to "act married" at a younger age than couples who marry directly. My study finds that when couples are compared by the age at which they move in together and start taking on the roles associated with marriage, there is no difference in divorce rates between couples that lived together before marriage and those that didn't.

It turns out that cohabitation doesn't cause divorce and probably never did. What leads to divorce is when people move in with someone—with or without a marriage license—before they have the maturity and experience to choose compatible partners and to conduct themselves in ways that can sustain a long-term relationship. Early entry into marriage or cohabitation, especially before age twenty-three, is the critical risk factor for divorce.

Council on Contemporary Families Expert Commentaries on Kuperberg's "Does Premarital Cohabitation Raise Your Risk of Divorce?"

BUT HOW DO THE RELATIONSHIPS GET STARTED?

Sharon Sassler, Cornell University

Clearly, the age at which one begins living with a partner, whether in marriage or cohabitation, is important. But perhaps more important is how long one is involved with a romantic partner before moving in together. And there are substantial variations in this, linked to education and socioeconomic status.

Among college graduates who enter into cohabiting unions, the process of entering into shared living is quite protracted. Half of college-educated women who enter into cohabiting relationships have been romantically involved for more than a year (an average of fourteen months) before moving in together. More than one-third were romantically involved for over two years before "shacking up."

By contrast, my qualitative research (with Amanda Miller), based on over 150 interviews with cohabitors, found that the majority of individuals with less than a college degree had moved in with their partners within six months of starting their romantic relationship. Nationally representative data from the most recent National Survey of Family Growth validate these findings: Of young women with only a high school diploma, the majority of those who cohabited had entered into shared living within about six months.

What causes many young adults to enter cohabiting unions so rapidly? Our interviews suggest that financial needs often precipitate the move into shared living among the less advantaged, while the college educated are better able to maintain separate homes while getting to know each other and assessing whether their relationship has a future. College-educated individuals also enter into shared living at older ages, on average—frequently after completing their degree. These differences undoubtedly contribute to the fact that less-educated cohabitors are more likely to break up before ever entering marriage, and more likely to divorce if they do marry, than their better-educated counterparts.

It may be premature, then, to assert that premarital cohabitation is not associated with an increased risk of divorce. Rather, knowing more about how relationships are formed and how they develop—such as how long couples are romantically involved before moving in together—may help us make better predictions about the chances that a relationship will dissolve, whether before the couple marries or after they do so.

Source: The research diwwwsed here comes from a book in progress about cohabitation among young adults in the United States.

WHAT CAN REDUCE UNINTENDED PREGNANCIES AND INCREASE STABLE RELATIONSHIPS?
Kristi Williams, The Ohio State University

As Sharon Sassler mentions in her commentary, early cohabitation—not just at a young age, but at an early stage in a relationship—is a risk factor for relationship stability. Arielle Kuperberg's new study shows that this is equally true for marriage. These findings suggest that efforts to promote marriage, a central goal of the 1996 welfare reform legislation, miss the point. Far more effective in helping Americans develop stable relationships would be to provide educational opportunities that discourage early marriage and to do a better job of preventing the unintended pregnancies that often trigger early marriage or cohabitation.

More than three-fourths of births to unpartnered women under the age of twenty-five are unintended. But marrying in response to an unintended pregnancy is hardly a recipe for relationship stability, especially for low-income women. A new study indicates that women who marry after the conception of a child but before the birth (the traditional "shotgun" marriage) are more likely to experience divorce in their first marriage than similar women who remain single at first birth. Postconception ("shotgun") cohabiting unions are especially fragile. They are almost three times more likely than postconception marriages to end by the child's third birthday. Unintended births also substantially increase the risk of union dissolution among those already in cohabiting or marital unions.

The Fragile Families and Child Wellbeing Study found that only 16 percent of low-income unwed mothers who married the child's biological father either before or after the child's birth were still married to him five years after the child's birth. In one nationally representative study, approximately 64 percent of the single mothers who married were divorced by the time they reached the age of thirty-five to forty-four.

Given that premarital sex has been nearly universal in the United States for more than forty years and that early marriage poses divorce risks, it is vital to provide teens and young adults with access to effective contraceptives and family planning services. Each year nearly 2 million unintended pregnancies are prevented by publicly funded family planning services, with savings of $4 on Medicaid-related pregnancy expenditures for every $1 spent.

Yet across the United States, efforts to restrict access to contraception are growing. Nine states currently ban or restrict abortion providers or affiliated organizations like Planned Parenthood from receiving public funds, and thirteen states restrict access to emergency contraception. Challenges to the contraceptive mandate in the Affordable Care Act are currently pending in eighty cases. These efforts fly in the face of a large body of scientific evidence showing that preventing unintended pregnancies strengthens the family.

WHAT ARE THE BENEFITS OF DELAY? WOMEN'S DELAYED ENTRY INTO FIRST MARRIAGE AND MARITAL STABILITY

Evelyn Lehrer, University of Illinois, Chicago

The age at which people enter first marriage has long been known to be an important factor in the stability of unions. The precise nature of the relationship has been the subject of some debate, however. An early study by Gary Becker and colleagues (1977) found that the relationship is nonlinear: at first, increases in age at marriage are associated with greater marital stability; but after a point, additional increases are associated with lower stability. The authors reasoned that this could be due to a "poor match effect": As women still single in their thirties or later begin to hear the biological clock tick, they may settle for a match that is less than optimal, resulting in a higher probability of a subsequent divorce.

In two studies using large-scale national data sets for 1995, 2002–2003 (Lehrer 2008), and 2006–2010 (Lehrer and Chen 2013), we found that women who enter first marriage at later ages do so having completed relatively high levels of schooling before the marriage, and the same is true of their partners. Their unions are often unconventional—for example, the spouses differ substantially in race/ethnicity, age, education, and/or religion, or the husband had been married before—traits that are typically associated with a higher probability of divorce. At first glance this would seem to support Becker et al.'s theory of a poor match effect. However, we found that these unconventional marriages contracted at late ages tend to be solid. The curve showing the relationship between women's age at first marriage and the probability of divorce is steeply downward sloping until the early thirties and flattens thereafter, without rising again.

Our statistical analysis of this puzzle found that although unconventional matches are indeed associated with higher marital instability—even in couples who have delayed entry into marriage—the stabilizing effects associated with older age at marriage and higher levels of educational attainment are far larger and outweigh the risk factors.

In sum, although women who delay marriage disproportionately enter unconventional matches that pose real challenges for couples, they and their partners also tend to have relatively high levels of human capital and maturity—and the unions they form therefore tend to be stable.

WHO KNOWS WHAT OTHER OLD RULES MAY BE SHATTERED IN THE NEXT FEW YEARS?

Stephanie Coontz, The Evergreen State College

Kuperberg's and other new studies of cohabitation and marriage provide more evidence of the unprecedented transformation now occurring in the dynamics of close relationships. Almost all the old sociological "rules" about who marries, what people want in a mate, what contributes to marital satisfaction, and what predicts divorce are in flux.

In the 1950s, for example, the average couple wed after only six months of courtship. But divorce rates were much lower than they are today, partly because marriages in that era were based on predefined, rigid gender roles. Both parties knew exactly what was expected of them. It was much easier to figure out how to make a marriage work than it is today, when there is so much more to negotiate.

Early marriage was already a divorce risk by 1960. But *early* meant something quite different when the average age of marriage for women was barely over twenty—still too young to legally drink a toast at their own wedding reception. And as Lehrer points out, in the 1960s marrying at a later than average age was also a divorce risk; that association has now disappeared.

In the 1950s, cohabitation was so stigmatized that the only people likely to live together were truly unconventional and unconcerned with social respectability. In that context, premarital cohabitation was associated with higher divorce rates, not so much as a cause but as a symptom of associated risky behaviors and values. Now that prior cohabitation is the normative route to marriage, and especially now that marriage requires more negotiation skills and deeper friendship than the past, the United States may well follow the same pattern that researchers found in Australia. In that country, in the 1940s and 1950s, premarital cohabitation significantly increased the risk of divorce. But the added divorce risk declined each year for marriages contracted up to 1988 and then it reversed, so that since then premarital cohabitation has reduced the risk of separation. Who knows what other old rules may be shattered in the next few years?

13

Growing Up with a Lesbian, Gay, or Bisexual Sibling

Amy Brainer

The seed of this analysis took root in my mind several years before I set out to interview people with lesbian, gay, and bisexual siblings. As part of my work with a queer advocacy organization, I was giving a talk about faith and sexuality at a Christian university that bans openly gay students. A young woman approached me after the talk and asked to speak confidentially. "My brother just told me that he's gay," she confided when the two of us had moved out of earshot of other students. As she poured out her family story, several things became very clear: her love for and loyalty to her brother, her anxiety about her parents' potentially harsh reaction should they find out her brother is gay, and her emerging role as a bridge between her brother and their parents. "Is there a group or something for people who have gay siblings?" she asked. The long list of resources I had prepared contained no such group. Instead, I took her name and e-mail address to put her in touch with one of my own siblings.

I recalled my conversation with this student some years later, as I was reading Gloria Filax's book about queer youth in Alberta, Canada.[1] One passage in particular leapt off the page: "Fear that siblings will be targets of harassment or that their families will be viewed as dysfunctional figure in many queer youth narratives." This was followed by a number of examples, such as a youth who said, "I have to be careful because my sister might suffer if the kids at school know [that I'm gay]."[2] These short quotes, largely unremarked on in the analysis, raised multiple questions for me: How do siblings of queer young people understand, experience, and cope with antigay bullying in their schools? How do these siblings cope with antigay policies and practices in other social spaces—for example, the sister I spoke to who attended a college with an antigay admissions policy? And a broader question that forms the basis of this analysis: What is it like to grow up with a lesbian, gay, or bisexual sibling?

I began combing sociology and family studies journals in search of research on straight people with gay siblings. I found very little. In previous research on straight and gay sibling pairs, researchers have used straight siblings as a control group to identify differences and similarities based on sexual orientation, often with a goal of figuring out what makes a person straight or gay.[3] I also found references to siblings peppered throughout lesbian, gay, and bisexual people's life stories. But the voices of these siblings themselves were missing from the literature.

In the midst of this investigation, I called my own sister to share my emerging ideas and questions about this topic. "I'd like to interview people who have gay siblings," I said. "What do you think about that?" It was as if I had unlatched a deep trunk filled to the brim with memories and feelings. My sister talked for more than two hours without stopping. I knew she had played an important role in our family after I told my Christian parents about my same-sex relationships, but I had no idea how profoundly these experiences had touched my sister's life and shaped her own sense of self. With both our phones low on battery, and the first of many such conversations drawing to a close, my sister said, "I've never really talked about that before."

Not everyone who grows up with a lesbian, gay, or bisexual sibling will be strongly affected by the experience, and certainly no two people are affected in exactly the same ways. For some, this may be a relatively minor characteristic of family life. For others, it may be something they like and appreciate about themselves and their family, a source of conflict, something else, or all of these things. By including people with lesbian, gay, and bisexual siblings in research on sexualities and families, we can begin to identify the variation and patterns in people's experiences.

In this chapter, I provide a preliminary theoretical framework for analyzing sibling identities and relationships across constructions of difference and inequality. I then draw from interviews with twenty-two heterosexual young adults (ages eighteen to twenty-nine) who grew up with a lesbian, gay, or bisexual sibling to expand what we know about this important but understudied population.

ASSOCIATIVE IDENTITIES AND "COURTESY STIGMA": BUILDING A THEORETICAL TOOLKIT

As discussed earlier, much of the literature on straight and gay siblings is comparative by design. While geneticists and other scientists have compared siblings' physiology, psychologists have compared straight and gay siblings on a battery of social indicators, including (but not limited to) religiosity, political affiliation, division of household labor, mental health, and suicide attempts.[4] At the conclusion of one of these studies, Esther Rothblum and her colleagues took a conceptual step back to ask why heterosexual respondents with LGB siblings continue to show highly "traditional" outcomes. They speculated that these respondents may be under extra pressure from parents to "remain faithful to [heteronormative] family values" due to having a known LGB sibling who cannot fulfill these expectations.[5] Although the survey data analyzed by Rothblum and colleagues cannot answer this question definitively, the framework they propose holds the possibility of an epistemological shift, from comparative research on straight and gay differences to research that generates more complex theories about interdependent sibling relationships.

A small number of researchers have pioneered work on how the "coming out" process affects sibling relationships.[6] Findings primarily focus on sibling responses to the LGB person's disclosure of same-sex attraction, and provide recommendations for clinicians who work with such individuals and families. In most cases explored, the LGB sibling came out after both siblings were adults and no longer living together. Questions remain about the impact of having a known LGB sibling while growing up in a shared home environment. Additionally, we know little about the experience of having a lesbian, gay, or bisexual sibling beyond the context of the home and family, and the experiences of people for whom "coming out" is not a relevant or primary framework. For example, in many families, sexuality is tacitly understood rather than openly discussed; it is important to understand how siblings get on under these circumstances as well.

Expanding on this small body of work, I found helpful theoretical innovations in the area of disability studies, where researchers have used concepts such as "family disability" and "disability by association" to describe how siblings of people with disabilities construct their identities and interact with others.[7] Gay identity and disability are neither conceptually equivalent nor mutually exclusive—siblings may differ from one another in multiple areas (gender, sexuality, dis/ability, race), and each of these axes of difference and inequality operates in distinctive ways. At the same time, theories of "family disability" and "disability by association" make an important contribution to our broader understanding of sibling ties and associative identities and have implications for the study of siblings in other populations.

In interviews with non-disabled children ages six to nineteen who had one or more disabled siblings, Stalker and Connors found that shared family biographies often took precedence over any perceived differences among family members. These children acknowledged that others viewed and treated their siblings as "different" although they recognized their siblings as "normal." Some children had been taunted by peers because of their association with a disabled sibling: for example, "Your brother's thick; it means you're thick."[8] As a result of their movement between disabled and non-disabled social worlds, these children developed a unique vantage point that enabled them to notice—and critique—societal definitions of difference and normalcy.

> These children inhabit the world of "normals" outside the family and they spend time at home with their disabled brother or sister: thus they are well placed to mediate difference both ways. They have access to society's view of difference, which tends to be equated with "abnormality," but also face the challenge of moving the boundaries of normalcy in order to include their sibling, if they choose to do so.[9]

As Stalker and Connors have noted, this unique position is not without its challenges. While non-disabled children with disabled siblings have access to multiple social worlds, they may also experience a sense of not quite belonging in all worlds.

Several scholars have used Erving Goffman's theory of "courtesy stigma" to analyze the identities and relationships of non-disabled people with disabled children and siblings.[10] Courtesy stigma is attached to individuals who are related through the social structure (in this case, through familial ties) to what Goffman calls a "stigmatized" individual, "a relationship that leads the wider society to treat both individuals in some respects as one."[11] Goffman anticipated that courtesy group membership would present some unique challenges with regard to insider/outsider status:

> The individual with a courtesy stigma may find that he [sic] must suffer many of the standard deprivations of his courtesy group and yet not be able to enjoy the self-elevation which is a common defense against such treatment. Further, much like the stigmatized in regard to him, he can doubt that in the last analysis he is really "accepted" by his courtesy group.[12]

What Goffman calls "self-elevation" may be a strong, positive identity, community, and support system that prepares individuals to face prejudice and discrimination. Siblings who experience prejudice and discrimination "by association" may lack access to these critical resources. For example, people with LGB siblings may deal with "standard deprivations" such as loss of friends or being picked on at school (as suggested by Filax's work on queer Canadian youth, discussed earlier in this chapter[13]) without access to an affirming LGB subculture from which to draw support.[14] Given the paucity of research about sibling relationships in general and people with LGB siblings in particular, theories of family disability and courtesy stigma provide us with some productive first steps toward understanding the experiences of heterosexuals who are growing up with lesbian, gay, and bisexual siblings.

Goffman's theory of courtesy stigma also has limitations. The word *stigma* may cast a negative shadow over the experience of having a disabled and/or LGB sibling. Neither the children in the studies described earlier, nor the people I interviewed, described this experience as wholly or primarily negative. And it's important to keep in mind that the "stigma" they did face originated from ableism, homophobia, and heteronormativity in culture and society, not from their siblings themselves. Burke notes that "disability by association" can empower people to make changes as they come to recognize and resist the social construction of normalcy, difference, and inequality[15]—something siblings with a unique insider/outsider status may be well equipped to do. With these caveats in mind, we can use "courtesy stigma" as one of several tools to deepen our understanding of how siblings' lives converge.

Notes on Data Collection and Analysis

In summer and fall 2008, I interviewed twenty-two people—sixteen heterosexual women and six heterosexual men—ranging in age from eighteen to twenty-nine. Thirteen have a gay brother, one has a bisexual brother, four have a lesbian sister, and five have a bisexual sister, with overlap due to one woman who has both a bisexual sister and a gay brother. To locate participants for this research, I advertised the study on Chicago-area university and community college bulletin boards and electronic listservs that serve general student populations. My call for participation specified that interviewees should be eighteen to twenty-nine, identify as heterosexual, and have a full, step, or half-sibling who identifies as lesbian, gay, or bisexual[16] with whom they shared a childhood home for one or more years (all twenty-two people who responded spent most of their growing-up years in the same home as their LGB siblings).

I chose not to recruit through LGB organizations first or primarily, because I felt that my data-collection strategy should reflect the epistemological shift I hoped to make, placing straight people with LGB siblings at the center of analysis from the outset of the research, rather than making their participation contingent upon their siblings. Relying on LGB siblings to connect us would have created a barrier for people who do not have a good relationship with their LGB sibling and/or do not discuss sexuality openly with their sibling, as was the case for some people in my sample. In addition, I hoped to reach people who were not already well connected to LGB communities and people who held more socially conservative views about sexuality.

Not surprisingly, most of the people who responded to my call for participation felt positively about having a lesbian, gay, or bisexual sibling. It is likely that people with less positive feelings would choose not to participate in research on this topic. However, there was a small amount of variation; for example, one person told me that her mother had custody of her nephews (her bisexual sister's sons) and that she thought it was better for her mother to raise these boys to prevent them from "developing signs of homosexuality" like their mother (her older sister). This differed markedly from the person who wiped tears from her eyes as she told me how hurt and offended she had been when someone asked her if she felt uncomfortable exposing her daughter to a lesbian aunt (her older sister). This kind of variation is important to note, and researchers should make ongoing efforts to hear from people who feel ambivalent or negatively about having a lesbian, gay, or bisexual family member.

One black, five Latino, and sixteen non-Hispanic white people participated in this research. The study includes three first-generation immigrants who moved to the United States from Russia, Israel, and Mexico in late adolescence. I categorized eleven of my participants as "working class" and eleven as "middle class" based on their parents' occupations and the median income in their neighborhoods. However, these categories should be taken with a grain of salt, since class is often far more complicated than a simple occupation and income matrix permits us to see—what is important here is the variation in the family backgrounds of the people who took part in this study. For example, one person lived in a two-story apartment with her parents, brother, uncle, and uncle's family, all of whom contributed to the family income through their work as restaurant waitstaff and bussers; another lived with his brother in a downtown condo while completing his law degree, supported by his lawyer father and doctor mother; and another lived in a suburb and was taking time off from school to care for her mother, who is a single parent on disability. My decision to advertise on university and community college campuses yielded an educationally privileged sample. Most of the people I interviewed were first-generation college students. As described earlier, the sample contains a disproportionate number of whites, women, and people with gay brothers. About two-thirds of the people who took part in this study grew up in cities, suburbs, or mid-sized towns in the Midwest; one-third hailed from other parts of the country and world, having moved to the Chicago area as young adults.

It is important to note that this study is not representative of people who have lesbian, gay, and bisexual siblings and should not be used to make generalizations about their lives. It is an exploratory study focused on emerging themes and the theoretical implications of those themes. Further work is needed to investigate the intersections of race, class, citizenship status, geographic location (including urban/suburban/rural areas) and other factors that influence the experience of growing up with a sibling who is lesbian, gay, or bisexual.

During the interviews, I asked people to talk about their sibling and family relationships at different life stages (childhood, adolescence, and adulthood) and in different social spaces; for example, home, school, work, neighborhood, places of worship, and any other space(s) where they spent a significant amount of time. I also asked people to reflect on their relationships with peers, significant others, teachers, coaches, clergy, core and extended family members, and any other relationship(s) that they considered to be important, with a focus on whether and how these relationships shaped and were shaped by the experience of growing up with a lesbian, gay, or bisexual sibling. In conclusion, I asked people to tell me about their own gender and sexual identities. The interviews took two hours to complete on average. I then transcribed the interviews and conducted multiple rounds of coding: open coding to identify themes emerging from the data, and focused coding to identify patterns and dissimilarities across interviews.[17] In this chapter, I'll discuss four key themes that emerged from the interviews: (1) emotion work in the family; (2) coping with antigay beliefs and practices; (3) straight siblings as gay by association; and (4) issues of belonging and group membership.

"My Role Is More or Less Mediator": Emotion Work in the Family

Sociologists use the term *emotion work* to describe the often invisible work required to socially manage our emotions and provide emotional support to others.[18] Participants in this research did a significant amount of emotion work to support their siblings and manage potential or actual family conflicts over gender and sexuality-related issues. For example, Gina[19] recounted a falling out among her family members over whether her gay older brother should be permitted to bring his boyfriend to Thanksgiving dinner. When her aunt said that a same-sex couple would "really make people uncomfortable," it was Gina who stepped in to handle the situation:

> So I talked to my aunt, who I have a decent enough relationship with, and I explained my brother's side without being mad about it like he would be. He was very mad and very hurt, and I didn't have as much of a passion about it. I was more level-headed. So just trying to mediate and be like, "Well, if you guys don't accept

it, that's fine. But I do, so I'm willing to spend my Thanksgiving with him and his boyfriend." . . . My role is more or less mediator. Like I said, the sibling loyalty is there. Probably before anybody else I would be there for him.

Gina was one of several people who arranged alternative holiday celebrations to accommodate their LGB siblings. For these women and men, emotion work involved going back and forth between family members, soothing hurt and angry feelings, reasoning with people in hopes of getting the family together, and sometimes hosting a separate holiday meal for their sibling and their sibling's partner.

Other participants were among the few or only family members who knew of their sibling's LGB sexuality. In these cases, participants worked to educate and prepare other family members for potential disclosure or discovery, and to make the family environment more welcoming for their LGB sibling. As Jillian shared:

> My grandma found out that I had gone to the gay pride parade. And so she was like, "Oh, I heard you went to that, that's disgusting." And I was like, "Why? Explain this to me." And she was like, "All those boys are kissing each other." And I said, "You know what? It would be disgusting if I was sitting on the corner and some guy and girl were kissing, were making out, were doing nasty stuff. It's disturbing no matter what. So the fact of the matter is, if you find someone you love and you're in a committed relationship, good for you." And she was like, "Yeah, I guess that's true."

Jillian also comforted her mom around the time her younger brother, Ted, came out as gay:

> My mom is one of those people that feels really guilty about everything. The fact that Ted is gay she thinks is her fault, another thing she screwed up. We talked about it, you know. And I was like, "No, it's not your fault. . . . Mom, how did you know you were straight? At one point you were attracted to boys, and at one point Ted realized that he was attracted to boys. It's not something you can change."

In these examples, Jillian's emotion work is taking place on several levels: she is paying close attention to her mom's feelings and tailoring her response to her mom's particular concerns, as well as normalizing same-sex attraction for her mom (who knows that her brother is gay) and grandmother (who does not yet know). Jillian also showed support for her brother by going to a public gay event and talking openly about this event with her family members.

Participants provided similar types of emotional support to LGB siblings themselves. For example, Edward supported his bisexual younger sister through active listening, expressing care and concern about her feelings (such as staying up late to talk with her about biphobic treatment she had experienced), and inviting her to LGB-themed events. Edward's sister continued to live in the rural community where the two of them grew up, while Edward had recently moved to Chicago for college and made an effort to share the new kinds of resources at his disposal:

> I invite her to these events, when there's say a speaker or something, posted on a campus, who's particularly receptive to the GBL and/or T community. Then I invite her, because my friends out here attend these events, and I figure, why not come down? Not as a token—"well, you're not heterosexual, you'll enjoy this." But more of, I'm enjoying this with my friends, and I'd love to have you here. Because it's not fair to you to be in an area with less resources at your disposal. So I'm trying to be that bridge.

Interestingly, Edward invokes the "bridge" analogy—used by other participants to describe their position as a mediator between their parents and sibling—to talk about bridging his sister to LGB resources. Such gestures were especially common among older brothers and sisters, who felt responsible for providing some kind of guidance to their lesbian, gay, and bisexual younger siblings, requiring them to do the work to learn about these things first.

In sum, emotion work for women and men in this research entailed mediating among family members, making an effort to include LGB siblings in family activities, educating family members about LGB issues, and listening to and helping LGB siblings in a variety of ways. I have focused here on emotion work in the family context. In the following sections, I expand my focus beyond the home and family to examine straight and gay sibling identities and relationships in other social and cultural spaces.

"DO I CHOOSE THE FAITH, OR DO I CHOOSE MY BROTHER?" COPING WITH ANTIGAY BELIEFS AND PRACTICES

Participants encountered antigay beliefs and practices in many different social contexts. In this section I will focus on faith-based institutions, not because these are singular or more important, but because they illustrate how associative identities operate when antigay beliefs inform institutional policies and practices. In addition, faith communities, and churches in particular, were the spaces cited most frequently by participants in this research as being inhospitable to people with LGB family members. Grace was among those who voiced this perspective, saying she felt "absolutely isolated" from her religious community after her older sister began to identify as bisexual. She recounted, with emotion, a chapel service she had attended at her Christian college, in which the chaplain said that no same-sex couple is capable of having a long-term, loving relationship, and made numerous other derogatory comments about LGB people:

> I was just sitting there, and I couldn't even believe my ears. I just felt my blood boiling inside me. And then I did the same thing [kept quiet], which is not something I'm proud of. I wish I had spoken up. I actually raised my hand, but right then the meeting was ending, so I didn't get to say what I was gonna say. And then I ran out of that building, and I could feel myself on fire. I was so hot and burning, and my heart was palpating inside me. And then I ran home, and I went to my roommate, and for an hour I told her everything I had heard, and how angry I was. How angry I was at all the people. I felt so irate about it, I threw a chair.

The depth of Grace's feelings—her physical distress in and after the chapel service, and her thick residual emotions when recounting this story to me some years later—highlight the extent to which these antigay teachings wounded Grace, not vicariously (i.e., she felt hurt because her sister was hurt—in this case, her sister was not even present, and Grace had never told her about the service) but directly and personally. Although Grace reported that church was very important to her, she had stopped attending her home church because of its inhospitality to LGB people and their families, and she had not yet found a new church to attend. She was looking for a more liturgical church (in contrast to the evangelical churches she attended as a child) because she thought highly scripted services might be less homophobic. However, participants who did attend liturgical churches were coping with equally hurtful antigay beliefs and practices in those spaces. For Sandra, who was raised Catholic, conflicts of religious faith and sibling identity began in childhood:

> It was confirmation. Seventh grade. And I remember I felt embarrassed to ask the question. So I had one of my good friends ask the question, that knew my sister was a lesbian. And I said, "Can you ask if it's OK if a homosexual is my sponsor? Or is that seen as wrong in God's eyes?" And the teacher said, "Well, I don't think the confirmation would be legitimate. I think that in God's eyes it would be seen as false. Because they need to go and confess their sin for being a homosexual and change their ways." And I could not believe they were saying this.

Like Grace, Sandra ultimately left the church, attributing her decision to the church's failure to welcome lesbian and gay congregants and, by extension, their siblings. Another participant, Kevin, put it frankly:

> When I started having a falling out with the Catholic Church was right around the time my brother came out. And it was basically because I thought, I still love

my brother; he's still an amazing person. And yet the faith we were raised in, he's not accepted. So do I choose the faith, or do I choose my brother? And it was a pretty easy choice to choose my brother. So I've had basically a falling out with the Catholic Church ever since. I'm trying to find a faith community that's more welcoming of gays.

These data show the far-reaching effects of antigay beliefs and practices in faith-based institutions, with implications for other social institutions, such as primary and secondary schools and clubs (e.g., Boy Scouts of America, which only recently voted to allow openly gay Scout members but continues to ban gay Scout leaders[20]). Beliefs and practices that exclude lesbian, gay, and bisexual people from full participation in community life are likely to alienate straight people with LGB siblings, for whom these practices exact a personal and familial cost.

"If Your Sister's a Lesbian, Then You Might Be a Lesbian, Too": Siblings as Gay by Association

Participants described many instances in which people suspected them of being "gay by association." This subject came up most frequently for those with same-gender LGB siblings (i.e., women with lesbian or bisexual sisters, and men with gay brothers).[21] Some friends and acquaintances limited or withheld intimacy from participants because of these associations. For example, Carmen recalled:

In high school, my friends, they didn't know if they should be comfortable around me. They felt like, oh, if your sister's a lesbian, then you might be a lesbian, too. You know? So it was always like, you get dressed here, and I'll get dressed over there, in a different room, or something like that.

High school friends also asked Carmen whether her own sister had tried to kiss her, and whether Carmen permitted her sister to see Carmen naked. Carmen's ex-boyfriend forbade her to spend time with her sister because "she might turn you into a lesbian." Other women participants talked about friends who refused to dance with or hug them, saying things such as, "I've been thinking about your sister, and I think you have it [lesbianism], too." One woman was interrogated about her own sexuality before she was permitted to pledge a sorority, after sorority sisters found out that she had a bisexual sister. Kevin described a situation at the pool where he worked as a lifeguard, where antigay attitudes were directed toward him and his gay older brother:

Whenever my brother and I see each other after a long time, we always give each other a hug and usually kiss each other on the cheek. So he snuck up behind me and gave me a hug and then kissed me on the cheek. I didn't think anything of it. And at the end of the day all the lifeguards were done, and I could hear all the rumors circulating. Everybody was like, "Is your brother gay? Why did your brother do that? Do you guys always do that?"

It is possible that Kevin's coworkers would have responded the same way to a hug and kiss between two brothers who both identify as straight. Kevin, however, connected their questions to his brother's sexuality and to derogatory comments about gay people that he dealt with at work on a daily basis. While Kevin's experience had no bearing on his employment, other participants hid their family lives at work for fear of being penalized by homophobic employers, and one participant changed careers entirely because of the antigay culture of his workplace.

In addition to being viewed as (potentially) gay themselves, several people had been the targets of antigay slurs and jokes. For example, Ashma shared this family story about her bisexual older sister (whom she describes here as homosexual and gay—like many participants, Ashma used these words interchangeably throughout the interview) and heterosexual older brother:

> I feel like a lot of people do judge you. Especially friends and stuff like that. I think my brother had to deal with that a lot, because they're only two years apart. And so growing up, they were very close, and their friends overlapped tremendously. So once people started finding out that she's homosexual, they'd talk about him. Like, "Your sister's gay, dog." Stuff like that. You know, it bothers him. Even though they're grown it's still the same kind of thing; you don't want people talking about your family like that. You don't want them being able to use that kind of stuff to degrade you or look at you in a light that you wouldn't want them to. I think that's why it bothered him so much.

Significantly, it is Ashma's heterosexual brother whom she describes as being judged and talked about not because of his own sexual identity, but because of his associative identity as someone with a bisexual sibling. Ashma also points out that age is an important factor—siblings who are closer in age are likely to have stronger associative identities, due largely to their overlapping social circles.

The stories shared by these women and men point to multiple ways that peers and others may view and treat straight people with LGB siblings as gay by association, including suspecting that they are actually or potentially gay and making them the target of derogatory remarks. These findings suggest that improving the status and treatment of lesbian, gay, and bisexual people in society will benefit straight people with LGB siblings not only in a vicarious way but also in a more direct and personal way.

"How Do I Fit into This Whole Community?": Dilemmas of Courtesy Stigma

Though participants felt a strong connection to lesbian, gay, and bisexual people, they had difficulty expressing why and how they were connected, and questioned the legitimacy of their membership in what Goffman called the "courtesy group." As Viktor put it:

> How do I fit into this whole community? How much should I really participate? I mean, I have a sibling; it's not like I'm gay. I am only able to tangentially relate to their concerns. . . . Just recently I did some research for the upcoming gay pride parade; I went to Boystown.[22] And I was wondering, how should I approach this? Because, as I said, I tend to be a bit self-conscious, because I'm afraid that people will wonder if I really know anything.

Viktor showed me clippings of newspaper articles he had written about gay issues, and told me about his decision to join a gay club on his university campus. Although he appeared to cultivate many gay-related interests and activities, Viktor worried that others would not see him as a legitimate member of this community. Also, despite telling me that he could only "tangentially relate to their [the gay community's] concerns," Viktor was in the process of making some huge life choices based on these concerns. His deliberation about whether to become a naturalized U.S. citizen was based, in large part, on how living in Russia, his country of origin, might be for somebody with a gay sibling (in his case, a younger gay brother):

> What's gonna happen if, say, we're walking down the street, and someone is gonna ask point blank [if my brother is gay]? . . . If they ask me, am I gonna be able to stand up for him? It just made me wonder, should I go back, how would I live my life there?

Making these decisions about where and how to live did not change Viktor's perception that he was only tangentially related to the gay community, or, as Carmen put it, "an outsider peeking in." Questions of insider/outsider status came up repeatedly in interviews, as people searched for the appropriate words to talk about their identities and relationships. Individualist notions of self made the expression of an associative or "courtesy" identity linguistically impossible for many participants, illustrated here by Hannah:

> [Having a bisexual twin brother] makes me feel a little more authentic, to hang out with gay and lesbian people, you know? That I'm . . . I'm sort of, you know . . . I'm

a friend, I'm a . . . I forget what the actual term is. But I'm a friendly, you know, accepting, supporting person. You know? I don't know. I don't ever bring it up as like, membership to the club. But I think it does make me feel a little bit more . . . you know, when speaking to my gay friends . . . that they know that I'm coming from a place. That I have a closer relationship to a gay man than I do with them. So that I'm not . . . I don't know what. I'm coming from a friendly place, and that I'm . . . I don't know. It makes me feel a little bit more included, maybe. In the culture. Well, not culture, but community. Community is such a weird word too. But in the [makes a wide circle gesture with hands]. It sounds stupid when I say it, but I guess I do feel that way. It makes me feel like . . . I'm not gay myself, but I like people who are. I don't know. You know?

Hannah never did find a satisfactory word to describe her relationship to lesbian and gay people, despite using a large number of them: *friend, friendly, accepting, supporting, coming from a friendly place, included, in the culture or community.* While Hannah struggled to name this connection, Grace struggled to understand the very desire for this connection:

When I would go to the store, I'd feel so stupid—but if I saw a lesbian couple, I would feel like I wanted to make eye contact with them. And I wanted them to see me. But I feel like they didn't, a lot of times. These people I would feel this desire to connect with wouldn't connect with me. Sometimes I found myself almost staring at them, and I felt like they would perceive it as, I was staring at them because of their orientation. But really I was staring at them because I wanted them to look at me and feel some sort of closeness to me. And it's really weird. And odd. Or, like, if I was in a restaurant and saw them, I would feel like, oh, I would like to be near them; I would like to be their friend.

Grace described her desire to connect with lesbians as stupid, weird, and odd. Yet her interview revealed that this desire had shaped Grace's social networks in meaningful ways, as she routinely sought out LGBT friends, connected with LGBT classmates and colleagues, and formed special bonds with gay and transgender patients in her work as a nurse. Many participants talked about their friendships with lesbian, gay, and bisexual people, which they felt exceeded those of most heterosexuals in number and intimacy. Additionally, many participants felt that LGB people understood their lives in ways that other heterosexuals could not. As Paul explained:

With the gay woman at my work, I did talk to her about my brother, and how it affects me and my family. Because one day we were riding together somewhere, and we just talked about experiences with family. Like how her family thinks of her, and how my family thinks of my brother. It was kind of nice to share some information. It was nice to hear that other people are out there, that have the same issues and problems.

Three people had chosen to live with lesbian or gay roommates, and four women had dated men who later identified as gay or bisexual. Reflecting on this, Gina said:

I think I identify with men in a different way because of being so close to my brother. People always say you marry somebody who's like your dad basically. But I really think I'm attracted to very flamboyant men, who sometimes end up being gay. I think that because I'm so close to my brother, I find his qualities to be attractive in other men.

Other women talked about striving for greater gender parity in their relationships with men, and connected this to having a lesbian or gay sibling. For example, Nadine shared:

I went for somebody [a boyfriend] that was more open and more liberal and more accepting because if they weren't, I wouldn't be with them. It was a prerequisite. Our relationship is more of a partner-partner thing than a female-male thing, which I think I get from living with Stan [Nadine's gay twin brother]. Which I think is better. It's more open and loving and what I think a relationship should be, instead of: do this because you're this, and do that because you're that.

In addition to cultivating friendships, living arrangements, and even romantic attachments to people who identify as LGB, and altering gender expectations in their heterosexual relationships, one participant was developing a physical therapy manual for a queer youth center; another was working on a research project about lesbian and gay health care; another was an active member of the Human Rights Campaign; another spoke on panels at his college about gay issues; another had decided to major in gender studies after finding out that her brother was gay; and another was considering going to work full-time for the Matthew Shepherd Foundation.[23] Clearly, the affinity with lesbian, gay, and bisexual people that participants struggled to articulate was not imagined. Yet they had very little language to talk about this affinity in ways that felt appropriate or comfortable to them.

A "Weird Gazelle" in the Gay Bar: Concluding Remarks

The women and men in this study described multiple ways that having a lesbian, gay, or bisexual sibling mattered in their lives. Many had educated people in their families about LGB issues, wrestled with the antigay positions taken by their faith communities, distanced themselves from friends who suspected them of being gay by association, formed close relationships with LGB people, and actively supported LGB causes. At the same time, they lacked words to name, understand, and legitimize their felt and desired connections to lesbian, gay, and bisexual communities.

As Goffman predicted, these individuals baffled "stigmatized" (LGB) as well as "non-stigmatized" (heterosexual) groups. They frequented gay bars with their siblings and "shocked" lesbian and gay clientele who (they surmised) "expect all straight people to be homophobic." Some lesbian and gay acquaintances told participants that they had never met a fully supportive family member. Richard encountered this point of view when he accompanied his younger brother to a gay club: "I gotta tell you, there were like, multiple gay guys who were just like, 'So, it doesn't bother you?' It was like I was a weird gazelle or something like that. They were like, 'You exist?!'"

Goffman's theory of courtesy stigma gives us some tools for making sense of this "weird gazelle" phenomenon. Courtesy group membership is a unique vantage point, a foot in both worlds (in this case, heterosexual and LGB social worlds) and, Goffman notes, an important vehicle for normalization. That is, courtesy group members may, as Stalker and Connors write, "[move] the boundaries of normalcy in order to include their sibling."[24] But it is also a precarious position, as courtesy group members may be viewed suspiciously for carrying "a burden that is not 'really' theirs."[25] In reality, the burdens, joys, pleasures, and frustrations carried by heterosexuals with LGB siblings do not belong to someone else—they are not reflections or kickbacks of what LGB people themselves experience; rather, they are qualitatively new, unique, and important in their own right.

At heart, this chapter is a call for the inclusion of people with lesbian, gay, and bisexual siblings in family theory and practice, and in queer community work. The women and men I interviewed perceived LGB family organizations like PFLAG (Parents, Families, and Friends of Lesbians and Gays) to be "for" parents rather than siblings. Some people felt no need for sibling-centered information and other kinds of support. But many others wished that they had known more at younger ages. Magdalena shared this about her experience of growing up with a gay older brother:

> I wish I had someone telling me, "There's other people like you." Or at least my brother telling me, "Oh, you know, Magdalena, I'm gay, but I'm still your brother."

But he didn't even tell me he was gay; I had to find out for myself. I don't think he's ever been like, "Oh, Magdalena, you know what? I'm gay" after all these years. But I wish someone had told me there's gay people. Because I went to a Catholic high school and even elementary school, so no one was like, "This is what gay is." All these things I've had to figure out for myself. And maybe that's why I've had my ups and my downs with this thing. I've sometimes felt really frustrated. I wish maybe my mom would have talked to me more about this. And she did, but she didn't tell me how to deal with it in the community or in the world. And I think that's what's needed—how to deal with it in the community or in different situations.

Magdalena touches on several issues raised in this chapter: how important it is to recognize the population of young people growing up with lesbian, gay, and bisexual siblings ("there's other people like you"); the alienation people with LGB siblings may experience in heteronormative spaces, such as Magdalena's schools; and the fact that people are dealing with different situations and community contexts that shape the meanings and experience of having a lesbian, gay, or bisexual sibling. For Magdalena, "coming out" is not the pivotal experience, because her brother never came out to her; nevertheless, his gay sexuality has shaped her life in meaningful ways.

Continued work is needed to contextualize the different kinds of experiences people are having, and to identify new theoretical insights and best practices for children, teens, and adults with LGB siblings. Including siblings in research and theory about sexuality and families promises to enrich our knowledge about this understudied group as well as our broader understanding of how sibling ties shape people's identities, relationships, and lives.

Notes

1. Filax (2006).
2. *Ibid.*, p. 61.
3. See Blanchard (2004); Hamer (2011); Sánchez, Bocklandt, and Vilain (2013).
4. See Balsam et al. (2005); Rothblum et al. (2004, 2005, 2007).
5. Rothblum et al. (2005, p. 84). See also Rothblum (2011).
6. Jenkins (2008); Hilton and Szymanski (2011).
7. See Burke (2004); Davis and Salkin (2005).
8. Stalker and Connors (2004, p. 223).
9. *Ibid.*, p. 227.
10. See Burke (2010); Green (2003).
11. Goffman (1963, p. 30).
12. *Ibid.*, p. 31.
13. Filax (2006).

14. Many lesbian, gay, bisexual, transgender, and queer youth also lack access to what Goffman calls "self-elevation" as a defense against anti-LGBTQ beliefs and practices.
15. Burke (2010).
16. I chose to use the words "lesbian, gay, and bisexual" because most of the heterosexual young adults I spoke to during the pretest phase of the research were most familiar and comfortable with them, even if their sibling identified in some other way (e.g., queer, femme, pansexual). I chose not to include the T in LGBT because of the small scale of the study and my focus on sibling variation in sexual orientation. Sibling variation in gender identity and expression is an important topic that fell beyond the purview of this research (importantly, "trans" and "LGB" are not mutually exclusive, as trans people also have a sexual orientation. I welcomed anyone with a lesbian, gay, or bisexual sib; by definition, this includes people with transgender sibs who identify as lesbian, gay, or bisexual, and heterosexual trans people with LGB sibs. At the same time, I recognize that such individuals may have been less likely to respond given the absence of the T on my recruitment flyer). In later research I conducted on LGBT family relationships in Taiwan, I did interview people with transgender siblings, and I hope to see more work in this area in the future.
17. For a description of open and focused coding techniques, see Emerson, Fretz, and Shaw (2011).
18. Hochschild (1989); Erikson (1993).
19. All participants have been given pseudonyms.
20. For NPR coverage of the Boy Scouts' decision, see Kathy Lohr, "Boy Scouts 'Moving Forward' to Allow Gay Members," May 24, 2013, http://www.npr.org/templates/story/story.php?storyId=186410401.
21. While I expect that the same would be true for men with bisexual brothers, I did not have any men with bisexual brothers in my sample.
22. Boystown is the district where the Chicago Pride parade is held, an area known for its high concentration of shops, bars, and other businesses operated by and for gay men.
23. People are more likely to volunteer to be in research about growing up with a lesbian, gay, or bisexual sibling if this aspect of their lives is important to them. Thus, these data should not be taken to mean that all people or even most people with LGB siblings experience the kinds of significant life changes I have described in this section. What's notable here is that even people who have experienced these and other significant changes—for whom growing up with a lesbian, gay, or bisexual sibling is very important—feel uncertain about how to describe their connection to LGB communities.
24. Stalker and Connors (2004, p. 223).
25. Goffman (1963, p. 31).

CCF Symposium

Why Interracial Marriage Is Good for Black Women, and Experts in Response

Ralph Richard Banks, Jackson Eli Reynolds Professor of Law, Stanford Law School | August 2011

More than two out of every three black women are currently unmarried, as are a majority of black men, and black women are three times as likely as white women never to marry.

College-educated black women are twice as likely as their white peers never to marry, and a majority of college-educated black wives have less educated husbands.

These figures are often blamed on the shortage of stable and employed men in low-income communities, and there's considerable truth in that explanation. But racial gaps in marriage span the socioeconomic spectrum. At every income level black men are less likely than white men to be married.

Indeed, by some measures, the racial gap is actually wider among affluent men than among their economically disadvantaged counterparts. In most racial-ethnic groups, increases in income consistently translate into a greater likelihood of marriage. But the most affluent black men—those who earn more than $100,000 a year—are actually less likely to marry than their lower earning but economically stable counterparts, men who earn, say, $50,000 or $60,000 a year.

One way to understand these features of the contemporary African American relationship scene is the gender imbalance at all income and educational levels. In lower-income groups, black men have fallen behind their female counterparts, victims of a criminal justice system that incarcerates them en masse, an educational system that fails them, and a labor market that offers few lawful economic opportunities for poorly educated men. At any given time, more than one in ten black men in their twenties and early thirties—prime marrying ages—is incarcerated.

But there is also a shortage of potential partners for middle-income and high-income black women. Many of the union jobs and other work that once allowed male high school graduates to earn middle-income wages have vanished, even as jobs that traditionally employ females have expanded. Only half as many black men as women complete college. The ranks of eligible black men are depleted further still by intermarriage: black men are two to three times as likely as black women to marry someone of another race, and economically successful black men are the most likely to do so.

While many black women don't marry because they have too few options, some black men don't marry because they have too many. In the relationship market, scarcity equals power: The better one's options outside the relationship, the more leverage one can exert within it. A desirable black man who ends an unsatisfying relationship will find many other women waiting. That's not true for black women, especially those who limit their relationships to black men.

When black women do marry, they are likely to marry men with less education or earnings than themselves. Half of all college-educated black wives have a husband with less education—often significantly less. In a world where successful marriages increasingly depend on shared interests rather than separate spheres, this incompatibility contributes to lower rates of marital satisfaction and higher rates of divorce in the black community. Some black men use their scarcity advantage, as men in other racial-ethnic groups and cultures have also done in similar situations, to maintain relationships that are sexually intimate but not monogamous. Research suggests that black men are more likely than any other group of American men to maintain relationships with multiple women. The end result is above-average rates of discord and distrust between black men and women.

Certainly, not all black men take advantage of the numbers imbalance. But when her partner's behavior is less than satisfactory, a black woman, recognizing that she is on the wrong side of a numbers imbalance, may feel she has few options and hence little power to demand a different arrangement.

The most common response to the waning of black marriage has been to redouble the pressure on black women to uplift the community by bonding with their brothers in need. Black women have been urged—by marriage activists, advice magazines, and often by their friends and families—to "save" black men. Interracial marriage has been cast as a form of abandonment or betrayal. Better to remain single or put up with a partner's bad behavior, the thinking goes, than to "betray the race."

Black women are further discouraged from looking elsewhere by the widespread belief that they have few options for forming relationships with men who are not black. Much has been made, for example, of an OkCupid website study finding that black women send the most messages and receive the fewest replies of any group, and that white men write back to black women 25 percent less frequently than they should based on the compatibility scores the website calculates.

But fixating on that finding underestimates black women's prospects in an integrated relationship market. In that same OkCupid study, Latino, Middle Eastern, Indian, and Native American men all responded to black women at rates substantially higher than did white men. In fact, some of these groups of men responded to black women at higher rates than did black men!

The scarcity factor works in black women's favor when they look beyond their own race. Black women constitute only 13 percent of the total female population, while nonblack men are roughly 87 percent of the male population. Even taking into account that some white men may not want to date black women, there are more white men who are willing to form a relationship with a black woman than there are black women available to date. When we include other racial-ethnic groups, the odds get even better. There are certainly three or more times as many nonblack men willing to date black women as there are black women.

In interviewing black women for my forthcoming book, I discovered many reasons that black women hesitate to cross the race line in their search for love. Many feel an understandable loyalty to their male counterparts, because they know all too well that racist indignities and injustices persist as part of the racist legacy in America. Some fear rejection by their partner's family or their own. Some assume that men of a different race, white men in particular, won't know anything about black women, black culture, or black history, and will lack the ability or desire to learn. Others worry that as a result of racist stereotypes, some nonblack men will view a black woman as a fetish object or an exotic adventure, someone to experience but not to love.

And some black women remain within the race because they want their children to identify as black and fear that if they are biracial, they won't. They don't want children whose complexion is so light that their black mother may be mistaken for the nanny.

These and other explanations given by the women I interviewed are all very understandable. Yet as interracial marriage becomes ever more accepted, black women willing to enter the integrated romantic marketplace will find considerable benefits. Some research suggests that black women who marry outside the race are less likely to divorce than those who marry within it. One reason for this is that, in general, college-educated black women may have more in common with their white, Asian, or Latino classmates and co-workers than with a black guy they grew up with who never went on to higher education. By marrying out, black women avoid the need to marry down.

If significant numbers of black women embark on interracial relationships, this will help counteract the power imbalance that diminishes the marriage rate and corrodes relationships in the black community. The more black women expand their relationship options, the less power black men will wield, and the greater ability black women will have to create the kind of relationship they desire. It is difficult to resist this paradoxical conclusion: If more black women married nonblack men, then more black men and women would marry each other.

Responses to Banks's Marriage Proposal

BELINDA TUCKER (UCLA) AGREES THAT BLACK WOMEN ARE WARY OF WHITE MEN, BUT TIES THIS TO A HISTORY OF WHITE MEN'S ATTITUDES TOWARD THEM

Our data from 21 large U.S. cities in 1996 showed that while nearly 90 percent of black men would marry someone of another race, 71 percent of black women also supported interracial marriage. When it came down to specifics, though, a differential reluctance emerged: only 57 percent of black women would marry someone who was white.*

This reluctance to marry white men comes from a deep knowledge of this society's historical and current views about black women, especially in regard to those elements of self that are most vulnerable in romantic encounters—physical features and sexuality. Societal physical standards essentially the opposite of those possessed by most African American women are made abundantly clear in the skin color, hair texture, hip size, etc., glamorized in television programs, ads, and magazines. Media portrayals of black women as either hypersexualized or Big Mommas continue to encourage exploitative attitudes. When I was in high school in the 1960s, one of my white male classmates casually quoted his father's assertion: "You cannot be a man until you split a black oak." That quote has remained embedded in my consciousness, and I'm certain it has affected my assessments of the motivations of white men who pursue African American women.

Though Professor Banks may believe the continued loyalty expressed by African American women for African American men is misplaced, the enduring embrace of African American men establishes a boundary that is, at the very least, safe from societal rejections of black womanhood (i.e., where standards of attractiveness and status are at least partially community defined). For, despite the near-universal acceptance among black men of interracial marriage, most married African American men have black wives.

*Taylor, P. L., Tucker, M. B., & Mitchell-Kernan, C. (n.d.). *"I Do" but to Whom: Differentiated Attitudes toward Intermarriage.*

Source: From M. Belinda Tucker, Vice Provost, Institute of American Cultures; and Professor of Psychiatry and Biobehavioral Sciences, Center for Culture and Health, University of California, Los Angeles.

SHIRLEY HILL (KANSAS UNIVERSITY) SAYS BANKS'S PROPOSAL HAS MERIT BUT "PUTS A LOT OF RESPONSIBILITY ON WOMEN"

Professor Banks's proposal that African American women confront the shortage of marriageable black men by becoming more open to interracial relationships has some appeal: It stands to broaden options for forming intimate partnerships and complicate racial categories for generations of children to come. The formula is simple: The bad behavior of African American men (in this case, their evasion of marriage and fidelity) can be tamed if black women reverse the scarcity advantage. It puts a lot of responsibility on women, however, implying that African American parents (mostly mothers) are not properly socializing their sons and that women in the broader community (e.g., girlfriends) must take up the task. As Banks notes, high rates of marginal (or no) employment and incarceration, coupled with low rates of educational attainment, explain many of the patterns he describes. Dealing with those structural issues gets us closer to the root of the problem.

Source: From Shirley A. Hill, Professor of Sociology and Director of Graduate Studies, Kansas University.

In the News

STANFORD LAW PROFESSOR ARGUES BLACK WOMEN SHOULD CROSS RACE BARRIER FOR MARRIAGE PARTNERS

San Jose Mercury News, September 12, 2011

Lisa M. Krieger

Black women are getting to the best universities, strongest corporations and top ranks of government offices.

But not to the altar.

A provocative new book by Stanford law professor Ralph Richard Banks examines why black women are so unlikely to marry—and proposes a solution that is arousing controversy in the African-American community: Cross the color line.

"Don't marry down. Marry out," says Banks in his campus office, busy with phone calls, emails and preparation for the new semester. The shared experience that once bound blacks together—segregation—is gone, he asserts. "So it all coalesces around this . . . whether black women will continue to be held hostage to the failings of black men."

Particularly in California, where only 6.2 percent of the population is black, "conditions are very conducive to interracial relationships," he says. "African-Americans are a very small group here. And everyone's moved away from home, so they're more likely to form nontraditional bonds."

Some welcome his book, "Is Marriage for White People?" because it has started an uncomfortable conversation they say is long overdue.

But others contend that he denigrates men and dispirits women, calling him a profiteer, a "racial pimp" and other names he says "that I can't repeat."

He speaks from a position that seems rarer every day: a black male who is highly educated (bachelor's and master's degrees from Stanford, '87, and one from Harvard Law, cum laude, '94), professional (14 years at Stanford Law School), married to a black woman (Stanford social psychology professor Jennifer Eberhardt, whom he calls "the most brilliant and beautiful woman I have ever met").

The project grew out of an intellectual journey that is part of his scholarship at Stanford Law School, focusing on two long-standing interests: racial equality and discrimination, and family and children. Many Stanford-based colleagues and friends helped him refine his arguments, and Stanford students helped with interviews.

"It's a good thing to get married, I think, if you find someone you want to be with," says Banks, who attended elementary school with Eberhardt in inner-city Cleveland. "I did find that person."

But most black women face a big problem, he asserts. High rates of incarceration and job-market discrimination against black men have created a gender imbalance. Then women confront the venerable economic model of supply and demand—scarcity creates excess demand for black grooms, tilting the terms of courtship to men's favor. Many simply sidestep commitment.

Yes, there are exceptions, he concedes—fairy tale couples such as Barack and Michelle, or Will and Jada, dubbed "nuptial eye candy" by *Essence* magazine.

Personal Experience

He speaks from personal experience; two of Banks' three sisters—"intelligent, beautiful and educated"—are unmarried. In fact, black women are the most unmarried group of people in our nation. They're only half as likely as white women to be married, and more than three times as likely as white women never to marry, according to his analyses.

"Black women face the thinnest pool of same-race partners of any group in the country," he says.

It wasn't always so. Through the middle of the 20th century, about nine out of 10 black women married. Now black women are about half as likely to be married as their 1950s counterparts. White adults are also more likely to be single today than in the past. But marriage has diminished more among African-Americans than among any other Americans.

And when they do marry, black women are more likely to marry men with substantially less education or less income, Banks says.

His message to black women: Stop settling for less than you deserve. Forget race loyalty. Quit thinking that white, Asian and Latino men don't find you attractive; it's not true. (Exhibit A: Beyoncé, Halle Berry, Jennifer Hudson.) Yes, there's a lot of bad history, but a modern white man's intentions may be entirely honorable.

He writes with a tone of encouragement, not blame or finger-pointing. Think Oprah, not Dr. Laura.

"It's not an advice book," he cautions. "The goal is to enable a conversation that has been squelched. And expand the freedom of black women to make choices that are right choices for them.

"A Stanford student will find more in common with the guy sitting next to her in a seminar, than some working-class guy in Oakland," he says.

"But there is a lot of policing of black women," he adds, "controlling them through pop culture messages—that you should 'stick with the black man first,' that 'the black man needs your help.' That leaves people feeling less free than they need to be."

Analysis Rings True

Oakland-based L. Jeanine Phillips, 28, who has a bachelor's degree in biology, a passion for reading and a rewarding career as an operations manager for an upscale firm, says Banks' analysis rings true.

"I have dated and even married a black man in the past," says Phillips, vice president of the Bay Area chapter of the Sistas Book Club. "After endless bad relationships—all seeming to stem from black men's egos and inability to keep their penis in their pants, also coming from broken homes—I have decided to go on hiatus from black men and only date out of my race.

"And thus far it has been a success. I am currently dating a great white man" with a degree from UC Davis, she says, "who seems to appreciate me, respect me, and we match equally educationally and culturally. We have the same religious beliefs. And it's a major bonus that we share the same family values."

Jethroe Moore, president of the San Jose chapter of the NAACP, also agrees with Banks—but says that efforts to improve the fate of black men could help solve the problem.

Experienced through his work with at-risk youth at San Jose's East Side Union High School District, Moore says that "the African-American man is endangered before he can get out of high school—either through incarceration or because he is his family's provider, and continuing school is not an option."

"Growing up in San Jose, we used to be able to come out of high school and get a job at a manufacturing company and work our way up to a management position," he says. "Now those possibilities are gone, because Silicon Valley has so little manufacturing.

"I can understand why women's choices are limited," says Moore, who met plenty of young women at college—but was introduced to his wife, Audrey, by her mother, an acquaintance at church. "No one wants someone who won't be successful. You want him to have something in common with you. Just because he's black—that's not much of a choice."

"Marry for Love"

Like Banks, Moore says, "I would tell my sister to marry for love," irrespective of race. "If that person makes you happy, you should pursue that relationship."

But the book's assumptions have come under attack by Howard University professor Ivory A. Toldson and Morehouse College professor Bryant Marks. They say they've looked at the same data—from the census and American Community Surveys—through a different lens, and found it less gloomy.

If the analysis is limited to blacks over age 35, the number of single women drops, they say. And in major cities such as Washington, D.C., and Atlanta, women with doctorates are more than twice as likely to be married as those with a high school degree. Finally, although black women have more degrees, that doesn't translate into high incomes: In fact, more black men than black women earn more than $75,000 a year.

"Entrepreneurial elements of America have found a variety of creative ways to benefit financially from black females' anxieties at the expense of black male egos," Toldson told the African-American online magazine the *Root* in a reference to Banks. "If you can show somebody that there is a really devastating problem, they'll pay more attention to you.

"He's not going to show you any evidence to the contrary because he wants his book to be found," she said.

Journalist and Middlebury College graduate Dori J. Maynard, president and CEO of the Oakland-based Robert C. Maynard Institute for Journalism Education, co-founded by her father, criticizes "a media-driven narrative—desperate black women seeking husbands—that flies in the face of a lot of people's realities." The widow of African-American architect Charles Grant Lewis, Maynard says, "This conversation would be a lot more helpful if we also included the experience of the 75 percent of black women who are happily married and raising children in two-parent families."

Conclusions Challenged

"This picture distorts the picture of African-American women who are happy, fulfilled and living good and productive lives," Maynard says. "It is also a distortion of black men, as well—portraying them as pathetic losers who we wouldn't want to be married to—which has not been my experience."

Banks' solution was also challenged by African-American scholars in a "virtual symposium" held by the nonprofit and nonpartisan Council on Contemporary Families.

There, Professor Micere Keels of the University of Chicago argued that black women don't rule out nonblack partners. Rather, studies show they receive fewer advances from whites, Latinos or Asians.

"The only viable solution for black women's low likelihood of marriage is to correct society's failure to educate all our boys," she concluded.

Similarly, Kansas University professor Shirley Hill said in the same symposium that "dealing with structural issues"—such as high unemployment and incarceration of black men—"gets us closer to the root of the problem."

There's a reason that black women are wary of white men: white men's attitudes toward them, said symposium participant Belinda Tucker, a professor at UCLA. "Media portrayals of black women as either hypersexualized or Big Mommas continue to encourage exploitative attitudes," she said. By dating black men, women are "safe from societal rejections."

And while interracial families are a potent symbol of a society that's healing its racial divide, raising multiracial children is a challenge that Banks doesn't address, said symposium participant Jenifer Bratter of Rice University.

"Biracial children often face racial difficulties from both sides of the racial spectrum, leaving parents to help their children to make sense of these experiences," she said.

Taps into Anxieties

Banks shrugs off such criticism with the confidence of an attorney used to sparring.

"There's resistance to an issue that seems fairly simple: If there are too few men in your own group, why not consider men of other groups?" he asks.

But he concedes that his suggestion taps into deep-seated anxieties that people have about race.

It's natural to fear assimilation, particularly if you're from a marginalized group, he says. And women—of all races—have greater concern than men about perpetuating their culture.

"Black women are the most loyal of all," he says. "But they pay a very high price."

Racial identities change, over generations. "It's fruitless to worry about it, as though you could preserve it," he continues. "It's like putting your finger in a dike. Your children will see the world differently than you or I do.

"The black experience is more varied now," he says. "Our children have grown up in an integrated Palo Alto or Orinda. They don't have the experience of living in the Jim Crow South."

For Banks, the song "Lift Every Voice and Sing" still makes his skin tingle, evoking memories of hearing the "Negro National Anthem" while growing up in an all-black Cleveland neighborhood.

But it means nothing to his sons, he observes, now students at Menlo Park's integrated Phillips Brooks School and Hillsborough's college-prep Crystal Springs Uplands School.

And when they bring home a date?

"I want them to be happy, whoever they're with," Banks says. "It's hard to make a relationship work. Compatibility now is more about class and background and experiences and aspirations and values than about race."

"I'd tell them: 'If you find someone who is purple, and it works, go for that.'" ◼

In Other Words

INTERRACIAL MARRIAGE AND THE MEANING OF MULTIRACIALITY

Sociological Images, July 13, 2011

Jennifer Lee

Rising Immigration and Intermarriage

Today we see both increased immigration and rising rates of intermarriage. In 1960, less than 1% of U.S. marriages were interracial, but by 2008, this figure rose to 7.6%, meaning that 1 out of every 13 U.S. marriages was interracial. If we look at only new marriages that took place in 2008, the figure rises to 14.6%, translating to 1 out of every 7 American marriages.

The rising trend in intermarriage has resulted in a growing multiracial population. In 2010, 2.9% of Americans identified as multiracial. Demographers project that the multiracial population will continue to grow so that by 2050, 1 in 5 Americans could claim a multiracial background, and by 2100, the ratio could soar to 1 in 3.

At first glance, these trends appear to signal that we're moving into a "post-racial" era, in which race is declining in significance for all Americans. However, if we take a closer look at these trends, we find that they mask vast inter-group differences.

For instance, Asians and Latinos intermarry at much higher rates than blacks. About 30% of Asian and Latino marriages are interracial, but the corresponding figure for blacks is only 17%. However, if we include only U.S.-born Asians and Latinos, we find that intermarriage rates are much higher. Nearly, three-quarters (72%) of married, U.S.-born Asians, and over half (52%) of U.S.-born Latinos are interracially married, and most often, the intermarriage is with a white partner. While the intermarriage rate for blacks has risen steadily in the past five decades, it is still far below that of Asians and Latinos, especially those born in the United States.

The pattern of multiracial identification is similar to that of intermarriage: Asians and Latinos report much higher rates of multiracial identification than blacks. In 2010, 15% of Asians and 12% of Latinos reported a multiracial identification. The corresponding figure for blacks is only 7 percent. Although the rate of multiracial reporting among blacks has risen since 2000, it increased from a very small base of only 4.2%.

The U.S. Census estimates that about 75–90% of black Americans are ancestrally multiracial, so it is perplexing that only 7% choose to identify as such. Clearly, genealogy alone does not dictate racial identification. Given that the "one-drop rule" of

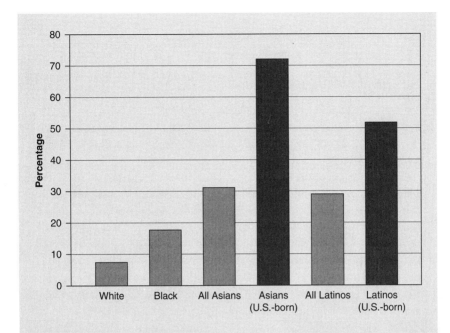

Figure 1 | Intermarriage Rates (%)

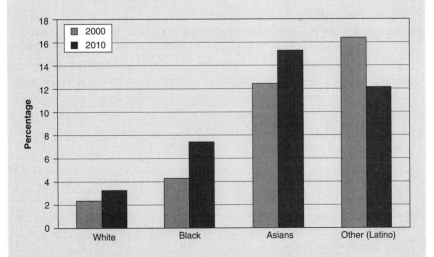

Figure 2 | Multiracial Identification by Census Racial Categories

hypodescent* is no longer legally codified, why does the rate of multiracial report-ing among blacks remain relatively low?

Patterns in Racial/Ethnic Identity

These are some of the vexing questions that we tackle in our book, *The Diversity Paradox*, drawing on analyses of 2000 Census data, 2007–2008 American Com-munity Survey, as well as 82 in-depth interviews: 46 with multiracial adults and 36 with interracial couples with children.

Turning to the in-depth interviews with the interracial couples, we found that while all acknowledged their children's multiracial or multiethnic backgrounds, the meaning of multiraciality differs remarkably for the children of Asian-white and Latino-white couples on the one hand, and the children of black-white couples on the other. For the Asian-white and Latino-white couples, they may go to great lengths to maintain distinctive elements of their Asian or Latino ethnic and cultural backgrounds, but they believe that as their children grow up, they will simply iden-tify, and be identified as "American" or as "white," using these terms interchangeably, and consequently conflating a national origin identity with a racial identity.

The Asian-white and Latino-white respondents also revealed that they can turn their ethnicities on and off whenever they choose, and, importantly, their choices are not contested by others. Our interview data reveal that the Asian and Latino ethnicities for multiracial Americans are what Herbert Gans and Mary Waters would describe as "symbolic"—meaning that they are voluntary, optional, and cost-less, as European ethnicity is for white Americans.

By contrast, none of the black-white couples identified their children as just white or American, nor did they claim that their children identify as such. While these couples recognize and celebrate the racial mixture of their children's back-grounds, they unequivocally identify their children as black. When we asked why, they pointed out that nobody would take them seriously if they tried to identify their children as white, reflecting the constraints that black interracial couples feel when identifying their children. Moreover, black interracial couples do not identify their children as simply "American" because as native-born Americans, they feel that American is an implicit part of their identity.

The legacy of the one-drop rule remains culturally intact, explaining why 75–90% of black Americans are ancestrally multiracial, yet only 7% choose to identify as such. It also explains why we, as Americans, are so attuned to identifying black ancestry in a way that we are not similarly attuned to identifying and constraining Asian and Latino ancestries.

On this note, it is also critical to underscore that a black racial identification also reflects agency and choice on the part of interracial couples and multiracial blacks.

Given the legacy behind the one-drop rule and the meaning and consequences behind the historical practice of "passing as white," choosing to identify one's children as white may not only signify a rejection of the black community, but also a desire to be accepted by a group that has legally excluded and oppressed them in the past, a point underscored by Randall Kennedy.

Black Exceptionalism

But regardless of choice or constraint, the patterns of intermarriage and multiracial identification point to a pattern of "black exceptionalism." Why does black exceptionalism persist, even amidst the country's new racial/ethnic diversity? It persists because the legacy of slavery and the legacy of immigration are two competing yet strangely symbiotic legacies on which the United States was founded. If immigration represents the optimistic side of the country's past and future, slavery and its aftermath is an indelible stain in our nation's collective memory. The desire to overlook the legacy of slavery becomes a reason to reinforce the country's immigrant origins.

That Asians and Latinos are largely immigrants (or the children of immigrants) means that their understanding of race and the color line are born out of an entirely different experience and narrative than that of African Americans. Hence, despite the increased diversity, race is not declining in significance, and we are far from a "post-racial" society. That we continue to find a pattern of black exceptionalism—even amidst the country's new racial/ethnic diversity—points to the paradox of diversity in the 21st century. ▮

---

*The one-drop rule was first implemented during the era of slavery so that any children born to a white male slaver owner and a black female slave would be legally identified as black, and, as a result, have no rights to property and other wealth holdings of their white father.

In Other Words

THE COOLEST THING ABOUT ONLINE DATING SITES

Cyborgology, December 3, 2013

Jenny L. Davis

Quartz, a business and marketing website, recently released data on the Facebook dating app Are You Interested (AYI), which connects singles within the confines of their direct and indirect Facebook networks. Quartz' data are based on a series of yes or no questions about who users are interested in, as well as response rates between users, once notified of a potential suitor. The data show that white men and Asian women receive the most interest, whereas black men and women receive the least amount of interest (see figure for the complex picture of racial preference by gender). The writers at Quartz summarize the findings as follows:

> Unfortunately the data reveal winners and losers. All men except Asians pre-
> ferred Asian women, while all except black women preferred white men. And
> both black men and black women got the lowest response rates for their respec-
> tive genders.

As a sociologist, I am entirely unsurprised that race matters, especially in such a personal process like dating/mating. However, these findings may come as a sur-prise to the (quite significant) segments of the population who identify as color-blind; those who label contemporary society post-racial.

And this is why dating sites are so cool. Social psychologists know that what people say and what they do have little empirical connection. Dating sites capture what we do, and play it back for us. They expose who we are, who we want, and of course, who we don't want. As shown by Quartz, "we" fetishize Asian women while devaluing blacks.

With a schism between what people say and what they do; between what they say and what they unconsciously think, surveys of racial attitudes are always already quite limited. People can say whatever they want—that race doesn't matter, that they don't see color—but when it comes to selecting a partner, and the selection criteria are formalized through profiles and response decisions, we, as individuals and a society, can no longer hide from ourselves. The numbers blare back at us, forcing us to presume uncomfortable cultural and identity meanings both person-ally and collectively.

Of course, what these sites tell us about ourselves does not stop at race. They also tell us that we care about things like income, physical (dis)ability and body size, exposing the range of isms that American prefer not to speak of in polite company, and certainly refrain from applying to themselves.

At an individual level, how someone fills in hir preferences and the way s/he engages (or refuses to engage) interested parties, tells that individual a lot about who s/he is. But dating sites, at a cultural level, are incredibly revealing even before the first user signs up. Indeed, before anyone has answered anything, the architecture of online dating sites say a lot. Namely, they tell us what we value. They tell us which characteristics are the ones about which we are likely to care; about which we *should* care.

More concretely, the moment a site prompts users to select racial identification and/or racial preference, an embedded race-based value system is both exposed and reinforced. As such, although the Quartz graph of user data is revealing, the presence of racial identification and racial preference on dating sites in general already demolish arguments about color blindness and post-racial culture. ■

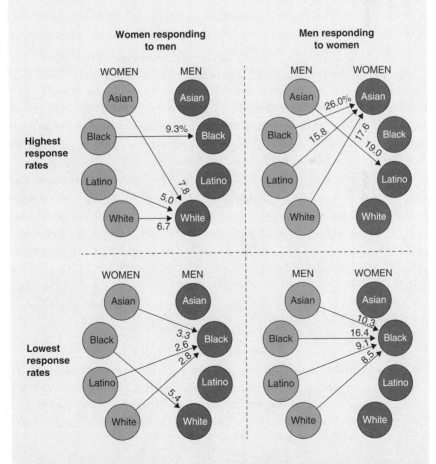

14

Life in a Dual-Earner Couple Before, During, and After the Great Recession

Shannon N. Davis and Brittany Owen

Juan and Elena are both professionals—he is an environmental engineer, she is a dietician—who make roughly $120,000 in combined household income. They have been married for eight years and have two children, Angela (age seven) and Lucas (age five-and-a-half). Juan works a standard day shift at the office, while Elena works part-time during the morning so that she can pick up the children from the bus. Richard (a construction worker) and Donna (a nurse) are a working-class couple who earn approximately $50,000 a year. They have been married for twelve years and have one child together. Richard works a rotating schedule—seven days on, seven days off—and Donna currently works the night shift full-time at the same hospital as Elena. Richard and Donna chose these alternative shifts in order to maximize the amount of time spent with their six-year-old son, Rick Jr. They would like a second child, but Richard is concerned about his job stability in the wake of the Great Recession.

Both of these couples are what would be considered dual-earner couples, where both partners are employed for pay. In this chapter, we investigate and review the research on some of the common concerns that arise in or seem to result from being in a dual-earner couple, with an eye toward recent research on how dual-earner couples are faring in light of the Great Recession. In each section, we come back to Juan and Elena and Richard and Donna, examining their experiences while taking into consideration what we learn from studies. While gay married couples and heterosexual and gay cohabiting couples are important, we focus here on married heterosexual couples because much research limits itself to them. In the section on housework, we highlight our new research on dual-earner couples with data analysis from the Work and Family Survey, 2010, a small, national, telephone-based survey.

WHO ARE DUAL-EARNER COUPLES?

Dual-earner couples are not a new type of family in the United States, although our cultural conversation about them suggests they were created in the 1960s.[1] The majority of married American couples likely have been dual earners at one point in their marriage (see Figure 14.1).[2] Before the Great Recession, married couples who were more likely to be dual earners were those in which the wives had postgraduate education, the wives were better educated than their husbands, and both spouses were black.[3] Dual-earner couples have historically had one primary breadwinner (typically the husband), although between 1970 and 2001, more wives have become the primary contributor to the total household income (where they earned 55 percent of their husbands' income).[4]

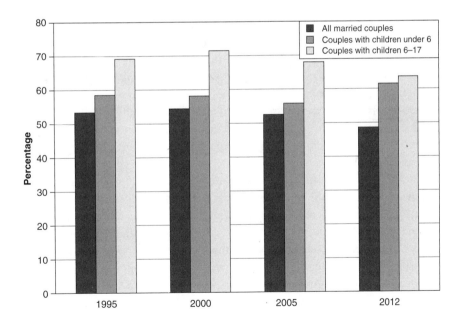

Figure 14.1 | Dual-Earner Couples

Source: Author calculations from Bureau of Labor Statistics (1997, 2001, 2006, and 2013).

Has the Great Recession influenced dual-earner couples? In the early stages of the Great Recession, men were disproportionately among the ranks of the unemployed.[5] Not surprisingly, then, wives' percentage contribution to the total household income increased 5 percent from 2006 to 2011, evidence that women have become more active as financial providers than they had been before the recession.[6] There seems to be little evidence, however, that the Great Recession *created* dual-earner families.[7] Wives who increased their employment from 2006 to 2010 tended to be those whose husbands were already working long hours rather than those whose husbands were working in industries that were hardest hit by the recession.[8]

CAREER PRIORITIZATION

Juan has been offered a career opportunity at GreenTech, a firm located in California. Relocating means that Juan could pursue his dream of designing more efficient windmills—but Elena will have to forgo her comfortable position at the clinic. Meanwhile, Richard is worried about construction job stability because of the real estate crash leading up to the recession; Donna's work as a nurse is far more stable. She has also been offered a promotion, but it will require Richard to change his work hours to look after Rick Jr. How would these couples' decisions play out in real life?

Dual-earner or dual-income couples may have two employed spouses, but odds are that the husband's job is considered more important than the wife's.[9] In looking at career-prioritizing decisions, research has shown that even when wives earn more than their husbands, there is no long-term pattern of favoring the wife's career within the marriage.[10] Further, when their spouse is offered a career opportunity, wives report higher levels of support for their spouses than husbands do.[11]

Higher levels of family involvement may lead workers to be less willing to disadvantage their family by relocating.[12] This theory suggests that financial considerations, rather than attitudes about gender and work, should be important to individuals highly involved in family life. We know that couples with traditional beliefs about gender tend to prioritize the husband's job/career.[13] Women are more likely to cite family considerations when thinking about whether to relocate for their own careers.[14] And husbands who have previously prioritized their wives' careers, or neither career, are significantly more supportive of potentially prioritizing their wives' careers in the future.[15]

There is a toll to career prioritization, and it tends to be economic. Wives benefit most in terms of wages from having their careers prioritized or from alternating prioritization patterns, and they suffer most when their spouse's career is prioritized.[16] This effect is compounded by wives' increased likelihood to have interrupted career paths due to child rearing, thus leading to lower salaries.[17]

Rather than choosing between one partner's career and the other, some couples instead turn to dual-household, or commuter, marriages. The U.S. Census Bureau reported in 2006 that 3.6 million married Americans, not including those separated, were living apart from their spouses. Such marriages allow couples to pursue their career interests and maintain familial stability by eliminating the economic and social strains associated with one spouse having to relocate in support of the other's job. Healthy commuter marriages are characterized by an acceptance of the situation and confidence in the relationship—not surprising, given the difficulties of maintaining two households and jobs while maintaining the marriage.[18]

There is some evidence that the Great Recession is having an effect on career prioritization. Researchers using the Work and Family Study found that while a quarter of respondents reported that they would expect to prioritize the husband's employment over the wife's employment, most married individuals reported equal willingness to relocate in support of either spouse's employment or reported greater willingness to relocate in support of the wife's employment.[19] These findings could be due to the Great Recession, as families may be indicating they are increasingly likely to be pragmatic in their responses to employment opportunities. These results could also be due to shifting gender norms and increasing equality between spouses.

CHILDBEARING AND CHILD REARING

Having a child can be one of the biggest milestones in a person's life. Juan and Elena waited to have Angela until they were thirty-seven and thirty-five, respectively. Meanwhile, Richard and Donna would like to have a second child but fear that Richard's job will not be stable enough. Instead, Richard takes advantage of his alternating shifts to spend more time with Rick Jr. during the day and on the weekends. Are these typical portraits of dual-career couples' fertility and parenthood decisions?

Dual-earner couples tend to have children later than do couples with a sole earner.[20] This later birth timing is typically seen as a result of dual-earner couples' greater likelihood of high levels of education among both spouses, but especially the wife.[21] Indeed, having a higher education increases the "opportunity costs" of having children.[22]

Employed women are less likely than are women out of the labor force to have as many children as they desire.[23] However, the explanation is not that women have higher levels of work-family conflict and choose not to have more children. Men in dual-earner couples who believe their wives have high levels of work-family conflict have lower fertility intentions than those men whose wives have low levels of work-family conflict. And yet, surprisingly, women's own levels of work-family conflict do not influence their fertility intentions.[24] Women who have difficulty balancing work and family do not tend to delay or forgo having additional children. Instead, they are more likely to reduce their working hours.[25] This reduction in working hours explains some, but not all, of the "motherhood penalty," a drop in wages that occurs for women after they become mothers.[26] Older, more educated, and African American women are more likely to stay in the labor force after having children and not experience the same reduction in work hours.[27] Because the Family and Medical Leave Act of 1993 (FMLA) protects leave of absence for only family or medical reasons, "formal, paid parental leave for both mothers and fathers is available only through the workplace policies of specific firms."[28] This lack of paid parental leave can result in the disruption of mothers' careers in particular.[29]

Children in dual-earner families spend less time with their mothers than do children whose mothers are not employed.[30] Dual-earner fathers are the most involved in child rearing when their wives work full-time and the parents work alternating shifts (as compared to families where mothers work part-time on the same shift as fathers).[31] Bianchi's review of the literature on time allocation of American fathers documents the increased time that dual-earner families are spending with their children, leading to more specific knowledge among fathers about their children's lives.[32] Both mothers and fathers are spending more time "with" their children rather than spending time on actual child-rearing tasks.[33] Lareau's research documents the ways middle-class (dual-earner) parents cultivate their children,[34] and despite the time "with" their children, dual-earner parents still say they want more time with them.[35]

While Sobotka, Skirbekk, and Pilipov document some research in the United States that implies an effect of the Great Recession on fertility intentions and births overall, they argue that it is unlikely for the United States to have an overall long-term reduction in fertility timing and number of children borne per woman as a result solely of the recession.[36]

DIVIDING THE HOUSEWORK: HOW FAIR IS THE SPLIT?

As a part-time worker, Elena does most of the housework in her household. Juan does discretionary tasks such as yard work on the weekend. Alternatively, Richard completes what housework he can on his days off, but still spends less time doing housework than Donna, who often cooks and cleans before leaving for work at night. How do these couples negotiate the division of labor?

Research has highlighted the creativity with which dual-earner couples combine work and family. In particular, the use of flexible work schedules and nontraditional work schedules allows dual-earner spouses to negotiate a tenuous balance addressing the needs of all family members by dividing labor.[37]

When we think about a division of labor, we tend to think about people splitting up tasks so that work can be done efficiently. Gary Becker, an economist, argued that economic efficiency, where individuals maximize their behavior in families to fulfill the needs of the family and thus create stability in the family, yields not only stable families but also more productive ones.[38] Under this economic argument, the most efficient households are those where individuals maximize their strengths, such as men's wage-earning potential, and divide work accordingly. Therefore, it is rational for men to focus on employment and women on homemaking.

Becker's argument about the economic utility of a gendered division of labor and specialization of market and nonmarket work predicted that dual-earner couples would be less happy, report less fairness, and would be more likely to divorce. Of course, those "rational choice" arguments also presumed a set of beliefs about the kinds of work husbands and wives should do. The rise of dual-earner couples across the United States would mean that both spouses should also be doing housework, under this economic theory. If everyone were entirely rational, and specialization by dividing home and family work could not occur, then equilibrium would occur through shared labor time across work and home.

We were not surprised to learn that couples do not rationally trade off employment hours for housework hours. Research shows that men still tend to specialize in paid labor, although women are catching up. American women and men may spend approximately the same amount of time per week working, but the kind of work they do differs.[39] Men tend to be employed more hours than are women, while women tend to do more housework (almost twice as much). Compared to 1965, in the twenty-first century men do more than double the amount of housework per week, while women's housework time has been cut almost in half.[40]

Maybe the reason women do more housework is that they work fewer hours. The time availability theory of the division of household labor argues precisely this—individuals who are employed more hours will do less housework, simply because they can work only so many hours in a week. This argument finds some support, although dual-earner couples do not have an equitable division of housework.[41] For example, Arrighi and Maume find that employed spouses with jobs that do not require long hours were more likely to participate in household labor and that spouses with longer work weeks were less likely to do so.[42]

Among dual-earner couples, wives do about two-thirds of overall tasks at home, although men tend to do discretionary tasks.[43] Discretionary tasks are those that can be done when time is available and whose non-completion would not disrupt others in the family (e.g., yard work, maintenance, trash removal). Husbands are doing more of the non-discretionary tasks like cooking and cleaning as well, but dual-earner wives continue to do these tasks at higher rates than do their husbands.[44]

It is possible that the Great Recession, which heavily affected men's employment (at least initially[45]), may have changed the distribution of household tasks within dual-earner couples. Husbands may be working less and wives may be working more. Figure 14.2 provides some evidence for the argument that the Great Recession has changed how dual-earner husbands and wives are spending their time,[46] as men report doing more housework after the Great Recession began.

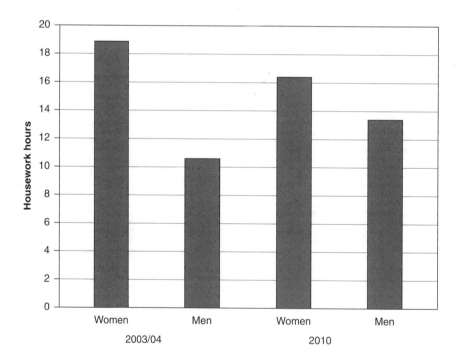

Figure 14.2 | Gender and Reported Housework Hours per Week

Source: For 2003–04, data from Bianchi et al. (2012, Table 1). For 2010, author calculations from *Work and Family Survey, 2010* (N = 145).

In Figure 14.3, we analyze data from dual-earner couples in the Work and Family Study, examining housework hours by gender and full-time employment status of both spouses. Women who worked part-time did the most housework, followed interestingly by men who worked part-time and women who worked full-time alongside their full-time employed husbands. Women in dual-earner marriages did more housework than men did, which is consistent with the data presented in Figure 14.2. Whether they have a partner who has full-time employment or not, when women work full-time, they did approximately 16 hours of housework. This pattern is the same among men. That is, when men work full-time, regardless of whether their wife works full-time, they did approximately the same amount of housework (about 12 hours of housework in this case). When only one spouse worked full-time, it appears that men and women report approximately the same number of housework hours.

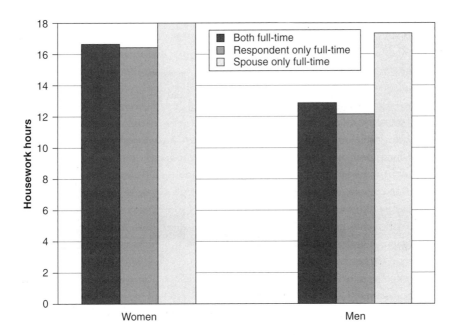

Figure 14.3 | Reported Housework Hours, Gender, and Full-Time Employment Status

Source: Author calculations from *Work and Family Survey, 2010*, reflecting differences in housework hours performed and whether respondent and spouse both worked full-time ($N = 145$).

When dual-earner couples do not do equal (or even somewhat more equal) housework, how do spouses feel about this inequality? Interestingly, most research finds that because most spouses expect that women will do more of the housework (even when the wife is employed), they report the division of labor as fair.[47] Wives are more likely than husbands to report unfairness, as are spouses with higher educations and those who do not subscribe to traditional beliefs about gender in relationships.[48] Indeed, when wives and husbands become more equal in their job status and income, there is a stronger association between the division of housework and perceptions of fairness.[49]

Given the difficulties that men faced early in the Great Recession, women began taking on more of a breadwinning role. How has this change influenced their sense of fairness with the division of household labor? In analysis not reported here, we found that in couples where both spouses work full-time, wives report more unfairness in the division of labor than do husbands, regardless of how much labor they actually perform. Women who work full-time seem to desire their husbands who work full-time to do more housework than the husbands currently do. Possibly such couples report more unfairness in the division of housework because the wives are doing most of the housework, regardless of the actual number of hours they spend. Wives might see this as unfair because both they and their husbands are contributing approximately the same amount of time to paid work; therefore, they should also contribute approximately the same amount of time to unpaid work. We explore the relationship between the relative amount of housework and perceptions of fairness in Figures 14.4 and 14.5.

We also found that women and men in couples where one spouse is employed full-time and one is employed part-time report similar levels of perceptions of fairness. Specifically, women who work full-time report about the same amount of unfairness as do men who work part-time, and men who work full-time report about the same amount of unfairness as do women who work part-time, regardless of the actual amount of housework these spouses do. We suspect that the similarity in the levels of unfairness is due to the creation of a shared sense of understanding around the division of paid and unpaid work in these families.[50] The spouses have accepted some specialization in their household and therefore are reporting levels of unfairness that reflect their shared sense of what is considered fair and appropriate given their specialization.

Respondents in the Work and Family Study were asked not only how many hours of housework they regularly do but also how many their spouse regularly does (this is a standard procedure in collecting data on the division of housework). Relative housework hours were calculated as one spouse's housework hours divided by the total of both partners' hours. We split the sample into two groups based on how much of the overall housework the respondent did. Figure 14.4 displays the reported unfairness of the division of labor among respondents

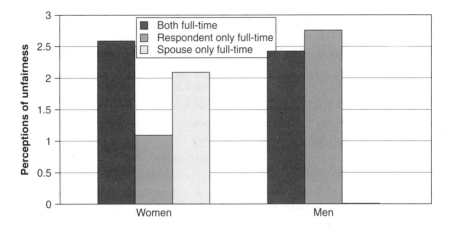

Figure 14.4 | Gender, Full-Time Employment Status, and Perceptions of Fairness of the Division of Housework among Respondents Doing 40 Percent or Less of the Housework

Source: Author calculations from *Work and Family Survey, 2010*, reflecting differences in perceptions of fairness by hours of housework performed and whether respondent and spouse both worked full-time. Higher perceptions of fairness scores means greater sense of unfairness (N = 67).

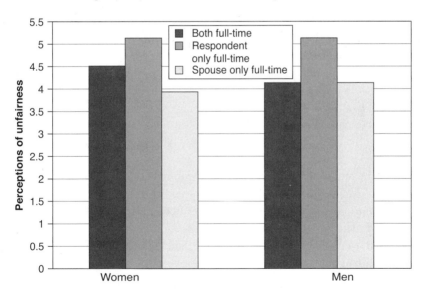

Figure 14.5 | Gender, Full-Time Employment Status, and Perceptions of Fairness of the Division of Housework among Respondents Doing More than 60 Percent of the Housework

Source: Author calculations from *Work and Family Survey, 2010*, reflecting differences in perceptions of fairness by hours of housework performed and whether respondent and spouse both worked full-time. Higher perceptions of fairness scores means greater sense of unfairness (N = 41).

reporting they did 40 percent or less of the housework, and Figure 14.5 displays the reported unfairness of the division of labor among respondents who said they did more than 60 percent of the housework. These groups allow us to see how people who do less of the overall housework feel about fairness in comparison to those who do most of the overall housework. (In the Work and Family Study, no respondents reported an "equal" split of the housework, where they did 41 to 60 percent of the housework; nor did any men say they did 40 percent or less of the housework when they worked part-time.)

As Figure 14.4 shows, individuals who do less than half of the housework report low levels of unfairness. We found gender similarity in the reports of unfairness when both the respondent and the spouse were employed full-time. Women working part-time whose husbands worked full-time report the lowest levels of unfairness. This result is likely because women who work part-time see the housework as their responsibility because they have more time to do housework than their husbands do. Men who are employed full-time and married to women who work part-time report more unfairness than do women who are employed full-time and married to men with part-time jobs; this is true even though the men who work full-time do 40 percent or less of the total housework. This may be a result of men continuing to expect that they will have to do little housework when they are the breadwinner. Any amount of housework to these men may seem unfair, a finding that would be consistent with their internalizing traditional norms about gendered behaviors.[51]

Comparing the perceptions of unfairness among individuals doing less than half of the housework (Figure 14.4) to those doing most of the housework (Figure 14.5) shows a stark contrast in the levels of unfairness. Across the board, all individuals in a dual-earner couple who report doing most of the housework report high levels of unfairness in the division of labor. In fact, there is little difference in the reports of unfairness between wives and husbands when they do most of housework.

Among the respondents who reported doing most of the housework, individuals working full-time while their spouses work part-time also report the highest levels of unfairness in the sample. In couples where both spouses are employed full-time, women report slightly higher levels of unfairness in the division of housework than do men when they do most of the housework (although the difference is quite small).

Individuals working part-time who have a spouse employed full-time report the lowest levels of unfairness among those respondents who do most of the housework. While these individuals may be willing to concede that they have more time to do housework than does their full-time employed spouse, the data suggest that the spouse working part-time would prefer not to be doing most of the housework tasks.

Washington State University
1500 North East Terrell
Mall
Pullman, WA 99163
509-332-2537

The Bookie

STORE:00500   REG:003   TRAN#:1273
CASHIER:FERNANDO R

RISMAN/FAMILIES AS
USED
2900393937670   T
(1 @ 46.35)   46.35
   APPROVED FINANC   46.35

Subtotal   46.35
 T1 Sales Tax (07.900%)   3.66
TOTAL   **50.01**
FINANCIAL AID   **50.01**

******** FINANCIAL AID DETAIL ********
ITEM   EVENT   AMOUNT
RISMAN/FAMILIES AS   000001   46.35 Y
******* FINANCIAL AID SUMMARY *******
AMOUNT DESCRIPTION   BALANCE   EXEMPT
50.01 30 WSU ATHLE   449.99

LUCERIS   SUAREZ PACHECO

ACCT #   XXXXXXX7

NOW HIRING!
Apply Online at www.bncollegejobs.com

V290.05   07/18/2023 12:31PM

CUSTOMER COPY

MARITAL SATISFACTION, WORK-FAMILY BALANCE, AND DIVORCE

Juan and Elena and Richard and Donna describe their marriages as relatively stable and happy. However, the two couples are not without their problems. Elena is frequently stressed about juggling a job, housework, and children, whereas Juan is experiencing pressure at his job to work overtime. Because their shifts have little overlap, Richard and Donna are not able to regularly spend time with one another, making communication difficult. Richard's job insecurity also affects their marriage, as at times he is afraid of not being able to support his family. How do these couples navigate marriage in the wake of the Great Recession?

People who feel that their relationship is not working may be thinking about ending that relationship. As we have seen, wives in dual-earner couples who experience inequality in the division of labor do report this inequity. Wives in these dual-earner marriages are often responsible for most of the housework and child care, resulting in increased marital stress and conflict.[52] This unequal division of housework between dual-earner spouses decreases marital quality and marital satisfaction.[53] Inequity in the division of labor also is associated with an increased likelihood of divorce.[54]

Why would the division of household labor influence the likelihood of divorce among dual-earner couples? Researchers have argued that wives in particular in dual-earner marriages experience role strain due to their balancing the demands of family life and employment.[55] Work-family balance and work-family conflict influence marital satisfaction,[56] which in turn influences the likelihood of divorce. Therefore, an increase in work-family balance and a reduction in work-family conflict should improve marital satisfaction and reduce the likelihood that a dual-earner couple will divorce.

Positive or negative feelings can "spill over" from work to marriage, leading to strain on the marital role and ultimately influencing marital satisfaction.[57] Positive spillover for husbands often occurs when they work in managerial/professional jobs. It is wives' levels of social support at work that seems to play an integral role in shaping both husbands' and wives' marital satisfaction.[58] Wives who report high levels of social support at work not only have a higher level of marital satisfaction themselves, but their husbands also report high levels of marital satisfaction.[59] Negative spillover increases role strain (which reduces work-family balance and increased work-family conflict) and is increased when couples overall work more hours, resulting in diminished marital satisfaction.[60]

Greater marital dissatisfaction also occurs when one spouse works a non-day shift.[61] Wives who work non-day shifts report more work-family conflict, and so do their husbands, especially when the wives work longer hours.[62] Interestingly, Galinsky, Aumann, and Bond found that dual-earner mothers' reports of work-family conflict have not changed substantively since 1977, but fathers in dual-earner couples are significantly more likely to report work-family conflict than they were in 1977.[63] In fact, they may be more likely than mothers to report work-family conflict.

Barnett reminds us that dual-earner couples do not generally describe their marriages as in trouble, and both women and men tend to report their marriages as rewarding.[64] In fact, in her research, Barnett found that women did not appear to be more susceptible to family role strain than did men. Her research also noted that wives' evaluations of their marriages were built on how much their husbands reduced the traditional work that wives performed (specifically child care tasks), while husbands' evaluations were tied to how they felt about their wives' earnings. Men who felt threatened by their wives' earnings (usually due to holding onto the breadwinning role as an identity) reported more marital unhappiness.[65]

Damaske's research on women's employment trajectories documents the role that work-family conflict plays in women's employment decisions.[66] Women's work pathways are a function of their experience of work-family conflict, which is explained simultaneously by the type of job acquired and how supportive their partner is (if they are married). Having a good job is a necessary but not sufficient condition to holding steady employment. Similarly, having a supportive partner is a necessary but not sufficient condition to holding steady employment. If a woman has a good job but her partner does not support her employment (e.g., by giving her encouragement and doing domestic labor), then she has a greater likelihood of pulling back out of the labor force.

Understanding work-family conflict is therefore a key component of understanding dual-earner couples, as it reflects role strain in particular for wives. This role strain influences marital satisfaction, women's employment decisions (including potentially leaving the labor market), and the overall health of the marriage. Early research on divorce found that wives' labor force participation was associated with the likelihood of marital dissolution.[67] One explanation for this association is women's increased economic freedom. Employed wives are more likely to be economically independent of their husbands and therefore do not see financial dependence as a reason to remain married.

Research in the United States and elsewhere has found that employment among wives, even part-time employment, increases the likelihood that couples will divorce,[68] although part-time employment among mothers reduces their likelihood of divorcing in comparison to stay-at-home mothers.[69] Marital satisfaction is a lynchpin in understanding this association. Women's employment does not seem to influence the likelihood of marital disruption in happy marriages, but does increase the likelihood of divorce in unhappy marriages.[70] In addition, other researchers have found that the relationship between wives' employment/

income and probability of divorce differs based on the women's beliefs about gendered relationships, so that employment and income have less influence on marital stability for nontraditional wives than for traditional ones.[71]

Research has started to investigate how the Great Recession has influenced marital dynamics, including work-family conflict, marital satisfaction, and likelihood of divorce. Cohen tests whether the economic hardship brought on by the Great Recession increased the likelihood of divorce (due to increased stress in relationships) or decreased the likelihood of divorce (due to a renewed commitment to one another by facing a hardship together).[72] He finds that living in a state with high foreclosure rates was positively associated with the odds of divorce, but only among the highly educated. There was scant other evidence in support of an influence of the Great Recession on the likelihood of divorce among the over 2 million women represented in his analysis. Morgan, Cumberworth, and Wimer find no evidence that the Great Recession influenced the overall divorce rate in the United States.[73] Indeed, some research has found that, at least among cohabitors, being able to blame the economy for household financial difficulties mitigates the negative effects of financial disagreements on relationship satisfaction.[74]

Concluding Remarks

Dual-earner couples like Juan and Elena and Richard and Donna are the norm in the United States; economic need and personal interest will continue to push both partners into the paid labor force. Instead of focusing on the potential negative outcomes of dual-earner couples, it may be more productive for us to think about how to help these families be more balanced, more satisfied, and happier.

One way to increase wives' marital satisfaction is to figure out how to get men to do more housework, something that sounds really easy but has been rather difficult to make happen. There are a lot of pressures on men *not* to do housework, and a lot of pressures on women *to* do (most of the) housework. Sociologists call this "doing gender"—behaving in a particular way because you know people will judge how good of a woman or man you are based on how you behave. But given how important the perceptions of fairness in the division of housework is to marital satisfaction among dual-earner couples, it important to consider how to encourage men to do more of the day-to-day work of keeping a house running.

Another approach is to reduce work-family conflict through "family-friendly" policies. Flexible workplace policies like telecommuting and flexible work schedules allow workers greater schedule control, one of the most important workplace influences on level of work-family conflict.[75] Therefore, finding ways for individuals to have greater schedule control, whether they are in a dual-earner family or not, will help workers find work-family balance and reduce the spillover of their role demands into other parts of their lives. Having greater schedule control will likely help dual-earner families the most. Given that dual-earner families are an integral part of the fabric of American life and are becoming more diverse (given more cohabiting heterosexual and gay couples and married gay couples), figuring out how to help families to live their best lives will benefit everyone.

NOTES

1. Coontz (1992).
2. See Figure 14.1; Bureau of Labor Statistics (1997, 2001, 2006, 2013).
3. Raley, Mattingly, and Bianchi (2006).
4. Pixley (2008).
5. Boushey (2011).
6. Payne and Gibbs (2013).
7. Landivar (2012).
8. *Ibid.*
9. Becker and Moen (1999); Davis, Jacobsen, and Anderson (2012); Pixley and Moen (2003).
10. Winslow-Bowe (2006).
11. Abraham, Auspurg, and Hinz (2010); Davis, Jacobsen, and Anderson (2012); Pixley and Moen (2003).
12. Markham and Pleck (1986).
13. Pixley and Moen (2003).
14. Bielby and Bielby (1992).
15. Davis, Jacobsen, and Anderson (2012).
16. Pixley (2008).
17. Han (2005); Lundberg and Rose (2002); Markham and Pleck (1986).
18. Magnuson and Norum (1999).
19. Davis (2012).
20. Coltrane (1990); Soloway and Smith (1987).
21. Raley, Mattingly, and Bianchi (2006).
22. Torr and Short (2004).
23. Brewster and Rindfuss (2000).
24. Shreffler, Pirretti, and Drago (2010).
25. Liu and Hynes (2012); Lundberg and Rose (2000); Mason and Goulden (2002).
26. Avellar and Smock (2003); Budig and England (2001); Lundberg and Rose (2000).
27. Boushey (2008).
28. Singley and Hines (2005, p. 397).
29. Avellar and Smock (2003); Han (2005); Lundberg and Rose (2000); Markham and Pleck (1986).
30. Bianchi (2000); Hofferth (2001); Sandberg and Hofferth (2001).
31. Brayfield (1995); Hofferth (2001); Meteyer and Perry-Jenkins (2010).

32. Bianchi (2011).
33. *Ibid.*
34. Lareau (2011).
35. Bianchi, Robinson, and Milkie (2006).
36. Sobotka, Skirbekk, and Pilipov (2011).
37. Garey (1999); Haddock et al. (2006).
38. Becker (1981).
39. Bianchi, Robinson, and Milkie (2006).
40. *Ibid.*
41. For reviews of this research, see Bianchi and Milkie (2010); Coltrane (2000); Lachance-Grzela and Bouchard (2010).
42. Arrighi and Maume (2000).
43. E.g., Bartley, Blanton, and Gilliard. (2005).
44. Bianchi et al. (2012); Sayer (2005).
45. Boushey (2011).
46. See also Berik and Konger (2012).
47. DeMaris and Longmore (1996); Gager (1998); Gager and Hohmann-Marriott (2006); Thompson (1991).
48. Bartley et al. (2005); Davis (2010); Greenstein (1996); Rosenbluth, Steil, and Whitcomb (1998).
49. Perry-Jenkins and Folk (1994).
50. See also Gager (1998).
51. Davis and Greenstein (2009).
52. Greenstein (1995).
53. Dillaway and Broman (2001); Piña and Bengston (1993); Stohs (2000); Suitor (1991); Voydanoff and Donnelly (1999).
54. Frisco and Williams (2003); Greenstein (1990); Spitze and South (1985).
55. See Hochschild and Machung (1989) for early discussions of this process.
56. Hostetler et al. (2012).
57. Schneider and Waite (2005).
58. Pederson and Minnotte (2012).
59. *Ibid.*
60. Hostetler et al. (2012).
61. Jacobs and Gerson (2004); Presser (2003).
62. Barnett, Gareis, and Brennan (2008).
63. Galinsky, Aumann, and Bond (2011).
64. Barnett (2002).
65. See Tichenor's (2005) work for similar findings.
66. Damaske (2011).
67. Becker, Landis, and Michael (1977); Booth et al. (1986); Spitze and South (1985).
68. Cooke and Gash (2010); Davis and Greenstein (2004); South (2001).
69. Cooke and Gash (2010).
70. Schoen et al. (2002).
71. Greenstein (1995); Sayer and Bianchi (1998).
72. Cohen (2012).
73. Morgan, Cumberworth, and Wimer (2011).
74. Diamond and Hicks (2012).
75. Kelly, Moen, and Tranby (2011).

15

From Outlaws to In-Laws

Gay and Lesbian Couples in Contemporary Society

Robert-Jay Green

In 2003, the U.S. Supreme Court overturned all remaining state laws that criminalized homosexual behavior between consenting adults. The following year (2004), the first same-sex marriages in the United States were performed in Massachusetts following a ruling by the Massachusetts Supreme Court. Thus, in the span of only eleven months, same-sex partners who literally had been outlaws in some states could legally become in-laws to one another's families in Massachusetts. By the end of 2013, eighteen states and the District of Columbia offered full marriage equality to same-sex couples. These momentous societal shifts and the psychological implications for same-sex couples, their families, and their communities are the focus of this chapter.

A THOUGHT EXPERIMENT

To set the stage for what follows, I invite you to engage in a little thought experiment. Imagine for a moment that you were asked to write a chapter on "heterosexual married couples" for this book. Where would you begin? What general statements might you make about heterosexual married couples in the United States? Thinking of all the heterosexual couples you have ever known, what do heterosexual married couples as a group have in common beyond the most obvious facts that they are composed of a woman and a man? How about these:

- Heterosexual married couples in the United States are a high-risk group for separation and dissolution of relationships. Their instability generally results from heterosexual attempts to resolve conflicts by using escalating anger or avoidance/withdrawal strategies, both of which fail to solve couple problems. In fact, almost half of heterosexual marriages end in divorce.

- The heterosexual married lifestyle is characterized by a distinctive division of household labor such that women do a significantly larger share of household work, child rearing, and caring for aging relatives, even when wives work outside the home as many hours as their husbands. Greater inequities in this regard are associated with higher levels of distress in wives and lower levels of marital satisfaction for both spouses. Given the negative effects of such unequal divisions of household and child-care labor, one wonders why heterosexual couples have maintained and sometimes extolled these imbalances for centuries.

- Heterosexuals are known for being preoccupied with sex and inconsistent in their use of birth control before and after marriage, casually producing offspring at such high rates that overpopulation is becoming a grave concern. One is forced to conclude that heterosexual couples are sorely lacking in impulse control and must be uncontrollably driven to engage in their distinctive manner of sexual relations.

- A significant portion of the married population partakes in a centuries-old heterosexual practice called "extramarital affairs." Although commonplace, other people's affairs seem to be a source of endless curiosity and highly animated gossip among heterosexuals. Even some of the most prominent and esteemed members of the heterosexual married community, including their highest-ranking politicians and leaders of their conservative religious groups, are notorious for grand acts of deception and hypocrisy when it comes to extramarital sexual behavior. Social scientists, who rarely have sex, remain perplexed as to why.

As these semi-humorous generalizations illustrate, it is arbitrary to select a few of a group's behavioral patterns to define or evaluate that group's overall functioning. It is even more arrogant to ascribe malevolent or pathological motivations to that group for having evolved group-specific patterns of behavior over the course of history. Lastly, in the absence of proving a causal link, there is no justification for attributing group members' actions solely or mostly to their sexual orientations rather than to other factors.

Yet an equivalent kind of negative stereotyping has been so commonplace in the public discourse about same-sex couples that it been given its own label in the social sciences: *heterocentrism*. This term may be defined as "viewing and evaluating the behavior of lesbian, gay, and bisexual people out of cultural and historical context and using heterosexual relations as the presumptive ideal."

Our little experiment above highlights a central point about the public debates concerning same-sex couples. In this domain of inquiry perhaps more than any other, one should actively counter the human tendency to engage in selective perception, categorical ("either/or") thinking, or the attribution of all things problematic to a group's differentness from the mainstream. Heterosexuality and homosexuality are not logical opposites. Counterpoising one against the other inevitably exaggerates their differences and minimizes their commonalities. Heterosexuality and homosexuality are most accurately viewed as variations on a common theme about romantic attractions and the human capacity for enduring love relationships.

SIMILARITIES AND DIFFERENCES BETWEEN SAME-SEX AND HETEROSEXUAL COUPLES

There is as much demographic and psychological diversity within these two types of couples as there is between them. In general, knowing a person's sexual orientation gives us much less information about that person than is often assumed. In many respects, same-sex couples may be more like heterosexual couples of their same social class, religious, racial/ethnic, or occupational group than they are like same-sex couples from markedly different demographic groups.

Research directly comparing same-sex and heterosexual couples reveals that they are remarkably similar to each other on most dimensions.[1] For example, regardless of the partners' sexual orientations, the same set of factors tends to predict relationship quality and relationship longevity across all types of couples: (1) partners' placing more value on security, permanence, shared activities, and togetherness; (2) partners' placing lower value on having separate activities and on personal autonomy; (3) higher expressiveness; (4) more perceived intrinsic rewards for being in the relationship; (5) fewer perceived attractive alternatives to the relationship; (6) more perceived barriers to ending the relationship; (7) less belief that disagreement is destructive; (8) higher trust in partner—viewing partner as dependable; (9) greater closeness and flexibility; (10) better problem-solving and conflict-resolution skills—less criticism, expression of contempt, and withdrawal during conflict discussions; (11) higher shared/egalitarian decision making; (12) greater perceived social support from sources outside the relationship.

However, group comparison studies also suggest that same-sex couples (especially lesbian couples) have an advantage in escaping the traditional gender role divisions that make for power imbalances and dissatisfaction in many hetero-sexual relationships. For example, in research by Green, Bettinger, and Zacks, lesbian couples described themselves as emotionally closer than gay male cou-ples who, in turn, described themselves as emotionally closer than heterosexual married couples.[2] Lesbian couples also reported the most flexibility in the way they handled rules and roles in the relationship, whereas heterosexual couples reported the least flexibility. It was noteworthy that higher levels of closeness and flexibility were associated with lesbian couples staying together versus breaking up over a two-year follow-up period. Overall, high levels of closeness and flex-ibility were reported by 79 percent of lesbian couples and 56 percent of gay male couples, but by only 8 percent of heterosexual married couples.

Same-sex couples' greater equality also was confirmed in studies by Gott-man, Levinson, and colleagues.[3] Based on observations of couples interacting in conflict situations, these scientists found that same-sex couples were better at resolving disagreements. They approached problems from a position of peer equality, using "softer" (less aggressive and accusatorial) starts when initiating conflict discussions and using more humor during the discussion to avoid escala-tion of hostilities. With married heterosexual couples, the researchers observed that there was much more of a power struggle in which one partner was being invalidated by the other.

SPECIAL CHALLENGES FOR SAME-SEX COUPLES

Despite the evidence above that same-sex couples may be functioning better than heterosexual couples in terms of closeness and equality within the relation-ship, it also is important to recognize that same-sex relationships tend not to last as long as heterosexual marriages. One explanation for this difference may be that because same-sex couples are less likely to be raising children together, they can more easily walk away from their relationships during periods of conflict. But same-sex couples also face three specific challenges unique to their position in society, which renders their relationships more vulnerable to breaking up:

- *Antigay Prejudice.* Partners in same-sex couples are subjected to and must continually cope with antigay prejudice and discrimination from their fami-lies, communities, and/or the larger society.

- *Ambiguity in the Social and Legal Definition of Relationships.* Due to the his-torical absence of social norms and legalized statuses for same-sex couples, these partners typically go through much more uncertainty about what it means to be a couple and commit to a relationship. Also, in the vast majority of states (where marriage currently is not available for same-sex couples), the partners face obstacles to protecting and providing for one another, including in times of serious illness or disability and after a partner's death.

- *Barriers to Forming Cohesive Social Support Networks.* Same-sex couples typically have more difficulty creating cohesive and lasting systems of social support because their families of origin, work settings, religious groups, and other community members tend to be less accepting and supportive of their relationships and because the gay and straight segments of their social networks tend to be segregated.

These three stresses are challenging to all (and detrimental to some) gay and lesbian relationships, and I will focus on them in the next sections of this chapter.

ANTIGAY DISCRIMINATION

The overarching difference in the lives of same-sex versus heterosexual couples is that the former must continually cope with the special risks of claiming a socially stigmatized identity.[4] In this section, I examine the historical and contemporary sociopolitical contexts in which same-sex relationships have been shaped. Then I discuss the psychological implications of these factors for the functioning of same-sex partners.

The Historical Context

For much of U.S. history, love and sexual behavior between two consenting adult women or men was against the law.[5] Depending on local norms and statutes, homosexual acts were punishable by fines, imprisonment, consignment to mental hospitals, dismissal from jobs, and extreme social ostracism of the individual and sometimes of other family members as well. In the 1950s, for example, unjustified police raids on bars serving gay and lesbian patrons were common, and newspapers frequently published photographs designed to shame the people who were arrested in these police sweeps. Careers and lives were ruined, and suicide rates were high. Lesbian and gay people feared being revealed or even blackmailed by vengeful former same-sex partners, confidants, or others who discovered their sexual orientation.

Thus committed relationships between two men or two women were extremely dangerous, because their ongoing nature made it more difficult for people to hide their sexual orientation. This was especially true for men. Although two "single" women could live together seemingly as "just friends" in order to share household expenses and companionship (and might even elicit sympathy from the community for never having married), two men living together after the age of thirty immediately raised suspicion.[6]

As a result, lesbians and gay men typically married heterosexual partners or lived alone, engaging in same-sex romantic encounters briefly and clandestinely. They remained closeted to almost all heterosexuals, living in fear of familial, social, economic, and legal consequences of being found out. The alternative of forming a continuing love relationship with a same-sex partner was too fraught with the danger of being exposed and becoming a social pariah.

In this way, throughout American history, the "closet" worked against ongoing same-sex love relationships and favored anonymous short ones. Such is still the case for most lesbian, gay, and bisexual people in the world, including in almost all of Asia and Africa, most of Latin America and Eastern Europe, all of the Middle East, in many U.S. rural communities, and in enclaves of recent immigrants in large U.S. metropolitan areas. Homosexual behavior between consenting adults is still punishable by torture and death in some countries and can lead to imprisonment in many more.

A paradoxical effect of this history is that having been precluded from forming committed same-sex relationships, lesbian and gay people simultaneously have been accused of not being able to create and sustain them. Imagine what shape heterosexual relationships might have taken over the last 200 years if heterosexuals had been socially and legally prevented from forming any kind of love relationships, let alone marriages, during that time.

Although a complete account of how same sex-couples went from being outlaws to in-laws over the last century is beyond the scope of this chapter, it is important to keep the above-mentioned history in mind during any discussion of contemporary same-sex couples. As we will see, even within the current population, there are marked generational differences in worldviews and life goals as a function of when in history the partners grew up. The different historical contexts in which these individuals came out to themselves and others helped shape their couple and family relationships and their political priorities for the future.

Contemporary Discrimination

A surprising number of Americans seem to believe that discrimination against lesbian and gay people is largely a thing of the past. According to an NBC/Wall Street Journal poll conducted in August 2008 (using a sample of 1,075 likely voters), 23 percent of respondents said they believed gay and lesbian people were "receiving too many special advantages," and 28 percent said they believe gays/lesbians are "receiving fair treatment." By contrast, 40 percent of respondents in the survey believed that gay and lesbian people were being discriminated against.

Thus a majority of voters (51 percent) as recently as 2008 thought that gay and lesbian people were not discriminated against in America, and this was well before 2013 when the U.S. federal government repealed its ban on recognizing same-sex marriages performed in some states and the District of Columbia.

Unfortunately, the majority's beliefs are contradicted by what gays and lesbians report about their own experiences. For example, based on an interview study of 528 New York metropolitan area (urban and suburban) youths ages fifteen to nineteen, D'Augelli and colleagues found that 80 percent reported receiving verbal taunts related to being gay or lesbian. Fourteen percent reported physical attacks. Overall, 70 percent of verbal victimization incidents and 56 percent of physical victimization occurred in schools. Nine percent of these youths (especially those who had experienced more physical victimization for being gay) met the formal psychiatric criteria for a diagnosis of post-traumatic stress disorder (PTSD).[7] In this context, it is noteworthy that most U.S. states provide no specific legal protection from discrimination for gay and lesbian youth in public schools, even though it is very clear from many surveys that such youth are disproportionately the targets of bullying.

In examining workplace discrimination, Ragins, Singh, and Cornwell surveyed 500 U.S. adults who self-identified as gay or lesbian.[8] Their data showed that 37 percent of workers reported having faced discrimination on the job because others suspected or assumed they were gay or lesbian. More than 10 percent said they had been physically harassed because they were perceived to be gay or lesbian. More than 22 percent said they had been verbally harassed. Nearly 31 percent said they had resigned from a job, been fired from a job, or left a job because they had encountered gay/lesbian-related discrimination. Surprisingly, most heterosexual Americans seem to think that gay and lesbian people are protected against such discrimination everywhere in the United States, but in fact most states have no laws that prevent employers from firing or not hiring employees simply for being gay or lesbian. There is no federal legislation providing legal protection against employment or housing discrimination for gays and lesbians in the United States except in the U.S. military (subsequent to the 2011 repeal of the "don't ask, don't tell" ban on openly gay and lesbian personnel serving in the armed forces).

In June 2013, the U.S. Supreme Court struck down Section 3 of the federal Defense of Marriage Act, which prevented our national government from recognizing legal marriages of same-sex partners. This new ruling allows same-sex couples legally married in any state (regardless of the marriage laws in their current state of residence) to receive all the federal benefits of marriage given to heterosexual spouses. Most notably, these benefits include Social Security income for surviving spouses, inheritance tax exemptions for surviving spouses, and immigration rights for international spouses married to U.S. citizens. Also on the basis of this Supreme Court decision, many same-sex couples have sued successfully for marriage rights in their states of residence. This has resulted in an even larger number of states now permitting same-sex marriage or seemingly on the verge of permitting it pending the results of ongoing federal court appeals.

Despite these advances, only eighteen U.S. states and the District of Columbia provided marriage equality for same-sex couples as of December 2013.[9] Most states continue not to offer legal recognition of any kind for same-sex couples. Most of them continue to have constitutional amendments prohibiting same-sex marriage or "Defense of Marriage" acts (DOMA) banning the recognition of same-sex marriages performed elsewhere. The arrival of these anti–same-sex marriage laws between 1998 and 2013 paralleled the rise of well-funded antigay groups in America—groups that seek to prevent the equal treatment of lesbian or gay people and their relationships.[10] Most prominent among these groups have been Focus on the Family, Family Research Council, Family Research Institute, American Family Association, and the National Organization for Marriage. Despite their seemingly innocuous and nonpartisan titles, these groups have explicitly antigay agendas to dismantle all equal protections for LGBT people in the United States.

Same-sex couples are still confronted daily with media statements by antigay groups that openly disparage gay and lesbian people and their relationships. Many of these public statements contain outright distortions of the social science findings on gay and lesbian issues. A typical example appeared in an invited commentary for *Time* magazine in December 2006, following the birth of a son to Mary Cheney (the former U.S. vice president's daughter) and her female partner. An essay titled "Two Mommies Is One Too Many," penned by James Dobson (then president of Focus on the Family), stated:

> With all due respect to Cheney and her partner, Heather Poe, the majority of more than 30 years of social-science evidence indicates that children do best on every measure of well-being when raised by their married mother and father. . . . We should not enter into yet another untested and far-reaching social experiment.

Although this kind of claim has been extensively repeated in the media by antigay groups, there has not been a shred of credible social science evidence that children raised by heterosexual mothers and fathers do better on any measure of well-being than children raised by lesbian or gay parents. All of the legitimate social science actually converges on the conclusion that there are no statistically significant differences in mental health outcomes, peer relations, academic achievement, and gender identity between children raised by lesbian or gay parents compared with children raised by heterosexual parents.[11] In fact, some researchers have found very small but statistically significant differences on a few dimensions that seem to favor children of lesbian and gay parents. For example, daughters of lesbian mothers seem to be somewhat more career-oriented, sons of lesbian mothers seem to be less objectifying in their approach to romantic partners, and lesbian parents report being closer to their child.[12]

EFFECTS OF ANTIGAY ATTITUDES ON SAME-SEX PARTNERS

Although same-sex couples do not encounter intolerance at every turn, they experience enough of it personally, vicariously (by identification with other lesbian and gay victims of discrimination), and through antigay political initiatives and media advertisements to remain constantly vigilant for its occurrence. It is impossible for a lesbian or gay person to grow up in this society without internalizing some negative attitudes and fears about same-sex orientation and the dangers of discrimination.[13]

Most relevant for formation of couple relationships, the difficulty accepting one's homosexuality (termed *internalized homonegativity*) and/or the fear of punitive social and economic consequences of coming out still discourage many lesbian and gay people from forming lasting couple bonds. In many parts of the United States, it still remains safer for gay and lesbian people to be closeted and to restrict their sexual/romantic involvements to brief encounters. To reach the level of "outness" necessary to form a same-sex couple relationship, lesbian and gay partners must have successfully challenged in their own minds the negative views they were taught about homosexuality and overcome their fears of being seriously harmed by discrimination.

Successfully countering internalized antigay attitudes requires attributing them to societal ignorance, prejudice, fear, and the human tendency to conform to dominant norms. It also requires exposure to, and social support from, other lesbian and gay people whose behavior counteracts negative stereotypes about homosexuality. Thus, when partners participate actively in lesbian and gay community organizations, whatever stereotypes they may have held about lesbian and gay people and relationships tend to fall apart because of the enormous diversity within the community.

Equally important, partners in same-sex relationships sometimes have to engage in much self-reflection and questioning to be able to step outside of traditional gender norms and accept the reality of their own love for one another. Typically, this involves a personal review of the many antigay social influences that pressure them to regard their capacity for same-sex love as bad, sinful, mentally disturbed, inferior, and so on. All the negative messages they have received about homosexuality over a lifetime have to be considered against their own personal experience of self, their observations of other lesbian and gay people, and sometimes the extensive social science evidence showing that most lesbian and gay people lead happy, fulfilling lives despite the discrimination they may encounter. Ultimately, to function well, lesbian or gay partners must come to view their love as a normal human variation—one that has always existed among a small percentage of the population in all societies, and always will.

In many cases, partners are at different levels of comfort about their sexual orientations or may face very different levels of acceptance at work or in their families. These discrepancies may create couple conflicts over whether or how safe it is to be "out" in various situations. Couples that successfully manage these conflicts tend to maximize their participation in situations where they can be safely out as a couple.

Depending on the kind of discrimination same-sex partners face, coping successfully with antigay prejudice may require (1) working actively for change in one's current social environment; (2) changing to a different social environment (literally relocating geographically or quitting one's job to escape an intransigent or dangerously antigay situation); (3) reattributing the cause of one's distress to different factors (e.g., attributing one's distress to external prejudice and ignorance rather than to personal inadequacy); or (4) recognizing that some discriminatory situations cannot be changed, and then instead focusing on other areas in one's life that are meaningful.

LACK OF A NORMATIVE AND LEGAL TEMPLATE FOR SAME-SEX COUPLEHOOD

In contrast to heterosexual couples, for whom there is a traditionally prescribed way of being a couple with explicit and implicit rules, there is no prescribed way of being a same-sex couple. For example, some of the socially prescribed rules of heterosexual marriage include expectations of monogamy, sharing responsibility for each other's aging relatives, combining financial assets, dividing instrumental/expressive and household roles somewhat along traditional gender lines, relocating for one another's career advancement, and taking care of one another in times of serious illness or disability. Because until very recently same-sex partners could not marry anywhere in the United States, it has been unclear whether or at what turning point these traditional expectations of couples might apply to same-sex relationships. Elsewhere, I have termed this kind of uncertainty relational ambiguity, and it tends to play a central role in same-sex couple relationships, especially in the early years of couple formation.

For example, committed heterosexual couples (typically within one to three years of starting to date) take a wedding vow to stay together "in sickness and in health till death do us part." This vow to take care of each other is also a promise to family members, friends, and other witnesses, including in most cases to "God as a witness."

By contrast, it is unclear when or if most same-sex partners can have the same expectations of their relationship if same-sex marriage is prohibited in their state. Do same-sex unmarried partners implicitly make this vow when they move in together? After being together for two years or ten years? Can there be equivalent vow-making for same-sex couples when they cannot get legally married in their own states or within some religious denominations? Is a vow made in private the same psychologically as one made in public? Is a promise made in a public "commitment ceremony" that is not recognized by the state and/or federal government the same as a promise made against the backdrop of legally enforceable state marriage laws? Do domestic partnerships or civil unions convey the same sense of transition to a greater level of commitment as is implied by getting legally married in one's state of residence?

Lacking a preordained prescription for what being a same-sex couple means, unmarried lesbian and gay partners often must develop their own basic ideals of themselves as a couple. Inevitably, they will rely to some extent on earlier observations of successful and unsuccessful heterosexual marriages. But the same-sex composition of the couple and the unusual position of lesbians and gays in society throw into doubt how relevant these heterosexual models might be.

Furthermore, the greater variety of relationship arrangements that are acceptable within the gay community (e.g., many such couples never live together, others have non-monogamous relationships by agreement, shorter relationships are normative, fewer same-sex couples are raising children) leaves open the possibility that a same-sex couple's commitment could be either quite similar to or quite different from that of most married heterosexual couples. Compared with the generally prescribed expectations of marriage in the heterosexual community, the broader acceptance of varied couple arrangements in the lesbian and gay community seems to thrust each same-sex couple into a longer period of uncertainty and negotiation regarding its definition of personal couplehood.

The advent of legal marriage in eighteen U.S. states and the District of Columbia and its recognition by the federal government should reduce relational ambiguity for couples who marry. But the fact remains that as of December 2013, there is no within-state equal status available to help anchor and give legal substance to same-sex relationships in most states. As a result, many same-sex couples, their families, and their state governments seem to be experiencing heightened ambiguity about their situations. They still cannot get married in their own states, but they can travel to other states to get married. Regardless of where they reside after getting legally married, the U.S. federal government will recognize their marriages, but their home state may not recognize same-sex marriages performed in other states. They may be treated as a married couple by the federal Internal Revenue Service but treated as single individuals for the purposes of state income taxes. Partners who are married in one state may be treated as unmarried when they cross the border into another state, even if the federal government regards them as married in any state.[14]

In addition, partners who make up a couple may be at differing points on a continuum of commitment clarity and relationship definition because of the rapid social changes in the last few years. Same-sex couples of a certain age are confronted nowadays with the same ubiquitous questions familiar to heterosexuals who have been dating each other for more than a year—"When are the two of you going to get married and start a family?" However, many same-sex partners are woefully unprepared to answer because they never could have imagined either possibility until very recently, whereas heterosexual partners have been anticipating marriage and having children virtually all of their lives.

There are no simple solutions for resolving these ambiguities in same-sex couple relationships, given that many of these uncertainties are the result of laws and tradition forbidding recognition and acceptance of same-sex couples. In general, however, a couple tends to function best when there are clear agreements about their commitment and boundaries and when the couple's relationship is a higher priority than any other relationship (in terms of emotional involvement, caregiving, honesty, time, and influence over major decisions).

For couples who view their relationships as entailing a lifetime commitment but who are unable to get married or to obtain other legal couple statuses in their home states, it is possible to get married in the eighteen states and District of Columbia that perform same-sex marriages. Because such marriages will be recognized by the federal government, they provide some measure of substantiation of the couple's legal existence for federal tax, health care, inheritance, immigration, and other purposes.[15] However, these out-of-state marriages still leave uncertain how their relationships will be treated in their home states in terms of recognition, benefits, and mandated obligations attached to marriage. If they break up, it is unclear what would happen to these couples in terms of legal divorce proceedings and division of community property. If your state of residence does not recognize your marriage, how can it process and recognize your divorce? And given that it is not possible to file for divorce in a state where you do not reside, how would such couples divorce without moving to states that perform same-sex marriages?

Regardless of marital status, when same-sex partners are able to clarify their expectations and create agreements in contested areas or in areas that have never been discussed (such as finances or monogamy), it helps reduce relational ambiguity. This, in turn, increases partners' feelings of secure attachment and belief in the permanence of their bond, grounding their relationship in tangible definitions of what it means for them to be a couple.

Marriage, on the other hand, carries with it "automatic" agreements on the financial side of life and many implied agreements on psychological and ethical issues in a relationship. A significant advantage of marriage is that it signals the desire and intent to spend one's life with the other person for better or for worse, for richer or for poorer, in sickness and in health, until death of one of the partners. It thus provides the highest amount of reassurance of love and acceptance that human beings can give to one another in the form of a verbal promise backed up by state laws protecting the partners' rights and obligations in relation to each other. Thus, to the extent marriage becomes available to same-sex couples, it will go a long way toward reducing their relational ambiguity and put them on par with heterosexual couples.

FRAGMENTED SOCIAL SUPPORT SYSTEMS

Unlike members of racial, ethnic, and religious minority groups in which parents and children usually share their minority status, children who become lesbian and gay only rarely have parents who share their same sexual minority status. Being different from other family members in this way has profound consequences for the development of almost every lesbian and gay person. For example, because heterosexual parents have never suffered sexual orientation discrimination themselves, even the most well-meaning among them is not able to offer the kind of insight and socialization experiences that would buffer their child against antigay prejudice and its internalization.

By contrast, when children and parents mutually identify as members of the same minority group (for example, African Americans, Jews, Muslims), the children are explicitly taught—and parents implicitly model—ways to counter society's prejudice against their group. Typically, such parents and children are involved together in community institutions (religious, social) that are instrumental in supporting the child's development of a positive minority identity, and parents take a protective stance toward their children's experiences of oppression.

Parents of lesbian or gay children typically are unaware of their child's minority status, however, and therefore are unlikely to seek out community groups that would support the development of a positive lesbian or gay identity in their child. In fact, rather than protecting their child against prejudice, heterosexual parents often show subtle or not-so-subtle signs of antigay prejudice themselves. Instead of being on the same side as their child against the external dangers, the parents' own antigay attitudes and behavior may be the greatest external danger of all for the child.

Large numbers of lesbian and gay adults in the United States, especially members of conservative religious families or of immigrant families with traditional values, still remain closeted from one or both parents if they perceive their parents as being antigay. For couple relationships, this secrecy requires either distancing from the family of origin lest the secret be revealed or forgoing couple commitments in order to stay connected with the family of origin.

Although most parents do not completely reject their lesbian and gay children after the disclosure, the level of acceptance that offspring receive is highly variable and usually somewhat qualified.[16] As a result, same-sex couples frequently turn to their lesbian and gay friends for greater levels of mutual support and identification. Ideally, these friends and selected family members are woven together into a so-called family of choice—an interconnected system of emotional and instrumental support over time.[17]

In general, same-sex couples tend to have less interconnected social networks than heterosexual couples. The tendency toward social segregation of the straight and gay worlds generally—and between the straight and gay segments of an individual's social network—usually requires that same-sex couples have to expend more deliberate effort to create an integrated social support system that has family-like qualities. This is especially true for same-sex couples of color, interracial couples, or couples in which one or both members are bisexual or transgender.[18] These same-sex couples often are subject to much higher levels of antigay discrimination from their families and their original communities and usually experience significantly more difficulty integrating their more segregated social networks into a coherent whole.

When a young adult or older lesbian or gay individual can accept his or her own sexual orientation and choice of partner, dealing with the family is emotionally much easier, and parents' antigay sentiments can be dealt with more dispassionately, assertively, and with fewer setbacks to the couple's functioning. In building a family of choice, couples must take a proactive stance toward the goal of developing an ongoing social support system consisting of about eight to ten individuals or couples. In building a personal support system, the couple has to take two basic steps: first, developing or maintaining a reciprocally supportive relationship with each person who would be a member of the couple's support system; and second, "knitting" these people together into an integrated system of support.

The best strategy is for the partners to become active in a well-established organization together, attend its events regularly to become familiar fixtures in the organization, and take on positions of leadership or active committee involvement that require repeated interaction with the same people frequently and over months or years. In smaller or rural communities with fewer lesbian and gay organizations, the Internet may be the best venue for starting friendship networks.

The great advantage of meeting new people through existing lesbian and gay organizations is that those organizations already will have some degree of "groupness" to them, so that the couple may be able to become an integral part of an already existing social support system. If the couple's closest relationships arose at different times from different settings, more effort has to go into knitting these disparate relationships into a more cohesive unit. The only way to increase the cohesiveness of a fragmented support system is for the couple to actively, frequently, and persistently take the lead in physically bringing together the disconnected individuals or subgroups. It generally takes about one to two years to link a disconnected collection of about eight to ten individual relationships into a functional social support system with family-like properties (a family of choice), but same-sex couples invariably find the effort worthwhile.

THE FUTURE OF SAME-SEX RELATIONSHIPS: A TALE OF TWO GENERATIONS

The U.S. Census Bureau's American Community Survey of 2010 revealed that there were approximately 594,000 same-sex-couple households in the United States. Many observers suspect that the number of same-sex couples may actually be significantly higher, because respondents (especially those living in more conservative regions) may be reluctant to reveal information about their sexual orientation to the U.S. Census Bureau. Among cohabiting couples, approximately 20 percent were raising children. Approximately 37 percent of all lesbian and gay adults in the United States report having had at least one child.[19]

What in general do lesbian and gay people want in terms of their couple and family relationships as well as public policies toward them in the future? In a survey of the legal and political priorities of 768 lesbian, gay, and bisexual people, Egan, Edelman, and Sherrill[20] found interesting generational differences. For adults age sixty-five and older, highest priorities were laws against hate crimes, followed by workplace discrimination protections. But for those ages eighteen to twenty-five, highest priorities were marriage rights, followed by parental and adoption rights. These findings seem to reflect the two age groups' different experiences historically.

When lesbian and gay people who now are over sixty-five first came out, it was inconceivable that marriage or parenting would be available to them, and their major concerns revolved around being physically harmed or fired from their jobs for being gay or lesbian. The younger generation, by contrast, seems to have taken a giant leap forward in raising expectations for equality, striving for same-sex marriage rights and for the same opportunities to adopt or conceive children (via alternative insemination or surrogacy) that heterosexual married couples enjoy.[21]

For example, in a study of youths, D'Augelli et al.[22] individually interviewed 133 self-identified gay or lesbian urban and suburban young people (50 females and 83 males in the New York metropolitan area) about their aspirations for couple relationships and parenting in the future. The participants were ages sixteen to twenty-two (average age was nineteen); 42 percent were Hispanic, 39 percent were people of color, and the rest were white non-Hispanic. In this sample, 92 percent of the lesbian youths and 82 percent of gay male youths reported that they wanted to be in a long-term monogamous relationship within ten years. Furthermore, 78 percent of the lesbian youths and 61 percent of gay male youths said it was "very" or "extremely" likely they would marry a same-sex partner if legally possible. In terms of parenting, 66 percent of lesbian youths and 52 percent of gay male youths said it was "very" or "extremely" likely they would be raising children in the future. These high percentages of gay and lesbian youths aspiring to marriage and parenthood are astonishing to older gay and lesbian adults, who could not in their wildest dreams have imagined a time where such equal freedoms would be available to them.

Moreover, despite indications of continuing prejudice and discrimination against lesbian and gay people, there is abundant evidence of change in the direction of greater acceptance. Illustrative of these trends, virtually all the national public opinion polls show that the American public now is in favor of same-sex marriage by a slight majority (ranging from 54 to 59 percent). However, opposition remains high, especially among voters who are older, more politically conservative, and endorse a more fundamentalist approach to religion.[23] The very strong link between younger age (especially under age thirty) and greater support for same-sex marriage has now shown up in all national opinion polls, suggesting that it is just a matter of time until a fairly large majority of the electorate favors same-sex marriage—unless, of course, the younger cohorts become markedly more socially conservative as they age.

In addition, recent polls show that about 49 percent of people in the United States say that they have a close friend or family member who is lesbian or gay;

and 87 percent say they "know" someone personally who is lesbian or gay.[24] Being close to someone lesbian or gay—and knowing more lesbian/gay people in general—are both strongly associated with more favorable attitudes toward same-sex marriage. For example, in a June 2013 Pew Research Center poll, 61 percent of respondents who said they have a close lesbian/gay friend or family member were in favor of same-sex marriage; but only 41 percent of those who did not have a close lesbian/gay friend or family member were in favor. Similarly, among those who said they knew a "lot" of lesbian/gay people, 68 percent were in favor of same-sex marriage compared to only 32 percent among those who did not know a lesbian/gay person.

Thus, to the extent that younger generations of lesbian and gay people create the kind of long-lasting couple and family relationships they aspire to and then become friends and acquaintances of heterosexuals, we are likely to witness more public support for marriage equality. Heterosexuals' attitudes toward same-sex couples are clearly a case where familiarity seems to breed positive impressions, and absence of familiarity is associated with contempt. To know thy neighborhood same-sex couple is tantamount to losing thy stereotypes.

Notes

1. Balsam, Beauchaine, Rothblum, and Solomon (2008); Fingerhut and Peplau(2013); Gotta, Green, Rothblum, Solomon, Balsam, and Schwartz (2011); Solomon, Rothblum, and Balsam (2004).
2. Green, Bettinger, and Zacks (1996).
3. Gottman, Levenson, Gross, et al.(2003a); Gottman, Levenson, Swanson, et al. (2003b).
4. Herek (1998).
5. Emilio (1998); Katz (1992).
6. Faderman (1991).
7. D'Augelli, Rendina, Sinclair, and Grossman (2006/2007).
8. Ragins, Singh, and Cornwell (2007).
9. As of December 2013, eighteen states (CA, CT, DE, HI, IA, IL, ME, MD, MA, MN, NH, NJ, NM, NY, RI, VT, UT, WA, and the District of Columbia) had full marriage equality for same-sex couples. Three states offered partnership rights that approach those of marriage in their states (civil unions in CO, and domestic partnerships in OR and NV). Wisconsin offered more limited domestic partnership rights. Thirty-eight percent of the U.S. population lived in a state that provided marriage to same-sex couples or recognized such out-of-state marriages. The U.S. federal government and its branches (such as the Internal Revenue Service, Immigration and Naturalization Service, and U.S. Military and National Guard) fully recognized same-sex marriages performed legally in any state regardless of the couple's current state of residence. Because the legal status of same-sex marriage is changing so rapidly in the United States and elsewhere, readers are advised to consult the following website for updated information: http://www.freedomtomarry.org.

10. For a description of the most prominent antigay groups, see Schlatter (2010).

11. Biblarz and Savci (2010); Crowl, Ahn, and Baker (2008); Patterson (2013).

12. Biblarz and Savci (2010); Bos and Gartrell (2010); Crowl, Ahn, and Baker (2008); Patterson (2013).

13. Madsen and Green (2012); Meyer (2003); Rostosky, Riggle, Horne, and Miller (2009); Ryan, Huebner, Diaz, and Sanchez (2009).

14. Herdt and Kertzner (2006); Herek (2006).

15. Castello (2013); Clifford, Hertz, and Doskow (2012).

16. Lanutti (2008); Pew Research Center (2013a).

17. Weston (1991).

18. For these topics, see especially Firestein (2007); Fox (2006); Lev (2004); Sanchez and Vilain (2013); Wilson and Harper (2013).

19. Gates (2013); U.S. Census Bureau (2011).

20. Egan, Edelman, and Sherrill (2008).

21. Bergman, Rubio, Green, and Padron (2010); Brodzinsky, Green, and Katuzny (2012); Mitchell and Green (2007).

22. D'Augelli et al. (2006/2007).

23. Craighill and Clement (2014); Langer (2013); Murray (2013); Pew Research Center (2013b); Saad (2013).

24. Pew Research Center (2013b).

In Other Words

SOME STATES SEE FIGHT FOR RIGHT TO SAME-SEX DIVORCE

Associated Press, December 1, 2013

Holbrook Mohr and David Crary

HERNANDO, Miss.—Lauren Beth Czekala-Chatham wants to force Mississippi, one of the America's most conservative states, to recognize her same-sex marriage. She hopes to do so by getting a divorce.

She and Dana Ann Melancon traveled from Mississippi to San Francisco to get married in 2008. The wedding was all Czekala-Chatham hoped it would be, the Golden Gate Bridge in the background, dreams for a promising future. She wrote the vows herself.

The couple bought a house together in Walls, a town of about 1,100 in northern Mississippi's DeSoto County in June 2009. But the marriage was tumultuous and, like so many others, it didn't last.

Czekala-Chatham, a 51-year-old credit analyst and mother of two teenage sons from an earlier straight marriage, filed for divorce in chancery court in September. She wants to force Mississippi to recognize the same-sex marriage for the purpose of granting the divorce.

"It's humiliating to know that you spend that money, that time to be in a committed relationship and for it to end. I mean, that hurts. But then to be in a state that doesn't recognize you as a human being, or recognize you for who you are, for who you love, it's hard," Czekala-Chatham said during an interview at her current home in Hernando. "I'm not treated like the neighbors next door. I'm treated like a second-class citizen."

She has plenty of company among gay and lesbian couples in other conservative states, although thus far only a few have pursued divorce cases in the courts.

Even as the number of states legalizing same-sex marriage will soon grow to 16, most states—like Mississippi—refuse to recognize such unions or to help dissolve them. Gay couples who move to those states after marrying elsewhere face roadblocks if they wish to divorce, as do couples from those states who make a brief foray out-of-state to get married.

Often, such couples in non-recognition states would have to move back to the state where they were married and establish residency in order to get divorced—an option that can be unworkable in many cases.

"The idea you can't go to your local courthouse and file for divorce is very disruptive," said Peter Zupcofska, a Boston lawyer who has represented many gay and lesbian clients in marriage and divorce cases. "It's an enormous waste of effort and time."

The right to divorce isn't as upbeat a topic as the right to marry, but gay-rights lawyers and activists say it's equally important.

"The marriage system is a way we recognize and protect the commitments people make to their partner," said James Esseks, director of the Lesbian, Gay, Bisexual and Transgender Project at the American Civil Liberties Union.

"Part of that system is creating a predictable, regularized way of dealing with the reality that relationships sometimes end," he said. "Those are the times people are the worst to each other, and that's why we have divorce courts. There's got to be an adult in the room."

On a recent evening, in the one-story brick house she shares with her two children, a new girlfriend and several pets, Czekala-Chatham sat on the edge of a leather recliner, shaking her head.

"Why should I be treated differently, you know?" she said. "When the courthouse is a few blocks from here, I should be able to walk up there and get married. I should also be able to go up there and get divorced."

She could get a divorce in California, but her lawyer argues that Mississippi wouldn't recognize the divorce and their marital property would remain "in limbo."

Melancon's lawyer, Chad Reeves, filed a motion to dismiss the divorce complaint based on the argument that Mississippi can't grant a divorce for a marriage that it doesn't recognize. However, Reeves told The Associated Press on Friday that the motion was withdrawn after the parties signed an agreement related to division of property and debts.

Reeves said he opposed the divorce because Czekala-Chatham asked for alimony, among other things, but those matters have been settled. He said Melancon will get the house, and won't have to pay alimony. Czekala-Chatham says she doesn't care, she just wants the divorce.

A hearing is scheduled for Monday.

Melancon, who now lives in Arkansas, declined to be interviewed. She said in an email that she wants the divorce, but the "avenues to pursue are vague and expensive." She did not elaborate.

The Mississippi Attorney General's office filed a motion to intervene on Nov. 15 that said the divorce petition should be dismissed.

Mississippi "has no obligation to give effect to California laws that are contrary to Mississippi's expressly stated public policy," the motion argues. "That legitimate policy choice precludes recognition of other States' same sex marriages for any reason, including granting a divorce."

Legal experts say getting Mississippi to recognize the marriage for any purpose is a longshot. Lawmakers amended state law in 1997 to say any same-sex marriage "is prohibited and null and void from the beginning. Any marriage between persons of the same gender that is valid in another jurisdiction does not constitute a legal or valid marriage in Mississippi."

In 2004, 86 percent of Mississippi voters approved an amendment placing a ban on same-sex marriage in the state constitution.

In his arguments for a divorce, Czekala-Chatham's lawyer, Wesley Hisaw, cites a recent ruling by the U.S. Supreme Court that struck down parts of the federal Defense of Marriage Act and ordered the U.S. government to recognize legal same-sex marriages. That has created a situation where same-sex couples "are married lawfully under the laws of the United States, but not under Mississippi law," Hisaw contends.

He also argues that bigamous and incestuous marriages are considered "void" in Mississippi, just like same-sex marriages, but bigamy and incest are also grounds for divorce.

"There can be no legitimate state purpose in allowing bigamous or incestuous couples to divorce and not allowing the same remedy to same-sex couples," he wrote.

Right-to-divorce cases have cropped up in some other states with constitutional bans on same-sex marriage. On Nov. 5, the Texas Supreme Court heard arguments about whether the state can grant divorces to gay couples married elsewhere.

The plaintiffs are couples from Austin and Dallas who married in Massachusetts and later filed for divorce in Texas. The Austin couple was granted a divorce, but Attorney General Greg Abbott intervened in the Dallas case and won an appeals court decision blocking a divorce.

In the oral arguments, Assistant Attorney General James Blacklock argued there's no way for Texas to grant a divorce because of the constitutional ban.

"There's no marriage here," he said. "So there can be no divorce."

A similar case has just commenced in Kentucky, where two women married in Massachusetts are seeking a divorce.

At least one same-sex couple has been able to get a divorce in a state that doesn't officially recognize same-sex unions. In 2011, the Wyoming Supreme Court ruled that two women married in Canada could get a divorce in the state, reversing a ruling by a district judge.

While the issue of same-sex divorce has drawn increasing attention, there is little in the way of comprehensive data to help draw comparisons between the divorce rates of gay couples and heterosexual couples.

One of the few large-scale studies addressing the question was conducted by Michael Rosenfeld, a sociology professor at Stanford University. He assessed the breakup rates among about 3,000 couples since 2009, and concluded there was little difference between gay couples and straight couples.

Depending on a couple's circumstances, a host of weighty matters can be affected by the inability to divorce—division of property, child custody, health coverage for a spouse, the ability to get remarried. In some cases, the inability to divorce could mean that an estranged spouse would continue to receive spousal benefits even though the other partner wanted those benefits halted so he or she could move on to a new relationship.

"It's really problematic for people in getting on with their lives, being considered single again," said Kenneth Upton Jr., an attorney in the Dallas office of Lambda Legal, a national gay-rights group. ▄

16

Independent Women

Equality in African American Lesbian Relationships

Mignon R. Moore

Researchers on lesbian and gay populations have tended to generalize the experiences of lesbian practice and gay sexuality from past research on white, middle-class, feminist women. But alternative histories and experiences of women from other racial and socioeconomic groups offer new information on the relationship among race, class, gender, and homosexual relationships. The present study covers three years in the lives of a population of gay women who are not often visible in public life—lesbians of color who are creating families. In this article, I offer an examination of the ways black gay women evaluate the concept of equality or egalitarianism in same-sex unions.

This research is drawn from my book *Invisible Families: Gay Identities, Relationships, and Motherhood among Black Women*, which argues that previously formed identification statuses, such as those based on race or class, influence how individuals perceive and enact later group memberships, like those based on sexuality. It does this by analyzing a group of women who, because of year of birth, geographic location, socioeconomic status, and other characteristics, came of age during periods of heavy racial segregation and entered into their gay identities with firmly entrenched black racial identities. The larger project from which this essay is drawn suggests there is value in analyzing the ways past experiences in families of origin influence the expectations individuals have for their own relationships, regardless of sexual preference.

In this essay, I examine the concept of equality in lesbian relationships by looking closely at the two primary aspects of egalitarianism: equal responsibility for paid work and housework. Past studies of lesbian households have emphasized the egalitarian nature of these couples vis-à-vis their division of family labor, which includes household chores such as cooking and cleaning as well as child care and supervision. This body of literature has had little to say about the other aspect of egalitarianism: how lesbian couples distribute paid work, evaluate its importance in their relationship, and construct ideologies about economic independence. These studies have also tended to understate the experiences of women of color and working-class and poor women.[1]

In this work, I examine the relative importance of both components of egalitarianism for black lesbians, looking at differences across socioeconomic background as one explanation for how women come to make decisions about what they value in their relationships.

EGALITARIANISM: ECONOMIC INDEPENDENCE AND AN EQUITABLE DIVISION OF HOUSEHOLD LABOR

Since the 1970s, feminist research on the division of household labor has conceptualized the gender specialization model of husband as primary wage earner and wife as primary caretaker as an indicator of gender stratification. This research generally defines egalitarianism as "joint responsibility for paid work, housework, and child rearing."[2] From 1989 onward, the social science literature on household decision making in lesbian-led families has tended to measure egalitarianism and equality in relationships by focusing on the ways couples distribute household chores and child care. It has not paid close attention to how much lesbian partners value, or the extent to which they enact, the other component of egalitarianism—economic independence and financial contributions from both partners in the relationship.[3]

Part of the problem has been the way research on lesbian-headed households has been conducted. Scholars who study lesbian families have been interested in addressing the literature on heterosexual couples that measured the distribution of and time spent on household chores by husbands and wives. Studies of gender in the heterosexual division of labor sought and revealed explanations for the greater responsibility of wives for household chores.[4] Studies of the division of labor among lesbian and gay couples sought to illuminate how these same issues played out in the absence of sex differences between partners.[5] After 1989, the emphasis in the family literature focused heavily on the domestic realm, and researchers of lesbian-headed households tended to follow suit.

Lesbian subjects have also persisted in emphasizing the egalitarian nature of their unions because of deep-rooted concerns about the public image of gay communities. Carrington's 1999 study of the ways gay couples assign various aspects of domesticity revealed this tendency. Even though the subjects of more recent scholarship on lesbian families may not take on a dominant identity as feminist, they hold significant ideological commitment to egalitarianism and form unions, with the principles of egalitarian feminism in mind.

Recent studies show evidence that lesbian couples tend to distribute housework, paid work, and child care duties across the couple using an "ethic of equality" that is drawn from lesbian-feminist ideologies.[6] Much of the research has focused on one component of this notion of equality—the distribution of housework. But as far back as 1983, Blumstein and Schwartz revealed that for lesbian couples, equal responsibility for household financial responsibilities was also a very important measure of equality. Partners' interest in each individual's economic independence was linked to an effort to avoid the breadwinner/homemaker patriarchy found in some heterosexual relationships.[7] In drawing attention toward domestic matters and away from the economic sphere, contemporary lesbian family scholars may have inadvertently shifted the definition of egalitarian ideologies too far in the other direction. I draw from a sample of women who do not use a lesbian-feminist framework to measure equality in their same-sex relationships, and I examine how experiences in the families they were reared in influence the expectations they have for their same-sex partners.

AFRICAN AMERICAN GAY WOMEN AND EQUALITY IN LESBIAN RELATIONSHIPS

There are several reasons why African American women are the focus of this inquiry. First, the family studies literature identifies several household patterns that are more common among black than white heterosexual couples, such as the greater importance black women place on their partner's economic contributions when they choose and evaluate a mate, more traditional gender ideologies among black wives and husbands relative to white wives and husbands, and a greater tendency for separate rather than joint financial bank accounts in black heterosexual unions.[8] It is instructive to see if these patterns of family life are also more likely to occur in a population where sexuality is experienced differently.

Black lesbians are also a useful population for studying the division of household labor, because historically as a group they developed a gay culture outside the ideology of lesbian feminism. While middle-class white women largely came to understand lesbian sexuality in the context of consciousness-raising meetings in the women's movement or women's studies classes on college campuses,[9] racial segregation in housing, education, and occupations as well as the very fabric of social life limited black women's involvements in these groups. Instead, black women were entering the lesbian world through parties and social events taking place in informal environments that were more distant from lesbian-feminist ideals. The racial segregation of these social and political environments influenced whether and in what form egalitarian ideologies would be incorporated into their self-images.[10]

A final benefit in analyzing household organization and feminist ideologies among black women in same-sex unions is that it grants us the opportunity to examine how past experiences connected to race and class background relate to the patterns of social organization lesbians use in the families they form. Analyses of unmarried partner households in the 2000 Census suggest significant differences between black and white female same-sex couples, including lower median household incomes, lower rates of homeownership, and lower rates of employment for black women. Black female same-sex couples are also significantly more likely to have children living with them in the home.[11]

INVISIBLE FAMILIES STUDY AND ASSESSING
EGALITARIAN ATTITUDES

The Invisible Family data consist of 100 women who identify as lesbian, gay, bisexual, in the Life, or women-loving-women. It includes women in committed relationships with other women as well as unpartnered mothers. To be eligible for the study, one person in the relationship had to identify as black. There are four types of data: participant-observation field notes collected over approximately thirty months, four focus groups, fifty-eight in-depth interviews, and a mail-in survey.

I used participant-observation methods at predominantly black lesbian social events to recruit women. Sixty percent of survey respondents were recruited directly through my attendance and participation in these social activities, 11 percent were recruited through announcements and presentations made at these events, 25 percent were obtained through referrals from those who were in the study (using a snowball sampling method of data collection), and 4 percent were recruited through referrals from nongay people. In total, 131 surveys were mailed and 100 were returned, giving the study a response rate of 76 percent.

The mean age of the sample in 2004 was 36.7 years, with a range of 24 to 61 years of age. Sixty-four percent of the sample identified as black American, 21 percent as West Indian or African, 10 percent as Latina, and 5 percent as white. Thirty-four percent completed high school and 62 percent received a four-year college degree or advanced degree. At the time of the interview, 45 percent were in working-class occupations, including construction worker, security guard, and administrative assistant.[12] Forty-two percent were considered middle class, in jobs that included teacher and human resources administrator. Thirteen percent of the sample were upper middle class, in occupations such as attorney and physician.[13]

The survey asked respondents to evaluate three statements that measured the strength of egalitarian attitudes: "Both mates in a relationship should divide evenly the household tasks (washing dishes, preparing meals, doing laundry, etc.)," "If both mates work full time, both of their career plans should be considered equally in determining where they will live," and "It is better if one person in the relationship takes the major financial responsibility and the other person takes the major responsibility of caring for the home." Responses to all three of these statements show that most of the respondents profess views that are consistent with feminist measures of equality or egalitarianism in relationships. Eighty-four percent agreed or strongly agreed that both mates should divide household tasks evenly, 89 percent agreed or strongly agreed that both partners' career plans should be equally considered when making decisions about where to live, and 84 percent disagreed or strongly disagreed with the specialization model of one person taking on the major financial responsibility and the other person primarily caring for the home.

Despite their ideological agreement with feminist egalitarian principles, however, survey, participant-observation, focus group, and in-depth interview data all suggest that respondents tend not to behave in egalitarian ways. In most households, one person spends much more time performing household chores. But while this is sometimes a source of frustration for the partner who does more housework, it is not the primary source of conflict in their relationships, it is not the primary measure of whether respondents believe their relationships are fair, and it is not related to the balance of power in the home.[14] Instead, the focus group, participant-observation, and in-depth interviews reveal that self-sufficiency and autonomy are highly valued, and respondents place a premium on economic independence rather than the division of family labor as a value and a behavior that is critical for relationship satisfaction. This importance is expressed through the belief that each partner should contribute her own financial resources to the relationship.

Class backgrounds and experiences growing up provide different explanations for why self-sufficiency is so important. Many of these background experiences relate to the socioeconomic status of respondents' families and their experiences around race and gender. These analyses focus on how family backgrounds of black women who grew up poor, working class, or middle class and who were interviewed in depth for the study influence their ideologies regarding the importance of women's economic independence in relationships. Thirty-two percent of these women grew up in poverty, 33 percent were raised in working-class families, and 35 percent lived in middle-class or upper-middle-class households during their childhoods.

POOR AND WORKING-CLASS FAMILY BACKGROUND: ECONOMIC INDEPENDENCE TIED TO PERSONAL SURVIVAL AND ABILITY TO MOVE OUT OF BAD RELATIONSHIPS

Karen Jabar[15] is a forty-two-year-old African American woman and mother of three who left her husband of twenty-one years when she came out as gay. Karen is also a child of two alcoholic parents whose addictions resulted in traumatic consequences for everyone in her family of origin. Under conditions of extreme poverty, homelessness, and constant instability, she and her ten brothers and sisters banded together to protect one another from the taunting and bullying they received from other children in their neighborhood. She says:

> My life was rough. We struggled. I would probably say that we were a poor family because I could remember eating sugar sandwiches, things like that. I remember mice and roaches being in the house, taking care of my brothers and sisters and not having electricity or the fact that we would plug in the TV cord or the extension cord into the hallway socket to get light into our apartment; having the door cracked and not really knowing who is coming into the building.

In 1974, when Karen was thirteen, her mother killed her father in self-defense during a fight that began after heavy drinking. After that incident, Karen and her siblings were separated from one another and placed in different homes. At that time, the New York child welfare services agency had not designed policies to keep siblings together after a family removal, so Karen found herself having to survive without the security of her brothers and sisters in a group home for girls. She describes her teenage years as a life of loneliness, vulnerability, and uncertainty about her day-to-day future.

Despite the dire circumstances of her childhood, Karen has been able to rise above some of the challenges she has faced. After several starts and stops, she received a four-year college degree and is the only one of her siblings to have achieved this level of education. Karen avoids drugs and is able to provide for herself economically. Nevertheless, she does not maintain close relationships with her family members, battles with depression and low self-esteem, and has a difficult time staying employed. She has held and lost positions in the U.S. military, New York State Department of Correctional Services, various security positions for private firms, and several civil service jobs in New York City.

While a snapshot of Karen Jabar at the time of her interview might have indicated a middle-class status (college education and a job as a supervisor for the Administration for Children's Services city agency), her family background of extreme poverty, her struggle to complete her education, and other factors in her personal life make her experience quite different from that of many of the middle-class lesbians usually studied by researchers. These background experiences have influenced several areas of her adult life, including the things she finds important in her intimate relationships. For Karen, economic independence, even through a succession of short-term jobs, allows her to maintain some type of control over her own life. She has had a series of negative, temporary relationships with women who have taken advantage of her financially and emotionally. Regardless of the status of the women she dates, she stays employed so that she will be able to care for herself and have the resources to leave unhealthy relationships when she is ready to move on. While she has taken on more than her share of the financial responsibilities with the women she has dated, she expects "equal sharing of all of the family responsibilities" with a partner in a serious relationship, and this includes paid work. For Karen, economic self-sufficiency rather than strict equality in the division of household chores carries the most weight in her satisfaction with her mate.

WORKING-CLASS FAMILY BACKGROUND: ECONOMIC INDEPENDENCE TIED TO CHILDHOOD EXPERIENCE OF WORK AND TO INDIVIDUAL SURVIVAL DURING TIMES OF MARITAL DISTRESS

Roberta "Ro" Gaul is a licensed electrician who was born in Jamaica, West Indies, in 1966. Throughout her adult life, her intimate relationships have only been with women. Ro was raised by her mother with her siblings in Flatbush, a working-class, largely West Indian community in Brooklyn, New York. When Ro was growing up, her mother worked as a nurse's aide and her father did not live with the family. Currently, Ro lives with her partner, Sifa Brody, and in separate interviews they both said that Sifa does most of the housework and that Ro does not do enough of it. But in their interviews, they each reported being very satisfied with their relationship. On separate surveys, they both reported spending equal amounts of time on the relationship and having equal power in it.

Ro's feelings on the importance of each partner's financial independence stem from her own experiences with work as an adolescent. When asked about the qualities she looks for in a partner, she said:

> They have to be working because I'm extremely independent and I believe people, everybody should work. I grew up as a young child working, and I am still working. So I believe that you must have a job. If it means that the job is paying you enough for you to maintain yourself or your own independence, you have to be working.

While Ro links her opinions about work to her experiences in her family of origin and the necessity of each person's income to the well-being of the household, other working-class women draw on an ideology of independence as a means of self-empowerment and protection against poverty. They believe in economic independence for themselves and their mates, and they have created a life that assures their own survival when a partner is not able to fulfill her or his own financial responsibilities.

Shelly Jackson is a thirty-eight-year-old bus driver. She was raised by her black American parents, grandparents, and great-grandparents, who have all shared a two-family house in Crown Heights, Brooklyn, since her parents married in 1962. She says her father took care of the family financially while her mother was "the homemaker." Before entering into a gay relationship, Shelly had been heterosexually married twice. At the time of the interview, she was legally separated but not divorced from her second husband, and she was living with her children and her female partner, Shaunte Austin, in an East New York housing project. She is emphatic that regardless of sexuality, each partner should bring her own resources to a relationship, saying, "I don't give a damn who you're with, you always need . . . to be independent and take care of yourself." She told us she learned the importance of financial independence by watching her father provide for the family, and knew she wanted to always be able to do that for herself and her children. When asked about some of the positive aspects of her life while growing up, she said:

> That my father was always there to take care and provide for us, and that's what made me who I am today. 'Cause even when I was married, I always took that role of being the provider. I was always the one to go out there and work and pay the rent and pay the bills and do this and do that. And not look for him to take care of

me—I've seen what my mother went through and that's not what I wanted to go through growing up, being an adult.

Shelly's first marriage was tumultuous largely because of an abusive husband. After five years of kicking him out of the house and then letting him back in, she ended the relationship. Her second marriage was characterized by significant drug use that involved herself and her husband. Although her own illicit drug use ended once she was pregnant, her husband continued to use and that eventually caused their relationship to end. Throughout both of these marriages, Shelly continued to work. Had she not remained financially independent, she would certainly have slipped into poverty. She defines a "provider" as someone who has the ability to take care of herself without the help of others.

Schwartz, in her 1994 study of egalitarian heterosexual marriages, defines the provider role or provider complex as a combination of roles that give one person the responsibility for financially supporting the family, and the other person responsibility for all the auxiliary duties that allow the first person to devote himself or herself to his or her work.[16] Schwartz's definition is different from the way Shelly Jackson uses the term *provider*, and this becomes clear as Shelly continues in her description of the financial contributions she expects from her mate. On separate surveys, Shelly and her partner, Shaunte Austin, each report that Shaunte spends more time on household chores and takes on much of the child-care responsibilities. Shelly often works the night shift or double shifts, and relies on Shaunte to feed and bathe the children, help them with their homework, and keep the house tidy. But when asked how happy she is with the way she and her mate divide household responsibilities, Shelly says she became much happier once Shaunte found a job:

> Don't get me wrong. She [Shaunte] has always been so good to me as far as helping me out with the kids, 'cause my hours [at work] is crazy and Shaunte is somebody I could depend on. But it was hard when she wasn't working. She wasn't having no income coming in, and I was like, "I'm not your sugar mama!"

Shelly's comment draws on negative images of a woman's dependence on a male "sugar daddy" and simultaneously emphasizes her expectation that her partner will contribute economically to the family. But she has also prepared to provide for herself and her children in the event that her mate cannot or will not contribute her share, or if their relationship comes to an end. For working-class lesbians raising families, economic independence provides a financial and psychological barrier against a step backwards into poverty.[17]

MIDDLE-CLASS FAMILY BACKGROUND: ECONOMIC INDEPENDENCE TIED TO UPWARD MOBILITY AND LEADERSHIP IN SOCIETY

Dr. Renee Martin is a physician. Born in 1967, Renee grew up in New Orleans with her parents and younger sister in a middle-class neighborhood that bordered two racially segregated areas of the community. One might characterize Renee's family background as upper middle class. Her father was one of the first African Americans in Louisiana to receive a doctorate in mechanical engineering. After having two children, Renee's mother continued to work as a college professor until her recent retirement. Although Renee's father earned more than her mother, throughout Renee's childhood she witnessed her mother thrive in a respectable, middle-class occupation that she found personally fulfilling. Both of her parents were active members of their church and other volunteer organizations, and they played important leadership roles in their African American community.

Renee currently lives in New York City, where she owns her own home, has considerable authority at work, and is advancing steadily in her career. Renee's partner, Naja Rhodes, has a master's degree in education. They report spending similar amounts of time on household chores, though Naja believes she spends about two additional hours per week taking care of the home. Renee also tends to perform more of the stereotypically male tasks like yard work, household repairs, and taking out the trash. Both say they are satisfied with the way they organize their household responsibilities and invest equal amounts of time and have equal power in the relationship. Renee's discussion of economic independence does not mention economic survival or a worry about being able to provide for herself in the absence of an employed partner. These issues are not part of her current life, nor are they part of her past experiences. Coming from a socioeconomically secure background and having a high status and economically lucrative occupation precludes Renee from experiencing many of the worries expressed by the working-class respondents in this study. She could easily take on the traditional provider role in her relationship, relieving Naja from any obligation to contribute financially to the household.

Instead, Renee's discussion of egalitarianism in her relationship involves ways of helping her partner achieve greater independence and fulfillment in her own career. Renee encourages Naja to build her finances and to own her own property, and she has shown Naja how to build wealth. When talking about Naja, Renee makes reference to the independence her mother has always had from her father's income. She is proud of the fact that her mother has always maintained her own financial accounts and used her income to create a mutual interdependence in her relationship with Renee's father. In turn, Renee wants to help her own partner achieve these things.

The structure and functioning of Renee and Naja's relationship has its parallel in the way Renee's parents organized their marriage, as described by Landry in his (2000) historical research on black working wives. Landry argues that for the black middle class, women's paid work was not simply a response to economic circumstances, but the fulfillment of women's rights to self-actualization. His evidence lies in the experience of black women who married men who could support them, yet continued to pursue careers throughout their marital lives.[18] For couples like Renee and Naja, egalitarianism is expressed not merely through each person's ability to contribute economic resources, but in the desire of each person to pursue a life of self-fulfillment in the economic sphere. It is reminiscent of the argument in Betty Friedan's *The Feminine Mystique* about middle-class white women in the 1950s. But Donna Franklin (Chapter 7 of this volume) shows how these beliefs were championed much earlier than the 1950s in African American middle-class families.[19]

Katrice Webster is a thirty-six-year-old attorney. She attended Ivy League institutions for college and law school and is employed at one of the top three law firms in Manhattan. Katrice was born and raised in Romulus, Michigan, a lower-middle-class, racially integrated small city just outside of Detroit. Her parents divorced when she was six, and she and her siblings were raised by her mother, who worked her way up from administrative assistant to office manager at her place of employment. After the divorce, the children lived with their mother, but they spent holidays and vacations with their father, who remained nearby. He was a business executive with a much higher income than Katrice's mother had, and he continued to contribute financially to their household throughout her childhood. An extensive extended family also lived in the area and served as an important source of support for the family. Katrice describes her childhood as happy.

When asked about the qualities she looks for in a mate, Katrice does not emphasize a college background or particular socioeconomic status. As a corporate attorney, her salary is higher than the salaries of women she has dated, and it is higher than what her current partner earns. Her interest in economic independence is not to ensure her own survival. She has obtained the education and occupational opportunities to secure that part of her life, and she is not reliant on her partner's income for her own upward mobility. Instead, she wants a partner who is ambitious, and Katrice is willing to help that person move toward the type of financial independence she has obtained for herself. When asked what she looks for in a mate, she says, "They just have to have a drive and want to be successful at something. If they own their own house-cleaning business, they just have to run it well."

Her partner, Caroline Tate, is a self-employed makeup artist. Caroline and Katrice each pay their own bills, but Katrice pays for a greater portion of their expenses and is the sole owner of the home where they live. Caroline is the mother of a seventeen-year-old daughter who was born in a prior heterosexual union. Caroline not only spends more time parenting, but she also takes on much more of the household chores like cooking and laundry. They hire a person to come in and clean. They report some disagreement over parenting and discipline, but they do not raise the issue of housework as a problem in the relationship. Katrice would like her partner to become more financially stable and to learn about different methods of building assets. She says, "I try to encourage her to save because I always like to think everybody needs to have a nest egg for a rainy day." For her, promoting self-sufficiency in her partner will not improve Katrice's economic standing, but is a way to uplift her mate and help her become more stable for her own personal gain.

Among black women born before 1970, it was uncommon to have parents whose lives represented the traditional patriarchal relationship that feminist egalitarian ideologies attempt to dismantle. Mothers and fathers both worked to provide (when they could find employment), and many households did not contain two married biological parents for a person's entire childhood. When looking at the family structures of the women in the study, we see that Katrice's single-mother household, though different because of its middle-class status, was quite similar to the family backgrounds of most women in the study. Just 36 percent of respondents were raised with two married biological parents, and only two of the black women reported having a stay-at-home mother. Forty-four percent grew up in single-mother households, and 42 percent of these single-parent families were multigenerational and included a grandparent or other adult female relative. Fourteen percent of the respondents were not raised with any biological parents, and they grew up in households with their grandparents or nonrelatives. In regard to community context, more than 90 percent were raised in predominantly black or well-integrated neighborhoods. These experiences suggest that the black heterosexual family, in all of its varied forms, has been the dominant model for expectations that African American lesbian women have for their families.

Linking the Experiences of African American Women to Feminist Principles of Equality

I find that the way lesbians think about partner responsibilities in their relationships is influenced by the social contexts in which they were raised. The women in this study ideologically support the equal division of paid work and housework like lesbians in previous studies, but in practice they more closely emphasize economic independence in their relationships. Unlike the respondents in other research, they do not necessarily draw from egalitarian feminist ideologies in their relationships. Insights from the literature on black feminist thought can shed light on why this is so. Historical documents outlining the tenets of black feminism reveal that the equal division of housework and market labor in male/female relationships was never a dominant component of black feminist frameworks.[20] Egalitarian relationships were certainly important to black feminists, but unlike white feminists who saw inequality as rooted in relationships between men and women in home life and in economic life, black women concentrated their platform on how to reduce the gender inequality they believed was connected to inequalities based on race and socioeconomic disadvantage.[21]

Patricia Hill Collins and Bonnie Thornton Dill both argue that, relative to whites, black family structures have historically been more varied.[22] Comparatively fewer blacks have spent time in nuclear family units where there is one male primary or solitary earner. Black women have had comparatively greater labor force participation, and their male partners have had less earnings advantage relative to white men.[23] Historically, black women have experienced competing sources of oppression, based not only on gender but also on race, socioeconomic status, and blocked occupational mobility.[24] These factors combine to focus the attention of black women on other problems and issues outside of the platforms white lesbian feminists were fighting for.

The poor, working-class, and middle-class family backgrounds of the respondents in this study shape the values they bring to their lesbian relationships. Their values are consistent with egalitarian ideologies, but they also add other dimensions to our analyses of equality and fairness in relationships. These women create families using their understanding of role expectations that were learned through their socialization in black family structures. While patriarchy is something they find oppressive, it is not often directly related to how and why they organize same-sex partnerships in a particular way. Instead, economic independence, survival, and mobility are most important to them. The economic contribution of partners does not have to be equal—they grant their partners some leeway to complete their education, to recover from illness, or to deal with various other extenuating circumstances. However, what is paramount is that both partners can contribute as well as take away their own financial resources.

Notes

1. Examples include work by Patterson (1995), Kurdek (1993), Carrington (1999), Gartrell et al. (2000), and Mezey (2008). But Maureen Sullivan's 2004 study is one exception. Although her sample is almost all white and middle-class, the family backgrounds of her respondents include both working and middle-class experiences, which are reflected in the way they conceptualize their lesbian relationships.
2. Walby (1990).
3. For example, in Sullivan's 2004 study of lesbian-headed families, economic independence is not a direct concern for her respondents because they are largely middle-class, dual-earner couples with relatively secure jobs and financial resources. A portion of her sample is working class, but the author's analysis of egalitarianism in these families concerns how the partners divide housework and child care and does not focus on the association between economic independence and relationship satisfaction. Sullivan finds that self-sufficiency is a trait some women from working-class families were raised to value in their relationships, but it is not a deciding factor in their decision making about family and work responsibilities (p. 108). Nelson's 1996 study of lesbian-headed households finds conflict around parenting authority among partners in blended families, but it does not provide an analysis of the way respondents feel about economic independence and self-sufficiency in their unions.
4. See, for example, Ferree (1991); Hochschild (1989); Tichenor (2005).
5. See, for example, Carrington (1999); Sullivan (2004); Kurdek (1993); Moore (2008).
6. See Kurdek (1993); Patterson (1995); Nelson (1996); Sullivan (2004).
7. Blumstein and Schwartz (1983), p. 60.
8. For differences between black and white heterosexual couples in the relative importance of economic contributions of partners, see Bulcroft and Bulcroft (1993). For the relationship between race and gender ideologies among women and men, see Ransford and Miller (1983); Hunter and Sellers (1998); Kamo and Cohen (1998). For understandings of married and cohabiting couples and their financial accounts, see Kenney (2006).
9. Wolf (1979).
10. I make this argument in my 2006 article, "Lipstick or Timberlands? Meanings of Gender Presentation in Black Lesbian Communities." Even many college-educated black lesbians first came into their gay sexualities in predominantly black social circles and predominantly black college settings. See Cornwell (1983); Abdulahad et al. (1983).
11. See Dang and Frazer (2004); Gates (2008).
12. Four percent of women in the sample might be considered "working poor" because they were single mothers and their income-to-needs ratio at the time of the interview put them below the poverty line for their family size. These women have been included in the working-class socioeconomic category in this study.
13. For details on the sample recruitment and other aspects of these data, see Moore (2008).

14. See Moore (2008) for an analysis of the division of household labor and the importance of economic independence in the Invisible Families data.
15. All names are pseudonyms. The ages given for the respondents are their ages in the year 2004.
16. See Schwartz (1994), p. 111.
17. Sullivan (2004) reports something similar among the portion of her sample that was working class. She found that women from working-class backgrounds were taught "not to depend on anyone for material or other support but to survive and make a life for oneself, by oneself, because no one would be there to help" (p. 107).
18. Landry (2000), p. 79.
19. Landry (2000) also makes this argument in his work.
20. See Combahee River Collective (1983).
21. See King (1988) and Combahee River Collective (1983).
22. See Collins (2004); Dill (1979).
23. See Kessler-Harris (2003).
24. See Crenshaw (1995); Collins (2004).

PART FOUR

Intimacy in the Twenty-First Century

17

Why Is Everyone Afraid of Sex?

Pepper Schwartz

In spite of the visibility of sex in the media and popular culture, despite a widespread acceptance of a variety of sexual practices, Americans still hold a deep-rooted fear of sex. In this article, I argue Americans are more sexually constrained than liberated, more miserable than happy, and more misinformed than informed in American society than it appears. The acceptance of abstinence-only sexual education and laws outlawing sexual toys designed for women's sexual pleasure point to the existence of a cultural fear of sex. The reasons for this fear and suggestions to overcome it are the topic of this chapter.

We all know that sexuality is a part of courtship and marriage. It goes without saying (I hope) to say it is critical, although I suppose not absolutely necessary, for reproduction. Eggs can be fertilized in a laboratory and inserted into a uterus, but most of us, if we can, prefer to become pregnant in the old-fashioned way. We flirt, we seduce, we touch, we make love in various ways, or sometimes we see sexuality as an appetite, which can be used merely to satisfy an urge. Most people think sex is most fulfilling when it is part of an expression of profound love. To put it another way, sexuality is an elemental aspect of being attracted to someone, choosing a partner, establishing or maintaining a relationship, and creating a family. It is part of our lives from childhood to old age. That said, *I believe sex is also something we are deeply afraid of. Why is that so?*

Before I begin my argument to support that statement and answer that question, I should admit that there is evidence to the contrary. Perhaps you think so too. You could, fairly, offer the following arguments.

First, look at popular culture. The media, print, Internet, movies, and television are saturated with sex. The Internet pushes the tolerance of community standards with access to exotic pornography and also allows smaller communities of people with specific sexual preferences (such as foot fetishists or swingers) to find and mingle with one another. Television titillates in almost every show, whether it is an adventure story, a soap opera ("is Brad *really* the long lost adopted brother of his lover?"), or just dancing (take a look at the costumes of the women competitors on *Dancing with the Stars*, for example). Advertising and marketing use sex both subliminally (such as showing a gorgeous woman stroking a car) or blatantly, such as Calvin Klein ads where sultry teenagers have their jeans unbuttoned to show just a little bit more of their long, lean torsos. And if that doesn't convince, you might remember the ads for Viagra and Cialis, where famous men endorse the erectile dysfunction product, or silver-haired men and women are able to be "ready when the time is right." The media doesn't seem too fearful, does it?

Second, what about actual behavior among young people? The statistics on premarital sexuality would seem to belie the title of this paper. A number of studies talk about the "decoupling of relationship status and sex" and the earlier entrance of young women into sexual intercourse, resulting in more sexual partners over a lifetime. Multiple short-term relationships and transitory cohabiting relationships[1] also help increase the number of sexual encounters in men's and women's premarital or nonmarital lives. Proponents of sexual freedom rather than restriction could also point out the relatively new phenomenon of "hooking up," a term adolescents and young adults use to describe brief and spontaneous interaction in noncommitted encounters that could encompass everything from just hanging out together to intercourse.[2]

Third, but isn't everyone doing everything? Yes, that's true too. There is a widening acceptance of different sexual behaviors, and a decrease in racial, age, class, and gender differences in terms of who is doing what.[3] There are many taboos that have been broached, not the least of which is the appearance of proudly "out" lesbians and gay men on national television, their relationships and sexual preferences interwoven into the story line of prime-time television (e.g., *Will and Grace*) and some indication that bisexual behavior is more acceptable and more common than it might ever have been, at least among young people.[4]

While I agree with all these points, I still believe that we are more sexually constrained than liberated, more miserable than happy, and more misinformed than informed in American society than it would appear. And here are the issues and circumstances that support my position: (1) a national policy that underfunds or ignores comprehensive sex education and supports abstinence education, (2) a number of laws across our country that specifically outlaw sexual pleasure, and (3) our continued queasiness about homosexuality and continued insistence on a dichotomous view of sexuality.

ABSTINENCE EDUCATION

With any luck, this will change, but at the present time, Congress has systematically increased funding for programs based on a philosophy that is not supported
by any credible research. Funding for abstinence started in 1997 at the cost of
$9 million. At the time of this writing, the government has spent over $1 billion
chasing a horse that left the barn so long ago that the manure has turned to topsoil.[5]

 Complaints about the government's abstinence programs have come from
Planned Parenthood, SIECUS (the Sexuality Information and Education Council of the United States), individual sex educators, state governments that resisted
taking abstinence money but needed funding for sex education, and parents who
want their children to hear more than "just say no." In 2004, Henry Waxman,
a congressman from California, chaired congressional hearings on the efficacy
of abstinence programs that, by definition, do not give any information on contraception, on sexual decision making once sexual behavior exists or is desired,
or in fact, accurate information on the consequences of sexual behavior. After
reviewing the abstinence materials gathered from many states, Waxman concluded, "Over 80 percent of the Abstinence Only curricula used by 2/3 of federally funded programs contain false, misleading or distorted information about
reproductive health."

Waxman relied on some excellent research to come to his other conclusion:
that the programs didn't accomplish their own goal—to keep young men and
women (indeed, all men and women) abstinent until marriage. A well-done and
well-publicized 2001 study by Bearman and Brückner looked at data on 20,000
students who had taken abstinence pledges and found that only 12 percent kept
their promise. They did wait longer to have intercourse, but since they were significantly less likely than people who had had a comprehensive sex education to
use condoms when they did have sex, they were as likely to get a sexually transmitted infection as people who had not made virginity pledges or had abstinence
education.[6]

So here we have a paradox. The majority of unmarried people are having
intercourse or some kind of genital sexuality before marriage. Only a small number of people intend to wait until marriage for sex, and most of them do not
accomplish that goal. Still, legislators vote for programs that have been found to
be ineffective because, I imagine, they believe this is the safest course for them to
pursue. Why would they do this when there is a tidal wave of research indicating
that abstinence education doesn't work? Why would they fund programs whose
material is full of falsehoods such as premarital sexuality is likely to cause psychological and physical problems and that abstinence from sexual activity before
marriage is the expected standard in the United States!?

My answer is that *American parents are extremely uneasy with the idea of young people being sexual and acting sexually.* Even though the parents of teenagers were unlikely to have been sexually abstinent themselves, they are uneasy about endorsing any kind of sexual behavior for their children. If this were not true, they would be fighting tooth and nail to get their kids really good sex education that included the proper use of contraception. I think adults in America still think that sex is dangerous for youth—emotionally, physically, and morally. While they "handled it" (or not) themselves, they do not feel their sixteen-year-old is capable of good sexual choices. Meanwhile, of course, their sixteen-year-old is making sexual choices anyhow (about half of them will already have had intercourse) but without proper education about what kinds of information and self-knowledge should go into decision making or physical and mental safety. While there is a lot of sexiness on television (some of which is directed at *very* young people), no network at this time will accept condom ads! Does this sound like a sexually sane or comfortable nation to you?

LAWS OUTLAWING SEXUAL PLEASURE

It is amazing that, in this period that allows so much sexual license and freedom of choice, there are laws prohibiting the way we become sexually excited. There are a number of ridiculous laws in this category, but for purposes of discussion, let me refer to the one that I find the most ludicrous. At present, though this may fluctuate since some of these laws are under attack, about six states outlaw the sale of vibrators. I know this is hard to believe, but legislators in the states of Alabama, Georgia, Texas, Mississippi, Arkansas, and Kansas have decided that vibrators are dangerous to American morality. I was an expert witness in cases in Alabama and Georgia, and I have followed the Texas case. Legislators denounced vibrators (or any nonhuman device used for sexual stimulation) as obscene and passed legislation to outlaw their sale. In these states, owners of small businesses that sold erotic toys, books, and lotions were persecuted and prosecuted. The Texas law was recently overturned, and after many twists and turns in court it looks like the Alabama law has also been overturned. (It is hard to know because some of these results are either under appeal or an appeal is being considered.) But the fact is that legally elected officials in these states felt that prosecuting sex shops would be a popular stance, and legislators who disagreed (or were afraid to come out in favor of vibrators) were in the minority.

Isn't this more than a bit odd? When I testified in favor of vibrators, I could not base my testimony on the mere fact that vibrating devices felt great or that women deserved to have better or quicker orgasms any way they wanted to as long as their sexual pleasure was not endangering minors or pressuring an unwilling adult. No, the astute legal team felt the best approach was to defend vibrators as medical devices because they were useful for nonorgasmic women who had to learn how to have an orgasm. We took that approach and ultimately had success with it. But it struck me, why would a sexually liberated society tolerate the control—and criminalization—of the lowly vibrator? Surely, this is in direct contradiction to other kinds of sexual license as portrayed in the media and as illustrated by sexual behavior. I could only come up with one hypothesis that seemed powerful enough to explain all the money and legal maneuvering that took place—a continuing fear of women's sexuality unless it related to either reproduction or men.

The idea of unpartnered sex is deeply frightening to many sectors of American society. Pleasurable sex is allowed if it is in the service of reproduction—or the attainment or maintenance of marriage. But when it allows women to have alternatives to men (or any partner) and, indeed, when there is the fear that the vibrator may not only be equivalent but perhaps superior to the pleasure produced by intercourse or other kinds of stimulation, then it becomes a public menace. We seem to believe in love and union, but not pleasure for its own sake. This prudish stance stands in the face of the obvious natural tendency of humans to masturbate and small children to touch themselves, unconsciously and happily, unless criticized. Most boys and a significant number of girls teach themselves how to masturbate to orgasm, often before puberty.[7] And yet this has long been a tabooed activity. Even in the history of the last 100 years of Western civilization, children have had their hands tied to prevent touching themselves and, at the turn of the century, clitorectomies (surgical removal of the clitoris) were recommended by doctors who feared that masturbation or sexual interest by young women was a form of insanity.[8] One would think we had progressed far from those days, but perhaps we have not come as far as it would seem. Not so long ago, Joycelyn Elders, surgeon general under President Bill Clinton, was dismissed by Clinton because she said that she thought children should be taught about masturbation so that they would delay the complications that could ensue from precocious intercourse. Do you think the outcome would be different if a current surgeon general said the same thing?[9]

ATTITUDES TOWARD HOMOSEXUALITY

While there is much more acceptance of homosexuality and homosexuals than there has ever been, opinion is still split over whether homosexual relations between consenting adults should be legal. More encouraging is the fact that a clear majority of the public is comfortable with a gay doctor or teacher.[10] Debate has been particularly acrimonious, however, when it comes to the issue of gay marriage and gay union, though somewhat less bitter for domestic partnerships, since rights for domestic partnership are not exactly the same as rights for heterosexual marriage and it is not called "marriage."[11] After decades of political activism by gay rights leaders and civil libertarians of various sexual orientations, there has been some political movement, such as fair housing and employment laws for homosexuals in various cities and states in the United States, and most recently, the legal right to get married in thirty-five states plus the District of Columbia as of December 2014.

Personal feelings about homosexuality retain a kind of fear far beyond expectation, particularly as stereotypes about homosexual predatory behavior have been dismissed or diminished. One of the interesting ways we deal with this fear is to ignore what we know to be true about the extent of casual or intermittent attraction to members of our own sex and instead create a dichotomous category (either homosexual or heterosexual) of sexual orientation, regardless of this information to the contrary. In the late 1940s, the famous study by Alfred Kinsey[12] created the Kinsey scale, a 0 to 6 scale of sexual orientation, with 0 being people who had absolutely no experience with homosexual relations and 6 being people who had absolutely no heterosexual experience. Later academic books (for example, McWhirter, Sanders, and Reinisch, 1990) have examined the scale and shown additional systematic ways to look at the breadth of same-sex experience (fantasy, love, identity). Still, the original contribution is important as created because it shows that there is a wide variety of homosexual experience that is not encapsulated in dichotomous terms. For example, Kinsey found that about a third of his male population had some kind of genital sexual experience with another man and about a fifth of the women had some kind of same-sex sexual contact.

Because homosexuality is stigmatized and used as a way of defaming individuals, it is not surprising that few men or women claim a middle place on the Kinsey continuum. Some women, particularly of late, have celebrated their bisexuality,[13] but few men feel safe in doing so. The politics of desire seems to offer some cover for female bisexuality but almost none for males. While females are thought to be sexually labile—that is, they can move back and forth between homosexuality and heterosexuality without having the latter impugned—men have quite the opposite situation. A man who has had one homosexual experience and fifty heterosexual ones is perceived to be in denial of his homosexuality. He is rarely seen as a bisexual or free sexual spirit.

The place of homosexuals in our society is still politically and personally unsafe; it can even be a life and death circumstance since strong fears and hatred of homosexuals have spawned violence and homicide. How can we begin to think of ourselves as a sexually secure nation when the mere mention of homosexuality or homosexual marriage ignites a firestorm of commentary, denial, or outrage?

SOURCES OF FEAR ABOUT SEXUALITY

These points lead me to turn to the bigger question: Why are so many individuals in the United States sexually frightened? I will discuss five of what I think are the main sources of fear: (1) religious indoctrination and tradition, (2) the double standard and patriarchal norms, (3) sexual transmission of disease, (4) cultural expectations about appearance and sexual competence, and (5) ostracism for not being masculine enough.

Religious Indoctrination and Tradition

Whatever the Bible says (and scholars differ on their interpretations), the teachings of most religious institutions vary from conservative to extremely conservative views about sexual behavior.[14] Sex outside of marriage is often condemned, even if it is almost universal. Masturbation is not mentioned, or if it is, it is seen as sick or weak. The best most parishioners can hope for vis-à-vis homosexuality is a policy of tolerance and compassion. Usually any kind of same-sex sexual contact, or even just desire, is immediately condemned as immoral. The result of this generally negative or hushed approach toward sexuality is widespread guilt, shame, blame, horror, and anger at various populations of "sinners." At the individual level, many people trace their inhibitions, and inability to enjoy sexuality, to their religious training or background.[15]

While some religions are somewhat more supportive of marital sexuality (for example, orthodox Judaism clearly sees marital sexuality as a mitzvah, a blessing), there is still no toleration in ancient religious books for masturbation or homosexuality.

Double Standard and Patriarchal Norms

Our society has watched women's sexuality change to mirror men's sexuality. Women are now more likely to buy sex toys, to have sex before marriage, to hook up, and to be overtly sexual in their presentation of self.[16] This drives a lot of people wild with apprehension and anger. To some, it puts the family, and even the nation, in jeopardy. Sexual freedom that includes sexual freedom for women is desired by men in the particular (i.e., personal access to sexually willing women), but it is decried in the general (social policy or public approval). In the United States, women are still threatened with the word *slut* or the amorphous "bad" reputation.[17] The double standard, greatly changed, still exists.[18]

In some parts of the world (particularly the Middle East), women are killed for sexuality outside of wedlock. These are called "honor killings" because the belief is that a woman who has had sex outside of marriage, even a woman who is raped against her will, creates a blot on the family name that can only be erased by her death. While this is not the practice in most of the world, it exists in Jordan, Egypt, Syria, Lebanon, Yemen, Iraq, Iran, Saudi Arabia, and a number of other countries, as well as among Israeli Arabs. For example, one 1995 government report in Egypt counted 52 honor killings out of a total of 819 murders. Yemen reported 400 such killings in 1997.[19] Until the mid-twentieth century in Texas, it was not illegal for a husband to kill his wife if he found her in bed with another man. No one suggested a reciprocal allowance for women. The idea of a free sexual life for women, equal to the privileges given to men, is still a very new, and to many people, troubling idea.

Association of Sexuality, Disease, and Death

Sexuality does require a certain amount of physical as well as emotional vulnerability. There is a sad history of sexually transmitted diseases.[20] Without prophylactic measures that could prevent transmission, centuries of sexually active men and women have suffered from debilitating and often fatal infections. Even when those prophylactic measures became more effective, availability, promotion, and consistent use of them has been limited.[21] When AIDS first emerged as a modern-day plague in the early 1980s, all the fears and hysteria of earlier periods of contagion reemerged, and frightened, angry moralists and policy makers reacted by blaming sex, gay men, and modern immorality for the deaths.[22] Influenza has also killed many people in its time, but when sexual transmission is added to a contagion, sex itself becomes the villain. Instead of concentrating on helping people avoid infection, policy makers, some religious leaders, and multiple moral entrepreneurs go on the attack, using the medical crisis to create a moral one. Instead of using the circumstances to create good public health initiatives such as helping sexually active people understand how to prevent most disease transmission, moral conservatives attack sex itself and condemn the very health practices that would make sex safer. Thus, in the very midst of an AIDS epidemic, government figures, religious leaders, and conservative action groups have condemned condoms, exaggerating their failure rate (which is actually quite small) and promoting the idea that condoms actually increase vulnerability to disease because they allow unmarried and gay people to have sex. Conservative forces do not want anyone but married, monogamous heterosexuals to have sex, and they refuse to accept the fact that teenagers, single adults, and gay and lesbian individuals are having sex, will continue to have sex, and need the best health protections they can get. The fact that sex is so obviously not restricted to the monogamously married anymore (if it ever was) has deepened the backlash of these morality police against all kinds of premarital and nonmonogamous sexuality.

Fear about Sexual Acceptability and Competence

We pretend that because sexuality is biological that it is easily accomplished. While some lucky people get sex education and, at a deeper level, advice and information about their own sexual quandaries and challenges, most of us learn, through trial and error, how to be what we hope is a good lover. At first it is just our attractiveness and acceptability that we worry about. Each period of recorded history has had normative evocations of what is beautiful, what is masculine or feminine, what is sexy.[23] The imagery is idealized, even iconic, rather than representative. Most female stars in movie scenes are tall, beautiful, and slim. Most male teenagers in ads have a six pack. It is hard for the average person, however, to fit the media and model standard for sexual attractiveness, and a huge industry has grown up trying to make us recognize our imperfections so that we can buy goods and services to correct them. An enormous number of young men and women, and many people throughout the life cycle, loathe their bodies, feel unlovable, and have no faith in their ability to make someone else sexually satisfied and emotionally faithful. As a result, there is often anger at all the sexual imagery—anger at how it makes us feel, anger at the standards we are oppressed by, and anxiety about whether we are sexually acceptable and whether we have a sex life that is "normal." As a result, we vacillate from condemning sex-saturated advertising and media content to trying desperately to have a harder penis, more perfect breasts, or more instant orgasms.[24] So many people feel that cultural expectations about appearance and behavior are beyond their capacity or desire that many act out their fear by condemning the sexual behavior of others or personally retreating from sexual or romantic engagement.

Fears about Sexual Orientation

People have a variety of fantasies, sexual experiences, and crushes before they settle on a primary sexual identity. Because we are given only two categories of sexual being—heterosexual and homosexual—the presence of anything indicating homosexuality is extremely scary to people, particularly to men. Men are not only punished for anything that indicates femininity; they are also punished for not being heroically heterosexual (dating a lot, having sex with a succession of women, sporting a six pack, etc.).[25] Anything, from being bad at athletics to choosing not to have premarital sex with a girlfriend, could cause a man to be called a "fag" or some other nasty put-down. A teen does not have to be homosexual to be called a fag. Rather, the word is often thrown at boys who are believed to be heterosexual but who are not enacting culturally adequate portrayals of masculine behavior in the way the peer group thinks "maleness" should look. Young men who not only fail at being heterosexual enough, but who are also believed to be homosexual, or who have stated that they are indeed homosexual, can still be in grave danger of ostracism.[26] Homophobic statements, and the fear that one might not be heterosexual, and the absence of any vision of another acceptable place on the Kinsey scale, creates a huge fear about one's sexual identity and performance of that identity. The literature on lesbians and gay men is consistent about how hard it is for young people with homosexual feelings to feel good about themselves and how much adult therapeutic work they often have to do to embrace their sexual selves. Fear about homosexuality and fear about any homosexual fantasies or experience creates fear in general about sexual identity, sexual preference, and sexual behavior.

CONCLUSION

For all the sexual imagery in American society, it seems clear that we are not at ease with our sexuality at either the policy or personal level. There are mixed signals in every realm. We sell everything from cars to toothpaste on television with sexual innuendo, but we cannot sell condoms during these same time slots. Women are now having almost as much sex as men before marriage, yet there is still a double standard. We have sex earlier, and it is normative to have sex before marriage, yet there is still guilt and shame and inadequate preparation for physical or emotional safety. We still have more trouble talking about sex than doing it. We have a policy that does not fund comprehensive sexual education, even though half of all American teenagers are having intercourse by age sixteen and most parents are in favor of comprehensive sex education.[27] Fear, not comfort, lies only a few centimeters under our bravado and long lists of sexual partners.

The answer to all this confusion and irrationality is clear but still oddly out of reach. We need to reduce sexual anxiety and ignorance through education. We can do that by using well-trained sex educators, researchers, and teachers to distribute scientific data and reassuring counsel to both children and their parents. This does not mean a sexual free-for-all. Far from it. It means giving valid sexual information and help in sexual decision making throughout the life cycle. It means recognizing that sexual desire is natural and that people of all ages need information and support to feel good enough about themselves, their bodies, and their sexual behavior, and to act responsibly and comfortably on their own behalf. It means legitimizing pleasure and giving people information about how to give it to themselves and others in honorable, honest, and safe ways. It means that we have to stop snickering about sex, or pontificating about it, and we need to make it part of our mental and social health curriculum from early childhood to late adulthood. This is not a new or brilliant idea; it is merely a rational one. Our culture is still afraid of sex, and it is in our individual interest, our family interests, and the interests of public health to quash the toxic tactics used to create sexual fears and instead to help make sexuality a source of happiness in our own life and in our intimate relationships.

NOTES

1. Laumann, Mahay, and Youm (2007).
2. Bogle (2008).
3. Laumann et al. (1994).
4. Baumgardner (2007).
5. Klein and Strossen (2006).
6. Bearman and Brückner (2001); Brückner and Bearman (2005).
7. Laumann et al. (1994).
8. Schwartz and Rutter (2000).
9. Klein and Strossen (2006).
10. Rom (2007).
11. Wilcox et al. (2007).
12. Kinsey, Pomeroy, and Martin (1948).
13. Baumgardner (2007).
14. Campbell and Robinson (2007).
15. Reiss and Reiss (2002).
16. Kamen (2000).
17. Tannenbaum (1999).
18. Carpenter (2005).
19. Jehl (1999).
20. D'Emilio and Freedman (1988).

21. Brandt (1987).
22. Shilts (1987).
23. D'Emilio and Freedman (1988).
24. Tiefer (1995).
25. Schwartz (2007).
26. Pascoe (2007).
27. Boonstra (2009).

18

First Comes Love, Then Comes Herpes

Sexual Health and Relationships

Adina Nack

S *hame. Stigma. Silence.* Every year, millions of Americans find out they have contracted medically incurable sexually transmitted diseases (STDs). Beyond the clinic walls, the U.S. public remains undereducated, underdiagnosed, and largely ignorant of the cumulative harm caused to individuals' bodies as well as their social and psychological well-being. The social significance of STDs for a variety of relationships can sometimes be neglected in favor of emphasizing the medical aspects alone. This chapter charts the paths by which highly contagious and chronic infections, like genital HSV (herpes simplex virus) and HPV (human papillomavirus), affect not only intimate relationships but also U.S. families. From dating to marriage, from pregnancy to parenting, sexual health shapes the way we live and love. This chapter draws on interview data and contemporary health policy debates to show readers why the destigmatization of STDs is at the heart of supporting healthy romantic and familial relationships in the twenty-first century.

A Personal Introduction

For readers who have contracted a sexually transmitted disease (STD), allow me to welcome you to the club! After being diagnosed with a cervical HPV infection when I was twenty, I focused my first research project on understanding women's and men's experiences with medically incurable STDs.[1] The topic continues to be timely: a number of STDs have reached pandemic proportions. The Centers for Disease Control and Prevention (CDC) estimates that almost 20 million people in the United States contract a new STD annually, and those ages fifteen to twenty-four account for 50 percent of all new STDs.[2] These infections range from easily curable to treatable but not curable to potentially fatal. So, statistically speaking, we are the norm, but most of us have felt deviant or socially stigmatized for having this infection. And our social and psychological experiences affect a variety of personal relationships.

Medically incurable infections make up a significant portion of the STD epidemic in the United States. The CDC identifies HPV as the most common STD: "Most sexually active men and women will get HPV at some point in their lives."[3] The American Social Health Association (ASHA) estimates that 20 percent of Americans have been infected with genital HSV—and up to 90 percent are undiagnosed.[4] High incidence rates result from these viruses having the ability to remain asymptomatic for long periods of time and a lack of health education campaigns to inform the sexually active public about the risk of skin-to-skin transmission: risks are reduced—but not eliminated—by the correct and consistent use of "safer" sex barrier methods (e.g., male condoms, female condoms, dental dams). In addition, there are no definitive tests for oral or genital HPV or HSV infections,[5] and public understandings of both diseases have been distorted by popular euphemisms (e.g., "cold sores" rather than "herpes lesions," and "abnormal Pap smear" rather than "cervical HPV infection"), myths about risks of transmission (e.g., many believe you're contagious only if you can see a herpes sore or genital wart), myths about modes of transmission (both HSV and HPV can be transmitted via kissing), and purposefully confusing marketing of HPV vaccines (more on this later).

Sexually transmitted HSV and HPV infections, while medically treatable, often have long-term health consequences. Therefore, these STDs have greater likelihoods of having long-lasting effects on the sexual aspects of STD-positive[6] individuals' lives: on their approaches to and experiences of (1) intimate relationships, (2) reproductive plans, and (3) parenting. However, these effects are not necessarily negative. As medical sociologist Arthur Frank noted, "Illness takes away parts of your life, but in doing so, it gives you the opportunity to choose the life you will lead, as opposed to living out the one you have simply accumulated over the years."[7]

When other scholars[8] and I[9] have interviewed and surveyed people about STDs, our many studies confirm that gendered double standards of sexual morality serve to stigmatize infected women more than infected men and also that STD stigma negatively influences individuals' sexual selves,[10] often resulting in social-psychological damage and serving as a barrier to testing and/or treatment.[11] In this chapter, I draw on a multidisciplinary body of scholarship focused on STDs, as well as on formal, in-depth interviews I conducted with over fifty men and women living with genital HSV and/or genital HPV infections. I also reflect on informal, unstructured interviews I have had with over 100 additional HSV-infected and HPV-infected adults. I found that women and men had learned, via formal and informal sex education, to see these diseases as "symbols of impurity, antithetical to feminine ideals."[12] In sum, a *good* man can be infected, but any STD-positive woman is assumed to be *bad*. Not surprisingly, all but one of the women from the in-depth interview sample experienced their STD diagnoses as highly stigmatizing (to their moral characters, sexual body parts, and social statuses). By contrast, only about half of the men described their STD as being moderately to highly stigmatizing.

Women and men experience these diseases differently, depending not only on their sex and gender but also on their age/generation, racial/ethnic identity, socioeconomic status, sexual orientation, and religious background. This is why individuals' sex lives are better understood when they are examined within relevant socio-historical contexts (e.g., generational cohorts come of age during distinct socio-historical contexts). For example, Americans born before 1946 came of age during a time of sexual silence—strong taboos against talking about sexual health. Then, baby boomers grew up when herpes was a growing threat but before HIV and HPV were widely discussed. Though pop culture narratives described "free love" clashing with traditional values, the advent of accessible/effective birth control likely became a reason to not use condoms. In contrast, gen X came of age during the highly publicized and publicly tragic early years of the HIV/AIDS pandemic. Condoms regained popularity, though mainstream America was slow to rally behind preventing a disease that had been wrongly stereotyped as a gay men's issue and remained focused on teen pregnancy as the top sexual risk. More recently, most of gen Y completed high school when U.S. federal funding supported abstinence-until-marriage (rather than comprehensive) sex education, leaving them undereducated about STDs.

While specific socio-historical contexts vary, overall, STD-positive individuals consistently note the ways in which stigma management becomes key to sex-related interactions (with potential or current sexual partners, family, and friends). Similar to sociologists Rutter and Schwartz,[13] I argue that these interactions are socially constructed in gender-specific ways; most women and men make meanings of these experiences on the basis of gendered, often heterosexist, social scripts about sexuality.

STD DISCLOSURES AND INTIMATE RELATIONSHIPS: HAVING "THE TALK" (PART I)

Just because you have a STD doesn't mean you stop wanting to find love, desiring sex, and craving intimacy. It does mean that you likely have concerns, worries, or even fears that differ from the ones you had before you became STD-positive. The women and men I interviewed represent the variety of relationship statuses. Medically, psychologically, and socially, STDs have the potential to alter the way individuals imagine sexual scenarios at the cultural level and how they experience sexual interactions at both the interpersonal and intrapersonal levels. When it comes to dating, their experiences reflect a spectrum of experiences throughout the different stages in creating STD-positively great sexual relationships.

Because skin-to-skin contact is a relatively easy mode of transmission for both HSV and HPV, many STD-positive individuals believe it is ethical to tell others about their STD statuses before they put those others at risk for contracting their infections. Research on individuals living with stigmatizing illnesses confirms that they often worry about what "others think of them and 'their kind' and about how these others might react to disclosure."[14] Given the negative connotations of STD infection—promiscuity, immorality, "dirtiness," irresponsibility—they understandingly worry: *How will this person view me once they know about my STD status?*

Many STD-positive individuals feel relief from cathartic disclosure.[15] Unfortunately, sometimes these disclosures may be received poorly: negative reactions range from a potential romantic partner opting to "remain friends," to ending the relationship altogether, to clear rejection (verbal and/or physical expressions of disgust and condemnation). As a sexual health educator, I have advised STD-positive people to view their disclosures as a sort of "litmus test": If a person rejects you, then they were not "the one." Some people may at first be surprised, confused, and/or somewhat distressed to find out about your STD. But a good partner will be open to (1) learning more about your medical condition, (2) getting themselves tested for STDs/HIV (including being open about his or her own STD status), and (3) learning how to practice safer sex in ways that allow you to experience physical intimacy, to give and receive sexual pleasure.

STD-POSITIVELY GREAT SEX

In the best cases, STD disclosure and negotiations demand (potentially uncomfortable) dialogues that open channels of communication about topics beyond sexual health: building trust, respect, strengthening nonsexual intimacy. When you enter into an intimate relationship with a partner who is interested in understanding, then you likely have questions about both practical and sensual aspects of safer sex. If only one of you is infected, or if you are each infected with a different chronic STD, then the first question is usually one of prevention: how do you have a sexual relationship without putting your partner or yourself at risk? With HPV and HSV, you have to reconcile the odds of your chosen treatment options' effectiveness with the types of sexual contact you wish to have with each other.

Sexual health educators talk about ways to practice "safer" sex, acknowledging the limitations of sexual health techniques as well as human error that can reduce the effectiveness of attempts to prevent STD transmission, HIV transmission, and unintended pregnancy. Now, we're living and loving in an age where research has found that chronic and sometimes fatal STDs (e.g., HPV-related oral/throat cancers result in thousands of deaths each year in the United States) are being transmitted via kissing. "Open-mouth" kissing is a documented—though likely rare—mode of transmitting potentially cancer-causing types of HPV.[16]

If even kissing can be risky, then how can we practice safer sex? Given what we know about transmission routes, clothes-on hugging and holding hands are very safe expressions of physical affection. Non-mouth kissing (kissing of earlobes, necks, backs, etc.) is also low risk, as is manual-genital stimulation (aka "hand jobs"). Then, safer oral sex (entailing the use of barriers, such as condoms on a male receiving partner and dental dams on a female receiving partner) are among low-risk behaviors because the partner giving the oral stimulation can hopefully avoid any mouth-to-skin contact around the edges of the protective barrier. Higher levels of risky behaviors include oral-vaginal and oral-anal sex with the use of condoms: the risk increases because not all skin-to-skin contact can be eliminated during penetrative sex (risk depends on exact location of infection and whether the barrier device completely covers that area). Then, the highest-risk behaviors include kissing, unprotected oral sex, unprotected penile-vaginal sex, and unprotected penile-anal sex. With any of these behaviors, healthy immune systems and appropriate medical treatment(s) can reduce the likelihood of transmission. In addition, the particular risk is shaped by the presence or absence of viral shedding/infected cells in the areas of skin-to-skin contact. With all this discussion of risk, it is important to note that individuals who are well educated about STD transmission may decide they are comfortable taking lower to higher degrees of risk in order to enjoy different types of sexual contact.

As a sexual health researcher and educator, I encourage people to (1) get tested for STDs (acknowledging that not all STDs have definitive tests), (2) disclose their STD status to any partner before engaging in behavior(s) that could put the partner as risk, (3) ask that partner to get tested and share her or his results,

(4) educate yourself about the particular risks, (5) and then decide which risk(s) you are each willing to take to enjoy the types of sexual contact that you desire.

Single, Again?

Whether it's the end of a long-term committed relationship or the death of a partner, many Americans find themselves back in the dating pool at a later stage of life, not sure if the "old" rules still apply. Often apprehensive, adults who find themselves dating and having new sexual partners after a long stretch of being "off the market" can benefit from sexual health education that emphasizes not only how to prevent contracting a STD but also how to live and love after becoming STD-positive. In recent years, better sources of sexual relationship advice are available for older people.[17] Over time, healthy sexuality education that serves to destigmatize STDs and HIV will inform new generations on how to better navigate sexual relationships at any age.

Reproduction

As chronic viral infections, HSV and HPV tend to become more symptomatic in individuals with compromised/weakened immune systems, such as those of pregnant women. In my interviews and conversations, all the women who hoped to become biological mothers also had concerns about their STDs being transmitted from mother to baby during delivery. In the case of herpes, medical experts agree that neonatal herpes transmission is rare[18] but potentially fatal:

> If a woman with genital herpes has virus present in the birth canal during delivery, herpes simplex virus (HSV) can be spread to an infant, causing neonatal herpes, a serious and sometimes fatal condition. Neonatal herpes can cause an overwhelming infection resulting in lasting damage to the central nervous system, mental retardation, or death. Medication, if given early, may help prevent or reduce lasting damage, but even with antiviral medication, this infection has serious consequences for most infected infants.

With genital HPV infections, the concerns are somewhat different. In cases of HPV 6 and HPV 11, the two types causally linked to about 90 percent of genital warts cases,

> neonatal transmission can occur in the absence of clinically evident lesions. HPV 6 or 11 may lead to Juvenile Onset Recurrent Respiratory Papillomatosis (JORRP).

TCA, liquid nitrogen, laser ablation or electrocautery can be used to treat external genital HPV lesions at any time during pregnancy. Cesarean section is recommended only if the lesions are obstructing the birth canal.[19]

For the types of HPV that cause cervical HPV infections (including those that progress to cervical cancer), several of the medical treatments can cause scarring and other types of damage to the cervix that some researchers have linked to fertility problems and pre-term delivery.[20] Primarily on the basis of this evidence, medical practitioners have become more hesitant to recommend medical treatments for women who hope to become pregnant and have mild to moderate *cervical dysplasia* (abnormal/precancerous cellular changes), in hopes that their immune systems will resolve the HPV infection. However, a 2012 study found that "no clear evidence emerged of adverse effects resulting from the [cervical dysplasia] treatment itself," and the researchers "did not discover any reduced incidence of pregnancy or livebirths both after treatment for [cervical dysplasia]."[21]

Finding an obstetrician or midwife with expertise in genital herpes and/or HPV can reduce risks of transmission, and having a Cesarean section delivery is considered safest when the woman has an active outbreak at the time of delivery. For example, I interviewed a woman (living with both genital herpes and genital HPV infections) who planned ahead to holistically strengthen her immune system[22] before becoming pregnant. She "really wanted to have a vaginal birth," so she had interviewed different ob-gyns and was happy to find one who would support her with additional checkups to detect any outbreaks: she was able to have an outbreak-free pregnancy and deliver a healthy baby vaginally without any complications.

PARENTING: HAVING "THE TALK" (PART II)

It used to be that having "the talk" with kids meant telling them about how babies are made. In a world where medically incurable STDs can be spread via kissing, I join many sexual health researchers in recommending that sex education focus more on defining *abstinence* to specify abstaining not only from behaviors that can result in pregnancy but also from behaviors that can transmit a STD.

In addition to talking about which partnered sexual behaviors may be safer than others, today's parents face new challenges. For instance, if you're one of the millions of STD-positive parents, if/when/how do you disclose your own STD status to your child? To date, research on this question of parental disclosure has not been done regarding parents living with HPV and HSV infections. But questions like this one are starting to arise in pediatricians' offices, where it is becoming more common for parents to be asked if they want their daughter *or* son to be vaccinated for HPV.

In the United States, from about 2006 to 2009, you likely saw an ad promoting a "cervical cancer" vaccine. While it was initially FDA-approved and CDC-recommended only for girls and women (ages nine to twenty-six), many of us HPV researchers knew that you didn't need a cervix to benefit from Merck's vaccine, trademarked as Gardasil. This vaccine was designed to protect against four types of HPV: types 16 and 18 (estimated to cause about 70 percent of cervical cancers) and also types 6 and 11 (estimated to cause about 90 percent of genital warts).[23] About a year after Gardasil's approval, GlaxoSmithKline sought FDA approval for Cervarix, a vaccine that protects against only HPV 16 and HPV 18.

Several health organizations were concerned that the American public's acceptance of the vaccine would depend on whether it was viewed as a cancer vaccine or as an STD vaccine. Given the strong, negative STD stigma specifically directed at girls and women, it made sense that their concerns became reality: Initial press coverage of the vaccine trials inspired protests from some conservative organizations. For example, the conservative Family Research Council (FRC) equated it to a "license" for young people to have premarital sex. However, recent research has concluded that there is no association between HPV vaccination and increases in sexual activity among vaccinated girls.[24]

About three years after seeking FDA approval for use in girls and women, Merck sought approval for Gardasil in boys and men (ages nine to twenty-six), and Gardasil could no longer be exclusively marketed as a cervical cancer vaccine. Initially approved only for prevention of genital warts in boys and men, FDA approval and CDC recommendations have increased as the evidence mounted: In addition to causing cervical cancer, HPV 16 and HPV 18 can also cause penile, anal, and oral cancers—all of which affect boys and men. In fact, the National Cancer Institute reports, "The incidence of HPV-associated oropharyngeal [throat] cancer has increased during the past 20 years, especially among men. It has been estimated that, by 2020, HPV will cause more oropharyngeal cancers than cervical cancers in the United States."[25] With low public awareness of the risks, types, and severities of HPV-related cancers, U.S. acceptance of HPV vaccination remains low: a 2011 national survey found that only 35 percent of girls and 1 percent of boys (ages nine to nineteen) had received the required three-dose series to complete HPV vaccination.[26] With regard to the ongoing development of HSV vaccines, researchers of infectious pediatric diseases have noted, "Once an efficacious herpes vaccine is available, its effectiveness will depend ultimately on vaccine acceptance by professional organizations, health-care professionals, and parents."[27]

CONCLUSION

Sexual attitudes and behaviors are shaped by the experiences—both the advantageous and disadvantageous ones—that accumulate over time. And those experiences come within contexts of relationships with partners—past, current, and future—with family members, and even with children whose STD-positive parents often struggle to decide how much is too much to share. Many of the women and men I have spoken with came to view their STD as a catalyst for positive change in sexual health attitudes as well as behaviors. With good education and social-psychological support, an STD diagnosis can motivate those affected to learn new techniques for safer sex and also to employ more assertive sexual negotiation skills. Though a medical cure for HSV and HPV infections remains a hope for the future, now is the time to correct our social values and norms so that all STDs are destigmatized. By doing so, we can free millions of infected men, women, and children from the damages caused by guilt, shame, and self-loathing.

NOTES

1. See my 2008 book, *Damaged Goods*, for more details.
2. See CDC (2013a).
3. See CDC (2013a).
4. See ASHA (2013).
5. While blood tests can detect antibodies for HSV-1 and HSV-2, the CDC cautions, "False positive test results may occur in some persons with a low likelihood of infection" (see CDC 2013b). The National Cancer Institute (NCI) also notes, "There are also no currently recommended screening methods similar to a Pap test for detecting cell changes caused by HPV infection in anal, vulvar, vaginal, penile, or oropharyngeal tissues" (see NCI 2013).
6. In this chapter, I use the shorthand term "STD-positive" to refer to someone who has been diagnosed with a genital herpes and/or genital HPV infection.
7. See Frank (1991, p.1).
8. For example, see East et al. (2010).
9. See Nack (2002, 2008).
10. See Nack (2000).

11. For example, see Lichtenstein (2003) and Melville et al. (2003).

12. See Nack (2002, p. 463).

13. See Rutter and Schwartz (2011).

14. See Schneider and Conrad (1981, p. 35).

15. See Adler and Adler (2006).

16. See D'Souza et al. (2009) and Kreimer (2009).

17. For example, see Schwartz (2008).

18. "Less than 0.1% of babies born in the United States each year get neonatal herpes. By contrast, some 25–30% of pregnant women have genital herpes" (ASHA 2013b).

19. See Singhal, Naswa, and Marfatia (2009, p. 71).

20. For examples, see Kyrgiou et al. (2006), Albrechsten et al. (2008), and Jakobsson et al. (2009).

21. See Kalliala et al. (2011, pp. 227, 234).

22. While there are three FDA-approved antiviral medications for treating genital herpes, many medical experts do not consider these to be safe during pregnancy. Many STD-positive individuals successfully manage outbreaks of herpes and/or HPV via immune-boosting behaviors, for example, "effective stress management, and getting adequate rest, nutrition, and exercise" (see ASHA 2013c).

23. See Temte (2007).

24. See Bednarczyk et al. (2012).

25. See NCI (2013).

26. See CDC (2013c).

27. See Rupp et al. (2005, p. 31).

CCF Facts

VALENTINE'S DAY FACT SHEET ON HEALTHY SEX

Adina Nack | February 2013

What do you plan to give your valentine this February 14th—a bouquet of flowers, a heart-shaped box of chocolates, a candlelit dinner? If celebration plans include any type of sexual activity, then perhaps it is worth considering how to avoid giving or receiving one of the most-unwanted gifts: a sexually transmitted disease (STD).

The reality is that several STDs have reached epidemic proportions here in the U.S. and have become pandemics throughout the rest of the world. Therefore, a day that celebrates love, romance, and sexuality is a good reason to focus on sexual health. While researchers have discovered a lot of useful information about STDs, many people continue to come up with reasons to avoid learning the truth about these socially taboo infections. So, whether or not sex is part of your plans for this Valentine's Day, consider these myths and facts about STDs:

1. *Virgins do not have to worry about STDs*. The validity of this argument depends solely upon one's definition of virginity. Many define virginity as not having had penile-vaginal intercourse, but this definition does not necessarily include abstinence from the full range of behaviors that can transmit STDs: oral sex, anal sex, and non-penetrative skin-to-skin contact. Recent studies of college students reveal that less than 50 percent consider oral sex to be "sex," and 24 percent consider anal intercourse to be an "abstinent behavior."

2. *Only certain types of people have STDs*. STDs are "equal opportunity" pathogens, infecting a wide range of people: from "technical virgins" to those who have had many sexual partners. However, researchers have documented the consistency and strength of the STD stereotype: people often link infection status with promiscuity and other undesirable traits (e.g., irresponsibility, unintelligence, immorality, and uncleanliness). Belief in this myth leads many to assume that "screening" their partners for these traits will automatically eliminate STD risk. Lynn Barclay, president and CEO of the American Social Health Association, recently warned against anyone thinking that "STDs happen to 'other' people" and reminded us that "[t]he stark reality is that 19 million new cases of STDs occur in the U.S. each year."

3. *People know if they are infected*. One might have no idea of her/his infection status because many STDs are asymptomatic. High school health classes typically feature slideshow photos of the worst-case infections, leaving many

thinking that the absence of an oozing sore or a cauliflower-shaped growth of warts means the absence of any infection. According to the CDC, each year in the United States, an estimated 820,000 people contract gonorrhea and 2.86 million contract chlamydia infections. These infections are usually asymptomatic and, if left untreated, may have serious consequences for women: pelvic inflammatory disease (PID), chronic pelvic pain, ectopic pregnancy, and, ultimately, infertility.

4. *Regular annual medical exams and HIV testing eliminate the need to worry about STDs.* Do not assume that you are being tested for all STDs when you go in for your exam. A survey of U.S. physicians found that less than one-third conducted routine STD screenings of their patients. In addition, many people treat a negative HIV test result like a clean bill of sexual health: Approximately 50 percent of U.S. adults (18–44 years old) have *only* been tested for HIV and not for any other STD. When one does go in for testing, it is important to understand the limitations: There are no definitive tests for either human papillomavirus (HPV) or herpes simplex virus (HSV) in the absence of noticeable symptoms. Even the most accurate HSV blood test is not able to distinguish between a genital or oral herpes infection, testing with HSV via viral cultures has a high rate of false negatives, and a Pap smear can only detect some cervical HPV infections. An in-depth visual inspection for genital warts, involving the application of acetic acid and use of a magnifying colposcope, is a practitioner's best way to detect smaller warts or lesions but may still produce false negatives. In other words, there is no way to be 100 percent sure of one's genital HSV or HPV infection status.

5. *Correct and consistent use of condoms eliminates the need to worry about STDs.* HIV/AIDS public health campaigns and educational programs have succeeded in promoting the use of latex (male) condoms as the "safer sex" norm. However, two medically incurable STDs, HPV and HSV, are transmitted by skin-to-skin contact, which can occur even when latex condoms are used correctly. So, how prevalent are these viruses? Estimates are that about 75 percent of adult Americans have genital HPV infections and about 20 percent have genital herpes infections. The ASHA predicts that will increase to 40–50 percent of all men and women being infected with genital herpes by 2025.

6. *Having the "STD talk" is unromantic.* Contracting a STD, especially a medically incurable one, is far less romantic than even the most uncomfortable conversation about sexual health. Communicating honestly with one's partner about past sexual experiences and sexual health issues is the foundation of a healthy sexual relationship. The "STD talk" is ultimately about sharing existing

medical information, determining what additional testing is needed, and talking through the health risks of different sexual behaviors.

Setting the stage for a romantic Valentine's Day requires more than flowers or chocolates—a sexually *healthy* celebration of love requires education, testing, and communication. Perhaps the best gifts for this February 14th are the gifts of *knowledge*, getting as thoroughly tested as possible for all STDs, and true *intimacy*—sharing test results and talking through ways to incorporate healthy behaviors into one's sex life.

In Other Words

CAN WE HAVE THE HPV VACCINE WITHOUT THE SEXISM AND THE HOMOPHOBIA?

Ms. blog, October 27, 2011

Adina Nack

I respect that some of you are anti-vaccines—or just anti-Gardasil—but I hope that some *Ms.* readers will join me in cheering what I consider a better-late-than-never decision by the CDC's Advisory Committee on Immunization Practices. It has officially recommended that boys and men ages 13 to 21 be vaccinated against the sexually transmitted disease HPV (human papillomavirus) to protect from anal and throat cancers.

There are many reasons this makes good sense. As I wrote in the Winter 2010 issue of *Ms.*, there's overwhelming evidence that HPV can lead to deadly oral, anal and penile cancers—all of which affect men and all of which are collectively responsible for twice as many deaths in the U.S. each year as cervical cancer. However, vaccines are a touchy topic, and I want to be clear that I'm not advocating in favor of or against anyone's decision to get an HPV vaccination. I do strongly advocate for boys and girls, men and women, to have equal access to Gardasil and any other FDA-approved vaccine. Private insurers are required to cover HPV vaccines for girls and young women with no co-pay under the 2010 health reform legislation, and with this decision, that coverage requirement will extend to boys and young men, effective one year after the date of the recommendation. And, whether or not you or your loved ones get vaccinated against HPV, we will all benefit from more vaccinations, considering the extent of this sexually transmitted epidemic/pandemic, which affects as many as 75 percent of adult Americans and can be spread by skin-to-skin genital or oral contact (yes, that includes "french kissing").

However, the media coverage of the recommendation includes a line of reasoning that I, as a sexual health educator and researcher, find offensive, ignorant, and inaccurate. The *New York Times* wrote: "Many of the cancers in men result from homosexual sex." Really? What counts as "homosexual sex"? Most public health experts and HIV/AIDS researchers view "homosexuality" primarily as a sexual orientation, sometimes as a social or political identity, but not as a type of intercourse. Anyone who studies U.S. sexual norms knows that oral sex and anal sex—the behaviors cited as increasing risks of HPV-related oral and anal cancers—are not restricted to men who have sex with men. In fact, the *NYT* article itself asserts, "A growing body of evidence suggests that HPV also causes throat cancers in men and women as a result of oral sex"—so you don't have to identify as a "homosexual" man to be at risk; you don't even have to be a man.

Nevertheless, the *New York Times* goes on to muse that "vaccinating homosexual boys would be far more cost effective than vaccinating all boys, since the burden of disease is far higher in homosexuals." Thankfully, the author also thought to check this idea with a member of the CDC committee, who seemed to grasp the ethical and practical challenges of making a recommendation based on a boy's or man's "homosexuality." Kristen R. Ehresmann, Minnesota Department of Health and ACIP member, is quoted as cautioning, "But it's not necessarily effective or perhaps even appropriate to be making those determinations at the 11- to 12-year-old age."

Still stuck on the question of sexual orientation, that *NYT* author seeks to console potentially "uncomfortable" parents of boys by reassuring them that "vaccinating boys will also benefit female partners since cervical cancer in women results mostly from vaginal sex with infected males." So, is the message, if you don't want to imagine your son having oral or anal sex with a male partner, then you can focus on the public health service you are providing for girls and women who have male partners?

Instead of contributing to a homophobic panic, I thought it might be helpful to field a few frequently asked questions:

Q: Do you have to have a cervix to benefit from the "cervical cancer" vaccine?

A: No. Despite its early branding, Gardasil has always been an HPV vaccine. Physiologically speaking, boys and men could have been benefiting from the vaccine since its initial FDA approval.

Q: Why are they recommending vaccinations for girls and boys as young as 11?

A: Vaccines only work if given before contact with the virus. Reliable data on age of first "french" kiss is not available, but recent surveys show that about 25 percent of girls and boys in the U.S. have had penile-vaginal intercourse before their 15th birthdays.

Q: Are you too old to benefit?

A: If you have not yet been exposed to all four of the HPV strains covered by Gardasil, then you can still gain protection. The more challenging question is: How would you know? The only ways to test for HPV (and then HPV type) is by tissue samples being sent to a lab. Most HPV infections are asymptomatic.

Q: What's the risk of not getting vaccinated?

A: We know that U.S. cervical cancer rates have dramatically decreased in recent decades due to improvements in screening, such as the Pap smear, and better treatment options. However, rates of HPV-related oral and anal cancers are reported to be increasing—and our screening options for these types of cancers are not as effective, affordable or accessible as those for cervical cancer.

Q: So, what can an unvaccinated person do to protect him/herself from a cancer-causing strain of HPV?

A: Abstain from behaviors that can transmit the virus, such as deep/open-mouthed kissing, and use barrier methods when engaging in vaginal, anal or oral sex.

If this last answer strikes you as unreasonable, then mobilize your political energies to advocate for increased funding for HPV research. We need and deserve better ways to be tested and treated for the types of HPV that have been linked to serious and potentially fatal cancers. And, as my own research has shown, we have to get rid of the harmful stigma surrounding HPV and other sexually transmitted infections. We also need to stop inaccurately linking STDs to gender or sexual orientation. You can help by making sure your community supports medically accurate, age-appropriate sexuality education. ▪

19

Orgasm in College Hookups and Relationships

Elizabeth A. Armstrong, Paula England, and Alison C. K. Fogarty

I s the sex in college hookups good? How does hookup sex compare to relationship sex? How often do men and women have orgasms in hookups and in relationships? Is the sex in some situations good for men but not so good for women, or the other way around?

We describe college student sexual experiences in hookups and relationships, with a focus on gender differences. We define hookups as sexual events that occur outside of an exclusive relationship, often without a prearranged date, involving varying degrees of interest in a relationship. Hookups sometimes involve just making out, or they may involve oral sex or intercourse.[1]

This report uses data from an online survey of 12,925 undergraduates at seventeen universities and qualitative in-depth interviews at two universities. Students taking the online survey were asked fixed-response questions about their experiences with hooking up, dating, and relationships.[2] Statistics presented in this paper are from responses to the online survey, taken by students at the seventeen universities between 2005 and 2008. Quotations in the paper are from approximately fifty in-depth qualitative interviews conducted at Stanford and Indiana University between 2006 and 2008. In this article, we discuss only heterosexual hookups and relationships, leaving same-sex encounters for future research.

While most students hook up, few know what others are doing in their hookups. Thus, we begin with an overview of college student sexual behavior to provide background for a closer investigation of sexual pleasure in hookups and relationships. Using orgasm as an indicator of good sex, we then describe how rates of orgasm differ for men and women in hookups and relationships. We find a gender gap in orgasm across both hookups and relationships, with men experiencing more orgasm in both. This gender gap is not constant, however. It is largest in first hookups, smaller in repeat hookups with the same person, and the smallest in relationships. In this paper we delve into how variation in sexual reciprocity by context contributes to the varying size of the orgasm gap. To foreshadow some of our findings, women are more likely to receive oral sex in relationships than in hookups, and this is associated with women reaching orgasm. These findings suggest that both women and men have absorbed a notion that women are entitled to sexual pleasure in relationships. Women and men are, however, more ambivalent about the importance of women's sexual pleasure outside of relationships. This ambivalence, supported by a stubborn double standard that stigmatizes women who have sex outside of relationships, lets men off the hook in terms of responsibility for sexually pleasuring hookup partners and makes it more difficult for women to actively pursue sexual satisfaction in hookups.

These empirical findings inform debates about the rise of the hookup culture. Sexual conservatives often argue that hooking up is damaging, particularly for women, counseling that it is better to limit sex to serious relationships (and in extreme versions of the argument, to marriage).[3] They see changes in gender and sexuality as having gone too far, and they advocate a return to more traditional arrangements. Their position is expressed in the "Take Back the Date" movement.[4] Like sexual conservatives, a number of feminist sociologists and activists have focused on the negative aspects of sexual culture on campus—particularly on sexual assault and sexual harassment.[5] In contrast to sexual conservatives, though, feminists tend to see gender and sexual change as having not gone far enough. This position is expressed in the annual "Take Back the Night" marches organized on many campuses in protest of sexual violence. Our focus on sexual pleasure—and our finding that college women enjoy sex, albeit not as much as men, and not equally in all contexts—leads us to see the situation as less dire than these two groups. Most college students—both men and women—see women as entitled to sexual pleasure in relationships and the reciprocity required to achieve it. This is a meaningful change from prior generations, where women were seen as entitled to sexual pleasure only within marriage.[6] That these norms of reciprocity and entitlement to pleasure have not fully diffused beyond relationships leads us to sympathize with both the conservative distaste for hookups—after all, sex is better in relationships, particularly for women—and with the feminist insistence on tackling sexual double standards. Hookup sex is not usually great for women. It could be a lot better. Further extension of egalitarian norms and practices would improve women's experience of hookup sex.

SEXUAL ACTIVITY IN HOOKUPS AND RELATIONSHIPS

Seventy-four percent of respondents—both men and women—reported at least one hookup by their senior year in college. Of these, 40 percent had hooked up three times or less, 40 percent had hooked up between four and nine times, and 20 percent had hooked up ten or more times.

In addition to asking students about how many hookups they had overall, we also asked them for details about their most recent hookup, including a question on the number of times the student had previously hooked up with this same partner. From these questions, we learned that multiple hookups with the same person were common. About half of the hookups reported were first hookups with that partner. Eighteen percent were cases where the student had hooked up with this same person once or twice before, and in 33 percent of the cases the couple had hooked up at least three times before. Fully 16 percent of these hookups involved someone the student had hooked up with ten or more times. The media often refer to higher-order hookups as "friends with benefits" or "fuck buddies."[7] Students know and occasionally use these terms, but they are more likely to refer to them as "repeat," "regular," or "continuing" hookups, or to not label them at all.[8] When we report below on what happened in these different kinds of hookups, we'll use the term *repeat hookup* when the hookup was with someone the individual had hooked up with three or more times before.

The rise of hookups has not meant the demise of relationships among college students. By their senior year, 69 percent of heterosexual students reported that they had been in a relationship that lasted at least six months while they were in college.[9] In interviews, we learned that many more have had shorter relationships. Our interviewees told us that, to them, relationships involved sexual exclusivity, spending time together, and frequently a talk to clarify that they had become girlfriend-boyfriend.[10] While college students still form relationships, the rise of the hookup has changed how relationships begin. Traditional dating has been largely replaced by hookups as the main pathway to relationships.[11]

The online survey asked students who had hooked up while in college to tell us about what happened on their most recent hookup. Students who had been in a relationship were asked to report on the most recent time they did something more sexual than kissing in that relationship. We classify events into four contexts: first hookups, second or third hookups (1–2 previous hookups), repeat hookups (3 or more previous hookups), and relationships. Figure 19.1 shows what happened sexually in these different contexts, categorized by the behavior that entailed going farthest, as students generally view it. For example, if a couple had oral sex and intercourse, it is classified as an intercourse event. Students did not go as far on first hookups as on higher-order hookups, and they went farther in

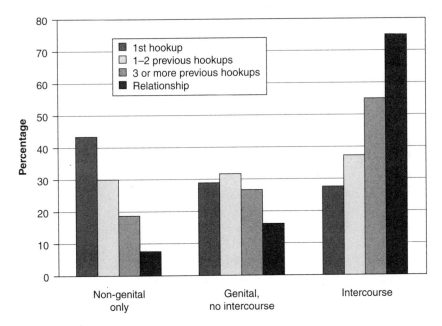

Figure 19.1 | Percentage Engaging in Various Sexual Behaviors* in
Four Sexual Contexts

*Respondents are classified in "Non-genital only" if they did not engage in oral sex, hand-genital
stimulation, or intercourse; in "Genital, no intercourse" if they did not engage in intercourse but
engaged in oral sex or hand-genital stimulation (irrespective of who gave or who received it); in
"Intercourse" if they had intercourse. Percentages for three behaviors within one context may not
add up to 100 percent because of rounding error.

relationships. In first hookups, 44 percent of students reported kissing and touching, but no genital contact (i.e., no stimulation of one partner's genitals with the
other's hand, no oral sex, and no intercourse).[12] In contrast, the percentage that
only had non-genital activity was 30 percent among those who had hooked up
one or two times before, 19 percent in repeat hookups, and 7 percent of those
in relationships. The percentage having intercourse was 27 percent on the first
hookup, 37 percent when they had hooked up once or twice before, 54 percent in
repeat hookups, and 76 percent of those in relationships.[13] In sum, most relationship events involve intercourse, while most hookups don't, but the more times
people have hooked up before, the more likely they are to have intercourse.

We also asked students what sexual acts they had ever done. Eighty percent
reported intercourse by senior year of college, so 20 percent graduated from college as virgins—a bit of information that some may find surprising. Of those who

engaged in intercourse by their senior year, students reported a median of four partners and 67 percent reported having intercourse outside of a relationship.

WHO HAS ORGASMS IN HOOKUPS AND RELATIONSHIPS?

The survey asked students whether they had an orgasm in their most recent hookup and in their most recent relationship sexual event.[14] While orgasm is certainly not the only indicator of sexual pleasure, most who have experienced it find it to be extremely pleasurable.[15]

Figure 19.2 shows what percentage of men and women had an orgasm in first hookups, higher-order hookups, and relationship sexual events. Both men and women experience orgasm more in repeat hookups than with a new hookup partner. And relationship sex is most likely to lead to orgasm for both men and women. This is partly a function of the fact that couples go farther sexually the more times they have hooked up, and they go the farthest in relationships. But

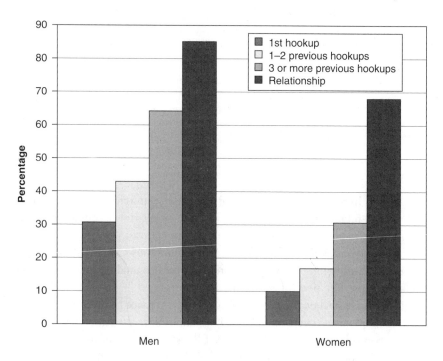

Figure 19.2 | Percentage of Men and Women Having an Orgasm in Four Sexual Contexts

this effect is not only driven by behavior. For both men and women, the same behaviors yield higher rates of orgasm in relationships than in hookups, and in higher-order hookups than in first hookups. Sex in relationships tends to be better in part because in any encounter, one has a greater incentive to treat one's partner well if a repeat is likely.[16] Also, good sex takes practice, as, over time, partners learn what turns each other on. The importance of partner-specific sexual skills was mentioned by numerous men and women in the qualitative interviews. For example, a man, when discussing why he believed women would be more likely to orgasm in relationships, explained, "Because a guy will already know how she likes it, where she likes it and how much she likes it." Similarly, a woman noted that in a relationship you are accustomed to communicating with your partner about everything, which means that "you're more open to talking about different things that you want out of the sex or if you want to experiment. You could explore more because you have knowledge about the other person. You trust the other person." Context matters for both men and women.

But, in an odd echo of the gender gap in pay, there is a gender gap in orgasm as well. This gap exists in all contexts, but it is less severe in repeat hookups than in first hookups, and least severe in relationships. If we take the percentage of women having an orgasm as a ratio of the male percentage, those ratios are .32 for first hookups, .39 if they've hooked up one to two previous times with this person, .49 on repeat hookups with the same person, and .79 in relationships. Comparing the two extremes, this means that women orgasm only 32 percent as often as men in first hookups, but 79 percent as often as men in relationships.

WHY IS SEXUAL PLEASURE MORE EQUAL IN RELATIONSHIPS THAN IN HOOKUPS?

Why is sexual pleasure more equal between men and women in relationships than in hookups, particularly first hookups? Some might find this a ridiculous question, viewing men's greater enjoyment of uncommitted sex as simply obvious. Others might explain this difference by evolutionary psychology—arguing that women need commitment to enjoy sex because of a "hard-wired" need to secure male resources for any offspring produced.[17] Some might argue that gender socialization leads women to be more relationally oriented than men, in sex as well as other arenas.[18] Others might argue that partner-specific experience matters more for women than for men because women's orgasm is more difficult to achieve. Still others might attribute the difference to a sexual double standard: women may feel guilty about casual sex and thus enjoy it less. These explanations are not mutually exclusive, but our data don't allow us to judge their relative merits. We can, however, demonstrate more immediate, proximate causes of some of the gap: behaviors especially conducive to female orgasm are more likely to occur in repeat hookups and relationships. Below we document variation in rates of cunnilingus and women's genital self-simulation across contexts, and their role in boosting rates of orgasm.

What Men and Women Give: Oral Sex in Hookups and Relationships

Cunnilingus (the woman receiving oral sex) is more likely to produce a female orgasm than is fellatio (the man receiving oral sex). Additionally, many women need direct clitoral stimulation along with intercourse to reach orgasm. This point, sensationalized by *The Hite Report* in the 1970s, has since become well-documented empirically in sex research.[19]

Cunnilingus, effective as it is for women's orgasm, is less well-represented in college student sexual repertoires than fellatio. Figure 19.3 illustrates for four sexual contexts the percentage of men and women receiving oral sex in sexual events without intercourse. If only one person received oral sex, it was more likely to be the man. But this disparity was shown less in repeat hookups and least in relationships. Men received oral sex roughly 80 percent of the time in all contexts (combining when men alone received oral sex and when both men and women mutually received it), while women received it (combining when women alone received oral sex and when both men and women mutually received it) 46 percent of the time in first hookups, 55 percent in second or third hookups, 59 percent in repeat hookups, and 68 percent in relationships.[20] Men gave oral sex to their female partners more in repeat hookups and especially in relationships. Women gave oral sex to their male partners in all contexts at higher rates than women received it in any context.

What about when the couple had intercourse? Our survey showed that when they also had intercourse, men received oral sex in 77 percent of first hookups, 82 percent of second or third hookups, 88 percent of repeat hookups, and 91 percent of relationship events. Women, on the other hand, received oral sex between 60 percent and 68 percent of the time in hookups, but in 84 percent of relationship events. And, sure enough, women's orgasm rates reflect the difference. In events that included intercourse and oral sex for the woman, she was generally more likely to report an orgasm than when intercourse was not combined with oral sex.[21] In repeat hookups with intercourse, she had an orgasm 40 percent of the time if there was no oral sex but 55 percent of the time when intercourse

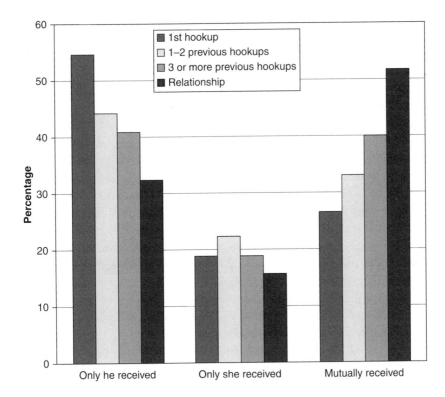

Figure 19.3 | Percentage of Men and Women Receiving Oral Sex in Events Where at Least One Received Oral Sex and Intercourse Did Not Occur, in Four Sexual Contexts

was accompanied by oral sex. In relationships, orgasms in women increased from 55 percent when there was intercourse but no oral sex to 80 percent when oral sex was combined with intercourse. Oral sex is important for some women to have orgasms, so the fact that women are much more likely to receive it in repeat hookups and relationships is part of why they have orgasms more often in those contexts.[22]

These findings suggest that women treat hookup partners with sexual generosity—often giving oral sex even in first hookups. Men, on the other hand, appear to be comparatively sexually selfish in hookups, particularly first hookups, and more sexually generous as they become more committed. This pattern is built into gendered sexual scripts: Men feel entitled to fellatio on a first or second hookup and women obligated to provide it, while women do not similarly feel entitled to cunnilingus, nor do men feel obligated to give it.[23]

This brings us to a good news/bad news story about gender equality in sex. Our culture continues to have a double standard that judges women's and men's sexual practices differently. In the past, women were expected to be virgins before marriage, while men were not.[24] Women were evaluated negatively for premarital sex, and they were certainly not viewed as entitled to sexual satisfaction in premarital sexual relationships. Over the course of the past forty years or so, among most groups the stigma associated with premarital sex within relationships for women has almost entirely disappeared. The removal of this stigma has the added bonus of making it not just acceptable for women to have sex in premarital relationships, but acceptable for women to enjoy it. Men and women agree that it is normal for women to expect sexual satisfaction in relationships, to ask for what they need to get it, and to be disappointed, and perhaps even end relationships, if they do not get it. Relationships have become defined as an appropriate space for unmarried women to express sexual desire and to engage in sexual exploration. Men and women also agree that it is expected that men in a relationship attend to their partners' sexual needs as well as their own. This is the good news, and it accounts for the greater reciprocity of oral sex in relationships, as many men now care about women's pleasure in relationships.

The bad news is that sexual double standards have not disappeared. Instead, what we see now is a new double standard, in which women who seek sexual pleasure outside of committed relationships are judged more harshly than men who do. Men and women at both schools told us that women perceived as hooking up too much, or going too far on hookups, are called "sluts" by both men and women.[25] Along with ambivalence about women's participation in sex outside of relationships comes ambivalence about women's pleasure in these contexts. The survival of a sexual double standard may be an important reason that men tend to treat hookup and relationship partners differently—in short, some men think that that it is acceptable to be sexually selfish with hookup partners, especially first-time partners. Men's lack of respect for women who will have sex outside of a relationship seems to translate into a sense that hookup partners are not owed the same level of sexual reciprocity as girlfriends—both in terms of what sex acts are engaged in (e.g., giving her oral sex) and in the care and attention to her sexual pleasure.

In interviews, men were upfront about expressing different levels of concern for hookup and relationship partners. For example, one man, after explaining that, with his girlfriend, "definitely oral is really important [for her to orgasm], you can do it for pretty much as long as needed," told us that in a hookup, "I don't give a shit." Another noted that, "I mean like if you're just like hooking up with someone, I guess it's more of a selfish thing." A third man explained:

> Now that I'm in a relationship, I think [her orgasm is] actually pretty important. More important than [in a] hookup. Because you have more invested in that

person. You know, when you have sex, it's more a reciprocal thing. When it's a hookup you feel less investment. You still want [her to orgasm] in that, sort of, "I'm a guy who's the greatest lover in the world and I want to, you should orgasm."

This man suggested that his interest in a hookup partner having an orgasm was primarily selfish, as her pleasure reflected on his sexual performance and sense of masculinity. A number of others noted that in hookups her orgasm just did not matter. In contrast, men's comments revealed universal endorsement of the notion of women's entitlement to sexual pleasure in relationships. For example, one man explained, with pride,

> [In my relationship] she comes every time and that's because I know what she likes and I make sure she does. And if I have to go down on her for a longer period of time, I'll do that. I've a pretty good idea of what she likes and it's been partly through trial and error, partly through explicit instruction. She definitely likes for me to go down on her and usually it goes both ways before we have sex.

This passage suggests—and this is reflected throughout the interviews—that college men understand the importance of oral sex to women's orgasm.

Some women complained about the lack of mutuality in oral sex, particularly in early hookups. One woman said, "When I . . . meet somebody and I'm gonna have a random hookup . . . from what I have seen, they're not even trying to, you know, make it a mutual thing." Another complained,

> He did that thing where . . . they put their hand on the top of your head . . . and I hate that! . . . Especially 'cause there was no effort made to, like, return that favor.

A third woman complained of a recent encounter,

> I just was with some stupid guy at a frat party and we were in his room and I gave head. And I was kind of waiting and he fell asleep. And I was like, "Fuck this," and I just left. It's degrading.

This woman did not consider hooking up to be degrading. What she felt was degrading was the one-sided nature of the encounter. Some women reported learning to turn the tables. For example, one assertive woman said,

> In my first relationship . . . it was very one way . . . and that just didn't do much for me in terms of making me feel good about myself . . . so . . . I hate it when a guy is like take your head and try and push it down, because I then just switch it around to make them go down first usually. And some guys say no and then I just say no if they say no.

Women provided descriptions of sexually attentive boyfriends, confirming men's self-reports. For example, in describing her boyfriend, one woman told us:

> I know that he wants to make me happy. I know that he wants me to orgasm. I know that, and like just me knowing that we are connected and like we're going for the same thing and that like he cares.

In general, students reported that their relationships were characterized by much greater mutuality than their hookups.[26]

WOMEN'S AGENCY: GENITAL SELF-STIMULATION AND ENTITLEMENT TO PLEASURE

It is not just men whose sexual practices may be affected by the new version of the sexual double standard. The double standard may also lead women to feel ambivalent about enjoying hookup sex, or not entitled to pleasure within it. While we typically think of the double standard as involving how men and women are differently judged for participating in sex, double standards also often involve gendered notions about appropriate degrees of enthusiasm, pleasure, or initiative. In interviews with adolescent girls, Deborah Tolman found that the expectation that it is girls' job to play the role of the "gatekeeper" interfered with girls' experience of bodily desire because they had to monitor and suppress their own physical responses in order to keep the sexual activity from going "too far."[27]

We found both quantitative and qualitative evidence that women feel less entitled to pleasure in hookup contexts than in relationships. In the survey data, the practice of women stimulating their own genitals with a hand as part of partnered sex, much as one would in masturbation, proved to be particularly interesting. Engaging in this practice clearly shows one's interest in one's own pleasure, and reveals to a sex partner one's familiarity and competence with masturbatory technique. We asked students if they had done this and learned that only 4 percent of women did this in a first hookup, 6 percent in second or third hookups, 10 percent in a repeat hookup, and 24 percent in a relationship. Examining only events where the partners had intercourse, it was also true that women were least likely to self-stimulate in first hookups and most likely in relationships. Like oral sex, self-stimulation helps women to orgasm. We found that among women having intercourse and receiving oral sex, there was still a big boost to orgasm from the addition of self-stimulation—a difference of 37 percent versus 63 percent having orgasm in first hookups, and a difference of 80 percent versus 92 percent in relationships (see Figure 19.4). In every context, the addition of self-stimulation made a difference to orgasm. But women were more likely to feel comfortable

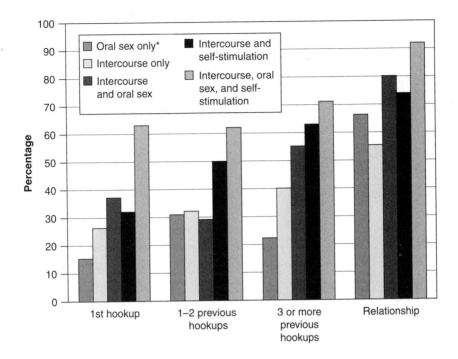

Figure 19.4 | Percentage of Women Having an Orgasm in Four Sexual Contexts, by Occurrence of Selected Sexual Behaviors

*Oral sex refers to receiving of oral sex.

enough to self-stimulate in repeat hookups, and most likely in relationships. Women's reticence about self-stimulation in hookups is another part of the reason that women orgasm less in these contexts.

Evidence that women feel more entitled to sexual pleasure in relationships was also present in interviews. This attitude was reflected in general discussions of rights and obligations. For example, one woman explained that, for her, "being able to communicate" about what she wanted and needed was important for good sex. But, she added,

I feel like when it's just a hookup, I just feel like I almost like don't have the right. Or not that I don't have the right but it's just not comfortable enough to be like, "You know, hey, this isn't doing [it] for me."

In contrast, a number of women stated their sense of entitlement to good sex within a relationship:

I think that I'm assertive enough of a person to know what it takes for me to orgasm and like be able to communicate that. I probably would try to work it out, try to give him more practice, more lessons, before I would ultimately break off the relationship. But I'm gonna say this very hesitatingly, I probably would end the relationship after having tried many, many things to fix it so that it's sexually pleasurable.

While she was willing to work hard with a boyfriend to improve sex to make sure she had orgasms, she viewed lack of success in this department as grounds to end the relationship. This sense of entitlement to sexual satisfaction was less evident in women's discussions of hookup sex—although there was variation on this issue. A number of women noted that they had gotten better over time about insisting on getting their needs met in hookups.

One woman, implicitly contrasting relationships with hookups, pointed to the more egalitarian nature of relationship sex:

I think also just because in a relationship, there's much more expected as far as like equality wise, like give and take sexually. If you're gonna be in a relationship, it's expected, like more equality. . . . You can explore more, be more fun and goofy and stuff like that, which I think is always fun too.

Her reference to exploring in a relationship hints at the way that relationships, by creating a zone in which sex is viewed as acceptable for women, give women license to relax (e.g., be "goofy") and experiment. One woman noted that she could imagine the conditions for good sex to be present outside of a relationship:

But for me, I feel that to have good sex there's a few qualities that need to be present. Like the desirability and that confidence in being able to ask for what you want or what you don't want. And if you can find that outside of a relationship, I think that's good. But I feel that [it] would be a lot more difficult to find those qualities with someone that you're not in a relationship with.

And some women did find the conditions necessary for good sex outside of relationships. The more times couples hooked up, the greater the degree of comfort and familiarity, and, consequently, the higher the rates of orgasm.

It is important, however, to emphasize that differences in rates of orgasm in hookups and relationships are not driven solely by the behaviors we were able to measure, such as whether the woman received oral sex or engaged in self-stimulation. We suspect that a sense of entitlement led to other behavioral changes by women in repeat hookups and relationships that our survey didn't measure—such as initiating changes in position. But as Figure 19.4 shows, at every level of sexual activity, relationship sex yields orgasm for women at higher rates than hookup sex (and repeat hookups at higher rates than first hookups).

This pattern is true for men as well as for women, although both context and behavior seem to matter more for women than for men. Women's rates of orgasm become nearly universal and almost converge with men's (92 percent compared with men's 96 percent) only in one situation—in relationships when couples engaged in intercourse and the women received oral sex and engaged in self-stimulation. This convergence suggests that a gender gap in orgasm is not inevitable, but it is largely a consequence of the social organization of sexuality.

Overall, our findings suggest that women's orgasm is strongly affected by how comfortable women are seeking their own sexual pleasure, how motivated men are to provide stimulation of the sort that a particular woman finds pleasurable, and the extent to which either partner engages in behaviors that provide plentiful clitoral stimulation for women. We strongly suspect that the sexual double standard is an important factor behind why women feel less entitled to sexual pleasure in hookups. The sexual double standard also permits men not to care about their partner's pleasure in hookups. Women would orgasm more in hookups if their sexual satisfaction were considered to be as important as that of their male partners.[28]

CONCLUSION

As measured by orgasm, relationship sex is better than hookup sex for both men and women, but especially for women. Similarly, sex is better in repeat hookups than in first hookups, particularly for women. The gender gap in orgasm is the lowest in relationships, in part because men are more likely to engage in cunnilingus—a practice strongly associated with women's orgasm—in relationships than in hookups. In contrast, women engage in fellatio at high rates across all contexts. The skewed nature of sexual reciprocity is in part a consequence of a new version of the old sexual double standard. In relationships, today's norms support women's right to sexual pleasure, whereas in hookups, especially first hookups, the double standard means that the man does not feel obligated to provide oral sex or to ensure his partner's sexual satisfaction. Women's behavior varies across these contexts too. In early hookups, women may feel they have to focus on limiting how far things go because of concerns about negative judgments if they go too far. Many don't feel comfortable enough to focus on their own pleasure through self-stimulation of their genitals, or to communicate what they want. In relationships women are freer of the effects of the double standard, and this decreases the orgasm gap between men and women.

If we think the current hookup culture doesn't foster gender equality or good sex for all women, what would be better? According to sexual conservatives, the sexual revolution has led men to have more access to sex, but it has also led women to be exploited by men who don't respect the women they have sex with and don't concern themselves with women's pleasure. In this view, women would be better off refusing to hook up, and instead holding out for relationships before they have sex.

In one sense our research supports this strategy. If college women want good sex without stigma, relationships make sense. This may help explain why college women report a stronger desire for relationships than college men.[29] Men, who are less stigmatized for having sex outside of relationships, may prefer hookups because they provide sex with orgasms, while not limiting their options to hook up with other people. Thus, one way to view gender inequality in college sex is as a gender struggle over hookups versus relationships as contexts for having sex. From this perspective, women try to form relationships while men try to avoid them. Some research suggests that women participate in lower-quality hookup sex because they can't get men to commit to relationships and in hopes that a series of hookups will turn into a relationship.[30] If this is the main reason why so much of the sex college women engage in does not lead to orgasm, perhaps a campaign to move all sex back into relationships could be seen as a move toward gender equality.

But moving college sex back into relationships would have some drawbacks. First, not all women want relationships with their hookup partners. We found that although more women than men reported an interest in a relationship with their most recent hookup partner, fewer than half of the women reported any such interest. At the same time, after a hookup, women reported high levels of enjoyment (even without orgasm) and low levels of regret.[31] These findings are inconsistent with the view that college women would prefer relationships as a context for all their sexual activity. Second, focusing exclusively on getting sex back into relationships would not improve the treatment of those women who choose to hook up. The woman who was annoyed with her partner who fell asleep after getting fellatio did not want a relationship with this man—she just wanted him to be considerate enough to return the favor. And third, while relationships are better contexts for sex than hookups, relationships involve a lot more than sex. Sometimes relationships lead women to withdraw from college or scale back on their career ambitions; even worse, they sometimes involve physical or emotional abuse.[32]

Our research suggests a second, complementary response to the poor quality of hookup sex for women. In addition to creating conditions that facilitate college relationships, we advocate addressing factors that degrade the quality of hookup sex for women—sexual double standards and lack of reciprocity. A challenge to the contemporary sexual double standard would mean defending the position that young women and men are equally entitled to sexual pleasure and sexual respect in hookups as well as relationships. To achieve this, the attitudes and practices of both men and women need to be confronted. Men should be challenged to treat even first hookup partners generously and with the respect and consideration that they treat their girlfriends. (They might find that if they did so, more women would want to hook up with them and that the hookups would be more fun!) Women should grow into adulthood with a sense of entitlement to sex and sexual pleasure. For women, a first condition is understanding their own sexual response (e.g., learning how to masturbate). A second condition is the confidence to ask for what they want in all contexts. This means assertiveness to say no as well as to say yes.[33] If this seems utopian at present, then it is evidence of how far we have to go to achieve gender equality in premarital sexual relations.

NOTES

1. Paul, McManus, and Hayes (2000); Glenn and Marquardt (2001); and Bogle (2007).
2. Participating universities include University of Arizona, Indiana University, Stanford University, University of California at Santa Barbara, State University of New York at Stony Brook, Ithaca College, Evergreen College, University of Massachusetts at Amherst, Ohio State University, Whitman College, Foothill College, Harvard University, University of Illinois at Chicago, Framingham State College, Radford University, Beloit College, and the University of California at Riverside. In almost all cases, respondents were recruited through classes. We did not employ probability sampling, so our sample is not strictly representative of college students at these institutions.
3. OCSLS data collection is ongoing. This uses the June 2008 version of the data. Anonymous, M.D., *Unprotected: A Campus Psychiatrist Reveals How Political Correctness in Her Profession Endangers Every Student* (New York: Sentinel HC, 2006); Glenn and Marquardt (2001); Kass (1997); Popenoe and Defoe Whitehead (2000): *The Social Health of Marriage in America* (2000); Sessions Stepp (2007); and Waite and Gallagher (2000).
4. Kasic (2008), Independent Women's Forum, available at http://www.iwf.org/campus /show/20122.html.
5. Boswell and Spade (April 1996); Yancey Martin and Hummer (1989); and Stombler (1994).
6. Evangelical Christians have not moved in this direction. See Freitas (2008) for a discussion of the ideal of purity among conservative Christian college students. Immigrant groups may also retain ideas of premarital chastity. See González-López (2005) for a discussion of sexual ethics among Mexicans immigrating to the United States.
7. Denizet-Lewis (2004).
8. See also Bogle (2008); Freitas (2008); and Hamilton and Armstrong (2009) for more discussion of repeat hookups.
9. Glenn and Marquardt (2001) also find high participation in relationships.
10. England, Fitzgibbons Shafer, and Fogarty (2007).
11. For discussions of the rise and fall of dating as a social form, see Bailey (1988); and Bogle (2008).
12. Men and women's reports of what happened in their most recent hookup differ slightly; men report a bit more action. This may be a result of men's over-reporting or women's under-reporting of sexual activity and/or of women more often than men classifying "making out" as a hookup. We combine male and female respondents' reports here.

13. While 76 percent reported intercourse in the last relationship sexual event, 84 percent reported intercourse ever in this relationship.
14. If a couple had never gone beyond kissing, they were not asked the question, but only 3 percent of those in a relationship of at least six months had not.
15. Orgasm is correlated with a subjective measure of sexual satisfaction for our respondents—and, contrary to common lore, more so for women than for men.
16. See Laumann et al. (1994); and Waite and Joyner (2001) for more detailed discussions of this perspective. Laumann and his colleagues found that married people reported higher levels of sexual satisfaction than single people. Waite and Joyner found that how long women thought their relationship would last and sexual exclusivity were associated with emotional and physical satisfaction with sex.
17. Buss (1994); and Townsend (1995).
18. Chodorow (1978).
19. Hite (1976); Darling, Davidson Sr., and Jennings (1991); Fisher (1973); and Mah and Binik (2001).
20. These percentages and those in the next paragraph use both men's and women's reports.
21. In these percentages, we excluded intercourse events that also included the woman self-stimulating her own genitals with her hand. Figure 19.4 shows that, in events with intercourse, when oral sex also occurred, it helped women's orgasm in three of the four contexts, but not in intercourse events in hookups where the couple had previously hooked up one to two times.
22. Richters et al. (2006) similarly found that the addition of oral or manual stimulation to vaginal intercourse provided a big boost to women's experience of orgasms.
23. See Gagnon and Simon (1974) for a discussion of the ways in which sexual scripts organize sexual behavior.
24. See Schwartz and Rutter (2000); and Crawford and Popp (2003) on sexual double standards.
25. See Bogle (2008); Freitas (2008); and Hamilton and Armstrong (2009) for discussions of the double standard among today's students. See Tanenbaum (1999); and White (2001) for discussions of how girls and young women get labeled as sluts, and the consequences of such labeling for their lives.
26. See Braun, Gavey, and McPhillips (2003) for a more critical view of the consequences for gender equality of the discourse of sexual reciprocity among heterosexuals.
27. Tolman (2002).
28. Our argument echoes that of Richters et al. (2006), who found that "the proximal cause—the sexual stimulation delivered to women in the typical, rigidly-scripted hetero-sexual interaction—has more to do with whether they reach orgasm (and, we suspect, enjoy sex) than with more obscure and distant causes" (p. 252).
29. See England et al. (2007); Bogle (2008).
30. Bogle (2008).
31. England et al. (2007).
32. Hamilton and Armstrong (2009); Holland and Eisenhart (1990); and Gilmartin (2005).
33. Feminist scholars often use the term *sexual subjectivity* to refer to women's feelings of ownership of their sexuality and feelings of entitlement to pleasure. See Martin (1996); Schalet (2004); Schalet (2009); and Tolman (2002).

In Other Words

HOOKING UP AS A COLLEGE CULTURE

Gender & Society blog, February 25, 2014

Rachel Allison

This month in *Slate*, Jessica Grose tells us that college hookup culture is a fiction, that despite a series of recent, high-profile media articles, hooking up, or casual, spontaneous sexual behavior outside of relationships, is far less prevalent than we might imagine. Research based on the Online College Social Life Survey with over 20,000 students nationwide backs this assertion. Elizabeth Armstrong and colleagues report in *Contexts* that "about 80 percent of students hook up, on average, less than once per semester over the course of college."

But what if instead of studying who does how much hooking up, we think about hooking up as a college culture? My own research with Barbara J. Risman shows that however much students are hooking up (if at all), there is widespread belief that if you aren't doing it, you are missing out on an important part of the "college experience."

We interviewed 87 undergraduates at the University of Illinois at Chicago, an urban, 4-year university where more than half of our students commute. Not surprisingly, we found that where you live matters. Although the majority of undergraduates we talked to reported at least one hookup, lively hookup scenes emerged where students lived in dorms and apartments independent from family, close to same-aged peers, and mostly among those who did not work as well as attend classes. What this meant is that middle class students, the majority of whom were white, were able to drink, party, and hook up far more than their working class peers. Working class and minority students were acutely aware of an existing on-campus party culture from which they were excluded.

In late 2010, I sat down with Amanda, a 23-year-old working class Latina college senior who lived with her parents in the city. Amanda worked part-time at a women's clothing store in downtown Chicago. Her daily travel between home, work, and school left her little time to take part in campus party culture. In addition, her parents imposed a strict curfew that Amanda respected. Amanda reported that she had seen evidence of an on- and near-campus party and hookup culture since her freshman year, and had always wanted to take part.

She said,

> So I remember for my [freshman] orientation it was pretty cool, you're a first comer and you're like, wow, a party life, college finally, ya know! I mean all the time

you see like flyers and requests on Facebook, like parties going on at UIC either in dorms or things like that. I remember the beginning of my freshmen year, it was just like, I wanted to go out but then I had school, you know, to handle, and things like that, but the temptation was there, it was always there.

For Amanda, the inability to take part in drinking, partying, and hooking up was connected to time, money, and familial constraints. However, the realities of her life did little to dislodge the dominance of partying, drinking, and hooking up in her cultural image of what college should be.

Where students live, as well as how many hours they work outside of class time, shape the peer groups and social opportunities of both men and women equally. However, families constrain women and men somewhat differently, with women's leisure time more closely policed by parents.

We find clear divides in college students' social lives, with white, middle class students at the center of hookup culture. Poorer students and students of color hover around the edges of what most believe would be the full "college experience," including hooking up. Let's move beyond the debate about how much hooking up goes on to ask just who is included and who is excluded from the hookup scene and why. Perhaps new research ought to study when and how hooking up came to be seen as the "real college experience." ◼

In Other Words

EVERYTHING YOU WANTED TO KNOW ABOUT SEX AND HOUSEWORK BUT WERE TOO BUSY TO ASK*

The Washington Post, February 10, 2014

Brigid Schulte

So husbands and wives who share work, housework and child care are sexless but equal? At least according to an explosive *New York Times* magazine article that is rocketing around the web like a heat-seeking missile in the ongoing Battle of the Sexes.

Psychotherapist and writer Lori Gottlieb tells the stories of couples who are striving to more equitably juggle all the competing demands of modern life, but dropping the ball when it comes time to turn out the lights. She writes of egalitarian couples saying they're bored in bed. Their sex lives mediocre and uninteresting. Or non-existent.

In contrast, Gottlieb cites a study that found that couples with more traditional marriages—she cooks and cleans, he mows and changes the oil—have more sex. And the wives in these 1950s-era unions report feeling more sexually satisfied—more turned on, apparently, by the site of a sweaty hunk swaggering around outside with a manly leaf blower than a milquetoast throwing in another load of girly laundry in the basement.

That study, "Egalitarianism, Housework and Sexual Frequency," was released to great hoopla last year. "Valentine's Day Tip for Men: Sex More Likely for Those who Avoid House Chores," trumpeted one headline at the time.

But men, don't put those vacuums away just yet.

As with anything related to sex and the human species, the truth is like that movie about love, lust, infidelity, power, and happiness: It's Complicated. And there are five things you need to know to understand why.

Here's the first: Constance Gager, a social scientist at Montclair University, and her colleague used the very same data and came up with a very different conclusion: Men who did *more* housework had *more* sex. Gager looked at men's *total* housework hours. The newer study Gottlieb uses looked at the *kind* of housework men did and labeled the tasks either masculine or feminine.

"When our study came out, people kept fighting us, they couldn't believe that if men did more housework they'd have more sex. Nobody wanted to hear it," Gager said. (Her study found the correlation was true for both men and women.) "But with this study, people can't get enough, saying, 'Men, stop doing housework and you'll get laid.'"

With a host of surveys showing that majorities of men and women around the world, particularly younger men and women, prefer more egalitarian marriages, Gager worries about the message that sends.

"Is the idea that we'd all be better off if men went back to bowling and women went back to playing canasta, and then we'd all have more sex?" Gager said. "That men get more sex when they go back to being cave men?"

Which brings us to the second thing you need to know: the data both studies use—collected from interviews with 6,877 couples—is *20 years old.* Attitudes have changed since then. In 1990, the Pew Research Center found that 47 percent of adults said sharing household chores was an important factor in a successful marriage. Now, 72 percent do, ranking chore-sharing as the third most important factor in a good marriage, just behind faithfulness and sex, and ahead of income and having adequate housing.

Other more recent studies have linked a father's housework to more feelings of warmth for their wives, and linked a wife's satisfaction with sharing chores with her husband's satisfaction in bed. (Some researchers call this a "tit for tat" exchange: he does housework in order to get sex.)

And new time diary data collected by the American Time Use Survey shows that while men's time spent doing chores hasn't changed much since the 1990s, men have *tripled* the amount of time they spend caring for children. According to time diary research by Suzanne Bianchi, Liana Sayer, Melissa Milkie and John Robinson, mothers spent four times more time with children than fathers in 1965, 2.5 times more in 1995 and 1.9 times more in 2009–2010.

So what does that have to do with sex?

Here's the third thing: With people working long hours and spending so much time with kids, never mind cooking and cleaning, they don't have much time for sex anymore. Or they're too exhausted. A roll in the hay can instead become just another nagging chore to be checked off the To Do list.

That theme runs throughout Gottlieb's provocative piece. "The modern marital tableau," she quotes someone at a dinner party quipping, "is two overwhelmed people trying to relax before bed: he on Pornhub, she on Pinterest. Then they kiss and go to sleep."

But is it just people in egalitarian marriages not having sex?

Point number four: The National Health and Social Life Survey estimates that one in every five marriages in the U.S. are what it deems "sexless"—engaging in sex less than ten times a year.

And anecdotes of lackluster sex lives abound, regardless of who's cooking dinner or mopping the floor. Just take a peek at the DeadBedrooms chat room on Reddit, a support group for people "who are coping with a relationship without any physical intimacy in it." It had 11,873 readers on a recent day.

Which leads to the fifth and final thing you need to know: We don't know as much about sex as we think.

Gottlieb writes that egalitarian marriages are dull between the sheets because the partners are too alike. And while it's nice to have a "kindred spirit," it's not hot.

"What's hot is being different, mysterious, unpredictable, and having power imbalance," a sex therapist explained to me, "all things that can make for a conflict-ridden marriage reminiscent of those depicted on Mad Men, where the men have all the power."

That sexy power imbalance, Gottlieb argues, may be why so many women were drawn to the erotic blockbuster Fifty Shades of Grey and its fantasies of male domination and female submission.

The sex therapist encouraged people in egalitarian marriages to "get creative" to spice up their differences.

But Sinikka Elliott, a sociologist who studies gender, sexuality and inequality at North Carolina State University, said, it was time, instead, to throw out outdated gender "sexual scripts."

"Here's a possible scenario: you have an exhausted husband who's put in long hours in paid and unpaid labor . . . and has consequently had less leisure time and less time to fantasize about sex, and is less likely to initiate sex. Meanwhile, his wife may not feel empowered to take over this role and he may not want her to because men are 'supposed' to initiate sex," Elliott wrote in an email.

So it's not that a man needs to do less housework, or drop the iron for the lawn-mower to get more sex, as the study Gottlieb writes about suggests. Instead, society needs to get over centuries of harshly repressing women's sexuality, Elliott wrote, "so that women and men can feel more confident and comfortable with women initiating sex and acting on sexual desire."

Natalie Angier, the New York Times science writer, in her fascinating book, "Woman: An Intimate Geography," takes on long-held assumptions that women just don't want sex as much as men do, and have to be pursued, won over with chocolates, wowed by manly wood chopping or obligated after a grudging bout of vacuuming.

"Men have the naturally higher sex drive, yet all the laws, customs, punishments, shame, strictures, mystiques, and anti mystiques are aimed with full hominid fury at that tepid, sleepy, hypoactive creature the female libido," she writes. "How can we know what is 'natural' for us when we are treated as unnatural for wanting our lust?"

After all, she writes, female primates, who share so much of our DNA, are pretty randy creatures.

In the end, what strikes me most about all the fury about sex and housework is just how much we are still on the bleeding edge of the first massive shift in gender roles since, oh, the Pleistocene era. It's not surprising that things are confusing. And the demands of modern life leave us little time to sort them out.

But rather than mourn the supposedly sexier unions of the past, with dominant men and submissive women, or lament that the current move to egalitarian partnerships leaves us sexless roommates, why not, as Elliott suggests, throw out the old sexual scripts. Why not begin to imagine something entirely new—not only a fairer division of labor, but a more honest expression of our human sexuality?

Now that's something to fantasize about. ▬

PART FIVE

Marriage and Divorce: Does Policy Matter?

20

The Marriage Movement

Orit Avishai, Melanie Heath, and Jennifer Randles[1]

A cultural development that has played a role in eroding the standing of marriage is that moderately educated Americans are markedly less likely than are highly educated Americans to embrace the bourgeois values and virtues—for instance, delayed gratification, a focus on education, and temperance—that are the sine qua nons of personal and marital success in the contemporary United States. By contrast, highly educated Americans (and their children) adhere devoutly to a "success sequence" norm that puts education, work, marriage, and childbearing in sequence, one after another, in ways that maximize their odds of making good on the American Dream and obtaining a successful family life.

—Brad Wilcox, *The State of Our Unions* (2010)

This quotation, from sociologist Brad Wilcox, comes from a report[2] used to stake claims and support something we examine in this chapter—the marriage movement in the United States. As the quotation suggests, at the center of the marriage movement is a belief in the "marriage cure": that we can reduce poverty by promoting and strengthening marriage. The early twenty-first century will be remembered as a time of contentious debates about marriage in the United States. Most Americans are familiar with demands to equalize the marriage playing field among heterosexual and same-sex couples. Less known is that the marriage equality debate was part of broader political and cultural conversations about the implications of changing families on sustaining a successful society.

The marriage equality debate has featured a vast gap between conservatives and liberals about desirable family models and the best contexts for raising children. But conservatives and liberals are more united in their concerns about other heterosexual marriage-related issues, including the implications of lower marriage rates and the rise of cohabitation and single motherhood, especially for poor and working-class Americans and their children who have a harder time following the "success sequence." While they agree on the existence of marriage- and family-related problems, conservatives and liberals vary widely in their assessments of the causes of these demographic shifts and desired policy responses. These different perspectives were all featured in the "marriage movement" that emerged in the late twentieth century, aiming to revitalize marriage and reverse the trends in family formation of the past few decades that saw fewer people start lifelong marriages before having children.

This chapter provides an overview of the marriage debates in the late twentieth and early twenty-first centuries, focusing particularly on one policy response to changing family demographics: efforts by a variety of faith-based, community, and government-funded organizations to promote marriage and educate American heterosexual couples about the benefits of marriage and healthy relationship dynamics. Each of us has studied marriage promotion policy and the marriage education movement. Avishai attended marriage education conferences, visited marriage education organizations, and interviewed dozens of individuals involved in marriage education around the country. Heath traveled to Oklahoma to do eleven months of ethnographic research on a statewide initiative that seeks to promote and strengthen marriage throughout the state. Randles studied twenty government-funded marriage education programs and spent eighteen months studying one program she calls "Thriving Families" that targeted low-income unmarried couples who were expecting or just had a new baby. All of us participated in and observed numerous marriage education classes, interviewed participants and instructors, and examined how marriage education unfolds on the ground.

We were struck by two similar puzzles. First, most sociologists, demographers, and historians agree that character-based explanations—such as individuals' failure to follow the "success sequence"—do injustice to persistent patterns of social and economic inequalities surrounding family formation. Yet the marriage education movement has largely ignored the patterns underlying inequality at the heart of shifting family forms. Second, while marriage education and promotion policies were billed as antipoverty measures, they had limited effect on poverty. Instead, our fieldwork pointed to a different likely explanation for the embrace of these policies: a moral battle against changing family forms. In what follows, we take you through the emergence and growth of the marriage movement to explain these puzzles, trace the debates and controversies over its philosophy and policies, and offer insight into how these debates played out on the ground.

EMPIRICAL REALITIES: THE MARRIAGE GAP

When scholars and activists refer to the marriage debates, they typically mean debates over marriage equality: the question of whether same-sex couples should have the right to legally marry. The political battle over same-sex marriage rights is an issue of equality and citizenship because marriage is associated with a variety of legal, social, and economic benefits, including rights to inheritance, hospital visitation, insurance coverage, and social recognition of one's intimate relationship, among numerous others. This important issue of marriage equality tends to garner the most public attention concerning what sociologists call "intimate inequalities."

Intimate inequalities is a phrase first coined by sociologist Ken Plummer[3] to describe how social and economic inequalities shape the most personal aspects of our lives. The term provides a useful analytic lens to assess other trends in contemporary American family life, because it emphasizes that our access to economic resources, social recognition, and political rights is affected by and reflective of our marital status. This is one of the main reasons legal battles over marriage equality are so significant. However, other changes in the structure of family life in the United States have also contributed to intimate inequalities. Changing patterns in family life have accelerated in the second half of the twentieth century and are contributing to class inequalities. Americans still almost universally aspire to marry, but their social class largely predicts whether they will marry. Sociologists find that Americans who live below or near the poverty line are more likely to delay or avoid marriage indefinitely compared to the more economically advantaged, or those who have more education, make more money, and struggle less with finding consistent, well-paying employment. Poor and low-income Americans are also significantly more likely to cohabit before marriage, have children outside of marriage, and have children with more than one partner.[4]

Social scientists refer to this social class disparity in marriage rates as the marriage gap. This gap is important because children who grow up in always-married families tend to benefit from the economic and relational stability that is often associated with marriage. There is evidence that, on average, children raised in two-parent families do better on a number of outcomes than children who grow up with just one parent. These outcomes include better educational achievement and fewer substance abuse and behavioral problems, among others.[5] In other words, the family as a social institution is a primary mechanism of inequality that perpetuates class divisions from one generation to the next, a cycle that sociologists refer to as *social reproduction*. The higher one sits on the socioeconomic ladder, the more likely she or he is to get married, stay married, and have children *after* getting married.[6] As we turn to consider the marriage movement's goals and strategies, it is important to keep in mind that social trends of concern to the marriage movement—cohabitation, nonmarital childbearing, and divorce—are significantly more common among socially and economically disadvantaged groups.

THE IDEOLOGICAL DEBATE: WHAT IS THE SIGNIFICANCE OF MARRIAGE?

Social commentators of all ideological stripes agree on the demographics of the marriage gap. However, they vary widely in their analyses of the causes of these gaps and their implications for individuals and American society as a whole. Sociologists such as Brad Wilcox, author of *The State of Our Unions* report cited in the epigraph, focus on individual *choices*—like the failure to follow the "success sequences." Others, like historian Stephanie Coontz and sociologist Andrew Cherlin, focus on demographic and cultural shifts that demonstrate that the marriage gap, like other changes in marriage and family life of the past half-century, is intimately linked to broader changes in American society. According to Coontz, in America and throughout much of the world, the social norms that once regulated decisions about heterosexual marriage have relaxed in favor of ones that privilege the emotional component of marriage.[7] Love, personal choice, and self-fulfillment compete with laws, religious sanctions, and economic constraints as the social glue of marriage and family.

Transformations in family and sexual mores have been centuries in the making, but they began to accelerate in the 1960s in tandem with other social and economic developments. Over a twenty-year period, between the 1960s and mid-1980s, the divorce rate more than doubled. By the early 1980s, one out of six births occurred outside marriage, and by the twenty-first century, this figure had grown to one out of three. Yet not all children are similarly affected by these changes. Most of the children born to unmarried parents are born into poverty or low-income homes, and African American and Hispanic children are more likely to be born to unmarried, low-income parents.[8]

Scholars disagree about the social and cultural meanings of these changes. Some argue that we are witnessing a family crisis because most people now deviate from traditional family-formation patterns that put lifelong marriage at the center of family and social life. They argue that excessive individualism is undermining the institution of marriage, as indicated by high divorce rates and the growing number of individuals who cohabit and have children outside of marriage. In other words, these changes are reflective of pervasive moral failures. Others claim that family life is not deteriorating but simply changing to accommodate more egalitarian gender dynamics, economic restructuring, and growing social acceptance of diverse family forms. Cherlin argues that we have a unique marriage culture in the United States, one in which marriage as a cultural ideal is stronger than elsewhere in the developed world. Americans have one of the highest marriage and divorce rates of all Western industrialized countries, a trend that can be explained in large part by the simultaneous and often contradictory commitments of Americans to stable and secure lifelong marriage and to individual fulfillment and self-expression that justifies ending marriages when they cease to be happy.[9]

These empirical realities, competing interpretations of the meanings of marriage in the United States, and divergent assessments of the implications had social activists, politicians, and academics scratching their heads about the best ways to respond. In the late 1990s a potential solution emerged in the form of a marriage movement that sought to encourage marriage, discourage divorce, and improve the relationships of American couples. The movement brought together an unlikely coalition of therapists, clergy and other religious leaders, community activists, politicians, think tanks, welfare agencies, and government officials. Its goal was lofty: to implement a renaissance of marriage in the United States.[10] Some in the movement were motivated primarily by the moral implications of what they viewed as the decline of the "natural" nuclear family; the "marriage decline" camp also tended to support legislation to define marriage as a union of one man and one woman. Others were more concerned about the empirical outcomes of changing family forms; they focused on structural patterns, such as unemployment and poverty, rather than individual failures. Though their ideological convictions varied widely—for example, the conservative Heritage Foundation and the centrist Brookings Institute were on board—movement participants were united by their belief that a reinvigorated marriage culture could address the range of social problems associated with single motherhood, prolonged cohabitation, and high divorce rates. Mirroring the diversity of actors, the marriage movement promoted a variety of initiatives, including introducing divorce reform (undoing no-fault divorce and expanding options such as covenant marriage through which couples agree to limited grounds for and restrictions on divorce, such as mandatory marital counseling); rejuvenating marriage culture; developing fatherhood initiatives; and opposing same-sex marriage.

MAKING A MARRIAGE MOVEMENT: PROMOTION AND EDUCATION

The marriage movement seeks to expand the role of government, schools, and social service agencies in reinstitutionalizing marriage—that is, revitalizing marriage as a key institution in American society. It was officially set in motion in 2000 with the release of "A Statement of Principles," whose 113 signatories included a number of prominent conservatives and a few self-identified liberals. The marriage movement sought to implement these principles through promotion of policies in state and federal legislatures and services such as relationship skills training and parenting classes.

The marriage movement ideologically and practically privileges marriage as the ideal way to shape one's intimate life and create a family. It intersected with several other national conversations and policy changes, in particular the growing debate about marriage equality and the enactment of the Defense of Marriage Act—subsequently declared unconstitutional by the Supreme Court in June 2013 as a violation of personal liberty protected by the Fifth Amendment— which explicitly defined marriage as between one man and one woman; President George W. Bush's Faith Based Initiative, which allowed federal funding of faith-based organizations[11]; the rewriting of welfare under President Clinton, which included provisions to directly promote marriage and two-parent families using public money; and the emergence of a range of state and community marriage initiatives, including one in Oklahoma that we describe later.

While the debate over marriage equality produced legislation and constitutional amendments to ban same-sex marriage, debates over changing family structures led to policies to promote heterosexual marriage. The cornerstone of these policies, the 2002 federal Healthy Marriage Initiative (HMI), paved the way for a patchwork of funding that added up to about $200 million for marriage-promotion activities. The 2005 welfare renewal legislation included $500 million for marriage programs through 2011. In 2011, under President Obama, Congress approved $75 million for marriage-promotion activities for that fiscal year. Individual states have also used portions of their federal Temporary Assistance to Needy Families (TANF) grants for marriage-promotion activities.

The idea was simple: State and federal funds would be used to both promote marriage as the best family context in which to raise children and provide couples with skills for succeeding at their relationships. This, in turn, would address high rates of divorce, cohabitation, and single motherhood, leading to reduced poverty rates. Oklahoma, which launched a statewide initiative in 1999, provided a blueprint for the national movement while community organizations, including welfare agencies and faith-based organizations, provided the boots on the ground to test out these new initiatives around the country. Yet, as we discuss later, over time, much of the federal and state funding has gone to programs that provide "marriage and relationship education," with the goal of preventing marital distress and divorce and strengthening relationships and marriages, without paying much attention to the specific needs of individuals living in poverty.

Marriage education involves classes and workshops based on the premise that marital success is rooted in couple dynamics and individual skills—such as how spouses divide household chores, fight, and spend their leisure time—and that such dynamics and skills can be altered and taught. Therapists, clinical psychologists, and other students of human relationship dynamics have amassed knowledge about how relationships work. Studies of such dynamics have coalesced into a relationship science—a multidisciplinary endeavor that draws on empirical work from psychology, sociology, communication studies, and economics to theorize the basic laws that shape satisfying interpersonal interactions. As evidence mounted that marriage failure or success hinges on predictable patterns of interpersonal interaction, relationship experts began to translate this knowledge into teachable skills. Marriage education is an applied extension of this work.

The logic, repeated by marriage educators we have interviewed and observed across the country, is deceivingly simple: having a healthy marriage is something one can *learn*. People who receive the information, practice the skills, and develop the attributes known to be linked to healthy marriages will be able to achieve marital bliss—or at least transcend the marital blah, or the everyday rut. Unlike couples therapy, which involves a single couple and a trained psychologist, marriage education is delivered to several—sometimes dozens—of couples at a time, typically by a team consisting of a male and a female educator (often a married couple). There are numerous programs on the market, though some industry favorites enjoy particular financial success and visibility. Programs typically include units that address communication and conflict resolution skills, goal setting, benefits of marriage, and financial management techniques such as budgeting. They deliver this content through alternating periods of instructor presentation, group discussion, and couple exercises. Educators typically need to be certified to teach a certain curriculum, but these requirements vary widely across programs.

While relationship-enhancing programs are not a novelty, government-funded marriage-promotion programs extend the basic premise of helping couples to enjoy better marriages into a new realm: these better marriages, the proponents hold, can alleviate poverty. The philosophy sees single parenthood as a *cause* of poverty, and supporters argue that strengthening marriage represents a plausible poverty-reduction strategy. For example, author Kay Hymowitz of the Manhattan Institute, a proponent of and key actor in the marriage movement, argues that marriage has become paramount in the transmission of class privilege from one generation to the next because highly educated, middle-class people prepare "for marriage by becoming self-sufficient and looking for the right partner to share a home and children."[12] Hymowitz believes that those in poverty who delay marriage neither value marriage nor make major life decisions with the goal of creating a stable married family life. Hymowitz's logic is strikingly similar to that articulated in *The State of Our Unions* report and is widely shared by others in the marriage movement. Put simply: Marriage makes you a better, happier, and healthier person, and marriage causes a reduction in poverty; therefore, marriage is good for people and good for society.

The real picture, however, is much more complicated. Sociologists Kathryn Edin and Maria Kefalas found that poor and low-income women highly value marriage but view it as a luxury they may never achieve, because they find it difficult to reach the high economic bar for marriage.[13] Like many Americans, they believe that to be ready for marriage, they and their future spouse must be financially secure first and need to accomplish certain economic and social milestones such as finishing school; getting a secure, well-paying job; and being able to afford a nice wedding.[14] In other words, poor and low-income women are well aware of the "success sequence" of which marriage proponents speak. But these pre-marriage milestones are significantly harder for them to reach because of economic and social hardships that have little to do with marriage.

Here's the catch: Marriage advocates view low-income people's lower rates of marriage as a failure that can and should be fixed by educating them about the importance of marriage—but neglect the economic and job-market realities that underpin people's choices about marriage and family. Meanwhile, marriage-promotion policy represents an unprecedented attempt to intervene with the marriage and childbearing decisions of Americans, and especially of low-income Americans. While it was heralded as a solution for a range of social problems such as teenage pregnancy, high crime rates, and low high school graduation rates, the policy has failed to achieve its goals of increasing marriage rates, reducing poverty, and significantly improving the relationships of couples attending government-funded programs. In 2012, researchers released final results from a government-funded healthy marriage evaluation project. Building Strong Families (BSF) is a relationship-strengthening program for low-income unmarried parents.[15] Of the eight BSF sites that participated in the study, only one—a BSF program in Oklahoma—had a positive impact on couples' relationship quality and stability. None of the programs affected the marriage rates of unmarried, poor couples. There are also no indications that marriage education programs have had an impact on rates of cohabitation, divorce, or single motherhood.

Our collective work provides insight into why marriage-promotion policies have not delivered on their antipoverty goals. As we unravel this puzzle, we also highlight the kinds of tensions, successes, and implementation challenges the larger marriage movement faces.

Good Communication, Not Marriage

Since 2002, the federal government has funded hundreds of relationship-strengthening and marriage education programs across the country, many targeting poor and low-income unmarried couples who are expecting or just had a new baby. The logic of targeting this particular social group is that couples might consider the time around a child's birth as a "magic moment" or unique window of opportunity to get married and create a more stable married family.

Yet, in her research on Thriving Families, Randles found that, in line with previous sociological research on the marriage gap between low-income and more affluent Americans, couples in this program delayed marriage because of a phenomenon she calls *curtailed commitment*—the belief that if a couple cannot live up to middle-class norms of family life, including meeting a specific economic threshold, they are not equipped for marriage.[16] Randles also found that parents responded positively to instruction in co-parenting and communication skills because they felt empowered and better equipped to be better partners and parents.[17] Couples viewed the classes as a rare opportunity to learn communication skills in an environment free of the material constraints that overwhelmingly characterized their daily lives and their intimate relationships. The classes offered parents in poverty a free and safe collective space to discuss romantic and parenting challenges, and this helped normalize the relationship conflicts that they experienced. Furthermore, the classes helped couples recognize that others shared their struggles and that their relationship challenges were not necessarily the result of personal or psychological shortcomings, but rather related to the challenges of trying to raise a family and keep a relationship intact while living in poverty. Mason, a twenty-four-year-old white father, told Randles during an interview that he really appreciated the relationship skills classes because:

> you figure out what your problems were. You have to know what your issues are before you can address them together. . . . And with everyone else in the classes, you're not the only one going through it. Everyone has the same problems. . . . Everybody was all in the same boat. They were all not married, having a baby, whether it was their first, second, or fourth kid. They were all there wanting to work on their relationship and help build a family.

While couples benefited from learning to better communicate and understand their situation in context, Randles also found that economic challenges significantly impeded the usefulness of the classes. Practicing the skills they learned in class required parents to have control over their time, living space, and finances. But the couples did not always have access to these advantages given their frequent need to work multiple low-wage jobs; live with many others in small, crowded apartments; and struggle with making financial ends meet. Thus, although Thriving Families staff and instructors effectively devised strategies that appealed to low-income parents, they were not always able to enact the strategies outside the classroom, in large part because of the same material constraints that tend to prevent them from realizing their marital aspirations.

Overall, the classes were unsuccessful at convincing parents of two of the main ideas behind marriage-promotion policy: that married families are healthier and that marriage is a precursor to economic self-sufficiency. Nor, significantly, did parents find helpful the financial management tips that are often part of marriage education for poor couples. Most parents told Randles that either they did not have money to manage or they already knew how to manage the little money they did have to the best extent possible by prioritizing necessary expenses. As Joshua, eighteen and white, told Randles, "Money's easy to manage when you have some." Similarly, one mother, Marcy, twenty-one and white, told her, "We already know how to manage our money to a 'T.' As soon as we get paid, [our son] comes first. His diapers, his wipes, soap, if he runs out, we get him more. Then we buy what we can from there."

Policies promoting marriage as a means to escape and avoid poverty prop up the ideology of marital self-sufficiency that links marriage to the socioeconomic opportunities of the shrinking American middle class. In the end, marriage education programs that are based on the "individual failure" logic (promoted by commentators such as sociologists Waite and Wilcox) have the potential to *exacerbate* rather than alleviate the intimate inequalities that often lead to curtailed commitments among couples in poverty who tend to find themselves deep within the marriage gap. While the federal government has funded many programs targeting low-income couples like the one that Randles studied, many of the government-funded programs have a different focus: providing marriage education to as many people as possible. Our research found that this strategy has the unintended consequence of diverting money away from needy families, another important piece in the puzzle of perpetuating intimate inequalities.

PROMOTING MARRIAGE AMONG THE MASSES

A number of individual states have used TANF (welfare) funds for the purpose of strengthening marriage. In 2000, Oklahoma became the pioneer of a statewide effort to do just that. Former governor Frank Keating declared his state's divorce and unwed childbearing rates to be social problems and committed an initial $10 million out of its TANF funds for the initiative. Heath, in her research on this controversial policy, asked: "What do state policies to promote marriage look like on the ground?" Her findings were surprising. For months, she attended marriage education classes for the general population that focused on strengthening communication skills. Unlike the classes studied by Randles that specifically targeted low-income couples, Heath discovered that most of the classes offered by the Oklahoma Marriage Initiative recruited white, middle-class couples. Interviews with leaders and staff of the marriage initiative confirmed that although they viewed low-income families as an important target for relationship-strengthening programs, privileged families were more likely to benefit from the services. During an interview with a staff member who described the new BSF program that would target unmarried, low-income couples at the "magic moment" around the birth of their child, Heath responded enthusiastically that this seemed a positive direction because it appeared that many of the current services were going to . . . Before Heath could complete her sentence, a staff member finished it: "the middle class."

While the state initiative provided marriage education to more privileged families, these classes were funded with money specifically meant to help needy families. This finding led Heath in search of an answer to what she called the "marriage initiative puzzle": What is the logic behind using TANF funds that are meant for needy families to offer marriage workshops to people who can afford to pay? The answer to this question offers a window into the complex debates over government policies to promote and strengthen marriage. The logic behind marriage promotion can seem compelling. Katherine Boo, a journalist who traveled to Oklahoma to study what is often called the "marriage cure"—marriage as a cure to poverty—wrote in her award-winning 2003 New Yorker story about the logic of marriage-promotion policy: "Marriage is probably the most cost-efficient antipoverty instrument a society possesses."[18] For a very small investment, the government can offer marriage education classes to poor single mothers. If these classes help them to marry, a combined income of husband and wife might presumably "remove both of them, in one fell act, from America's poverty rolls." Yet, as Randles discovered in her research (and as the recent BSF study confirmed), these classes missed the mark in convincing unmarried couples to marry.

Heath's finding that most of the classes are not serving the population for which the funding is targeted raises an important question concerning the goal of marriage promotion, and points to a second tension that characterizes the marriage promotion goal of the marriage movement and the policy response it has helped generate. Marriage advocates worry about the problem of unwed motherhood and poverty, but they also worry about ensuring that marriage is upheld by law and public policy as the best institution for raising children. In other words, they are motivated by a moral belief that marriage is the best kind of family for society. This focus on strengthening marriage throughout society helps explain why the marriage initiative in Oklahoma would redistribute resources meant for needy families to offer marriage education to the general population. Ultimately, the goal of many participants of the marriage movement is to reinstitutionalize marriage among *all* populations and not just the needy. Yet, the redistribution has its own moral consequences, siphoning money away from poor women and their children. A director of one program in Oklahoma had this concern:

> I tell you that the amount of money that is spent on [the marriage initiative] really, really bothers me. I think it was $2 million this year! So, it was money that was taken away from poor women, and it hasn't been targeting poor women. In February on Valentine's weekend, there's a Sweethearts Getaway, and all these people come, and then you have the PREP [Prevention and Relationship Enhancement Program] spin-off for [adoptive] couples and high school kids. Not that those things are not important, but they are being paid for with funds that were set aside for poor families.

The lack of a social safety net and the low monthly payments for women on TANF (in 2003 when the program was newly underway, an Oklahoma family of three could receive a maximum benefit of $292 a month) underscores the punitive nature of redistributing welfare money, whether intentional or not.[19]

While marriage workshops have been ineffective at reducing poverty, the lack of real efforts to devise antipoverty programs at the state level has also occurred on a grander scale. Like the general marriage movement of which it is a product, the marriage education movement prides itself on taking a "big tent" approach to the range of stakeholders who comprise it. The movement was emboldened by its ability to draw into its ranks a variety of stakeholders and sought to straddle the welfare and cultural goals of marriage education. Over the past decade and a half, it has generated organizations that have professionalized the field, streamlined delivery of services, provided legitimacy through certification programs, and ensured its longevity through lobbying. The movement has also given rise to movement leaders and a reliable pool of industry experts who help set its tone and chart its directions. Despite the marriage education movement's emphasis on its big-tent approach, it ultimately remains focused on the cultural implications of changing family forms and on helping individual couples change their behavior—rather than on eradicating poverty. In this final section, we consider the larger marriage education movement and show that its focus and agenda are not antipoverty based.

The "Aha" Moment: The Marriage Education Industry

A key player in the marriage movement was family therapist Diane Sollee, who in 1996 founded the Coalition for Marriage, Family, and Couples Education (CMFCE). The CMFCE served as a clearinghouse for the movement and sponsored the annual Smart Marriages conference from 1996 to 2010.[20] These conferences drew thousands of therapists, educators, clergy and other religious leaders, researchers, and couples to a yearly gathering where they could catch up on the latest research, train to become marriage educators, learn about new programs and curricula, network with other marriage educators, and collaborate on legislative initiatives. The organization continues to maintain a Listserv that reaches thousands of marriage educators.

The Smart Marriages organization, and its yearly conferences in particular, were crucial to the melding of the marriage education movement. With the addition of $100 million in federal support a year starting in 2006, the conference became an important site for curricula developers to market their products. Some of them, along with several other industry experts, became movement stars who were featured regularly in the conference's listings and keynote addresses.

The success of Smart Marriages may have been the source of its own demise. By 2010, when it featured its last conference, a new organization emerged from the ranks: the National Association for Relationship and Marriage Educators (NARME). This group was launched at the 2010 Smart Marriages conference by leaders of successful marriage education organizations across the country who networked through Smart Marriages. The organization billed itself as "a relentless champion for marriages, families, and children" that seeks to "provide relationship education for healthy marriages, responsible fathers, and strong families." While its initial key mission focused on ensuring the movement's success through legislative action, it soon also took over the reins from Smart Marriages and started organizing its own yearly conference.

NARME claims to be an ideologically neutral organization that seeks to professionalize the field and guarantee its future. Its membership includes marriage educators from a variety of organizations ranging from local Head Start and social service agencies to large, federally funded organizations to faith-based grassroots organizations. Member organizations in NARME as well as the organization itself refuse to partake in larger political battles pertaining to marriage and family, most notably the debate over marriage equality. Leaders of marriage education around the country, interviewed by Avishai, emphasized that "[same-sex marriage] is not our issue." In addition, although many (but definitely not all) of the educators and administrators at the organizations that Avishai studied told her they became involved with marriage education because of their personal unease with the breakdown of the family, they also emphasized that when it came to working with their clients the emphasis is providing them with "all those wonderful tools that we know work to improve marriages."

Despite these earnest aspirations, it is difficult to escape the perception that the movement is ultimately invested more in the cultural and moral, rather than the antipoverty, aspects of marriage education. The term *marriage* in the movement remains unqualified; it is taken for granted that the term applies to heterosexual marriages only and does not account for how children can thrive in various kinds of families—even single-parent families—especially if they are stable. In the wake of the Obama administration's restructuring of marriage education funding to include a jobs-training component, many marriage educators Avishai interviewed were at a loss as to why "the one program that focuses on marriage should spend some of its measly dollars on jobs training. Aren't there enough programs that already do that?" This logic is on full display at the conferences of the movement. Although the welfare imperative was the one that persuaded lawmakers to fund marriage education, Smart Marriages and NARME conferences have featured only a handful of speakers who addressed the economic and structural aspects of the changing nature of family dynamics in the United States. Most keynote speakers at these conferences are industry insiders who promote marriage education for the sake of helping individual couples overcome their marital woes. Significantly, none of the social scientists widely recognized by the social science community as experts on family demographics (including Stephanie Coontz, Andrew Cherlin, Kathryn Edin, and Sara McLanahan) was ever invited to speak at these conferences, nor is their work known among marriage educators.

The rare speakers who do emphasize the structural aspects of family formation receive a lukewarm reception from this audience. For example, the 2012 NARME conference featured a speaker from the Annie E. Casey Foundation, a private nonprofit organization invested in building better futures for disadvantaged children. The speaker walked the audience through well-known facts: children from single-family homes and disadvantaged backgrounds were much more likely to drop out of school, be incarcerated, and get pregnant; and they were less likely to attend college. Yet the narrative this speaker offered strayed from the much-rehearsed narrative in these gatherings: Rather than emphasizing the "breakdown" of the family as the key culprit, the speaker surveyed the range of cultural, historical, and economic shifts (discussed earlier in this chapter), and suggested policy solutions that deemphasized marriage education. Not surprisingly, the speaker's departure was not accompanied by thunderous applause, and many conference attendees Avishai later spoke to said they were "disappointed" with this speaker.

None of this is surprising. Nothing in NARME's charter or public materials discusses the welfare aspect of marriage education. On its website the organization explains that NARME was started because leaders of successful community-based organizations "realized that if they did not step up to the plate, more children would grow up in broken homes, and more families would be shattered by divorce and out-of-wedlock childbearing." This rhetoric is echoed in the logic that structures the mission statements and origin stories of many of the organizations Avishai studied. Perhaps most telling is the marriage education movement's flat refusal to accept the outcomes of recent research clearly showing that marriage education is not delivering on the welfare front. Although organization leaders Avishai interviewed were very familiar with social science research about the correlation between family structure and the range of social outcomes they hoped to address through marriage education, they routinely dismissed lack of evidence for the efficacy of marriage education. Instead, they cite anecdotal evidence, testimonies from individual couples who were supported by the programs, or research generated by industry insiders (most prominently the Prevention & Relationship Enhancement Program [PREP] lab) about program efficacy.

Ultimately, the best indicator of where the movement's deepest concerns lie goes back to the original "aha" moment that prompted Diane Sollee to found Smart Marriages in her kitchen. The "origin story," as she tells it, was her rude awakening that marriage therapy was failing to address marital crises, caused by a reporter who asked her why divorce rates have not plummeted despite the growing circle of trained family therapists.[21] Marriage therapy, like marriage education, does not account for structural aspects of family formation. It seems as if marriage education was doomed from the start as an antipoverty measure—or perhaps it was never really intended for that purpose.

This is not to say that the marriage education movement and marriage education organizations are not doing good work or helping some couples achieve happier and more stable relationships. They are to a degree, as indicated by studies that measure outcomes such as relationship quality and satisfaction.[22] But when we try to understand why marriage education has failed as an antipoverty measure, the movement's own logic, founding documents, and directing rationales provide excellent clues.

CONCLUSION

Is it a surprise that the antipoverty goals of marriage education have failed to deliver? Not to social scientists or, for that matter, to anyone who has taken an introductory course in sociology. The philosophy behind marriage education and the policies of marriage promotion ignore the demographics of marriage and divorce. Relationship experts have looked to individual skills, psyches, experiences, and relationship dynamics to explain marital success and failure, while sociologists such as Waite and Wilcox have focused on individual failings and character traits. In contrast, economists, sociologists, and demographers have looked to social factors, such as class and education. From them, we know that the United States is characterized by a class-based marriage (and divorce) gap: highly educated and middle-class women and men are more likely than poor and struggling Americans to get married, stay married, and enjoy a stable relationship. In other words, at the macro level, the most important predictors of marriage and divorce (and the range of outcomes associated with marriage) are not whether an individual has mastered good communication skills, but whether one has a stable job and a college degree. This is not because more privileged Americans understand the "success sequence" or because less privileged Americans choose to ignore this sequence, but rather because race, class, and education differences make the success sequence plausible, rational, and accessible in the first place. This failure to account for macro dynamics of family formation is central to why marriage educators miss the mark in offering marriage education to low-income couples, whose relationships will remain precarious in the face of severe economic insecurities. It also explains why it is so easy for the marriage education movement to obscure antipoverty goals. It is much easier to strengthen relationships and marriages among couples who are not struggling to make ends meet.

The important question from a policy perspective is whether the government should fund these programs, even in the face of growing evidence that the policy has little value as an antipoverty measure. Given the research of sociologists Kathryn Edin and Maria Kefalas showing that low-income women do value marriage but find it a difficult institution to enter,[23] we argue for the need to provide low-income couples with the economic supports that could give them a shot at a future of married stability.

Marriage-promotion policies get at the heart of tensions over the ability of these policies to recognize and support diverse family forms and practices. Our research points to the need to direct our attention away from the idea of promoting marriage and toward policies that can alleviate the intimate inequalities that persist in American society.

NOTES

1. Authors are listed alphabetically and made equal contributions to the chapter.
2. Wilcox (2010).
3. Plummer (2003).

4. Pew Research Center, Social & Demographic Trends Report (2010a).

5. Cherlin (2009).

6. Conger, Conger, and Martin (2010).

7. Coontz (2005).

8. Pew Research Center, Social & Demographic Trends Report (2010b).

9. Cherlin (2009).

10. Brotherson and Duncan (2004); Heath (2012).

11. Sager (2010).

12. Hymowitz (2007).

13. Edin and Kefalas (2005).

14. Pew Social & Demographic Trends Report (2010a).

15. Wood, Moore, Clarkwest, Killewald, and Monahan (2012).

16. Randles (forthcoming).

17. Randles (forthcoming).

18. Boo (2003).

19. Heath (2012).

20. *Ibid.*

21. Waters (2004).

22. Hawkins and Fackrell (2010).

23. Edin and Kefalas (2005).

In the News

HOW TO STAY MARRIED

The Times of London, November 30, 2006

Stephanie Coontz

As married couples become a minority, our correspondent argues that the best way to keep a marriage strong and healthy is to retain a close network of friends.

Now, for the first time, married-couple households are a minority in both the UK and the U.S., outnumbered by single-person households and cohabiting couples. In the U.S. 49 percent of all households contain married couples. In the UK it is even fewer—45 percent in 2005, a drop from 54 percent in 1996. This has caused consternation among people who believe that we could restore the primacy of marriage in modern life if we could just get couples to invest more energy in their marriages. But the idea that a romantic partner can meet all our needs is a very recent invention. Through most of history, marriage was only one of many places where people cultivated long-term commitments. Neighbours, family and friends have been equally important sources of emotional and practical support.

Today, we expect much more intimacy and support from our partners than in the past, but much less from everyone else. This puts a huge strain on the institution of marriage. When a couple's relationship is strong, a marriage can be more fulfilling than ever. But we often overload marriage by asking our partner to satisfy more needs than any one individual can possibly meet, and if our marriage falters, we have few emotional support systems to fall back on.

Men are especially vulnerable after divorce, because they pay less attention to maintaining social ties outside marriage. But women also fall prey to the fantasy that once they find their "soul-mate" they can retreat to an isolated island of marital bliss.

Even the best-matched couples need to find gratification and support from sources other than their partner. When they don't, notes Joshua Coleman, a therapist and author of *The Marriage Makeover,* they have less to offer each other and fewer ways to replenish their relationship. Often the marriage buckles under the weight of the partners' expectations that each will fulfill all the other's needs.

For almost 20 years, Richard Lucas has been studying the self-reported happiness of more than 30,000 individuals. He finds that feelings of happiness increase around the time of marriage, but after a few years people return to their original happiness "set point." People who marry and stay married are slightly happier, on average, than people who never marry, and significantly happier than most people who marry and then divorce. But such individuals already reported higher-than-average happiness before they married. They didn't depend on marriage to make them happy—and that's one reason why they didn't become discontented once the honeymoon wore off. Couples who expect to find the greatest happiness from marriage are prone to the greatest disappointments.

Putting all our emotional eggs in the basket of marriage is a particular problem now that people live unmarried for longer periods of their lives than in the past. When we make romantic love our only source of commitment and obligation, we neglect the wider interpersonal ties that knit society together. This impoverishes the social lives of single and married individuals alike.

Several studies in the U.S. reveal how couples ask love and marriage to meet too many of their interpersonal needs. Over the past two decades, according to research by three American sociologists, the percentage of people who said their spouse was a close confidante rose from 30 to 38 percent. It's good news that more couples are now close friends. But the flip side of this trend is more disturbing. Using U.S. national data from 1992 to 2004, the sociologists Naomi Gerstel and Natalia Sarkisian found that modern married couples are less likely to visit, call, or offer support to parents and siblings than their single counterparts.

Apart from activities with other families when their children are young, married couples are also less likely to hang out with friends and socialise with neighbours. They often distance themselves from single or divorced individuals, even if they were once close to these people. This pattern can come back to haunt them if their own marriage breaks up.

Even as more spouses reported being each other's close confidantes over the past two decades, the number of neighbours, co-workers, club or church members, and extended family with whom Americans discussed important matters dropped sharply. The number of people who reported having four to five confidantes was halved between 1985 and 2004, falling to just 15 percent of the population. And almost half of all Americans now say that there is just one person, or no one at all, with whom they discuss important matters.

In the UK a British social attitudes survey in 1996 found that almost two-thirds of married people or those living together said that their first port of call when depressed was their spouse or partner. Thirteen percent said they would turn to a friend first. Roughly the same number said they would turn to extended family.

Popular culture is full of advice on how to take our romantic relationships to a deeper level. One common warning is to avoid letting ties to friends or family "interfere" with the time we spend with our spouse. But trying to be everything to one another is part of the problem, not part of the solution, to the tensions of modern marriage.

Through most of history, it was considered dangerously antisocial to be too emotionally attached to one's spouse, because that diluted loyalties to family, neighbours, and society at large. Until the mid-19th-century, the word "love" was used more frequently to describe feelings for neighbours, relatives and fellow church members than spouses.

The emotional lives of Victorian middle-class women revolved around passionate female bonds that overshadowed the "respectful affection" they felt for their husbands. Men, too, sought intimacy outside the family circle. A man could write a letter to his betrothed recounting his pleasure at falling asleep on the bosom of his best friend without fearing that she might think him gay. When couples first began to go on honeymoons in the 19th century they often took family and friends along for company.

But as modern economic and political trends eroded traditional dependencies on neighbours and local institutions, people began to focus more of their emotions on love and marriage. Society came to view intense same-sex ties with suspicion. Psychologists urged people to rebuff family and neighbours who might compete with the nuclear family for attention. In the postwar "Golden Age of Marriage" people began expecting their spouse to meet more and more of their needs.

The weaknesses of this marriage model soon became apparent. Housewives discovered that they could not find complete fulfillment in domesticity. Many men also felt diminished when they gave up older patterns of socialising to cocoon in the nuclear family.

The women's movement of the 1960s offered a better balance—fairer, more intimate marriages combined with social engagement outside the home. But in the past few decades, our speeded-up global economy has made balance harder and harder to attain, leading us to seek ever more meaning and satisfaction in love and marriage.

I am not suggesting that we lower our expectations of intimacy and friendship in marriage. Instead, I propose that we raise our expectations of other relationships. Emotional obligations to people outside the family can enrich, not diminish, our marital commitments. Society needs to respect and encourage social ties that extend beyond the couple, including those of unmarried individuals, as well as ties between the married and the unmarried.

Taking the emotional pressure off marriage is a win-win situation. The happiest couples are those who have interests, confidantes and support networks extending beyond the twosome. And such networks also make single and divorced people better off.

The best protection against the atomisation of modern life is to structure our workplaces and communities in ways that allow people, whatever their marital status, to sustain commitments beyond the couple relationship and the nuclear family. As Coleman notes, "Having friendships and social activities other than marriage is not only good for the self and for society, it's also good for the marriage." ◼

CCF Brief

PROMOTING MARRIAGE AMONG SINGLE MOTHERS: AN INEFFECTIVE WEAPON IN THE WAR ON POVERTY?

Kristi Williams | January 2014

The rapid rise in nonmarital fertility is arguably the most significant demographic trend of the past two decades. The proportion of births to unmarried women grew 46 percent over the past twenty years, so that more than four in ten births now occur to unmarried women. Nonmarital fertility is quickly becoming a dominant pathway to family formation, especially among the disadvantaged. This is worrisome because decades of research show that children raised in single-parent homes fare worse on a wide range of outcomes (e.g., poverty, educational attainment, nonmarital and teen childbearing) than children raised by two biological parents. The poverty rates of single-parent households are particularly striking. According to recent data from the U.S. Census Bureau, approximately 46 percent of children in single-mother households were living in poverty in 2013 compared to 11 percent of children living with two married parents.

How can we improve the lives of the growing numbers of unmarried mothers and their children? So far, a dominant approach has been to encourage their mothers to marry. At first glance, the logic makes sense. If growing up in a two-parent home is best for children, then adding a second parent to a single-mother home should at least partially address the problem. The 1996 welfare reform legislation and its subsequent reauthorization institutionalized this focus on marriage by allowing states to spend welfare funds on a range of marriage-promotion efforts.

The flaw in this argument is the assumption that all marriages are equally beneficial. In fact, however, the pool of potential marriage partners for single mothers in impoverished communities does not include many men with good prospects for becoming stable and helpful partners. Single mothers are especially likely to marry men who have children from other partnerships, have few economic resources, lack a high-school diploma, have been incarcerated, or have substance abuse problems. The new unions that single mothers form tend to have low levels of relationship quality and high rates of instability. A nationally representative study of more than 7,000 women found that approximately 64 percent of the single mothers who married were divorced by the time they reached age thirty-five to forty-four. More importantly, single mothers who marry and later divorce are worse off economically than single mothers who never marry. Even marriages that endure appear to offer few health benefits to single mothers unless they are to the biological father of their first child.

The hope of the marriage-promotion campaign was that marriages in low-income communities could be made more stable and beneficial through skills training and support. Although one program in Oklahoma City slightly increased relationship stability, the most rigorous evaluation of the programs in eight cities found that, overall, they created no long-term improvements in new unwed parents' relationship quality, marriage rates, or children's economic well-being, and they actually resulted in modest *decreases* in fathers' financial support and parental involvement.

Our recent research adds to the growing body of evidence that promoting marriage is not the answer to the problems facing single mothers and their children. Analyzing more than thirty years of data on a nationally representative cohort of women and their children, we found no physical or psychological advantages for the majority of adolescents born to a single mother whose mothers later married. We did find a modest physical health advantage among the minority of youth whose single mother later married and stayed married to their biological father, compared to those whose mothers remained unmarried. However, such unions are exceedingly rare. Only 16 percent of low-income unwed mothers in the Fragile Families and Child Wellbeing study were married to the child's biological father five years after the child's birth. Marriage may matter, but only a little, and only in very specific and relatively rare circumstances.

There is growing consensus among researchers that it would be more beneficial to convince women to delay childbirth rather than to promote marriage. But even this seemingly uncontroversial policy is more complicated than it sounds. For African Americans in the United States, later ages at birth are associated with higher rates of neonatal mortality, perhaps because the stress of chronic disadvantage and racial discrimination accelerates biological aging for this group. More recent evidence from Britain indicates that delaying births to the early twenties offers few advantages for children's later educational and socioeconomic attainment, and our ongoing research suggests that such delays may even pose long-term health risks for African American women. Ultimately, attempts to influence highly personal decisions such as fertility timing and context will likely have limited success, especially when early or nonmarital fertility is sometimes adaptive compared to the alternatives.

A more promising approach is to focus on reducing *unintended* or *mistimed* births. Approximately 79 percent of births to unpartnered women under the age of twenty-five are unintended, and these appear to have the most negative consequences for women. Our research suggests that, among African American women, nonmarital childbearing is associated with negative mental health outcomes only among those who did not expect to have a nonmarital birth. Unlike broader efforts to convince women to delay childbirth or to marry, reducing unintended births does not require changing attitudes or preferences. Instead, it involves providing women most likely to be negatively affected by a nonmarital or early birth (i.e., those who do not intend to have one) with the resources and knowledge to carry out their intentions. These include comprehensive and early sex education and expansive and affordable access to birth control and family-planning services.

If the goal of marriage-promotion efforts is truly to lower poverty rates and improve the well-being of unmarried parents and their children, then it is time to take a different approach to this goal. Fortunately, numerous models of success exist. International comparisons indicate that single mothers and their children fare substantially better in countries with supportive social and economic family policies. A recent cross-national comparison indicates that the 51 percent poverty rate of U.S. single-parent households is nearly twice the average in sixteen high-income comparison countries, even though U.S. single-parent households have higher rates of employment. Another recent study identifies three family policies associated with substantially lower poverty rates among single-parent households: (1) family allowances (direct payments to parents of dependent children), (2) paid parental leave, and (3) publicly funded child care for children under age three. For example, in countries like the United States with the least generous family transfer policies among the twenty high-income countries included in the study, single-parent households are more than twice as likely to be in poverty than are those in countries with the most generous policies. Paid parental leave and publicly funded child care for children under age three appear especially advantageous in reducing poverty among single mothers, largely by increasing their employment rates—a primary goal of the 1996 welfare reform legislation. Such policies benefit all families and are likely to be more effective than marriage promotion in reducing poverty and improving the lives of the growing number of single mothers and their children.

In the News

NO, MARRIAGE IS NOT A GOOD WAY TO FIGHT POVERTY

ThinkProgress, January 9, 2014

Bryce Covert

In a speech marking the 50-year anniversary of the War on Poverty meant to offer up his ideas on how to address the problem today, Sen. Marco Rubio (R–FL) laid out some new ideas, such as consolidating all federal anti-poverty programs into one agency and doing away with the Earned Income Tax Credit to instead give people "wage enhancement." But he also offered up a very old idea: promoting marriage as a way to drastically reduce poverty:

> Social factors also play a major role in denying opportunity. The truth is that **the greatest tool to lift people, to lift children and families from poverty, is one that decreases the probability of child poverty by 82 percent. But it isn't a government program. It's called marriage.** Fifty years ago today, when the War on Poverty was launched, 93 percent of children in the United States were born to married parents. By 2010, that number had plummeted to 60 percent. It shouldn't surprise us that 71 percent of poor families, poor families with children, are families that are not headed by a married couple.

Unfortunately for him, though, there is new evidence that marriage is not in fact the panacea for poverty that some may think. Kristi Williams, associate professor of sociology at Ohio State University, did some research and found that more than two-thirds of single mothers who married ended up divorced by the time they were 35 to 44. On top of that, marrying and then later divorcing leaves them worse off economically than if they had just stayed unmarried. And marriage promotion campaigns don't seem to help. An evaluation of programs in eight cities found that they didn't lead to a lasting improvement in marriage rates, relationship quality, or children's economic wellbeing. On the other hand, they "resulted in modest decreases in fathers' financial support and parental involvement," she writes.

Yet even the marriages that last don't end up offering women much of a lifeline. Firstly, Williams and her fellow researchers found that the pool of potential partners in low-income communities doesn't offer single mothers many chances for finding stable partners with economic resources. "The new unions that single mothers form tend to have low levels of relationship quality and high rates of instability," she writes. Meanwhile, those who do marry and stay together still don't see a lot of pay off. "[W]e found no physical or psychological advantages for the majority of adolescents born to a single mother whose mothers later married," she reports.

So what might help them? Williams points to greater access to "comprehensive and early sex education and expansive and affordable access to birth control and family planning services" to help women avoid unwanted or mistimed births. Contraception can be a potent tool in helping women achieve a higher economic status. In one study, the majority of women reported that contraception allowed them to support themselves financially, complete their education, and either keep or get a job. And family planning doesn't just benefit mothers: it benefits their future children. Research has found that it can increase their children's likelihood of completing college and getting a job while boosting their wages decades later. But it can also be costly, which can limit access. One in three women have struggled to afford prescription birth control at some point, and more than half of young women experienced a time when they couldn't afford to take it consistently.

But even with greater access to contraception, some women will still be single mothers. So what can we do to help them stay out of poverty? It turns out that while marriage may not offer much help, better policies could. American single mothers are worse off than their counterparts in 16 other high-income peer countries thanks to a thin social safety net. Single moms in this country have the highest rates of lacking health insurance, put up with the stingiest income support programs, have to wait longer than in other countries for early childhood education to begin, aren't guaranteed paid time off of work for a new child or if they or their kids fall sick, and have a low rate of receiving child support. They also are much more likely to be employed in low wage work.

There are ways to solve the problems they face: universal preschool and more support for childcare could help them get to their jobs and know their children have somewhere to be; raising the minimum wage would lift many out of poverty; guaranteed paid sick days would give them the ability to care for a child when he or she falls ill without losing wages or risking a job; paid family leave would mean they wouldn't have to quit, go into debt, or go on public assistance when a new child arrives; welfare, or the Temporary Assistance for Needy Families, could be updated so that it reaches more families and the benefits could be enhanced so that they are worth more than in 1996.

If part of Rubio's plan is to focus on helping single mothers survive financially, there's little evidence to back up his idea that marriage promotion is the way to go. But we may have to wait a while for him to espouse greater access to family planning and a more robust social safety net. ▪

21

The Case for Divorce

Virginia E. Rutter

requently in public and academic debates about the costs and benefits of marriage and divorce, evidence about health or economic consequences is used to support various perspectives. The book *The Case for Marriage* is a familiar example of this, and so we consider here "The Case for Divorce." This chapter offers evidence about when divorce leads to health benefits, rather than to more often reported negative health consequences. In particular, research shows that there are negative health consequences to remaining in a distressed marriage. The chapter also offers advice about the three things any reader of marriage and divorce research should look out for when trying to understand how useful or generalizable the claims are. Readers should consider whether marital quality has been considered—and how it has been measured; whether domestic violence and other pathologies have been examined; and whether "selection effects," or forces that occurred prior to marriage and that don't have anything to do with the marriage or the divorce itself but that make people more likely to divorce, have been tested. Finally, the chapter asks how we can explicitly—rather than implicitly—express values and beliefs when talking about the case for divorce.

Starting in 1880, when U.S. divorce statistics began to be recorded, the rate of divorce increased steadily for eighty years and then increased dramatically from 1960 to 1980.[1] By the end of that period, about half of all marriages ended in divorce. Since then, our 50 percent divorce rate has leveled off, and we haven't seen much change.[2]

Divorce policy has changed in that time. In the 1970s, there was a shift in divorce laws to allow unilateral divorce ("no-fault divorce") in the United States. Since that time, rates of wife's suicide, domestic violence, and spousal homicide have declined.[3] Meanwhile, the number of children involved in any given divorce has gone from 1.34 children to less than 1 child per divorce[4] because of the declining birthrate.

Increases in divorce have made it a fixture in family life—and a "problem" to be understood, interpreted, analyzed, and fixed.[5] But what exactly is the problem? A better understanding of divorce—and divorce research—clarifies the case for divorce, and by extension informs us about life as it really is in contemporary families. The case for divorce asks: Are there some cases where divorce is a *better* outcome than remaining married? Three decades of research on the impact on adults and children points to yes.

RESEARCHING THE IMPACT OF DIVORCE

While discussion of research methods leaves some people cold or in wish of a nap, the consistent hallmark of the best research on the impact of divorce is that it makes a logical and reasonable comparison. Some studies do this. But some don't. It is as simple as this: if my now-divorced parents had been happily married, life would have been different, and a divorce would have been a big loss to them, me, my brothers, and the community. But that wasn't the case. They treated each other with contempt, led parallel lives, lived through their children (and also did a lot of good things). Then they were divorced.

The logical comparison for divorce versus not divorce in my own biography is a comparison between having unhappily married parents or divorced parents who moved on. My parents' post-divorce lives were up and down, but ultimately a lot more sensible for all involved, and (crucially) better than the life that preceded the divorce. Research that asks "compared to what?" is designed to do a what-if exercise—not just with one person's story—but with the stories of many.

When researchers carefully examine "divorce compared to what?" they are sometimes searching for *selection bias*—a particular kind of problem that shows there is something about the people who get divorced that happened before they got into the current situation that makes them more likely to divorce. Some attributes that existed before the marriage may affect who divorces. So when we compare divorced people to people who stayed married, the question is whether selection bias has influenced the results. There is selection bias if the divorced group was already different from the stably married group. For example, getting married at a younger age, living in poverty, and not having a college degree are all associated with divorce. Already we see that selection bias plays a role in divorce. But how have researchers answered the question about how or whether divorce *causes* problems for adults or their children? Selection bias may explain some, but certainly not all, of today's divorces.

The case for divorce includes research on children as well as research on adults. In the first section below, "Resilient Children of Divorce," I show how the research on the impact of divorce on children teaches us two important lessons. First, most children of divorce do well. And second, children who remain in high-conflict families, where the parents have a distressed marriage, are at greater risk for problems. When parents divorce, children have already been subject to their distressed marriages, and that is what puts these children at greater risk for problems. In the second section—"Does Divorce Make You Happy?"—I discuss how research on the impact of divorce on adults follows a similar pattern: the consequences of a harsh or conflictual marriage exceed the consequences of divorce. In the third section, "Measuring Divorce's Impact with and without a Comparison Group," I show new evidence about how neutral the impact of divorce really is on children. At the same time, I remind you of the problems of research that fails to have a logical comparison group. As the research shows us, the case for divorce is straightforward. The consequences of remaining in a distressed marriage for children as well as for adults are myriad and long-lived. In those cases, perhaps the line shouldn't be "stay together for the kids," but "get divorced for the kids," not to mention for the health and well-being of the parents, on whom the children depend.

Resilient Children of Divorce

In 1989, psychologist Mavis Hetherington presented her research at the American Association for Marriage and Family Therapy, showing that most children of divorce fare just as well as children from intact families. She had established a comparative rate of distress among children: while 10 percent of children in the general population have behavioral or school-related problems, 20–25 percent of children from divorced families have these problems (but about 80 percent of the children of divorce do not have such problems). Numerous research papers provided more detail and supported the finding in her research.

Hetherington reported on specific kinds of distress that parents and children experience with divorce. She found a "crisis period" of about two years surrounding the divorce. She learned that, depending on the timing of divorce, boys and girls have different responses: when boys have problems, they tend to "act out"; when girls have problems, they are more likely to become depressed. But what Hetherington saw overall was the *resilience* of children of divorce.[6] Most children did fine. They were able to use personal resources and social networks in their family and community to cope.

Another study came out that year that refuted these findings, but also differed in terms of how the research was conducted. Psychologist Judith Wallerstein reported her research finding that children of divorce experienced more mental health problems than children of nondivorced, married families. She found that these children sometimes suffered a "sleeper effect"; their difficulty emerged as adults—hence the phrase "adult children of divorce"—keeping us ever vigilant for some lurking form of damage that could pop up like a dormant cancer.

To judge between these two pieces of research, we need to look at how these psychologists collected their information.

Wallerstein's methods: She studied a *clinical* sample of young, white, upper-middle-class teenagers whose parents had been divorced and who sought treatment at a mental health center in Northern California.[7] A clinical sample involves people who want help. They are a sample of folks who are, by definition, troubled. While a clinical sample can teach us much about the course of mental disturbances or adjustment problems, it cannot inform us about the prevalence or origins of a problem in the population, or reveal why some people end up doing well in the face of adversity while others do not. Wallerstein provided cases full of rich detail, but they were not *representative*. Her study has the strength of being *longitudinal* (that is, she tracked her subjects over time), but her evidence couldn't tell us whether these problems occur consistently in the population, or if they were due to selection bias. Children of divorce who are troubled are, by definition, the ones who seek therapy.

Hetherington's methods: Researchers obtained a population-based sample of stably married families with a four-year-old and followed them over time. It was a *prospective*, longitudinal study. *Prospective* means that the study started before any divorces happened. Using a series of observations, parental reports, and teacher reports, Hetherington tracked these children in their everyday lives. Some children's parents went on to divorce; others remained together. We can't do experiments where we randomly assign some children to divorced parents and others to married parents, but this gives us a quasi-experimental design that helps us evaluate the impact of divorce compared to no divorce. In the comparison, all the children started off the same in the sense that they weren't showing up in the study because they already had "problems." Not only did this design allow researchers to compare children whose parents divorced versus those whose parents stayed together, it also enabled the researchers to see how children fared before the divorce versus how they were doing after the divorce. Hetherington had built-in comparisons.[8]

As research progressed, Hetherington learned more about divorce and children. Because she had detailed information about both kinds of families, she was able to compare married families with divorced families. Sometimes the married families were extremely distressed; sometimes they were civil. Hetherington was able to analyze the well-being of children in extremely distressed married families versus children of divorce and children in harmoniously married families. By adding comparisons about the level of distress in all the families, she observed that children in harmonious married families fared better than children in divorced families *and* in distressed married families. Here's the punch line: The worst kind of family for a child to be raised in, in terms of mental health and behavior, was a *distressed married* family.[9]

Several key pieces of research extended Hetherington's results by using comparison groups and a prospective design. In 1991, demographer Andrew Cherlin and his colleagues wrote about longitudinal studies in Great Britain and the United States in the journal *Science*. The studies included data from parents, children, and teachers over time. At the first time point, age seven, all the children's parents were married. Over the study period, some went on to divorce, and some did not. Cherlin confirmed Hetherington's findings: While about 10 percent of children overall are at risk for adjustment and mental health problems, children of divorce are about 20–25 percent at risk for problems. Seventy-five to 80 percent of the children are fine.[10]

Cherlin also found that the difference between the children of divorce versus children in stable marriages existed *prior* to the divorce. These were *predisruption effects*, and here's how it makes sense: Parents who end up divorcing are different from parents who don't end up divorcing. They relate to each other differently; they relate to their children differently; and their children relate to them differently. Cherlin had identified selection bias, or a case of selection for who divorces.

In 1998, Cherlin and his colleagues offered an update on their continuing research.[11] Respondents analyzed in the 1991 study had gotten older, so he had more information. While the 1991 paper highlighted predisruption effects, this one reported that there were *postdisruption* effects (negative effects after the divorce) that accumulated and made life more difficult for children of divorce. Financial hardship and the loss of paternal involvement were key culprits. He called this phenomenon the "cascade of negative life events" and emphasized, as he had back in 1991, the importance of social and institutional supports for children in disrupted and remarried families.

A similar longitudinal study by Paul Amato and Juliana Sobolewski replicated these results in 2001.[12] They studied stably married, distressed but married, and divorced families over the course of seventeen years. They observed that grown children whose parents had divorced during their childhood had more adjustment problems. Although these adjustment problems were associated with predisruption effects—in other words, trouble in the family that preceded the divorce—postdisruption effects accumulated, too. Finally, the researchers found that children who grew up with married parents in distressed unions were more likely to experience psychological distress in later life, in contrast to their counterparts with nondistressed, stably married parents.

Starting with Hetherington in the 1980s, and following through Cherlin's parallel work in the 1990s, research designs that included comparison groups helped bring to light three points. First, using a population-based rather than a clinical sample provided a rate of distress among children of divorce that exemplified their *resilience*: approximately 80 percent were doing well versus 90 percent of children in the general population who were doing well. Second, difficulties—predisruption effects—found in longitudinal, prospective studies, indicated that children in families where their parents were headed for divorce were having troubles prior to the breakup. Postdisruption effects—and the cascade of negative life events—also played a role. Third, distressed marriages were harder on children than divorces. This last point foreshadowed the results in the studies of adults that I describe next.

DOES DIVORCE MAKE YOU HAPPY?

People who divorce do not go through such a costly and difficult process just to "feel good" or in some casual way to be happy. As you'll see below, research shows us just how difficult living in a distressed marriage is. The research shows us that divorce makes people feel better in the same way that the cessation of pain or illness makes them feel better.

In 2002, Linda Waite, a demographer at the University of Chicago, and several of her colleagues, released a study titled "Does Divorce Make People Happy?" At the same time, I was completing research at the University of Washington for a paper that would be titled "The Case for Divorce: Under What Conditions Is Divorce Beneficial and for Whom?"[13]

Our results were completely divergent. We both asked: How does people's level of well-being change when they divorce (versus when they stay married)? Both projects relied on the same data set; they both used a longitudinal design where all the people were married at the first time point, and some of them went on to divorce by the second time point. I found that adults who exited unhappy marriages were less depressed than those who stayed. According to Waite, there were no differences in happiness between those who stayed in their marriages and those who divorced.

What is the point? Should we throw up our hands and claim that research is merely a Rorschach test, a projective test that displays and reveals our deep-seated values and biases? For goodness' sake, no!

Instead, ask: "Divorce compared to what?" Were people who divorced compared to those who stayed in a happy marriage, or compared to those who stayed in a stressed-out marriage? One difference between Waite's study and mine was that I used a more stringent measure of marital distress. I was able to detect the people who were in seriously distressed marriages. (I also took severe domestic violence into account, and I measured depression rather than "happiness.") The contrast makes all the difference. When comparing how markedly unhappily married people fare compared to people who divorced, the divorcing people were less depressed, and the unhappily married people were more depressed. My additional statistical tests ("fixed effects," discussed below) confirmed that marital distress, not other factors, accounted for the differences between the unhappily married and divorced groups. In other words, what made the married people in distressed marriages more depressed was *being in a distressed marriage*, not their risk of depression.

Other longitudinal studies, including a study by Daniel Hawkins and Alan Booth,[14] found similar results regarding marital distress: the more carefully marital distress was measured, the more pronounced were the psychological advantages of leaving over staying. Again, a better comparison between married and divorced people was accomplished by using a thoughtful measurement of marital quality. A study by Pamela Smock and her colleagues assessed the economic costs of divorcing and also used methods that took into account selection bias. Smock and her colleagues found that divorced women experience economic disadvantages but that some of that economic disadvantage would have existed even if they had remained married.[15] With psychological distress, as with economic distress, people who divorced were different for reasons *other* than divorcing, not *because* of divorcing.

More recent research has examined how the accumulation of marital transitions—a divorce, a cohabitation, a breakup, perhaps a remarriage—may be an additional important way to examine the impact of divorce. The approach is to examine "relationship trajectories." Sarah Meadows and her colleagues[16] examined the consequence of such multiple transitions for women who started as single mothers, and found that for women who face continuous instability—rather than a single transition—their health was negatively affected. Such research allows for even more complexity, and requires that we compare higher levels of disruption with lower levels of disruption, including divorce.

Why Marital Quality Matters

Marital quality makes a difference when we ask whether divorce is better than staying married. The benefits of marriage accrue only to people in happy and well-functioning marriages; the benefits of happy marriages are, indeed, robust. The same is not true for people in distressed marriages, and we save those marriages at our—and our partners'—peril. For example, studies on the "psychophysiology of marriage" show that when men and women are in distressed marriages—where they may experience contempt, criticism, defensiveness, and stonewalling—their immune systems decline over time.[17] These people are less healthy and less happy. Troubled marriages have immediate costs; they also have downstream health costs as the years of distress accumulate.

Research has demonstrated how high those costs are. Weissman used community mental health samples to assess the impact of marriage and marital distress on rates of major depression.[18] While the study found that depression was reduced for people in happy marriages, depression for men *and* women in unhappy marriages was *twenty-five* times more likely than for people in happy marriages. Another study found that marital dissatisfaction a year earlier is associated with a 2.7 times greater depression risk for women and with an elevated rate of depression for men. Even more alarming is a study that showed that, among married women who were more depressed than average, by far the most common explanation was domestic violence. In my research, women who were victims of domestic violence—severe enough to have been injured in the past year—were different in their response to distress and divorce from those in nonviolent distressed marriages, likely because the problems domestic violence victims have to solve are different from the problems of those who are in distressed but nonviolent marriages. This suggests that clear research on divorce should always seek to identify victims of abuse because these cases follow a different story line.[19]

When researchers measure marital distress in terms of level of conflict, or they use multiple measures of distress and find high conflict and distress, they find that divorce is a relief to those couples. This parallels what Hetherington found for children—that divorce is better than living in a high-conflict family. It is easy enough to ask, "How was marital distress measured?" in order to learn whether a measure of general happiness that merely captures transient feelings of satisfaction was used, or whether a measure of serious distress or conflict, which tends to identify which couples are "candidates" for divorce, was used.

On Happiness

Other measures matter, too: My study and the Waite study both looked at the personal costs of divorcing. While Waite measured "happiness," I measured "depression." It matters how we measure "personal well-being." While van Hemert and colleagues have found that happiness and depression are correlated, there's a big difference between them. Out of hundreds of correlational studies catalogued by Veenhoven in the World Database of Happiness, there are scarcely any gender differences in happiness. Nor does happiness have the major correlates to race or poverty that have been well established for depression.[20]

All these differences suggest that "happiness" is measuring something psychologically different from "distress" or "depression." The societal implications are quite different between these two measures. Greenberg and colleagues have found that unhappy people are not usually functionally impaired, but that depression involves costs in terms of lost wages, productivity, and negative impact on children.[21] The lesson of these studies is that what we measure, as well as whether we include a good comparison, will help us better understand when and how divorce has consequences.

MEASURING DIVORCE'S IMPACT WITH AND WITHOUT A COMPARISON GROUP

In April 2008 the questions about the impact of divorce and its costs continued to be alive and well. Two studies were released the very same week on the topic. These studies asked: What is the impact of divorce? A release from the Council on Contemporary Families was based on demographer Allen Li's research. The other paper, by economist Ben Scafidi, was released by the Institute for American Values. Li's paper pertained to the emotional impact of divorce on children, while Scafidi's paper addressed the economic impact of divorce across America.[22]

The results in the two papers were completely divergent. Li asked: What is the impact of divorce on children? He found that divorce itself does not explain the differences between children with divorced and married parents. He did find differences between the two groups (on average)—just as researchers have been finding since the 1980s. With increasingly refined research techniques, however, Li was able to show that *selection bias*—or a case of improper comparisons—is what accounts for the differences.

Li's technique included testing for "fixed effects"—a statistical tool used in economics and biomedical research with longitudinal data. Fixed-effects models tell us if there are aspects of the individuals that are not measured explicitly but that account for results. The children in Li's study whose parents ended up divorcing were getting a different kind of parenting all along the way when compared with the children whose parents stayed married.

Meanwhile, Scafidi asked: What does divorce cost the general public? Hold on to your hats. By his calculations, divorce—plus single parenthood—costs taxpayers $112 billion a year. To calculate this, he assumed that divorce and single parenthood *cause* poverty. In other words, he neglected the notion that selection bias could play a role in who ends up as a single parent or who gets divorced. In a 2002 report, historian Stephanie Coontz and economist Nancy Folbre examined the problems with assuming that divorce and single parenthood cause poverty by taking into account selection bias.[23] While there is a correlation between single parenthood and poverty, the correlation does not mean that single parenthood *causes* poverty. *Causation* is complex and challenging to establish, but the evidence that causality flows in the other direction—that poverty often *causes* or precedes single parenthood—is to many analysts a lot stronger. As Stevenson and Wolfers point out, Scafidi neglected comparisons in another way as well: while some women end up losing financially following divorce, others actually *gain*.[24] Scafidi did not include these economic gains in his equations.

The results were divergent because of their fundamental differences in thinking about "what causes what?" While Li's article asks, "divorce *compared to what?*" Scafidi did not assess the costs of divorce relative to, for example, remaining in a distressed, tumultuous, or violent family situation. Scafidi didn't test the premise that divorce (and single parenthood) causes economic problems. He assumed that it did.

Meanwhile, other researchers continue to find that selection bias accounts for some if not all the differences between children whose parents divorce and children whose parents remain married to each other. For example, in 2007 Fomby and Cherlin found that the characteristics of the mother that precede the divorce helped explain the reduced cognitive outcomes for children of divorce.[25] In their study, they also found that postdisruption effects of the divorce, rather than just selection bias or predisruption effects, also were associated with behavioral problems sometimes seen in children of divorce. Just as research on relationship trajectories may help us better understand how and when divorce is difficult on adults, this same promising line of research may further explain the postdisruption effects of divorce on children. It turns out that children exposed to multiple transitions—a divorce, then a cohabitation and breakup, then perhaps another marriage—may be at elevated risk relative to children exposed to only one transition. In a 2007 study that focused on single parents, Osborne and McLanahan[26] found that the accumulation of a mother's relationship transitions leads to hardship for her children.

Lessons Learned

Divorce researchers who use comparison groups and control for selection bias, who measure marital quality carefully, and who take domestic violence into account may still disagree about just how different children of divorce are from children of married parents. (Are 20 percent affected? Are 25 percent affected?) But they agree about the resilience of children in the face of divorce. Researchers may disagree about whether the impact of divorce is neutral, as Allen Li argues, or whether some of the impact of divorce is due to preexisting factors, or whether some of the impact of divorce should be attributed to postdisruption factors, or whether relationship trajectory research is an important piece of the puzzle about the circumstances under which divorce is harder on children. Scientists agree, however, that comparing married families to divorced families without taking selection bias into account is a case of comparing apples to oranges and will get us nowhere in terms of helping families. As Rutter, Hawkins, and Hetherington all show, failing to take the quality of the marriages seriously is like ignoring the elephant in the room! The distressed marriage is where most people considering divorce start. And this distress is highly costly to the health and mental health of parents and their children.

If you are reading research on marriage and divorce—or listening to some-one's conclusions about it—always remember to ask, "Did this study include a comparison group and take selection bias into account?" and "Did the researchers measure things—especially marital distress—carefully?"

When I ask these questions—and when I look at the role of divorce in U.S. history—I see a complicated story. Above all, I have discovered that there is a case for divorce. There are times and situations when divorce is beneficial to the people who divorce and to their children.

NOTES

1. See Ruggles (1997).

2. See Heuveline (2005).

3. Discussed by Stevenson and Wolfers (2006).

4. Reported by Cowen (2007).

5. See Coltrane and Adams (2003).

6. See Hetherington and Stanley-Hagan (1997).

7. See Wallerstein and Blakeslee (1988).

8. A complete, accessible review of Hetherington's longitudinal research is in Hetherington and Kelly (2002).

9. See Hetherington (1999).

10. Cherlin et al. (1991).

11. Cherlin et al. (1998).

12. Amato and Sobolewski (2001).

13. See Waite et al. (2002); Rutter (2004).

14. Hawkins and Booth (2005).

15. See Smock, Manning, and Gupta (1999).

16. Meadows, McLanahan, and Brooks-Gunn (2008).

17. See Gottman (1994); Kiecolt-Glaser et al. (1988); and Robles and Kiecolt-Glaser (2003).

18. See Weissman (1987).

19. See Whisman (1999) on depression and Campbell (1998) on domestic violence.

20. See van Hemert, van de Vijver, and Poortinga (2002) and Veenhoven (2004) on the World Database of Happiness.

21. Greenberg et al. (1993a, 1993b).

22. See Li (2008) and Li (2007); also see Scafidi (2008).

23. See Coontz and Folbre (2002).

24. See Stevenson and Wolfers's note in Li (2007) and Ananat and Michaels (2008).

25. Fomby and Cherlin (2007).

26. Osborne and McLanahan (2007).

In Other Words

SILVER LININGS DIVORCE TREND

Family Inequality, January 29, 2014

Philip N. Cohen

In yesterday's *LA Times* story on my divorce paper, "Recession and Divorce in the United States 2008–2011," reporter Emily Alpert Reyes and her editors focused on the rebound, headlining it, "Divorces rise as economy recovers, study finds." I had been focused on whether the drop from 2008 to 2009 could really be attributed to the recession. Their decision made good journalistic as well as analytical sense.

So what does the increase say about the "silver linings" interpretation of the divorce trend? That was the idea, pitched by Brad Wilcox, that the drop he observed in 2008 from 2007 (using vital statistics data) reflected the fact that "many couples appear to be developing a new appreciation for the economic and social support that marriage can provide in tough times." There was, and is, no evidence for this that I am aware of.

I think that the rebound in divorce undermines the silver linings theory. However, I can't swear the theory is wrong. It hasn't been tested.

But when I was Googling for stories on this yesterday I found this 2009 CBS news report, which accidentally illustrates the problem with silver linings. The story was called "Recession Bright Spot? Divorce Rate Drops." It featured the Levines, in which the husband lost his job, and the marriage suddenly was in trouble (like a block building suddenly collapsing).

Then, the couple pulls together, and it looks like they're going to make it: "If they can get through this, they can get through just about anything."

The story was a Wilcox plant, featuring him saying, "What we're seeing is some people are postponing divorce because home values have dropped. For others, the recession has led to a new sense of togetherness." (In my paper, incidentally, divorce was more common in states with higher foreclosure rates.)

And the reporter noted, as evidence, "There were almost 20,000 fewer divorces in 2008 than 2007." As I noted at the time, divorce fell at least that much in most years, so that's meaningless manipulation of reporters' demographic ignorance by Wilcox. Anyway, that's not the point. The point is, this couple was doing fine *before* the recession! So the recession caused him to lose his job, and then their marriage was in trouble, and then they pulled through. So how, exactly, was the recession *reducing* divorce?

And yet my analysis shows the recession probably did reduce divorce in the aggregate (just not in their case). My suspicion remains that the recession increased stress and conflict within marriages, like CBS's couple. It probably raised the Levines' odds of divorce, even if not quite up to 1.0. There is just a lot of evidence at the individual level that job loss increases the odds of divorce. Lots of people—and relationships—had to have been made miserable by the recession.

If that is true, then was the drop in divorce rates good or bad? Was it a silver lining? You have to think about the continuum of marriages—from happy to sad—and who is affected. People who are bouncing around between kinda happy and kinda sad aren't likely considering the cost of a lawyer yet. Not like those who have hit bottom. But if the cost of divorce—legal fees, real estate, relocation, or whatever—actually delays or forestalls some divorces, it's probably the ones that are closest to actually occurring for which the outcome changes. That is, the almost-most miserable marriages.

If the recession made more people miserable, and yet fewer got divorced, divorce was more selective. Think of grant funding: when times are tight, more people apply but fewer are funded, so the ones that do are the best of the best (ideally). And the number of good ones not funded goes up. With marriages in a recession, more are miserable, yet the bar for divorcing is raised (or lowered) by the costs relative to income. So there are more miserable marriages not ending in divorce. Obviously, God thinks this is good, because he has no patience for our petty divorce excuses (which explains Wilcox's interpretation).

One obvious possibility is that family violence increases when more miserable marriages produce fewer divorces. There was a spike in intimate partner violence in 2008 and 2009, the years men's unemployment rates jumped.

It is very common, yet wholly unjustified, to always assume falling divorce rates are good. As I argued before: We simply do not know what is the best level of divorce to maximize the benefits of good marriage while mitigating the harms caused by bad marriage. ▄

22

Stepfamilies as They Really Are

Neither Cinderella nor the Brady Bunch

Marilyn Coleman and Lawrence Ganong

C onsider this: "She was beat like a red-headed stepchild." "Software is the stepchild of the computer industry." These quotations support the widely believed notion that stepfamilies are bad for children: Stepmothers are wicked and uncaring; stepfathers are abusive. The flip side is that stepfamilies are like the Brady Bunch, who never met a family problem they couldn't solve in thirty minutes or less in the 1970s situation comedy. A recent national survey reported that more than half of respondents under age thirty had a close step-relationship (stepparent, stepchild, step-sibling), so it is likely that you are either in a stepfamily or know someone who is. Despite their prevalence, stepfamilies and stepfamily members continue to be seen in these stereotypical extremes (Cinderella, Brady Bunch). In this chapter we present research on stepfamilies as they really are. We share research about stepfamily relationships and how parents' remarriages affect children. We examine what is known about stepfamilies formed by gay and lesbian couples, and we look at unmarried (cohabiting) couples as well as married ones.

STEPFAMILIES AS THEY REALLY ARE

Americans have the highest rates of marriage, divorce, and remarriage in the industrialized world. Cohabitation, while not as frequent in the United States as in some European nations, is also a common experience. As a result of these trends, there are large numbers of stepfamilies in the United States. In a 2011

Pew Center national poll, 42 percent of all respondents and 52 percent of those younger than age thirty reported that they had a close step-relative (i.e., a stepparent, stepchild, step-sibling).[1]

Despite the prevalence of step-relationships, there is still confusion and misinformation about stepfamilies. On the one hand, there are widespread beliefs about the dysfunctional nature of stepfamilies, with stereotypes about wicked stepmothers, abusive stepfathers, and unloved, neglected stepchildren. But on the other hand, some people see remarriages as "recreating" the nuclear family, and they expect new stepparents to serve as substitutes for absent biological parents ("Isn't it great that you have a new daddy now?").

CINDERELLA, THE BRADY BUNCH, AND OTHER STEPFAMILY STEREOTYPES

Nearly all cultures have a version of the Cinderella story, and many of the centuries-old fairy tales featuring stepfamilies were Grimm indeed (pun intended). The story of Cinderella has been traced back to ninth-century China, and other age-old fairy tales, such as Hansel and Gretel and Snow White, featured wicked stepmothers. The plot is similar in these tales—a child's mother dies, the father remarries a woman who is jealous of her stepdaughter and is cruel and/or murderous toward her. A question seldom raised is why the biological father was so hapless in these stories, but it is certainly no wonder that people have often opted to hide their stepfamily status—nobody wants to be the wicked "stepmonster," the neglected and unloved stepchild, or the weak bioparent from these widely known fairy tales.

Current versions of tales featuring wicked stepparents are offered by some evolutionary psychologists. Daly and Wilson, for example, have argued that stepmothers truly are mean because they want to privilege their own children, so they are more likely to abuse or neglect their stepchildren.[2] These two scholars also have indicated, however, that it is stepfathers rather than stepmothers who are most likely to abuse stepchildren. And, according to the U.S. Department of Health and Human Services, the family member most likely to abuse children is the biological mother and not the stepmother or stepfather. Daly and Wilson have been accused of using Darwinian explanations to marginalize and stigmatize stepparents, similar to how Darwinian explanations have previously been used to target gays and lesbians, people of color, and Jews.

Stepparents also may invest fewer material goods and resources in their stepchildren than parents invest in their children. Again, evolutionary arguments are given for why stepparents spend less on stepchildren than parents do on children, but there are other explanations—stepparents may be supporting their biological children living elsewhere as well as stepchildren they live with, many stepfamilies experience greater poverty, or nonresidential bioparents may be sending child support to residential stepchildren, giving a stepparent less need to provide resources.

It is perhaps not surprising, considering the stereotyping of stepfamilies, that they have sometimes elected to hide their stepfamily status (like the Brady Bunch did in the old TV show). Stepfamilies have hidden their status in multiple ways, including having all members of the stepfamily use the same last name (sometimes legally, often not), having stepchildren call the stepparent "mom" or "dad," and generally presenting themselves as a nuclear family to outsiders. When all parents agree to it, stepparents may legally adopt their stepchildren in an effort to change their family/relationship status and therefore avoid the "step" stigma. In fact, stepparent adoptions of stepchildren lead all other types of adoptions in the United States. For a child to be adopted by a stepparent, however, a biological parent has to give up all claims and rights to the child; in some states, the name of the parent is actually changed on the child's birth certificate.

Clinicians and researchers have attempted to de-stigmatize stepfamilies by calling them *blended*, *reconstituted*, or *reformed*. The problem with some of these attempts is the lack of family labels or names for the various members of the stepfamilies. The designations *stepmother*, *stepfather*, and *stepchild* are usually understood in our culture, but introducing a stepmother as "my blended mother" or a stepfather as "my reconstituted father" sounds ridiculous. We believe that these attempts to hide stepfamily status reflect a rather simplistic understanding of family diversity.

What are the truths about stepfamilies as they really are? It is good to start with a definition of whom we are writing about. We define stepfamilies as families in which at least one adult has either biological or adopted children from a previous relationship. Within this simple definition lies a huge amount of diversity and complexity. Some of this diversity is structural (i.e., Which adult in the household is a stepparent? Are there step-siblings in the family?), and some of it is related to social and cultural variability—stepfamilies are from all walks of life.

Some scholars refer to the concepts of *stepfamily* and *stepfamily household* as if they were interchangeable, but they are not always the same. The membership of many stepfamilies extends beyond a single household, and consequently many stepfamily members do not live in the same household as other family members, at least not all the time. "Simple" stepfamilies are households consisting of a stepparent (usually a stepfather), a biological parent (usually a mother), and the parents' children from earlier unions. Researchers consider a stepfamily household to be "blended" or "complex" when each adult brings children to the household from previous relationships. Some simple and complex stepfamily households also contain children born to the remarried (or cohabiting) union, so there truly are children who are his, hers, and "ours." Some stepchildren end up with full-, half-, and step-siblings spread across several households.

The number of stepfamily structural combinations seems almost endless. Some of the complexity may lead to confusion about stepfamilies and stigma on the part of those who live in far less complicated families. We often stigmatize that which we do not well understand.

WHO LIVES IN STEPFAMILIES?

Stepfamilies are formed by individuals from every social class, from diverse racial and ethnic backgrounds, and across the life span. However, the chances of being in a stepfamily are somewhat greater for Americans who are young, black, and do not have a college degree. These days, young adults have more step-relatives than older adults do because of their parents' generation's high divorce rate and because increasing numbers of never-married parents later partnered with someone other than the parent of their child. Sixty percent of the black adults interviewed in the Pew survey indicated that they had at least one step-relative, compared to 46 percent of Latino/as and 39 percent of white adults. Americans who never attended college or had some college credits were similar to each other in their likelihood of having a step-relative (45–47 percent). Of those with a college degree, 33 percent had a step-relative.[3]

While much imagery and myths about stepfamilies invoke heterosexual unions, stepfamilies are headed by gay and lesbian parents as well as heterosexual couples. Most stepfamilies headed by gay men were formed in similar ways as heterosexual stepfamilies, in that children were born to a married couple, the father came out as gay, was divorced from the child's mother, and formed a new union with another man. In the past, most lesbian stepfamilies also were formed when one partner brought children from a previous heterosexual union to the family. Recently, however, growing numbers of lesbian couples have used various means of assisted reproduction so that one partner bears a child; although they usually consider these children as belonging to both partners, the nonbiological parent, like a stepparent in a heterosexual union, lacks legal recognition as a parent in most states. If a lesbian stepfamily dissolves, the partner who did not give birth to the child usually has no legal access to the child. This is true of those couples who used an assisted reproductive technique as well as those who brought children from a previous relationship to the marriage. As gay and lesbian legal marriages become increasingly common in the United States, it will be interesting to see how the legal system deals with the dissolution of these unions and their children. To date, however, much of the available research on stepfamilies focuses on opposite-sex couples.

Stepfamilies are also formed later in life because of increasing numbers of formerly married older adults who are on the dating and marriage market due to longer life spans and the continued high level of divorce in the United States. Although there are many reasons why remarriage is not an attractive option for older adults, many do remarry. But growing numbers of healthy older adults also are in cohabiting relationships, committed unions that may or may not be sharing residences. Some older stepfamilies, of course, are long-term unions of couples that re-partnered when they were much younger. Consequently, the number of older stepfamilies is the largest it has ever been.

Men remarry in old age more often than do women, and older women with adequate finances are the least likely to remarry. Older women who were previously in marriages where they did most of the household work and caregiving of other family members may be unwilling to take on those responsibilities again. Although often interested in a partner to spend time with, they do not want the obligations associated with marriage.

As the baby boomers move into old age, rates of cohabitation likely will increase, as will LAT couples. LAT, or living apart together, refers to those who are in committed relationships but who live in their own, separate homes. The baby boomers were the first age group to separate sex from marriage in large numbers (thanks in part to the invention of the birth control pill) and to cohabit in high numbers. These behaviors will likely carry over into old age. If the thought of widowed or divorced grandparents becoming sexually active is startling, keep in mind that re-partnering in old age has some significant benefits, especially for older men. Older divorced or widowed men who don't re-partner are more likely to become isolated and depressed.

SOME STEPFAMILY HISTORY

Although the study of stepfamilies did not really begin until the final quarter of the twentieth century, stepfamilies have always been rather common. Life spans were fairly short until well into the twentieth century, so parents of young children often died while children were still in the home—women died in childbirth, men were killed in work accidents and wars, and diseases were not well understood or effectively treated. Parents who lost a spouse were motivated to remarry quickly because replacing the deceased parent was necessary for family survival. Widowers who worked on farms or in factories had no time to care for an infant or for young children and needed immediate child-rearing help. Widows with young children often would end up poverty stricken after their spouses died, with no viable options other than remarriage. Post-bereavement stepfamilies, therefore, were quite common.

Not until the last quarter of the twentieth century, when divorce passed bereavement as the leading "cause" of remarriage, were societal concerns about stepfamilies raised. Remarriage following divorce became viewed as a social and familial problem rather than as a solution to a problem, as was true when remarriage followed bereavement. Because remarriage was viewed as a problem, clinicians took notice of stepfamilies before researchers did. As a result, early knowledge about stepfamilies was problem oriented because it came out of clinical practice with stepfamilies having difficulties adapting to their new family structure. Research-based knowledge about stepfamilies was minimal, and as late as 1979, only eleven studies on remarriage and stepfamily living had been conducted, including dissertations and master's theses. These studies were based on data from only about 600 stepfamily members.

It is little wonder that Andrew Cherlin wrote in 1978 that stepfamilies formed after remarriage were "incomplete institutions" lacking formal societal supports and guidelines for family roles and behaviors.[4] Cherlin noted that English had no words to describe some stepfamily relationships (e.g., what are stepfathers and fathers to each other?), suggesting that the lack of terminology made it difficult for stepfamily members to imagine the existence of such relationships. The absence of formal institutional support meant that stepfamily members experienced greater stress because they lacked aids to help them figure out how to be a family. In the absence of such norms, many assumed that stepfamilies were reconstituted versions of first-marriage families. The TV show from the early 1970s, *The Brady Bunch*, was an example of a reconstituted version of a first-marriage family. Fondness for this simplistic version of stepfamilies was evident by the numerous *Brady Bunch* remakes that appeared in the 1990s and 2000s.

How Stepfamilies Differ from First-Married Families

While clinical perspectives on stepfamilies typically focused more on problems rather than strengths, important information flowed from their experiences working with stepfamilies. In particular, they developed a greater understanding of the differences between first-married families and stepfamilies. A grasp of these differences can be helpful in understanding some of the adaptations and adjustments that face stepfamily members in the beginning phases of stepfamily life. The following are some of those differences.

1. Unlike first-married families, stepfamilies are usually preceded by several types of losses. How these losses are handled have implications for the success of the stepfamily. When remarriage (or re-partnering without marriage) follows the death of a partner or a parent, grieving accompanies that loss of a loved one. People grieve at different rates, so some family members may be ready to move on with their lives and possibly into new relationships much sooner than other family members. In divorce, too, there is grieving—for the end of the marriage, for the loss of the family as it had been known, for the time lost with nonresidential parents—and this grieving also is not done at the same rate by all family members. For example, what anthropologist Paul Bohannon referred to as the "emotional" divorce, that period when one or both members of the couple have given up on a no longer satisfying marriage, typically occurs much sooner (sometimes years sooner) for one member of the divorced couple than the other.[5] Because parents often do not keep their children apprised of their crumbling relationship (which is mostly a good thing!), children may be surprised by the ending of their parents' marriage and thus have had less time to grieve and accommodate to the changes of their previous family. Adults who ended a marriage often enter a remarriage seeing it as a second chance at happiness, but children may resent the remarriage and the stepparent, and they are not likely to view the remarriage as a second chance at happiness.

2. In remarriages, the parent-child relationship predates the marriage. This may seem like a minor point, but it is not. Remarriages begin with the closest emotional ties being between the parent and the child rather than between the members of the couple. In first marriages, the couple has some time to adjust to each other, develop rituals, and settle into a life together before children arrive. In remarriage, there is no such adjustment period. The children are already there, they may be resentful or still grieving over losses, and they may have different ideas than the stepparent about family rituals, rules, and roles. Nearly everything about everyday family life has to be negotiated, which may seem really difficult and stressful. Renowned stepfamily therapist Patricia Papernow calls this negotiating process establishing a *middle ground*, a necessary step in stepfamily development.[6] The middle ground is that area where everyone in the family can agree. Papernow says that too much middle ground leads to boredom, perhaps, with routine (seldom a problem in stepfamilies). However, establishing such middle ground makes

life much easier. Having to negotiate such everyday activities as what time you will eat dinner, what you will eat for dinner, where you will eat dinner, and who has to be present at dinner can be exhausting and stressful. As family and household behaviors become more routine (more middle ground), there is more emotional space for stepfamily members to bond.

3. Children in stepfamilies often are members of two households because of widespread legal preferences for joint physical custody. This increasingly means a constant coming and going of children into and out of the household, which is difficult for some family members to adjust to. When children are members of two households, it represents more than moving back and forth between those households, however. It means that the family in one household cannot plan a family vacation without checking with the child's parent in the other household. It may mean that a parent can't afford to provide a biological child with dance lessons because a stepchild in the other household needs braces. These boundaries are physical (e.g., different households in different communities), but they are also emotional, and they represent abstractions such as power and control. If the divorced couple is unable to civilly and effectively communicate, the child is caught in the middle, carrying messages from one household to the other ("Tell your dad he needs to pay his child support") and back ("Tell your mother that I am picking you up early next Friday"), a position that most children deeply resent.

4. Unlike the relationship between parents and their children, there are no (or few) legal ties between a stepparent and a stepchild. This matters very little unless the family re-divorces. When the stepfamily splits up, the stepparent generally no longer has rights (or responsibilities) regarding the stepchild. Even for stepfamilies that have shared a household for years, in some cases stepfamily members have not been allowed to visit other stepfamily members in the hospital's intensive care unit because they are not considered "immediate family." Schools have become more aware that stepparents may lack legal ties to a child, but that they may be important family members. This is evidenced by the change in recent years of most school forms. Newer school forms are now more likely to have more than two lines for students to list their parents, avoiding the child's dilemma (and guilt) of deciding which parents they should list.

5. Unlike first-married families, stepfamily members do not share a history. The stepparent will not know things such as that their stepchild slept with a pink plush rabbit until they were five, or fell off a horse when they were seven and are deathly afraid of horses. In this example, the lack of history can account for a child's puzzling hostility toward a stepparent's attempt to get the stepchild on a horse while on vacation. It may feel awkward for children and their

parent to talk about things that happened in the previous family in front of a stepparent, which contributes to children's feelings of loss. Some stepparents who have taken their stepchild to the doctor have been embarrassed about not knowing whether a child has had vaccines or what allergies she or he might have. These feelings of awkwardness sometimes interfere with feelings of family cohesiveness that seem to come naturally to first-married families.

6. The lack of institutionalization of stepfamilies is often confusing and uncomfortable for stepfamily members. Stepfamilies do not have a legal structure or a history that gives them a set of rules and traditions to follow. In the absence of norms to guide behaviors, some stepparents and their spouses try to act immediately as if they were a first-marriage unit. This works well only when stepchildren are so young they do not remember when their biological parents were together or when older stepchildren are willing to have the stepparent functionally replace their absent parent. If stepchildren are not willing to follow this "first-marriage family model," then problems are more likely to arise. For instance, most stepchildren call their stepparent by their first names; remarried couples trying to emulate a first-marriage family, however, may insist on a stepchild calling the stepparent "mom" or "dad," a request often met with resistance. Some stepparents try to avoid uncomfortable ambiguity by having the stepparent adopt the stepchild. This, of course, is feasible only if the biological parent is willing to give up all rights to the child, and if the child accepts this adoption.

REMARRIAGE AND STEPFAMILY RESEARCH

The early stepfamily research was rather unsophisticated. For instance, data were collected from anyone who lived in a stepfamily—biological parents, stepchildren, stepparents, stepsiblings—and then analyzed together as though everyone—parents, stepparents, children—experienced stepfamilies similarly. The wide variety of stepfamilies usually was ignored, and samples often included only white and middle-class individuals.

The perspective of most early researchers was what we have referred to as a *deficit comparison* approach.[7] Deficit comparison studies are primarily cross-sectional comparisons of stepchildren to children in two-parent, first-marriage families, although the studies sometimes include children living with a single parent or children whose parents are divorced but not remarried. The prevailing assumption in these deficit comparison studies is that stepchildren will fare more poorly on outcome measures when compared to children living with both of their biological parents.

These study designs are essentially snapshots of family life, offering little consideration of the personal histories of the individuals that led them into living in stepfamilies, or single-parent households, or first-marriage families. A variety of topics have been studied with this deficit approach (e.g., children's self-esteem, externalizing behaviors such as getting in trouble, and grade point averages) and consistently found that, on average, stepchildren did not fare as well as children in first-marriage families, but they were similar to children living with never-married or divorced single parents. Although the developmental and behavioral differences generally were very small among these groups of children, some researchers and the general public have tended to perceive these findings as large and absolute—that *all* stepchildren do less well on all measures of well-being than do children whose parents are still married, which simply is not true. In fact, most stepchildren function well, and their development is not damaged permanently by their parents' re-partnering.

Researchers have become more sophisticated about comparing family structures, and most research on stepchildren has followed the trend toward research designs that follow changes in families over time, pay greater attention to family process variables (such as relationship quality, everyday talk, and relationships with non-household kin), and involve more nuanced theorizing about stepfamily effects on children. For example, fewer researchers look only at family structure as the sole, or even main, explanation for children's and adults' well-being. More structural variables are also being included, such as the number of marital (or partner) transitions, the current and past marital statuses of parents and stepparents, and the presence of non-household stepfamily members.

In addition, some scholars have moved from a deficit comparison model to a *normative adaptive* approach that assumes that divorce and remarriage are often normal lifestyle choices rather than the result of personal psychopathology or maladaptive interpersonal or social problems. In using a normative adaptive approach, some researchers conduct longitudinal studies so that they can follow individuals and their families over time and across family transitions, yielding a more complete picture of the contexts in which stepfamilies live. Conducting research this way is like taking videos rather than still photos of stepfamily interactions. In addition, more normative adaptive researchers are using qualitative methods that involve in-depth conversations with stepfamily members to understand their experiences living in stepfamilies more holistically than is possible from questionnaires in anonymous surveys. We have found that some notable stepfamily researchers have never actually talked to any members of a stepfamily. They study stepfamilies using large data sets collected by other people, or they collect their own data using survey questionnaires. While large data sets are a valuable and informative research tool, using multiple methods that include observations or interaction with stepfamily members has deepened and made more reliable our understanding of the diversity as well as the resources within stepfamilies.

Normative adaptive perspectives include the study of resilience in stepfamilies. For instance, researchers have investigated stepchildren who are doing well in stepfamilies to see how they and their families differ from those that are struggling, as a way to determine what individual, interpersonal, and social factors contribute to successful adaptations. These studies also examine the context of successful stepfamily relationships as well as how stepfamily members build and maintain positive relationships.

WHAT HAVE WE LEARNED FROM RESEARCH ON STEPFAMILIES?

Over the past four decades, stepfamily scholarship has gone from less than a dozen studies to thousands of studies based on data from tens of thousands of stepfamily members from around the world. So what has been learned from the explosion of stepfamily research over the past three decades? Here is what we have learned:

1. "If-then" statements, as is true of most research, are necessary in drawing conclusions from the study of stepfamilies. For example, "*If* a child gains a stepparent when younger and *if* the remarriage lasts during most of the years that the child still lives at home, *then* the relationship is likely to resemble that between a biological parent and child." "*If* the stepparent invests in activities that the stepchild enjoys (as opposed to the stepparent engaging in activities they think the stepchild *should* enjoy, *then* the relationship will more likely resemble that between a biological parent and child." "*If* the child is close to all of their parents (biological and step-), *then* they will likely experience greater well-being."

2. Remarriages are less stable than first marriages, ending in divorce somewhat more frequently. Reasons for higher divorce rates for remarried couples include financial problems, issues involving raising children from prior unions, and what have been called *selection factors*. This latter point means that divorced individuals probably have different attitudes about divorce as a potential solution to marital problems than do never-divorced individuals. They know they can cope with a marital breakup, so divorce holds less fear for them, and they see fewer barriers to ending a marriage.

3. Remarriages tend to be more egalitarian than first marriages. This is primarily because women want more power and control in remarriage than they had in their previous marriage. Women who have been divorced and on their own, effectively managing their income and their children, are reluctant to

give up that hard-earned control. Men in remarriages seem to be more willing to share power with their wives, and when they do so, remarriages are more satisfying for both partners.

4. Even though stepchildren tend to do slightly less well, on average, than children in continuously married families on a number of dimensions of well-being, these differences often relate to factors that have less to do with stepfamily dynamics than with more general issues. For instance, conflict between the children's biological parents, household and family stressors, poverty, the experience of multiple family transitions, and even genetic factors such as mental illness and addiction are found to be more relevant than parents' marital status in many studies of stepchildren.

5. The relationship between stepchildren and stepparents is heavily influenced by the stepchild's judgments about the contributions the stepparent is making (or has made) to the family. These judgments generally are affected somewhat by input from the stepchild's biological parents and by other kin (e.g., siblings and grandparents), but other factors are also important. Other contributing factors include the stepchildren's ages when the relationship between their parent and the parent's partner began, the amount of time the stepparent and stepchild have spent together (heavily determined by custody arrangements), and the gender of the stepchild and stepparent. It may be especially important to stepchildren that the stepfather bring financial resources to the household rather than reducing resources. To many stepchildren, a stepfather who does not financially contribute to the household is merely taking away valuable time with their mother.

6. Stepparent-stepchild relationships generally work best when stepparents support the parent rather than taking parental roles, especially disciplinary roles. Over time, stepparents may become more like parents to stepchildren, but for this to happen, the stepparent has to do a great deal of what is called *affinity building* (i.e., engaging with the stepchild in activities that the stepchild enjoys). In response to these efforts, stepchildren need to engage in relationship-building actions with the stepparent as well. In one study, stepfathers who were observed making efforts at the dinner table day after day to connect with stepchildren who ignored their efforts eventually gave up. Although it is painful to stepparents to try to bond with a stepchild who responds with rudeness or disinterest, they should not give up. The stepchild may eventually succumb to a stepparent's efforts if they believe that the stepparent is sincere. Some children may not be able to begin bonding with their stepparent until they have finished grieving for their previous family.

7. Stepmothers, especially nonresidential ones, have a more difficult time than do stepfathers. Residential stepmothers may be forced to engage in parenting

behaviors simply because they are there with the stepchildren day in and day out. Most stepmothers do not share a residence with stepchildren full-time, however, and those who do not spend much time with their stepchildren struggle with determining what roles they should take. Some have even wondered if they should be in the home when the stepchildren visit, because the children often make it clear they are there only to see their father. Following old-fashioned gender scripts, sometimes more traditional fathers push the care of their children onto the stepmother, assuming that she will enjoy the "mothering" role and that his children will accept her in that role. Stepmothers and stepchildren, however, seldom feel that way. Some non-residential stepmothers have described their positions as "mothering but not a mother" or as "an additional mother." Because the role of mother is such a powerful one, most stepmothers are very careful to avoid encroaching on the biological mother's territory, even though in describing what they do with and for their stepchildren, they are defining mothering behaviors. The role that a stepmother is able to take with her stepchildren, however, is basically determined by the biological mother. If she does not like the stepmother, the children are likely to engage in such behaviors as refusing to eat anything the stepmother cooks, ignoring her, or making fun of her.

8. A number of patterns typify how stepparent-stepchild relationships develop and are maintained.[8] Given the complexity of stepfamilies, it should not be surprising that there are many types of step-relationships.

    a. Stepchildren who were raised by a stepparent from infancy are likely to accept that stepparent as a parent. The stepparent may be a replacement for a deceased parent or for one who has abandoned the child, or the stepparent may be an additional (third) parent with all the pluses and minuses of a biological parent. Stepchildren representing this pattern often do not remember a time when the stepparent was not a part of their family. This does not necessarily mean, however, that the stepchildren do not also have a relationship with their nonresidential parent: some children have positive relations with more than two parent figures.

    b. Some stepchildren like their stepparent from the beginning (but do not necessarily accept them as a parent or parent-figure). These relationships usually develop quickly and form around shared interests, similar personalities, or common values. These stepchildren notice early on that the stepparent treats their parent well and also does not put the stepchild in a loyalty bind by trying to replace their biological parent. Stepparents who are accepted from the beginning usually are accepted because they engage in a great deal of affinity-developing behavior.

c. Some stepchildren (often adolescents) accept their stepparents into the family, but with ambivalence. They really are not interested in having another adult telling them what to do. It is developmentally appropriate for adolescents to begin disengaging from their families, and if the remarried partners are trying to make things "feel like a family" and force an adolescent to take part in stepfamily activities, conflicts may develop. Stepchildren who accept their stepparent with ambivalence do not invest much energy in developing a relationship with him or her. Some stepchildren may feel they have little in common with their stepparent and see the stepparent as an unnecessary family member. Ambivalence is a common characteristic of nearly all step-relationships, though its extent is variable.

d. A fourth pattern consists of stepchildren who either become more or less accepting of the stepparent over time. Stepparents who keep engaging in affinity development with their stepchildren often will eventually win them over. Stepchildren, as they mature and become less self-focused, may begin to appreciate that the stepparent makes their parent happy. These new insights may lead to greater acceptance of the stepparent. On the other hand, stepparents (mostly stepfathers) who "courted" the stepchild along with the stepchild's mother sometimes quit engaging in those behaviors after the remarriage. In these circumstances, stepchildren observe that the stepfather was nice—took them to movies, out to eat—until the remarriage and then everything changed. Other stepchildren indicate that despite spending considerable effort being nice to a stepparent (often a nonresidential stepmother), the stepparent continually rebuffs them or is rude. Even if she makes the father happy, the relationship between the stepchild and stepmother is soured.

e. A fifth pattern is stepchildren who disliked and rejected the stepparent from the start. Many reasons were given for this. Some blamed their nonresidential stepmother for the distant relationship that they had with their father. Some thought the stepparent moved into a disciplinary role too quickly and resented taking direction from the stepparent. Others saw the stepparent as taking away from the quality of their parent's lives (e.g., stepfathers who did not contribute financially to the household or who were alcoholics who treated their mothers poorly; stepmothers who interfered with or were jealous of the relationship between the stepchild and their parent).

f. Stepchildren who coexisted with their stepparent (usually a stepparent acquired after the stepchild was an adult or nearly an adult). Sometimes coexisting relationships were the norm because the parent had been married multiple times and the stepchild assumed that the relationship would not last long enough to bother investing time in it.

9. Stepchildren can be close to both a mother and stepmother and to both a father and stepfather. In fact, there is evidence that stepchildren develop better when they get along with and are close to all of the parents and step-parents who are raising them. Clinicians have long pointed out the damage to children when placed in the middle of loyalty binds between parents, or between a parent and a stepparent, or between their two step-households, and researchers' findings have supported the notion that allowing children to bond with all of the adults in their lives is helpful to their development. Of course, some stepchildren are close to only one parent, and some do not get along with any of their parents or stepparents.

There are all types of stepfamilies—some are happy and satisfying, some are grim and stressful. Most stepfamilies, like most other family forms, fall some-where between these extremes. In the past few years, family researchers have learned a lot about how stepfamily members relate to each other, but many ques-tions remain to be answered, such as how do gay and lesbian couples experience stepfamily life? Do interracial stepfamilies have distinct resources or challenges that same-race stepfamilies do not? How will our aging population experience stepfamily issues—including caregiving responsibilities—which are increasingly prevalent? Our understanding of stepfamilies is growing, and both the questions and answers about them are better when the varieties of experiences are recog-nized by researchers, practitioners, and even by stepfamily members themselves. Sociologist Judith Stacey has called stepfamilies "brave new families," and we have long contended that learning about stepfamily resilience processes yields valuable lessons that can be helpful to members of all family forms.

NOTES

1. Pew Research Social and Demographic Trends (2011).
2. Daly and Wilson (1998).
3. Pew Research Social and Demographic Trends (2011).
4. Cherlin (1978).
5. Bohannon (1984).
6. Papernow (1987).
7. Ganong and Coleman (2004).
8. Ganong, Coleman, and Jamison (2011).

23

Beyond Family Structure

*Family Process Studies Help to Reframe Debates
about What's Good for Children*

Philip A. Cowan and Carolyn Pape Cowan

Ever since 1992, when Republican Vice President Dan Quayle criticized a fictional television character, Murphy Brown, for having a baby without being married, family values and family policies have assumed an important role in political debates between those with a liberal or conservative bent. Should single parenthood be discouraged and marriage encouraged? Should marriage between same-sex partners be legalized or forbidden? Should divorces be made more difficult or easier to obtain? Should poor families receive income supplements or tax breaks? These questions frame the discussion of family issues in terms of categories or typologies. Most often, the focus is on family structure—are the biological parents married, divorced, cohabiting, separated, or single? In this chapter, we argue that what is left out of too many contemporary family policy discussions is a concern with family process—the quality or pattern of the interactions among family members.

We are concerned with family policy debates, not only because government regulations affect the lives of many families but also because the debates in themselves have the power to influence what ordinary families actually do. Conclusions about single parenthood and divorce, for example, propel at least some toward marriage and others to preserve their marriage despite misery or domestic violence. It would be well, then, to make sure that both the logic and the evidence cited on both sides of family policy questions actually support the position held by each of the advocates.

We see some difficulties with the evidence cited by both liberals and conservatives who describe families in terms of categories or types. Both sides typically justify their policy positions by pointing to social science research that purports to show that their view would lead to children's enhanced development and well-being, whereas the opposing view would fail to help children and might place them in harm's way. Some examples:

- Those who advocate policies to encourage marriage note that single mothers are more likely to be poor, and their children more likely to be at risk for academic difficulties and behavior problems.[1] Marriage, they argue, could bring the family out of poverty with resulting benefits to children.

- Opponents of same-sex marriage often claim that children will suffer from the absence of both male and female role models. Supporters of same-sex marriage point out that, contrary to stereotype, children of lesbian parents are not significantly different than children of heterosexual parents on a number of developmental measures.[2]

- In a book entitled *The Case for Marriage: Why Married People Are Healthier, Happier, and Better Off Financially*, Waite and Gallagher summarize large numbers of studies showing that, on average, in comparison with non-married couples, married couples are better off.[3] Although the authors mention that many of these advantages accrue to happily married couples, they continue to minimize that distinction throughout the book. This is an important omission, because they do not cite a good deal of evidence that married couples in high conflict are less healthy than couples who can regulate negative emotion in the course of an argument and that the children of unhappily married couples suffer from their parents' heated or unresolved conflicts.[4]

We live in a time when polarized public discussions are the norm. The proponents of a particular view assume that they can be right only if they prove the other side wrong. In our attempt to highlight the importance of family process, we will not argue that categorical descriptions of families in terms of structure or demographics are irrelevant to discussions of family policy. There are often important differences in outcomes for children whose parents are married, divorced, or single, and these facts can help us fashion appropriate policies or interventions. But we intend to add a relatively neglected perspective to the discussion—by focusing on the quality of relationships within the family. Our own view is that (1) all of these ways of describing families are important in understanding children's well-being; and (2) a consideration of information about family processes will lead to policy recommendations for governments, social service agencies, and families themselves that differ from typical conservative and liberal approaches to American family policy.

Due to the constraints of chapter length, we have chosen to focus our discussion of family process and children's well-being primarily on issues concerning the involvement of fathers in family life, and the quality of the relationship between the parents. This choice leads us to ignore other equally important family decision-making and policy questions such as whether both partners should work outside the home and use local child-care facilities, whether the government should regulate workplace practices to provide support for workers' family lives (e.g., through family leave), or whether it is the government's responsibility to provide high-quality child care.

We begin by briefly summarizing the voluminous data on the association between categories of family structure and children's well-being. We then summarize the research on family process guided by a family systems model, which demonstrates that a combination of data regarding five family risk or protective factors provides the best explanations of children's level of development, adaptation, and problematic behavior. We discuss the model's implications for how both parents and social service agencies should think about the kind of interventions that can improve family environments. We then explore the implications of this family systems model for family policy. We conclude that, in contrast with conservative thinkers who advocate inducements to poor single parents to marry and liberal thinkers who advocate family income supplements to poor families, the data suggest that interventions to strengthen couple relationships and involve fathers more centrally in family life—regardless of whether the parents are married—have the potential to provide important benefits for children's social, emotional, and academic development.

FAMILY STRUCTURE, FAMILY DEMOGRAPHICS, FAMILY VALUES, AND CHILDREN'S WELL-BEING

As Stephanie Coontz points out in Chapter 5 of this volume, a great many changes in family structure and demographics have occurred over the past century, although the amount of change depends in part on the beginning and end points of our historical search. We focus here on the fact that over the past sixty years, there have been marked increases in the rates of single parenthood and divorce and a decline in marriage rates and birthrates. The central question for family policy is how to interpret these changes. If they are interpreted as evidence of a decline in the quality of family life, then we should consider what kinds of family arrangements, social services, and government policies might alleviate the negative impact or reverse the effects. If the changes are interpreted as evidence of family variety, resilience, and a response to historical and economic shifts, then proposals that would affect marriage and divorce rates through government regulation or the provision of social services may not be necessary.

Controversies about the Impact of Divorce

The question of how divorce affects children remains one of the most contested areas of family research. There is not room to describe the controversy here, but the issue has been well described elsewhere in both U.S. and U.K. publications.[5] There is no doubt that, at least in the short term, parents and children are affected when parents separate. Most children of any age are extremely upset by the divorce of their parents, and a substantial number suffer at least temporary setbacks in social and emotional development and academic achievement. In the long term, however, the negative effects dissipate for most children, so that "only" about 20 percent of children suffer in lasting ways.[6] This means that although some children may be suffering some consequences of their parents' divorce, it is also true that the vast majority will go on to develop healthy and productive lives. In our view, the sociologist Paul Amato has a sensible perspective on the issues surrounding divorce.[7] He suggests that the usual framing of the question "Does divorce hurt children: yes or no?" is misleading. He suggests a more differentiated approach:

> Divorce benefits some individuals, leads others to experience temporary decrements in well-being, and forces others on a downward trajectory from which they might never recover fully. Understanding the contingencies under which divorce leads to these diverse outcomes is a priority for future research.

As we will see later in this chapter, some important contingencies can be found in the research on family processes, especially based on how conflict between parents both before and after divorce is handled.

Controversies about the Impact of Single Parenthood

Similar conclusions can be drawn from research on the impact of single parenthood on children. There is no doubt that if you are an actuary interested in predicting negative outcomes, you can rely on the myriad of studies showing that, on average, a large list of behavioral and school problems appear more frequently in children living with only one parent.[8] Again, the question is how to interpret the correlational finding. Some senior policy makers treat the correlational data as causal; if single parenthood increases poverty and produces risks for children, then provide incentives for single parents to get married and the lives of children will improve.[9] Of course, it is impossible to do a randomized clinical trial of this hypothesis by assigning some women randomly to a "get married group" and others to a "stay single" group. But we lack even correlational data to show that when poverty declines and single parents marry, their children's well-being increases.

Some researchers argue that the correlation between single parenthood and negative outcomes for children reflects a selection effect—parents with more financial, intellectual, and social resources are more likely to marry and less likely to divorce. In a careful summary of the literature, Cherlin concludes that even after selection effects are considered, there is a small but statistically significant effect of family structure (married vs. single) on children.[10] That is, family structure plays some role in determining outcomes for children, but most of the children reared in single-parent homes fare quite well. It is necessary, then, to examine other factors to explain the finding that children of single parents are more likely to have cognitive, social, or emotional difficulties.

These brief accounts of research on divorce and single parenthood serve to make our main point. "Family decline" proponents who pay attention only to family categories and report only the statistically significant differences among family types overstate the magnitude of the effects; their presentation makes it appear as if nontraditional family structures account for the major proportion of social problems and psychopathology in children and youth. These overstatements are then used to justify recommendations to parents, social service providers, and policy makers: to protect children, we should encourage married parents to stay together, make divorces harder to obtain, and encourage single parents to marry. We will use the same data and other studies to come to a different conclusion: to protect children and prevent parents' divorce, we could profitably provide services to strengthen couple relationships before they become so problematic and painful that separation and divorce become reasonable options.

Are Family Values to Blame for Historical Changes in Family Life?

Most social observers who assert that families are in decline place the blame for this decline on an erosion of family values.[11] They argue that changes in single-parent, divorced, and dual-worker families result from individual decisions about family life that reflect a lack of investment in the importance of becoming responsible parents devoted to the care of their children. It follows from this analysis that to protect children, we need interventions that will remind parents of these important family values and convince them to reinvest in them.

There are two puzzling aspects of this argument. First, the idea that a change in family values triggered the social trends we have been discussing is not based on any data we know of that (1) assess changes in family values over time, and (2) show that values held by individual men and women are in fact correlated with the family arrangements they have constructed. One counterexample can be seen in an interview study of low-income unmarried women[12] suggesting that they hold rather traditional family values concerning the importance and desirability of marriage and of the financial responsibilities involved in making that commitment, and that these ideals lead them to be wary of entering into marriages they believe are doomed to failure.

A second response to the focus on family values as explaining negative family trends comes from newly emerging studies with quantitative data. One of the major sources of stress on contemporary families is financial.[13] Financial circumstances often affect family decisions about marriage, divorce, and whether both partners need to work outside the home. Not only do families feel external stress from lack of money and little workplace flexibility, but social service resources are limited for direct services to families in difficulty. Even fewer resources are available for preventive services to offer assistance to families before their dysfunction reaches a level that is difficult to treat. From this perspective, what is needed to protect children is not an exhortation to parents to adopt more positive family values (a relatively inexpensive approach) but rather serious governmental commitment to change the economic circumstances that play havoc with the lives of mothers, fathers, and children. We return to this issue later.

Family Process and Children's Well-Being: A Framework Based on Five Family Risk and Protective Factors

The family structure and demographic approach represents an outsider perspective on family life. One can categorize a family as, for example, low-income or high-income, married or not married, on the basis of the kind of information gathered in the census. By contrast, the family process approach pays attention to the characteristics of each family member and especially to how the members behave with each other. What are the central factors in a family process approach? Elsewhere, we have summarized our own research and many other studies that support a five-domain family systems risk model of children's adaptation.[14] This model demonstrates that a child's cognitive, social, and emotional development can be explained by information concerning five kinds of risk or protective factors that affect children's development:

1. The level of adaptation of each family member, his or her self-perceptions, and indicators of mental health and psychological distress

2. The quality of both mother-child and father-child relationships

3. The quality of the relationship between the parents, including communication styles, conflict resolution, problem-solving styles, and emotion regulation

4. The patterns of both couple and parent-child relationships transmitted across the generations from grandparents to parents to children

5. The balance between life stressors and social supports outside the immediate family

Each Parent's Level of Adaptation

Beyond the questions of whether parents are married or poor, a family process approach looks at whether either or both parents are suffering from depression, anxiety, personality disorders, or serious mental illness. The task here is not to place parents in a particular diagnostic category, but to discover whether their difficulties interfere with or affect the quality of their relationships with each other and their children. Not surprisingly, evidence suggests that parents who are depressed, antisocial, or schizophrenic are less effective at solving their problems as a couple and function less effectively to provide nurturance, guidance, and limit setting appropriate to the age of their children.[15]

Parent-Child Relationships

People have many different ideas about what constitutes effective parenting. It is noteworthy that the proliferation of self-help books on parenting present widely different prescriptions for parenting behavior, most without systematic evidence to support the author's recommendations.[16] The picture brightens somewhat when we turn to systematic studies of parenting styles. There is reasonable agreement in the research literature on children's development that authoritative parenting—a combination of parental warmth, structure, limit setting, and appropriate demands for maturity—provides a context in which children are more likely to develop effective cognitive skills, better relationships with peers, and fewer behavior problems.[17] Other parenting styles are less effective. Authoritarian parenting is harsh and structured. Permissive parenting is warm but laissez-faire, with few if any limits. Neglectful or uninvolved parenting is neither warm nor structured and demanding. It is probably obvious that parental harshness and neglect are not good for children. The lesson here for modern parents who both work and tend to see their children for shorter times during their waking hours is that warmth without some form of limits and maturity demands is not helpful in stimulating children's growth or the development of social and cognitive skills and self-regulation.

A serious limitation of both the popular and social science literatures is that *parent* has generally meant "mother."[18] Only in the past few decades have there been systematic studies of father-child relationships,[19] and an even smaller body of information examines how the combination of two parents' styles of parenting affects children's development. Yet, it should be no surprise that systematic studies find that when fathers are more positively engaged with their children's daily lives, the children, the mothers, and the fathers themselves are more likely to be competent, form more positive relationships with peers, and show fewer signs of emotional distress. Furthermore, information about the quality of the father-child relationship enhances our ability to account for children's adaptation, over and above what we know about the quality of the mother-child relationship.

We should make clear what we are not saying here. We do not mean to imply that fathers should be encouraged to be involved with their children when they are abusive to the child or the mother. And we are not arguing, as some do,[20] that having a father is essential to raising a well-adjusted child.[21] We are simply stating that a second, positively engaged parent or parent figure can make an additional and unique contribution to children's cognitive, social, and emotional development.[22] So far, the research that makes this point has been done with heterosexual couples as parents; we await further study but believe that studies of families with same-sex parents will show very similar findings.

The Couple Relationship

Another conspicuous omission from popular books on raising children is the conclusion from a growing body of recent research based on family systems principles about the effect of the parents' relationship on their children. With few exceptions,[23] the popular books focus almost entirely on how mothers relate to their children. What recent family systems research studies reveal, however, is that the quality of the relationship between the parents, whether they are married, separated, or divorced, is consistently correlated with how children fare. When couples are unable to resolve their disagreements and either escalate their anger or withdraw into freezing silence, their children are at risk for difficulties in every developmental domain.[24]

We describe later some intervention studies that help answer the question of whether conflict or withdrawal in the relationship between parents plays a causal role in children's development. Here we briefly summarize two speculations to explain the correlations. First, parents' behavior can have a direct, anxiety-provoking effect on children. When parents' anger toward each other is out of control or they fail to talk with each other for hours or days, many children become increasingly frightened, anxious, and vulnerable. Second, when parents fail to provide a nurturing environment for each other, it is difficult to provide a caring environment for their child; the metaphor of "spillover"—anger overflowing from the relationship between the parents to one or both parent-child relationships—is used to explain the link between couple conflict and children's problematic outcomes.[25]

Intergenerational Transmission of Family Patterns

Substantial evidence exists to support the widespread belief that family patterns tend to be repeated from one generation to the next.[26] We are not suggesting that difficulties in our family of origin doom us to repeat the maladaptive patterns of our forebears. We are simply reporting the finding that mental illness in individuals, harsh or neglectful treatment of children, and dysfunctional couple relationships in one generation increase the risks of similar negative outcomes in the next generation.[27] Fortunately, although positive patterns do not guarantee good outcomes, they function as protective factors that raise the likelihood of good outcomes.

During the transition to first-time parenthood, patterns from the parents' relationships in their families of origin become particularly salient. Each parent has some patterns he or she wishes to repeat and some he or she wishes to change in this new family. Coordinating these potentially different dreams is a challenge faced by many new parents. If neither parent has positive models, the challenge is even greater.

In raising the topic of intergenerational transmission, we are not simply playing the blame game—that is, explaining or excusing problems in current families as having been passed down from the grandparents. Rather, we are pointing to the finding that attempts to change current family relationship quality almost inevitably involve increasing the consciousness of both parents about the patterns they wish to carry over or avoid.

Life Stress and Social Support Outside the Family

What happens inside the nuclear family is affected by the external environment and the family's relationship to it. Families tend to fare better when outside stressors are few or at least balanced by adequate support from kin, friends, and social institutions. Evidence from McLoyd and colleagues' summary of research on African American families[28] and Conger and colleagues' research on white farm families during a recession[29] indicate that poverty affects children through its corrosive effects on the quality of both couple and parent-child relationships. Stress in the workplace has a similarly disruptive spillover effect on family relationships.

The Full Model

Most studies of children's development focus on one or at most two of the five family risk and protective domains at a time. Elsewhere we have shown that each of these domains contributes uniquely to predicting children's academic and social competence as well as their internalizing and externalizing problem behaviors in early elementary school.[30] Child rearing is not simply a matter of "good parenting." Children are also affected by their parents' psychological adjustment and their ability as a couple to resolve problems and disagreements between them, by the repetition of cycles across generations, and by the availability of people and institutions to provide support when the culture, country, and neighborhood impose pressures that are difficult to avoid. Data from studies based on this model imply that when family interventions focus on only one of these aspects of families' lives, they may have limited effectiveness.

For example, there is currently a large public and private industry devoted to "parenting classes." For a long while, the news was disappointing; the few evaluated programs amassed very little evidence that the classes had direct positive effects on children's behavior.[31] But more recently, parenting classes embedded in university-based research programs have shown some signs of success.[32] The importance of thinking in terms of more than one domain during a parenting intervention is supported by studies showing that therapeutic treatment for mothers of aggressive children often fails to work until fathers are involved and the relationship between the parents is addressed directly.[33]

We have only begun to test the hypothesis that family processes play a causal role in children's well-being. The correlational findings are suggestive but not conclusive. It can be argued that some of the links between family process and children's well-being are genetic[34] and that genetic transmission is not subject to interventions that can change family relationships. But newer formulations of the interaction of genes and the environment[35] indicate that even when personality characteristics are highly heritable, changes in the family relationship environment still affect how and whether heritability leads to negative outcomes in the children.

The correlations between marital conflict and children's outcomes suggest that interventions focusing on the relationship between the parents will be helpful to children, but we cannot use correlational studies as proof of our claim. We need to provide some data from intervention studies that have used randomized control designs to demonstrate that when the interventions were followed by more effective couple relationships, parenting effectiveness and the children's behavior were affected in positive ways.

THREE EXAMPLES OF PREVENTIVE INTERVENTION STUDIES BASED ON OUR MULTI-DOMAIN MODEL

The reason for our emphasis on couple relationships when we consider children's well-being lies in an unfortunate fact. In addition to marital dissatisfaction leading to a high divorce rate (around 50 percent of marriages), more than twenty-five studies in Western industrialized societies[36] find that, on average, men's and women's satisfaction with their relationship as a couple declines over at least the first fifteen years of marriage (we know of no longitudinal studies beyond that point). This trend is significant not only for the well-being of couples but also for the well-being of their children, because other studies show consistent connections between marital dissatisfaction and unresolved couple conflict, and children's and adolescents' achievement, aggressive behavior, and depression. Given these links, interventions that help couples maintain satisfaction with their relationship would be an important goal.

Over the past thirty-five years, we have conducted three studies of interventions in the form of couples groups led by clinically trained co-leaders. All three studies used randomized clinical trials in which some couples were randomly chosen to participate in the intervention while others were not. The male or female co-leaders met with the couples weekly over at least four months, and assessments were made before and after the group interventions to evaluate the groups' effectiveness. The couples were not seeking family treatment but responding to an invitation to meet with our staff around a key family transition or during their children's early development. Our goal was to create a preventive intervention to enhance family relationships when the children were early in their development and to prevent small problems and strains from becoming more serious. We did not attempt to teach couples specific skills, but to help them become the kind of couples and parents they wanted to be. We hoped to do this by providing a safe environment in which they could consider issues concerning their needs as individuals and as a couple. Our interventions and assessments also focused on their ties with their parents and children, and on how to cope with stress and distress and enlist supports inside and outside the family.

Working with Couples during the Transition to Parenthood

In the Becoming a Family Project, we followed ninety-six couples regularly over a period of five years: seventy-two entered the study when pregnant with their first child, and twenty-four were not yet parents and not pregnant.[37] All ninety-six couples completed regular interviews and questionnaires until their first child had completed kindergarten. Some of the expectant couples, randomly chosen, were offered the opportunity to participate in a couples group that met with their co-leaders for twenty-four weeks (six months). Each group session included some open time to discuss personal events and concerns in their lives and a topic that addressed one of the aspects of family life in our model.

Relevant to the focus of this chapter, we found that while there was a decline in satisfaction as a couple in the new parents without the intervention, as expected, the new parent couples who took part in a couples group maintained their level of satisfaction over the next five years until their children finished kindergarten. Although expectant couples in both conditions were initially quite happy, five years later, the average scores of couples in the control group had descended into the range where half of them resembled couples already in therapy. Five years after the groups for the parents ended, the quality of the couple relationships and the parent-child relationships in all the families during the pre-school period predicted the children's adaptation to kindergarten as their teachers rated it—academically, socially, and in terms of problematic behavior. This finding seemed especially strong since the teachers (in many different schools) did not know which children were participants in the study.

Couple Relationships and Children's Transition to School

A second intervention study, the Schoolchildren and Their Families Project, followed another 100 couples from the year before their first child entered kindergarten until the children were in eleventh grade.[38] There were three randomly assigned conditions—an offer to use our staff as consultants once a year (the control group), a couples group that emphasized parent-child relationships, or a couples group that focused more on the relationship between the parents during the open-ended part of the evenings. That is, we were comparing the effects of a more traditional parenting intervention (although it is unusual to have fathers attending with mothers) with a group in which leaders focused more on the relationship between the parents. The families were assessed when their children were in kindergarten and first grade. Parents who had been in a group emphasizing parent-child relationships had indeed improved in the aspects of parenting we observed in our project playroom, whereas the parenting style of parents in the control group showed no improvement.[39] By contrast, parents who had participated in a group in which the leaders focused more on couple relationships showed significantly less conflict as we observed them, and their parenting became more effective.

In this study, both variations of the ongoing intervention groups had an effect on the children. The children of parents in the parenting-focused groups improved in positive self-image, and they were less likely to show shy, withdrawn, and depressed behavior at school. Children of parents in the couples-focused groups were at an advantage in terms of higher scores on individually administered achievement tests and lower levels of aggressive behavior at school. The interventions continued to have a significant impact on the families over the next ten years—in terms of both self-reported and observed positive couple relationship quality and low levels of behavior problems in the students. The impact of the couples-focused groups was always equal to or greater than the impact of the parenting-focused groups.

Enhancing Father Involvement in Low-Income Families

Based on the results of the first two studies, the California Department of Social Services Office of Child Abuse Prevention asked us to design and evaluate an intervention that would enhance and maintain the positive involvement of low-income fathers with their children. Along with Marsha Kline Pruett from Smith College and Kyle Pruett from Yale University, we completed the first phase of the Supporting Father Involvement Project, in which ninety-six couples attended a single-session workshop that presented material about the importance of fathers in children's lives (the control group), ninety-two fathers attended a sixteen-week fathers group, and ninety-five fathers and their partners attended a sixteen-week couples group.[40] Again, the assignment was random, the groups were led by clinically trained male/female co-leaders, and the curriculum for both fathers and couples groups focused on the five family risk and protective factors we have been describing.

At the beginning of the study, children ranged in age from in utero to seven years. The project was mounted in Family Resource Centers in four California counties; two-thirds of the participants were Mexican American and one-third were European American; 75 percent were married and 20 percent were living together; and two-thirds of the households in both ethnic groups had incomes below twice the federal poverty line. Assessments (in English or Spanish) at baseline, two months after the groups ended, and again one year after the groups ended revealed the positive impact of participation in one of the intervention groups. In both fathers and couples groups, fathers' involvement in the day-to-day activities of caring for their children (feeding, playing, taking to the doctor) increased significantly, and the children's level of aggressive and depressed behaviors remained stable, in comparison with the children in the control group, whose parents described them as increasingly aggressive or depressed over the same period of time. In addition to these positive effects in the fathers-group participants, fathers and mothers from the couples groups showed a significant decline in parenting stress, and they maintained their satisfaction as couples, in contrast with both controls and parents assigned to the fathers group, whose parenting stress rose and relationship satisfaction declined.

A second trial of the Supporting Father Involvement study was conducted with a new cohort of 236 Mexican American, African American, and European American families.[41] This time, because the participants in the earlier single-session meeting changed negatively, we did not include a control group; and because the couples group had stronger effects, fathers and mothers were enrolled in that condition. The positive changes over the eighteen months of the study were very similar to those we obtained earlier. A third trial that includes families referred by the child welfare system because of domestic violence or child abuse or neglect is also showing positive results in preliminary analyses.

In sum, we have shown that the preventive intervention groups, especially the groups for both mothers and fathers, had positive effects on father involvement, parenting stress, couple relationship satisfaction, and children's problematic behavior. All these aspects of life are related to children's well-being, and all function as either risk or protective factors for child abuse and neglect. On the strength of these positive findings, the Office of Child Abuse Prevention has supported an extension of the study to a broader sample of another 300 families and created an infrastructure to disseminate the project by providing technical assistance and training in the intervention to staff in family agencies beyond those in the original counties in our study. New groups are now being conducted in Alberta, Canada (funded by a private foundation), and in England, funded by the British government.

IMPLICATIONS OF RESEARCH FOR PARENTS

What are the implications of the research on family process for parents? We emphasize what this perspective adds to current debates that have focused primarily on family structure.

Father Involvement

In our view, the current political dialogue on the risks associated with single parenthood has resulted in an unproductive conversation about the role that fathers play in children's development. Taking their cue from research on family structure, some observers argue for encouraging single mothers to marry so that fathers can be in the home providing income and setting examples, especially for young boys. And in fact, there is now substantial evidence that relationships with fathers are important for girls' well-being also. In reaction, others argue that this goal represents a conservative position that privileges traditional heterosexual family arrangements and denies the vitality and resilience of diverse family forms. From the structural perspective, then, single parents, especially mothers, are given two choices: find a man to marry or remain confident about their single state.

A new set of findings makes the structural perspective a little more complex. The very large Fragile Families Study taking place in twenty American cities follows about 5,000 children, of whom about 75 percent were born to parents who were not married. The study found that around the time of childbirth, more than half of "single mothers" had the biological father as a romantic partner living in the home, and a large majority of these mothers were in a romantic relationship with the biological father, who wanted to play an active role in his child's life.[42] That is, the existing categories in the family structure perspective vastly underestimate the participation of men, at least in the early stages of family making.

The family process literature adds an important point for parents in all family structures to consider. If there is a second parent (studies here have examined only heterosexual families), positive engaged fathering can make a unique, positive contribution to children's development, regardless of whether the parents are married, unmarried, separated, or divorced. Even though cultural stereotypes about men's roles in the lives of their children have been moving toward a more egalitarian ideal of equal participation in housework and child care, the realities are still far from this ideal. Men need to know that fathers are important. Women need to help men challenge the stereotype, and avoid the kind of "gatekeeping" that keeps men out if they engage the child in ways that are different from what mothers do.

Beyond Current Books on Parenting

Clearly, the research data and the intervention data we have cited suggest two important topics that are missing in most popular books on parenting. First, as we have noted, fathers are rarely referred to in parenting books, or they are acknowledged in a single chapter devoted to dads. This trend reinforces cultural stereotypes about the centrality of mothers and gives the mistaken message to fathers that they matter little to their young children's development. We need to find ways to get the word out to parents in two-parent families that both the mother and the father matter, so they can make their own decisions about how they will arrange their parenting responsibilities.

Second, how both fathers and mothers treat children is very important both on the negative end, in terms of abuse and neglect, and on the positive end, in terms of providing warmth and structure. Equally important is what happens between the parents. A key obstacle to keeping couple relationships alive is time, especially in dual-worker families. We find that modern working parents typically feel they should devote most of their nonwork time to their children. The research findings indicate that it is not "selfish" for parents to focus on their relationship as a couple, enjoy time together, or make space to resolve disagreements and difficulties to both partners' satisfaction. Improvements in the quality of the relationship between the parents will have a direct payoff for the children.

Should We Stay Together for the Sake of Our Children?

Authors of a number of books and articles that draw heavily on social science research conclude that, except for situations of domestic violence or abuse, parents in unhappy marriages should attempt to stay together to avoid the negative impact of divorce on their children. Almost all the research they refer to adopts a family structure perspective, simply following children of divorce over time[43] or comparing them with similar samples of children whose parents did not divorce.[44] In both cases, stories from youngsters and teenagers recounting long-term distress about their parents' divorce imply that if only the parents had stayed together, the children would not be having problems. The voluminous data, from which we have selected only several reviews and examples, suggest strongly that a second comparison group is necessary—children of high-conflict parents or low-conflict but unhappy parents who stay together. Studies of families in which the parents are unhappy indicate that keeping the family structure intact without regard to the quality of the key family relationships does not guarantee children's well-being.

None of the divorce studies can provide conclusive advice for a mother or father contemplating divorce, because there are risks for children no matter which decision is made. Two major questions are important to answer: If the partners stay together, can they find help from a therapist, clergyman, family member, or friend who would help them to improve their relationship? If they separate or divorce, can they still be positive co-parents who support each other in regard to caring for the children? Clearly, including information about family process makes for a more complex but, we suggest, more nuanced discussion of how to think about parents' and children's well-being when parents are unhappy.

IMPLICATIONS OF RESEARCH FOR FAMILY SERVICE PROVIDERS

What are the implications of the research on family process for family service providers?

Making Fathers Welcome

The current interest in involving fathers more in family life is echoed by family service providers who want to include fathers but complain that men are hard to reach and resistant to the services they offer. In our view, the problem of resistant men is exacerbated by the lack of father friendliness in many family service agencies. As we began the Supporting Father Involvement Project in California communities (described earlier), our visits to existing family resource centers revealed few signs that fathers were wanted or welcome—in the physical environment (colors on the walls, pictures, magazines), the social environment (mostly women staff), and organization of services or programs (few services or programs for fathers, little flexibility in terms of times when they are offered, little outreach to men). We believe that the problem of resistance to services is much too easily attributed to the men, when an equal share of the problem stems from the resistance of the staff to reaching out to fathers. The Supporting Father Involvement Project has shown that "if you build it, they will come." By now more than 900 men have participated in the program over the last three years, most of them meeting in groups for eleven to sixteen weeks. Staff dedicated to changing the environment of the agency made that happen.

The Importance of Couple Relationships for Father Involvement

We have stated that one of the best predictors of whether a father will become and stay involved with his child is the quality of the father's relationship with the mother. Ronald Mincy and Hillard Pouncy observe that the few existing systematic evaluations of fathers groups composed of low-income men show dis-appointing outcomes.[45] Most of the fathers groups attempting to increase father involvement occur long after the parents have separated or divorced and after the fathers have lost contact with their children. Not surprisingly, the mothers of the children were not supportive of their ex-spouse or ex-partner's attempts to take an active role in their child's life. Our own family intervention study shows stronger effects for couples groups than for fathers groups. Father involvement, then, emerges not simply from men's decisions to be involved in the family but from the ways in which family relationships enhance or interfere with men's relationships with their children.

Beyond Parenting Classes: Couples-Based Interventions for Parents

Both correlational studies and the intervention studies we have cited suggest that the many classes for parents offered in community colleges and social service agencies require some rethinking. First, the classes need to make stronger efforts to recruit both parents and provide experiences that will help them want to stay. Second, the classes need to pay much more attention to how the partners work together—or fail—to deal with co-parenting and other disagreements. We recog-nize that this raises the issue that leaders of parenting classes rarely are trained to work with parents on their issues as a couple.

POLICY IMPLICATIONS

Father Involvement

In the Deficit Reduction Act of 2005 (which reauthorized the welfare reform law of 1996), one-third of the $150 million annual budget for family work was to be directed to promoting fathers' involvement with their children. The Promoting Responsible Fatherhood website (http://fatherhood.hhs.gov/index.shtml) recog-nizes that the goals of marriage promotion and father involvement are directly connected. As in the case of funds allocated to promote healthy marriage, some of the funds were to go to research institutions. But in the case of promoting father involvement, most of the money has been allocated to statewide and local secular and faith-based organizations (faith-based organizations have very detailed instructions that the content of the programs must not include religious material). As of this writing, no systematic evaluations of these programs have appeared.

Marriage Promotion versus Couple Relationship Enhancement

In its growing concern over the erosion of marriage and the problems of children whose parents dissolved their marriage, the U.S. Federal Administration for Children and Families (ACF) used research-based findings from the Fragile Families Study[46] as a rationale for government intervention. The finding that most unmarried biological fathers have an ongoing romantic relationship with the mother when their child is born but fade from their child's life over the next few years[47] was used as a justification for promoting marriage, especially among low-income populations. Starting in 2005, this policy objective was supported by more than $150 million per year for five years with money from the Deficit Reduction ("welfare reform") Act.

While some of this money has been used in direct efforts to encourage marriage, a substantial amount has been allocated to two very large research projects funded by the ACF to test the effectiveness of "marriage education." One large intervention project (more than 4,000 couples)—Building Strong Families, conducted by Mathematica—focused on unmarried low-income couples having babies.[48] Although the results of this study were disappointing, indicating no overall effects of the intervention when contrasted with a randomly assigned no-treatment control group, there were significant effects for African American couples. A flaw in the implementation of this project was the very low attendance rate (around 35 percent). Another equally large random assignment study, Supporting Healthy Marriage, conducted by MDRC, focused on married low-income couples, most of whom were already parents.[49] This study, with attendance rates around 70 percent, did find small but statistically significant effects on both self-reported and observed couple relationship quality and on child outcomes for the youngest participants.

The policy implications of these activities are complex and controversial. For distinctly different views, see Johnson's critique[50] and Hawkins and colleagues' response.[51] Some critics focus on these large government-funded studies and ignore smaller couple relationship and father involvement studies. The effects of these interventions are not large, and we have yet to determine whether achieving small effects yields benefits that are worth the costs. Some colleagues argue that if one goal of the enterprise is to improve conditions for low-income families, why not supplement their incomes directly or at least provide job training, since unemployment is so directly linked to low income? Because we are not aware of evidence that income interventions have improved distressed couple relationships or parent-child relationships, we suggest that it seems reasonable to give relationship approaches that have been evaluated a chance to show whether they work and for whom they could provide the most benefit. Anecdotal reports from the staff conducting these large national projects, along with our own results with both middle- and low-income couples, give at least some hope that this approach to preventive intervention by strengthening couple and parent-child relationships has promise for strengthening families.

Training and Costs

Family systems research and our own intervention experiences have led us to emphasize the importance of couple relationships for children's well-being and the need to provide services to enhance those relationships. That is, we are calling for increased resources for training as well as for the provision of services that support mothers and fathers in the challenging task of balancing work and family demands during their children's formative years.

We are aware that these increased resources require funding. We are not aware of cost-benefit analyses of this kind of family work. It seems to us that the costs of providing services need to be compared with the costs of not providing services—in terms of family disruption, violence, parents' and children's psychological and physical health problems, and children's and young people's behavior problems.

CONCLUSIONS

Our goal in this paper has been to show that research on family processes can add new dimensions to current discussions about how to foster the well-being of children. We have shown that in addition to considering the structure of the family, what fosters children's healthy development and adaptation is having (at least) two parents who are positively involved in the children's lives and in maintaining a satisfying and effective relationship with each other. We believe that while children can grow up healthy in a one-parent household, they can also benefit from positive relationships with an additional co-parent or co-parenting figures.

In particular, we have highlighted how positively involved fathers and parents who nurture the quality of their relationship as a couple and as co-parents contribute to their children's emotional, social, and academic competence. Furthermore, studies of family process provide important messages for parents, family service agencies, and government policy makers about the need to go beyond attempting to persuade parents to "be responsible." If the policy makers are truly concerned with making a difference in children's well-being, they will need to provide more support for individual mothers and fathers and for the relationship between the parents or parenting figures. Rather than starting family policy discussions with attempts to influence family structure and hoping that children will benefit, we recommend starting with programs that enhance the quality of family relationships, with the expectations that improved family relationships will ultimately make family structures more stable and supportive of the development of all family members.

NOTES

1. See Fagan, Patterson, and Rector (2002).
2. See Stacey and Biblarz (2001).
3. See Waite and Gallagher (2000).
4. See Davies, Cummings, and Winter (2004).
5. For reviews of the research, see Ahrons (2004); Amato (2001); Hetherington and Kelly (2002); Pruett and Barker (2009); Rodgers and Pryor (1998); Wallerstein, Lewis, and Blakeslee (2000).
6. See Hetherington and Kelly (2002).
7. See Amato (2000).
8. See Moore, Jekielek, and Emig (2002).
9. A good example is Haskins and Sawhill (2003) of the Brookings Institute.
10. See Cherlin (2005).
11. For example, Blankenhorn, Bayme, and Elshtain (1990).
12. See Edin and Kefalas (2005).
13. See Conger et al. (1994).
14. See P. A. Cowan and C. P. Cowan (2006).
15. See Belsky and Barends (2002); Seifer and Dickstein (2000) for reviews.
16. Even very good ones; see, for example, Brazelton and Sparrow (2001); Faber and Mazlish (1995).
17. See Baumrind (1980); P. A. Cowan, Powell, and C. P. Cowan (1998).
18. See Luchetti (1999).
19. For reviews of fatherhood research, see P. A. Cowan et al. (2008); Lamb (2000); Tamis-LeMonda and Cabrera (2002).
20. See Blankenhorn (1995) and Popenoe (1996).
21. Silverstein and Auerbach (1999) have a useful discussion of this issue.
22. See Bronfenbrenner and Ceci (1994).
23. Parke (1996) and Pruett (2000) are among them.
24. See Cummings, Davies, and Campbell's text (2000), which presents a family systems view of child psychopathology.

25. See P. A. Cowan and C. P. Cowan (2002); Cui and Conger (2008).

26. See Cicchetti, Toth, and Maughan (2000).

27. See Caspi and Elder (1988).

28. See McLoyd (1990); Mistry et al. (2002).

29. See Conger et al. (1994).

30. See P. A. Cowan, C. P. Cowan, and Heming (2005).

31. See review by Durlak and Wells (1997).

32. See Powell (2006).

33. An example can be seen in Dadds, Schwartz, and Sanders (1987).

34. See Plomin (2003).

35. See Tully et al. (2004) for an example of how family process and genetic vulnerability interact.

36. See Twenge, Campbell, and Foster (2003).

37. The study is described in detail in C. P. Cowan and P. A. Cowan (2000).

38. The study is described in detail in P. A. Cowan et al. (2005).

39. The observers did not know which couples were in which condition.

40. See C. P. Cowan et al. (2007) for an early report.

41. See P. A. Cowan et al. (2014).

42. McLanahan et al. (1998).

43. Wallerstein et al. (2000).

44. Marquardt (2005).

45. Mincy and Pouncy (2002).

46. Harknett et al. (2001).

47. Mincy and Dupree (2001).

48. Wood et al. (2010).

49. Lundquist et al. (2014).

50. Johnson (2012).

51. Hawkins et al. (2013).

CCF Brief

WAS THE WAR ON POVERTY A FAILURE? OR ARE ANTIPOVERTY EFFORTS SWIMMING SIMPLY AGAINST A STRONGER TIDE?

Philip N. Cohen | January 2014

Half a century ago, on January 8, 1964, President Lyndon Johnson declared an "unconditional war on poverty in America." His goal was "to help that one-fifth of all American families with incomes too small to even meet their basic needs." The "chief weapons" he pledged to use were "better schools, and better health, and better homes, and better training, and better job opportunities." He also proposed more libraries, public transportation, and food relief for the poor.

Following Johnson's declaration, the government embarked on a major push to address various aspects of poverty and economic hardship. Medicare and Medicaid were launched in 1965, extending health coverage to millions of older Americans and poor families and alleviating a key source of hardship and insecurity for their families.

With the passage of the Food Stamp Act of 1964 and the Child Nutrition Act of 1966, food aid to the poor ramped up rapidly. The percentage of children getting free or reduced-price lunches at school jumped from 6 percent in 1969 to 27 percent by 1981. In the same year, the Food Stamp program reached 10 percent of the total population by 1981 (see Figure 1). The school aid program that became known as Title I passed in 1965, giving federal money to schools and districts with high proportion of poor students.

In the 1960s, the government also established the Department of Housing and Urban Development, initiated an extensive federal loan program for college students, and increased Social Security payments. Johnson's policies were continued under President Nixon. One of the most important programs, Aid to Families with Dependent Children (AFDC), provided cash assistance to a growing proportion of single mothers, until more than 35 percent were participating at the program's peak in 1975.

The suite of social welfare programs introduced or expanded in that era moved millions of people out of poverty and improved the lives of millions more who remained income-poor. In that sense the War on Poverty was unquestionably successful, demonstrating the continued ability of the government to direct the great wealth of the country to the improvement of public welfare.

Many of the improvements in American living standards are not reflected by the official poverty rate. That measure compares families' money income to their consumption needs, disregarding any benefits they might receive (especially health care and tax credits) and also any costs that sap their resources (especially health care and child care). A poverty measure that factors in both these benefits and costs gives us a better sense of where the War on Poverty has and has not worked.

The War on Poverty succeeded most dramatically for older people. Taking into account both changing costs and non-cash resources, the poverty rate for people age sixty-five and older fell from close to 50 percent in 1967 to 20 percent by the early 1980s. The improvement for children was more modest but still substantial.

In recent years, however, poverty has been rising once again, and the top and bottom of the income distribution are being pulled further and further apart. What happened?

In the early 1980s, the country hit a turning point. That decade experienced several recessions and a steep decline in the manufacturing industry, accompanied by stagnating wages, weakening unions, and increasing poverty rates. As it became more expensive to counter these unfavorable trends, politicians abandoned their

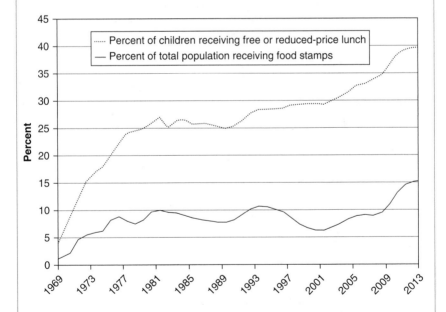

Figure 1 | Percentage of U.S. Population Receiving Free or Reduced-Price Lunch and Food Stamps: 1969–2013

Source: U.S. Department of Agriculture.

commitment to continue the struggle. President Reagan cut the budget for public housing and rent subsidies in half and slashed federal assistance to local governments by 60 percent. Just as U.S. cities faced their hardest times under the weight of industrial restructuring, the federal government withdrew much of its support. With budgets collapsing for schools, libraries, hospitals, and other public services, local governments were unable to stop the decline of urban areas and the concentration of poverty there. The official poverty rate in central cities spiked up to 22 percent by 1993, more than 1.6 times the national average (Figure 2).

To make matters worse, the minimum wage wasn't raised during the 1980s, even as inflation chipped away at its value. As a result, one worker in a minimum wage job could no longer keep a small family out of poverty (Figure 3). In 1965, a person working 2,000 hours during the year earned just enough to reach the poverty line for a family of three. By the end of the 1980s, he or she could make only 68 percent of the poverty line.

There is no doubt that government programs still help tremendously, especially in the wake of the Great Recession. Some 49 percent of households receive support from one or more programs. In addition to the 16 percent on food stamps, 27 percent receive Medicaid, 16 percent receive Social Security, and 15 percent receive Medicare. And these programs do alleviate poverty. Without these programs,

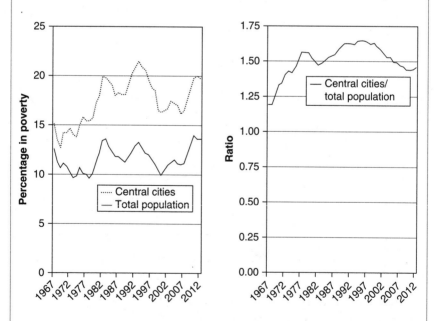

Figure 2 | Poverty in Central Cities versus Total Population: 1967–2012

Source: Author calculations from Census data.

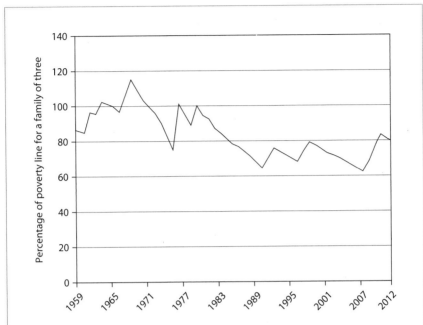

Figure 3 | Earnings for 2,000 Hours at Minimum Wage, as a Percentage of the Poverty Line for a Family of Three: 1959–2012

Source: Author calculations from Department of Labor and Census data.

according to researchers at the Columbia Population Center, poverty rates would have risen by 5 to 6 percentage points between 2007 and 2012, meaning about 15 million more people in poverty.

Focusing on children, our most vulnerable citizens, highlights both the strengths and the limits of our current antipoverty programs. By breaking out costs such as out-of-pocket medical bills and child care, and benefits such as government assistance and tax credits, as the Census Bureau now does, we can see what factors lift children above the poverty line and which pull them down below it. This "supplemental poverty measure" shows 18 percent of children living without enough resources to meet their basic needs—lower than the official rate of 22 percent but still higher than in other countries with comparable wealth and resources.

Figure 4 shows how the most important elements beyond employment income affect that rate, by adding or draining resources that prevent poverty. Tax credits for low-wage jobs and dependent children—which come as cash refunds to many poor families—reduce child poverty by 6.7 percent. Food stamps bring the number down 3 percent. Those are effective government programs. On the other hand, the medical payments low-income families make, and the cost associated with employment for their parents (mostly child care and transportation), each drive about

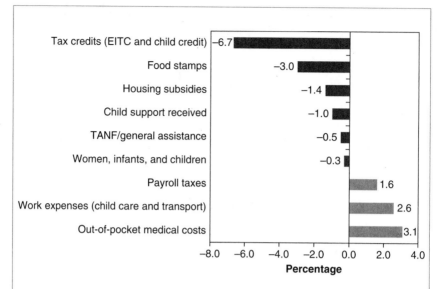

Figure 4 | Effect of Programs and Expenses on Percentage of Children in Poverty

Source: March 2013 Current Population Survey.

3 percent of children below the poverty line. Payroll taxes push 1.6 percent of children below poverty. The lack of policies to curtail health costs and provide affordable child care and public transportation exposes more of our children to poverty.

The high rates of child poverty in America highlight a basic feature about the U.S. system, and its principal vulnerability: ours remains predominantly a market-based system of care. As Janet Gornick has shown, U.S. inequality in earned income is not higher than that of most European countries, but the inequality that remains after taxes and government transfers is the highest; we do less to redistribute resources to counter inequality in employment income. So getting and keeping a good job is what divides the haves from the have-nots in America. This may sound like a reasonable principle, until we realize that many people cannot find livable-wage jobs in today's economy while others have to leave such jobs to raise children or provide care for other family members.

A key problem of our market-based system of care, as the economist Nancy Folbre has explained, is its failure to compensate care work and facilitate investment in the next generation. Most parents must either privately purchase child care, which can in some areas exceed the cost of college tuition, or stay home from work to care for the children. For breadwinner-homemaker families that share an adequate income from one earner, that may work (unless the couple divorces or the breadwinner becomes unemployed). And single parents with good incomes may be able to piece together a care regimen with paid child care. But for those with low-wage jobs, the market system falls short, and the resulting poverty undermines the upward mobility of their children.

And the multiplication of low-wage jobs that has come with widening inequality is a formidable obstacle to reducing poverty today. That is the gap that our antipoverty programs attempt to reduce, and the growing difficulty of that task has forced the programs to swim against the tide. A simple illustration of changing earnings for workers by education level underscores this point (Figure 5). Over the last two decades, earnings for those working full-time and year-round increased substantially only for those with bachelor's degrees or more education—about 7 percent. For everyone else, earnings have declined substantially or been flat. In a system where good jobs and personal income are the primary source of security and well-being, this widening inequality presents an increasing challenge.

The rise of single parenthood has been another tide that antipoverty programs have had to swim against. Single-parent families have fewer adults to earn incomes, and the vast majority of those adults are women, whose earnings remain lower than men's.

Yet single-parent families—principally single mothers—are not the main cause of child poverty today. Through the 1960s and 1970s, single-parent families represented a growing share of the poor. But since the mid-1980s, a fairly stable 34 to

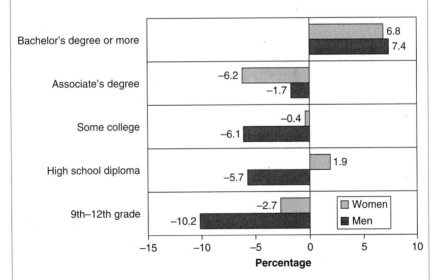

Figure 5 | Change in Real Median Earnings for Full-Time, Year-Round Workers by Gender and Education: 1992–2012

Source: Author calculations from Census data.

39 percent of poor families have been headed by a single mother. Nevertheless, although single parenthood is not driving recent increases in child poverty, the poverty of single parents is especially acute. This finding illustrates the weakness of counting on the labor market to solve poverty in the absence of programs that subsidize parental caregiving so low-income parents of young children can stay home, and/or provide affordable, high-quality child care so they can work without risk to their children.

In 1996 Congress replaced AFDC, the program Johnson expected to provide cash assistance to single mothers with children, with a program entitled Temporary Assistance to Needy Families (TANF), which combined new work requirements with a strong push to promote marriage among single mothers. As I show elsewhere, the attempt to promote marriage among poor parents and would-be parents has been an abject failure. The strong job market in the late 1990s and the expansion of the Earned Income Tax Credit (EITC) did lead to increases in employment for poor single mothers, and child poverty improved. But since the employment boom of the late 1990s ended, there has been no further reduction in child poverty, and in the last decade the problem has grown worse, not better. Today, government policies force single parents to choose between marriage and employment as their means of supporting their children. For many parents, neither option provides adequate security, as discussed in Kristi Williams's CCF Brief at the end of Chapter 20.

Much better options are available to us. One promising approach is a guaranteed income program. People often forget that President Richard Nixon actually proposed such a plan back in 1969, at a time when our political leaders seemed much more serious about waging war on poverty—and the House of Representatives passed a minimum income plan in 1970, though it died in the Senate.

A guaranteed income program could be accomplished by expanding the Child Tax Credit for those with children or using the tax code to ensure a minimum income for everyone, presumably in combination with a program of government jobs. Alternatively, a variety of separate improvements might reduce either the poverty level or its harms. These include a higher minimum wage, state-provided child care, paid family leave, part-time wage protection, and of course health care.

All these possibilities should be on the table, because we know for sure, despite frequent claims to the contrary, that government can play a key role in reducing poverty. In 1999, Great Britain had an even higher child poverty rate than we do today. At that point the British embarked on their own war on poverty, as described by Jane Waldfogel. The government introduced new work requirements for welfare, but also established a minimum wage more generous than the U.S. one. As a result, more single parents got jobs, and the jobs they got paid better. At the same time, family leave for new mothers was extended to one year, and half of that time was paid. Legislators also put in place a system of income support for all but the richest parents, not conditional on employment, intended to increase investment in children's well-being. Finally, the government introduced free preschool for all three- and four-year-olds, and made it easier to switch to part-time or flexible employment. Along with educational investment and school reform, the initiatives amounted to an increased investment in children of 1 percent of Britain's gross domestic product. The result of such a concerted effort was a decline in child poverty of about one-quarter to one-half in a decade, depending on the measures used.

The British example highlights the limits of our own policies. Despite undeniable progress since the declaration of our own War on Poverty in 1964—and even with the many lives improved through current programs—today's antipoverty efforts cannot be described as an "unconditional war on poverty." At best, we have been fighting with one hand tied behind our back. We could do much more.

PART SIX

A Generational Dance: How Parents and Kids Relate

24

Parenting Adult Children in the Twenty-First Century

Joshua Coleman

The past century has witnessed a profound change in our perception of children and how they should be parented. Prior to the twentieth century, parents viewed children as resilient and robust, and they also believed that the rigors of life would make children stronger and more capable. For a variety of reasons, including smaller family size, the prevalence of divorce, the advent of parenting experts, a decrease in opportunities after college, and a perception of an increasingly dangerous world, today's parents believe that children are fragile and vulnerable, requiring a close and carefully managed childhood in order to succeed. Since the 1960s, there has been a gradual blurring of the boundaries between parents and children as families moved to a more democratic structure where the child's opinions and feelings became far more valued. Parents' expectations of what they wanted from their children also underwent an enormous change.

When I was growing up, my friends and I couldn't stand our parents' music, clothing, and more than a few of their friends. We would have no sooner put on a Bing Crosby record than they would have worn a tie-dyed T-shirt, smoked a bong, or waxed poetic about the intensity of a Jimi Hendrix solo. They were the ADULTS—foreign, unfathomable, living in a world we scarcely deigned to penetrate except to get the keys to their cars.[1]

In addition, our parents had little interest in our music and weren't terribly concerned with what we thought about their taste in clothing. They expected us to respect them and didn't spend a lot of time worrying whether their parenting mistakes would ruin our love for them. They also didn't spend endless hours reading parenting books or watching experts on television, and they weren't terribly concerned about respecting our rights or infringing on our autonomy.

While these generational boundaries still exist in poor and working-class families, a very different world greets today's middle-class children and their parents.[2] In many ways, the generational markers that were common as recently as three or four decades ago have largely disappeared. While the twentieth century has seen unprecedented improvements in the quality of children's lives, today's middle-class parents are freaked out. They obsess over the slightest error in parenting and worry that they may have forever blighted their child's life with a comment made in anger or exhaustion. The constant broadcast of parenting advice causes new mothers to feel as though they and their husbands are practically committing child abuse if they don't obsessively read every available book on pregnancy, early childhood development, and acing the SATs. Both parents worry that if they don't closely monitor the academic implications of every grade from preschool through high school, their child will get crowded out of the increasingly tight bottleneck of colleges and the ever-shrinking opportunities for employment.[3] They are terrified of doing something to turn their child against them or of losing their love for good. Parents of all classes worry about drug and alcohol addiction, Internet porn, ADD, sexual predators, and a whole slew of psychiatric disorders.[4]

While prior generations of parents felt that their job was finished once children left home, many of today's parents continue to worry long afterwards. As a psychologist in private practice, I see a large number of parents struggling to understand their adult children and many are fighting to find ways to keep them in their lives. The confusion about how to remain close to adult children has spawned an explosion of new self-help books in just the past few years with titles such as *Walking on Eggshells, You're Wearing That?, Don't Bite Your Tongue, Setting Boundaries with Your Adult Children*, and my own book, *When Parents Hurt*.

FROM RESILIENCE TO FRAGILITY

In prior generations, the task of children was to prepare themselves for adult work by following the instructions appropriate to their class, race, and gender. As Steven Mintz points out (in Chapter 6 of this volume), at the end of the nineteenth century Americans began to see children as independent beings with their own needs and rhythms of development. In addition, Americans began to shift from believing that it was the obligation of children to meet the family's needs to believing that the family should meet the children's needs.[5]

From the 1920s to the 1970s, Americans steadily changed their child-rearing emphasis from valuing conformity, church attendance, loyalty, and obedience to focusing on children's autonomy, tolerance, and the ability to think for themselves.[6] This change was accompanied by a transformation in the family climate of the middle class from authoritarian to more democratic and permissive. Children went from being quietly kept in the background to being loudly and proudly paraded into the foreground. In many households, children became the axis upon which the household turned.[7]

Freud and the experts who followed him popularized the idea that parents could be a corrupting influence on the fragile psychological development of the child. According to Freud, children could be easily led into neurosis, if not psychosis, by parents who failed to adequately address the challenges posed by each stage of development.[8] This perspective put an enormous amount of pressure on parents and made them worry that a small mistake would forever consign their child to a life spent in a therapist's office, or worse.

Nevertheless, for the first half of the twentieth century, parents continued to believe that children could not only handle the stresses created by struggle, adversity, and competition, but that these would strengthen and prepare them for the challenges they would later face.[9] Phrases such as "building backbone," "strengthening character," and "improving moral fiber" were all used to characterize the outcome of a childhood and adolescence exposed to these elements.

Over the past forty to fifty years, however, our view has slowly changed to perceiving children as fragile and requiring a kind of "hothouse parenting" in order to thrive.[10] Sociologist Annette Lareau describes this type of middle-class parenting as "concerted cultivation." It is characterized by the parents' active organization of children's leisure activities and the frequent engagement of verbally intensive interactions geared to increase a sense of entitlement and mutuality with adults. One of the goals of concerted cultivation is helping children understand the parents' decisions and assisting children to understand their own inner worlds.[11]

This angle on parenting is new. Historian Steven Mintz writes that with the notable exceptions of the Quakers and Native Americans, strategies that relied on guilt, shame, or pain dominated American parenting up through the Victorian era. During the twentieth century, these strategies gradually gave way to approaches that emphasized negotiating with children to help them understand their behavior and motivation.[12]

As a result of this shift, parents began to feel tremendous pressure to produce a child who was self-aware, but who was not unduly fettered by the corrosive effects of guilt, self-consciousness, and the burdens of "codependency" (the inclination to worry so much about the well-being of the other that you consistently put their needs above your own).

PARENTS AS PROBLEMS

This new focus on raising self-aware children created a slew of relational and parenting experts to help people overcome the guilt, anxiety, and fear that came as they began to wrestle with this new kind of identity. One of the central obstacles to this individualistic perspective became the problematic parent. Parents began to be viewed as potential baggage to be contained, if not eliminated, in the quest for self-esteem, psychological health, and personal fulfillment. A visit to any bookstore shows the success of this enterprise.

In fact, the field of psychology has probably done more to create parental, especially maternal, anxiety and guilt than any other institution. For example, in the 1960s, the influential child psychologist Bruno Bettelheim wrote that childhood autism was caused by mothers who couldn't relate to their children.[13] Psychologist Jay Haley and colleagues, along with anthropologist Gregory Bateson, argued that schizophrenia resulted from mothers who communicated in contradictory, "double-binding" fashions with their children.[14] Both theories, popular at their time, have been disproved or shown to be highly flawed.

Parents' capacity to provide their children with entertainment became an effective and guilt-inducing tool to market products to parents. In addition, it became another way that children could later fault their parents. The statement "I'm bored" grew to be a statement that reflected on the parents' adequacy and worth. Children could now judge parents by how well they provided opportunities and, therefore, how deserving they were of the child's love and respect. Children could later, rightly or wrongly, blame parents for the ways that they turned out or failed to turn out.[15] They could attribute the failure to provide "formative opportunities" as being far more central than they may have been.

For example, in Steven Spielberg's movie *Hook*, a remake of *Peter Pan*, Captain Hook attempts to curry favor with Michael by arranging a baseball game. When Michael is up to bat, Hook motivates him by saying, "This is for all of the baseball games that your father never attended!" The child snarls in righteous anger and hits a home run.

This is a major reversal in polarities. Where prior generations of children were expected to earn the *parents'* love and respect, today's parents are worried that they won't have their *children's* love and respect because they're not good *enough*: not psychological enough, not sensitive enough, not fun enough, not "there" enough.[16] They're worried, often correctly, that their real or imagined mistakes in parenting may one day come back to haunt them. And in comparison to the past, parents have far fewer support systems of kin and neighbors to help them strike the right balance in raising their child.

THE ISOLATED FAMILY

In the past few decades, the financial and emotional resources that were once exchanged with extended kin, neighbors, religious institutions, and friends have become increasingly concentrated in the nuclear family. Only half as many people said that they had four to five confidants in 2004 compared with those who had that number of confidants in 1985, and the number of people stating that there is *no one* with whom they discuss important matters has tripled in that same time frame.[17]

Whereas the family and the identity of its members once existed in a rich eco-system fed and nourished by a community of supports, American families have more and more begun to stand alone. Much of the time and energy that once went into socializing with neighbors and kin has been transferred into parenting. According to sociologists Suzanne Bianchi, John Robinson, and Melissa Milke, today's mothers spend twice as much time with their children and fathers three times as much time as they did in the supposedly halcyon days of the mid-1960s. Parents, especially mothers, achieve this by giving up time for themselves, sacrificing sleep, friendships, and time with their spouses.[18] At the same time, there has been a 40 percent reduction in the amount of time that children play outside, leaving parents with much more time under the same roof with their children.[19] These changes, combined with smaller family sizes, have increased the demands on parents to play the emotional, educational, and socializing roles that siblings, neighbors, and friends once filled.

On the one hand, these changes have benefited some families. A greater amount of time spent between parent and child offers the potential for more intimacy, understanding, and shared meaning. Many of today's parents are able to have long-term friendships with their children after they leave home that are enriched by the close and involved years that they spent together before the children moved out.[20]

Yet, this intensive parenting environment may test the limits of what couples can reasonably ask of each other and may place an undue burden on the parent-child relationship. When parents spend less time with their friends and communities, many of them may turn to their offspring for fulfillment, intimacy, and long-term security. More time and more involvement create the possibility for more conflict, resentment, and disappointment on the part of both parent and child. In addition, a close, intimate relationship with a parent may make it harder to separate from that parent and, as a result, may tempt the adult child to push away more aggressively in order to launch her own adult life.

While parents are expected to provide an even greater investment in child care, entertainment, protection, college, and after-college care than prior generations of parents, there are few guidelines for what they might expect in return. Parents may feel betrayed if they do not get the love and gratitude they look forward to and believe that they deserve. But children can also review their childhoods from the calculus of how supportive or affectionate their parents were and may declare the relationship null and void if they evaluate it as something less than they needed or deserved.

SOUL-MATE PARENT

The combination of the democratization of the family form, fewer opportunities after children leave home, a culture that blames parents for child outcomes, a more dangerous world, and an increase in parental guilt and anxiety have together created an environment where parents believe that they have to be everything for their children. From this perspective, the modern middle-class parent has much in common with another cultural icon, the soul mate. For example, in soul-mate ideology, one's future spouse is supposed to be sexy (though not insatiable), independent (but not too independent), intimate (but not cloying), funny (but not obnoxious), well-educated (but not arrogant), and sensitive (but not wimpy).

In the ideology of the soul-mate parent, mom or dad is supposed to be sensitive (but not intrusive), tolerant (though not neglectful), forgiving (though not weak), current on child development (though not a pedant), a good playmate (but not trying to live their life through the child), and a good mentor (without using the word *mentor*). Parents are also supposed to be enthusiastic fans of whatever artistic, sporting, or academic endeavor is pursued by the child.

Both the ideology of the romantic soul mate and the soul-mate parent suffer from fundamental problems: (1) most individuals don't have the bounty of traits, attitudes, and attributes to bring to any one relationship, (2) what we want and need from a person at one point in time is often quite different from what we may need from him at another, and (3) our own character flaws, genetics, and moods may cause us to wittingly or unwittingly shut down or greatly inhibit the other's capacity to provide the interaction that we may so desperately crave.

WHEN THE CHILD REJECTS THE PARENT

In the past decade, I have seen an explosion in my clinical practice of parents who have come to me because they were cut off by their grown children. While some of these parents made terrible mistakes, many of them were loving and reasonable. If there is an increase in the rejecting of parents, why is it occurring?

Divorce seems to be one common factor. The ideology of family life now places affectionate choice at the center of family relationships, and the voluntary nature of relating as the central governing principle. Parents are more concerned than in the past about their children's individual happiness, but they are also looking out for their own. As a result, they increasingly feel free to leave marriages that are insufficiently supportive, meaningful, or affectionate.

In some circumstances, a divorce creates the ability to be a more involved, less distracted parent.[21] Numerous studies show that children are benefited by a divorce if their parents had a high-conflict marriage.[22] In this situation, a divorce may allow the children to have better relationships with their parents if the divorce ends their conflict. Constance Ahrons found that many adult children felt that their relationships with their fathers had either improved or remained stable over time after a divorce.[23]

But divorce also offers a variety of ways for parents and children to become distant or estranged. Numerous studies show that the relationship between father and daughter is more at risk than the mother-daughter relationship after a divorce.[24] These feelings may become especially inflamed after a parent remarries, or with increased interparental conflict, early father remarriage, or low father involvement in the early post-divorce years. And in their old age, divorced fathers usually get much less care and attention from their daughters than do mothers.[25] Divorce increases fathers' vulnerability to anxiety and depression.[26] Mothers or fathers who feel angry or hurt by the divorce, and who use their children as a way to punish the other parent, often alienate adult children. Mentally ill parents may successfully cause the adult child to believe that closeness with the other parent is a selfish or disloyal act.[27]

But divorce is not the only source of tension between parents and their adult children. Many of the causes, as the previous discussion has shown, are built into today's high expectations of parent-child relations and the greater isolation of nuclear families. Both high expectations and greater isolation create more possibilities for disappointment and fewer places to turn to compensate for problems in the parent-adult relationship. These tensions have been exacerbated in the past thirty years by a decline in the prospects for youthful economic independence. Adult children have become more economically dependent upon parents, and parents are less able to understand the lives and decisions of their young adult children.

"When I Was Your Age . . ."

Prior to the 1970s, a young man could reasonably expect to leave high school and, even without a college degree, marry and support a family. College grads were likely to get permanent work shortly after graduation and could expect to send their kids to an even better university. Women did not have the same opportunities, but they expected to marry and, for most, marriage seemed the best economic investment in their future.

As historian Stephanie Coontz notes (see Chapter 5 of this volume), many of the young men starting families after World War II were eligible for veterans' benefits that allowed an unprecedented number of them to enter the middle class. The federal government was also active in helping families by underwriting low down payments and long-term mortgages to boost home ownership. This, in combination with well-paid union jobs, allowed many working-class families to gain entry into the middle class. Women and minorities also began to believe that they might claim their fair share as a result of the women's movement and the civil rights struggle of the 1950s and 1960s.[28]

This is radically different from the opportunities that greet today's high school and college graduates. Deindustrialization and economic restructuring during the past thirty years have altered the educational and vocational requirements needed to support a family. Whereas a high school degree was once the basic requirement for successful employment, now a college degree is considered the baseline.[29] But, even a college degree may not be enough to manage the vagaries of today's changing economic market.

These recent economic changes may strain the relationship between parents and their adult children because many parents fail to understand or sympathize with the very different social and economic world that greets their newly minted adults. They may believe that the economic problems of their young adult children stem more from a lack of character than a new social reality. A *New Yorker* cartoon illustrated this dynamic. It showed two parents standing over their twentysomething, who was watching television in their living room. The caption, addressed to the reclining son, read, "When I was your age, I was an adult." The cartoon reflects the sentiment that many parents feel and often express to their adult children.

Yet, many of today's parents are unaware of the extent that the job market has changed. While prior generations of children could assume they would one day outearn their parents, this opportunity appears to be dwindling except around a fortunate few. An article in the satirical paper *The Onion* says it all with the headline, "Most Americans Falling for 'Get Rich Slowly Over a Lifetime of Hard Work' Schemes."[30] Prior generations of parents could rely on their children's higher earnings to help provide for those parents in old age. But due to skyrocketing costs for health care and housing, low pay for entry-level jobs, and the erosion of job benefits, many of today's young adults find themselves barely able to support themselves, let alone help support their parents. These changes in the economy have also removed an important way that adult children shared a sense of obligation and connection to their parents over the life span of both.

Of course, many young people do go on to earn very good wages, but the lengthening transition to adulthood means that their ability to do so often depends on their parents' willingness and ability to subsidize them. A study by the Institute for Social Research at the University of Michigan found that 34 percent of young adults between the ages of eighteen and thirty-four receive financial assistance on a regular basis from their parents. According to government statistics gathered in 2005, middle-income parents can expect to spend $190,980 on each child through the age of seventeen. But parents can anticipate spending an additional 25 percent of that amount again over the next seventeen years—an average of $1,556 yearly on children as old as thirty-three and thirty-four. Even parents who cannot afford these expenditures are helping out more than in the past. Today's parents spend nine weeks of their time each year helping adult children aged eighteen to thirty-four with babysitting, transportation, and laundry.[31]

So just as tensions may rise when parents are not able to understand why their kids aren't self-supporting, young adults may resent their parents, either because they can't help, or because they feel that there are strings attached to the help their parents give. They may also be tempted to blame parents for their difficult circumstances because they were raised in a culture that views parents as the most important causal agent in child development.

INDIVIDUALISM AND DEPRESSION

Less than one-fifth of Americans see class, race, or gender as important in getting ahead in life. The majority believe that what matters most is individual initiative.[32] But what happens when individual initiative is insufficient to support a family? Psychologist Martin Seligman has shown that individualistic attributions of causality that focus on enduring, personal traits can be useful in creating feelings of optimism and happiness when events go well. But they can generate feelings of depression and pessimism when events turn out poorly because of the self-blame that they engender.[33]

One of the strategies to defend against feelings of self-blame is to blame someone else—what psychologists refer to as externalization. Externalization can be a healthy defense mechanism and, as a result, most therapists work hard to help their clients find reasonable explanations that direct blame away from the self. Unfortunately, in today's culture, this often occurs by blaming the parents.

While parents are clearly important in how children turn out, they are less so than our current culture leads us to believe. As historian Stephanie Coontz writes, we live in a culture "that expects us single-handedly, or at most two-parently to counter all the comic ups and downs, social pressures, personal choices, and competing demands of a highly unequal, consumption-oriented culture dominated by deteriorating working conditions, interest-group politics, and self-serving advertisements for everything from toothpaste to moral values."[34] An overemphasis on parental responsibility ignores compelling evidence that children are also affected by peer group, neighborhood, class, genetics, and siblings.[35] Yet, most of the stories that end up in the media feature parents who are (or were) selfish, abusive, neglectful, alcoholic, drug addicted, intrusive, or weak.

While the system of psychotherapy provides a way to externalize blame onto parents, there are fewer culturally prescribed ways for parents to externalize their feelings of guilt and inadequacy when they feel, rightly or wrongly, that they have caused their child to suffer or to fail. This is probably why so many parents suffer from depression when their children don't thrive as adults, or when their children cut off contact with them.[36] While a certain level of selfless devotion comes with the job of being a parent, we need a more accurate lens for people to evaluate the outcomes of their adulthoods other than whether mom or dad did a good-enough job. Perspectives that blame child outcomes on parents are especially problematic when applied to the poor since the social dynamics of poverty make it harder for parents to protect their children and provide them with the assortment of educational, enrichment, and therapeutic opportunities that are available to parents with greater resources.[37]

Increasing the Understanding

It is unlikely that the social foundation of the tensions between parents and their adult children will become part of the public dialogue anytime soon. For this reason, I advise parents who have been cut off or consistently criticized by their adult children to work toward not being defensive, to try to understand their children's complaints, to take responsibility for their parenting mistakes (large and small), and to continue to reach out to their adult children.

Many parents feel challenged by these suggestions. For example, I recently worked with a sixty-three-year-old mother who was frustrated by her thirty-five-year-old daughter's complaints that she wasn't encouraging enough of her when she was growing up. "When I was a child, you got what you got and you were glad for it," she told me. "I wouldn't have even *thought* about my mother not encouraging me enough." Many older parents feel confused and resentful, like this mother, when their parenting is held to the ideal of today's much more intensive parenting standard.

They struggle not to say any one of the following to their complaining adult child:

"Your childhood was a dream compared to mine."

"After everything that I sacrificed for you, this is what I get in response?"

"I didn't have all of the information about parenting that you have these days. It's unfair to have expected me to have known things that weren't part of the culture at the time."

"You had your own contributions to make to our relationship. You weren't an easy child."

I discourage parents from saying any of these statements, because they sound defensive. As with marriage, communication is the most effective when people work to understand, reflect what was said, and empathize. I also let parents know that even if it feels as though an adult child has all the power, the parent is still a powerful figure in the adult child's mind, even if the parent feels impotent.

There are many reasons why an adult child might cut off or criticize a parent. As with marriage, it is now a game negotiated between equals, and as such, it requires more patience, more respect, and less reliance on the invocations of parental authority. From adult children, it requires an understanding that much more is being asked of today's parents than was asked in prior generations. In the same way that there are numerous forces that affect a child's development, there are many forces affecting an individual's capacity to parent. The more parents and their adult children can empathize with the separate realities of the other, the more closeness and shared understanding can occur going forward.

Notes

1.   Coleman (2003).
2.   Lareau (2003).
3.   Coleman (2007).
4.   Stearns (2003).
5.   Zelizer (1994).
6.   Coltrane (1996).
7.   Stearns (2003).
8.   Freud (1926).
9.   Stearns (2003).
10. Marano (November/December, 2004).
11. Lareau (2003).
12. Mintz (2004).

13. Bettelheim (1967).

14. Bateson (1980).

15. Stearns (2003).

16. Ehrensaft (1997).

17. Coontz (2006); Putnam (2000).

18. Bianchi, Robinson, and Milke (2006); Sullivan and Coltrane (2008).

19. Mintz (2006).

20. Pew Research Center (2006).

21. Mavis Hetherington and Kelly (2002).

22. Amato and Booth (1997); Hetherington and Kelly (2002).

23. Ahrons (2004); Ahrons and Tanner (2003).

24. Nielsen (2004); Hetherington and Kelly (2002).

25. Lin (2008).

26. Amato and Sobolewski (2004); Baum (2006).

27. Hetherington and Kelly (2002); Nielsen (2004).

28. Coontz (2008).

29. Flanagan (2006); Danziger and Gottschalk (2005).

30. "Most Americans Falling for 'Get Rich Slowly over a Lifetime of Hard Work' Scheme," *The Onion* 41(49), December 7, 2005, p. 2.

31. Lacar, "The Bank of Mom and Dad," *New York Times*, April 9, 2006.

32. Lareau (2003); Schwartz (2004).

33. Seligman (1996).

34. Coontz (1997).

35. Dunn and Plomin (1990); Harris (1999); Reiss, Neiderhiser, Hetherington, and Plomin (2000).

36. Knoester (2003).

37. Coontz (1997).

In the News

LEAN TIMES FORCE MANY BAY AREA "BOOMERANG KIDS" TO RETURN HOME AS ADULTS

San Jose Mercury News, July 19, 2011

Hannah Dreier and Paul Burgarino

A word to Bay Area parents: You may want to hold off on converting those empty bedrooms into offices and exercise spaces.

High unemployment and changing social norms are guiding young—and not-so-young—adults to move back home, new census data shows.

"It's almost becoming a normal step," said Joshua Coleman, a Bay Area psychologist who is a co-chairman of the Council on Contemporary Families. "Children leave home and go away to college—or don't—and then move back in with the parents for a while."

Almost 31 percent of all children living at home in California are 18 or older—up 7 percent from 2000 and reflecting a national trend. Over the past decade, the number of adult children living with their parents grew by 21 percent in the East Bay and 14 percent in Silicon Valley.

This is puzzling to parents who, in their time, couldn't possibly envision moving back in with mom and dad.

"We all worked," said Linda Hodges, 49. "The minute we could, we got apartments to live the single life."

Two of Hodges' five adopted and biological children have moved back to her San Leandro house; a third recently lost his job and may return home as well.

"The job market is just so tight," Hodges said. Many of her sons' friends also live with their parents, she said.

Nearly every Bay Area city saw a rise in "boomerang kids" over the past decade. Adults now account for more than a third of children living at home in San Leandro, Hayward, Union City, Hercules, San Bruno and San Francisco, among other cities.

The U.S. Census Bureau attributed the trend mostly to economic factors in a report this spring, noting that adults who are poorer or less educated have the greatest odds of living in what is called a "doubled-up household."

Henry Kelly's youngest son returned to the family's Brentwood home two months ago. The 22-year-old had moved in with a friend last year, but he wasn't able to make rent with his paycheck from a retail hardware store job.

"Life is still life at the Kellys'. Luckily, we did not downsize or change his room or anything like that," said Kelly, who is also a pastor at an Antioch church.

Not Just Financial

Not everyone who moves home is desperate. About half of grown children who live in their childhood home have full- or part-time jobs, according to a 2009 Pew Research Center survey.

Josh Rose, director of the Richmond- and Antioch-based Family Works Community Counseling, says he sees adults moving home for psychological support or to transition between jobs or relationships. Some even move back to support their parents or protect them from threats such as domestic abuse.

"The decision is rarely only a financial choice," he said.

It was the promise of free baby-sitting that helped persuade Anna Cordrey to move back into her parents' Fremont home with her husband and toddler last year. The couple says they've become closer as a family and that their son loves the constant attention.

Still, it's a balancing act. Cordrey's parents are not always thrilled to see their grandson's bottles and toys lying around, and his bulky stroller takes up space by the front door.

"They'll be like, 'First of all, you don't need a stroller—we didn't have strollers in Vietnam,'" said Cordrey, whose parents are Vietnamese immigrants. "It becomes a whole conversation about 'Where to put your things, Anna.'"

Ingrid Alonso, 29, who lives with her two sons in her parents' East San Jose home, said she is happy to let her parents pay the mortgage and keep house while she works on advancing her career. In addition, they are happy to help her out.

It is partly due to Latino culture, she said. "It's that traditional notion of 'What kind of woman leaves her house?'" Alonso said. "With guys, it's more like, 'Eh, he's leaving,' but with women it's like you've got to be home until you're married."

She recently went through a divorce and says living with her parents helps to stave off loneliness. She also loves her mother's home-cooked meals. However, she sometimes clashes with her father when he scolds her children.

"I like the home-cooked meals. I cooked before, but it's nice to be able to have that from the parents," she said.

Parents and children alike say it can be difficult to negotiate life under one roof. The past few years have seen a proliferation of guides from outlets such as AARP and Newsweek advising parents on how to cope with children who have not moved away.

Cleaning, financial contributions and length of stay are common points of contention.

Hodges thinks that time away from their San Leandro home did her sons good, teaching them the value of a free crash pad and the hard work it takes to pay for it. She also loves being able to keep an eye on her boys and make sure they're safe.

Her son Nick, 23, however, worries that he is missing out on his time to explore and grow.

"It's a weird balance," he said. "My mom is my biggest supporter and I have the amazing luxury of staying for free while I'm looking for a job. But I feel like I'm being contained a little bit."

"Exit Strategy"

In his Oakland and San Francisco psychology practices, Coleman cautions families that an "exit strategy" with a "firm timetable" is imperative for families negotiating life under one roof for a second time.

Jaclyn Hutchins, 27, opted to move back home after graduating from college and accepting a job teaching high school English in San Ramon.

But what started as a temporary arrangement stretched on for two years. Hutchins eventually left to pursue a master's degree in the Midwest, but returned home this April to start her job search.

Hutchins would like to move out of her parents' home soon—if only to avoid the bane of every boomerang child's existence: mom and dad checking up on where she's going or what her plans are.

However, she doesn't feel much social pressure. Like the Cordreys, she considers her position enviable.

"I think before, when the economy was stronger, people judged when you moved home," she said. "Now there's people in their 40s that are moving home—I just don't feel out of place." ■

CCF Facts

MYTHS OF LATER MOTHERHOOD

Elizabeth Gregory | July 2012

Today, almost 40 percent of all babies in the United States are born to women over 30, and almost 15 percent—1 in 7—are born to women 35 and over; birth rates to women aged 15–24 have fallen significantly since 1970, while birth rates for women aged 30–39 have risen significantly.

The recession has accelerated the trend toward older births. While the overall U.S. birth rate fell more than 7 percent between December 2007 and December 2010, the birth rate for women ages 40–44 *rose* by 8 percent in the same period, continuing a trend that has been mounting since 1983. The sharp decline in births to younger moms—teen birth rates fell by 17 percent, and births to women aged 20–24 by 16 percent—presages an added rise in the number of later mothers in the future.

Having children later in life is nothing new. When women routinely had four or five children, many bore their last child in their thirties or even forties. What is new is the increasing trend toward postponing first births into that later age range. In 1970, one in 100 first births was to a mother 35 and over. Today, the figure is 1 in every 12. And 1 in every 4 first births is to a woman over 30.

But is it risky for women to delay first births, as the mass media incessantly warns? This fact sheet explores three myths that impede women's ability to make informed decisions about when to embark on motherhood.

Myth 1: Women Who Delay Motherhood Past Age 35 Are Unlikely to Ever Get Pregnant

According to one 2010 news story, a 30-year-old woman has only 12 percent of her eggs left. The author conveniently left out the fact that this is in comparison to the number of eggs in a 20-week-old fetus. In fact, a 15-year-old woman has only half the egg cells of a female fetus and a healthy woman of 25 has only 22 percent. Since there is no major fertility decline at 30, apparently 12 percent is all you need. It is true that fertility declines after 35, and it often takes longer for a couple to conceive. But studies suggest that about 90 percent of 35-year-old women can get pregnant without aid, roughly two-thirds can do so through age 39, and about half at 41. Rates plummet thereafter, and few women have children after age 44 with their own eggs.

Myth 2: Women Who Do Get Pregnant after Age 35 Are Putting Their Children at Risk

Though the risk of autism does increase with maternal age, the rate of increase is often blown out of proportion. The increased risk attributable to mothers' age appears to be *one half of 1 percent*. Older fathers, often partnered with older mothers, have been linked to a somewhat higher risk. But while reported cases of autism increased by 600 percent in the 1990s, less than 1 percent of the total rise was due to maternal age. Not only has the risk of older motherhood to children been exaggerated, but the benefits have been ignored. For example, children's test scores improve with each year of motherhood delay.

Myth 3: Older Parents Will Not Have the Health or Energy to Really Enjoy Parenting

Although all mothers have a spike in happiness around the birth of a child, this spike is particularly strong for moms who start their families after 35 and is not followed by the steep and sustained decline in happiness and satisfaction that occurs among younger mothers. Mothers who choose to delay childbirth actually live longer than other mothers, on average (due to a combination of physical vitality, better access to health care, and perhaps a will to stick around to see their children through).

Establishing oneself in a career before having a child makes sense to many women, and in the absence of the family-friendly work policies adopted by every other major industrial democracy (see Heymann & Earle, 2007, for CCF), delay is also a shadow-benefits system, minimizing the motherhood penalty that women accrue when they interrupt their careers early. For example, female college graduates earn substantially more—roughly 12 percent more in long-term salary—for each year they delay having children. Thus a college graduate who had her first child at 30 would make twice as much in annual salary over her lifetime as she would have if she'd had her first child upon graduation at 22.

This fact sheet is based upon *Ready: Why Women Are Embracing the New Later Motherhood* (Basic Books, 2012).

In the News

NUMBER OF "OLDER" WOMEN HAVING BABIES CONTINUES TO GROW

Deseret News, July 28, 2012

Lois M. Collins

SALT LAKE CITY —It seems to Mandy Krell that she has been waiting for a long time. The Lansing, Mich., native didn't meet a man she wanted to marry and with whom she'd like to have a child until she was 39, a bit later than she expected. Now she is waiting for that longed-for child who has not, so far, arrived.

What has come into her life is a bad economy that left her unemployed and fearful about being able to afford a child on one income. And she worries that her opportunity to have a child may have passed.

If Krell does manage to have a baby in her 40s, she will be less alone than she would have been in decades past. The number of births, particularly first-time births, to older mothers is growing. First-time maternity for "older women"—and this may be the only area besides sports where women in their late 30s and 40s are considered "old"—is becoming less uncommon. But women who have or are trying to have children then, naturally or with assistance, agree it is a journey filled with both challenges and joys.

"Forty is the new 20 when it comes to having babies," wrote Susan Newman, social psychologist and author of 15 books on family issues and parenting, in a *Psychology Today* blog. The Council on Contemporary Families said 40 percent of babies are born to women over 30 and that 1 in 7 babies is born to women over 35, while the Pew Research Center in 2010 reported that more babies were born to women older than 35 than to teenagers. It is a change, Pew said, driven by medical advances, later marriages and new views on motherhood.

In Good Company

June's National Vital Statistics Report said the pregnancy rate for women 40–44 has increased steadily since 1991 to 18.8 pregnancies per 1,000 women in that age group. It didn't count women who have babies beyond 44, but that number is growing, too.

The National Center for Health Statistics reported that nearly 40 percent of women who had a first baby at age 35 or later between 2006 and 2010 went on to have at least one more, compared to 26 percent in 1995.

Research gives mixed reviews, but there is much good news among the bad for older moms: Children born to moms over 40 tend to have higher IQs and more impressive early vocabulary, according to a study from the Institute of Child Health, University College London and Birkbeck College in London. Those children are less apt to need hospitalization or have accidents. The researchers theorized older moms are either more cautious or are better able to identify and help children avoid risks.

Different research showed that women who delay motherhood live longer than those who give birth at younger ages, perhaps even to 100. And studies consistently show that older moms are typically better educated than young moms.

But researchers have found a downside, too. Older moms are more prone to health problems linked to childbirth. While most women in their late 30s and early 40s will have healthy pregnancies and babies, the March of Dimes said, the moms' older age confers greater risk of high blood pressure, diabetes, miscarriage, delivery complications, prematurity and stillbirth than younger women face. Autism numbers rise. And the chance the baby will have a genetic disorder increases with maternal age. So does the possibility that fertility has declined or gone away.

Still, numbers are sometimes misinterpreted. A report that a woman at 30 only has 12 percent of her eggs didn't note it was comparing a woman that age to a 20-week-old female fetus. By that measure, a girl of 15 only has half the egg cells and a healthy woman of 25 only 22 percent. While fertility declines, and it may take longer for a couple to conceive after 35, studies say about 90 percent of women at 35 can conceive without aid, as can 75 percent of those through age 39 and about half of those who are 41, said Elizabeth Gregory, director of women's studies at the University of Houston, in a fact sheet prepared for the Council on Contemporary Families. "Rates plummet thereafter, and few women have children after age 44 with their own eggs," she said.

Having Babies

Jocelyn Nager joked that by the time she looks at colleges for her daughters, Pearl, 5, and Sarah, 8, she'll get the AARP discount. Nager, a lawyer from New York City, got married late and didn't think she'd be able to have children. It was not, it turned out, a problem for her.

Pushing 40 with the first birth, she was established in her career and now enjoys the flexibility to set some of her own hours, with financial stability enough to send the girls to a nice school and summer camp. "There are a lot of extras I could not provide for my kids if I was in my 20s or 30s," Nager said. She still rides bikes with her girls and is very active.

"I think I'm not a typical 48-year-old," she told the *Deseret News*. "But really, what is typical these days?"

Different Challenges

Amy Wasserman, a Palham, Mass., artist who sells her work through Amycreates
.com, always knew she'd want to have a baby. After she married Scott Plotkin at
age 38, she learned she couldn't become pregnant. They eventually became foster
parents and when she was 44, in 2003, they adopted their 2-year-old foster child, Lily.

As a mom, she said, what she lacks in stamina she makes up for in patience and
wisdom.

She is sorry she could not experience pregnancy herself. But she has no regrets
about having a child in her 40s instead of her 20s. Wasserman is confident she recognizes her daughter's long-term needs—including how important it is to be inspired
by successful, hard-working women, she said—more than she would have when she
was younger.

Paula Pant is 28, but plans to wait until her mid-30s to have children, unfazed by
statements like "older parents won't have the energy to play with their children," or
"they'll never live to see their kids grow up."

Pant, who was raised in Cincinnati and lives now in Atlanta, was adopted when
her folks were 43. "They played with me and kept up; 40 is not that old." The quirk
that came with her parents' age, she said, was that much of her childhood she saw
them plan their retirements. Pant doesn't think it's a coincidence she now writes a
financial-issues blog, "Afford-Anything.com," with lots to say about retirement.

The biggest drawback to older parents was that generational differences
were "amplified." Some things she wanted to do that were common with her peers
were very foreign to her parents, two generations removed. Still, she will wait, too,
she said, "half for economic reasons, but half because I want the freedom to travel
the world, to move on a whim, to do the fun things you can do when you don't have
the responsibility."

She won't push it, though, she said. She doesn't want increased risk of genetic or
physical complications that come after 35, however small that chance.

Jennifer Archer is 40, married just shy of 15 years, and contemplating whether to
have children. Her baby right now is her Shiba inu dog, Koho, on whom she dotes.
Real babies are a great deal more daunting, she said.

Her own parents had her when they were 20, which they told her is too young.
They encouraged their own children to get an education, to work and travel and
grow up first. Now, after years of doing what they want without children, she and
her husband, Tyler, wonder what kind of parents they would be and if they're ready
for that. "I think we're at a stage where we've agreed to give it a good go and see
what happens," said Archer, who works for KSL in Salt Lake City. "But it scares me
a little, too."

Experts and Experience

On her 40th birthday, Angel LaLiberte, the sound of her biological clock pounding in her ears, gave up on finding Mr. Right. She remembers being in a "dark place, deeply depressed," as she realized she'd likely not marry or have children.

The Santa Cruz, Calif., woman was packing up those dreams and moving on when he walked into her life and her heart two weeks later. The problem was, Bill Cozzens had been told that he couldn't have children. At a fertility clinic, he had been handed a shiny brochure, its cover sporting a cup-half-full photo of an old couple, no kids but a burgeoning retirement account and a still-good life.

When they married a decade ago, Cozzens and LaLiberte decided to try for kids anyway, and with the help of a medical procedure for him she was carrying their baby, Leo, five months later.

She'd grown up with siblings and wanted Leo to have that, too, so a miscarriage when she was 43 was devastating. They went to another doctor, who told her to forget it; she was too old, Cozzen's previous fertility problem too complicated. She wept in the parking lot. They didn't know then that medicine sometimes gets it wrong. She was already pregnant. When Isabella was born, six years ago, they thought about sending the doctor a photo.

She calls herself a flower power mom and has a blog by that name, a meeting ground for older moms who share experiences. "We are the shock troops, if you will, for a demographic and a future where no woman or mother as a minority collective has gone before. It's both scary and fascinating."

Older moms definitely get more tired, she said, and have to learn to pay attention to their own health. It's part of giving kids "the energetic mom they're entitled to." A drop in fertility is real. So is the criticism some people feel emboldened to offer about an older mom's choices. And it's harder to find pals among the moms of kids' friends, since they're 20 years younger.

But the pluses are quite lovely, she said, including studies that prove later mothers cope as well as younger ones with newborns, don't feel more stress and tend to be more patient with their children. "That younger mom might have more energy, but I have discipline, experience and knowledge," she said. "And I'm more financially secure. That matters. It's an expensive venture to have kids."

By the time she became a mom, she'd worked a couple of decades, honing skills. "I had been a homeowner, I knew how to manage things, I'd trained to handle tough decisions."

As for older mothers dying before their children are grown, life happens. Her own mom was not an older mom, but died when she was 24. Besides that, she added, these days, 40 is midlife, with decades to go. ▰

25

"This Is Your Job Now": Latina Mothers and Daughters and Family Work

Lorena Garcia

livia slips off the padded shoulder straps of her backpack and sets it on the table with a loud sigh. Smiling at her mentor, she pulls out two heavy textbooks—trigonometry and U.S. history—along with a worn notebook and a couple of pencils. Within a few minutes, the seventeen-year-old high school junior is already at work trying to solve trigonometry problems with the assistance of her mentor, a thirtysomething Latina professional who is there at the community organization through an employer-run volunteer program.[1] Many of Olivia's peers are still settling down, chit-chatting with each other or with mentors about compliments on outfits, school-related gossip, or just complaints about homework—small talk that most often draws in any person, including myself and other mentors. But Olivia remains focused on her work, occasionally looking up as she thinks about a trigonometry problem. Often described by Hogar del Pueblo youth program staff as a "good student" and "smart," the slender young Puerto Rican woman does not join in any of these conversations until she has completed her homework, which is usually the remaining ten to fifteen minutes of the two-hour tutoring session.

It is not until my interviews with Olivia that I am able to fully appreciate her ability to be so disciplined during the weekly tutoring program. With both her parents working full-time jobs—her mother as a downtown hotel housekeeper and her father as a factory worker in a nearby suburb—Olivia, the eldest of three children—is "in charge of helping at home." She walks me through her typical weekday: When she leaves school around 2:30 pm, she picks up her eight-year-old sister from an after-school program. At home, Olivia gives her sister a snack; and while her sister watches cartoons, she handles some cleaning since her parents do not arrive home until around 6:00 pm. Counting off each task on her fingers, she explains:

> I wash the dishes, sweep and do [make] the beds, but only my parents' bed and my bed [which she shares with her sister]. I don't do it for my brother [who is fifteen years old] anymore 'cause he can do that himself. And if I don't have to clean anything else, like the bathroom, maybe I'll try to do a little bit of homework.

But she really is unable to begin her homework until around 8:00 pm, after her family has a quick dinner together that her mother usually prepares. Olivia works at the kitchen table as her mother cleans up after dinner and watches *telenovelas* (soap operas) on a small portable television. The tutoring session is the one weekday she can have an uninterrupted block of time to do homework, and Olivia takes advantage of it. "I don't have time to mess around when I get there, especially when I have questions about trigonometry or need help with other stuff. I only socialize after I finish, if I have time," she explains to me.

Olivia's experience, like that of other young women in my study, suggests that our discussions about who cleans the home and cares for family members and the time spent doing such work often fail to consider how children are incorporated into this central aspect of family life. Generally, the division of household labor is primarily regarded as relevant only to couples. White heterosexual married couples' experiences receive the most attention, though we are witnessing more consideration of how a wider range of couples, such as same-sex and immigrant couples, sort out the work that needs to be done in the home.[2] One key pattern that interests many of us and generates heated debates about men's and women's "roles" in their families is that work to maintain the home and meet the various needs of family members is organized by gender. For instance, we know that women tend to do more of the repetitive labor necessary to their family's day-to-day functioning, such as washing dishes, laundry, and cooking, whereas men's work is likely to be more infrequent, such as mowing the lawn and taking out the trash.[3] And we are also intrigued by how and under what conditions families move away from relying on gender expectations to determine the division of household labor.[4] But we really do not know much about how this plays out between parents and their children. What are parents and children's experiences of the work they do for their families? And how do parents and their children negotiate and make sense of this work?

This chapter draws on interviews and ethnographic fieldwork with second-generation Latina girls and a subset of their mothers to consider these questions. The findings presented here are from my research for my book *Respect*

Yourself, Protect Yourself: Latina Girls and Sexual Identity, in which I explore how Latina girls experience their emerging sexuality and their approaches to safe sex.[5] Though I did not ask about it, girls and their mothers often discussed how they contributed to their family. Mothers focused on what their paid labor allowed them to do for their families, and daughters talked of the unpaid labor they did for their families. Most mothers worked full- or part-time jobs outside the home, which they deemed to be relevant to their parenting practices and identities as good mothers. They saw their employment as necessitating that other family members do more family work, and it was especially young women who were expected to take on this responsibility.

The young Latinas I got to know encountered a "second shift," a term introduced by the sociologist Arlie Hochschild to describe the additional and unpaid labor done by some family members when they arrive home from work, such as grocery shopping, cooking, and caring for children. Generally, it is women who do a disproportionate share of such work, even among those heterosexual couples in which both individuals work outside the home. I found that Latina girls also grappled with juggling the demands of the family work assigned to them with that of their schoolwork, and sometimes brought their own ideas to their families' division of labor.

The narratives of this group of mothers and daughters provide us with further insight into how they make sense of what family work is and how this relates to their formation of their identities. Following what I learned from these interviews, I explore three major themes in this chapter: women's paid work as part of their mothering identity; daughters' contributions to family work; and generational change in gendered expectations for boys and men.

IT'S WHAT MOTHERS DO

Most mothers were initially noticeably self-conscious about their daughters' sexual behavior and how it reflected on them as mothers. Forty-six-year-old Lilia, for instance, stated at least two times within thirty minutes of our first interview that most people would think she had insufficiently supervised her sixteen-year-old daughter, Eva, because she was no longer a virgin. But as the interview progressed, she asserted, "I am still a good mother, even if people don't think so!" Lilia's initial embarrassed demeanor, like that of other mothers, gave way to an unapologetic determination to continue to provide guidance to her daughter. Refusing to be classified as "bad mothers" on the basis of what were deemed to be daughters' sexual transgressions, they highlighted how they fulfilled what was expected of them. One theme that emerged in these conversations was how their employment outside the home fit into their assessments of their parenting.

Nearly all mothers believed that working outside the home was not incompatible with their identities as mothers.

Rather, as conveyed to me by Julia, this was understood as integral to what it meant to be a "good mother." The busy Mexican mother of three invited me to her home one early afternoon for our second interview. Sitting in her small kitchen, I watched as Julia washed dishes and checked on a pot of beans simmering on the stove. A full-time laundry attendant, she was already in her uniform and would be heading to work in about an hour. She explained that she would leave the beans on very low heat and her sixteen-year-old daughter, Inés, would then monitor the beans until they were fully cooked when she arrived home from school—about thirty minutes after Julia left for work. According to Julia, her daughter would finish making dinner for her two younger siblings and herself by preparing some rice and quesadillas to serve with the beans. Tiredly sitting down on the kitchen chair across from me she told me, "I wish I could be here to do that for them more when they get home from school. And I think they would like that, too. But there is a necessity to pay bills and the rent. As their mother, I want to give them everything they need." Julia then went on to list the things she worked hard to procure for her children, such as food, clothing, and school supplies.

As a single mother, Julia was the only wage earner and believed that her ability to financially provide for her children made her a good mother. But talk of the necessity of employment due to family economic struggles was not just confined to single mothers. Most mothers, whether single, married, or cohabiting, described their families as barely making ends meet. Women who were married or cohabiting sought to avoid relying on only their partners' income. They saw their employment as a safety net in the event their partners lost their jobs, recognizing the instability of some work, such as in landscaping and construction. They also wanted to meet particular financial goals, such as buying a home, paying off a debt, sending money to relatives in Mexico or Puerto Rico, and/or being economically self-sufficient women. The last reason—economic independence—was particularly relevant to their parenting, because they also viewed their employment as a teaching tool for financially educating their children.

Mothers believed their employment made them good role models for their children because it facilitated how they taught their children two important lessons about work. The first was about one's approach to labor, namely, that one works for the things one wants or needs. Elsa recounted a conversation she had with her daughter when she stole a small toy from the store:

> Arely was eight years old. . . . I walked her back to the store and made her return it. It was a good thing the owner knew us and did not get mad. At home, I asked her if she ever saw me or her father take anything from the store without paying for it.

She said no. And then I told her that I wanted a lot of things, but if I didn't have the money then I can't get them. I said to her, "That is why we work, to pay for things. And sometimes we still can't get what we want, but the things we do have are paid for with the money we worked for."

When Martina's teenage son wanted an expensive pair of Nike basketball shoes, she told him, "That is too expensive! We aren't rich. I wish we could buy them for you, but we're unable to. We have to work hard to earn the little money we have! You will see what it is like when you have to work and pay for the things you want."

And while proud of the economic subsistence they provided for their families, another message for their children was that they should strive for better jobs than those held by their parents. As im/migrant women with low levels of education, their opportunities for employment were generally confined to factory or service work. Working at physically demanding jobs, they stressed to their children the importance of an education to avoid such work.

Emma attributed her chronic back pain to the repetitive bending and heavy lifting she did for her factory job. She often remarked to her children that what she did for a living was drudgery and that she did not want that for them.

When I think they aren't focusing on their studies, I say to them, "Do you want to end up like me?! You think I like to work like a donkey every day?! I don't have a choice. I can't find too many jobs. But you do have opportunities, *prepararse para una carrera* [prepare yourself for a profession]!"

And as a way to further promote the lesson about the value of an education, Lilia took her sixteen-year-old daughter, Eva, to work with her at her factory. On her spring break, Eva spent the week working on an assembly line in a packaging factory.

She hated it! But I wanted her to see how hard my job was so she stays in school. I told her, "That's why you need to go to school and study so that when you work, you will get paid for using your head and not have to do what I do."

Though they did not point their children down particular career paths, this group of mothers made it very clear what they should endeavor to avoid in their future employment.

These lessons about economic self-sufficiency were for all their children. But for their daughters, it was also layered with a message about how to navigate gender inequality.[6] As they did with their sexual education of their daughters, in which they advised them to respect themselves and take care of themselves, they communicated to them the importance of personal responsibility for their finances in the near future. Although nearly every mother expected marriage for their daughters and/or assumed that daughters wanted this in the future, they did not want them to be economically dependent within the marriage. Gina expressed this when she considered the experiences of her cousin at the hands of her abusive man.

> She doesn't work so she really can't leave him because he has all of the money. My daughter says she should just leave him, as if it is just that easy! I tell her, "That is why it is important for a woman to have her own money, so she is not stuck with a man who thinks he can mistreat her whenever he feels like it."

Jasmine stated that she often told her daughter:

> You have to go to school to get a career so that you can always take care of yourself. That way no matter what happens with your husband, you won't need to depend on him or other people for money.

She spoke from her experience of moving in with her sister's family in an already overcrowded apartment after her children's father broke up with her and moved out of state, very rarely communicating with them. Jasmine's children were seven and ten years old at the time. Jasmine initially struggled to find a job, and it took her almost two years to save enough money to move out of her sister's place. She used her experience to illustrate to her daughters the importance of a woman's economic independence.

These Latina mothers did not describe their employment as a "temporary" situation or themselves as "helping" their husbands or partners or "supplementing" their earnings. Prior to their arrival in the United States, the mothers explained that as young girls, they and their own mothers had participated in their family's ability to economically and reproductively maintain itself by hand washing clothes, making and selling different types of food, or caring for younger siblings. And as with their families of origin, they expected that they would participate in economic activities for their own families and understood employment outside the home and family work as connected to each other and relevant to their roles as mothers rather than as two separate spheres.[7] Seeing themselves as legitimate economic providers for their working-class families, this group of Latina mothers drew on this role to further validate their perceptions of themselves as good mothers and as a valuable resource in socializing their children on the advantages of an education and economic independence. Thus, their employment outside the home was not at odds with their identities as mothers.

EVERYONE HAS TO MAKE SACRIFICES

Aracelia, who worked full-time as a cashier at a local grocery store, talked of wanting to "dedicate more time to her children" and her children's frustration when she was required to work a double shift. Speaking of what was required of everyone in the family, including children, she said matter-of-factly, "But we all have to make an effort and sacrifice a little to get ahead." Aracelia and other mothers reasoned that they and their children might need to forgo time with each other in the interest of meeting their family's financial needs. And for daughters, this might necessitate relinquishing some of their own interests and time to do more in the home—as was the case for Inés, whose mother relied on her to head home right after school to finish prepping and serve dinner to her younger siblings. Like their mothers, Latina girls were initiated into "women's work" in the home at a young age and were expected to assume more responsibility for it as they grew into young women.

Proudly claiming that her enchiladas were better than her mother's enchiladas, seventeen-year-old Isela shared with me the secret ingredients in the dinner she had prepared for her family the evening before. When I inquired as to how she learned her enchilada-making skills, she rolled her eyes and explained,

> My mom's been having me help her make them since I was like eleven or twelve. When she first started showing me how to make them she said I should know how to make them 'cause I'm a girl and I could make them for my husband and stuff.

Similarly, sixteen-year-old Yvette recounted how her father and her uncle communicated this to her at the age of ten:

> I was outside playing tag with my friends and they (her father and her uncle) were hanging out in front of our house, too. After awhile they told me to go inside and help my mom finish cooking and cleaning. I was like, "Why?" They told me because I was a girl and that I needed to start knowing how to do stuff like that and help her more. I ignored them and kept on playing. Later that night, I guess my dad told my mom that I didn't listen to him about helping her and she whooped (spanked) my ass!

Like Isela and Yvette, young Latinas spoke of being enlisted into family work at a young age. The primary explanation was that they "needed" to learn how to do tasks such as cleaning, cooking, and/or caring for young or older family members because of their gender.[8]

And when mothers described how they introduced their daughters to household work, they also framed it as something that they "needed" to do because of the gender identities they claimed for themselves and their daughters that intersected especially with their racial/ethnic identities. It was a way they assisted their daughters in learning to be women, but more concretely, Mexican or Puerto Rican women. And it was also another practice that affirmed their presentations of themselves as good Mexican or Puerto Rican mothers. Take for example, Carmen's interaction with her seventeen-year-old daughter while at her niece's birthday party:

> Minerva was just sitting in the living room and I told her to go in the kitchen and offer to help. She responded that the boys didn't have to do it. I told her not to worry about that, to just worry about what she has to do. Later on at home, I told her that she should always offer to help with stuff like serving food, cooking or washing dishes. I told her it didn't look right if a woman doesn't do that. That is how we were taught in Mexico and that is what you should be accustomed to doing. And I didn't want anyone to think she was *mal educada* [not well-mannered].

Carmen's vigilance over her respectability as a good mother reminds us of the pressures felt by mothers in general in a larger culture of mother blaming in our society. Assumed and expected to be the primary caretakers of children, they are primarily the ones we blame when something goes "wrong" with their children. And since mothers are expected to model normative gender behavior for their daughters (as fathers are to do for their sons), the misbehavior or failure of a daughter is read as a shortcoming of her mother's own femininity. In talking to me about what they wanted for their daughters, mothers acknowledged that their daughters were not growing up in Mexico or Puerto Rico, as they had done. But they still believed their daughters shared their gendered racial/ethnic identity. They wanted and insisted that their daughters maintain a gendered identity that was grounded in their identities as Mexican and Puerto Rican women.

Even before becoming aware of their daughters' sexual behavior, mothers warned them not to behave like white young women, who they described as having too much freedom. Mothers sometimes accused their daughters of acting like white young women when they disapproved of their behavior, a characterization that daughters adamantly rejected because they did see themselves as Mexican or Puerto Rican despite growing up in the United States. One key site in which they negotiated this identity was within their families. As U.S.-born daughters of Mexican immigrants or Puerto Rican migrants from poor and working-class backgrounds, they were expected to contribute to their families' economic efforts, most often in the form of reproductive labor. But unlike their mothers, the young Latinas I spoke with never used the word *sacrifice* to talk of their work in the home. Instead, they tended to describe themselves as "helping" their family.

For those with younger siblings, "helping out" often required that they forgo some extracurricular activities. Such was the experience of Minerva, who felt unable to attend a campus visit to a university about one hour from Chicago that was organized by Hogar del Pueblo. This trip would require one overnight stay—something that Minerva felt was out of the question for her. Assuming she would be joining the group of students leaving for the campus visit the next day, I asked her if she had already packed for the trip. Giving me a half-hearted smile she shook her head, stating, "What for? They [her parents] ain't going to let me go." She added,

> They never let me sleep over anywhere—not even my cousin's house. Anyways, I can't go cause they need me to help out with my brother and sister cause there's no one else to watch them after school. It would just be too hard for them to deal with all that right now.

Minerva shared with me that she had not even asked her parents for permission to go on the trip. Resigning herself to the situation, she stated that she would still apply to the school, but just "check it out on the website." I later found out from some of the youth program staff that they had strongly encouraged Minerva to go and even offered to speak to her parents about it, but she insisted that they not approach her parents out of her concern that it would "cause a fight or something."

However, my interviews with Minerva's mom, Carmen, led me to think that she would have tried to make it work so that her daughter could go on the trip. Carmen, like most other mothers I spoke with, did describe restricting her daughter's time outside the home to sexually "protect" her as well as to have her "help out" at home. But mothers were flexible about their daughters being outside the home if it was for educational activities.

As discussed earlier, mothers stressed educational success as a way for their daughters to gain more independence and avoid economic reliance on men. One way they promoted this message was by encouraging daughters to seek additional educational opportunities such as tutoring or summer enrichment programs at community centers, even when they encountered opposition to daughters' participation in these types of activities from other family members or were criticized for allowing their daughters *demasiado libertad* (too much freedom) outside the home. Some mothers, for example, stated that their daughters' fathers were worried that daughters would not be properly supervised in such contexts.

Young Latinas expressed awareness of these tensions in their interviews and spoke of how they wanted to do well academically, especially so as not to disappoint their mothers. They also commented on their family's limited finances and/or child care resources and their parents' efforts to economically provide for their family, as Minerva did when she conveyed her concern over how her parents would manage child care for her siblings if she went on the college tour/visit. Their mindfulness of the pressures facing their family and the impact on family relations, as well as their efforts to minimize some of their family's stress through their labor in the home, suggest that these Latina girls were also doing emotion work.[9] In other words, they sought to sustain their family's emotional well-being through their emotional support of family members, particularly their parents. Therefore, their family work also encompassed emotion work.[10]

Reflected in these Latinas' accounts of their labor for their family are their understandings of what it means to "do gender" appropriately.[11] A key component of this for them was their willingness to "give up" something to better their family's circumstances—for mothers, it was especially the "sacrifice" of more time with their children; for their daughters, it was extracurricular activities to "help out" at home. Informing their commitment to their family's ability to sustain itself in the midst of economic struggles was their integration of their gender and racial/ethnic identities.[12] Mothers took primary responsibility for recruiting their daughters into family work at a young age, seeking to demonstrate their competency as "good" Mexican or Puerto Rican mothers, but also to provide their daughters with lessons about what femininity required of them.

Evident in my interviews with Latina girls was their attentiveness to the needs of their family in relation to what they wanted or needed for themselves as young women coming of age. Their cognizance of their family's financial circumstances and their cautiousness to minimize and/or not add tension may be why they approached their labor within the home as providing support to their families. Not one young Latina I spoke with described her work within the home as "chores," nor did she mention expecting some type of financial compensation for it (i.e., allowance). As their mothers articulated what their employment outside the home meant for their identities within their families, their daughters also negotiated what their participation in family work meant for their sense of themselves as young Mexican or Puerto Rican women. At this point in their lives, their development of gender identities and practices was closely linked to their racial/ethnic identities as well as to their family's needs.

CHANGING IT UP

Latina girls' contribution to the work of family life did not mean that they uncritically assumed their "place" in the gendered division of household labor. Their enactment of the work expected of them was also about protecting the little freedom they had outside the home. Seventeen-year-old Carla conveyed this to me when she described the various household tasks she handled, "It's annoying to do some of it, but I just do it 'cause if I don't, she would never let me go anywhere! Man, I can't really go anywhere now, so imagínate [imagine]!" And sixteen-year-old Asuzena explained that her parents allowed her to go to the Centro Adelante youth program so long as she "behaved," which included "not getting in trouble, like cutting school or hanging around with boys all crazy, and like cleaning and stuff like that in the house."

One crucial way this group of Latina girls carved out some freedom for themselves was through youth activities at community organizations. For more than half of them, this was the only after-school activity they were permitted to join. Feeling that their parents restricted their time outside their home as their bodies began to develop, these young women were cautious about jeopardizing what little autonomy they did have away from their families. They believed it was already limited by household work that was required of them because their mothers worked outside the home. Thus, through their family work, they also sought to demonstrate that they were "good girls" deserving of permission to at least hang out with other youth at community organizations.

Some young women also attempted to reduce the uneven distribution of family work, particularly between themselves and their brothers. For those with younger brothers, this was done purposefully by incorporating them more into family work routines. This is how sixteen-year-old Gloria introduced her ten-year-old brother to his cleaning responsibilities:

> He would leave everything lying around. Toys, shoes, clothes, dishes, whatever! One day I was starting to pick up his toys that were on the floor and I was like, "Hold up, uh-uh, this ain't my mess. He is big enough to take care of this himself." I made him clean it up. Then I was like, and he should start doing more around here. So I was like, this is how you sweep the floor and this is how you clean the table. This is your job now when you get home from school. If you don't do it, you ain't watch TV or play your stupid little video games.

That Gloria and some of the young women were able to obtain the cooperation of their younger brothers was most likely related to their age—they were older and had probably garnered some respect from their brothers because of the care they provided for them. It is difficult to ascertain whether their parents supported them in this effort because I did not have an opportunity to ask mothers about it (given the focus of my research), though some girls' narratives suggest that mothers were comfortable with it. And studies on parents' gender socialization of their children indicate that these young women's mothers and/or fathers might have agreed that developing sons' household-related knowledge and skills was a good idea.[13]

Latina girls' interactions with older brothers on household work were a more trying experience. Some reported that when they criticized their brothers for failing to clean up after themselves or help out, their older brothers would claim their male privilege by replying that it was not required of them. Declaring, "My brother gets on my nerves!" Sara shared that her brother often "left a mess on purpose" for her to clean up. Sometimes he taunted her by telling her, "I'm not a woman, that's what you're supposed to do, so just shut up and do it!" These brother-sister interactions often led to very heated arguments that mothers or both parents intervened in and tried to resolve.

Such was the experience of eighteen-year-old Alicia, who told me that although she often did the family laundry, she folded everyone's clothes except those of her brother (who was nineteen). Without my asking as to why this was, she explained, "He can fold his own clothes. He's a big boy." When Alicia's brother complained about it, her mother scolded her, but Alicia still refused to fold his clothes. "I told her, 'Just cause he's a guy, don't mean he don't gotta do anything up in this house!'" After this "fight," Alicia was no longer obliged to handle that task for her brother. And although he was now expected to assume responsibility for his own clothes, she noted,

> He usually doesn't do it anyway, just once in awhile. He just leaves his clothes on the bed or throws it on the floor. But they don't say anything to him for that. But if it's me, they'll be like, "why is your room like that?"

Like Alicia, other girls took up these frustrations primarily with their mothers. These types of interactions, in which daughters justified their efforts to get brothers to do more household work or their refusal to do certain things for them, also led some mothers to revisit their approaches to teaching sons and daughters about their roles in the work of family life. Emma recalled how her daughter, sixteen-year-old Miriam, recently challenged her expectations of her eighteen-year-old son when Miriam asserted that her brother should iron his own shirt and refused to do it for him:

> I reminded her that he didn't know how to iron, so she should help him. She said, "Well, isn't it time for him to learn how to do it?" I started giving some thought to this and decided that she was right. Arturo [her son] should know how to do something like that for himself. I guess I just thought she should do it for him because that is the way my mom taught me. We get used to doing certain things, but sometimes we need to ask why we do them, you know?

As reflected in Emma's narrative, these kinds of mother-daughter interactions sometimes presented opportunities for mothers to reflect upon their beliefs about household work required of men and women and to consider alternative ways of teaching their children to engage with family work.

These young Latinas' strategies to address the inequality in their family's gendered division of labor entailed interactions with brothers and mothers. Even though these were the interactions that they spoke of with me, it is likely that they were not just limited to those family members. The exchanges with brothers and mothers they described underscore that lessons about "doing gender" in the context of family work is not just passed down from older generations to the younger generations, but are also sometimes transmitted in the other direction and across generations. These exchanges hopefully can invite collaboration across various generations to "undo gender" in the organization of family work.[14]

CONCLUSION

Culture is almost always the starting point for popular and academic discussions of gender and sexuality among Latinas/os. *Familismo, machismo,* and *marianismo* are three concepts that tend to consistently surface in attempts to make sense of some of their "attitudes and behaviors" as well as some of their "outcomes." Described as placing a strong emphasis on the family, Latinas/os are generally understood as having a deep sense of loyalty to their families that requires their appropriate embodiment and practice of gender to demonstrate the centeredness of their families in their lives. For Latinas, *familismo* is explained as requiring a self-sacrificing femininity and a mindfulness to avoid behavior that could be shameful to one's family, which as some argue, is in line with their *marianismo*.[15] This "cultural trait" is also seen as complimenting and sustaining Latinos' *machismo*, which is commonly conceptualized as a strong and exaggerated sense of masculinity specific to Latinos. There are certainly aspects of Latinas' cultural backgrounds that privilege men, but this is not unique to Latinas/os. Therefore, we should be cautious in interpreting the behaviors, attitudes, and outcomes of Latinas/os as if they solely originate from a "Latino culture," which is already contested as homogenizing of a diverse group.

Though it is clear from my interviews with Latina girls and their mothers that their families were indeed important to them, their narratives of how they made sense of the work they did for their families and how it related to their identities tell us that simply attributing this to culture is insufficient. We have a very limited view of their worlds if we just start and end with culture as *the* explanation for how their family lives unfold. In my in-depth interviews with this group of women and ethnographic fieldwork, I specifically concentrated on their meaning-making to move beyond and complicate cultural frameworks as they relate to Latinas/os.[16] In doing so, I was able to uncover some of the ways in which their families' socioeconomic positioning, their work in the labor market, their educational barriers and opportunities, and their generational status informed their perspectives and approaches to their labor for their families as well as how this connected to their formation of their intersecting identities.

Notes

1. The Chicago nonprofit community organization Hogar del Pueblo provides comprehensive services to Chicago's low-income families. Most clients of the organization are predominantly Latina/o immigrants. One of the youth-focused services is a mentoring/tutoring program that connects high school students with Chicago-area professionals for weekly one-on-one sessions centered on academics, college preparation, and life skills.

2. See, for example, Carrington (1999); George (2005); Hondagneu-Sotelo (1994); Moore (2011); Nelson (1996); Sullivan (2004).

3. See, for example, Coltrane (2000); Hochschild (1989); Shelton (1992).

4. See, for example, Risman (1998); Gerson (2010); Sullivan (2006).

5. Garcia (2012).

6. Messages about the importance of women's economic independence have also been found in other studies on Latinas that consider lessons that mothers transmit to their daughters (Ayala 2006; Fine, Weis, and Roberts 2000; Hurtado 2003; Lopez 2003; Villeñas and Moreno 2001).

7. This is relevant particularly to working-class women of color in the United States (Collins 1987; Collins 1994; Dill 1988; Glenn 1994; Hondagneu-Sotelo 1997; Segura 1994).

8. Other studies have also found this; see, for example, Ayala (2006); Hurtado (2003); Lopez (2003); Souza (2002).

9. Emotion work, also referred to as emotional labor, most often is discussed in relation to paid employment with a significant amount of interaction with customers, such as that of teachers, health care workers, sales clerks, and flight attendants. Such workers often perform emotion work such as smiling, thanking, and providing undivided attention. This is work that is invisible and can be taxing for workers (Hochschild 1983).

10. Erickson (1993, 2005) points out that emotion work within families has been understudied and that family work should be reconceptualized to include emotion work (and not just thought of as household work and child care).

11. Rather than conceptualize gender as traits and behaviors that individuals possess, the "doing gender" framework concentrates on gender as a situated accomplishment that is influenced by accountability. That is, social interactions are viewed as central to how gender differences are created and come to be seen as natural rather than socially constructed (West and Zimmerman 1987).

12. Segura and Pierce (1993) argue that it is necessary to account for how unique social contexts may produce particular family configurations of various groups, which may also mean different gender identity development processes for girls. In their article, they specifically focus on working-class Chicanas to illustrate how their family relationships

and dynamics inform their intertwining of gender and race/ethnic identities. One such way this occurs is through their commitment to improving their families' and communities' circumstances.

13. See, Berridge and Romich (2011); Hill (1999); Kane (2006); Penha-Lopes (2006).

14. While research on how gender is "done" has been critical to understanding how gender inequality is created and maintained, we must also focus on how it is challenged, from the level of individuals' gender identities to broader institutional practices (Chafetz 1990; Deutsch 2007; Lorber 2005; Ridgeway 2011; Risman 1998).

15. This is a gender ideology that refers to women's passiveness, submissiveness, and self-sacrificing. It is assumed to be unique to Latinas' gender identities and practices.

16. For more on scholars' concerns of an overreliance on cultural frameworks as it relates to Latinas/os' gender and sexual lives, see Cantú (2000); Carrillo (2002); González-López and Vidal-Ortiz (2008). And for further discussion of meaning-making as it relates to cultural perspectives and practices, see Lamont (2002); Swidler (1986); Young (2004).

26

Adoptive Parents Raising *Neoethnics*

Pamela Anne Quiroz

I ncreasing attention to the formation of families through transnational adoption raises the question as to whether transnational adoption is in the public interest because there are unresolved issues about human rights and social justice. On the one hand, children gain material and social advantage through adoption. On the other hand, many, if not most, of these children lose their name, contact with family and community of origin, native language, and culture. Both sending and receiving countries have raised issues about the commodification of children and child trafficking, erosion of national interests, and damaging of children's identity.[1] Perhaps the most powerful critique of transnational adoption has emerged from adolescent and adult adoptees, whose narratives reveal the profound effects of being raised by ethnic "others."[2] Their stories compel us to examine the processes that produce the problems they describe in their lives and how culture and race were dealt with by their adoptive parents.

In this article, I combine analysis of parent interactions in three online adoption forums with observations of five transnational adoption workshops. I show how parents interpret race, ethnicity, and culture to their children. Practices described by parents help us understand how the symbolic ethnicity of adoptive parents affects the identity formation of their adopted children. *Symbolic ethnicity* is typically associated with white Americans who have a great deal of choice in terms of their ethnic identities and who bear little social cost for their identification with different white ethnic groups (Irish or Polish).[3] Forum interactions also provide a firsthand account of adoptive parents, who are typically white ethnics, as selective participants in the cultural socialization and racial assignment of their adopted children. It is through these practices that transnational adoptive families produce a unique group of migrants that I call *neoethnics*, people whose identities have literally been recreated through the act of adoption. These identities reflect the intersectionalities of race, class, gender, sexuality, citizenship, adoptive status, and sometimes even a disability. Like symbolic ethnics, neoethnic adoptees are socialized to choose their individual affiliations and to embrace racial identity as voluntary, flexible, and symbolic. Yet research on adoptees tells us they live on the margins of multiple worlds.[4] In this paper I explore how parents and adoption professionals deal with these complicated issues. I end with some suggestions for future practices for parents and professionals alike.

TRANSNATIONAL ADOPTIVE FAMILIES: A NEW FRONTIER

Between 1989 and 2009, adoptive parents in the United States, who are predominantly white, adopted more than 270,000 children from other countries. During this time, 50–75 percent of transnational adoptions came from four sending countries: China, Russia, Guatemala, and Korea.[5] This resulted in a substantial number of children who have been raised by parents whose race is different from theirs. Transnational adoptions have now declined significantly (from 22,290 in 2004 to 8,668 in 2012) because improved economic conditions of sending countries, reports of child trafficking, and highly publicized incidents of child abuse have shifted sentiment in sending countries to opposing transnational adoption.[6] It is also possible that biases toward marital status and sexuality have played a role, as single women accounted for a third of adoptive parents by the late 1990s. Subsequent and additional restrictions by China and other countries have eliminated adoption by single persons, and Russia has eliminated all adoptions by U.S. citizens. Indeed, in the past twenty-five years, over 40 percent of all sending countries either completely shut down or temporarily restricted their transnational adoptions.[7] Whether one views transnational adoption as a global gift or a neocolonialist mistake, the consequences for children deserve serious attention.

The large number of transnational adoptions to the United States, and the fact that most transnational adoptees occupy a different status from their adoptive parents in the U.S. racial hierarchy, have stimulated researchers to pay special attention to the impact of adoption on racial/ethnic identity formation.[8] Some studies have found positive indicators of adoptive parents' interest in promoting a bicultural orientation for their children, while others have highlighted discrepancies between parent and adoptees' perceptions of parents' attempts at cultural socialization. Still, the link between our knowledge of how parents address race and cultural socialization and how these processes affect adoptees' experiences remains limited.

Table 26.1 | U.S. Transnational Adoptions from Top Four Sending Countries

FY	China	Russia	Guatemala	Korea	Total Adoptions
1993	330	746	512	1,775	7,377 (45%)
1994	787	1,530	436	1,795	8,333 (55%)
1995	2,130	1,896	449	1,666	9,679 (63%)
1996	3,333	2,454	427	1,516	11,340 (68%)
1997	3,597	3,816	788	1,654	13,621 (72%)
1998	4,206	4,491	911	1,829	15,583 (73%)
1999	4,101	4,348	1,002	2,008	15,719 (72%)
2000	5,053	4,269	1,518	1,794	18,857 (67%)
2001	4,681	4,279	1,609	1,870	19,647 (63%)
2002	5,053	4,939	2,219	1,779	21,378 (65%)
2003	6,859	5,209	2,328	1,790	21,654 (75%)
2004	7,044	5,865	3,264	1,176	22,990 (75%)
2005	7,903	4,631	3,783	1,628	22,734 (79%)
2006	6,492	3,702	4,135	1,373	20,680 (76%)
2007	5,453	2,303	4,727	938	19,609 (68%)
2008	3,911	1,857	4,122	1,065	17,475 (63%)
2009	3,001	1,586	756	1,080	12,753

Sources: Bureau of Consular Affairs, U.S. Department of State. Intracountry Adoption, Statistics. http://adoption.state.gov/about_us/statistics.php (accessed September 23, 2010); and The Donaldson Adoption Institute, Annual Reports, http://adoptioninstitute.org/supportus/annual-reports/ (data from 1993–2005).

Exploring Parent Practices through the Use of Internet Data

Because many people now look to the Internet as a means of creating identity and a sense of community, I elected to explore adoptive parent practices involving race and culture by looking at interactions in adoption forums. Some of the advantages of using forum interactions to explore identity formation are that they are "public by default, but private through intent," as participants speak to people they believe are similarly situated. In these virtual spaces, parents discuss a variety of topics that range from the mundane to the highly sensitive. These interactions (forum posts) are unscripted, and the topics of discussion (threads) are generated by participants' concerns. Because they are speaking to one another, parents may use greater candor in these discussions than they would with researchers conducting interviews or surveys. Consequently, participants serve both as framers of identity and as audience for identities presented by other participants.

Table 26.2 | Adoptive Families in the United States*

- 2.5% of children in the United States are adopted (1.7 million children)
- 18% of these households contained members of different races (308,000)
- 71% adopted children under 18 lived with a white (non-Hispanic) head of household
- 1.8% of households have adopted children
- $56,000 = median income of households with adopted children
- 43 years = average age of parents of adopted children

*U.S. Census Bureau (2003); Pew Internet and American Life Project (2006).
Source: Census 2000 PHC-T-21. Adopted Children and Stepchildren: 2000. http://www.census.gov (retrieved on October 3, 2003).

As with all data collected by social scientists, there are limitations to understanding adoptive parenting using forum data. During the time frame of this study (2006–2008), the U.S. adoptive parent population was relatively small (3–4 percent), and adoptive parents who participated in forums were likely to be an even smaller and self-selected group. Additionally, online posts for any particular topic may number in the hundreds, but the actual number of participants can be quite small. For example, threads revolving around ethnoracial consciousness in the Guatemalan forum generated 805 posts, but the actual number of different people who participated in these discussions was only 85. This kind of analysis also fails to capture the nonverbal cues available in face-to-face interactions. Finally, because thread topics are discrete, it is not possible to determine whether the practices conveyed by parents represent a coherent and consistent set of practices or whether they are unique to a particular situation or moment. Therefore, modal orientations of forum posts are analyzed rather than individual parents. Nevertheless, patterns found in these forums mirror patterns found in other qualitative studies of adoptive parents, and the insights into cross-racial parenting are valuable as participants provide a way to gauge how they negotiate race and culture in transnational and transracial families.

I used archived threads from adoption forums posted on Adoption.com, the largest online adoption directory. Adoption.com's home page provided the parameters for interaction in the forums and generated literally thousands of interactions across a vast array of topics. The majority of participants self-defined as either parents or prospective parents. The large number of threads and lengthy discussions necessitated a circumscribed, two-year period of study (2006 to 2008). Forums for three of the four largest "sending" countries between 1989 and 2009 were selected: China, Russia, and Guatemala. These countries have also been the subject of a number of studies on adoption.[9]

An independent coder assisted me with interpreting forum contents, and we engaged in multiple iterations of coding that began with thread topics generated by participants and resulted in identifying four parenting processes related to racial assignment and cultural socialization. Interactions were sometimes brief but typically extensive: while a few participants posted only once, threads often included a small number of participants who posted multiple times, giving the interaction a conversational tone. Different threads tended to generate greater involvement by different subsets of participants. It was not possible to quantify participants by race, ethnicity, or gender, as they did not always state either or all those identities. However, most of those who did identify themselves in these forums indicated that they were white, which reflects the majority of U.S. adoptive parents. Because women more than men tend to use the Internet to seek and form relationships, I inferred that most of the participants in these adoption forums were white women. Because different parents posted in each thread, individual parent orientations cannot be assessed. What can be assessed is the number of different people posting on each topic. Frequent overlap in discussion threads and individual posts occurred. When this happened, the post was categorized under the dominant theme. For example, a thread about family acceptance included posts about color blindness or color consciousness. However, because the dominant focus of the thread was family acceptance, the post was placed in this category.

In addition to analyzing Internet data, I also observed five transnational adoption workshops offered by private adoption agencies. Three workshops were observed in Illinois and two were observed in Texas. Though they were located in different states, workshop formats were similar, and each workshop lasted approximately two hours. Workshops consisted of presentations by facilitators, followed by either a panel of adult adoptees or some mix of adoptive parents and their adolescent and adult children who presented their perspectives on transnational adoption. Presentations were typically followed by a question-and-answer session with prospective and adoptive parents. Notes were taken during these sessions, and a variety of brochures, pamphlets, articles, and guides (e.g., adoption language guides) were also gathered and examined. These observations supplement the analysis of forum posts and offer a look at the role of adoption agencies in shaping parent involvement. They also reveal discrepancies between parents and adoptees.

Using both kinds of data, I identified four general and overlapping activities regarding identity: choosing, avoiding or cultural distancing, keeping, and purchasing. *Choosing* refers to which children adoptive parents were willing to adopt and how they arrived at their decisions. Choosing also refers to the variety of decisions parents made that directly and indirectly affected identity. These decisions include minor and substantive decisions, such as where to live, which schools to attend, learning language, and other practices, such as circumcision. *Avoiding* refers to cultural distancing and the silence surrounding children's birth origins, culture, and race, as most of the posts in each forum indicated that parents either did not address their child's origins or addressed them in a perfunctory manner. *Keeping* refers to parents who subscribed to and engaged in activities to help their children retain a sense of native group identity. *Purchasing* refers to the use of cultural symbols, activities, media, and artifacts as a means of providing the basis of racial/cultural identity for adopted children.[10] I noted the frequency of posts within each category by participants who explicitly identified as parents and the number of people posting on each topic. Posts used here are presented verbatim and typify the modal set of responses within each category. Only spelling or punctuation is modified to clarify comments. Posts suggest well-intentioned efforts to understand and accommodate children while at the same time balancing parents' preferences and the demands of the complex social contexts within which they lived.

Dominant Practices Involving Cultural Socialization and Racial Assignment

Choosing

The practices described by forum participants are presented here as separate, but in fact, each represents one aspect of the cultural socialization process, and they overlap with one another. Tensions between these practices became apparent as many parents struggled to achieve a balance between their values and the interests of their children. The practice of choosing refers to the variety of decisions made by adoptive parents regarding their adopted child.[11] Parents described how they chose their adoption program or country, and even their child's gender, race, and health status. These choices were embedded in parents' constructions of their ideal child and their own identities, as well as their views and their family's views on race and culture. For example, many parents in the Russian forum found that the Russian cultural practice regarding circumcision conflicted with their own practice, so they weighed the emotional consequences for their adopted sons against their personal preferences and the perceived appropriateness of engaging in this practice. Most of those who posted on this topic elected to circumcise their adopted sons; however, discussions were not without some debate as parents moved between choosing, distancing, or avoiding the norms of their sons' culture of origin.

> Boys in Russia are almost never circumcised. Same with Eastern Europe. But for you, since it won't likely have been done, make your decision just as if you were having your own newborn. Circumcision is quite trivial at any age. It really is! It doesn't matter if it's 2 weeks, 2 months, 20 months or 4 years or older. I know

because I've been there, not only with my adopted son (at 4 y/o), but also with an adult friend who did it at 21 and a Jewish friend's ceremony for their newborn son. After several months, when he was settled, I easily obtained a referral from my pediatrician to a Urologist, and the Urologist told me they do about one circ (circumcision) a week and I shouldn't be uptight (I wasn't) because it's so common. (http://forums.adoption.com/russia-adoption, 11/25/2008)

I think often it is tempting for A-parents (adoptive parents) to try and erase a child's past and heritage in their efforts to make him more of *their* child. Please be assured that no matter whether your child's genitalia match your husband's or not, he will be completely your child. I sincerely hope that unless it is medically necessary you will not subject your son to an additional trauma, as he will already be going through a tremendous period of adjustment and acclimation. (http://forums .adoption.com/russia-adoption, 11/25/2008)

Several studies have shown how the process of choosing takes place in a racial system that defines which children are more acceptable and most likely to be integrated into extended families, so it is not surprising that this was reflected in adoption forums.[12] As Kazuyo Kubo[13] said, adoptive families not only provide "a space where racial integration can be created, they also tell us that it is a space where racial preference can be practiced."

I knew for me the Hispanic culture would have worked because I love it. I knew Russia would work because most of my family is from Russia. And I knew Africa would work because I live in an area with a large population of African Americans. I knew the Asian cultures had not fascinated me in the ways that the other cultures did. I had 9 years of infertility and adoption tribulation so it gave me an opportunity to educate my family on those things that would allow me to create my family. Not being willing to adopt certain nationalities may be a sign of bigotry but it may also be that parents have thought through the process and its consequences, and decided that certain things just would not work for them. (http://forums.adoption .com/Guatemala-adoptions, 11/2007)

Cultural Distancing

Across all forums, the dominant or modal practice described by parents was that of distancing themselves from their adopted child's birth origins by either failing to substantively address their child's race or culture or addressing it in a perfunctory manner. Such practices often occur when people are confronted with information that generates personal dissonance, a disjunction between current ideas, relations, and knowledge or beliefs. Transracial and transnational adoptions frequently result in personal conflicts and anxiety on the part of adoptive parents as intimate associations are disrupted by these adoptions. Conflicts may occur with extended family members who disapprove of an adoption, or even with close friends, neighbors, church members, or others who may not accept the adopted child or who may marginalize the adoptive family. It may also occur because of anxiety about how to navigate racial boundaries. Cultural distancing is an index of the feelings about the self and others, and in the case of adoption, how the child's "otherness" gets defined. Parents often alleviated this dissonance by promoting the child's engagement in choosing his or her own relationship to the culture of origin once he or she was grown.

> If we as parents decided to make contact, then we leave our children with the potential burden of the effects and outcomes of that contact. Suppose we choose to offer some type of financial support; then our children may feel pressured to continue that support down the road. I absolutely agree that the decision should be made by the adoptee when he or she is ready. . . . But as adoptive parents, we should always let our children know that we are there and will support and assist them if they choose to make contact. (http://forums.adoption.com/guatemala -adoptions, 3/2008)

Other distancing activities involve emphasizing the child's sameness with the adoptive family instead of discussing his or her difference, keeping silent about the child's birth family, and avoiding or downplaying the significance of racial incidents such as name-calling or bullying at school. Whether by design or default, these rhetorical strategies allowed parents to relinquish responsibility for keeping culture, assured distance from birth families and birth origins, and left the burden of racial identity to adoptees. It was apparent that the identities of parents were as much a focus of these processes as were the identities of their children.

Keeping

Many parents claimed a desire to achieve some degree of cultural literacy and to support their child's identification with his or her native culture, as described in Heather Jacobsen's book *Culture Keeping*.[14] Activities that involved *keeping* include retaining the child's birth name, learning about their child's country and culture of origin, learning their child's native language, visiting the sending country, and engaging in cultural activities such as ethnic celebrations.

> We take language lessons with our daughter because we want to be able to be part of her culture, at least as much as we can. It does take driving a ways to get there, and of course, it would be easier to just say, well she's in America now, but

it's one of the many things that brings us closer and makes us a family. We consider ourselves a Chinese American family, not an American family with a Chinese child. (http://forums.adoption.com/China adoption, 11/20/2007)

Rarely did parents describe a sense of "shared fate" with their children or profound alterations in lifestyles on behalf of their adopted children (e.g., changing churches, learning a language, or moving to a new neighborhood or city). Learning what it means to be Chinese, Guatemalan, or Russian did not seem to involve having friendships with members of their child's birth group. Instead, parents helped their child to construct a racial and cultural identity through a set of practices that involved other adoptive parents and by purchasing cultural artifacts and "ethnic" experiences. Participants in both the forums and the workshops spoke about relying on adoptive parent support groups such as *Red Thread* or *Raising China Children*. Parents typically looked to each other, adoption agencies, and adoption experts to help them with culture keeping. Even more pronounced was parents' use of cultural artifacts to mark inclusivity.

Purchasing

Purchasing was a natural outgrowth of two features of adoption: parents' limited knowledge of their child's culture of origin and the fact that adoptive parents are the primary consumers in the adoption industry. Consequently, adoptive parents purchased products sold by the adoption industry, such as books, artwork, toys, music, clothes, food, bedroom decorations, and experiences such as ethnic folk dancing, culture camp, and "Roots" or Heritage trips instead of engaging in more authentic ongoing cultural practices, such as making attempts to meet members of their child's country of origin.

In general, forum interactions presented cultural socialization as an opaque set of practices as parents engaged in balancing conflicting identities, reserving some decisions for themselves and deferring others to their adopted children. Whether acknowledged or even recognized, these processes reflected adoptive parents' position as symbolic ethnics as parents were allowed to selectively engage culture and ethnicity for themselves, and also to select their adopted child's race/ethnicity and the cultural representations, practices, and contacts made available to him or her.

PARENT-CHILD INTERACTION IN ADOPTION WORKSHOPS

Parent-child interactions in adoption workshops augment our understanding of these processes, as adoptive parents' perceptions of successful socialization differed significantly from their adopted child's perceptions. Two examples of these discrepancies extend our observations of forum interactions. In the first, the facilitator of a transnational adoption workshop who was also an adoptive parent of a child from India provided a moving rendition of her family's successful negotiation of culture. The social worker/mother offered examples of what she deemed to be culture keeping, such as learning about the history of India, learning to cook Indian food, and enrolling her daughter in Indian folk dance classes, which she claimed that her daughter loved. After this discussion, her daughter (in her late twenties) participated on a panel with three other adult adoptees and completely contradicted her mother's narrative. The daughter assessed her experiences as lacking real cultural understanding. She also contradicted her mother's positive version of the cultural activities in which she was placed and described them as difficult and isolating. Far from feeling accepted, the daughter claimed that the other Indian children in her folk dance class regarded her as white, and therefore, she was socially ostracized. Struck by these contrasting narratives, I observed the social worker/mother while her daughter spoke but saw no perceptible response regarding the discrepancies between their narratives.

A similar situation occurred between an adoptive mother and adolescent son (fourteen years old) in a workshop where three families presented in separate thirty-minute sessions. Again, the mother presented first and described the family's various efforts at culture keeping. These included decorating her son's room with artwork, piñatas, and artifacts brought home from Guatemala. It even included a photograph of the son's birth mother and siblings, whom the adoptive mother had met. Because at least some effort had been made to learn about her son's circumstances, this adoptive mother believed that her family had created and sustained a link to her son's family of origin and that through other efforts his culture was being honored. Unlike the daughter in the prior example, this son did not directly contradict his mother. However, he did express feelings of marginality with respect to both his adoptive siblings and biological siblings. Instead of confirming his mother's description of successful cultural socialization, this adoptee talked about his struggle to handle knowing that he was the only one of his biological siblings who had been placed for adoption.

Raising Neoethnics

Interactions in these adoption forums and workshops help us understand that the lack of strong cultural/racial identities among adult adoptees is partially the result of the sources of identity construction, the identities of adoptive parents, and the tools they use to socialize their children. I refer to these adoptees as a rather unique group of involuntary migrants, *neoethnics*. Neoethnics are people whose identities have been literally recreated through the act of adoption and who typically do not experience direct links to their culture and ethnicity of origin. They are socialized as symbolic ethnics who choose their individual affiliations, yet neoethnics also continue to be defined by their group affiliations. Recent research tells us that adult transnational adoptees typically experience everyday life as members of U.S. minority groups even though they may not identify with these groups, primarily because their lives do not mirror their native group or even the transplanted cultural group. Identification with these groups may be more a function of adoptees' racialized experiences in their adopted country.

Tobias Hubinette's study of Swedish adult adoptees of color found that they did not claim the same status or economic position of their adoptive Swedish parents, who were typically of high socioeconomic status.[15] Instead, adoptees of color typically occupied low socioeconomic status, did not marry, and remained childless. Though research on adult adoptees of color in the United States lacks the detail of the Swedish census to make similar comparisons, we also find adoptees to perceive themselves as members of a marginalized group. Adoptees are both involuntary migrants and members of minority groups who may be schooled in the performance of whiteness, but whose experiences continue to be influenced by race. Neoethnics are not likely to visit their countries of origin, to speak their native language, or to establish or sustain intimate relationships with members of their first family or country, or even to form close social ties to members who have migrated from their communities of origin. We know from numerous autobiographical accounts that those who do try to reclaim their past must often engage in this process alone or with the help of friends rather than family or other institutional supports.[16]

THE NEW NEOETHNICS?

In the past few years, we have witnessed a precipitous decline in the number of U.S. transnational adoptions to a fifteen-year low in 2012 (8,668). Recent restrictions in primary sending countries and new social movements against transnational adoption have shifted the attention of adoptive parents in the United States to new locations. Since 2007, adoptions from Africa have nearly tripled, as parents adopted children from Ethiopia, South Africa, Liberia, Nigeria, and Madagascar. Between 2003 and 2010, more than 35,000 children were adopted from African countries, with the majority (22,282) from Ethiopia.[17]

The Obama administration's detainment and deportation of over 400,000 Latinos has resulted in another group of children who have been affected by foster care and adoption. According to Race Forward: The Center for Racial

Table 26.3 | Changes in Transnational Adoptions from Primary
Sending Countries

Country	Peak Adoptions	Adoptions in the U.S. (2012)
China	7,903 in 2005	2,697
Russia	5,865 in 2004	748
Guatemala	4,727 in 2007	7
Korea	2,008 in 1999	627
Ethiopia	2,275 in 2009	1,568

Adoption statistics for 2007 = number of adoptions from October 2006 through September 2007
(the timeline for yearly visa count).
Source: Bureau of Consular Affairs, U.S. Department of State. Statistics. http://travel.state.gov/
content/adoptionsabroad/en/about-us/statistics.html (accessed November 2013).

Justice Innovation, more than 5,000 Latino children are currently in foster care
or in the process of being adopted because their parents have been detained or
deported. Race Forward projects that another 15,000 children will be in this situation within the next five years.[18] African adoptees and Latino children caught in
these processes will face the dilemmas of cultural socialization as they become
the newest neoethnics.

The United Nations Convention on the Rights of the Child guarantees children
the right to preserve their identity and cultural heritage, yet adoption forums
remind us we cannot assume that complex issues of race and cultural assignment
have been either addressed or transcended merely by the act of adoption.

DISCUSSION

Forum interactions and observations of workshops add a nuanced understanding
of adoptive parent practices regarding cultural socialization. They also illustrate
the processes through which parents' views are expressed, debated, and potentially
modified, and provide the link to understanding adolescent and adult adoptees' challenges with group identification and feelings of racial exceptionalism. Forum interactions illustrate how parents convey the guidelines for adoptees' racial subjectivity.
Choosing, cultural distancing, keeping, and purchasing are the processes by which
adoptees learn the scripts for their new social position within the adoptive family
and society. Despite survey results that indicate the willingness of adoptive parents
to discuss race and culture with their children, qualitative studies have found considerable variation in the manner, degree, and quality of these discussions.

It is not possible to know how long forum participants had been adoptive parents or how long they had been involved in these processes. However, studies suggest that perspectives on race and culture shift over time as adoptive families engage in everyday life. Online, some parents described incidents they initially regarded as uneventful as shifting them to awareness of the new niche they were carving as multiracial families. Though adoptive forum interactions indicate cultural distancing as the modal response by parents, this was not always their perception: many genuinely felt themselves to be doing what was best for their child and claimed efforts at acquiring cultural literacy. For a small number of parents, self-perceptions modified dramatically and shifted into a new identity that incorporated their child's identity of origin. Forum and workshop participants may not be representative of the full range of attitudes, and cultural socialization behaviors are not systematically captured here (i.e., how often and when parents engage in behavior), but the volume and time frame of posts suggest a link between parent practices and the profound impact of physical, legal, and social relocation on adoptees.

In transnational adoptive families in the United States, cultural socialization is predominantly in the hands of white adoptive parents who rarely describe living in or interacting within the "other's" domain. A significant number of online parents indicate that acceptance comes at a price because children are divorced from their culture, and we begin to see how families formed through transnational adoption may simultaneously reflect race-mixing while allowing the current racial hierarchy to remain firmly in place. As adoptees have increasingly demanded to be included in the conversation about transnational adoption, we are becoming aware of the complexities of this family form. To contribute to the debate about the impact of adoption on identity formation, one has to believe that as a set of symbolic, social, and material resources, *culture matters*. If one accepts this, then perhaps adoption forums and workshop interactions provide a way of understanding that something is uniquely lost to transnational adoptees.

RECOMMENDATIONS

Because parents typically look to each other, adoption agencies, and adoption experts for guidance on how to navigate culture keeping, we must address these areas to honor the social policies that aim to secure the rights of children. The ways that providers help shape the practices of adoptive parents are typically ignored. Unlike biological parents, adoptive parents require the approval of an agency social worker and the state, which must be willing to designate them as worthy, competent, and in the case of transnational adoption, *culturally literate*.

However, this designation relies primarily on a home study, an intercountry workshop, and parent education. Therefore, adoption professionals need to help adoptive parents move beyond a banal understanding of transnational adoption to an understanding of the political and social realities of the families and countries from which children are adopted. Aside from providing home studies and workshops on intercountry adoption, adoption agencies also promote reading adoption books as part of the ongoing education of adoptive parents. And while it is probably impossible to find a modern adoption book that completely ignores race or culture, it is rare to find a book that addresses these issues in any substantive manner, or that incorporates all the voices of adoption participants (parents, birth parents, children, and siblings of adopted children). More importantly, these books frequently invoke race and culture as a "dilemma" rather than as a value-added experience. Adding different perspectives and different voices (birth parents and members of the child's community) can help adoptive parents understand the enormous complexity of crossing race and culture. So long as adoption education focuses uniquely on symbolic acceptance of the "other" and fails to address how the positioning of adoptive parents and their adopted children affects members of the adoptive family, the dilemmas on which adoption books focus will remain.

Adoptive parents also need workshops that address the conditions of power and privilege in the formation of family, as those who adopt and those who are adopted occupy radically different cultural, economic, social, and racial spaces. These workshops should include multiple voices and multiple perspectives. Finally, we need to consider modeling transnational adoption after U.S. domestic open adoption, where children maintain some degree of contact with their biological families, and remind adoptive parents that culture keeping is a child's right and an enriching experience for both parents and children. In short, we are in need of an adoption policy framework that provides for more substantive practices regarding power, privilege, and their intersections with multiple dimensions of inequality (race, culture, sexuality, disability, gender). As Fonseca suggests, the meaning of adoption and family are largely defined by Western standards and may require creating more spaces for a plurality of views and practices to achieve true social justice.

NOTES

1. Cardello (2009); Hearst (2010); Leifson (2008); Smolin (2005).
2. Brian (2012); Lee et al. (2010); McGinnis et al. (2009); Samuels (2009); Tuan and Shiao (2011).

3. Waters (1990).

4. Hubinette (2012); McGinnis et al. (2009); Palmer (2011).

5. Quiroz (2012).

6. Briggs (2006); Fonseca (2002); Leifson (2008); Meier and Zhang (2008); Smerdon (2008).

7. Smolin (2004).

8. Lee et al. (2010); Tuan and Shiao (2011); McGinnis et al. (2009).

9. Dorow (2006); Gailey (2009); Jacobsen (2008); Rotabi et al. (2012).

10. Quiroz (2012).

11. Sweeney (2013).

12. Brian (2012); Dorow (2006); Ortiz and Briggs (2003); Sweeney (2013).

13. Kubo (2010).

14. Jacobsen (2008).

15. Hubinette (2012).

16. Trenka, Oparah, and Shin (2006).

17. Selman (2012).

18. Race Forward: The Center for Racial Justice Innovation (2011).

27

Parents as Pawns

Intersex, Medical Experts, and Questionable Consent

Georgiann Davis

D̲ id you have a boy or a girl? New parents are routinely asked this question. The assumption is that boys have penises and girls have vaginas, making the question seem simple when, in fact, gender is far more complex than what is between our legs. To start with, gender and sex are not synonymous. Gender is a culturally specific phenomenon expressed in different ways, for example in our clothing choices. Baby boys are routinely dressed in blue jumpers, whereas baby girls are more commonly spotted in pink dresses. These displays of gender are meant to signal a baby's sex, which is commonly understood through strict biological definitions. Males are assumed to have penises, testes, and XY sex chromosomes, while females are said to have vaginas, ovaries, a uterus, and XX sex chromosomes.

However, this line of thinking simultaneously oversimplifies gender and sex. Correlating them with each other is flawed, especially when one considers those born with intersex traits that surface as "ambiguous" external genitalia or sexual organs, and/or as sex chromosomes that do not match normative expectations. For example, those born with complete androgen insensitivity syndrome, an intersex trait, have vaginas, but they also have XY sex chromosomes and testes (usually internal and undescended). Historically, individuals with intersex traits were referred to as "hermaphrodites," but today, that term is considered derogatory by some in the intersex community. Terms less contentious include *intersex* and *intersexuality*. More recently, some have embraced new medical terminology—disorders of sex development, DSDs for short—to name their condition. I explore these terminological tensions in my forthcoming book.

441

Regardless of the terminology one uses, intersex traits make it explicitly clear that the "boy or girl" question is deeply problematic.

In this chapter, I draw on sixty-five in-depth interviews I conducted from 2008 to 2011 across the United States with parents of intersex children, adults with intersex traits, and medical experts. Most of my participants were recruited from the Androgen Insensitivity Syndrome Support Group-USA,[1] Organisation Intersex International, Accord Alliance, and the Intersex Society of North America. I rely on these interviews to describe the complexities of parental experiences within the medical management of intersexuality. I begin with a brief history of intersex medical care and the birth of intersex activism. I discuss how medical professionals present intersex traits to parents of newly diagnosed children as medical emergencies that can be fixed only with irreversible surgical treatments. I then describe how parents of children with intersex traits understand their child's diagnosis. I argue they often consent to medical recommendations with minimal hesitation because the condition is presented as a medical emergency. However, when parents eventually learn more about intersex traits, they often regret consenting to medical interventions that they come to realize were elective procedures rather than medically necessary interventions.

A Brief History of Intersex Medical Care

The medical community views individuals born with intersex traits as needing medical care, even though many of these traits rarely pose a health threat.[2] Since medical professionals have had the technological tools to discover and rid the body of intersex traits, they have surgically and/or hormonally erased its existence. There simply is no room for the intersex body in a world that assumes male and female bodies are mutually exclusive and must be neatly categorized. For example, we now know that testosterone isn't only present in the male body, just as we know that estrogen isn't found only in the female body. If we took a sample of men, we would find lots of variation in their genitals. We would also find genital variation if we examined women's bodies. Penises and vaginas are not one size fits all. Despite this obvious overlap in male and female bodies and natural variations across penises and vaginas, bodies around the world continue to be categorized as male or female.

Since medical professionals also categorize bodies as either male or female, their first response when encountering an intersex trait usually involves "treating" it by surgically erasing it. Medical professionals are not evil people who run down hospital corridors with scalpels in hand searching for "abnormal" genitals. But this does not mean that their actions should not be carefully examined, nor does it mean that their actions are appropriate. Rather, it means that their decision to medically treat intersex traits by erasing them is much more complicated than it appears. Because ideologies about sex maintain we must be either male or female with absolutely no overlap, medical providers justify their treatment of intersex traits as helping individuals born with these conditions fit into society.

In the early 1990s, everything seemed to change. Feminist critiques of the medical treatment of intersex bodies fueled the birth of the intersex rights movement. An individual with an intersex trait by the name of Cheryl Chase, who was angry about how the medical profession treated her when she was young (notably surgically modifying her body and lying to her about her condition as she got older), met similarly bodied others.[3] They shared criticisms of the everlasting effects of medically unnecessary interventions including loss of sexual pleasure and emotional harm caused by the absence of full disclosure. The U.S.-based intersex rights movement was fueled by these connections, which turned into newly formed activist organizations and peer support groups. Intersex activists organized protests at medical association meetings, and when possible, relied on the media to raise awareness about how they were treated by the medical community. Feminist scholars, such as Suzanne Kessler and Anne Fausto-Sterling, were standing with intersex activists as they offered similar critiques from a scholarly platform in ways that legitimized the intersex rights movement.[4] With such collective activism, medical professionals could no longer operate under the radar as they performed irreversible procedures on the basis that they were helping individuals unfortunate enough to be born with such "abnormalities."

With a decade of protests by adult intersex activists and scholarly critiques from feminist scholars, medical experts were under public scrutiny. The American Academy of Pediatrics issued a formal statement on the medical management of intersex conditions,[5] which at first glance seemed to be evidence of progress. The document had a number of recommendations, including that intersex infants "should be referred to as 'your baby' or 'your child'—not 'it,' 'he,' or 'she.'"[6] The guidelines advised doctors to inform parents that their baby's "abnormal appearance can be corrected and the child raised as a boy or a girl as appropriate."[7] Surgery was still an option. The guidelines also stated that a number of factors should be considered when determining which "gender assignment" should be recommended for a given intersex child. Most notably, these factors included "fertility potential" and "capacity for normal sexual function."[8] The medical definition of normal sexual function assumed that there is only one way to experience sexual pleasure—penile-vaginal penetration. This is inaccurate. Oral sex gives many people pleasure, as do other kinds of sexual activity that do not rely on penile-vaginal penetration. The medical community approaches gender assignment and the interventions that follow with the belief that one's genitals (internal and/or external) must match gender expression. The standard of medical care that dominated intersex treatment before the birth of intersex activism continued despite increased public attention and scrutiny from those born with intersex traits and feminist scholars.

In 2006, there once again seemed to be a ray of hope. The American Academy of Pediatrics revised its policy on intersex medical care due to "progress in diagnosis, surgical techniques, understanding psychosocial issues, and recognizing and accepting the place of patient advocacy."[9] The organization offered new recommendations in this policy revision, including introducing the option of avoiding unnecessary surgical interventions and the implementation of new nomenclature—disorders of sex development (DSD)—which I have shown in other scholarly work has replaced "intersex" language in virtually all corners of the medical profession.[10] However, despite this formal revision of the 2000 protocol, evidence suggests that medically unnecessary surgeries continue.[11]

Between October 2008 and April 2011, I set out on a journey to understand how intersex was treated and experienced in contemporary U.S. society. As a feminist who was born with an intersex trait, this journey was especially close to my heart. Before I started this project, I had met only one other person with an intersex trait who was as secretive about her condition as I was. Today, after traveling all across the country meeting so many individuals with intersex traits, their parents, and medical experts, I feel liberated and not at all ashamed about my intersex trait. In fact, it has become a central component of my identity.

During this methodological journey, I interviewed sixty-five individuals affiliated with four key organizations in the intersex community: the Intersex Society of North America (ISNA), Accord Alliance, the Androgen Insensitivity Syndrome Support Group-USA (AISSG-USA), and Organisation Intersex International (OII). I targeted these four organizations because, based on my initial assessment of their websites, each organization appeared to be involved in the intersex rights movement in a different way. For instance, ISNA and OII are activist organizations, while AISSG-USA is a support group, and Accord Alliance is an organization that seeks to distribute educational resources to medical professionals. I also asked participants to refer me to others who might share different views from their own—a methodological recruitment process known as snowball sampling. In addition to the in-depth interviews, I spent over 300 hours in the public meeting spaces of intersex organizational meetings recording informal observations.

In the sections that follow, I rely on this qualitative approach to understand why parents usually consent to these medically unnecessary interventions—especially irreversible surgery. I found that when doctors describe the condition to parents as a medical emergency, they are likely to defer to medical expertise and consequently willingly consent to medically unnecessary interventions. There is one exception, however. If parents connect with the intersex community before they consent to medically unnecessary interventions, they are likely to delay or even refuse such recommendations after hearing of the pain and suffering such procedures cause in one's life.

A Medical Emergency

When a baby is born, parents immediately want reassurance that their child is healthy. Since medical professionals are health experts, new parents often turn to them for such reassurance beginning with the all too familiar decision (especially in the Western world) to medicalize the entire pregnancy process from prenatal laboratory tests to ultrasonography to labor and delivery. In this section, I take you on a walk into medical consultation rooms, where we hear how medical providers describe intersex traits to parents who, of course, want nothing more than for their child to be healthy. What you will hear when reading these accounts is that when a medical professional discovers a child has an intersex trait, the provider usually presents the trait as a medical emergency that needs to be corrected.

Imagine your friend has just given birth to a baby. After a routine labor and delivery, it is discovered that the new baby has atypical genitalia. There are many possibilities for how the intersex trait could be discussed with the parents. For example, a doctor could describe the intersex trait as a natural and normal variation of the body. During this discussion the doctor could reassure the parents that the presence of an intersex trait, in most cases, does not mean there is an immediate health concern. However, this is not what typically happens in medical consultation rooms. Instead, the focus tends to be on whether the baby is male or female, as if biological sex is simple and the most important question. Medical professionals could approach intersex in a way that problematizes the sex binary. Instead, they tend to use the sex binary to problematize intersex.

When I asked Dr. D. to describe what happens when she encounters a baby with an intersex trait, she explained:

> We try to find out as much biochemical and genetic data as we can, *as fast as we can* [emphasis added]. We look at the phenotypic appearance of the exterior of the child. We try to figure out . . . if we know their biochemical basis or what we think it is, what is likely to happen to them at puberty.

Dr. I. elaborated:

> The family is aware that we are getting additional data. We have to wait for labs to come back, karyotypes to come back. We let the family know that the emergency, which would have been a salt-wasting CAH, is or is not the concern. Once you say there's no medical emergency here, then we say, let's get some more data.

Although Dr. I. explained that the possible "medical emergency" in this situation is salt-wasting CAH (congenital adrenal hyperplasia), which could potentially be life-threatening, it is important to note that ruling out this possibility neither ends nor postpones the need for immediate investigation. Rather, as Dr. I. explained, the search for "more data" continues, which reinforces the assumption that intersex is a medical emergency rather than a natural biological variation.

This search for hard scientific data about one's body is supposed to help decide if the child born with the intersex trait should be assigned a male or female gender identity. However, gender identity isn't so neatly tied to biology. Gender, itself, is culturally and contextually specific. Young women who grew up in the 1950s, for example, were expected to wear dresses and skirts. Today, teenage girls can be perfectly girly wearing the ever-so-popular "boyfriend" jeans. Neither genes nor jeans are perfectly correlated with gender identity.

Since medical professionals construct the emergency, they also create a situation that only they have the authority and power to address. For example, when a dentist tells us at a routine cleaning that we have a cavity that needs to be filled that we didn't even know we had, she reestablishes herself as the expert who is exclusively capable of fixing the cavity. Of course, we already view the dentist as an expert, but the fact that she uncovered a problem we didn't even know we had reinforces her authority and reestablishes the power she has to fix the problem that she has discovered. In the case of intersexuality, the emergency response involves a number of modern medical techniques designed to force the baby into the sex binary and disallow the existence of intersex bodies even though, as Dr. F. shared, there is not "a good scientific way to make a choice. I don't think it matters what the chromosomes are, I don't think you can tell [gender identity] from the hormones." The question this raises is why do medical professionals continue to search for medical markers of gender, when they themselves acknowledge such markers can't easily be predicted?

Although there is no clear medical marker in the body that can predict one's gender identity—how could we even expect such given gender is culturally specific and changes over time and context?—the authority that resides within the medical profession still justifies medical investigation. For example, Dr. A. was convinced that their "obligation as healthcare providers is to provide people with very complete information about what we know about the biology of DSDs, about the implications of DSDs for later development of sexual preference and sexual identity." Yet the allegedly "very complete information" that is delivered includes no social explanations of sex, gender, or sexuality, nor does it involve connecting individuals and their families with peer support groups. Instead, a "case conference," as Dr. F. called it, is held, where the medical professionals rely exclusively on medical markers to justify and necessitate their interventions on the intersex body.

Dr. I. describes the goal of these case conferences as follows:

> [We] meet as a team and think about what are the options, which option we feel is medically in their best interest, and then we present the options to the family. And then we help the family reach a decision as soon as possible.

The problem with such an approach is that by the time the medical team meets with parents, they have already made decisions about which interventions are "medically in [the child's] best interest." For example, Dr. I.'s comments indicate that a decision has already been made for the intersex child *before* medical professionals meet with the parents. Parents are not included in the team meetings. They are included in discussions only *after* the team has reached their decisions. Although the medical experts are clearly the decision makers here, they assume no responsibility for the decisions they recommend. Instead, they shift all the responsibility onto parents.

DOCTOR KNOWS BEST

Think back to the last time you were being treated by a medical professional. Maybe you were getting a physical, had a cold, or were simply under the weather and sought medical care to feel better. I recently sought out medical care hoping to get some relief from uncontrollable allergy symptoms: sneezing, itchy eyes, scratchy throat, and headaches. The symptoms were so debilitating, I could hardly get any work done. I made an appointment with my primary care physician, who during my visit wrote me a prescription that promised relief. After my visit, I drove directly to the pharmacy, where I anxiously waited for my prescription to be filled. Soon thereafter, I was medicated and waiting for the relief I had been promised.

I'd argue my experience with something as mundane as seeking care for my allergy symptoms is relevant to intersex medical care. Why? To begin with, it is an obvious example of how we defer to medical expertise. When was the last time you questioned the prescription a doctor was writing for you? When was the last time you did your own independent research before following your doctor's recommendations? Hardly ever, I'd imagine. And, if you have questioned a medical provider's recommendations, you likely faced some pushback. In part, there is a shared understanding that medical professionals are the experts. They did go through all that school, after all. They are body experts. We, on the other hand, tend to defer to their expertise, and perhaps we should in some cases.

In the case of intersex medical care, when irreversible and medically unnecessary interventions are being performed on children's bodies, it is important to present the most complete information to parents—which ought to include the fact that it is acceptable to do nothing. A child with an intersex trait that is not life threatening is perfectly healthy as born. There is no need to immediately perform any type of intervention. Yet, the birth is presented as a medical emergency, and parents defer to medical expertise. In this section, I highlight how doctors shift all the responsibility for medical interventions onto parents, who in turn, explain they were following medical recommendations with little hesitation under the assumption that *doctor knows best*. Medical professionals do not usually accept primary responsibility for performing unnecessary interventions on healthy intersex bodies. Rather, they present treatment options to the parents of intersex children in ways that appear to be exclusively informational.

For example, in explaining that medical intervention was performed out of respect for parents' wishes, Dr. A. said:

> [S]ome families, for cultural, religious, or psychological reasons, may feel very strongly about the importance of trying to have their child look more typically male or female. Under those circumstances, I would counsel them to defer surgery; I wouldn't oppose surgery.

While Dr. A. seems to be taking some responsibility by counseling parents to delay their decision about surgical intervention, he still makes it appear to be exclusively their decision. However, Dr. A. is involved in the decision-making process and, as a medical expert, in a very important way. He could have, for example, informed the parents that the surgical interventions they desire may down the road be emotionally or physically harmful. Instead, he only counseled parents to defer, rather than avoid, surgery. While deferring surgery is a better alternative than going forward with immediate surgical interventions, it still frames surgery as an appropriate medical response.

When I asked the medical professionals how they justified irreversible and medically unnecessary interventions, they tended to explain that they were fulfilling parents' beliefs that sex, gender, and sexuality ought to be perfectly correlated. For example, Dr. G. shared:

> The hard part [for this family] is that every time this mom changes the diaper of her baby girl, she sees these testes. . . . It's this daily reminder. Some families could accept that, but for this family, it's just really getting debilitating."

Dr. D. further explained that "parents [of intersex children raised as boys] complain to me that they wanna wear their sister's dresses and play with the dolls; they don't wanna go out and play with other boys." Dr. A., on the other hand, shifted the responsibility to parents more directly by citing their beliefs about sex, gender, and sexuality:

> I generally think it's up to parents to pick [a sex and ultimately a gender] based upon what information we have available at the time. The most important counseling that we can give to people is help them understand that the gender of rearing may or may not turn out to be much related to sexual preference and behavior later on. And parents need to appreciate the ambiguity involved.

When consulting with parents, medical professionals like Drs. G., D., and A. do not challenge the idea that sex, gender, and sexuality must be neatly correlated even though they acknowledge the "ambiguity involved." This is likely because they too hold narrow understandings of such phenomena and a deep desire to see two, and only two, sexes.

Let us not forget that medical professionals present the intersex trait to the parents of newly diagnosed children by inundating them with medical information. For example, Dr. B. explained:

> I feel like we pretty immediately—when we do the initial education with families— talk about what we know about the sources of these problems, and we talk a little bit about what we know about what determines sexual orientation and what determines, and what would determine, sexual function.

If medical professionals believe the sex, gender, and sexuality of an infant can be captured by diagnostic testing, and they are the experts who discover and then disclose the intersex traits to parents, we cannot reasonably expect parents to challenge their recommendations for how to "treat" the intersex trait. Medical professionals did acknowledge the difficulty parents face when making their decisions. Dr. B. described the process: "We kind of go through, here are the two choices, and get parents pretty actively involved. I think sometimes we overwhelm them a little bit with information, but I don't know how else you do it. I'm not sure." Dr. I. further explained:

> So for family, it's hard. They are forced to make certain decisions—not all decisions—some decisions with the best available data we have at this time. And that's hard. That's what parents do all the time. We just do the best we can [in our recommendations] with the data we have.

But although it was common for the medical professionals to acknowledge that decision making could be a difficult process for the parents, they still placed the responsibility for the decision entirely on the parents—thereby escaping any responsibility. When Dr. B. was asked what could be done to make the decision-making process easier for parents, she suggested that "better" data could help parents to make their decisions: "I mean, I'm really saying that we could give better information to parents 'cause they make the decision."

There were a few medical professionals who acknowledged that at least some parents were resistant to medical intervention. Describing one particular case, Dr. F. explained, "The mother is really torn about which sex to raise this child." Dr. F. further articulated the problem:

> [S]urgeons want to do a surgery to repair the hypospadias and make the child look more typically male now, and the mother is concerned that if she does that, that the child may somehow later in life reject that, or may want to change to a female sex of rearing, and [would] have gone through all this surgery unnecessarily. So the mother is disinclined to do any surgery, and the surgeon is trying to hint her into the direction of doing surgery.

Dr. E. similarly shared with me that "parents are really pressured . . . from doctors" to raise their intersex children to "conform to a gender role."

What happens when parents resist medical recommendations? Although such is not common given most parents defer to medical expertise, what I learned is that the parents who do challenge medical recommendations are likely to face harsh criticism from medical providers. For example, Dr. C. recounted a recent consultation with a family that was very critical of his recommendations:

> The father said, "[Doctor], can I ask you a question?" I said, "Absolutely, this is your forum. I'm at your disposal. You're hiring me." He said, "Why should we do anything?" And I acted physically surprised, I'm sure I did. And I said, "Well, I'm concerned that if you raise this child in a male gender role without a straight penis, he's not going to see himself as most other males and he's not going to certainly be able to function as most other males." And the father said, "Well, in our family we like to celebrate our differences and not try to all be the same and feel the social pressure to do everything like everyone else does." . . . I said, I do have to say one thing, and I think it's of key importance, that you both see a psychiatrist.

This harsh criticism is evidence of the pushback parents experience if they are brave enough to question medical recommendations. While the 2000 and 2006 medical statements introduced earlier warned against performing medically unnecessary interventions on intersex bodies, these surgeries continue. In the section that follows, we hear directly from the parents and learn that when they connect with the intersex community, they question the necessity of medical interventions, delaying and in some cases denying consent for such procedures.

ADVICE FROM THE COMMUNITY

I think it is fair to assume most parents are guided by their own life experiences and the best of intentions when they make parenting decisions. For most parents of children with intersex traits, they face an important parental decision—to consent or refuse to consent to irreversible medical interventions—without, in most cases, any of their own life experiences to guide their decision. For many parents, intersex is something they've never heard of before their child's diagnosis. This is further complicated when we are reminded that, as described earlier, medical professionals frame intersex as a medical emergency that demands immediate action. Some parents do question the necessity of acting immediately, and in turn, usually find themselves connected with the intersex community and diverse viewpoints from other parents, adults with intersex traits, and professional allies from both within and outside of medicine. They are not inundated with more medical diagnostics. Instead, they hear personal accounts in ways that shape how they understand intersex medical care. More specifically, parents connected to intersex communities learn about the consequences of irreversible medical interventions, and as discussed below, are less likely to allow medical providers to perform suggested procedures. The parents who connect with the intersex community after they've allowed medical professionals to perform irreversible medical interventions are also affected by the personal accounts, but since they've already consented to such procedures, they are left feeling responsible for earlier decisions they've made.

As described earlier, in the 1990s the intersex rights movement was formed. In many ways, the movement has been so successful in its formation because it formed as the Internet was gaining momentum and becoming more affordable for the average person to access. If one has access to the Internet, a simple Google search of "intersex," for example, would lead you to a number of intersex activist/support group organizations throughout the United States and even the world. Today, intersex activist organizations and support groups exist all over the Internet, allowing many parents of newly diagnosed children—and even adults with intersex traits—to get connected to the community and learn about the condition by communicating with those also personally affected.[12]

Parents who connect with the intersex community learn quite quickly that most adults with intersex traits are openly critical of unnecessary medical interventions. This criticism offers insight into the consequences of medically unnecessary interventions that most medical providers seem to ignore or not care to share. For example, Pidgeon, a young adult with an intersex trait, offered this advice that many in the community share:

> [N]ever let them touch you in terms of surgery. That's number one. If they ask about surgery or ask your opinion, don't do that. Don't do surgery, no matter what they say. . . . You'll love your body somehow, some way, and you don't need surgery to love your body and love yourself. . . . If you fuck with your body, you can never change that. But if you don't fuck with your body, you can change your acceptance of your body.

Parents in the community tended to offer similar advice geared to other parents. Hope explained:

> Just breathe. Take a deep breath and don't feel like you have to rush into anything. . . . Let [your child be]. Get all the information you can and then wait. Don't feel like you have to rush and make your decisions.

One of the reasons for the criticism from community members about medically unnecessary surgical interventions is that it creates an incredible amount of trauma in one's life. Ana, an adult with an intersex trait, shared:

> When I was 12 . . . I was told [by my parents and doctors] that my ovaries had not formed correctly and that there was a risk of cancer and that they needed to be removed. And I had lots of examinations including of my genitals, but I was never made aware [prior to surgery] that anything was going to be taken away [from down] there. So it was a big shock to me [when I woke up after surgery]. And I really had some work to do when I was eventually ready to do it . . . from the trauma that I had from waking up from my surgery to realize that what was between my legs was gone.

As you might imagine, parents are deeply moved when they hear these personal accounts from adults with intersex traits and their parents. In turn, this influences how parents who are faced with the decision to consent or refuse to consent to suggested medical interventions respond. For those who are contemplating their consent, they usually end up refusing or, at the very least, delaying consent to medically unnecessary interventions. Laura, a parent of a child with an intersex trait, explained:

> [My husband] wanted [anything male] gone. Anything male, he wanted it out of our daughter 'cause he considered it male, and our daughter a separate entity. . . .

But the more I was reading, and I guess on the [intersex support group] webpage and then on the parent group talking about it. . . . "Your daughter's natural hormone maker [should be left alone]. . . . It's better than being on a pill all your life. Sometimes kids with the pill have a difficult or more difficult puberty." There wasn't any doubt about it that I wanted to keep [her as is after that]. I think it was . . . it took me a little while to convince [my husband] we needed to keep it.

Shelby and her husband, Drew, parents of a young baby with an intersex trait, shared a similar experience. Drew explained:

When we met [an adult with an intersex trait], he said . . . "Hey, keep them in as long as you can." I think I'm going to listen to a guy like that a little bit more. . . . It sounds like there's probably more benefits to having them than less benefits.

However, Shelby and Drew experienced pushback from some medical experts. One doctor told them that their daughter "would be very psychologically damaged if [they] don't remove her testes immediately."

Michelle, a parent of a teenager with an intersex trait, had a comparable experience with medical professionals:

[T]hey told us that they needed to remove the gonads at one month. So she had surgery because they said "this is what you do" and we had no clue. Now I wish that we would've waited just because of all the information that we have now.

Jeff, a father of a young adult with an intersex trait, stated, with obvious emotion, that medical professionals advised:

Basically immediate surgery, for certain things . . . and you know we found out that that wasn't really necessary. . . . They didn't get into whether [she] would need surgery or not need surgery. . . . The big fear right away is . . . this is the fear that the pediatric endocrinologist put into us, is "Oh, she's got to have it taken out right now or she's going to have cancer. Right now." And then when you start finding out [from] people who've dealt with these situations for a long time, over many, many years . . . they're like "That's not true." The risk is no different than anybody else.

Laura, a parent introduced earlier, shared,

My big turnaround was when I met you guys [in the support group]. It showed me that it all works out in the end. It does all work out. You guys all lead great lives and you're not so worried all the time.

Drew had a similar experience:

> I think the [intersex support group] conference reassured me the most. To see . . .
> I mean, those girls, it seems like they're all accomplished people that are doctors,
> people that are whatever they want to be. Nothing's going to hold them back.

With respect to parents who found the intersex community after already consenting to such procedures, there appears to be some guilt, albeit with an understanding that their decision was anything but informed. For example, Susan, a
parent, shared "parents aren't making an informed decision" when doctors treat
it "like, oh, you got to do it right now." Jen, a parent, explained:

> The only reason we did [the surgery] then was that was what we were told eleven
> years ago. Oh, you have them taken out because . . . you either make a decision,
> or you wait for [your] teen to decide. . . . [The] word 'cancer' came up enough and
> that did it. So we took them out.

As I've shown in this section, parents could benefit in the decision-making process
if they were connected to the intersex community. However, for this to happen,
medical experts need to be willing to refer parents to intersex support groups.

PARENTS AS PAWNS

Parents seem to be pawns in the case of intersex medical care because medical
professionals tend to place all the responsibility for unnecessary surgical interventions on their shoulders. Medical professionals rarely accept responsibility in
the decision-making process. Instead, as I've shown, they tend to inundate parents with *medical information* and myths about cancer risks associated with intersex traits. While it may be the case that some intersex traits have the potential to
increase one's risk of developing gonadal (or other related) cancer,[13] these claims
have inconsistent support. It is also true that the mere risk of developing cancer
should not be reason enough to surgically modify healthy bodies. We don't, for
example, go around removing breast tissue from newborn babies to eliminate
their possibility of developing breast cancer.

What parents could benefit from is not more *medical information* but rather
personal experiences from those in the community—especially adults with intersex traits. When parents learn that irreversible medical interventions are not
always necessary and can even cause emotional and in some cases physical pain
for those who have been surgically modified, they choose to delay or even refuse

such procedures. Those who are exposed to such personal experiences after already consenting to irreversible interventions, on the other hand, are left with some guilt even though they were acting with the best of intentions and merely following medical recommendations.

Given parents are affected by the personal experiences of those in the intersex community, shouldn't doctors want to connect parents with similarly situated others as they contemplate irreversible interventions? Wouldn't this approach, coupled with the medical information doctors provide, offer parents the most complete pool of information and assist them in their decision-making process? If medical professionals do not begin to refer parents to support groups when there is evidence such connections influence the parental decision-making process about medical interventions, they are, on these grounds alone, acting *irresponsibly* and might even be *legally liable* for their actions. Medical professionals must present parents with a diverse pool of information even if some of that information resides outside of medicine—otherwise, parents will continue to be played like pawns in a chess game of medical authority and jurisdiction over the intersex body.

Notes

1. Androgen Insensitivity Syndrome Support Group-USA was recently renamed AIS-DSD Support Group.
2. See Cools et al. (2006); Pleskacova et al. (2010).
3. Chase (1998).
4. Some of the first feminist scholarship on the medical management of intersex traits is as follows: Fausto-Sterling (1993); Kessler (1990). For more contemporary feminist scholarship, see Karkazis (2008); Preves (2003).
5. Committee on Genetics: Section on Endocrinology and Section on Urology (2000).
6. *Ibid.*, p. 138.
7. *Ibid.*, p. 138.
8. *Ibid.*, p. 141.
9. Lee et al. (2006).
10. Davis (2011).
11. *Ibid.*
12. Preves (2004).
13. See Cools et al. (2006); Pleskacova et al. (2010).

In the News

OP-ED: HEY, FOX NEWS, INTERSEX IS NOT A PUNCHLINE

The Advocate, February 26, 2014

Sean Saifa Wall and Georgiann Davis

Everyone loves a good joke with a creative punchline. However, when well-known Fox News hosts Clayton Morris and Tucker Carlson took a cheap shot at the entire intersex community in a story about Facebook's move toward offering folks more gender options to choose from earlier this month, many people were left hurt and frustrated, especially our intersex friends.

Facebook's more expansive gender options aren't perfect, but they are a step in the right direction toward inclusivity. Because of this development, individuals in our community are now able to publicly claim their intersex identity on their respective Facebook profiles. We should be thankful to the LGBT community for pushing Facebook toward creating these options that will create not only a national but a global dialogue around gender identity. This ought to be a time of celebration, however, Fox News has used this development to poke fun at intersex.

No, Fox News, you don't get to laugh at the thought of being intersex.

Intersex refers to a variety of traits in which a person is born with a reproductive or sexual anatomy, internally and/or externally, that doesn't seem to fit the typical definitions of female or male. Medical providers often respond to people born with unique bodies such as ours by performing irreversible surgeries on our internal, and sometimes external, genitalia. That's right. They usually cut intersex bodies to make them look and feel "normal." What's worse is that when children like us are rolled into operating rooms, they are rarely, if at all, told the truth about their bodies and the medically unnecessary and irreversible surgeries that they are about to endure. Instead, they are lied to about their diagnosis.

Not surprisingly, these medically unnecessary surgeries cause more harm than help. They tend to leave folks with a lack of genital sensation, sexual struggles, and even emotionally deep and dark scars. Medical interventions are often bodily violations that impact people with intersex traits for the rest of their lives. Many people with intersex traits feel ashamed by their bodies. Folks like us often keep their diagnosis secret from their closest friends. Many are stigmatized and made to feel like "freaks."

While there are many sources that feed these feelings of abnormality—for example, the medical profession's treatment of our bodies—the media's portrayal of our bodies is a big part of the problem. How did Fox News think people with intersex traits would feel when they made a laughing matter of our bodies? Did the newscasters even care?

Maybe Fox News doesn't care about our community or the media's role in emotionally harming individuals, but surely the network's higher ups care about ratings or they'd all be out of a job. Intersex is not rare. For example, hypospadias, a trait where the urethral opening is located toward the base of the penis, affects 1 in every 250 male births, making it almost as common as being born with red hair! Given this fact that intersex traits are actually quite common, we are sure at least some folks in our community are, or at least were, supporters of Fox News. Surely the network wouldn't want to intentionally alienate its audience.

Chances are many of the employees of Fox News know someone in their personal lives who was born with an intersex trait. At the very least, with this letter, we are assured that they know at least two people born with an intersex trait who are regularly made to feel abnormal because of their unique bodies. Before laughing at folks like us and the intersex community to which we belong, we encourage Fox News to exercise caution over this very serious issue. ▇▇

28

The Power of Queer

How "Guy Moms" Challenge Heteronormative Assumptions about Mothering and Family

Raine Dozier

Recently, a friend of mine joked that she was going to nominate my YouTube channel for *Best YouTube Channel* in the TransGuys Community Awards. These awards are designed to honor excellence and achievement by transgender men on the Internet.[1] She said she thought my channel shows the real life of a trans[2] person that, rather than detailing my transition from female to male (common on YouTube), consists of my daughter's piano performances and a few vacation videos.

Human beings are complex, and I am no exception. I have multiple identities—I am a sociologist who studies gender and inequality, a mother, a single parent, a butch lesbian, and a transgender-identified person. My trans identity is relatively uncomplicated: I internally feel like a man and don't identify with being a woman. However, I have chosen not to take hormones or have surgeries, so, to the average observer, I am generally perceived as a masculine woman. Because there is not yet a body of research that investigates social locations such as "guy mom," my position offers insight into areas typically examined within a heterosexual framework, specifically gender and its relationship to mothering and the family. In this chapter, I combine some of my own vantage point with existing studies on same-sex parenting and my own research on gender and transmen. Doing so highlights the opportunities that guy mom, like other gender-transgressive categories, brings to those who seek to understand and transform gendered family structures. Examining motherhood and the family through this lens both adds to our understanding of LGBTQ parents and allows us to reconsider notions about mothering in families.

Much of the sociological research about gender focuses on what it means to be a man or woman in a particular society and how gender affects our interactions, position in the social structure, access to power, and life outcomes. This type of research often assumes that our sex (whether we are male or female), our gender identity (man/woman), our gendered behavior (masculine/feminine), and our sexual orientation (gay/lesbian, heterosexual, or bisexual) all align in one expected configuration. In addition, it assumes that each of these categories is binary—you are either one or the other. A smaller body of work considers gender within the context of marginalized identities such as transgender and gender-queer[3] people, lesbian and gay individuals, or feminine heterosexual men.[4] Often the purpose of this work is to "trouble the waters," calling into question our assumptions about binary categories and their "natural" existence and alignment with each other. Whether focusing on typical or marginalized identities, examining gender in the context of social institutions like the family can help us see more clearly how gender is not biologically determined, but socially constructed.

Doing Gender

The concept "doing gender" views gender as something created in interaction with others, and a performance for which we are all held accountable.[5] We all learn to do gender in childhood, but also learn, relearn, and revise how we do gender over time and depending on the social situation. For example, how boys express masculinity at five years old might be very different from how they perform it at fifteen. In addition, how we do gender at work might be very different depending on whether our job is in an office, on a construction site, or at a strip club. Individuals who parent also become accountable for their children's gender performance, as evidenced by studies that document some parents', especially fathers', angst over children playing with cross-gender toys (e.g., boys playing with Barbies), dressing gender atypically, or claiming to be the other gender.[6] Same-sex parents feel particularly accountable for their children's gender performance because lesbian and gay individuals are often viewed as a threat to their children's heterosexual orientation.[7]

In addition to our own performance of gender, others interpret our behaviors through the lens of gender. For example, if I am grocery shopping with a toddler and perceived as a woman, my behavior is relatively unremarkable. However, if I am perceived as a man, then my behavior is worth remarking on—and, in fact, people do. For example, gay fathers report that, when out with their children, people approach them to commend them for "giving their wives a break."[8] When men care for children, especially if they are doing more than playing, they are perceived as generous and remarkable while women are expected to provide the same level of care as a matter of course. Tasks associated with maintaining the family are often gendered, making the family an important site for creating and maintaining both gender and gender inequality.

Parents do gender in a variety of ways, ranging from how they choose to dress their children to how they divide the work involved in running a household. As they become parents, men and women in heterosexual couples increasingly specialize,[9] with women doing the lion's share of child care and housework. Some people argue this division of labor is natural, based on a mother's need to be at home with an infant due to the physical demands of breastfeeding and the recovery process from childbirth. Yet, as mothers in heterosexual[10] couples are increasingly in the labor force rather than at home, they still do most of the child care and housework—even when working full-time.[11]

Trying to decipher what is driven by physical necessity and what is doing gender can be difficult. Studies that look at the division of labor among lesbian and heterosexual parents find that lesbians have a more egalitarian distribution of housework and child care even when one of them has physically given birth, implying that gendered ideas about family participation might play a part in inequality among heterosexual parents.[12]

In an effort to control for the biological aspects of new parenting, one study investigated changes in the division of labor among different-sex and same-sex couples who recently adopted infants. While no member of these couples was nursing or physically recovering from birth, the study still found inequality in child care and household tasks, especially among heterosexual couples. For all couples, the more the primary parent[13] worked, the more equitable the distribution of child care, yet heterosexual couples still had a greater discrepancy relative to same-sex couples. Heterosexual couples also had far greater discrepancy in household tasks such as cleaning, cooking, doing laundry, washing dishes, and running errands. Among both same-sex and different-sex couples, the parent who made more money (not worked more hours) was less likely to engage in housework relative to the primary parent. This was especially true for heterosexual parents. Having economic power, then, means the primary earner is less obligated to do menial labor at home.[14] This study illustrates that the unequal division of labor in families is not based on biology, but on a combination of behavioral expectations based on gender and power inequities between a primary earner and a primary parent.

HETERONORMATIVE VIEWS OF FAMILY LIFE

Families are a significant site for the manufacture of heteronormative values and practices. Heteronormativity can be conceptualized as assumptions and practices grounded in the belief that heterosexuality is the norm and that an individual's sex, gender, sexual orientation, and gendered social roles are congruent. Heteronormativity asserts the primacy of certain lifestyles, such as the nuclear family (i.e., being heterosexually married with children) and delineates expectations about appropriate gendered behavior (e.g., women solely exhibit behaviors, attitudes, and interests associated with females and femininity). In the arena of family, heteronormativity also privileges biology—viewing "real" parents as those who have a biological connection to their children.

Heteronormativity not only suggests the "norm" for behavior, but also organizes social, political, and economic structures. If the heteronormative view of family is a nuclear heterosexual family where the woman stays home to "serve" the family, then even as structural realities change, women are still held accountable for this idealized norm. For example, women nearly equal men in the workforce, and more than half of women with infants work for wages.[15] Despite this remarkable growth in women's labor force participation, they still bear the brunt of what is termed the "second shift,"[16] doing the great majority of household labor in addition to their paid job.

Heteronormativity doesn't just inform how heterosexual-headed families are organized, it can also penalize LGBTQ[17] families in a variety of ways, including denying their existence on school, medical, or other official forms; excluding them from everyday activities; and denying them legal rights, sometimes with devastating results. For example, a lesbian mother, Lisa Pond, spent her dying hours alone after collapsing from an aneurysm in Florida on vacation with her family. Even with legal documents, including adoption papers and a health care proxy, her partner of eighteen years, Janice Langbehn, and their three children were not allowed to be with her for the majority of her final hours. As the hospital social worker told Janice, "This is an anti-gay city and an anti-gay state, and you are not going to get to see her or know her condition."[18] Heternormativity, then, organizes social life, leading not only to norms and expectations about family structure and appropriate gendered behavior, but to sanctions when individuals and families do not comply.

QUEERING FAMILY AND MOTHERHOOD

Any aspect of social life that is gendered can be "queered" when unexpected individuals participate in gendered social positions. Queering is "whatever is at odds with the normal, the legitimate, the dominant."[19] Queering involves a transgressive position or something that might deconstruct and destabilize accepted ideas about "the way things work." Queering motherhood, then, describes any act of mothering that is transgressive or deconstructs norms around mothering. If we accept this definition, then single motherhood, mothering in extended families or transracial families, mother as primary earner, and many other types of mothering are queer. The danger of defining *queer* as generally at odds with the dominant form, though, is that it removes the notion of queering motherhood from the realm of sexual orientation and gender identity. Mothering as a gay, lesbian, bisexual, transgender, or queer person is a particular position, at odds in a specific way, relative to the heteronormative institution of motherhood and family, which can both illuminate and deconstruct what is assumed normal and natural in family life. Even if same-sex-parent families are quite mainstream in family structure (i.e., two parents with children living in a household together), they still challenge heteronormative views of motherhood and the family.

Families with same-sex parents challenge what we assume is natural and necessary for mothering and families. They destabilize what is considered essential to creating a family: biology, one father, one mother, and the gendered division of labor. Some families with same-sex parents may have no interest in radicalizing the family structure; instead they might aspire to marriage, the white picket fence, PTA meetings, and all the trappings of a conventional family existence. Regardless of intention, though, having two mothers—or, in the case of gay men, having no mother at all—queers the family. Whether LGBTQ families seek to challenge heteronormative assumptions about the family as a deliberate political act or seek a fairly heteronormative life, they disrupt notions of family and motherhood simply by engaging in everyday family life.

As a parent, every time I edit a school form that asks for the names of "Mother" and "Father," it challenges the gender order in the same manner as when I check "Male" on forms that mistakenly ask me to identify my gender (rather than sex). It is a small but deliberate act that makes visible unexamined notions about motherhood and family structure. The now numerous lesbian and gay parents who have had their children rejected from Catholic schools or prohibited from participating in Boy Scout activities have queered the family, drawing public attention both to heteronormative assumptions about family and caring for children and to the marginalization of nontypical families. These everyday acts can lead to significant political change.

For example, after an eight-year-old boy was rejected from a Catholic elementary school in 2010 because of his lesbian mothers, the archdiocese of Boston clarified policy. In response to public outcry, the archdiocese's new admissions policy states that Boston's parochial schools must not "discriminate against or exclude any categories of students."[20] In another example, children of same-sex couples who are applying to college have had to negotiate the Free Application for Federal Student Aid (FAFSA), which until recently was bound by the language of the federal Defense of Marriage Act (DOMA), defining marriage as between one man and one woman. Although same-sex couples have not been, until recently, recognized at the federal level, new laws in a growing number of states allow same-sex couples to marry while other states allow second-parent, same-sex adoptions. This meant that a person with two legal, same-sex parents (who may or may not be married at the state level) could not report them both on the FAFSA. One student reports, "It was so stressful and so frustrating to try to fit our family into those forms when so clearly it wasn't going to fit. . . . You feel like you are lying no matter what you do."[21] Through their attempts to participate in everyday social life, same-sex couples with children challenge the heteronormative framework of major social institutions. Even the relatively conservative act of enrolling your child in parochial school can disrupt heteronormative assumptions about parenting and generate a broader societal conversation about LGBTQ families and inequality. At times, this leads to social change.

QUEERING FAMILY STRUCTURE

Due to biological factors, queer family formation challenges the nuclear-normative family model. Because a transwoman or transman cannot procreate within the sex they identify with[22] and same-sex couples need a third party to procreate, reproduction in LGBTQ families often involves more than two people and a radical disruption of gender in the case of pregnant transmen. While heterosexual couples can decide whether and when to disclose that an egg or sperm donor was involved in their child's conception, same-sex couples do not have this choice—the lack of biological connection between family members is visible. As a result, families with same-sex parents are constantly engaged with a variety of individuals and systems in discussions about biology, legitimacy, and the definition of motherhood and family.[23] For example, same-sex families are called upon to explain their family configuration to strangers at the playground, at the doctor's office or preschool, to acquaintances who want to know how their family was formed, and to extended family members who contest the legitimacy of nonbiological family connections.

The relationship of a same-sex couple to an egg or sperm donor or a surrogate or birth mother can take many forms. When children have a significant relationship to a donor dad or a shared parenting arrangement with a biological parent who is not romantically involved with the same-sex couple (or queer single parent), it illustrates possibilities for family structure beyond the nuclear family. It also sheds light on assumptions about biology, physical pregnancy, and what constitutes a mother. For example, if one person in a same-sex couple donates an egg and the other person carries and births the baby, who's the "real" mother?[24] The biological mother is often referred to as the "real" mother in situations such as adoption, yet in the case of egg donation, the biological mother's claim is less certain.[25]

Some studies address the issue of "realness" among lesbian parents, illustrating how biology is privileged in the social definition of family. Among lesbian couples, the nonbiological mother's role is often contested by relatives and devalued by individuals in other institutions such as schools and health care settings.[26] Sometimes relatives seek to "heterosexualize" the family by treating the sperm donor as a more significant family member than the nonbiological mother. Often in public and social situations, people attempt to ascertain who the "real" mother is through intrusive questioning.[27] Although these situations can be uncomfortable, frustrating, and demeaning for lesbian mothers, the visible lack of biological connection among family members destabilizes a basic tenet of heteronormative family structures—the biological basis of family connections and the gendered family structure.

Lesbian and gay individuals have a long history of creating "families of choice." As people who have historically faced family and community rejection, they developed strong, family-like relationships with people unrelated by biology or marital ties.[28] A de-emphasis on biology and a privileging of social connection may make same-sex couples an especially good fit for foster and adoptive parenting. Evidence suggests that same-sex couples are more likely to adopt, and to adopt transracially, relative to heterosexual couples.[29] Perhaps the inability to base a family on biological connection leaves room for other visible disruptions of biology, encouraging alternative family forms and offering opportunities to children who might otherwise remain unadopted.

Because lesbian- and gay-headed families are more likely to have atypical configurations—often with adults beyond the two-parent norm and family members who are not related biologically, they queer notions of family when engaging in everyday activities. When queer family configurations interact with institutions like schools, health care, and the legal system, they draw attention to unexamined beliefs about family and mothering, including the biological basis for mothering and family formation as well as the "naturalness" of the gendered division of labor. For example, when gay fathers are parenting, the unspoken policy for schools to contact the mother when a parent is needed is not possible, potentially weakening the role schools play in perpetuating gendered social norms. Whether they want to assimilate or not, a queered family configuration does not fit into heteronormative boxes available on forms and within social institutions, destabilizing the gender order.

THE POLITICS OF SAMENESS

Because same-sex parents are more vulnerable to legal challenges to their parenthood, there has been a heavy investment in showing that they do not differ from heterosexual parents. Families that include one mother, one father, and their biological children are assumed to be the "gold standard"[30] to which LGBTQ families must measure up. Multiple studies, particularly of lesbian mothers, find few differences between children of same-sex and heterosexual families in their mental health, school outcomes, sexual behavior, substance abuse, peer victimization, or family relationships.[31]

Unfortunately, the investment in asserting sameness has made it difficult to investigate potentially meaningful differences in LGBTQ parents, families, and their children.[32] Overall, evidence suggests that there are small but significant differences in children and families that favor lesbian-headed families[33] relative to families headed by heterosexuals.[34] Several studies find lesbian mothers have greater parental investment in child-rearing and fewer parenting disagreements with their co-parent relative to heterosexual parents.[35] One study examining lesbian mothers' parenting goals found they aspired to instill respect for others, honesty, and self-esteem in their children and prioritized education, cultural experiences, and family time together.[36] One of the most notable differences is the lack of abuse among lesbian-headed families; in contrast, over one-quarter of children in heterosexual families report physical abuse and 8 percent report sexual abuse.[37] Lesbian-headed families are also more likely to foster connected, open relationships with their children and pro-social, egalitarian behaviors in their children. Adolescents of planned lesbian families have greater social and academic competence, fewer social problems and externalizing behaviors, and a greater sense of connection to people at school relative to their counterparts with heterosexual parents.[38]

Although multiple studies suggest some differences between gay- and lesbian-headed and heterosexual-headed families, the politics of sameness seeks to de-emphasize difference. Since previous research has been used to legally discriminate against LGBTQ parents, it creates pressure to quash diversity in lifestyle, family structure, and gender expression and identity in new studies. For that reason, it is difficult to know what measurable and interesting differences researchers might find if they did not have to worry about their investigation endangering LGBTQ families. For example, no studies examine gender—that is, masculinity and femininity—in same-sex relationships (e.g., butch-femme relationships) and its influence on mothering and families. In addition, very few studies engage transgender parents, and none examines potential differences in trans individuals' parenting styles or their children's outcomes.

The need to measure up to heteronormative standards also creates enormous pressure for same-sex couples to be accountable for their children's gender performance, sexual orientation, and general functioning. One of the main themes in research on families with same-sex partners is whether their children are more likely to be lesbian, gay, or bisexual than other children. In addition, LGBTQ parents feel extra pressure to raise children who are "perfectly normal," especially in gender presentation, in order to justify their participation in parenting. One gay father reports,

> We make sure our girls' hair is done nice. We put them in dresses or nice dress shoes. Especially with the girls, I make sure that they see that a father can do the "mom thing" and dress their kids up. . . . I paint their fingernails.[39]

The "mom thing," then, includes socializing children into the gender binary, and LGBTQ parents are especially held accountable for creating appropriately gendered adults.

The politics of sameness creates pressure for researchers to focus on whether LGBTQ families "measure up" to heterosexual families even though evidence suggests that lesbian, and possibly gay, couples may demonstrate more positive parenting outcomes. In addition to influencing research, the pressure to measure up to heterosexual standards creates pressure for LGBTQ-headed families to toe the line, encouraging gender compliance in their children.

Homonormativity: The New Normal?

As same-sex couples and families become more visible and gain access to more rights and privileges such as gay marriage, their families may become more "normalized." Gaining social acceptance, however, increases the pressure to assimilate to heteronormative practices and structures. *Homonormativity* refers to societal acceptance of gays and lesbians based on their ability to express heteronormative values and behaviors.[40] Gays and lesbians are legitimized and included as long as they are "gender conventional, as long as we link sex to love and marriage-like relationship, as long as we defend family values, personify economic individualism, and display national pride."[41]

The strategy of emphasizing sameness appears to have been successful in light of recent legislative victories regarding same-sex marriage and the repeal of the military's "don't ask, don't tell" policy. However, homonormativity also orders who is an acceptable and unacceptable sexual orientation or gender minority. The "new normal" is affluent, white, monogamous, and conventional in every way except for sexual orientation. The closer a couple and family resemble a heteronormative family, the more valuable and less sanctioned they are. For example, gay men who are not feminine, mothers who are not masculine, and families with two and only two significant adults will reap social and legal rewards and privileges. As privileges become available to LGBTQ families, it is likely that socioeconomic status, immigration status, race/ethnicity, and gender identity and expression will begin to dictate who among LGBTQ people gains access to privileges and who does not, as it does in other areas of social life.

TRANSGRESSIVE MOTHERING

Some families and mothers hold a more radical conception of gender, sexual orientation, and family either as a conscious political act or because they are far from "the new normal." Their masculinity, femininity, gender identity, or relationship status does not align with hetero- or homonormative standards. Their inability to assimilate, whether by choice or not, queers all their interactions with the social institutions of mothering and the family. Surprisingly, there is little research engaging these individuals and families.

One important aspect of queering (and queer theory) is its focus on "deviant" cases of gender, sexual behavior, or identities that do not neatly fit into assumed categories, especially the binaries of sex, gender, and sexual orientation.[42] When considering mothering and families, queer positions are rarely represented in the research literature, yet they have much to offer. Looking at motherhood and families through a queer lens is useful not just in thinking about LGBTQ parents, but in examining accepted notions of how we do the work of mothering in families. My social position as a "guy mom"—a masculine (or butch), trans-identified mother—queers the concepts of mothering, nurturing, families, and the "natural" division of labor. Because of this, I would like to share some of my thoughts derived from personal experience, using my "deviant" or queer standpoint to discuss common conceptions of gender and mothering.

As a guy mom, I believe my participation in everyday mothering queers notions of gender, motherhood, and the family. When I wake up in the morning, pull on men's underwear and clothing, then rush around preparing breakfast and making a school lunch, it's queer. Lucal suggests that gender-atypical individuals who position themselves in gender-typical situations challenge the gender binary by their very existence.[43] In her case, she is referring to public bathrooms and whether, as a gender-atypical person, the act of using the female bathroom challenges the gender order. In my case, I am referring to the institution of motherhood and whether simply participating in it as a masculine female disrupts the sex/gender binary.

When I walk into ballet lessons or the mother-dominated PTA meeting with a tray of brownies, it disrupts notions of both masculinity and femininity. I do not identify as a woman: I appear masculine, yet I am existing in space predominantly occupied by women. When I explain that I am not in the wrong bathroom to other mothers at the middle school, it dislocates their assumptions about the natural and normal alignment of sex, gender, and mothering. I visibly don't look feminine, yet I am doing women's work. My inability to conform to the gender binary creates constant "gender trouble" for individuals interacting with me, especially in sites dominated by mothers and focused on children.

Gay men are in a similar situation. Their mere presence in everyday parenting life challenges heteronormative beliefs regarding gender, sexual orientation, and the "natural" gender order of the family. Consider the meaning of the phrase "fathering a child"—gay fathers are doing far more than fathering children (and in fact they may not have fathered their children at all); instead, their everyday parenting activities look very much like mothering. In one study, more than half of gay male parents "considered themselves mothers and were comfortable accepting the title"[44] not because they felt like women, but because their social role most closely resembles that of a mother.

When a gender-atypical person does mothering, everyday actions in public space require reexamination of commonly held notions about gender, biology, and mothering by both individuals and institutions. In one blog, a mother recounts her observations of her genderqueer partner in the public pool with their son.[45] The juxtaposition of a genderqueer person, shirtless with a surgically modified chest, being called "Mommy" and playing rough-and-tumble games with children disrupts our unexamined beliefs about sex, gender, and social participation in the binary that includes "mother" and "father." In another post, the genderqueer partner explains:

> "Mommy" is the word I used as a kid to describe the person who could take all the pain away or support me when I needed it. . . . So, when our son . . . was born, I chose "Mommy" as a name because I loved the idea of being that force for someone in this crazy world of ours. . . . I love to hear the word "mommy" and to be called "mom" sometimes. But that has no real bearing as to how I feel in my body.[46]

Interacting with mothers who are not clearly women calls for a radical reconsideration of gender and the family, including the division of labor and beliefs about the "natural" ability to mother as well as broader assumptions about sex, gender, and the organization of social life.

Trans-identified, genderqueer, or masculine mothers disrupt the idea that femininity and motherhood naturally align and that women, particularly feminine women, are uniquely qualified to engage in mothering. My particular case also challenges the overreliance on femininity or womanliness as a signal for reproductive ability. I have been asked countless times whether I adopted my children, because it is difficult for some individuals to separate the biological category of sex (male/female) from the behavioral/appearance categories of man/woman or masculine/feminine. In another example, a female-to-male (FTM) transman I interviewed for a study on gender and transmen had a baby after transitioning. The social impossibility of this meant that no one saw past his facial hair to interpret his body as pregnant. He explained, "When you have facial hair you can pass regardless of what your body looks like. I mean, I was nine months pregnant walking around and people were like, 'Ooh, that guy's fat.'"[47]

These examples illustrate that masculine appearance coupled with mothering behaviors disrupts the "natural" correlation of reproduction, mothering, and femininity. On a broader level, it illuminates the fallacy of gender. Although gender is socially created, people often rely on biology to explain why men and women behave in particular ways. Masculine female, gay male, and trans primary parents challenge biological explanations for the ability to mother and, more broadly, the innateness of masculine and feminine behaviors and interests.

GUY MOMS, GENDER, AND SINGLE MOTHERHOOD

In my previous research with transmen, I asserted that gender is a balancing act between perceived sex (i.e., perceived as male or female) and masculine and feminine behaviors.[48] I have come to realize that my conceptualization of gender as a combination of behavior and appearance is not completely accurate. It misses a crucial aspect of gender—our various social positions. Social position refers to the statuses one has in relation to individuals and institutions such as employers, family, school, or the legal system. My social position as a mother affects my personal life far more than my gender identity, appearance, or behavior. Gendered social positions—social positions generally ascribed to one sex—inescapably influence our lives. When a social position is highly correlated with being male or female, social policy, laws, and culture develop in response and have the effect of creating and sustaining structural inequality.

"Mother" and "single mother" are specific social locations; the words evoke particular expected behaviors in families as well as in interactions with social institutions such as schools, the labor market, and the legal system. The physical and economic constraints of single parenthood and the legal status of a primary parent with fewer assets is a uniquely gendered situation. Single parenthood is generally women's work and comes with the attendant hazards of poverty, legal troubles, and strained resources as the crises and costs of parenting fall dispropor-tionately on one set of shoulders. The gendered social position "single mother" affects individuals not because they are feminine or identify as women, but because there are gender differences in access to power and resources.[49]

I identify as transgender in the most stereotypical of ways—I feel like a man and don't relate to being a woman at all. Yet even with this relatively black-and-white conception of gender identity, I do not think of myself as a father, but as a mother within the context of particular political, social, and legal systems. For example, recently I have been engaged in a legal dispute over child support. These disputes are commonplace; whether the noncustodial parent is a man or a woman, masculine or feminine, influences the predicament less than the social structural position of the custodial parent. Currently, the label describing this position is "single mother." Regardless of gender identity, then, as a primary par-ent and a single parent, I find myself strongly allied with the plight of mothers, a distinctly *female* social position associated with less power in many major social institutions, including the family, the economy, and the legal system. I proudly claim the identity of "single mother" and all that entails in resources, time use, legal history, oppression, resistance, and life chances while retaining my mascu-line and male gender identity. Surely, this is queering motherhood.

QUEERING CHILDHOOD—UNEXAMINED POSSIBILITIES

Although research suggests that children raised by lesbian mothers differ in small but meaningful ways regarding gender (e.g., less gendered toy choices and more empathetic boys), it is difficult to know what effects radical departures from heteronormative attitudes and structures might have. Based on my own observa-tions, I would like to suggest a few areas for consideration that could be better understood with additional research.

The Necessity of Male or Female Role Models

A common concern raised by relatives, strangers, and even same-sex parents themselves is whether a child can have healthy development without a male role model and, in the case of gay male parents, a female role model. Some claim this fixation on a male role model for children in lesbian-headed families "seems to suggest that any model of maleness is preferable to none."[50] It is widely believed that male and female role models are necessary to socialize children into gender. The fear appears to be that without a male role model, boys won't grow into "real men." Evidence suggests this may be true to a certain extent; boys raised by lesbians are more empathetic and more open to difference and value egalitarian relationships.[51] However, are these differences we would like to inhibit or foster in boys and men? If we identify them as strengths, might we want to investigate how these characteristics are developed and try to replicate them in boys from heterosexual families?

The definition of a desirable male role model can vary based on culture, subculture, and personal values. For example, in one study, Swedish lesbian couples articulated a very different view of male role models when describing their process for choosing a sperm donor (donors are often involved in parenting in Sweden). The couples viewed gay men as healthier role models because they challenged stereotypical notions regarding manhood and masculinity. As a result, parents believed gay donor dads would be less likely to engage in sexist behavior, providing a positive male role model for children.[52]

The oft-voiced concern that children need both male and female role models within the family also implies that children do not foster meaningful relationships outside the family, ignoring children's significant involvement in schools and communities. Recently, after learning of my daughter's lack of a father, an individual said reassuringly to her, "Well, I'm sure you have male role models though." Confused, she quietly replied, "Not really." Later, as she was thinking over the incident at home, she quipped, "I should have told that guy, 'Sure I have male role models—Strangely (a not-typically-masculine circus performer), Gabe (a young trans guy), and my mom!'"

If I am responsible for doing "guy things" with the children—going to stock car races, showing them how to put brakes on the car, and playing football—am I an adequate male role model? What about a man who does not hold typical masculine interests and shows my daughter how to knit and apply makeup—is he a male role model because he has a male body? Although the unspoken assumption is that a male or female role model will teach a child how to grow up appropriately gendered, it is unclear what they must do to assure this.

The Lie of Gender Differentiation

Parents often seek role models for their children in the belief that behavior observed by children can influence their future behavior and development. For example, while the unequal division of household labor in heterosexual couples remains tenacious, there is evidence that viewing a different model in childhood can have enduring effects. One study found that men who had working mothers in early childhood spent more time on housework as adults relative to other men,[53] suggesting that early exposure to disruptions in the gender binary may have long-lasting effects on behavior. This finding implies that childhood exposure to the decoupling of masculinity and femininity from sex and gender identity could result in adults with more diverse sets of behaviors and interests and altered world views. For example, I recall an incident illustrating my preschooler's attempts to articulate the complexities of gender. She was amused that I was wearing her sister's flowery flip-flops. "Look, George," she exclaimed to a neighbor, "my mom looks like a drag queen!" In this case, she recognized there were gender differences, yet they were complex and unassociated with sex—a feminine person could include both her sister and a drag queen, but not her mother. As she has grown up with increasing exposure to trans and gender-nonconforming people, she learns both that gender is not binary and that appearance does not disclose identity, sex, behavior, or social position. This consistent exposure to queering sex and gender may leave her with a less gendered framework relative to girls raised in heteronormative family structures, offering her a greater sense of possibilities over her lifetime.

When speculating about the effects of queering motherhood, the little evidence available suggests that explicitly discussing gender and inequality (which is more likely in same-sex families) may result in children who are more aware of gendered scripts and feel less accountable to gender. Men and women who grew up with lesbian and gay parents report more diverse, less gender-typical interests, which they attribute to their upbringing.[54] In my personal experience, this leads to an ongoing awareness that gendered behaviors and social roles are optional, not inevitable. My adult daughter reports,

> When I went through puberty, I remember being really conscious that shaving your legs was a choice and that other girls didn't feel this way. I chose not to shave my legs. There are many things like that that have come up over the years—where I realized I had a choice to do or not to do something. It wasn't as automatic.

Although there is risk in drawing conclusions from personal experience, the lack of research demands some initial thoughts about the possible effects of radical departures from hetero- or homonormative parenting. Clearly, this is an area that calls for further investigation, both in how families who exist far outside the sex/gender norm differ in child rearing and in what enduring differences might be found in their children as a result.

CONCLUSION

While theoretical discussions help advance our understanding of both gender and family, it is important to note that, in everyday life, queer motherhood, lesbian motherhood, and heterosexual motherhood look fairly similar. The majority of mothering life involves basic tasks such as supervising homework, transporting children, cooking, and cleaning—our other social identities do not come into play. As I'm fond of saying, "It doesn't matter whether I feel like a man changing diapers or a woman changing diapers—I'm still changing diapers." Although various sex and gender identities may not affect the daily process of many mothering tasks, they do influence who does them, how they are interpreted, and the value placed on them by society. For this reason, upending expected gendered behaviors and family structures forces both individuals and institutions to examine heteronormative systems that create and perpetuate gender inequality.

NOTES

1.   Retrieved May 10, 2013 (http://transguys.com/features/transguys-of-the-year).

2.   *Trans* is an umbrella term that can include individuals with a variety of transgender identities. Generally, individuals with transgender identities do not solely identify with the gender (man/woman) associated with the sex (male/female) assigned to them at birth. They may or may not take hormones, have surgeries, or be socially recognized as the gender they identify with.

3.   The term *genderqueer* includes a variety of identities, but generally describes individuals who identify as outside the gender binary. They may identify as neither gender, both genders, as blurring gender categories, or as having a fluid gender.

4.   Dozier (2005); Heasley (2005); Schilt (2009); Shotwell and Sangrey (2009).

5.   West and Zimmerman (1987).

6.   Kane (2006).

7.   Lev (2010); Reich (2013).

8.   Giesler (2012, p. 128).

9.   Baxter, Hewitt, and Haynes (2008); Kluwer, Heesink, and van de Vliert (2002).

10.   To avoid confusion for the reader, I am choosing to primarily use the term *heterosexual couples* rather than different-sex couples in this chapter. However, it is important to note that not all individuals in different-sex couples are heterosexual—one or both of the members could identify as bisexual. In addition, if one of the members has a trans identity, then they might identify as a gay or lesbian couple rather than heterosexual.

11.   Bartley, Blanton, and Gilliard (2005); Bianchi and Milkie (2010).

12.   Goldberg and Perry-Jenkins (2007).

13.   A primary parent is the parent who has the primary responsibility for caregiving.

14.   Goldberg, Smith, and Perry-Jenkins (2012).

15.   Cohany and Sok (2007); U.S. Bureau of Labor Statistics (2013).

16.   Hochschild and Machung (2003).

17.   LGBTQ refers to individuals with lesbian, gay, bisexual, transgender, and queer identities.

18.   James (2009, para 7).

19.   Halperin (1995, p. 62).

20.   Wangsness (2011, para 1).

21.   Bernard (2011, para 2).

22. I am oversimplifying the term *trans* for the sake of brevity. Trans people can include a variety of individuals with a variety of identities—not necessarily only those who identify as the sex other than which they were born.

23. Chapman et al. (2012); Lindsay et al. (2006); O'Neill, Hamer, and Dixon (2012).

24. Grant (2009).

25. Dempsey (2010).

26. Chapman et al. (2012); Kitzinger (2005); Lindsay et al. (2006).

27. O'Neill et al. (2012).

28. Dempsey (2010); Weston (1997).

29. Goldberg (2009); Lev (2010).

30. Stacey and Biblarz (2001, p. 162).

31. Bos, van Balen, and Van den Boom (2007); Golombok (2007); Patterson (2006); Wainright and Patterson (2006); Wainright, Russell, and Patterson (2004).

32. Johnson (2012).

33. Most of the research on LGBTQ families has focused on lesbian-headed households because, historically, they have been much more common than families headed by gay men.

34. Biblarz and Stacey (2010).

35. Chan et al. (1998); Gartrell and Bos (2010); Johnson and O'Connor (2002); Vanfraussen, Ponjaert-Kristofferson, and Brewaeys (2002).

36. Johnson and O'Connor (2002).

37. Gartrell, Bos, and Goldberg (2011).

38. Gartrell and Bos (2010); Johnson (2012); Wainright and Patterson (2006).

39. Giesler, (2012, p. 130).

40. Duggan (2002).

41. Seidman (2002, p. 189).

42. Valocchi (2005).

43. Lucal (1999).

44. Brinamen (2000, p. 67).

45. Schilt (2012).

46. Schilt (2009, para 4).

47. Dozier (2005, p. 305).

48. Dozier (2005).

49. Cooper (1995); Elizabeth, Gavey, and Tolmie (2012).

50. Saffron (1996, p. 186).

51. Goldberg (2007); Johnson (2012); Lev (2010).

52. Ryan-Flood (2005).

53. Gupta (2006).

54. Goldberg (2007); Goldberg, Kashy, and Smith (2012); Tasker and Golombok (1997).

In Other Words

DRESS SHOPPING AND GENDER BENDING: WHY I'M WEARING A SUIT AND A VEIL

Offbeat Bride, March 4, 2014

Ashir Leah KaneRisman

I went to try on dresses. Me—in all my genderqueer/butch/transmasculine glory—in a traditional bridal salon, trying on wedding gowns. And it was fabulous. I got to have fun with my fiancé and my best friend. I got to look beautiful and revel in my feminine side. I was treated like I was special, and got compliments from random strangers. It was bizarre and surreal, and simultaneously it felt like the most natural thing in the world.

I fell in love. I found "The Dress." It was a simple form-fitting satin sheath dress with a strapless sweetheart neckline, a keyhole back, and a lace overlay that extended into a chapel-length train. It showed off my ass and my hips amazingly, it was light and comfortable, the train felt special, and I looked gorgeous. I felt sexy, and paradoxically I felt really butch. The incongruity of my short spiky hair, muscular arms, and boyish posture with a feminine gown was really cool.

But I didn't buy The Dress. I'm not going to wear The Dress or any other dress. That's not the point.

Finding The Dress, and loving how I looked and felt in it, actually put me more at peace with my decision to wear pants. Falling in love with a dress helped me examine what sort of self-presentation is important to me for my wedding day. It helped me assess what feminine aspects of the dress I liked most, and figure out how to incorporate them into my attire.

I'm sticking with my original idea of a white waistcoat-style vest and men's dress slacks. I'm going to splurge and have both vest and pants custom made for me so they fit right and show off my curves. I also decided I'm not going to wear a men's button up shirt and tie under the vest; instead I'm going to wear a tank top with a bit of lace showing on my chest. I think that bare arms and a hint of lace under the vest will make me look much more androgynous than would a shirt and tie, and besides, I like my arms!

And since the thing I loved most about The Dress was the dramatic flair of the lace overlay with a long train, I'm going to incorporate that into my look by wearing a chapel-length lace veil.

The TLDR (you know: too long; didn't read) version: I fell in love with a dress, but I definitely still want to wear men's pants and a vest. And I'm buying a chapel-length lace veil to wear with it. ▬

In Other Words

THE CLASS AND RACE DEMOGRAPHICS
OF LGBT FAMILIES

Sociological Images, December 7, 2011

Lisa Wade

Sonita M. sent in a report from the Movement Advancement Project about the state of lesbian, gay, bisexual, and transgender (LGBT) families.

LGBT families are more likely to be poor than non-LGBT families. Nine percent of married cis-gender different-sex couples live in poverty, compared to 21% of gay male couples and 20% of lesbian couples:

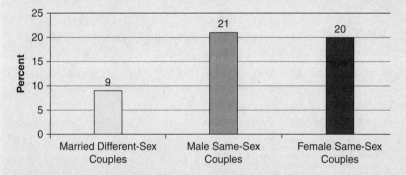

Figure 1 | Percentage of Families Raising Children Who Live in Poverty
Source: Randy Albelda, M. V. Lee Badgett, Alyssa Schneebaum, and Gary J. Gates, *Poverty in the Lesbian, Gay and Bisexual Community* (The Williams Institute, 2009).

LGBT couples may be more likely to be in poverty in part because of wage differentials between gays, lesbians, and their heterosexual counterparts. Research shows that gay and bisexual men earn significantly *less* money than heterosexual men, whereas lesbians make somewhat *more* money than straight women. Gay men would be more likely than heterosexual men to be in poverty, then. But what about women? Women in same-sex couples face the same wage disadvantage that all women face, but also are not married to the heterosexual men that are making so much money (making it so that heterosexual women can make less money than gay women but still be less likely to live in poverty). Make sense? I hope so.

The second reason that LGBT couples with children are more likely than cis-gendered different-sex couples with children to live in poverty is that black and Latino LGBT people are more likely than white LGBT people to be parents, and blacks and Latinos are disproportionately poor to begin with:

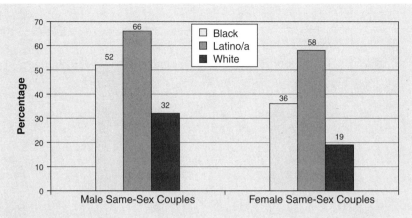

Figure 2 | Percentage of Same-Sex Couples Raising Children, by Race/ Ethnicity

Sources: Jason Cianciotto, *Hispanic and Latino Same-Sex Couple Households in the United States: A Report from the 2000 Census* (National Gay and Lesbian Task Force Policy Institute and National Latino/a Coalition for Justice, 2005); and Alain Dang and Somjen Frazer, *Black Same-Sex Households in the United States: A Report from the 2000 Census,* 2nd ed. (National Gay and Lesbian Task Force Policy Institute, 2005).

Among same-sex couples, being a parent is also correlated with immigration status, which also correlates with class. Non-citizens are more likely to be parents than citizens:

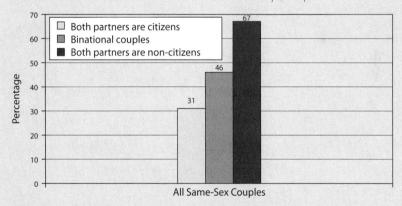

Figure 3 | Percentage of Same-Sex Couples Raising Children, by Immigration Status

Source: Gary J. Gates, *Binational Same-Sex Unmarried Partners in Census 2000: A Demographic Portrait.* (The Williams Institute, 2005).

The 2 million children in America being raised by LGBT parents, then, are more likely to suffer from class disadvantage. The authors of the report go on to discuss the ways in which formal policy and informal discrimination contribute to this state of affairs. ▬

PART SEVEN

Unequal Lives: Families across Economic and Citizenship Divides

29

The Immigration Kaleidoscope

Knowing the Immigrant Family Next Door

Etiony Aldarondo and Edward Ameen

This chapter is based on the twin premises that we are all stakeholders in the well-being of immigrant families and that we pay a high price for not having a good understanding of the facts about immigration. We use research findings to address some of the most insidious characterizations about immigrants in our country. We then focus on the immigration and acculturation processes, highlighting both the strains experienced by immigrant families and their strengths. We conclude the chapter with a description of immigrants' attitudes about the United States and how they experience life in this country.

It is 10 a.m. I (the first author) approach the hotel counter for help in printing a copy of the presentation I will be making later that day. A young woman comes to assist me, and we begin a casual conversation that quickly turns into a conversation about what we do, where we come from, and our aspirations in life. I begin telling her about the work my students and I do with immigrant children and families when Jenny cuts in and says:

> You know, I worry that we are losing hope. My friends are losing hope. I see it happening a lot. We are the hard-working people and they think we are here to do nothing. They think we are nothing. Ever since I was a little girl I had this feeling inside telling me that something was not right. I mean, how could it be that they don't see that we are here to work and take care of our families, that we are good people. How could it be that they don't see that we want the same things that they want—a good house, food on the table, peace, and good schools?

The printer was not working properly so we waited for the technician to fix it. In the meantime Jenny goes on to tell me about her life as a Mexican immigrant living in the United States since age five, going back and forth across the border for weddings and *quinceañeros*, being scolded by teachers for speaking Spanish among friends, keeping the house in order while her mother worked two shifts, getting pregnant at the age of thirteen, raising a child while completing high school with academic honors, and so forth.

So many of us know so little about the immigrant next door. The ones we want to take care of our children; cut our lawns; grow, pick, cook, and serve our food; clean our cars; paint our homes; fix our clothes; teach our children; be at our bedside at the hospital; run the local ethnic restaurants; join our police and military forces; support the local economy; and assimilate to our preferred ways of being. Instead, slowly and passively we appropriate from media outlets and other relevant contexts in our lives (e.g., government, politicians) a narrative about immigrants as criminal, lazy, violent, and uneducated people who don't pay taxes, exploit our community resources, do not want to learn English, are here illegally, take away our jobs and drive wages down, spread epidemics like tuberculosis and AIDS, are threats to our national security, and so on.

But the immigrant next door is nothing like the demonized and toxic caricature many of us submissively come to endorse. We know so much about what we want from them—shouldn't we know more about them? After all, we are a nation of immigrants, and many of our ancestors were immigrants who came to this country looking for opportunities, freedom, and safety.

That we are a nation of immigrants can hardly be denied. In 2006, the immigrant and children-of-immigrants population was estimated to be about 60 million or close to one-fifth of the total population of the United States.[1] Over two-thirds of the immigrants in this country are here legally. Among the estimated 12 million unauthorized immigrants in the country, two-thirds have been here for ten years or less, while 40 percent (4.4 million) of this population have been in the United States for five years or less.[2] What do we really know about the immigrants and their families living in our neighborhoods? What is the price we pay for not having a good understanding of the immigrant family next door?

The answers to these questions are embedded in history, politics, psychology, and economics. They are worth exploring, for as we learn about immigrant families, we begin to understand why many Americans adopt a limited and negative view of immigrant families in a context where state and federal governments often favor criminalization and deportation over support for the development of immigrant families and their integration into society. In this chapter, we attempt to help you see immigrant families differently. As the eminent family therapist Salvador Minuchin said,

> We live our lives like chips in a kaleidoscope, always part of patterns that are larger than ourselves and somehow more than the sum of their parts. . . . When we look at human beings from this perspective, whole new possibilities open up for exploring behavior and alleviating pain.[3]

We have divided the chapter into three main sections. In the first, we present research on immigration, and in doing so we address some of the most insidious characterizations about immigrants in our country. Rather than focusing on specific immigrant groups, we talk about immigration issues as they relate to foreign-born people of various ethnicities living in the United States. In the second section, we focus on the immigration and acculturation processes, highlighting some of the strains experienced by immigrant families. Closer attention to the immigration process helps us appreciate the resources and strengths of immigrant families while giving us a better idea about the conditions that promote and hinder their development. We conclude this chapter with a description of immigrants' attitudes about the United States and their experiences in this country. If we are to know the immigrant next door better, it seems prudent that we listen to what they have to say about living next to us.

RESEARCH ON IMMIGRATION

A large segment of the American public believes that there are too many immigrants in this country, that most immigrants are in this country illegally, and that the level of immigration should be reduced.[4] This perception appears to be fueled in part by the increased movement of immigrants to small towns and suburbs, where immigrants do not blend in as easily with the general population as they do in large urban areas of traditional immigration states like California, Texas, and New York.[5] The reality, however, is that the proportion of immigrants in this country is about the same as it has been for over 150 years. In 2007, there were 37.9 million immigrants in America (12.4 percent of the country's population).[6] Comparatively, immigrants made up 9.7 percent of the population in 1850 and 14.7 percent in 1910.[7] As a matter of perspective, "the rise in immigrant population from 1990 to 2000 was much less dramatic than the one from 1901 to 1910, when the population was just 92 million and the number of immigrants had jumped by 8.8 million."[8]

In terms of documentation status, over two-thirds of immigrants have proper legal documentation to work and live in this country.[9] Interestingly, documentation status varies widely between children and parents in immigrant families: Under the age of six, 93 percent of children are citizens, but only 19 percent have one or both parents with citizen status.[10] Far more children are citizens than their parents.

Public preoccupation about the number of immigrants in this country is linked to an array of perceived detrimental effects of immigration on the well-being of the nation in the areas of health, mental health, civic life, work and the economy, education and language use, and crime. Not surprisingly, many in the public see immigrants as burdens on the country.[11] If there were fewer immigrants around, the logic goes, the nation would be better off in these critical domains of life. However, research suggests these judgments to be based on incomplete or inaccurate information.

Health

According to health statistics, immigrants have a life span that is 3.4 years longer (80.0 compared to 76.6 years) than that of native-born people, they experience lower mortality rates, and they have better health statuses and behavioral outcomes.[12] Immigrant children are less likely than their native counterparts to experiment with illicit substances, engage in other risky behaviors, and be obese.[13]

Due to financial, cultural, linguistic, and documentation barriers (e.g., proper identification), immigrants have been shown to access health services at a lower rate. Although some see immigrant health insurance as a "taxpayer expense" because immigrant labor has "limited value," there is conclusive evidence to the contrary: immigrant children cost $270 a year in health care, compared to $1,059 for native-born children.[14] Examination of health-care expenditures "refutes the assumption that immigrants represent a disproportionate financial burden on the US health care system."[15] For example, when immigrants made up 10 percent of the population in 1998, they only accounted for 7.9 percent of health-care costs. Additionally, immigrants without Social Security numbers contribute $8.5 billion a year in taxes toward Medicare and Social Security, which they are not eligible to redeem.

Mental Health

Researchers have yet to reach a consensus about the mental health status of immigrants compared with that of natives, especially after taking into consideration the toxic effects of poverty.[16] For both immigrant and native adults, poverty is the best predictor of mental health problems. Thus, the more financially strapped immigrants are, the more likely they are to experience mental health problems such as anxiety and depression. But data from studies of foreign-born and first-generation immigrant teenagers suggest that foreign-born youth are more psychologically sound than their native peers. Although the journey of migration is difficult, many immigrant teens have the benefit of protective factors that promote better health, including higher levels of parental supervision, lower levels of parent-child conflicts, involvement in religious practices, and greater satisfaction with the support offered to them by relatives, friends, and significant others in their social network. Unfortunately, the protective power of some of these factors fades away during the acculturation process.[17]

Civic Life

Given the disproportionate amount of airtime occupied by anti-immigrant voices in television and radio outlets, it is hardly surprising to find people who think immigrants are bad for American society and that whatever contribution they may make to the quality of our civic life is minimal compared to the damage they cause. The data, again, do not support this view. Over 45,000 immigrants are serving in active or reserve capacity with the military, and over 26,000 recruits have been naturalized as citizens since September 11, 2001.[18] (The immigration process for undocumented servicemen and -women was expedited under President Bush and through the proposed DREAM Act in Congress.) As Emilio T. Gonzalez, former director of U.S. Citizenship and Immigration Services, testified in front of a Senate committee, "America gave these men, and their families, home and hope and they reciprocated with distinguished service, exceptional leadership, and boundless patriotism."[19]

Immigrant citizens are very motivated to participate in the democratic system of voting, and nearly half of all Hispanic registered voters are foreign born.[20] The Democratic presidential debate that aired in 2007 on Univision, a Spanish-language television network, drew substantially more viewers than debates aired on English-speaking networks around the same time. Matthew Dowd, chief pollster for President Bush, said in the *Wall Street Journal* that the Hispanic vote has grown 400 percent in the last twenty years.[21] When the House passed the "Sensenbrenner Bill" in 2005, branding undocumented immigrants as criminals, the following spring saw a huge mobilization and some of the "largest civic demonstrations in the U.S. in more than a generation"[22] and resulted in the alienation of the Hispanic community from the Republican Party.

Contribution to civic life can also be thought of in terms of how often families access the resources in their community and participate in functions and events. Although accurate reporting of these data is hard to obtain, some figures suggest that immigrants may be less likely than their native counterparts to volunteer in a religious, school, or community organization.[23] To be sure, the relative lack of involvement of immigrants in broader community life is not surprising when considering that poverty; demands of physical labor; and cultural, linguistic, and documentation barriers are formidable obstacles to civic engagement and disproportionately affect immigrant families in this country. When thinking about the civic engagement of immigrant families, however, it is also important to consider that significant numbers of immigrants continue to be actively engaged civically and politically in their native countries even years after immigrating to this country. Interestingly, research suggests that this group of immigrants often translates the skills, commitments, and networks they developed in their native countries into valuable resources for civic life in the United States.[24]

Work and the Economy

We are currently experiencing what researchers call a "bimodal migration wave," in which large numbers of immigrants have either low levels of education and work-related skills or are highly skilled and educated. Combined, both groups contribute $50 billion a year in human capital to the U.S. economy.[25] In the workplace, immigrants have frequently been met with barriers due, in part, to difficulties applying skills developed in their countries of origin to the working conditions in this country. This may explain why immigrants seem to earn less than natives; nearly 2 million immigrants earn less than the minimum wage, and the average yearly income in 2001 for a low-wage immigrant parent was $14,400,[26] almost $4 less per hour. A family is in poverty when it makes below 200 percent of the federally determined income level measured according to family size. In 2007, 40.1 percent of all immigrant families and 28 percent of all native families were in poverty.[27] Compared to native families, immigrant families are not as easily lifted from poverty by having an additional working parent in the home. In fact, there were double the number of two-parent immigrant families in poverty compared to two-parent native families in 1999 (22 percent and 44 percent, respectively).[28] Thus, it seems reasonable to assert that wages rather than employment levels account for much of the income disparity between immigrant families and native families.

A second factor determining family income is education at the time of arrival. The current discrepancies in wages are best explained by significant differences in education levels, particularly at a time when recent waves of immigrants are less educated than their predecessors.[29] Immigrant families, in particular those starting at low-pay, entry-level positions, take ten to twenty years to earn good incomes, become homeowners, and catch up to their native counterparts. The poverty rate for given cohorts of immigrant families decreases incrementally over time. Some argue that children who come from disadvantaged schools and live in poor and minimally educated households—regardless of their aspirations or English fluency—will continue to bear the consequences of this profile.[30]

Fortunately for these families, there appears to be negligible to no difference in wages between documented and undocumented immigrants,[31] as nearly 96 percent of undocumented immigrant men are in the labor force.[32]

Some immigrants move up the economic ladder by starting their own small businesses. Recent census reports indicate that "immigrant entrepreneurs are the fastest-growing segment of small business owners today,"[33] outpacing non-immigrant business owners. In Los Angeles, the number of Hispanic-owned businesses increased by 700 percent in twenty years, outpacing Hispanic population growth at 200 percent.[34] Furthermore, immigrants do not tend to concentrate in a few occupational sectors, as compared to native-born workers.[35] The popular image of immigrant men as farmworkers and women as housekeepers is a poor match for the significant spread among managerial, professional, technical, sales, administrative, service, laborer, and farming occupations of the 18.9 million foreign-born workers in the United States in 2002.

Some wonder if immigrants have adverse effects on the labor markets for native job seekers. Aviva Chomsky[36] alerts us to the fact that this question is based on the assumption that there are only a fixed number of jobs. In fact, increases in population create more demand for products, and thus for workers to make them, whereas decreases cause the shutting down of businesses, stores, schools, and hospitals. Historically, unemployment rates have fluctuated independently of immigration rates, including during the Great Depression in the 1930s, when very few immigrants arrived in America. Rather than insinuate cause and effect from coincidence, it is important to investigate factors that are related to both changes in immigration and changes in employment. Writes Chomsky, "The same global economic restructuring that exacerbated inequality in the United States [where the wealthiest 5 percent control 60 percent of the money] also contributed to increasing immigration."[37]

In 2007, the Executive Office of the President released an economic impact statement indicating that working immigrants make the market more competitive, helping raise native-born wages by up to 1.8 percent since 1990, and increasing total U.S. native-born wages by $30–$80 billion annually.[38] Succinctly, immigrants help the economy now, and are expected to contribute in positive ways in the future.

Education and Language Use

Four out of five immigrant families speak a language other than English at home.[39] Nonetheless, there are still notably high levels of English language use within immigrant families. For example, California census data show that more than 71 percent of Latino families and 89 percent of Asian families speak English very well or exclusively at home.[40] In spite of differences in the use of language at home, children of immigrant parents "receive grades in school that are equal to or even higher" than non-immigrant peers.[41] In fact, children of immigrants account for a disproportionally large number of high-school valedictorians in this country.[42] Overall, the immigrant population is on a par with their native-born peers in the proportion with college degrees (27.3 percent and 27.2 percent, respectively)[43] but is markedly behind in terms of high-school graduates in the workforce (64.5 percent and 92 percent, respectively).[44] Foreign-born students often have more favorable views about school than their peers and drop out of school less often—half as often in Miami and one-third as often in San Diego.[45]

Many might also be surprised to learn that, while immigrant children have lower verbal and reading achievement scores on standardized tests, these discrepancies fade away after considering factors such as the trajectory an immigrant family may have taken to arrive in the United States, language proficiency, and the quality of the schools they attend. We know that English-language proficiency is a strong predictor of scores on standardized tests, much more predictive than family factors.[46] We also know that more immigrant children compared to native-born children improve their English-language skills as they move into adolescence.[47] But higher levels of English-language proficiency do not shield immigrant children from the adverse effects of attending failing schools. Education experts argue that immigrant children often attend schools that not only obstruct learning and engagement but may be toxic to healthy learning and development, making the school itself "the single best predictor of academic achievement" for this group of children.[48] Schools have the potential to educate children in a way that complements their ethnic heritages as opposed to assuming that these heritages interfere with their learning. Additive, as opposed to subtractive, schooling can boost students' confidence and connect them with their school.[49]

Most ignored in the educational system are undocumented immigrant children. Without legal status, they can rarely complete basic schooling, apply to colleges, and find stable work. In fact, only 5 to 10 percent of undocumented high school graduates go on to college.[50] This has unintended consequences on the economy and sends a clear negative message to immigrant families about the importance of education for all in this society. Meanwhile, researchers have noted that school revenues would increase and tax payments would go up if undocumented immigrant children were able to enter college.[51]

Crime

Analyses of crime in immigrant populations make it clear that anecdotal impressions of immigrants as criminals are not backed up by scientific evidence. "For every ethnic group without exception, incarceration rates among young men are lowest for immigrants, even those who are the least educated."[52] Interestingly, these findings mirror the conclusions of a study commissioned over 100 years ago that evaluated and discredited the negative stereotypes of criminal immigrants and a crime-ridden society of immigrants.[53] The available data suggest that an influx of immigrants over the last three decades may have indeed contributed to lower crime rates, even in cities like Los Angeles, New York, and Miami that have larger-than-average immigrant populations. Without evidence to support the view of immigrants as criminals, we must wonder if ignorance, xenophobia, and nativism—the belief that native-born people are superior and more entitled than immigrants—are the true operating forces in myths such as these.

IMMIGRATION AND ACCULTURATION PROCESSES

Immigration

The immigration process is one of separation, loss, dislocation, discovery, adaptation, integration, and growth. This is a process packed with excitement, ambiguity, possibility, and stress that requires a fair amount of flexibility and skill to navigate successfully. In addition to changes in socioeconomic status and cultural life, immigrant families must negotiate the differences between their native and host environments. Most often, these differences pertain to gender roles, the various expectations of multiple generations (i.e., grandparents, parents, children) in family life, differences in the pace of acculturation of various family members, and social isolation.[54] As is to be expected, immigrant families vary in their ability to meet these challenges.

Because children typically have fewer strings attached to specific cultural beliefs and practices and have greater access and opportunity to interact with their host culture, they tend to adapt more quickly to the new environment than their parents do. Often, immigrant parents respond to this discrepancy by rigidly holding on to ways of thinking and doing consistent with their cultures of origin. This causes discord and stress for family members attempting to find their way in the new culture. As youth spend time at school, develop social bonds, and undergo their own personal development, they often mirror and embrace the new while questioning and rejecting parts of the old culture. Adolescents in particular may question the utility of their parents' culture-based beliefs, values, and practices as they form individual identities and put pressure on their parents to conform to what they perceive to be the dominant ways of being in this country. Within this context, grandparents become "defenders of traditional values and preservers of the family's ethnic identity,"[55] often clashing with their acculturating grandchildren and putting additional pressure on parents to fulfill traditional cultural expectations.

Much of the discrepancy between an immigrant's new and old cultures rests on an oversimplified representation of what counts as traditional or normal family life in this country. "The use of monolithic images of the 'Normal American Family' as a stick against which all families are measured is pervasive in the family wars."[56] Inherent in this normalized image is a code regarding what the family can be—generally white, middle class, heterosexual, headed by a breadwinning dad, and a mother who cares for the children—and what values, norms, and beliefs are acceptable—generally that families should be democratic, open, flexible, and forgiving. This image creates challenges for immigrant families that hold differing conceptions of family life. Problems arise when immigrant children internalize this ideal and when society isolates families who are different. The bridge between the immigrant family's lived reality and the prevailing family codes in this country consists of systems that allow immigrant families to maintain their traditions and values while experimenting and integrating new beliefs, values, and practices into their ways of being.

Often overlooked in the experience of immigrant families is their loss of major supportive social networks from their country of origin. Virtually all immigrant families are overwhelmed when they immigrate because the functions once taken on by extended family members and friends are now the work of the family and particularly the parents. "This increase in needs and reciprocal expectations takes place precisely while the [family member] is in turn most overloaded and less able to fulfill the other's need."[57] Because there are established connections between one's well-being and one's social network, it is understandable that immigrant parents and children will experience distress over this loss of network. Apart from relying on each other more, the challenge for many families is to reestablish a broader network of community participation. Moreover, support from host communities, positive attitudes toward immigrants, work opportunities, affordable housing, and a "general level of community wealth and support services" are crucial for immigrant families to successfully navigate this process.[58]

The above-mentioned pressures notwithstanding, the typical immigrant family appears to offer a supportive and caring environment for its members. Compared to native-born households, immigrants have been found to have higher marriage rates and lower divorce rates.[59] Greater marital harmony appears to be one of the reasons why children in immigrant families are 50 percent more likely than their native-born peers to be living with both parents.[60] The 2000 U.S. Census also shows that immigrant families with children tend to have larger household sizes. Grandparents, older siblings, and other relatives are commonly found in immigrant family homes. To be sure, an expanded family household offers greater opportunity for intimate bonds, social support, and adult supervision for children, but it can also lead to overcrowding, which is known to adversely affect child development. "Nearly half of children in immigrant families live in over-crowded housing, compared to only 11 percent of children in native-born families."[61]

Acculturation

Should we encourage immigrants to let go of their native identities and adopt a more generic set of American cultural beliefs, values, and practices? If you believe this to be the case, you share what was once a popular view of the accul-turation and assimilation process in the United States, which was commonly referred to as "the melting pot." This notion that immigrants eventually lose their cultural identity and fully adopt American values and ways of being has been shown to be both inaccurate and unhealthy for many families. Some refer to this process as "straight-line assimilation," whereby immigrants irrespective of cultural background learn to take on dominant American values and attitudes with similar results.[62] Instead, a growing number of immigration experts are now proponents of other approaches. Portes and Rumbaut describe the concept of "segmented assimilation," leading to three profiles that can exist within contem-porary immigrant families.[63] The first is consonant acculturation, where children and their parents both become full parts of the mainstream at approximately the same pace. This is contrasted with dissonant acculturation, where the chil-dren and parents acculturate at different paces (typically the children acculturate much faster), and which may lead to intergenerational conflict. The third type is selective acculturation, where both familial generations adapt to aspects of the new culture and retain parts of their native culture. With this type of accultura-tion, there is little conflict among family members, and the children are often bilingual. Naturally, families that differ in education, age, social support, stress, income, cohesion, and other characteristics will fall into different types in this segmented model.[64] Particularly problematic is dissonant acculturation, where gaps in the family's adaptation to life in the United States can produce tensions and even put them into a trap of downward mobility.

John Berry examined the relationship between how people acculturate and how well they adapt to their host society.[65] Dividing immigrant youth into four clusters—integrated, national, ethnic, and diffuse—he found that integrated youth, who showed favorable affiliations toward their native and host societies, had the best adjustment in terms of psychological and sociocultural outcomes. On the other hand, diffuse youth—those with ambivalent and relatively weak native and host identities—had the poorest rates of adaptation. He found similar results at the family level: the soundest families were those that maintained their cultural heritage and identity and participated in the everyday life of the larger society. These findings suggest that policy makers and mental health professionals ought to consider the benefits of integration over the rejection or singular preference for any one particular cultural orientation.

Moderate levels of acculturation appear to be protective for immigrant youth in most circumstances, but both high and low levels of acculturation put them at risk for substance abuse and mental health problems.[66] Moderately acculturated youth from immigrant families often do better psychologically, physically, and academically relative to their native-born peers, even those peers with the same socioeconomic and ethnic background.[67] Thus, contemporary thinking in this area suggests that it is important for the well-being of children in immigrant families to maintain some form of integrated, bicultural identity.

Interestingly, researchers have reported that the protective effects of acculturation decline over time. Referred to as "the paradox of assimilation,"[68] "the immigration paradox,"[69] or "the healthy migrant phenomenon,"[70] the issue is that there is a powerful connection between the number of years lived in this country and the catching up of immigrants to the same levels of risk that their American peers are exposed to. These risks include health problems, crime, drug use, depression, anxiety, and other factors. For example, as immigrant children adopt the high-fat diets that are popular in this country, they experience a sharp increase in obesity.[71] Similarly, in the area of education, it has been noted that "immigrant children become less willing to work hard in school the longer they are in this country."[72] Thus, it seems that while some aspects of acculturation—including American educational attainment and English language acquisition—are important predictors of successful families, other elements of the acculturation process may have negative consequences.

IMMIGRANTS' PERCEPTIONS OF LIFE IN THE UNITED STATES

The mismatch among public perceptions about immigrants, research data on immigration, and the many challenges faced by immigrant families as they integrate into American society gives us cause to wonder how immigrants experience life in the United States. Do they feel welcome in this country? Why, in spite of the many vicissitudes they experience and the pressures of anti-immigrant forces, do they stay? What do they think about American citizens? Fortunately for us, a recent national survey of over 1,000 immigrants in the United States provides answers for these and many other interesting questions.[73] Here we highlight the findings of the study most relevant for the purposes of this chapter.

It turns out that the overwhelming majority of immigrants consider the United States a special place to be (80 percent) and report being relatively happy living in this country (96 percent). They value the economic opportunities afforded to them in our society (88 percent), our commitment to promoting women's rights (68 percent), our democratic system of government (62 percent), and the freedom to choose how to live their lives (40 percent). They consider our legal (67 percent), health care (67 percent), and education (60 percent) systems to be better than what many of them had in their countries of origin. About three-quarters of immigrants indicate that they want to make the United States their permanent home, and approximately eight out of ten say that they think of themselves as Americans or as acting like Americans outside the home while keeping their own culture and traditions at home. This bicultural identity is reflected also in the finding that many immigrants keep close contact with family and friends in their country of origin (59 percent), send money back to relatives (44 percent), keep abreast of current events in their home country (47 percent), and hold dual citizenship (32 percent).

In terms of how they are treated by others, immigrants are somewhat more guarded in their judgments—a little over half (53 percent) believe that as a group, immigrants are not treated well by Americans. The majority (68 percent) indicated that Americans are not nice to each other. As indicated by the authors of this report, this last finding is consistent with data from general population studies showing that many Americans believe lack of respect and rudeness are on the rise in this country. Interestingly, most immigrants (63 percent) in this survey report having been treated well by government immigration officials.

Concerning other issues raised earlier in this chapter—for example, education, English language use, work, and civic life—reports by immigrants are fairly consistent with other research data. For example, the majority of immigrants believe that they have an obligation to learn English (65 percent) and find that learning English is essential for their personal and economic prosperity (87 percent). Nearly half (47 percent) of those coming to the United States with limited English take classes to learn the language and say they can read and communicate well (49 percent). In terms of attitudes toward work, immigrants profess a strong work ethic with a solid majority (73 percent) indicating that it is very important to work and stay off welfare. In reference to civic life, many immigrants believe that it is very important to become a citizen (68 percent), serve in the military (49 percent), and volunteer for community service (47 percent). "For an overwhelming majority, their connection to the U.S. is neither tenuous nor solely economic."[74]

Concluding Remarks

It is now about 11:30 a.m. I (the first author) have been talking with Jenny for over an hour. She is so articulate and clear about who she is as an immigrant and as an American that I am left hoping that more people could listen to her. I wonder what it would be like if we could find ways to include the voices of immigrants in the national conversation about immigration in this country. Jenny has just been accepted to college in a city far away from her border hometown and far away from an abusive partner who disapproved of her desire to go to school and become a professional. She told me that she had thought hard and long about what to study and had decided to become a lawyer.

> Frankly, I am better at the sciences. I was always good at math and science and for a while thought about studying to become a doctor or a nurse. But I see what is happening and have decided we all need more people fighting for us. I think as a lawyer I would be able to do that.

I think Jenny is right. But the fight is not only hers to fight. Now with the copies of my presentation ready, and reluctantly getting ready to go, I ask her if she would mind if I shared her story with others. She replies, "I don't know that there is anything special in my story—it is just like thousands of others. But if you think it would help someone, go ahead."

Shortly after this encounter with Jenny, we received an invitation from the editor of this volume to write a chapter on immigration to be included in a book for college students. Rather than offering an academic treatise, we thought it would be better to try to loosen the grip that the current anti-immigrant climate holds on our collective imagination by providing readers with an opportunity to reflect about immigration from the interrelated perspectives of content, process, and worldview. Each of these perspectives is offered here as an antidote to the myopic and demeaning characterizations of immigrants rampant in popular media outlets. Together, they offer us a better appreciation of the lived experience of our immigrant neighbors and their contribution to American society.

All of us are stakeholders in the well-being of immigrant families because they are part of our kaleidoscope: Together we eat in the same restaurants, work in the same offices, learn in the same schools, and worship in the same churches. If we agree to build a shared community, benefits abound:

> The mastery of different languages, the ability to cross racial and ethnic boundaries, and a general resiliency associated with the ability to endure hardships and overcome obstacles will clearly be recognized as a new cultural capital that will be crucial for success in a modern diversified society, not a handicap.[75]

Immigrant families do well and make significant contributions to our economic and community well-being when we offer them the minimal supports to so do. However, "choices to develop more empowering narratives are sorely limited by the larger culture's negative views of immigrants."[76] Consequences abound from these discriminatory processes, as our nation's complex history of immigration has shown. Individuals who experience the greatest amounts of perceived discrimination also show the poorest psychological and cultural adaptations.[77] Additionally, immigration stigma can cause decreased performance in multiple domains and problematic social interactions.[78] The very thing we come to fault is something we've created.

If the one shared hope among all stakeholders is that immigrant families will contribute positively to American society, then conditions and attitudes must align to reach that goal. Otherwise we risk ending up blaming the victim while watching our distorted views turn into self-fulfilling prophecies. The challenge is not easy, considering that the majority of national magazine covers published in the last four decades of the twentieth century portrayed overwhelmingly alarmist depictions of immigration[79] and that immigrants themselves do not have much of a voice or presence in our national conversation about immigration. With more accurate portrayals of immigrant families, we are hopeful that ordinary citizens, policy makers, and service providers will be better equipped to promote the well-being of the immigrant family next door.

NOTES

1. Hirschman (2006).
2. Passel (2006).
3. Minuchin (1984), p. 3.
4. Gallup/CNN/USA *Today* (2002).
5. See Espenshade (1997).
6. Camarota (2007).
7. Briggs (2003).
8. Guskin and Wilson (2007), p. 19.
9. Camarota (2007).
10. Fix and Capps (2004).
11. Gallup Poll (2000).
12. Singh and Hiatt (2006).
13. Suárez-Orozco, Suárez-Orozco, and Todorova (2008).
14. Mohanty et al. (2005).
15. *Ibid.*, p. 1431.
16. Hao and Johnson (2000), p. 602; Fennelly (2006).

17. Harker (2001).

18. Gonzalez (2006).

19. *Ibid.*, p. 6.

20. New Democrat Network (2007).

21. *Wall Street Journal* (2006, April 3). Matthew Dowd, chief pollster to President Bush, quoted in "Republicans Fear 'Amnesty,' but They Should Fear Losing Hispanics," The Journal Editorial Report. Included in New Democrat Network Presentation (2007).

22. New Democrat Network (2007), p. 17.

23. Reardon-Anderson, Capps, and Fix (2002).

24. DeSipio (2008).

25. Camarota (2007).

26. Capps et al. (2003).

27. Camarota (2007).

28. Reardon-Anderson, Capps, and Fix (2002).

29. Allen (2005).

30. Koepke (2007).

31. *Ibid.*, p. 16.

32. Passel, Capps, and Fix (2004).

33. Institute for the Future (2007).

34. Mutti (2002).

35. Migration Policy Institute (2004).

36. *Ibid.*, p. 13.

37. Chomsky (2007).

38. Executive Office of the President (2007).

39. Greico (2002).

40. Allen (2005).

41. Fuligni (1998), p. 99.

42. Suárez-Orozco and Suárez-Orozco (2001).

43. Singh and Hiatt (2006).

44. Camarota (2007).

45. Rumbaut (2002).

46. Suárez-Orozco, Suárez-Orozco, and Todorova (2008), p. 52.

47. Leventhal, Xue, and Brooks-Gunn (2006).

48. Suárez-Orozco, Suárez-Orozco, and Todorova (2008), p. 52.

49. Allen (2005), p. 19.

50. Gonzalez (2007).

51. *Ibid.*

52. Rumbaut and Ewing (2007), p. 1.
53. *Ibid.*
54. Hernandez and McGoldrick (2005).
55. *Ibid.*, p. 178.
56. Pyke (2000), p. 240.
57. Sluzki (1998), p. 13.
58. Chapman and Perreira (2005), p. 106.
59. Singh and Hiatt (2006).
60. Hernandez (2004a).
61. Hernandez (2004b), p. 24.
62. Portes and Rumbaut (2001).
63. *Ibid.*
64. Levitt, Lane, and Levitt (2005).
65. Berry (2007).
66. Chapman and Perreira (2005).
67. Fuligni (1998).
68. Portes and Rumbaut (2001).
69. Chang (2003).
70. Fennelly (2006).
71. *Ibid.*
72. Allen (2005), p. 20.
73. Farkas, Duffet, and Johnson (2003).
74. *Ibid.*, p. 38.
75. Trueba (2002), p. 7.
76. Falicov (2002), p. 291.
77. Phinney, Berry, Sam, and Vedder (2006).
78. Deaux (2006), pp. 84–85.
79. Chavez (2001).

In the News

THE PICTURE-PERFECT AMERICAN FAMILY? THESE DAYS, IT DOESN'T EXIST

The Washington Post, September 7, 2008

Andrew J. Cherlin

With the debut of the Palins before a nationwide audience, a presidential campaign that was supposed to be about the economy, Iraq or even race has unexpectedly become—for a little while, at least—a conversation about family. But even before the surprising news of 17-year-old Bristol Palin's pregnancy, the Obamas, Bidens and McCains had spent an inordinate amount of precious convention time introducing us to their loved ones: videos, scripted shout-outs, smiling tableaus as the confetti came down. Both parties clearly thought that it was crucial for the candidates to show how deeply they value their family lives.

But if the candidates wished to convince viewers that their families were just like ours, they were undone by a 21st-century reality: There is no typical family anymore—at least not in terms of who lives in the household and how they are related. Alaska Gov. Sarah Palin noted as much on Wednesday. While introducing her clan to a cheering crowd of the Republican faithful, the GOP vice presidential nominee said: "From the inside, no family ever seems typical. That's how it is with us."

In fact, the diversity of American households was the unspoken lesson of both conventions, as four strikingly different kinds of families came into view. First, the Obamas. The Democratic nominee's half-sister, Maya Soetoro-Ng, spoke to the Denver crowd, highlighting his biracial family background, dominated by an often single mother and a largely absent father. Obama's wife Michelle also took a powerful turn at the podium, focusing on her husband's biography but also playing up her own high-powered career and modest roots. The Bidens were introduced to a national audience that week as well, a stepfamily formed after the tragic death of the senator's first wife. With the McCains, we see another stepfamily, formed this time after the senator's divorce. Their family also includes Bridget, a daughter adopted from Bangladesh. And the Palins bring to the stage two working parents with five children, including a pregnant teenager and an infant with Down syndrome.

Divorce itself is not new to the presidential politics—Ronald Reagan and John F. Kerry both campaigned with second wives by their sides—but never has such an extraordinary range of family histories been center stage.

A half-century ago, when the two-parent, breadwinner-homemaker, first-marriage family was at its peak, all of the candidates would have conformed to the same mold. In the 1950s, iconic TV shows—the ones that you can still find while channel-surfing—celebrated the Cleavers and their ilk. Ward went to work and earned enough so that his single paycheck could keep June, Wally and the Beaver happily provided for at home. Sentiment against divorce in public life was so strong that New York Gov. Nelson Rockefeller's presidential aspirations were stymied in 1964 because he had recently divorced and remarried.

But the Cleavers are only available in reruns now, and the prominence of the breadwinner-homemaker family rapidly declined in the last third of the 20th century. Married women moved into the workforce, divorce rates rose, and more children were born outside of marriage.

That traditional family unit has been replaced by a wide variety of living arrangements. Today, only 58 percent of children live with two married, biological parents. Many others live with stepparents or with single parents. Even having a pregnant teen in the home is not that unusual: About one out of six 15-year-old girls will give birth before reaching age 20, according to the National Center for Health Statistics.

The candidates seemed to realize that none of their families is typical in the old sense. None of them tried to look like the '50s family. Instead, they focused on being "typical" in a different, 21st-century sense: They worked hard to show us how emotionally close they are.

Over the past few decades, the emotional rewards of family life have become more important to Americans, as compared to the rewards of bringing home a paycheck or raising children. In a 2001 national survey conducted by the National Marriage Project, more than 80 percent of women in their 20s agreed with the statement that it's more important "to have a husband who can communicate about his deepest feelings than to have a husband who makes a good living."

Personal satisfaction, the feeling that your family is helping you grow and develop as a person, communication, openness: These are the kinds of criteria people use in evaluating their family lives. Practical concerns still matter, but if that's all that holds your family together these days, people may view it askance. Given the demographic diversity of American families, emotional closeness, not who the Census takers find in your home, has become the new gold standard.

And so all four aspiring first and second families, despite their differences, appealed to the voters in much the same way. Each wanted to show how much support and warmth they provide to one another. What matters here is not whether your current wife is your first or second but whether you draw emotional strength from her. So Obama refers to his wife as "my rock" and McCain says of his wife, Cindy, "she's more my inspiration than I am hers." What matters is not whether your teenage daughter is pregnant but whether you provide loving support to her. So Palin and her husband issued a statement assuring the nation, "As Bristol faces the responsibilities of adulthood, she knows she has our unconditional love and support." What matters is being a loving, devoted father, even after the tragedy of losing one's spouse. So Biden's son Beau introduced his father to the Democrats in Denver as "my friend, my father, my hero."

This is not to say that the modern family is a free-for-all, choose-your-own-Thanksgiving-guest-list adventure for everyone. Social conservatives, for instance, still hold the family to stricter moral standards. In 1998, sociologist Penny Edgell asked all of the pastors in four upstate New York communities whether they agreed with the statement, "There have been all kinds of families throughout history, and God approves of many different kinds of families." Eighty-eight percent of pastors from the more liberal Protestant denominations agreed; none of the pastors from conservative denominations did. Social conservatives tend to disapprove of divorce except in cases of infidelity or desertion. They teach their children to abstain from sex until after marriage. But the religious right's reaction to the news of Bristol Palin's pregnancy shows they are willing to embrace a family that deviates from their ideals if the parents are willing to support each other and their children through difficult times. As former Baptist preacher, Arkansas governor and GOP presidential candidate Mike Huckabee said last week, "People of faith aren't people of perfection."

What is important today, in other words, is not who you live with—and how you're legally bound to them—but rather how you feel about them.

This is a barrier-breaking election in so many ways. But apart from the race and gender hurdles being trampled, the 2008 campaign has also shown that Americans, whether from red or blue states, have embraced a broad definition of what constitutes a family. Some traditionalists may lament the decline of the first-marriage, single-earner households. But diversity, in this case, has clear virtues. Would we really want to go back to an era when a divorce disqualified a person from running for president? Come November, it is unlikely to bother many voters that McCain is on his second marriage or that Michelle Obama had a demanding career or that Palin's daughter is facing what used to be called a shotgun wedding.

Of course, Americans' tolerance for family diversity still has limits; many voters, for instance, find it difficult to accept gay and lesbian unions. In 2004, Mary Cheney, the lesbian daughter of Vice President Cheney, sat in the audience with her partner as her father delivered his acceptance speech at the Republican convention. But the couple did not join the rest of the Cheney family on stage afterward and did not sit with the vice president when President Bush delivered his speech the following evening.

If the trend toward embracing greater diversity continues, however, convention stages a generation from now could easily look quite different from this year's. We could all be watching as a gay or lesbian candidate shouts out to his or her "rock" or "inspiration": a same-sex partner, smiling from the VIP box. ■

30

When Men Stay Home

Household Labor in Female-Led Indian Migrant Families

Pallavi Banerjee

⎡n today's global society, you may have heard the term *immigrant visa*. There are
⎣ many different types of visas, for students, work, families, and tourists. There
are a variety of reasons why immigrants/migrants need visas. For example, many
people who migrate to the United States each year come to work for U.S. employers. In 2012, a total of 334,291[1] people arrived in the United States to work; 40 percent (135,530)[2] were issued H-1B visas, or workers' visas. In this chapter, I report
on my study of migrant nurses from India who come here on skilled workers'
visas due to a shortage of nurses and later bring their families with them.

   The United States does not produce enough doctors, nurses, computer engineers, analysts, and programmers to meet the country's needs. As a response to
the rising demand for skilled workers, and their scarcity among U.S. residents, the
Immigration Act of 1990 introduced the distinctive category of non-immigrant
skilled workers' visas or the H-1B visas. While Indian male high-tech workers
have been the largest recipients of the skilled workers' visas, they are not the only
Indians who come to the United States on such visas. Less attention has been
paid to the migration of Indian nurses, who have been migrating to the United
States since the 1970s. Indian women nurses have been migrating to the United
States since the 1990s on skilled workers' visas and have been bringing their
husbands and children on the "dependent visa" or the H-4 visa. The dependent
visa puts many restrictions on the spouses of skilled workers. Men or women
who enter the United States on a "dependent visa" are not allowed to work for

pay until their husband or wife has gained permanent residency in the United States, a process that can take anywhere between five and fifteen years. Mostly women are the recipients of these visas, creating families that look like the 1950s nuclear family where dad goes off to work and mom stays home to care for the children. When foreign women move to America to work, however, their husbands also hold these visas. These visas have created families where men stay home as dependents and women, like the nurses in my study, are the main wage earners. Policy makers very rarely think about how different kinds of visas affect lives and gender relationships in migrant families. The gender dynamics become particularly complex when the skilled working migrant is a woman who is joined by her husband as a dependent. In my research, I ask: How do gender dynamics in the family change when women are the ones leading migration as the primary providers in the home? What do the family dynamics look like when men are legally defined as dependents?

In this chapter, I present findings from in-depth interviews with Indian migrant female nurses and their male spouses. To foreshadow my results, I find that in these families, despite the visa-enforced status reversal, the traditional gendered division of labor changes only in terms of child care. The traditional family division of labor, including housework, cooking, and patriarchal power remains. The women nurses ignore their own economic power and accept male dominance within the household because they feel intense guilt for being absentee mothers and nontraditional wives. They voluntarily[3] work a double shift, as a nurse and then at home, and emphasize the masculine role of their husbands in the family to overcompensate for what they perceive as their own inadequacy for not being a "dutiful woman."

The men use different strategies to reassert male privilege as heads of households and maintain their masculinity. The dependent husbands refuse to take on any purely "wifely" or "househusband" role. They don't clean or cook or support their wives' careers, except that they do take on the role of the primary caregiver for the children. They adopt this role out of necessity more so than desire. I show how, framed this way, men are able to justify their "nontraditional" role in the family by describing themselves as "sacrificial fathers." A paradox exists because caregiving and nurturance are at the very core of what defines stereotypical femininity. I suggest that even though the wives are ashamed and the husbands refuse to become domestic partners, they still are somewhat disrupting gendered norms by becoming caring nurturers, despite their unwillingness to acknowledge that role.

Indian Nurses Migrate to the United States: Pull and Push Factors

U.S. health care organizations have systematically hired foreign professional nurses in response to the cyclical shortage of nurses in U.S. hospitals and nursing homes.[4] With the elderly population in the United States projected to grow exponentially in the coming years, the demand for nurses will likely increase as well.[5] Countries with a large English-speaking population—such as the Philippines, Canada, Ireland, India, and the West Indies—have been the main suppliers of qualified nurses for the U.S. market since the Immigration Act of 1965.[6] Foreign-educated nurses increased from 9 percent in 1990 to 16 percent in 2006.[7] While Indian nurses have been migrating to the United States since the 1970s, in the early 2000s, U.S. recruiters increased their efforts to hire Indian nurses as other sources started drying up.[8]

In response to rising demand from wealthier nations and the global market for well-trained, English-speaking Indian nurses, Indian health care industry and nursing schools have developed themselves as business process outsourcing (BPO), producing nurses trained for the foreign markets.[9] In 2004 there were more than 1,000 accredited nursing schools in India, which collectively graduated 1,422,452 nurses. Many of these graduates receive further training by the BPOs to be foreign nurses. Out of all the nurses trained each year, about 75 percent immigrate to different parts of the world. Most of these nurses immigrate to the Gulf countries, the United States, Australia, New Zealand, Singapore, Ireland, and the United Kingdom, in that order.[10]

The licensing and visa processes governing migration in these different countries vary markedly and require significant knowledge on the part of the BPO hospitals. For example, the waiting period for migrating to the United Kingdom is as short as six months, whereas for the United States it is up to two to three years. The training and recruitment of nurses for the international health care industry occurs across all the big cities in India. However, most of the nurses are from one southern state in India called Kerala, and most of them are Christians.[11]

The BPOs are heavily invested in the training and recruitment of nurses for the foreign markets, but their recruitment practices are not always fair and sometimes result in extremely difficult situations for the nurses.[12] The women who talked to me corroborated past research with their description of how Indian nurses are hired by contracts and often sent to hospitals in rural areas for three years with relatively low pay. In these first assignments, they are not allowed to bring their families. Some of my participants described the isolation, fear, and pain they felt for the period of their contracts (ranging from three to six years) when they were separated from their families, including sometimes their children. When they tried to break their contracts, they often had to pay up to $60,000 in fines to the recruiters.

I asked these nurses why, despite these difficulties, they decided to migrate instead of working in India. I received three overlapping responses[13]: First, nursing is a low-paid profession in India with low occupational prestige and slim chances of upward mobility. Most of my participants cited the "much higher pay" as a foreign nurse as one of the primary reasons to emigrate. Second, in India, nurses are looked down upon as women who engage in dirty work of touching unclean bodies. This codification of nursing as dirty work is culturally related to two dominant religions in India, Hinduism and Islam, which both consider working with bodies as impure. Third, and most important, the nurses in my research told me about the severe lack of opportunities in their home state of Kerala. Kerala has been governed by the Communist Party of India for the last twenty years and has seen very little foreign investment or industrialization. The economy is predominantly agricultural, and there are very few jobs outside of agriculture. Most of the nurses and their husbands come from poor, rural farming families. Christian women in Kerala for years have taken up nursing to lift their immediate and extended families from poverty. This has been women's attempt at upward social mobility for forty years.[14] With the demand for Indian nurses from wealthier nations, migration has become the most viable economic options for nurses and their families. As one of my nurse participants put it:

> I only became a nurse so that I could get a job abroad and give my family, my children a chance to live better. It was very hard to leave, but now my parents, my brothers and sisters, my husband's family all are doing better, and my children will have a better future than me or my husband.

VISAS: MORE THAN A TRAVEL DOCUMENT

All the nurses in my research arrived in the United States on H-1B or skilled workers' non-immigrant visas. Their husbands joined them on dependent visas, specifically the H-4 visa. The formal definition of the skilled worker's temporary non-immigrant visa as put forth by the U.S. Immigration and Citizenship Services is, "H-1B applies to people who wish to perform services in a specialty occupation, services of exceptional merit." The H-4 or dependent visa is defined as "spouse and unmarried children under 21 years of age of H-1B workers may seek admission in the H-4 nonimmigrant classification. Family members in the H-4 nonimmigrant classification may not engage in employment in the United States."[15] These definitions or the clauses of the visa laws do not specifically mention husbands or wives, so they are legally gender neutral. My research, however, shows that the ways in which immigration experts (such as lawmakers, lawyers, activists) and the general public understand these laws are gendered. In my discussion about the H-1B visas with immigration experts, they often implied that the recipients of these skilled workers' visas are mostly men. As one immigration activist, in talking about high-skilled workers, put it: "We offer these *men* the opportunity to come develop their skills." The general assumption therefore is that the migrant high-skilled workers are men, and hence their spouses on dependent visas are women. While it is statistically true that most recipients of the H-1B visas are men,[16] as my research and other research[17] has shown, nurses also arrive in the United States as high-skilled migrants.

In talking about dependent visas, the default assumption among immigration experts (including legal opinions) and the public is that the dependent visa holders are women. When the proposal[18] for making changes to H-1B skilled workers' visa laws was floated in Congress in 1996, one of the additions proposed was to ease the process of procuring H-4 dependent visas, particularly for high-tech workers to allow "the *wife*" to migrate as it is "important for the well-being and productiveness of the transnational high-skilled employee." Given that men have also been arriving on dependent visas, my research asks how this gender reversal affects the well-being of families. I am also interested in how institutional policies translate to the everyday lives of transnational families.

DATA AND METHODS

This chapter is part of a research project that involved two and a half years of extensive qualitative methods. I did in-depth interviews, ethnography, and archival research between summer 2009 and winter 2011. My fieldwork for this paper primarily involved conducting observations in the communities of Indian nurses in and around Chicago for a year. Most of my nurse participants migrated to the United States from the southern state of Kerala. They are called Malayalees and are usually Christians.

I began my fieldwork in three different Malayalee churches in the suburbs of Chicago. However, access to this community was not easy. I learned that my being Indian was not enough to gain access into this community because of my regional and religious identities. I am from north India and non-Christian, and this made me an outsider in their community. However, with the assistance of an undergraduate at the University of Illinois at Chicago (UIC) who was originally from Kerala, I was eventually welcomed into this community.

The undergraduate student became my research assistant. She gained field research experience as part of UIC's undergraduate research training, and as her mentor, I gained a junior partner in my research. It was a win-win situation. She accompanied me to church every Sunday for about six weeks. I approached the church pastor, who announced my research from the pulpit and asked his flock to cooperate. Both the presence of my Malayalee research assistant and the pastor's support changed how the nurses and their families reacted to me.

After three months of attending church every Sunday and participating in community events, I finally was accepted into this community. Nurses and their husbands were more inclined to talk to me now, though given my gender and status of being a sociologist, the nurses were more forthcoming than their husbands. In the year I spent in the communities of nurses, I conducted hours and hours of observations when I was participating in community events. The participant observations were conducted mostly in public events such as social gatherings at the churches or at nurses' homes.

During the participant observations, I focused on two questions. First, how did family gender dynamics work? I observed who had control over what aspect of the social events, the division of household labor among spouses at the events, discussions that men and women had about their work and family lives, and how men and women interacted with each other. I also observed and listened for talk about immigration status or visa status. I took detailed field notes of my observations and my emotional reactions during the observations.

I also conducted in-depth interviews with nurses who were primary family breadwinners and their dependent husbands. I asked them about their lives before migration, their experiences with the migration process, their work experiences, their household division of labor, and their views and understanding of visa policies. After interviewing each of the spouses separately, I interviewed them together. I interviewed twenty-five nurses and their husbands, fifty individuals total. I also interviewed ten immigration experts, including lawyers, activists, and policy makers, to understand their views on visa policies and immigration of high-skilled workers.

In this chapter, I discuss three key themes, all related to the struggles about gender expectations, that emerged from the analysis of my data: (1) nurses wrestling with how to accept themselves as main providers and not primarily as wives and as their children's primary caretakers; (2) men struggling with their masculinity; and (3) the division of household labor within families. In each of these areas, the families struggled with role reversals. The one arena where men accepted their new responsibilities was as primary caretakers of their children.

Nurses Wrestling with Gender

It was a hot summer Saturday afternoon in a Chicago suburb. I was in the house of Shija, a floor nurse in a suburban hospital. I sat on a bar stool across the kitchen counter, sipping on chilled coconut water, interviewing Shija while she cooked for her family for the week. Saturday was Shija's only day off, and she asked me to come at that particular time because her children had a play date in a local park where her husband had taken them. Shija had four burners on a stove and an oven, and all were on. The air-conditioning was off. In the sweltering heat, the aroma of the Keralite food filled the house. As she cooked, she offered me a taste of what she was cooking and I happily accepted. During the interview, she told me that even though it was hard on her to spend her only day off cooking, she felt good doing it. She explained:

> This is the only, most real way I can show my kids and my husband that I care for them. Also, I want my kids to grow up eating Malayalee food. It is big part of who we are. I grew up eating my mother's home cooked meals and so should they.

This was a regular occurrence in their household. Only when Shija didn't have a day off from work to cook for the week would her husband take care of meals. Shija went on to explain that her husband didn't do much of the cleaning in their large four-bedroom suburban house. I could see it had a spacious living room and large kitchen. She explained: "He sometimes does, but because he does everything for the children, I try to do the other things myself."

This was the story in nearly every family. Although the household division of labor had the nurses doing housework and cooking, they also worked full-time while the husbands either did not work or had minimal part-time jobs. While the men refused to count the hours they spent doing household labor, the nurses told me they were doing about thirty to forty hours of housework every week. Like Shija, all of my nurse participants said that they did most of the cleaning and cooking for their family on their days off. Some of the nurses (eight out of the twenty-five in my sample) had either parents or in-laws living with them who often helped out, but even then the nurses emphasized that cooking was primarily their responsibility. When I asked if this was something the family expected of them, most said they felt good cooking for their families. Rosa, one of the nurses, told me, "This is the least I can do for my children and my family—give them food cooked by mom. I work so much that I am never home. This is the only way I can give them mother's touch." Another nurse, Alma, told me that it would be hard to teach her husband to cook because "he's never cooked or done anything in the house. It would be more work teaching him to cook so I prefer cooking myself." Many of the nurses even opted for night shifts so that they didn't appear to be absentee mothers for the children during the day.

Given the hours that nurses were required to put in at work, they felt they were not fulfilling their mothering duties. In talking about their children and motherhood, many of the nurses broke down in tears, saying that they were "bad mothers" or that they were "losing out on the children's childhood." In a heart-wrenching remark, Jenny said:

> I picked this life so that I have a better life than my mother, but now I am losing my children. I like it that they are close to their father, but my heart bleeds every time they run to their father when they need something and don't come to me even when I am there. It is like I am the person who makes money but is never there for them. That is not what a mother is. [trails off in sobs]

The nurses also expressed a deep sense of guilt and shame when their husbands had to accompany them to the United States on dependent visas. In their guilt, the nurses often tried to overcompensate. Alma shared that she has been doing night shifts for three years "so that the kids don't think their mom brings money and dad sits at home." Gina, another nurse whose husband was on a dependent visa, said:

> I was only able to come here because my husband decided to support me. It was more his decision to move here. It is because of his sacrifice that I am here and I am being able to work. I have two kids, five and eight. If it were not for my husband, I would not be able to do anything. We are all in it together—we just want our family to live better. I am very lucky to have Joseph as my husband.

Like Gina, other nurses whose husbands were dependents—either from their visa status or from being stay-at-home husbands and dads—tried to assert that the husbands were still the heads of the household despite their economic dependence. In all the families with men on dependent visas, the women handed the reins of the family finances to their husbands. Many of the nurses told me that they did not even know their salaries and that their husbands "managed all money issues." Gina explained: "I only bring in the money, the rest is up to him." When I asked Lily what her income was, she said:

> I am not quite sure; you have to ask my husband. He is the one who handles all the money things. My salary goes into our account and then he manages it—does what he thinks best. We are still a traditional Indian family. He is still the master of the house. Any major decisions about the kids or money, he makes those decisions.

It is important for us as a family to give him that respect. Just because he cannot work because of the visa we don't want him to feel he is not the head of the family.

The nurses' emphasis on the men being the "head of the family" shows desire to maintain the semblance of the patriarchal familial structure that the visa laws threatened to alter. The insistence on cooking for the family shows internalized gendered cultural beliefs. In raising an immigrant family, the nurses felt it was important to impart the ethnic/regional food culture to their children even though they were growing up in the United States. The nurses construed "cooking for their children" as an essential part of motherhood. Opting for night shifts at work, engaging in second shifts[19] at home, and handing over finances to the husbands were all attempts to maintain the image of a normal traditional Indian family.

Almost all the nurses downplayed and often refused to even acknowledge their contribution toward their children and family—that is, providing material existence—home, food, education, and medical care. This behavior reveals a deeply internalized gendered understanding of what a family should look like.

Dependent Men Battle with Masculinity

The dependent husbands told me how they found it hard to cope with and resisted their loss of status as head of the household. Many of the men refused to come to the United States on dependent visas and preferred to live in India. Rather than compromise their masculine status by being labeled a dependent spouse, they visited their wives in the United States once a year. When they did come, they tried to negate their dependency by emphasizing that it was because of their "support," "insistence," and "permission" that their wives were able to accept the jobs and come to the United States. George, a husband on a dependent visa, said:

When my wife got this opportunity, she was not sure if she should take it because you know for a while I won't be able to work. But I knew it was important for our children and family. I gave her permission to take the job and then we moved here. It is easier because I can keep a watch on the children and while this is a bad policy, it is the way. What can we do?

Another husband on a dependent visa said:

As a man I needed to make sure my family is OK, and my wife was getting this opportunity to help our family, and for that I would have to sacrifice a little and I was ready for that. I don't think about these things. Government does what it has to—it is no point getting depressed about this. I am doing my duty of keeping my family secure. That is what a man should do.

This attempt to establish maleness in the family context by the dependent men could be interpreted as both a deep-seated gendered belief about a man's role in the family and also as a mechanism to cope with the perceived emasculation they experienced as dependent men. When they claimed to contribute to housework as the dependent spouse, they expressed resentment for having to do so. Shijo, a husband who was on an H-4 visa but now had a work permit, stated:

My wife works 40 to 60 hours depending on how much she is on call. She only has time to cook. I have to do the rest. No choice *nah* (no)? When you marry a nurse, you know you will be servant of the house (laughs). But see I can never say this to my friends and family in Kerala because they laugh at me, say "you became a woman or what?" But what will you do? If I earned like her, we would get a maid, but my English is not strong and my diploma is not good here. So I stay home. I don't want to work in gas station like others. I want to start a business later. But for now I am being houseboy.

The resentment expressed by Shijo about his changed role as the keeper of the house upon migration was a common sentiment among most of the husbands even when they were eligible for employment. However, it was more pronounced among the few husbands who were on H-4 dependent visas. Johnny, an unemployed, separated husband of a nurse, who had been on H-4 for five years (but was now a permanent resident) and was drunk at the time of the interview, shared:

I agreed to marry Maria without dowry because I thought she was my ticket to being rich and escaping from Kerala poverty. But when people have power even a lamb acts like a tiger. That is what happened to Maria. It was the biggest mistake of my life, you better write that down [trailing off].

Johnny's drunkenness might discount his views, but I found similar if less aggressive rhetoric in my other interviews with men on H-4 visas. When I asked George what his day looked like, he responded angrily:

Why do you even ask, to shame me? . . . I am like the wife, OK? I wake up in the morning, make tea, feed breakfast to my son, get him ready for school and then drop him [off]. My wife does night shift so by the time I come back, she is home and I warm breakfast for her—you are thinking, it should be the other way round, not in this house. And then she sleeps. I warm lunch, eat, clean the house and do laundry and then it is time to go pick up my son and take him for soccer and then drop my wife at the hospital and do the evening chores and go to bed. That is my life, not what a man's life should be. But I see it as a sacrifice for my family, my son. You know if you are woman in Kerala and a nurse you can do much more for the family. If you are man, you have nothing. It was my decision that we come here, but I should not have come, like some of the people in my village did. They stayed back till they got green cards. But I did not want my son not to have a good life so I came, so it is all for him. I am learning to be dependent, but it is not easy because you can't talk about it to anyone. Not many of the men are on this visa. Even if you don't work, but if you are not on this visa you have prestige. And it is not Mary's fault. She tries a lot . . . but what can she do. I did not ever drink or smoke—I have to now. It's bad but what to do. Please don't tell her anything. Please. I talked a lot with you.

George's unhappy confession, that he has taken to drinking and smoking to deal with his dependent status or, as he calls it, his role of "wife," shows the extent of internalization of gendered norms about masculinity among the men. The dependent men deeply lamented their loss of male privilege within the household even when their working wives strived against their own well-being and interests to maintain the patriarchal status quo.

HOUSEHOLD LABOR: GENDERED INTERACTIONS WITHIN THE FAMILIES

It was about 9:30 p.m. on a breezy fall Saturday night in a northwestern suburb of Chicago. I was leaning over on the kitchen counter at Amy's house, chatting with Amy's friend and colleague Rosa. Amy is a petite woman of thirty-eight, a nurse in an inner-city hospital. That particular night, all the women were clad in colorful silk saris. The men wore shirts and trousers. Amy owned a large five-bedroom house, which the family bought new about six years ago. It had a spacious kitchen with granite countertops, aluminum-finished gadgets, a large living and dining area, and a fully finished basement that served as a children's playroom. The house was spotlessly clean and had heavy, ornate furniture.[20] Adjoining the kitchen was a living area with a fifty-inch plasma television and couches. Amy's house was typical of most of the nurses' houses I visited for my interviews and observations, including the layout, the furniture, and the family pictures that hung in the living room.

On this weekend night, about fifteen families were having a get-together. All the families had nurses as the lead migrant and the main breadwinner. Three of the husbands in this group were on dependent visas. The rest of the husbands had work permits or were legal permanent residents or citizens, but very few had full-time jobs. Six were entirely stay-at-home fathers. I was invited by Amy to this party to conduct observations as well as interviews.

Like all other community events in the Malayalee community, this event was distinctly gender segregated. The men gathered at one area of the house—in this party, it was in the living space adjoining the kitchen, where some drank beer and chatted while watching Malayalee programming on TV. The women gathered in the kitchen or the living room. The children were often sent to the basement to play. The women usually took charge of warming and serving the food. Multiple dishes (seven to ten) were served, most of them cooked by the host family and a few brought by the guests. The women (nurses) cooked most of the food, but the husbands often declared that they had cooked the meat dishes. Cooking meat was understood to be a mark of masculinity. As I helped Amy[21] lay out the food, she whispered to me with a chuckle that her husband usually helps around the kitchen, but when he is with other men in the community "it is not the done thing to help in the kitchen." If the men helped in the kitchen at social gatherings, it was seen as a sign of not being man enough.

This scenario presents the various forms of gendered interactions that occur among couples in families of nurses and in the Malayalee communities. Gender-segregated social gatherings were common in the community. Dependent men and their wives were very protective of the men's male privilege in the presence of community members. The performance of masculinities among the nurses' husbands that fit gendered expectations of male heads of households was common in public and social events, including at the church.[22]

BREAKING GENDERED EXPECTATIONS: DADS AS NURTURERS

Within the family, nurses did a major share of the household chores. The men, however, were responsible for child care. All the couples I interviewed had at least one child, and given that these working mothers had highly demanding jobs and long hours, the fathers had to do child care. They could not afford paid child care, and parental care was considered more culturally appropriate. As one of the men put it, "Someone has to feed the child and put him to bed. If the mother is not there, I have to do it. The child can't go hungry." The men often took care of feeding the children, putting them to bed, dropping them off and picking them up from school and other extracurricular activities like music and dance lessons, arranging and taking them to playdates, reading to them, drawing with them, taking them to parks, or doing other recreational activities. Mothers stayed informed about what was happening in their children's lives, but joined in the activities only on their days off. Nurses who taught Sunday school at the church had more time with their own children at community and church events.

While men shunned housecleaning and cooking, the men assumed the responsibility of child care without much complaint. Some of the men even took pride in the fact that their children were closer to them than their mothers. John shared:

> My children really love me. If they need anything or if they have to share anything, the first person they run to is me, not their mother. It makes me feel important. It is a wonderful feeling to be loved by your children.

The nurses also felt that the children were closer to the fathers and shared regret and pain for being what they believed were absentee mothers. Some of the nurses were vocal in saying that it was important that the men contributed equally in the household chores. Missy, a floor nurse in a suburban hospital who is married to a mail sorter in the local post office, thought it was very important that he shared equally in the household labor. She explained:

> We are not living back in days and not living in the village in Kerala. It is impossible to run a family when both people are working, and in our families, we as nurses work more, to say that the women will still take care of the house. I now know how much hardship my mother had to go through because of this attitude, and I am happy that has changed. Arun (husband) does a lot in the house—takes of the children and that is very good if you ask me. I don't think Arun is unhappy. (Arun nods in consent).

In a similar story, Jenny shared that she decided to marry Thomas, who was less educated than her and came from a humble background, because she did not want to end up like her mother. She tearfully said:

> I only wanted to become a nurse and leave my village so that I could help my mother and save her from my father. You know she was the one, worked like a donkey both for the family and at the farm and yet my father would yell at her, push her around, sometimes even beat her. I did not want that for me, which is why I married Thomas even if he was lower status than me. I wanted a man who would be understanding and would take care of my home and children and not be like my father. Thomas is a great husband and I am happy that he does not think it is bad to take care of children and family.

Indeed, Thomas was one of the few men who did not complain about doing household chores.

In terms of social interactions and emotional work, the men in the families of nurses assumed more public responsibilities, such as organizing events at the church or organizing community picnics and games. The men said that while the church played an important role in their lives, they also unanimously complained that neither church nor community provided the same sort of social support they had in India. Yet, when it came to keeping in touch with family and friends in India, it was still the primary responsibility of the wives. In fact, the men avoided talking to family and friends in India—perhaps one way for them to protect their already vulnerable masculinity from being further challenged.

The social and political expectation that a worker with a dependent spouse would be able to delegate household duties to the spouse was trumped by the gendered cultural beliefs and expectations that the nurses and their husbands held for traditional Indian heterosexual families. The only time they willingly overcame these gendered cultural expectations was in nurturing their children. The dependent men jumped in to take charge of the children, and many of them enjoyed it and took pride in their relationships with their kids.

Discussion and Conclusion

In this chapter, I presented an analysis of the consequences of visa policies for female-led Indian migrant families. I have showed that female-led migration disrupted the traditional gender order: women were the breadwinners; men became caregivers. The story wasn't that simple, however. Instead, what emerged was a set of complicated gender dynamics within these families. Challenges to traditional expectations disrupted men's comfort with their own masculinity. Female primary breadwinners were still expected to cook and clean and give as much care to their children as they could fit into their schedule.

The husbands of the nurses resented being dependents. Most of these men from rural Kerala believed in strict rules about men's and women's positions in the family, and in their homeland, men were always the head of their households. The nurses, too, described the family structure in Kerala as strictly patriarchal with the father as an iron-fisted patriarch. The men still believed that male honor rested in being a provider and the head of the household. Visa-imposed dependency therefore meant loss of male privilege and honor for the men. They were often resentful and depressed about this loss of status.

The dependent husbands of the nurses refused to take on any purely "wifely" or househusband role. But they did not resist adopting the role of a caregiver for their children, because they believed their children needed care in the absence of their mother. These families, husbands and wives, were very child oriented.

The most common reason the families had moved to the United States was to provide a better and brighter future for their children. The men see the logic in taking the reins of child care, claiming they are strong, able, and sacrificial fathers. The paradox of the situation is that most sociologists and psychologists view child care, including caregiving and caretaking, to be the very definition of femininity. It seems, then, that the men are challenging gender norms by becoming caring nurturers, even if they would shy away from admitting it. Their behavior shows us how society has socially constructed the meaning of gender itself.

Still, most of the dependent men assert their male privilege as heads of households. They and their wives actively perform traditional gender by insisting that their families remain patriarchal. Husbands continue to be the symbolic heads of the household, even though without their wives, their families could not survive economically or remain in their homes.

The nurses emphasized that becoming a nurse was their way to escape the life of poverty and patriarchal oppression in rural Kerala. They saw a career in nursing in a developed country as a means to improve the lives of their children and families, both here and in India. They, however, still held onto traditional gender beliefs. They believed that household work is women's work. The nurses felt guilty for being the reason for their husbands' migration as dependents. They also felt intensely unhappy at being employed mothers with long and erratic hours. Their long working hours made them feel as if they were absentee mothers. But as the main family breadwinners, they felt compelled to abide by any and all demands of their employers. They did not feel they had the option to refuse these demands and better balance their work and family lives. The gender identity of mother remains strong among nurses as they envy the time fathers have with their children. The belief that men and women should have distinct family roles leaves nurses uncomfortable with reversed roles and keeps them from insisting household labor be more equitably divided.

Even though they were written in gender-neutral language, the institutional constraints of the visa structures are based on gendered presumptions that men bring wives with them. Visa laws, no matter how gender neutral they may seem, have gendered consequences for the families. The nurses and their husbands hold on to traditional gendered beliefs about male providership and motherhood, so that the nurses work for a living and then do most of the work in their households.

Seemingly gender-neutral visa policies have oppressive gendered consequences for individuals and for patterns of interactional expectations. I've shown the unintended consequences of visa laws on immigrants: rather than creating stable families, these visas create families full of anxiety and despair. If we are truly concerned with the interests of migrant families, visa laws must seriously be revised. We can no longer assume that partners of those on working visas are women or that immigrants' spouses of either sex should be forced into economic dependency or domesticity.

NOTES

1. http://travel.state.gov/content/visas/english/law-and-policy/statistics.html.

2. http://travel.state.gov/content/visas/english/law-and-policy/statistics/graphs.html.

3. Most nurses resented doing housework but avoided asking their husbands to do it.

4. See Aiken (2007); Aiken, Buchan, Sochalski, Nichols, and Powell (2004); Brush and Berger (2002); Polsky, Ross, Brush, and Sochalski (2007).

5. Brush, Sochalski, and Berger (2004).

6. Aiken (2007); George (2005); Khadaria (2007).

7. *Ibid.*

8. Rai (2003).

9. Khadria (2007).

10. *Ibid.*

11. *Ibid.*

12. Pittman, Folsom, and Bass (2010).

13. See George (2005); Kurien (2002); Walton-Roberts (2012).

14. *Ibid.*

15. The definitions are taken from the U.S. Citizenship and Immigration Services (USCIS), website at http://www.uscis.gov.

16. Xiang (2005).

17. See Dicicco-Bloom (2004); George (2005); Khadria (2007).

18. The proposal was to add fixed quotas of H-1Bs for each sending country, limiting the number of years on the visa to three years and then a continuation for three years and making the process of procuring H-4 dependent visas easier.

19. Hochschild (1989).

20. Most nurses had similarly designed suburban houses and similar ornate wood furniture bought from a suburban furniture store.

21. I did not address most of the nurses by their first names. I added *chechi* (the Malayalam term for "big sister") after their first names for the women and *chettan* (the Malayalam term for "big brother") for the men. The community viewed me as a younger woman though I was not markedly younger than most of the women and men I interviewed. But I learned quickly that it was disrespectful to address my participants by their first names.

22. See George (2005).

In the News

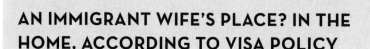

AN IMMIGRANT WIFE'S PLACE? IN THE HOME, ACCORDING TO VISA POLICY

Ms. blog, June 19, 2013

Pallavi Banerjee

Do most of us still live in a 1950 nuclear family where dad goes off to work and mom stays home to take care of the family? Not in real life. But that lifestyle is enshrined in the United States' dependent visa policies. According to the Immigration and Naturalization Service, the *Leave It to Beaver* way of life is the only way skilled workers' migrant families ought to live.

It all begins with one simple fact. There is a shortage of high-tech workers in the United States. We don't produce enough computer engineers, analysts, programmers, engineers, and doctors, to meet the country's needs. The United States tries to solve this problem by allowing U.S. businesses to hire high-tech workers from other countries by granting H-1B non-immigrant visas to individuals from other countries seeking temporary work in "specialty occupations."

These visas allow a U.S. company to employ a foreign individual for up to six years with the possibility of permanent residency. To further entice migrant high-skilled workers to leave their homeland and come to the U.S., they offer H-4 dependent visas to their spouses and children. In 2010, from India alone, 138,431 high-skilled Indian immigrants and the 55,335 Indian immigrants on H-4 dependent visas.

But the "dependent visa" puts many restrictions on the spouses, usually women, of the skilled workers who have an H-1B visa. The dependent visa holder is not allowed to work for pay until the lead migrant has gained permanent residency in the U.S., a process that can take six years or more. In some states, the dependent visa holders are not even allowed to drive.

When I studied families with an H-1B/H-4 dichotomy I found that most adult recipients of the H-4 dependent visas are highly qualified women. They experienced a loss of dignity and self-deprecation. Some women told me they felt they were thrown back into a model of the "traditional family" where women are not valued at all outside of the home. They talked about being rendered invisible, feeling lost, and for some, suicidal.

One of my study informants described her H-4 visa as a "vegetable visa meant to make you vegetate." Others called it a "prison" or "bondage" visa. Another woman told me, "You lose your individuality and in time all your confidence—and one day suddenly you realize you are just reduced to being a visa number in your head. It is scary—it's like losing your head."

Gaining permanent residency in the U.S., which would allow spousal employment, could take many years for H-1B workers. This means these women will be legally unable to work for years on end. Some of the women I spoke to simply could not handle their situation and decided to return to India. One high-tech worker who recently went through divorce told me, "We had absolutely no problem as a couple. It's this visa situation. . . . She was unhappy and depressed and it was not going to get better. We had to take the very hard and cruel way out—the many pains of being a foreign worker."

As the U.S. debates comprehensive immigration reform, and considers increasing the number of "high skilled foreign workers," lawmakers should reconsider the constraints on spouses embedded within dependent visas.

Immigration policies designed to bring high-skilled workers and their dependents to the U.S. fill a need in the high-tech industry, but they fall short in building gender equal, stable, happy, and viable families. The 1950s are long gone. It is time to let wives work. Why force migrant families to live in the past? ▰

31

Diverging Development

The Not-So-Invisible Hand of Social Class in the United States

Frank F. Furstenberg Jr.

The advantages and disadvantages associated with social class position build up over time, creating huge developmental differences in the course of growing up. This chapter discusses how development is shaped by social class position and how the processes associated with class position are either mitigated or amplified over the early part of the life course. By early adulthood, gaping disparities exist between children growing up in disadvantaged and advantaged families. I discuss how these trajectories pose special problems for less advantaged youth making the transition to adulthood due to the need for resources to pay for higher education.

America has never been a class-conscious society by the standards of the rest of the world. The notion that social class determines a person's life chances has always been anathema to this country's democratic ideology. Some of the earliest observers of American society, most notably Alexis de Tocqueville,[1] noted the disdain among American citizens for class distinctions compared with the acceptance of stratification in France or the rest of Europe. Although social class was far more prominent and salient in the United States when Tocqueville visited in the 1830s than it is today, from the country's very inception, the seemingly boundless possibilities of land ownership and the ideology of upward mobility softened its contours. The idea that any American by dint of good character and hard work could rise up the social ladder has long been celebrated, no more clearly than in the great American myth of Horatio Alger. That "rags to riches" parable instructed young men—and it was men—how to make their fortunes in nineteenth-century America.

Curiously, the United States, long regarded as the land of opportunity, has never entirely lived up to its billing. Studies comparing social mobility in the United States with that in our Western counterparts have failed to demonstrate that social mobility is higher here than in other industrialized nations.[2] Yet Americans seem as oblivious to class gradations today as they have ever been. Most of us declare that we are middle class, and finer distinctions such as working class and upper middle class have all but vanished in the popular vernacular and even in social science research. Yet as the salience of social class has declined during the past several decades, we have witnessed a huge rise in economic inequality.[3]

When I was entering academic sociology more than four decades ago, the social world was described very differently than it is today. Even while recognizing the muted notions of social class held by most Americans, social scientists were keenly attentive to, if not obsessed with, distinctions in values, lifestyle, and social practices that were inculcated in the family and linked to social mobility.[4] Indeed, the idea that parents in different social strata deliberately or unintentionally shaped their children's ambitions, goals, and habits, which in turn affected their chances of moving up the social ladder, was widely supported by a large body of literature in psychology, sociology, and economics. These studies showed how families at different rungs on the social ladder held distinctive worldviews and adhered to different ideas of development.[5] Most of all, social scientists believed that life chances were highly constrained by values and skills acquired in the family and by the structures of opportunity in the child's immediate environment that shaped his (and it usually was his) chances of economic success. Fine gradations of social class could be linked to virtually everything from toilet training to marriage practices.[6]

Social class, not so long ago the most powerful analytic category in the researcher's conceptual toolbox, has now been largely eclipsed by an emphasis on gender, race, and ethnicity. Socioeconomic status has been reduced to a variable, mostly one that is often statistically controlled, to permit researchers to focus on the effect of determinants other than social class. With relatively few exceptions, we have stopped measuring altogether the finer grade distinctions of growing up with differing resources. True, we continue to look at poverty and economic disadvantage with no less interest than before, and we certainly understand that affluence and education make a huge difference. Yet, most developmentalists view economic status as a continuum that defies qualitatively finer breakdowns. Consequently, working-class, lower-middle-class families, or even families in the middle of the income distribution are concealed rather than revealed by combining income, education, and occupation, without regard to the particulars of status combinations.[7] In short, the idea of social class has largely been collapsed into rich and poor, marked by education and earnings—above and below the poverty line. Think of the way we currently treat "single-parent families" as an example. They have become almost a proxy for poverty rather than a category of families that experience life differently than their two-parent counterparts do.

The contention that contemporary developmental research downplays the influence of social class in no way is meant to imply that professional attention to gender or race or ethnicity is unwarranted or should be diminished. Without a firm grasp of social class differences in contemporary America and how they affect men and women and people of different races and ethnicities, however, much of the current research on gender and ethnicity may not give us a full understanding of how the two shape social reality and social opportunities. Just as we have come to recognize the hazards of lumping together all Hispanics or Asians, I would suggest we need a more nuanced understanding of how individuals' levels of education, occupation, and income alter and shape their worldview and life course.

In this essay, I outline a research agenda for examining social class in greater detail. Beginning with a brief discussion of developmental theories, I point to some of the methodological obstacles to studying social class that must be attended to. Then I turn to developmental processes that expose research questions that warrant greater attention by social scientists, particularly developmental sociologists and psychologists. My work nicely complements observations put forth by Sara McLanahan[8] in her 2004 presidential address to the Population Association of America on inequality and children's development, although my attention is devoted primarily to how developmental processes are shaped by stratification. I examine a series of natural occurrences associated with social class that work in tandem to fashion a developmental course for children from birth to maturity that is pervasive, persistent, and far more powerful in the United States than Americans generally like to acknowledge.

SOCIAL CLASS: A PROBLEMATIC CONSTRUCT

One reason why attention to social class has faded can be traced to the academic controversies surrounding the very idea that social classes exist in this country. If what is meant by a social class system is a tightly bounded and largely closed hierarchical set of social strata that determines the life chances of its members, then surely most social scientists would agree that America is a classless society. But social class has been used in a different way to mark the structure of economic and social opportunities affecting individuals' behaviors and beliefs, networks and associations, and, ultimately, knowledge about and access to social institutions such as the family, education, and the labor market.

Viewed in this way, social classes are not tightly bounded categories; they are fuzzy sets created by experience and exposure to learning opportunities and selective social contacts that derive from resources that can be marshaled by individuals and their kinship networks. In this respect, the fuzzy nature of social class appears to differ from the constructs of gender or ethnicity, although in truth both of these constructs, too, have been appropriately critiqued as "socially constructed" statuses and are not naturally unambiguous. Still, there are no certain markers that identify individuals as belonging to one class or another; social class is probabilistically constructed and measured by constellations of economic and social opportunities. Thus, we might say that someone who has low education and works at a menial job that pays poorly is lower class, a term that admittedly has become virtually taboo in the United States. Nonetheless, we easily recognize that those possessing these attributes are more socially isolated, excluded from mainstream institutions, and limited in their access to mobility than their better educated and better paid counterparts. Whether we refer to such individuals as lower class, poor, disadvantaged, or socially excluded, we must still admit that their opportunities for advancement or their ability to confer such opportunities to their children are far more restricted than the opportunities of their more advantaged counterparts—a classic example of a class-based world.

I will dodge the question in this paper of whether it makes sense to identify a particular number of social strata such as was common in social science a generation ago, designating four, five, or seven classes that possessed different family practices, values and beliefs, or lifestyles and cultural habits.[9] Instead, I merely want to observe how the neglect of social class has created a void in attention by developmentalists to how stratification structures the first several decades of life. I refer to "several decades" because toward the end of this paper, I report on what my colleagues and I on the MacArthur Network on Transitions to Adulthood[10] have learned about how social class shapes the transition to adulthood in myriad ways that have profound implications for the future of American society.

A DEVELOPMENTAL THEORY OF SOCIAL CLASS

Human development involves an ongoing interaction between individual-level biological potential and social processes shaped by children's multiple and changing social environments. Sometimes developmentalists make distinctions between maturation, regulated in part by biology, and socially arranged learning through institutions such as the family or school, the process that we generally refer to as socialization. One of the important legacies of late-twentieth-century developmental science was to put an end to the fruitless and misleading debate between nature and nurture. Researchers reoriented theories designed to explore ongoing interactions from birth to maturity in varying and often nested contexts—families, child-care settings, schools, communities, and the like—to investigate how social context afforded or denied opportunities for optimal development. In doing so, they understood that optimal development can vary both by children's innate abilities or biologically influenced capacities and by their varying exposure to learning environments. Indeed, it is the ongoing interaction between biology and environment that shapes the course of a child's development.

No one understood this scheme better or promoted it with more vigor than Urie Bronfenbrenner,[11] who, as it happens, was one of the pioneers in psychology to examine the influence of social class on children's development. Bronfenbrenner's theory of development located the individual in an embedded set of contexts that extended from the intimate and direct to distant and indirect as they socially impinged on and shaped the course of human development over the life span. Bronfenbrenner's ideas about development in context loosely parallel a tradition of sociological theory stemming from the work of George Herbert Mead and of Charles Cooley,[12] which has come to be known as "symbolic interaction." Like Bronfenbrenner, both Mead and Cooley conceptualized human development as an ongoing process of engagement and response to social others—that is, social exchange guided by feedback from the surrounding social system. As sociologists applied these ideas in practice, they quickly realized how sensitive children are to varying contexts and cultures, a lesson that is closely aligned with Bronfenbrenner's theory.[13]

It was, and I believe still is, just a short step from this general theory of human development to seeing the pervasive influence of social class in shaping the course of development. That step involves a careful appraisal of how learning environments such as families, schools, and neighborhoods set the stage for a socially orchestrated life course. These more distal social arrangements are carefully regulated in all modern societies by gatekeepers who exercise presumably meritocratic standards based on a combination of talent, performance, and sponsorship.[14] In modern societies, parents cede direct control of their children's fates at increasingly early ages to other agents (for example, teachers), who become instrumental in guiding children through an age-graded system of opportunities. Resourceful parents are able to train and coach their children, select and direct choices in this system, advocate when problems arise, and try to arrange for remediation when their children are not following an optimal path. As I have argued elsewhere,[15] parents' managerial skills have become increasingly important in modern societies, influencing how adeptly children navigate the institutional arrangements that affect their opportunities in later life.

Of course, parents themselves are also embedded in different opportunity structures; specifically, they are more or less privileged in the knowledge, skills, and resources they can provide to their children. Expressed in currently fashionable parlance, parents possess different amounts of human, social, cultural, and psychological "capital" to invest in their children, and hence their managerial resources and skills reflect their social position. But parents are not the only agents who matter in a child's development. All caregivers of children also possess different levels of resources and, generally, the higher the status of the children, the higher the level of social and cultural resources these caregivers possess.

Of course, children possess different capacities to learn, relate, and procure support and sponsorship during childhood. These capacities influence their access to kin, friends, neighbors, teachers, and peers who can and do promote or diminish their chances of socioeconomic attainment. And even small differences in the abilities of parents and other caregivers to manage children's development can accumulate over time if they consistently are more positive or negative.

A century ago Max Weber used a powerful metaphor of loaded dice for how history operates.[16] Each throw of the dice, he imagined, is weighted by the result of the previous throw; constraints increase with repeated tosses of the dice, leading to progressively more skewed outcomes. Social class can be conceptualized as just such a mechanism, establishing a set of life chances that become more sharply pronounced as they play out over time. Micro-interactions accumulate in a patterned and successively more consequential pattern, etching a probabilistically preordained trajectory of success.

The outcome of these interactions is always affected by how the child comes to interpret and act in the immediate contexts. This might be an operational definition of resiliency or vulnerability as described by psychologists such as Rutter, Garmezy, and Werner[17]—the idea that some children are able to defy the odds. Interestingly, developmentalists in recent years have given at least as much, if not more, attention to research on beating the odds as on developing a careful understanding of how the structure of opportunities creates systematic advantage or disadvantage over time—or, we could say, why and how growing up in a certain social location establishes strong or long odds of departing from an expected pattern of success.

Recent data as shown in Figure 31.1 indicate that 42 percent of children born into the bottom fifth of the income distribution will remain there as adults. Only 7 percent will make it into the top one-fifth of the income distribution. For those born into the top one-fifth of the income distribution, 40 percent will remain there, while just 6 percent will fall into the lowest quintile.[18]

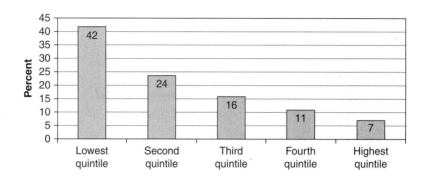

Figure 31.1 | Percentage Moving from Lowest Quintile

Methodological Obstacles to Study

Until very recently, we lacked the data and the methods to observe how social stratification shapes the course of human development. Longitudinal research really only became widely available in the latter decades of the last century, although pioneering studies were done on relatively small samples, such as Glen Elder's now classic work on the life course of youth in Berkeley and Oakland, California.[19] Not until the introduction of the computer could social scientists thoroughly analyze the large-scale samples necessary to examine variation in children's lives over time. Today, it is a relatively simple matter to merge and analyze multiple waves of interview data, administrative records, blood samples, and the responses to modern surveys of children that allow investigators to explore the numerous contingencies and pathways that constitute the course of children's development from conception to maturity.

Barriers based on disciplinary specialization may also have diverted attention from the potential influence of social class. Psychologists have been actively discouraged in many departments from working on large existing data sets and instructed instead to collect their own data, thus restricting the range of problems that could be examined. Beginning in the 1960s, sociologists turned away from studying children, ceding much work on socialization to psychologists. Disciplines have been organized to encourage work on specific life periods, and younger researchers have been encouraged to become specialists in infancy, early or middle childhood, or adolescence. Exceptions abound, of course, and I would be remiss if I did not acknowledge those researchers such as Eleanor Maccoby, John Clausen, Doris Entwisle, Emmy Werner, and others, who broke out of the mold or, one might say, beat the odds of doing research in disciplines that discouraged such efforts.

Added to the problems stemming from data availability and disciplinary constraints are the methods themselves that are required to examine how trajectories of development unfold over time. Today, a host of novel techniques are packaged in software for analyzing and interpreting longitudinal data. No doubt, many more techniques and tools will be coming in the future as new and more powerful ways of understanding career contingencies, transitions, and the evolution of trajectories of development are invented and refined. The tools are now available to describe and explain how advantage and disadvantage along many dimensions configure and crystallize the developmental pathways from birth to maturity.[20] I would contend that data availability and methods have outpaced our theoretical and substantive understanding of how social class influences human development.

THE ORIGIN OF SOCIAL CLASS DIFFERENCES

More sensitive analytic techniques must take account of several features of social class known to influence development. First and foremost, once set in place, early patterns of development may be difficult to surmount for several different and perhaps overlapping reasons. At this stage, we are only beginning to learn about brain development during infancy and early childhood, but it is entirely possible that the architecture of early development could well preclude or, at least, compromise subsequent patterns of development. There is growing evidence that cognitive and emotional capacity formed early in life may be foundational, providing a template or structure for later advances.[21]

Exposure to these developmental influences begins before the child is born and is shaped in no small way by mothers' prenatal experiences—their exposure to toxins, their diet, and the quality of health care received during pregnancy—and then by the neonatal health care provided to the newborn infants. Most mothers experience a normal delivery and their children are born in good health, but steep differences exist across social classes in all these factors.[22] Thus, children enter the world endowed unequally, even if we discount any genetic variation by social class.

The families into which they are born provide vastly different opportunities to build on that endowment. Whether children are planned or unplanned, whether they must compete for limited family resources or have enough, and whether they will receive steady and sufficient attention from parental figures are but a few of the contingencies known to vary by social class.[23] What is less understood is how these early influences combine and accumulate to create developmental divides with lasting effects on children's prospects later in life. The consequences of social attachment, for example, have not been traced long enough to understand whether or how it affects later transitions in adolescence and early adulthood.

The remarkable research by Charles Nelson and his colleagues on institutional care of children in Romania under the Communist regime provides evidence that a critical period exists for emotional development that, if breached, can lead to permanent impairment.[24] Children reared in a collective setting with little or no opportunity to develop attachments with stable emotional figures were emotionally incapacitated. Nelson and his colleagues discovered that if these children were placed in families with emotionally engaging surrogate parents by certain ages, the pattern of emotional disfigurement could be repaired, and perhaps even reversed if the placement occurred early in life. An interesting question, relevant to the discussion here, is whether stimulation and human interaction in early childhood is dichotomous or multitiered—that is, whether and how much early interaction sets the parameters for later growth by establishing a critical level or by operating in a more graduated fashion that may still fall below the optimal amount. Few children in American society are impaired by lack of stimulation, but there seems little doubt that many children get less stimulation or fewer opportunities for emotional engagement than is optimal.

A series of experiments in neuropsychology conducted to determine barriers to reading reveals fascinating and perhaps parallel findings on brain development.[25] It seems that middle-class and working-class children with reading difficulties may exhibit different neural responses when faced with a task of decoding words. The researchers hypothesize that the amount of exposure to reading and remediation affects neural responses and could account for the differences by social class, suggesting that the causes and the remedies for reading problems might vary for children by social class.

Both these studies bring to mind an impressive qualitative study by Hart and Risley.[26] Home observation of family interactions among children and their families revealed gigantic variations in the range of words, expressions, and interaction styles, creating, in effect, a continuous and mounting difference in verbal environments that appeared to be linked to the vocabularies that children acquired early in life.[27] These varying cognitive contexts were later linked to reading skills and, accordingly, to school success.

This study leads to a second observation relevant to developmental trajectories of children in different social classes. Small differences, if persistent, become larger and more consequential over time. A process of psychological and social accretion operates both at an internal and external level as children develop self-concepts, styles of thought, and habits that shape their motivation and social interactions in ways that harden over time. If, for example, children are exposed to very modest differences in, say, language, reading practices, or interaction styles over long periods of time, the cumulative effects could be quite striking and large. Thus, if years of education, on average, are linked to small differences in parental skills or practices, they could create significant effects, on average, in children's cognitive and emotional skills. These psychological and social styles create impressions on others that are reinforced and reified in informal and formal social settings. To answer the question of how parents' educational levels affect children's development, we need stable measures of social patterns that have been established inside the home, and these patterns must be measured with sufficient frequency to permit us to examine growth curves of emotional and cognitive development that extend into middle childhood, adolescence, and early adulthood.

The cognitive and behavioral styles that emerge in the home, and that are shaped to a great degree by class differences in child-rearing practices, establish what sociologists once referred to as "anticipatory socialization," advanced training for social roles outside the home, particularly the role of student. These class-related habits of speech, thought, and behavior affect perceptions of the child and entrance into preschool programs that foreshadow and initiate placement and social tracking within the school system. Modest or perhaps not so modest differences within families are unlikely to be offset or compensated for by learning that takes place outside the home. To the contrary, these differences are greatly amplified by parents' capacities to locate, gain access to, and monitor settings outside the home and by institutional practices that selectively recruit children from families with resources and children who exhibit the capabilities to perform well.

Parents in all social strata are well aware that beginning at an early age, children require and benefit from experiences outside the home, opportunities that can offset or reinforce patterns established in the family. We have rightly paid a good deal of attention to child care settings,[28] but we have much less information on the impact of peer interactions[29] or experiences with skill-enhancing facilities such as recreational centers, libraries, museums, and the like. The likelihood of a steady and stable exposure to these social institutions varies tremendously by social class.[30] Qualitative studies have demonstrated large differences by social class in children's exposure both to the number and quality of these settings. The reasons why are pretty obvious. Parents with more education are both more knowledgeable of, and therefore usually more discriminating in, locating high-quality settings. They also have greater resources to gain access to those settings. Finally, they have the ability to organize and take action on their children's behalf and to monitor ongoing engagements, whether they are with the right kind of peers, better classes, or high-quality teachers, coaches, or caregivers.

The other side of the coin is no less influential in channeling children from different social classes into more or less favorable settings. Settings find and recruit children from families of different social classes with varying levels of energy and enthusiasm. In other words, the availability of resources establishes to a large extent the social class distribution of families who participate in social institutions in American society. In many instances, settings regulate their clientele by the cost of services: the most expensive attract mostly or exclusively children from affluent families, whether they are prenatal health programs, child-care facilities, after-school programs, summer camps, or Ivy League colleges. Those who can pay the cost of admission typically can afford better teachers and can attract peers who are more motivated and prepared. We have relatively little research on the social class networks of children that emerge over time, but it is certainly plausible that most children in the United States grow up with little or no exposure to peers outside their social class. Thus, their opportunities to acquire cultural and social capital are tremendously influenced by the social class composition of kinship and peer networks. And we have every reason to believe that money and education are playing an ever larger role in regulating the level of cross-class exposure and the composition of children's social networks.

THE IMPORTANCE OF PLACE

Most parents are well aware that where one lives matters. Indeed, the primary way to manage opportunities for children is choice of the neighborhood where children are brought up. Interestingly, we have all too little information on social class and residential decision making. Given that schooling is generally determined by neighborhood, however, parents with more knowledge and resources can select neighborhoods that offer better schools, better peers, and often better recreational facilities. In the study that my colleagues and I did in Philadelphia on how families manage risk and opportunity, we discovered that parents were acutely aware of the opportunities attached to choice of neighborhood, though that awareness did not necessarily mean they were able to exercise much discretion in where to live.[31]

Most working-class families in Philadelphia could not afford to live in affluent sections of the city, much less move to the suburbs, where they knew that they would find better schools and more desirable peers. They often resorted to the second-best option: sending their children to parochial schools, where children were monitored more closely, had a longer school day with more after-school activities, and attended school with like-minded peers.[32]

Schools in turn were able to select families that enabled them to produce higher test scores and hence greater academic success. A good portion of these outcomes were predetermined by the selection of parents and their children, although clearly more able, prepared, and motivated students may help schools to recruit higher-quality teachers and administrative staff. As I sometimes like to say, economists want to rule out selection as a methodological nuisance, while sociologists regard selection as a fundamental social process that must be studied as a central feature of how things happen. In any event, social life is created by multiple and interacting influences that generally come in packages rather than operating as particular or singular influences, as they are commonly studied in experimental designs.

This package of place-based influences is one of the larger lessons learned from the Moving to Opportunity Program, which gave families in public housing the chance to move to lower-poverty neighborhoods. Moving to these neighborhoods was not an event, as the researchers tended to regard it from the onset, but a succession of adaptations and interpretations. This succession affected family members differently, depending on experiences prior to moving, new and old social networks, and demographic and unmeasured psychological characteristics of the movers and those who chose to remain. The net effects, always important to policy makers, conceal a huge range of varied responses that unfortunately are only dimly understood.

SOCIAL REDUNDANCY IN MULTIPLE CONTEXTS

Perhaps what I have written thus far is leading to the impression that opportunities at the family, school, and neighborhood levels are strongly correlated—that is, that the various contexts of social class operate closely in tandem in shaping the lives of children. But important work by Tom Cook and his colleagues in their study of families in Prince George's County, Maryland, reveals that, at an individual level, most children experience a mixture of social opportunities.[33] They found that there is only a modest correlation among the quality of parental resources, school resources, and neighborhood resources—surely the opposite conclusion from the idea that children grow up in an environment of class-congruent settings.

Yet, the research by Cook and his colleagues reveals that at the population level (when family characteristics, school, and neighborhood quality are considered in the aggregate), there is a much more powerful correlation among these arenas of social stratification. On average, children from better endowed families are very likely to attend better schools and live in better neighborhoods. It is as if the playing field for families is tilted in ways that are barely visible to the naked eye. Another way of looking at the stratification of social space is to imagine that families with more resources are able to arrange the world so that their children will have to be only ordinarily motivated and talented to succeed. Those with fewer resources must make more effort or have greater talent to succeed. Those with limited or meager resources must be highly gifted and super-motivated to achieve at comparable levels. Developmentalists have often implicitly acknowledged the way the world works by valorizing the families and children who do manage to swim against the current, but we should be measuring the current as well as the swimmer's efforts, particularly when there is every reason to believe that the current has become stronger in recent years.

Opportunity structures, made up of multiple and overlapping environments shaped by social position, are not accurately perceived by individuals from different vantage points in the social system. They can only be understood by examining simultaneously what families see and respond to in their familiar settings, what they do not see but what can be seen by other observers, and most difficult of all, seeing what is not there. Take, for example, how much parents or children know about colleges and how they work. Most children in affluent families know more about this topic at age twelve, I would guess, than children in working-class families know when they are ready to enter college. Cultural capital—knowledge of how the world works—is acquired, like vocabulary, in the family, schools, and from peers in the community.[34] Class differences result from a process of social redundancy that exposes children to information, ideas, expectations, and navigational tools that lead some children to know what they must do to get ahead and others merely to think they know what to do. Developmentalists have surely studied cultural knowledge of how the world works, but we have a long way to go before we have a good map of what is and is not known by parents and children about the stratification system and how this knowledge changes over time as young people's impressions of how things work run up against how they actually work. With relatively few exceptions,[35] we lack the kinds of recent cultural studies that have peered inside the family, looking at the operating culture of families.

THE SOCIAL CLASS DISTRIBUTION OF NEGATIVE EVENTS

Social class not only opens or shuts doors for advancement, it also influences the probability of negative events and circumstances in the lives of children and their families. The likelihood of bad things happening to people varies enormously by social class, although we know this more from inference and anecdote than we do from systematic studies of children's experiences in the course of growing up. Take, for example, psychological stressors, including death, poor health, accidents, family dissolution, residential changes, job loss, and so on. Virtually all these events occur much more frequently in highly disadvantaged than moderately advantaged families, and least of all among the most privileged. Negative events are more likely to happen to families who lack educational, cultural, and social capital, which are the protective resources associated with social advantage. Lower-income families are more vulnerable than higher-income families to a host of troubles, including credit loss, health problems, transportation breakdown, criminal victimization, divorce, mental health problems, and the list goes on. They also have fewer resources to prevent problems from happening in the first place by anticipating them or nipping them in the bud (preventive and ameliorative interventions). And, when these problems do occur, social class affects a family's ability to cushion their blow.

Anyone who has studied low-income households, as I have for so many decades, cannot help but notice a steady stream of these events that constantly unsettle family functioning, requiring time, energy, and resources that often are in short supply or altogether unavailable. Life is simply harder and more brutish at the bottom, and, I suspect, it is more precarious in the middle than we ordinarily imagine. As developmentalists, we have not done a very good job of evaluating how such events affect the lives and life chances of children. They create wear and tear on families and often ignite a succession of subsequent difficulties. The problems may begin with job loss, which in turn results in marital strife or dissolution and finally settles into long-term mental illness or substance abuse. Or this chain of events can just as easily be reversed. The point is that in the ordinary course of life, children at different social strata face vastly different probabilities of bad things happening to them and their parents, and these events often spiral out of control. Social scientists are accustomed to describing these behaviors as "non-normative" events, but they may only be "non-normative," at least in the statistical sense, in the lives of affluent families.

CLASS DIFFERENCES IN PROBLEM PREVENTION AND REMEDIATION

The distribution of negative events, as I have suggested, is negatively correlated with social class, just as the distribution of means to prevent and remediate troubles is negatively related to class. Affluent families have access to a tremendous range of strategies for prevention. They purchase and practice preventive health care, they situate themselves in environments free of toxins, and their homes and streets are safer. When and if their children experience problems in school, they can take a range of actions—from changing schools to procuring help in the form of tutoring, assessments, therapy, medication, and so on. If their children happen to get in trouble in the community, they have means to minimize the consequences by tapping informal contacts or legal interventions. We know much about how families employ these preventive and remedial strategies, but we have yet to put together a comprehensive picture of how troubles are avoided and deflected for children in different social classes. If we examined a sample of problem behaviors among adolescents, what would be the likelihood of adverse outcomes occurring from a series of incidents?

The criminological literature provides ample evidence that social class (and race and ethnicity as well) accounts for much of the variation in delinquency outcomes, for example. It is not that adolescents from affluent families do not commit delinquent acts, use drugs and alcohol, and engage in risky sex. Indeed, the evidence suggests that so-called problem behaviors are fairly evenly distributed by social class. But families with greater assets and social connections can minimize the significance of troubles even when they occur, particularly the more extreme sanctions, such as going to court and being incarcerated.

Social advantage provides a form of cover from negative events when they do occur. It provides for the privileged a social airbrush that conceals mistakes and missteps that invariably occur in the course of growing up. The management of problem behavior by families, and their ability to access and use professional delegates (doctors, lawyers, tutors, social service workers) varies across different social classes and represents a neglected topic in adolescent development.

SOCIAL CLASS, SOCIAL CAPITAL, AND SPONSORSHIP

We would miss much about the use of professional and nonprofessional agents in children's lives among different social classes were we to confine our attention to their role in problem intervention and remediation. It is also important to study the role of adult sponsors in promoting children's positive behaviors, skills, and talents. This topic represents a broader exercise of what has come to be called social capital, the social resources that families can use to promote children's positive development as well as to prevent or correct negative courses of action. Recently, there has been considerable interest in mentoring and the roles that mentors play in children's development, especially in helping children who have limited access to positive role models, advisers, advocates, and sponsors.[36]

Sponsors, of course, can be family members, but we generally think of them as agents outside the family who act on behalf of children. They can be gatekeepers in institutions that allocate resources and access to programs, services, and opportunities. More often, they are individuals who have connections to a range of different gatekeepers. Students of child and adolescent development should learn more about how sponsorship operates in everyday life because it undoubtedly plays an important part in channeling children into successful pathways.

We know only a little about how various adults help to cultivate skills, talents, and special abilities such as in art, music, theater, sports, and so on, and we know much less about how sponsors promote children's chances of getting ahead by nonacademic means or in combination with formal schooling. This topic merits greater attention because sponsors can play an important role in facilitating social mobility. Less visible, but perhaps equally important, is the role that sponsors play in helping to guarantee that children in the more affluent classes retain their privileged position.

Some research exists on how young people enter the world of work and the role that families play in using contacts and connections to place adolescents in training, service, and work opportunities.[37] Privileged parents understand that their children need to build portfolios of experience—résumés—to get ahead. Research in a Philadelphia study on the less advantaged and the disadvantaged suggests much less understanding on the part of these parents as to how to connect their children to select institutions.[38] Usually, it appears that sponsors identify children from less-advantaged families by dint of their good efforts in school or perhaps through community organizations. Affluent parents do not passively wait for sponsors to find their children. They actively recruit sponsors or place their children in social arenas where sponsors are present and looking for motivated and talented prospects. Schools with well-developed extracurricular programs, after-school activities, summer camps, and advanced educational courses are part of the stock-in-trade of growing up well off. Children in affluent families become accustomed to relating to adults and appreciating what adult sponsors, mentors, and coaches can do for them in middle childhood and adolescence. Increasingly, the role of sponsors figures prominently in young people's ability to navigate successfully as they move from adolescence into early adulthood.

Early Adulthood: The Extension of Investment

Early adulthood, the period of life when youth enter adult roles and assume adult responsibilities (entering the labor force and becoming economically self-sufficient and forming families), has in recent decades become a less orderly and more protracted process than it was a half-century ago. The driving force in this extended passage to adulthood has been the perceived need for a college education and, for the more privileged, an advanced degree often accompanied by a lengthy apprenticeship in a professional career. Related to this trend, but not wholly because of it, young people put off more permanent relationship commitments and, generally, parenthood as well. Commitments to marriage and children, public opinion tells us, have become almost a second stage of the adult transition, often put off until education has been completed and some measure of job security has been attained.[39] Social class differences are no less prominent in this new stage of life than they are during childhood or adolescence. The current demands on young adults to attain higher skills, be better prepared to enter the labor force, and postpone family formation play out quite differently in advantaged, middle-class, and disadvantaged families.

Let's begin with the obvious: the costs of higher education have become less affordable as grants and loans have not kept pace with college tuitions, much less the cost of professional education. Among low-income families, the debt taken on by parents and young adults can be crippling, even though the long-term pay-off theoretically makes borrowing for education economically rational.[40] Add to these economic problems the academic liabilities from years in low-performing schools that many, if not most, youth from disadvantaged families face, and it becomes obvious that a very small proportion are academically, much less financially, prepared to tackle a lengthy period of working and attending school (usually beginning with community college). Graduation happens, but relatively rarely. Instead, other events intrude: the lack of support staff and assistance in two-year colleges makes it harder to catch up if they fall behind academically, financial crises siphon off needed resources, parents cannot or will not offer aid or require support themselves, and so on.

These hurdles are one reason for the stark differences in graduation rates by social class. As Figure 31.2 shows, among seniors in high school who are likely

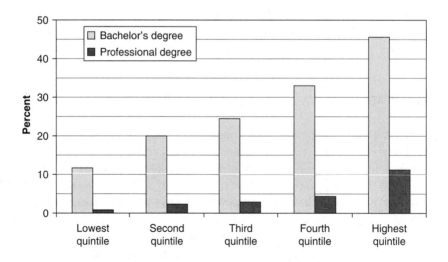

Figure 31.2 | Postsecondary Attainment of Twelfth-Graders (1992) by Income Quintile (2000)

Source: *Postsecondary Attainment, Attendance, Curriculum and Performance: Selected Results from the NELS:88/2000 Postsecondary Education Transcript Study*, Table 1 (2000, NCES 2003-394).

to go to college, approximately one in eight of those from families in the lowest income quintile completed college compared with nearly one in two of those from families in the highest quintile. Only one in four of those in the middle quintile completed college.

Among middle-class families, here the third income quintile from $43,400 to $65,832 in 2004,[41] few young adults can afford higher education without working to help pay for it. Balancing school and work commitments in early adulthood is not an easy task, often leading to high rates of school "stop out" and dropout. Thus, even when preparation for college is adequate and grants and loans can be managed, the process can be arduous and lengthy, partially accounting for the exceptionally high rates of college dropout in the United States. Many young people who enter college settle for, willingly or not, what amounts to postsecondary technical training, often restricting their mobility in their adult years.

The financial position of affluent families permits much greater latitude in helping out their children during the long period of college and professional training. The prospect of attaining a high-income job in the future, along with assistance offered by parents, more than likely sustains young adults through college and into professional careers. No doubt, too, young adults from affluent families who are generally better prepared academically are far more likely to qualify for scholarships based on academic merit and accordingly required to take on less debt.

Of course, this class-based profile is stereotypical to some degree. Talented individuals do rise from the bottom and untalented youth drift down. There may even be some disadvantages associated with the high-investment regime of child rearing more common in affluent families if children respond poorly to parental pressures for high achievement. The social class mechanisms that I have described in this paper continue to affect young adults during their twenties and thirties. The accumulation of debt, the likelihood of problematic events, the availability of social capital and sponsorship continue to tilt the playing field as youth enter institutions with different levels of selectivity or work situations that permit or thwart opportunities for attaining further human capital.

I cannot leave the topic of early adulthood without mentioning how social class exposure in childhood, adolescence, and early adulthood affects partnerships and family formation. We have always known that social class is linked to the quality and stability of marriage, though there was a time when divorce (not separation or marital unhappiness) occurred more frequently among the better off. This has not been true for some time. Lower human capital is related to lower social, cultural, and psychological capital—the skills, knowledge of the world, social networks, and sponsorship that play some part in the ability to manage and sustain emotional relationships. Striking differences emerge in marriage, its stability, and in the incidence of nonmarital childbearing by social class.[42]

These family patterns, so closely linked to class-based experiences in growing up, figure prominently in public discussions about the retreat from marriage among Americans. Curiously, the retreat has not occurred at all among the privileged, and it has occurred less often among the middle class than among the economically disadvantaged. Marriage is increasingly a luxury good attainable only by those with the social, psychological, and material goods that make it happen and make it work.

CONCLUSION

Social scientists have a strong interest in poverty and social disadvantage but have largely ignored gradations of disadvantage that occur beyond the least fortunate in our society. We firmly hold the view that, after all, we share a middle-class status with all but the least and most fortunate. This way of looking at the world is distorted by our own privileged circumstances that lead us to ignore relevant distinctions operating to keep most Americans in positions that are becoming economically and emotionally more precarious with each passing decade.

As social scientists and especially as developmentalists, we must begin to ask ourselves whether we are accurately describing the social and psychological worlds of most Americans who are far less privileged than we are. Are we adequately portraying this world in our professional writings to show how the social system is arranged to allow a small number to flourish while others with equal talents and motivations never reach their human potential? To put it simply, we are not telling it like it is.

Doing a better job requires that we take advantage of the new data sources and novel techniques for analysis to tell a more in-depth story of class-differentiated childhoods, adolescences, and early adulthoods. Doing a better job requires giving much more attention to opportunity differences in the so-called middle class. Doing a better job means doing more comparative research on social class differences and examining alternative possibilities of growing up in a less class-skewed society. It requires that we devote more attention to developing policies that restore some measure of balance and equity to our social system. We must begin to tackle the question of why our children are not doing well (by international standards) in so many important domains of health and education, why our young adults are falling behind in college completion for the first time in American history, and how our families, wanting to do the best for their children, are unable to measure up to the task.

Notes

1. See de Tocqueville (1835).

2. See Bendix and Lipset (1966); Goldthorpe and Erickson (1993).

3. See Danziger and Gottschalk (1995); Levy (1999); Wolff (2002, 2004).

4. See Hollingshead (1949); Lynd and Lynd (1929); Warner (1949).

5. See Bernstein and Henderson (1969); Gans (1962); Komarovsky (1987); Miller and Swanson (1958).

6. See Blood and Wolfe (1960); Mead and Wolfenstein (1955).

7. For exceptions, see Kefalas (2003); Lareau (2003).

8. See McLanahan (2004).

9. See Hollingshead (1949); Warner (1949).

10. See the MacArthur Network on Transitions to Adulthood website: http://www.transad .pop.upenn.edu.

11. See Bronfenbrenner (1979).

12. See Mead (1934); Cooley (1902).

13. See, for example, the work of anthropologists and sociologists such as Inkeles (1968); Kluckhohn and Murray (1948); Mead and Wolfenstein (1955); Miller and Swanson (1958).

14. See Buchmann (1989); Heinz and Marshall (2003).

15. See Furstenberg et al. (1999).

16. See Weber (1949).

17. See Rutter (1985, 2000); Garmezy (1991, 1993); Werner (1995).

18. See Hertz (2005).

19. See Elder (1974).

20. See Wagmiller et al. (2006).

21. See Danziger and Waldfogel (2000); Haggerty, Sherrod, Garmezy, and Rutter (1994); Shonkoff and Phillips (2000).

22. See Case, Fertig, and Paxton (2005); Conley and Bennett (2000).

23. See Brown and Eisenberg (1998); Joyce, Kaestner, and Korenman (2000).

24. See Nelson (2000); Nelson et al. (2005); Smyke et al. (2007).

25. See Noble, Norman, and Farah (2005).

26. See Hart and Risley (1995).

27. See Bernstein (1971); Bernstein and Henderson (1969); Farkas and Beron (2004).

28. See Chaudry (2004); Magnuson and Waldfogel (2005).

29. See Corsaro (2005).

30. See Medrich, Roizen, and Rubin (1982).

31. See Furstenberg et al. (1999).

32. *Ibid.*

33. See Cook, Herman, Phillips, and Settersten (2002).
34. See Bourdieu (1973, 1986); Lamont (2000); Lareau (1989, 2003).
35. See Edin and Kefalas (2005); Newman (1993); Burton and Stack (1993).
36. See Rhodes (2002).
37. See Mortimer (2008).
38. See Furstenberg et al. (1999).
39. See Furstenberg et al. (2004); Settersten, Furstenberg, and Rumbaut (2005).
40. See Rouse (2004).
41. Census Historical Income Tables, 2004, Table F-1.
42. See Ellwood and Jencks (2001); Goldstein and Kenney (2001); Wu and Wolfe (2001).

CCF Brief

UNEQUAL CHILDHOODS: INEQUALITIES IN THE RHYTHMS OF DAILY LIFE

Annette Lareau | March 2007

The intersection of race and class in American life is an important but often vexing subject for sociologists. The power of social class is often obscured by the visibility of race. I wrote *Unequal Childhoods: Class, Race, and Family Life* (University of California Press, 2003) in part because I wanted to make class real by showing how it works in everyday life. I hoped that by capturing the day-to-day rhythms of life in different kinds of families—those of middle-class, working-class, and poor whites and African Americans—I could help bring the seemingly intractable problem of inequality into clearer focus.

Most of the eighty-eight families my research assistants and I interviewed during the first stage of research had children in the third or fourth grade in elementary schools in a large northeastern city and its suburbs. From this initial pool, we selected twelve families, six African American and six white, for more intensive study. Nearly every day for three weeks we spent time, usually a few hours, with each family. We went to baseball games, church services, family reunions, grocery stores, beauty parlors, and barbershops. We even stayed overnight with most of the families. We saw siblings squabble and heard parents yell. We joined kids as they sat around watching TV and as they played outside in the yard or the street. By the standards of social science research, this was an unusually intensive study.

What we found was that although all parents want their children to be happy and to thrive, social class makes a very substantial difference in how this universal goal is met. Middle-class parents promote what I call concerted cultivation. They actively foster their children's talents, opinions, and skills by enrolling the children in organized activities, reasoning with them, and closely monitoring their experiences in institutions such as schools. The focus is squarely on children's individual development. As a result of this pattern of concerted cultivation, children gain an emerging sense of entitlement. Most of the middle-class families in the study were extremely busy; this pattern held for white and African American middle-class families. Children attend soccer games, go on Girl Scout trips, do homework, and go to birthday parties; parents need to arrange these activities as well as get children there and back. Despite the busy schedule, most parents worked full-time and some had job-related overnight travel. In addition to meeting their workplace responsibilities, parents had to manage the details of family life: they had to go grocery shopping, prepare dinner, do laundry, monitor homework, oversee children's showers, and participate in bedtime rituals. I detail in the book what children's schedules mean for family life. In describing the middle class, I use the term *the frenetic family*. Things are so hectic that the house sometimes seems to be little more than a holding space for the brief periods between activities.

The differences we observed between these middle-class families and those of working-class and poor families are striking. Parents in working-class and poor families promote what I call the accomplishment of natural growth. These parents care for their children, love them, and set limits for them, but within these boundaries, they allow the children to grow spontaneously. Children do not have organized activities. Instead, they play outside with cousins and siblings; they watch television. Parents use directives rather than reasoning with children. And children generally negotiate institutional life, including their day-to-day school experiences, on their own. The working-class and poor parents in the study often were very distrustful of contacts with "the school" and health care facilities. They were fearful that professionals in these institutions might "come and take my kids away." Rather than an emerging sense of entitlement, children in these families developed an emerging sense of constraint. Working-class and poor families struggled with severe economic shortages (including lack of food in the poor families) that often led to additional labor or complexity (long bus rides, missed appointments), but the pace of their daily life was much less hectic than that of the middle-class families.

Unquestionably, the families we studied differed in how they raised their children. But are these differences important—do they really matter? Neither the approach of concerted cultivation nor the accomplishment of natural growth is without flaws. Both have strengths and weaknesses. Middle-class children, for example, are often exhausted, have vicious fights with siblings, and do not have as much contact with their extended families as working-class and poor children do. But when children are in settings such as schools and health care facilities, middle-class parents' strategy of concerted cultivation coordinates much more closely with the current standards of professionals than does the accomplishment of natural growth strategy that working-class and poor parents rely on. Middle-class parents routinely make special requests of teachers, asking, for example, that they provide their children with individualized instruction. These parents expect the institution to accommodate them, and this expectation typically is met. Middle-class children are taught to ask doctors questions and to feel that they have the right to challenge people in positions of authority. Thus, the data suggest that middle-class children gain advantages, including potential benefits in the world of work, from the experience of concerted cultivation. Working-class and poor children are not taught these life skills, and thus they do not gain the associated benefits. In short, class matters.

What about race? We found that in terms of children's time use, parents' methods of talking to children, and parents' interactions with schools and other institutions, African American middle-class children had much more in common with white middle-class children than with African American poor or working-class children. Still, race does matter in other respects: most of the children lived in racially segregated neighborhoods, middle-class African American parents complained of race-based difficulties in the workplace, and African American middle-class parents were very worried about their children being exposed to racial insensitivity at school. These parents also tried to promote a positive racial identity for their children (for example, by taking them to a predominantly middle-class African American church). But in terms of the overall rhythm of children's family lives, and in the ways that parents address their own and their children's concerns, class emerged as much more important than race. Other studies also show substantial divisions between middle-class African Americans and working-class and poor African Americans.

The findings presented here, and in much greater detail in *Unequal Childhoods*, are based on an intensive study of only twelve families. Can we trust these results to tell us anything of significance? I believe that we can. The book's conclusions support established findings in social science research, which, using statistical techniques and nationally representative data, have shown important differences in how parents raise children. Rather than using numbers, *Unequal Childhoods* uses the stories of real families to highlight important social patterns. Moreover, American society is in a time of change. Children are being raised differently today than in earlier decades: middle-class children have more organized activities than in the 1950s and 1960s, for example. This shift has important implications for family life that our research helps expose by providing detailed insight into intimate details of daily life in families with young children. It gives us a chance to step back and reflect on how we are spending our time in family life as parents, and how we are choosing to raise our children. It also reminds us of the fact—all too often neglected—that there are important differences across social groups in the contours of childhood.

The arguments and evidence in *Unequal Childhoods* also point us toward new directions for social science research. The study suggests that while African American middle-class families do face some child-rearing problems that have no counterpart in white middle-class families, African American parents draw on a set of generic class resources to manage these problems. We can do better research and gain a deeper understanding of the intersection of race and class by showing how all families draw on class-based resources as they negotiate their daily lives. Put differently, we need to move beyond studying variables; it's time to focus on families.

32

Not Just Provide and Reside

Engaged Fathers in Low-Income Families

Kevin Roy and Natasha Cabrera

Thirty years ago, fathers were considered to be the "forgotten contributors" to children's lives.[1] Recently, however, social scientists have recognized dramatic changes in men's fathering due to shifts in cohabitation, marriage, divorce, remarriage, and nonmarital childbearing.[2] Often these demographic changes have impacted low-income families disproportionately.[3] Low-income fathers have emerged as a diverse group of men who are engaged with children, not simply as providers and co-residers, but as caregivers who transition in and out of children's lives. In this chapter, we provide a brief overview of literature on low-income fathers' involvement with their children. We explore social and cultural contexts for men's involvement. Finally, we examine processes of fathering and patterns of change in fathering over the life course.

FATHER INVOLVEMENT AND CHILD DEVELOPMENT

We now recognize that positive father involvement with their children enhances the children's physical, cognitive, and socioemotional development.[4] Even with recent demographic shifts in the way that families organize themselves due to remarriage or cohabitation, employment, immigration, and the global economy, engaged fathers have continued to shape their children's lives in positive ways. We have focused our attention on how fathers act as residential co-parents with mothers, although this family context may be more common for middle-class married men than for low-income minority men. However, we have shifted away from a discussion of "absent" or "deadbeat" dads and toward fathers' "presence," even if men do not live with their children. Whether or not they live with their children, unmarried and low-income fathers can positively impact their children's lives.

Recent studies show that sensitive, responsible, and accessible disadvantaged men who are engaged with their children enhance cognitive and socioemotional development in their children from the first year of birth up through pre-K.[5] Contrary to popular belief that low-income fathers are harsh disciplinarians, absent, or insensitive, fathers are often as sensitive and engaged as mothers across developmental periods.[6] Fathers and mothers both have high levels of engagement (i.e., sensitivity, positive regard, and cognitive stimulation) and low levels of negative aspects of engagement (i.e., detachment, intrusiveness, and negative regard). Moreover, low-income children with involved fathers acted out less and had fewer problems with negative social interaction. There is great diversity among low-income families in terms of education, parenting behaviors, and overall well-being. This is an important insight, because stereotypes of low-income minority families focus primarily on challenges to children rather than on the strengths in these families, which can offer a window for intervention for policies and programs.

It is also true that children living in poverty are at risk for harsh negative parenting and poor outcomes as they grow. These outcomes may be due to living in single-parent households with few resources, maternal stress, poor neighborhoods, and lack of social support. But if low-income parents are married or cohabiting, the combined effect of mothers' and fathers' sensitivity to the children, positive regard, and cognitive stimulation lead to better cognitive development during early childhood.[7] Children in low-income families benefit from involved and caring mothers, but they benefit additionally if their fathers are also supportive of them, and if their fathers have completed years of education beyond high school. In effect, low-income fathers can contribute their own critical, additional piece of the puzzle for their children's development. For low-income children who are at risk because of poverty, two involved parents may make an important difference.

Although evidence suggests that fathers matter, we do not understand how disadvantaged fathers actually shape their children's lives.[8] Fathering studies are no longer frozen in assumptions about fathers as providers or living in residence with their children. Instead, studies have examined how fathers transition in and out of children's lives—over time and across different social contexts.[9]

DIVERSE CONTEXTS FOR MEN'S INVOLVEMENT

Being an involved father is not simply determined by the choices of an individual parent. How men father their children depends on men's relationship with their own parents, race and ethnicity, biological factors, demographic background and personality traits, mothers' and children's own unique characteristics, community networks, mother and father's relationship, and even the economic situation in local neighborhoods.[10] With such a strong focus on co-residential, biological fathers, we often overlook the experiences of cohabiting partners, stepfathers, nonresident fathers, and grandfathers. If we carefully "break open" the assumptions of nuclear family households, we can reveal how fathers are embedded in complex family configurations that shape their parenting.

In particular, research with low-income and minority families has identified a range of flexible roles for fathers and father figures. In African American families, biological fathers, boyfriends, godfathers, uncles, brothers, cousins, and "ol' heads" (community elders) all serve as significant father figures in communities and kin networks with flexible expectations for men's participation as caregivers of children.[11] Grandfathers affect kin relationships between generations—in particular, they influence their sons' parenting through the earlier childhood experiences their sons have had with them.[12] Paternal grandmothers have been identified as key figures in both making sure that their sons play a role as fathers (particularly for young nonresidential fathers) and caring for their sons' children.[13] Men's place as caregivers in kin networks is also clear across other racial, ethnic, and class groups in which the men serve as critical family care providers for children.[14]

Low-income men's relationships with the mothers of their children directly shape how they are involved with their children. While mothers are important contributors to men's involvement with their children, who exactly is responsible for poor men stepping up as involved fathers?[15] This is a complicated question, and we need to pay closer attention to how men and women negotiate parenting and working in their families. Over the past three decades, fathers have been doing slightly more child care and more work in the household, although this is likely due to a shift in the proportion of work that women do with children and at home, as women's work hours have increased.[16] Cooperative co-parenting is better for children, especially if it is characterized by more responsive parenting behaviors, higher-quality relationships, and more frequent contact.[17] On the other hand, heightened conflict between parents, whether or not they co-reside, can threaten children's well-being in families.

Some men talk about the "package deal" for fathers—a set of expectations that society has for men to be fathers who both provide for and give care to their children.[18] Disadvantaged men try to live up to these ideals, just as middle-class or privileged fathers do. There may be a larger gap for these men, however, as they try to live up to expectations with limited opportunities and resources. For example, many would assume that men who are not breadwinners are not responsible fathers. For low-income men, however, "being there" for their children may be just as important—that is, by securing their children to a family legacy, linking them to family members, and fulfilling care obligations.[19]

Race or class-bound stereotypes about "good" fathers tend to dissolve when we look at actual paternal involvement in their children's daily lives. In studies of married or cohabiting parents across race and class, African American and Latino fathers are often more likely to monitor and supervise their children than white fathers, and Latino fathers often spend more time with their children than white or black fathers do.[20] Black fathers tend to be less engaged and less warm, but they take more control and more responsibility than white fathers, whereas Latino fathers take less control but more responsibility than white fathers, and they are as warm as white fathers. In effect, race differences in fathers' control and responsibility appear to be linked to parenting attitudes, but men's engagement and responsibility are more closely linked to economic factors, such as living in poverty.[21] Further, black and Latino nonresidential fathers are often more involved than nonresidential white fathers, a pattern explained in large part by the quality of their relationships with their children's mothers.[22]

Even within racial and ethnic contexts, men parent in very different ways.[23] For example, we acknowledge that many Latino families in low-income (and other) communities highly value family networks—a value called *familismo*.[24] But fathers and children have different experiences as they shift from one cultural context to another. They are often caught between cultures, one packed with traditional expectations of men as patriarchs and providers, and another filled with fluid and ambiguous expectations of men as friends, contributors, and co-parents. For Asian and Asian American fathers as well as Native American fathers in low-income communities, making a place in American culture may be at the very heart of relationships between fathers and children.[25] Often, families move across physical contexts too, leading them to confront the challenges of immigration, even as it can alter men's roles in families.

DYNAMIC CONTEXTS FOR MEN'S INVOLVEMENT

We need to be aware of diverse settings for men's parenting in low-income families, but we also need to grow more aware of how these settings are constantly changing over time.[26] Disadvantaged men are more likely to move in and out of intimate relationships, residences, and jobs, and their fathering may become transitory and attuned to the nature and duration of such transitions. For example, mothers may both encourage and discourage men's involvement over time, and in different contexts. Men describe "babymamadrama," or conflict with mothers of their children, and how they negotiate involvement with their children even when they are incarcerated.[27] We should give more attention to the process of low-income mothers' recruitment of fathers and father figures to care for their children.[28] These mothers may call on men for their contributions of material resources and time, but they also have children's safety as their highest priority. These mothers, then, may also seek social fathers and other kin as fathers, if biological fathers present too many risks to their families over time.

Similarly, multi-partner fertility is a common status associated with poor outcomes for children in low-income families.[29] But multi-partner parenting is a complex process that unfolds over time across multiple families. Men change their behavior as fathers on a daily basis, often by sitting down at the same table with mothers of their children to rearrange contact. Instead of swapping involvement in a prior family for involvement in a subsequent family, low-income fathers often attempt to reestablish relations with older children from previous partners.[30]

It is difficult to remain involved as disadvantaged men navigate these transitions in their families. Fathers must become resilient to barriers and challenges of poor employment options, environmental risks, and changing family relationships.[31] They often rely on family members to help secure their place as fathers. It seems that "beginnings matter," as men who were engaged to the mothers of their children when the women were pregnant are likely to maintain some kind of positive involvement with the children after the birth. Continuity matters, too. Support from other family members over time can help low-income fathers to boost their involvement and to avoid the extreme effects of disruptions in work and family relationships.

Finally, fathers' involvement changes over time, as men and children age. Men's involvement changes as fathers themselves age, especially as their residential status shifts.[32] A common pattern of involvement for low-income African American fathers is "flux"—in effect, if we take snapshots of men's residence with children, we find that a majority of men are involved with children, but they move in and out of children's households.[33] Involvement may also shift across generations. Men are socialized to being fathers when they are young themselves. Their experience with their own fathers can be a strong motivator for paternal involvement.[34]

Fathering in low-income families has changed historically as well. Globalization has transformed men's parenting as it has remade employment opportunities for families. For example, among a small group of forty low-income black fathers in Chicago, older fathers were two to three times more likely than younger fathers to find stable employment and establish co-residence with their partners and children in their early twenties.[35] More broadly speaking, across all income levels, men of child-rearing age spent 40 percent less time in families with children in 1980 than they did in 1960. In 1980, fewer young adult men lived in environments with children present.[36]

The Future of Fathering in Low-Income Families

Given the dramatic changes in families and men's lives that have been in the making for the past twenty-five years, where do we find fathers at the end of the first decade of the millennium? While there are large numbers of men who are increasingly disengaged from their children, there are also increasing numbers of men who are more involved than ever before. Just as American society has witnessed growing gaps in income inequality, there are growing gaps between the "highs" and "lows" of father involvement with children.

In past decades, being a low-income father was not synonymous with being disengaged from family life. But perhaps more than ever before in American history, if a father is poor in 2009, he is likely to live apart from his child as an unmarried parent. The income inequality gap has important implications for the future of these men's fathering. Even as we have expanded our notions of "new" fathers to include men's efforts to care for children—even if they live apart from children and their mothers, or are under/unemployed—we must acknowledge that men's engagement with children does not emerge solely from a change of heart or a value commitment. Families need resources—housing, health care, jobs with good wages, education—to stabilize men's involvement over time, and to stem the rapid and jarring transitions of men moving in and out of their children's lives.

Notes

1. Lamb (1975).
2. Eggebeen (2002a). LaRossa (1997) asserted that there is a culture of "new fatherhood" with expectations that men provide and care for their children. He noted, however, that men often do not live up to these emerging expectations—in effect, that there is a gap between the cultural ideal and the actual conduct of "new" fathers. Another perspective on "new" fathering was offered by Townsend (2002) with the notion of "the package deal." Again, middle-class men in his research saw that marriage, parenthood, employment, and homeownership represented a cluster of roles that went beyond traditional and outmoded sole breadwinner expectations.

3. Coley (2001).

4. Black, Dubowitz, and Starr (1999); Lamb (2004); Shannon, Tamis-LeMonda, London, and Cabrera (2002).

5. Cabrera et al. (2004); Shannon, Tamis-LeMonda, and Cabrera (2006); Tamis-LeMonda, Shannon, Cabrera, and Lamb (2004).

6. Cabrera, Shannon, and Tamis-LeMonda (2007).

7. *Ibid.*

8. Palkovitz (2002a).

9. Pleck and Masciadrelli (2004) confirm this redirection in father involvement research over the past five years. They write: "[This] increase in supportive evidence has been accompanied by increased awareness of methodological and conceptual complexity of association between paternal involvement and children's development. The research agenda has thus shifted from whether paternal involvement has positive consequences to questions about the *context* in which and the *processes* by which paternal effects occur" (p. 256).

10. Few models of father involvement have followed Bronfenbrenner's theoretical framework (1979) and considered human development in multiple contexts. Cabrera, Fitzgerald, Bradley, and Roggman's model (2007) is a step forward, with an explicit developmental approach to how men's involvement shapes child well-being over time.

11. Jarrett, Roy, and Burton (2002); Waller (2002).

12. Roy (2006).

13. Roy, Dyson, and Jackson (2013).

14. Nelson (2005); Hansen (2005).

15. Doherty, Kouneski, and Erickson proposed a model of father involvement (1998) that placed mothers as central figures in men's involvement with children. This model was critiqued by Walker and McGraw (2000), who questioned whether we should assume that women are responsible for men's engagement with children.

16. Pleck and Masciadrelli (2004).

17. Sobolewski and King (2005). Further, couples' marital expectations and changes in status are important predictors of men's involvement with children in low-income families; see Carlson and McLanahan (2002, 2004); Waller and McLanahan (2005).

18. Townsend (2002).

19. This is relevant particularly in research with African-American fathers (Allen and Connor, 1997; Jarrett et al., 2002; Roopnarine, 2004). As Cabrera and Garcia Coll (2004) argue, the "form and meaning of [father involvement] are culturally dependent and have not been explored widely."

20. Toth and Xu (1999).

21. Hofferth (2003).

22. Cabrera et al. (2007).

23. For example, Roopnarine (2004) contrasted subtle differences in parenting between African American and African Caribbean fathers and argued that less emphasis on family

structure would draw focus to "areas in which men from different socioeconomic backgrounds and familial arrangements mature and succeed as parents in raising socially/intellectually competent children—and which factors are responsible (such as cultural beliefs or practices, processes and changes in paternal involvement at different stages of the life cycle with different age children, quality of coparenting relationships, extrafamilial support, education, and income)."

24. Cabrera and Garcia Coll (2004).

25. Kwon and Roy (2007); Shwalb, Nakawaza, Yamamoto, and Hyun (2004).

26. Eggebeen (2002b) suggests that "we need data that is sensitive not only to the diverse settings of fatherhood, but also to its dynamic and constantly changing nature" (p. 205). Spaces and places, social relationships and family configurations, local or national cultural contexts, and social policies and institutions all shift in ways that must be accounted for within developmental research.

27. Roy and Dyson (2005).

28. Roy and Burton (2007).

29. If men have multiple children, they are likely to see less of their children and to contribute less financially (Carlson and Furstenberg, 2006).

30. Roy, Kaye, and Fitzgerald (Under review). Most low-income fathers in our study did not perceive themselves as having children across distinct family systems. Instead, they saw themselves as "pivot points" in a father-centered family system.

31. Roy, Palkovitz, and Fagan (2007); Fagan, Palkovitz, Roy, and Ferrie (2009).

32. Building on Hogan's (1981) work on early work transitions in men's lives, Palkovitz (2002b) discerned specific stages of men's involvement as they aged—and the impact that such involvement had on men as individuals. With men as the focal point of the study, Palkovitz raised the issue of reciprocal developmental effects, as children also shape men's developmental trajectories.

33. Mott (1990).

34. Hofferth et al. (2012). Roy (2006) finds that for low-income African-American men, experience with their own father—whether as a stable presence, a transitory figure, or even a complete absence—is a strong motivator for paternal involvement. In this study, low-income African-American men tied their own fathering to the barriers and dynamics that they had experienced with their own fathers.

35. Roy (2005).

36. Eggebeen and Uhlenberg (1985).

In Other Words

MORE SIMILARITIES THAN DIFFERENCES IN STUDY OF RACE AND FATHERHOOD

Sociological Images, January 11, 2014

Lisa Wade

The Centers for Disease Control have released new data comparing the involvement of black, white, and Latino fathers. The study found more similarities than differences. Men of all races were more likely to be living with their children than not. Defying stereotypes, black fathers were, on average, more involved in their children's daily care than white and Latino fathers.

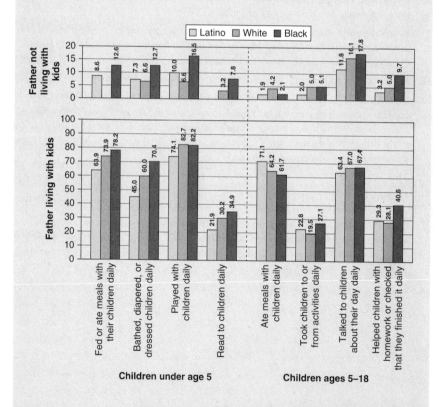

33

Mass Incarceration and Family Life[1]

Bryan L. Sykes and Becky Pettit

You have likely read or studied about high incarceration rates in the United States—and in this book, you have read extensively about changes in family life. We ask, how does the high number of people who are imprisoned—and who have been imprisoned—in the United States affect our families? American families have experienced tremendous demographic and economic change since the mid-twentieth century. Scholars of the American family have drawn attention to how increases in women's labor market involvement, the decline in manufacturing, wage stagnation, suburbanization, and other important large-scale economic, social, and political changes influence family life.[2] Four decades of growth in the prison and jail population represents a critical institutional intervention in the lives of American families, but one that has attracted relatively little scholarly attention.

Crime is at historic lows, yet the number of people in prison and jail remains near record highs. Close to 2.3 million Americans are behind bars—representing 1 percent of the adult population in the United States.[3] Sociologist David Garland has coined the term *mass incarceration* to characterize the uniquely modern American social phenomenon of extraordinarily high incarceration rates.[4]

Incarceration is highly concentrated among men, African Americans, and Hispanics, as well as those with low levels of education. Moreover, inequality in incarceration among adults is mirrored in inequality in parental incarceration among children. Black and Hispanic children are three to six times more likely than white children to have had a parent in state or federal prison for at least a year.

This dramatic impact brings us to this chapter, where we investigate race and class inequality in incarceration and its effects on families and children. We begin by reviewing trends in crime and punishment and illustrate inequality in exposure to the criminal justice system and incarceration. We then consider the consequences of incarceration for family life and child well-being. Parental incarceration is linked to family instability, economic insecurity, and an increased risk of behavioral problems, especially among boys. Children of incarcerated parents are overrepresented in foster care, and high rates of incarceration in disadvantaged communities negatively impact educational attainment even among children who themselves do not have an incarcerated parent. Finally, we consider how inequality in exposure to incarceration creates and exacerbates race and class inequalities in family life.

Trends in Crime and Punishment

Trends in crime in the United States bear only modest resemblance to trends in incarceration. Crime is down significantly from its peak, by any measure. However, different measures of crime and victimization have risen and fallen at different rates and to different levels over the past few decades. Figure 33.1 displays crime rates since 1960. Violent crime rates grew from the early 1970s through 1981 during the early years of the penal buildup. As Figure 33.1 shows, violent crime rates ebbed and then grew into the early 1990s. Violent crime rates exhibited steep declines after 1993. The most reliable measure of violent crime—the murder rate—peaked in the United States in 1980, fluctuated through the 1980s, but has been on the decline since 1991. The murder rate continues to hover near historic lows.

Figure 33.1 also shows trends in property crime rates. Like violent crime rates, property crime experienced surges in the 1960s through the 1980s. Property crime is more common than violence; the rate of these incidents is nearly seven times as high, as indicated by the main scale. Also like violent crime rates, property crime rates began to decline in the early 1990s. Despite some discrepancies in the time series across measures, the trend in crime rates over the last forty years is unmistakable. There were crime surges by most measures in the early 1980s and 1990s, but all measures of crime are down from their historic heights. Despite the economic downturn that started in the last quarter of 2007, current crime rates are on par with levels observed in the late 1960s and early 1970s.

At the same time, contemporary incarceration rates are at historic highs. Figure 33.2 documents the incarceration rate in the United States since the early 1970s. When statistics on the size of the prison population were first recorded in 1925, seventy-nine of every 100,000 Americans were held in federal or state prisons, generating an imprisonment rate of .079. The imprisonment rate, or the

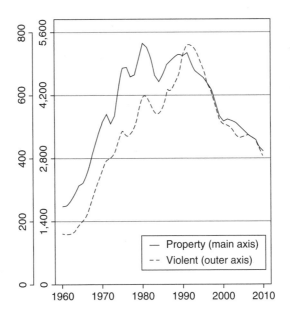

Figure 33.1 | Crime Rates per 100,000, United States, 1972–2010

Source: Author calculations using data from the Survey of Inmates, Current Population Survey, and Bureau of Justice Statistics.

percentage of Americans housed in federal or state prisons, hovered close to .1 (or 100 in 100,000) until the mid-1970s. The long-term stability in the imprisonment rate prompted some well-known criminologists to claim the existence of a "natural" or stable incarceration rate.[5]

Theories of stable incarceration rates were upended during the prison expansion that began in the mid-1970s. Between 1975 and 2009, the U.S. imprisonment rate grew an average of 4.7 percent annually. This is a stunning increase considering the imprisonment rate adjusts for population growth over the period. The incarceration rate, which includes inmates housed in local jails, grew almost as briskly. Figure 33.2 shows the steep increase in the incarceration rate in the United States that continued, unabated, even after the onset of declines in the crime rate in the early 1990s. Contrasting trends in Figures 33.1 and 33.2 illustrate the decoupling of crime and incarceration in the United States by the mid-1990s.

Currently just under 2.3 million Americans are behind bars—representing approximately 1 percent of the adult population in the United States. Nearly 5 million more men and women are under the supervision of the criminal justice system through parole, probation, or other forms of community-based corrections.[6]

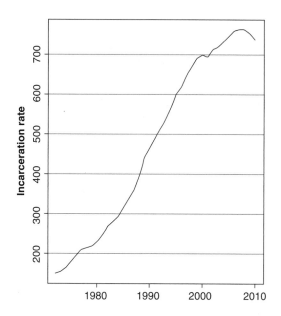

Figure 33.2 | Incarceration Rate per 100,000, United States, 1972–2010

Source: Author calculations using data from the Survey of Inmates, Current Population Survey, and Bureau of Justice Statistics.

That means approximately 3 percent of the U.S. population—or one in 31 adults—is under some form of correctional supervision or criminal justice surveillance.

Mass incarceration is not only a contemporary development, it is also distinctly American. Until the mid-1970s, the incarceration rate in the United States was similar to the incarceration rate in France and Germany, among other industrialized nations.[7] Now, after close to four decades of penal expansion, the United States is the world leader in incarceration.[8] Table 33.1 shows that in the late 2000s, the United States incarcerated a higher fraction of its population than any other advanced-industrialized country. In fact, the incarceration rate in the United States is over ten times the incarceration rate in Sweden, Norway, Slovenia, Finland, and Denmark.

The decoupling of crime rates and incarceration rates suggests that the growth in the penal population cannot simply be explained by large-scale changes in crime or criminality. Instead, shifts in policing, prosecution, and criminal justice policy at the local, state, and federal levels are important for understanding the expansion of the prison system. Over the past few decades, law enforcement agencies have stepped up policing, prosecutors have more actively pursued convictions, and a host of changes in sentencing policies now mandate jail or prison

Table 33.1 | Prison Population and Incarceration Rates by Country per 100,000 population, 2009–2010

Country	Number of Inmates	Incarceration Rate
United States	2,239,751	716
Russian Federation	681,600	475
Georgia	10,202	225
Belarus	31,700	335
Greenland	170	301
Ukraine	137,965	305
Lithuania	9,729	329
Estonia	3,186	238
Poland	83,610	217
Czech Republic	16,257	154
Slovakia	10,152	187
Turkey	137,133	179
Hungary	18,388	186
Spain	68,220	147
England/Wales	84,430	148
Scotland	7,855	147
Luxembourg	656	122
Romania	33,015	155
Bulgaria	10,996	151
Canada	40,544	118
Portugal	14,264	136
Italy	64,835	106
Austria	8,273	98
Greece	12,479	111
Ireland	4,068	88
Belgium	12,126	108
France	62,443	98
Netherlands	13,749	82
Northern Ireland	1,851	101
Germany	64,379	79
Switzerland	6,599	82
Sweden	6,364	67
Denmark	4,091	73
Norway	3,649	72
Iceland	152	47
Finland	3,134	58

Source: Walmsley, Roy. World Prison Population List, 10th ed. Retrieved on October 31, 2014, from http://www.prisonstudies.org/sites/prisonstudies.org/files/resources/downloads/wppl-10.pdf.

time.[9] Recent claims of decreased federal involvement in the lives of Americans[10] are at odds with the expansion of the criminal justice system; mass incarceration, as a policy intervention, has *increasingly* affected millions of adults and their families. In the following sections, we document inequality in exposure to the criminal justice system and its implications for American family life.

PATTERNS IN EXPOSURE TO THE CRIMINAL JUSTICE SYSTEM

Although explanations for contemporary prison and jail growth remain a source of debate, growth of the criminal justice system itself is indisputable. Even in the face of steep crime declines through the 1990s, the penal system continued its historic expansion into the twenty-first century. While women and Hispanics represent some of the fastest-growing segments of the incarcerated population, spending time in prison or jail continues to be most heavily concentrated among men, African Americans, and those with low levels of education.[11] Incarceration rates among black men are about seven times higher than those for whites. In 2008 the civilian incarceration rate among black men ages eighteen to sixty-four was 8 percent, compared with 1.2 percent among non-Hispanic whites. Among young men between ages twenty to thirty-four, the incarceration rate of African American men was 11.4 percent, compared to 1.7 percent for non-Hispanic whites. Among those with the lowest levels of education, 37.2 percent of black men and 12 percent of white men were incarcerated.

The lifetime risks of imprisonment have also grown during the period of prison expansion. Moreover, the risks of imprisonment are increasingly concentrated among African American men without a high school diploma.[12] Five percent of white men and 27 percent of black men born between 1989 and 1993 spent at least a year in prison before reaching age thirty-five. The risks of spending time in prison for this birth cohort were significantly higher among high school dropouts: 28 percent of white and 68 percent of black dropouts had spent at least a year in prison by 2009.

Exposure to imprisonment now rivals or exceeds exposure to other social institutions long thought vital to the transition to adulthood, such as the completion of schooling, employment, or marriage. Young, black, male high school dropouts are more likely to spend at least a year in prison than they are to get married, and spending time in prison has become more common than completing a four-year college degree or serving in the military.[13] In short, among some groups of black men, spending time in prison has become a normative life event.

Just as the number of adults who are incarcerated has grown, so has the number of children with a parent incarcerated. Figure 33.3 shows the number of

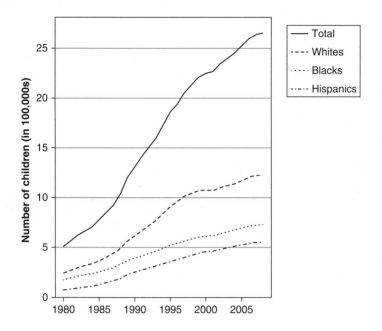

Figure 33.3 | Number of Minor Children with a Parent Incarcerated by Race, United States, 1980–2008

Source: Author calculations using data from the Survey of Inmates, Current Population Survey, and Bureau of Justice Statistics.

minor children with a parent incarcerated, by race. In 1980, roughly half a million children had a parent behind bars. By 2008, nearly 2.6 million children had at least one parent in prison or jail. While the number of children with a parent incarcerated has increased for all racial groups, black children experienced the fastest and largest growth in parental incarceration. In 1980 there were 245,000 black children with a parent in custody; by 2008, that figure had more than quintupled to over 1.23 million children, only slightly less than the combined total of white and Hispanic children.

Figure 33.4 illustrates how racial inequality in incarceration among adults is mirrored in racial inequality in children's chances of having a parent incarcerated. The figure shows the percentage of minor children with a parent incarcerated, by race. Between 1980 and 2008, the percentage of children in the United States with a parent behind bars increased from 0.8 percent to 3.6 percent. Yet, there is enormous racial inequality in parental incarceration for children. By

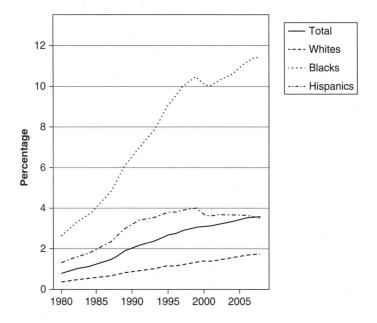

Figure 33.4 | Percentage of Minor Children with a Parent Incarcerated by Race, United States, 1980–2008

Source: Author calculations using data from the Survey of Inmates, Current Population Survey, and Bureau of Justice Statistics.

2008, nearly one in eight black children (roughly 12 percent) had a parent behind bars, compared to one in fifty white and one in twenty-five Hispanic children.[14]

Increases in the jail and prison population are largely attributable to nonviolent offenses. Figure 33.5 shows the percentage of minor children with a parent incarcerated, by offense type. While the percentage for any race-year group is the same as reported in Figure 33.4, we can investigate how much of parental incarceration is due to violent, drug, property, and other offense types. Several points are worth noting. First, violent offenses comprise no more than one-third of the total offenses for which parents are incarcerated. Second, the share of parents incarcerated for drug offenses has increased considerably since 1980, particularly for nonwhite parents. Drug offenses now explain one-third of parental incarceration for black children.

The risk of having a parent imprisoned at some point during childhood has also grown over time. Table 33.2 compares the risk of parental imprisonment by age seventeen for children born before penal system expansion and for children

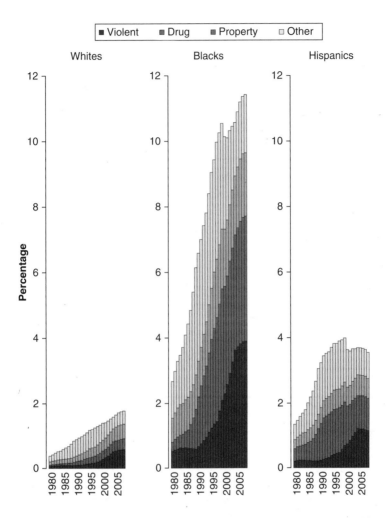

Figure 33.5 | Percentage of Minor Children with a Parent Incarcerated by Offense Type and Race, United States, 1980-2008

Source: Author calculations using data from the Survey of Inmates, Current Population Survey, and Bureau of Justice Statistics.

born during its height. In 1980, less than one-half percent of white children and less than 3 percent of black children experienced parental imprisonment by age seventeen. By 2009, those numbers had increased dramatically. Table 33.2 shows that approximately 4 percent of white children and about 25 percent of black children had a parent in prison at some point in their childhood. The numbers

Table 33.2 | Cumulative Risk of Parental (Paternal and Maternal) Imprisonment by Age Seventeen, by Parents' Educational Attainment, Percent of Children (in the Presence of Mortality)

	All	Less than High School	HS/GED	College
1980				
NH–White	0.44	1.27	0.49	0.14
NH–Black	2.89	5.52	2.23	1.17
Hispanic	1.72	2.31	1.26	0.99
1990				
NH–White	1.27	3.40	1.46	0.52
NH–Black	8.16	15.09	6.53	4.38
Hispanic	4.79	5.64	3.83	4.38
2000				
NH–White	3.02	7.49	3.37	1.26
NH–Black	19.97	37.64	16.73	9.39
Hispanic	10.34	13.32	8.76	5.37
2009				
NH–White	3.95	14.56	3.68	1.35
NH–Black	24.19	62.05	16.12	9.85
Hispanic	10.68	17.35	6.80	4.78

Note: NH stands for "non-Hispanic." The 1980 cohort is born 1960–1964; the 1990 cohort is born 1970–1974; the 2000 cohort is born 1980–1984; the 2009 cohort is born 1989–1993.

are staggering for children with poorly educated parents. Among recent cohorts of children of high school dropouts, 14.5 percent of white and 62 percent of black children had a parent who went to prison before the child reached age seventeen.

Other research has documented similar levels, and racial inequality in, exposure to parental incarceration. Data from the National Longitudinal Survey of Adolescent Health (Add Health) indicate that as many as 12 percent of recent cohorts of children have had a biological father in prison or jail at some point in their childhood.[15] And these findings are consistent with Wildeman's analysis of the risk of parental imprisonment, which finds that one-quarter of recent cohorts of black children can expect to have a parent imprisoned during their childhood.[16]

Mass incarceration is a uniquely modern American phenomenon that has disproportionately affected the lives of black men with low levels of education.

However, the reach of the criminal justice system extends well beyond offenders and now infiltrates the lives of children and other family members. Thus, mass incarceration has become an increasingly important institution to consider in the study of American family life.

The Collateral Consequences of Incarceration for Children and Families

A large and growing body of research investigates the consequences of criminal justice contact for individuals who have been incarcerated, their families, and their communities. Mass incarceration affects an inmate's community as well as an inmate's wages, employment, health, and political participation, as well as national election outcomes.[17] The impact of parental incarceration on children and families may be the least well understood, yet most consequential, implication of mass incarceration.[18]

Regardless of the crime committed, parental incarceration is likely to contribute to instability in family life. Over half of all prisoners have children under the age of eighteen, and about 45 percent of those parents were living with their children at the time they were sent to prison. In addition to the forced separation of incarceration, the post-release effects on economic opportunities leave formerly incarcerated parents less equipped to provide financially for their children. Incarceration is known to depress marriage and cohabitation among unwed parents.[19]

Many qualitative studies have effectively demonstrated how incarceration affects the family lives and children of those involved in the criminal justice system. By spending extended periods of time with inmates, former inmates, and their families, and conducting intensive interviews, researchers have gathered an impressive body of evidence documenting the effects of incarceration on families and children, carefully considering the pathways through which incarceration influences family life. Research draws attention to how removing individuals from their families, and the associated economic hardship and social stigma, influences parenting and partnering.

Hagan and Dinovitzer argue that the loss of a father to incarceration changes the family's status to that of a single-parent family, ushering in effects similar to those brought on by the death of a parent or divorce, such as financial instability as well as emotional and psychological effects on the children and partner.[20] These issues are examined in Donald Braman's book *Doing Time on the Outside*.[21] In the book, Braman provides an account of how mass incarceration affects family and community in Washington, DC. He demonstrates that incarceration levies financial costs that extend well beyond the individual incarcerated and that the psychological and social stigma associated with having a family member in prison or jail undermines the social fabric of urban communities.[22]

In *Doing Time Together*, Megan Comfort details the experiences of women attempting to maintain relationships with men at San Quentin State Prison.[23] Although the women she studied were free to leave San Quentin after their visits, the prison—and the men they loved who lived there—shaped their experiences and opportunities, burdening them financially and psychologically. Using the Fragile Families and Child Wellbeing Study, Amanda Geller and colleagues confirm, with quantitative data, the extent to which incarceration incapacitates fathers from the labor force, making them unable to contribute financially to their partners and children.[24]

While the financial effects of paternal incarceration may be greatest during periods of incapacitation, financial hardship affects previously incarcerated inmates and their families long after release.[25] In her book *My Baby's Father*, Maureen Waller demonstrates how men's poor economic opportunities—shaped by previous contact with the criminal justice system—structure their involvement in their children's lives.[26] Fathers' involvement in their children's lives may be curtailed, she argues, by their limited employment prospects and inability to contribute to the financial well-being of their children. Geller and colleagues also demonstrate that fathers' ability to contribute to the financial well-being of the family is curtailed even after release from prison or jail.[27]

Evidence suggests that fathers who have been incarcerated are much less likely to be cohabiting or married a year after their babies' birth.[28] Incarceration can also trigger higher risk of divorce or separation. Drawing on data from the National Longitudinal Survey of Youth (1979), Lopoo and Western find that the likelihood that a marriage will fail in the year a man is incarcerated is over three times higher than that for a man who is not incarcerated (13 percent compared to 4 percent).[29] Incarceration is thought to affect cohabitation and marriage directly through its incapacitative effect and indirectly through its implications on economic opportunities and social stigma.[30]

The effects of incarceration on children's well-being are only beginning to be understood. Children of incarcerated fathers are more likely to receive public assistance and more likely to experience material hardship, disruptive residential mobility, and greater risk for developmental outcomes such as aggressive behavior.[31] Children of incarcerated parents are commonly pushed into kinship care or formal foster care.[32] Arditti and colleagues find that families of inmates were at risk for financial and mental health instability even before incarceration, emphasizing how incarceration elevates the risks of hardship among the already vulnerable.[33]

Comfort finds that seeing a father arrested, visiting him in prison, and dealing with parental absence traumatizes children.[34] Children of incarcerated fathers,

Comfort argues, witness parental disempowerment and must contend with the emotional and psychological effects of their parent's abrupt removal as well as the quasi-imprisonment associated with the many rules and procedures involved in visiting a parent in correctional facilities. Nurse illustrates that incarcerated fathers' involvement in their children's lives is shaped by the children's mother and that hostility between young parents can have negative implications for children.[35] Wildeman demonstrates that recent and prior paternal incarceration is associated with significantly higher levels of physically aggressive behaviors for boys at age five.[36] In a review of existing research, Wakefield and Wildeman find that children who have had a parent incarcerated experience increases in mental health and behavioral problems as well as increases in the level of their physical aggression.[37]

Despite important insights gleaned from existing research, the social scientific and policy communities have been slow to respond to shifts in family life associated with mass incarceration and collect nationally representative data designed to investigate the implications of incarceration for families and children. Few national surveys collect information about reasons for father absence, and no national statistics exist on the number of children living in single-parent families because of parental incarceration. While data from Add Health and the Fragile Families and Child Well-Being Study have advanced our understanding of the effects of incarceration for families with young children, there is still much we do not know and cannot understand from existing large-scale data sources.

Children of incarcerated parents, particularly boys, are at greater risk of developmental delays and behavioral problems.[38] Paternal incarceration is associated with increased physical aggression for boys, thereby contributing to the intergenerational disadvantage fathers and sons are likely to experience. The effects of paternal incarceration are not confined to increased aggression; children with fathers incarcerated also exhibit increased attention problems, and the experience of parental incarceration is very different and more pronounced than other forms of father absence.

Children of incarcerated parents are also at significant risk of homelessness and food insecurity. A research brief on fragile families in America by *The Future of Children* shows that father incarceration is associated with increased odds of child homelessness even after accounting for a multitude of important social background characteristics like family income, social welfare support, characteristics of the mother, and other measures of housing insecurity.[39] Race differences in child homelessness are an artifact of increasing racial inequality in imprisonment. The risk of homelessness for black children is particularly high. Compared to children who never experienced paternal incarceration, the odds of black youth experiencing housing instability are 144 percent higher if they have a father incarcerated. Cox and Wallace show that the likelihood for food insecurity increases by 4 to 15 percentage points in households with adults and children where at least one parent has been incarcerated.[40]

CONCLUSION

A growing body of research implicates the criminal justice system in structuring and reproducing social inequality in the lives of American children. Almost half of all youths in the correctional system have a parent in the adult system,[41] and the likelihood of incarceration is five to six times greater among children with a parent in prison than it is for children of never-incarcerated parents.[42] Father absence is associated with increased aggressive behaviors and attention problems for children who have fathers incarcerated.[43]

The intergenerational effect of having a parent behind bars disrupts and alters the life-course trajectories of children. Parental imprisonment decreases the educational attainment of children in emerging adulthood.[44] Youth from these families are cumulatively disadvantaged. The social exclusion they face includes homelessness, lack of health care coverage, and political nonparticipation, all of which severely disconnects these children from important means of transitioning to adulthood.[45] Mass incarceration, particularly for nonviolent offenses, reproduces social inequality, thereby ensuring a vicious cycle wherein criminal justice contact does not diminish across generations.[46]

Current and former inmates constitute a Weberian status group: in particular, their social and economic differentiation, due to a lack of power and prestige to alter their current and future lives, solidifies them as a social class whose life chances have been fundamentally altered due to criminal justice contact.[47] Because of reduced opportunities for employment and housing, the children of inmates and former inmates are indirectly implicated as "legal bystanders" subjected to the effects of the legal system.[48] This invisible inequality produces a number of negative familial and community outcomes, especially as over half of all fathers expect to live with their children and families when they exit the criminal justice system.[49] While the long reach of the criminal justice system affects inmates and their families, newer research suggests that parole supervision may generate significant residential mobility. Harding and colleagues find that, among Michigan parolees, less than one-third of former inmates return to an address within half a mile of their pre-prison residence, indicating that intermediate sanctions—jail, treatment programs, and residential facilities for parole rule violators—produce upward mobility in the lives of these disadvantaged men and women.[50] Despite this positive and promising side effect of criminal justice contact, the overwhelming experience of incarceration is largely negative for families and communities.

The marked status of having criminal justice contact extends into the lives of children and lowers the quantity and quality of social capital they will receive. Scholars of social inequality have documented a host of negative educational and social outcomes for children associated with different parenting styles. Lareau shows that "concerted cultivation"—practices and opportunities that promote, and stimulate, the cognitive and social development of children—is largely exercised by middle-class families, ensuring the solidification of their social advantage.[51] Lower-class families, however, follow a path of "natural growth" that allows children to structure their own time and resources and does not imbue them with the same levels of social capital enjoyed by middle- and upper-class families. (You can learn more about Lareau's approach in the CCF Brief at the end of Chapter 31.) Because incarcerated men and women are marked and stigmatized for having a criminal record long after their sentence is completed,[52] the social inequality associated with parental incarceration will affect children during their formative years. Social policies are needed to address and to mitigate the disruptive effects of parental imprisonment in the lives of disadvantaged children.

NOTES

1. Please direct correspondence to Bryan Sykes (bsykes1@depaul.edu) and Becky Pettit (bpettit@u.washington.edu).
2. Wilson (1987).
3. Pew Charitable Trusts (2008).
4. Garland (2001).
5. Blumstein and Cohen (1973).
6. Glaze (2010); Guerino, Harrison, and Sabol (2011).
7. Whitman (2003).
8. Walmsley (2011).
9. Mauer (2006); Tonry (1995); Western (2006).
10. Western (2006).
11. *Ibid.*
12. See also Pettit and Western (2004).
13. *Ibid.*
14. Pettit, Sykes, and Western (2009).
15. Foster and Hagan (2007).
16. Wildeman (2009).
17. Alexander (2010); Clear (2007); Johnson and Raphael (2009); Massoglia (2008); Pettit (2012); Rosenfeld et al. (2011); Sykes and Piquero (2009); Uggen and Manza (2002); Western (2006).
18. Hagan and Dinovitzer (1999).

19. Edin, Nelson, and Paranal (2004); Lopoo and Western (2005); Western and Pettit (2005); Western, Lopoo, and McLanahan (2004); Wilson (1987).

20. Hagan and Dinovitzer (1999).

21. Braman (2004).

22. *Ibid.*

23. Comfort (2008).

24. Geller et al. (2009).

25. Comfort (2008).

26. Waller (2006).

27. Geller et al. (2011).

28. Western et al. (2004).

29. Lopoo and Western (2005).

30. See, for example, Edin and Kefalas (2005).

31. Geller et al. (2012).

32. Freudenberg (2001).

33. Arditti (2012); Arditti, Smock, and Parkman (2005).

34. Comfort (2008).

35. Nurse (2004).

36. Wildeman (2010).

37. Wakefield and Wildeman (2011).

38. Geller, Garfinkel, and Western (2011); Geller et al. (2012); Wildeman (2010).

39. Wildeman (2014).

40. Cox and Wallace (2013).

41. Mumola (2000).

42. Springer, Lynch, and Rubin (2000).

43. Geller et al. (2012); Wildeman (2010).

44. Cho (2010); Foster and Hagan (2009); Hagan and Foster (2012).

45. Foster and Hagan (2007).

46. Wildeman and Western (2010).

47. Wakefield and Uggen (2010).

48. Comfort (2008).

49. Foster and Hagan (2009).

50. Harding, Morenoff, and Herbert (2013).

51. Lareau (2003).

52. Pager (2007); Alexander (2010).

In Other Words

DOING TIME = DOING GENDER

Girl w/ Pen!, November 15, 2010

Virginia E. Rutter

We love to puzzle over the rise in employment for women vs. the decline in employment for men. Is it about psychology? (Leads to speculation about men's feelings of inadequacy.) Is it interpersonal? (Ends in "What does this mean for marriage?" ... or "How can we relate this to attachment parenting?").

But the big, giant, huge social forces of racism plus capitalism might help too: to wit, today the Center for Economic and Policy Research (CEPR) has published an analysis of Bureau of Justice Statistics data that indicates that incarceration in America reduces our male employment rate by 1.5 to 1.7 percent. The paper,

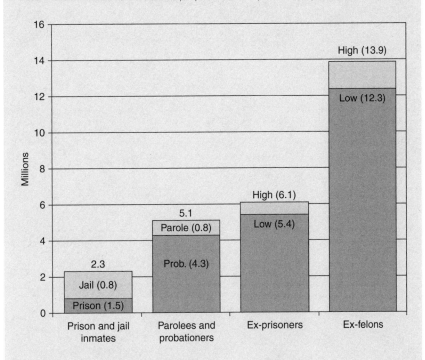

Figure 1 | Estimates of Correctional Populations, 2008

Source: CEPR analysis of BJS data.

"Ex-Offenders and the Labor Market," follows the CEPR's paper "The High Budget-ary Cost of Incarceration" that was released last June.

Each year we produce around 700,000 "ex-offenders" . . . and those people's prospects on the job market are undermined. Meanwhile, more than 90 percent of those ex-offenders are men. And a disproportionate number of them are African American.

"It isn't just that we have the highest incarceration rate in the world, we have created a situation over the last 30 years where about *one in eight men* is an ex-offender," said John Schmitt, a senior economist at CEPR and a co-author of the report with Kris Warner, also from CEPR.

Consider this: When you are thinking about gender and trends in employment, consider that in America, *doing time* is a social institution we've organized for doing gender. It is another one of our "man laws." ▐

PART EIGHT

Unfinished Gender Revolution

34

Betwixt and Be Tween

Gender Contradictions among Middle Schoolers

Barbara J. Risman and Elizabeth Seale

This research is based on interviews with middle-school children in a south-eastern city of the United States. In this paper, we ask whether the gender revolution has freed these children from being constrained by stereotypes. We find that both boys and girls are still punished for going beyond gender expectations, but boys much more so than girls. For girls, participation in tradition-ally masculine activities, such as sports and academic competition, is now quite acceptable and even encouraged by both parents and peers. We find, indeed, that girls are more likely to tease each other for being too girly than for being a sports star. Girls still feel pressure, however, to be thin and to dress in feminine ways, to "do gender" in their self-presentation. Boys are quickly teased for doing any behavior that is traditionally considered feminine. Boys who deviate in any way from traditional masculinity are stigmatized as "gay." Whereas girls can and do participate in a wide range of activities without being teased, boys consistently avoid activities defined as female to avoid peer harassment. Homophobia, at least toward boys, is alive and well in middle school.

Today parents and educators tell children that they can be whatever they want to be. Children are taught that women and men and whites and blacks are equal.[1] Changes in gender norms have created opportunities for girls that never before existed. For instance, in school, Title IX has encouraged girls' participation in athletics. But are boys and girls actually free to construct personal identities that leave behind gender stereotypes, even when their parents and teachers encourage them to do so?

How free are middle-school boys and girls to form identities outside the constraining gender expectations that have traditionally disadvantaged girls in the public sphere and repressed boys from exploring their emotions? We approached this subject by interviewing forty-four middle-school children in a mid-sized southeastern city. They were not yet teenagers but were already adapting to pressures to view the world through the eyes of their peers. Middle school is a time when peers become a crucial reference group. Conformity to group norms becomes central to popularity, fitting in, and self-image.[2] What do the experiences and perceptions of these preadolescent kids (tween-agers) tell us about growing up in contemporary society? How much have their expectations and self-images transcended traditional gender norms?

Peers become centrally important as tween-agers face new and complicated situations in which they must negotiate friendships, issues of sexuality, self-image, conflict, stratification, cliques, and the like. In this so-called "tween" culture, these kids try to make sense of things in their daily lives by using new tools as well as old ones taken from "cultural tool kits." The lives of tween-agers provide a glimpse into how contemporary definitions of race and gender are shaping the next generation, and what new realities the children themselves may be creating at a time when their core identities are developing.

Our data suggest that American middle-school children, at least in the mid-sized southeastern city we examined, have adopted an ideal of equality. Nearly all the kids say that men and women are equal, and that race no longer matters, or at least that it shouldn't. These children have been raised in a society that posits the ideals of gender and racial equality, and the kids seem to accept and believe in those ideals, at least when you scratch the surface of their opinions. But that ideal of equality is not what they experience in their real lives, and at least half of them recognize and identify contradictions between what should be and what is.

Despite their acceptance of the rhetoric of gender equality, these tween-agers hold very gender-stereotypical beliefs about boys, although not about girls. Any male gender nonconformity, where boys engage in behaviors or activities traditionally considered female, is taken as evidence that the boy is "gay." As a result, boys are afraid to cross any gender boundaries for fear of having that stigma attached to them. By contrast, the lives of girls are much less constricted by stereotypes about femininity. In fact, girls are more likely to be teased for being "too girly" than for being a tomboy. Girls still police each other's behavior, but the rules of femininity that they enforce now seem to focus almost exclusively on clothes, makeup, diet, and bodily presentation. The girls in our study still "do gender,"[3] but mostly by how they look.

RESEARCH ON GENDER AND YOUTH

Research on how traditional femininity constrains girls is contradictory. Some studies suggest that girls are viewed as less feminine if they participate in sports. Others argue that athleticism is no longer seen as incompatible with femininity and may indeed be part of the "ideal girlhood" package.[4]

In their study of middle-school cheerleaders, Adams and Bettis also point to fundamental contradictions in the contemporary ideal of girlhood. Traditional feminine characteristics like passivity and docility, they argue, have been replaced by independence, assertiveness, and strength, and participation in sports is considered an "essential component of girl culture today."[5] At the same time, when it comes to popularity, attractiveness trumps all other attributes. Cheerleading, in keeping up with changing gender expectations, has incorporated the new ideals of girlhood, including "confidence, rationality, risk-taking, athleticism, independence, and fearlessness."[6] But it continues to attract girls who value feminine looks and who are interested in attracting boys. Becoming a cheerleader is one way to cope with the contradictions of girlhood because it allows girls to be athletic and adopt some desired masculine traits, while retaining feminine characteristics that the girls enjoy and that make them desirable to boys.[7]

A few studies address how race and class differences among young women affect their standards of femininity. Bettie found class- and race-specific versions of femininity among high-school girls.[8] Lower-class white and nonwhite girls adopted a more sexualized style of femininity than white middle-class girls. Bettie suggested that *las chicas*, the Latina girls, adapted a style of femininity that emphasized their ethnicity, preferring darker and more visible makeup and tight-fitting clothes. Working-class white girls also generally wore more makeup than middle-class students. While school officials and middle-class peers commonly interpreted these bodily expressions as evidence of "looser" sexual morals, Bettie found that these girls were less interested in romantic attachments than outsiders supposed, and that their styles of bodily presentation had more to do with incorporating racial and community markers into their gender displays. For example, working-class white girls expressed resistance to middle-class culture by "dressing down" in torn jeans, whereas Mexican American girls, feeling that their brown skin was already perceived as a "dressed down" appearance, would dress "up" in an effort to deny any link between color and poverty. Bettie also found that although these girls presented a very sexualized version of femininity, they did not want to or expect to lead traditional lives as at-home mothers and wives and they were in favor of gender equality for adults.

Many studies of middle- and high-school girls find strong evidence of pressures to be attractive to boys.[9] Lemish finds that widely different modes of femininity are acceptable among preadolescent girls, as long as the girl is also "pretty." One of the paradoxes of contemporary girlhood is that there are confusing and conflicting messages about what a girl should be like, as well as what type of girl should be (de)valued.

There is very little latitude or tolerance for boys to behave in ways that have been traditionally labeled as girlish. Engaging in any traditionally feminine activity, from dancing well to knitting to playing the piano, opens boys up to being taunted as gay. Usually it is boys who tease other boys, but sometimes girls do as well. Researchers suggest that homophobia is not merely antihomosexual prejudice. It also reinforces sharp gender divisions through the deployment of fear. This is seen particularly at the high-school level, but some research suggests it is also evident in elementary school and in middle school.[10] Thorne found that by the fourth grade, "fag" is sometimes used as an insult. But Plummer points out that homophobic insults used in grade school do not actually carry sexual meaning.[11] Rather they are used to tease boys who are different, including boys viewed as effeminate. The use of homophobic terms as insults, Plummer maintains, increases with adolescence. Eder and her coauthors discuss homophobic insults among middle-school boys as a ritualistic way to assert masculine dominance, as a way to insult and further isolate the lowest on the peer hierarchy, and as a self-defense mechanism in identifying oneself as heterosexual and normal.[12] Their research illustrates the intense anxiety over peer approval and acceptance, and how that fosters bullying in middle school for both girls and boys, although more so for boys. By middle school, any sign of gender boundary crossing by boys is taken as signifying homosexuality and elicits strong homophobic teasing.

As boys grow older, the gender expectations appear to become more rigid and regulated. Among high-school youth, masculinity is defined as toughness: a potential if not an inclination for violence, lack of emotion, and sexual objectification of girls. By high school, it is a major insult for a boy to be called gay, and the label may be applied to any boy who is different from his male peers in some way, any boy who is considered feminine or unpopular, any boy who is a target for being bullied. Among young people, the word *gay* has acquired such a negative connotation that it is commonly used to describe anything that is bad, undesirable, or "lame."[13]

Pascoe (2005) identifies a "fag" discourse through which high-school boys use the term as an epithet on a daily basis. Any boy, she notes, may be temporarily labeled a "faggot," and so all boys continually struggle to avoid being stigmatized. With the possibility of being called a faggot only an insult away, constant work is required to be sufficiently masculine to avoid the label. In fact, the primary use of homophobia in policing the activities of boys is not to root out, expose, or punish potential homosexuals, but rather to regulate gender behavior and narrowly channel boys toward accepted activities and away from others.

It is not clear whether or how this use of homophobia to police boys' gender varies according to race. In Pascoe's (2007) study of fag discourse among high-school boys in a working-class California school, she found that behaviors that incur a fag stigma for white boys, such as attention to fashion, or dancing with another man, are accepted as normal by nonwhite boys. She suggests that the use of homophobic insults is more common among white than nonwhite teenagers.

Froyum studied an underclass African American summer program in a large East Coast city, however, and found heavy policing of heterosexuality among both boys and girls.[14] She argues that these impoverished urban kids use hetero-sexuality to carve out some self-esteem from the only stratification in which they can feel superior to someone else, that they take solace in the fact that "at least they aren't gay."

Methods

The authors and several graduate students interviewed forty-four middle-school students. We asked the children a set of questions, told them stories and solicited their responses, and had them draw pictures and write poems in order to find out what these boys and girls thought about their own lives, their friends, and their interactions with peers at school. We wanted to delve into middle-school students' expectations around gender, to examine how it feels to grow up in a society that proclaims gender equality and encourages "girl power."

We wanted to find out if children today still see limitations based on their sex, or if they really feel they live in a post-feminist world. We asked about family life, friendship, popularity, cliques, pressures to conform to stereotypes around being a boy or a girl, what "girl power" means, and attitudes regarding racial inequality. This was a diverse group of children, mostly white and African American, and we paid careful attention to whether the answers to our questions differed by race and/or ethnicity.

The interviews took place between the fall of 2003 and the summer of 2004. They typically lasted between one and two hours and were recorded. Respon-dents were in the sixth, seventh, and eighth grades and ranged in age from eleven to fourteen. The children were recruited at a racially integrated magnet middle school, a diverse YWCA after-school program and summer camp, and an urban, mostly black Girls' Club. All attended public middle schools in a mid-sized city in the southeastern United States. Because we did not get data on many topics of interest from two of the middle schoolers, we reduced our sample to be discussed here to forty-two. The pseudonyms and specific demographic information for each student are listed in a chart in the appendix at the end of this chapter. Most were middle class, although a few were from working-class or upper-middle-class professional families. We paid careful attention to any racial differences in the responses. But having only four nonwhite boys, two of whom were black, hampered our ability to examine racial or ethnic differences among boys. We hoped to learn something about what it is like to grow up in today's world. Interviewers asked the children many questions. How are you similar to other boys/girls? How are you different from other girls/boys? We also asked about likes and dislikes, activities, friendship groups, cliques at school, and favorite subjects. Many of our questions dealt specifically with the children's perceptions of gender. What does it mean when someone is called a "girly-girl"? What does it mean when a girl is called a tomboy? Is there a word (like *girly* for prissy boys) that refers to boys who are really tough or macho? Is there a word for a boy who is quiet and thoughtful and likes to do arts and crafts, one who likes the kinds of activities that girls more often like to do?

Using a hypothetical scenario to draw them out, we asked students to describe what their lives would be like as the opposite sex. We asked: "If an alien with supernatural powers came into your bedroom one night and turned you into a boy/girl, how would your life be different in the morning?" We also asked: "How would your life be different if an alien made you gay?"

We asked students to write a poem or paragraph beginning with "If I were a boy/girl . . ." If they preferred, they could draw a picture elaborating on that theme. We also explored their acceptance of nontraditional gender behavior by using vignettes and asking how they or their peers would react to a person who crossed a gender boundary.

To understand the boundary of female behavior, we used this hypothetical story: "Pretend for a moment that there is a girl in your grade named Jasmine. Jasmine is very athletic and loves competition. She decides that she wants to start an all-girls football club at your school. She places posters all over student lockers and the hallways promoting the girls' club and asking for players. Then she approaches the principal and asks if she can start the team." For male gender nonconformity, we constructed this story: "Imagine that there is a boy in your grade named Marcus. He loves to dance. He has taken gymnastics since he was little, and is very good. Now that he is older, he wants to be a cheerleader. He knows that [Name of University] has male cheerleaders and he wants to join that squad when he goes to college." Students who seemed mature enough were asked about homosexuality, including how they and their peers would react to a gay student.

Due to time constraints, variations in maturity levels, and the occasional tape malfunction, we do not have responses to all of these questions from every student. Although we do have a wealth of information from almost every student to utilize for analysis, with such open-ended qualitative data it is very challenging to compare responses across kids for interpretation.

There were several limitations to the methods we employed. Because we did not directly observe interactions between the middle schoolers, we had to rely on what they told us, and how they explained their thoughts on boys, girls, gender nonconformity, gender expectations, homosexuality, heterosexuality, and life in general. Nonetheless, we believe the method is useful because the thoughts and feelings of these preadolescents help us understand how they experience and react to peer pressure. Moreover, in one-on-one interviews, children and adults may reveal more about their thoughts and feelings than they would if others were present.

CONTRADICTIONS AND EQUALITY RHETORIC

When we asked these students questions about gender or race, their responses indicated that most have assimilated both the feminist-inspired ideology that women and men are equal and the post-civil rights ideology that all races are equal. Nine out of twelve male students and seventeen of twenty-two female students (for whom we have appropriate data) professed some belief in gender equality. For example, Molly finished the phrase "If I were a boy" in a poem that read: "If I were a boy, / Nothing should be different, / Because all people are equal." For the same exercise, another student, Marney, wrote that "I think I would be treated mainly the same by parents, friends, teachers." Brady similarly argued that "all people should be treated the same," although he felt life would be "very freaky" if he were turned into a girl. Micah told us that girl power means that girls now have every right that men do. The kids appeared to believe that males and females either were equal in reality or ought to be.

Despite this equality rhetoric, there were serious inconsistencies in their responses. For example, when the kids answered questions about what would happen if they were turned into the opposite sex, most expressed a belief that gender stereotypes were based in biology, despite earlier declarations that "we are all the same." With these questions, we found that many kids were well aware of the consequences for not conforming to gender norms.

This contradiction between the rhetoric of equality and more experience-biased appraisals of gender inequality was further revealed when we asked the children to place cards with occupations written on them under the categories "men," "women," and "both." They were first asked to place their cards according to whether men or women are more likely to hold each job, and afterward according to how they think it should be. This activity showed us whether students felt there was occupational segregation by sex and how they judged it. None of the boys and only five out of twenty-three girls thought that men and women were equally distributed among all occupations. Six of twelve boys and ten of twenty-two girls told us that all occupations should be distributed equally among men and women. The others, who believed gender segregation was appropriate, usually explained that men and women were different. In most cases, when asked how it should be versus how it really is, students put more occupations under the category of "both." Nurse, secretary, and librarian were commonly thought to be women's jobs, whereas police officer, firefighter, mechanic, and engineer were often seen as men's jobs. Sixteen out of thirty-four students expressed the belief that men and women were or should be "equal" and that girls and women should be able to do anything they want.

These children, even those consistently committed to equality in theory, however, often expressed contradictory views in other parts of the interview, displaying a belief in the essential differences between boys and girls or holding their peers to gendered expectations. In many cases, advances in ideology were not consistently guiding reported behavior.

BETWEEN TOMBOY AND GIRLY-GIRL

We asked boys and girls to answer questions about what girly-girls and tomboys are like, how girls think they are similar to and different from other girls, and what boys thought would be different if they were "turned into a girl."

Nearly all the students could describe a typical girly-girl and a tomboy. Many boys and girls alike defined girly-girls as preoccupied with appearances, in contrast to tomboys. One female student, Kay, described girly-girls in these terms: "'Oh my gosh!' totally into stuff like that. Always having their hair, you know, down like that, you know, kind of prissy. Want to wear high-heeled shoes all the time. Laughing and flirting and stuff like that." Marney, who stated that she did not consider herself a girly-girl, responded that "they're afraid to get dirty, you're obsessed with your hair, you like to wear makeup a lot." Kay indicated that girly-girl meant being obsessed with boys or talking about boys. Although this description was less common than references to appearance in characterizing girly-girls, romance-centered behavior (e.g., being "boy-crazy" or obsessed with boys, flirting, talking about boys, or gossiping about relationships) was mentioned by four girls and two boys as characterizing girly-girls. Several more mentioned such behavior when discussing "typical" girls in general.

Nearly 80 percent of those who responded provided what we interpret as a negative description of a girly-girl, and the rest gave neutral responses. Of the nine males, five gave negative descriptions and four gave neutral descriptions of girly-girls. A neutral response, for instance, might refer to girly-girls as wearing pink often, without indicating that wearing a lot of pink is objectionable.

There was not a single overtly positive definition of a girly-girl. No one told us, for instance, that girly-girls are kind, looked up to, or even desirable to boys. We did not count the suggestion that girly-girls are the most popular as being positive in itself, because such comments were often paired with expressions of disdain for the "popular" kids.

Common descriptions of girly-girls included fear of getting dirty, breaking a nail, or getting sweaty. Seven girls and two boys used the word *prissy*. Samantha suggested that a girly-girl is "prissy," wears makeup every day, and is obsessed with hair. She mimics such a person: "'Oh my gosh, it has to be perfect. I have to put hairspray in it.' Glitter, gel, whatever. Like, always running around scream-ing [high-pitched], 'Oh my God, a spider! Oh my gosh, my nail broke!' Just little things that are like your nail breaking. Crying over it or something. That's a girly-girl."

Girls were, overall, more censorious, but boys sometimes described girly-girls in a similarly contemptuous fashion. With a disgusted expression on his face, Jason told his interviewer, "To me, it means makeup and a whole lot of other girlie perfumes and . . . lipstick and mascara and eye shadow and other makeup that they put on that I don't even want to mention."

At the same time, when researchers asked explicitly whether "being a girly-girl is a good or bad thing" the kids were divided. Karlin, for example, initially por-trayed girly-girls in a contemptuous fashion, saying that they are girls who would say, "'Guys are better. I don't do sports. I might get my shoes wet.' Or like, 'I can't kick a ball. I try to look good but I don't have any specific talent.'" But when asked directly whether being a girly-girl is a bad or good thing, her response was that it depends on the person. If they are selfish, that is bad, but if this is just how they were brought up, then "it's fine."

Several kids indicated that being girly made a girl popular, whereas others (and sometimes even the same respondents) suggested that it was annoying, or that they themselves did not like these people. Mona talked about the "bad preps"—girls who dye their hair blonde, wear too much makeup, wear revealing clothes, and draw their eyebrows in after waxing them. She reported that she and her friends despise this group and frequently make jokes about them. But in other parts of the interview she associated girl preps with playing a lot of sports. Girly-girls were often defined in the abstract as girls who do not play sports, but in actual references to peers, being a girly-girl and playing sports were not always incompatible.

Although students tended to associate girly-girls with being popular and being more feminine, stereotypical girls were subject to substantial ridicule by girls and boys alike in these interviews. None of the female respondents identified themselves to the interviewer as exclusively girly-girl. And all three of the girls who did say they thought of themselves as at least part girly, also described themselves as partly or occasionally tomboyish (and none of these girls considered herself a "typical girl"). This reflects the negative connotations associated with being a girly-girl, which was usually defined contemptuously or with reference to activities and concerns generally seen as narcissistic and trivial (e.g., wearing too much makeup too often, afraid of breaking a nail, excessive shopping).

These disdainful descriptions of what it means to be a girly-girl tell us that too much emphasis on femininity is looked down upon at this age level. No matter where they fell on the girly-girl/tomboy continuum, the girls saw themselves as different from the category of the prototypical feminine girl, who was seen as narcissistic, vain, and silly. They did not want to be identified as that type of girl. But in the process of rejecting this stereotype for themselves, they sometimes conferred it upon others as the prototypical teenage girl.

The girls in our study also felt that girls should display some level of femininity, especially when it comes to looks. Several girls, black and white, indicated that being too much of a tomboy could be a bad thing. Karlin, for instance, chastised tomboys who fail to "recognize the fact that they're a girl." According to her, playing sports should not get in the way of "being a girl."

Kerri indicated that it is okay to be girlish if one is athletic as well. She asserted that "there are a lot" of girly-girls, although she did not personally know very many:

> Yeah, there are a lot. I don't know a lot of girly-girls. I know I don't mind wearing skirts and I don't mind wearing makeup but I'm not a girly-girl. And I know what a girly-girl is. It's when you're all obsessed with makeup and looking good and I mean all the girls I know play at least two sports and they own makeup, and they're, I mean, my room is blue and pink and yellow but you'd have to look around and see all my soccer pictures and all my basketball trophies. And I mean if you just looked in my room, didn't see any trophies, you'd think I was a really big girly-girl.

At least five kids indicated that being a tomboy was positive in some respects, but no one indicated that tomboys were considered the popular or privileged girls. One female middle schooler suggested a tomboy might have difficulty getting a boyfriend. In the interviews, being a tomboy was associated with being athletic, although girls could be athletic without being seen as a tomboy. It is also noteworthy that only three girls identified themselves as tomboys but not at all girly, although this was more than the number who considered themselves "girly-girls."

Most girls clearly do not place themselves in either of these two extreme categories, although they often suggest that they have characteristics associated with both. These two extremes bracket the entire spectrum of gender meanings for girls, but do not represent the majority of identities. Some girls embraced the label of tomboy (often while simultaneously embracing aspects of bodily femininity) as a strategy to avoid negative associations with being female. For example, one girl told us "we've actually made up, like those ten girls, we've made up the tomboy club because we don't mind competing against the guys for stuff, and we, I mean I actually liked being called a tomboy because then I knew people didn't just look at me as a girl. That they could actually see me as doing something more than being just a ballet dancer."

Most girls do adopt some aspects of traditional femininity. They wear makeup or lip gloss, enjoy shopping for and dressing up in gendered clothes, or like talking about boys. This became apparent in the interviews where girls discussed how they were similar to other girls, what they liked to do, and how they spent their time. It was also apparent in some of the field notes written by interviewers, who noted details about how the students dressed and presented themselves.

The female middle schoolers criticized only extreme forms of this femininity, such as wearing lots of makeup every day, dressing in too revealing a fashion, worrying about looking good all of the time, and especially having a girly-girl identity. Jamie, for example, said she is similar to other girls in that she likes clothes and guys, but says she is not girly like the ones who are "prim" and "afraid to get dirty, to get down and goof around."

When it comes to untangling the gender expectations that these middle schoolers hold and perceive, contradictions abound. In one part of her interview, Lola said:

> There's just some traits that all girls have in common. . . . Ability to accessorize [laughs]. Just stuff. You can always tell who's a boy and who's a girl. It's different. Like boys like video games and girls like makeup. . . . Boys are rougher. Girls are more into sitting and talking. And boys are more into going outside and playing Frisbee or something.

But she also asserted that girls would love to have their own football team. It is clear that girls perceive pressures both to be identifiably feminine and to take on some traditionally masculine characteristics like assertiveness, fearlessness, rationality, and independence in order to be taken seriously.

While girls face less restrictive norms for gender-appropriate behavior, there still seem to be limitations, especially in regard to ideals of beauty. Girls are still expected to demonstrate a type of femininity, although one that is no longer threatened by participation in traditionally male-dominated activities. Our story about a girl who wants to start a football team elicited a few worries that she might be teased because she did not play well, but there was little concern that Jasmine would be teased for violating norms of femininity. As Malcom pointed out in her study of softball players, girls who play sports run the risk of being seen as or teased for being incompetent as athletes rather than for displaying behavior inappropriate for girls.[15]

The girls in this study felt a girl can ignore many gender boundaries (in fact playing sports is no longer even considered a gender boundary). But in their view, girls are still expected to display some markers of traditional femininity. Put another way, appropriate femininity does not require avoidance of traditionally masculine activities, but it is accomplished through attention to how the girl displays her body. Femininity has become very body-centered and many respondents simply equate femininity with "looks." But it is interesting that even on this dimension, girls tend to look down on and avoid extreme femininity. For example, several girls criticized pop stars for dressing in tight, revealing clothing, although they also saw this as a requirement for celebrity.

We only have very suggestive data in our sample on how gender norms varied by race. But in three interviews, white girls criticized black girls for overly emphasizing the sexualized aspects of femininity—dressing in tight, revealing clothing, wearing inappropriate makeup, and engaging in inappropriate bodily display. Kerri related the following story about a black peer:

> And the girls, we won't really make fun of her but we just [ask] "Why? Why is she wearing that?" Because like if she combed her hair and put on some makeup and wore pants she'd be very pretty. But she doesn't. She has to wear the tightest skirts. She never combs her hair. She'll put on makeup but she doesn't put it on right. She'll put on like this dark blue and like gold mascara and she doesn't look right and she's trying, but she's not using the right stuff. So all of us got together one recess and we, not to be mean, but to say okay we could give her a makeover and this one girl, who could really draw. We said okay, we're gonna give her—if we could give her a makeover this is what we'd do. Some girl said okay I'd pick out all her makeup and I'd tweeze her eyebrows and I'd like shave her legs or something. And one girl said, I'd get her on Slim-Fast. And all this stuff. And like she drew a picture of what she'd look like if we all worked with her and she looked kind of looked a lot like me,

but kinda, it looked like all the girls had given a part of themselves to her so that was really fun and we thought if she did all of those things she'd look like that.

We also have suggestive data that African Americans girls sometimes try to adapt "white" beauty norms. Three black or biracial girls indicated that they wished they had physical traits more often seen in Caucasian women. For example, Joleesa, an African American sixth grader, wished she had long, soft, smooth hair and blue eyes. We do not have a large enough sample to have strong evidence of racialized femininity, but we do find suggestions that white and black girls value white markers of femininity, and that black girls are criticized by white girls if they exhibit more sexualized forms of femininity.

When boys were asked how they would be different if turned into a girl, several indicated they would act the way girly-girls are described. Four boys thought they would act "girly" in some way. Boys spoke of girls with stereotypical language. Tyrone drew a picture of a woman's makeup table and explained:

> I drew a vanity, which is a mirror with bulbs around it, and it usually has makeup and perfume around it, and then I drew a little girl stretching since it's been a long day and she's about to go out to the movies with her friends. . . . I drew the vanity because they like wearing tons of makeup.

By referring to an exaggerated, abstract notion of femininity when asked to imagine themselves as a girl or to describe girls in general, boys are implicitly defining masculinity as the opposite of this girly-girl femininity. Girls as well as boys distance themselves from this feminized, stereotypical "other" when they try to construct valued images of themselves.

POLICING MASCULINITY

Our respondents described preadolescent masculinity in very narrow and uniform ways. The most common response was that boys like sports (sometimes specific sports like football and basketball were emphasized). Other responses included competitiveness, hating losing to a girl, playing video games, general rowdiness, and being different from girls in that girls want to "really impress people and boys want to have their own way." When boys talked about their interests, they commonly emphasized sports, video games, and competing with male friends. But they almost never mentioned "liking" girls, flirting with girls, or talking about girls. It appears that at this age, romantic interests figure prominently among girls, but not among boys.

A boy who is perceived as too feminine is subject to much more ridicule than a girl who is seen as either overly masculine or overly feminine. If a boy tends to be quiet, shy, bookish, artistic, and/or nonassertive, his sexuality is called into question and he loses respect among other boys. We saw this in the way students made sense of our hypothetical story about Marcus, the boy who wants to be a cheerleader. We asked students whether Marcus should be allowed to join a cheerleading squad when he gets to high school, whether he would be teased by others, and whether the student her/himself would remain friends with Marcus, even if he were teased.

Many pointed out that Marcus would be the target of substantial ridicule because not many boys are cheerleaders.[16] In Lorenzo's opinion, "yeah [Marcus should be allowed to join a cheerleading squad], but um, he's probably gonna get made fun of by like a lot of boys." Asked what the boys would say, Lorenzo responded, "Like um, they're like homosexual or something." Krista told us that "people think that a male cheerleader is always gay, and, I mean, people would make fun of him. Or if he does stuff that people only think girls should do." Deirdre replied that the kids would call Marcus a sissy, and the boys especially would "call him gay." She also suggested that even if they had been friends, she would not stay "close friends" with him because "everyone [would be] calling him gay, and if I hang around him, they'd be like, ew you're gay too." Other questions also revealed the middle-schoolers' fear of peer disapproval. For instance, when we asked Samantha if she would still dance if she were turned into a boy, she responded "probably not" because she would be "made fun of."

Deviating from masculine norms inevitably led to teasing, according to student reports. While only two kids suggested that a tomboy might have her heterosexuality questioned, many suggested that a boy who liked girl-type activities would be called gay. Some of the terms the students applied to girlish boys were *wimps, tomgirls, weird, geeks, weak,* and *punk.* Because of the stigma associated with being considered feminine in any way, it is not surprising that some girls described themselves as tomboys, but not a single boy described himself in any way as girly. A few female students, however, indicated that some of the girls would appreciate such a boy, even though other boys would make fun of him. The threat of being stigmatized as gay or a faggot plays a big part in policing and enforcing masculinity.

POLICING HETEROSEXUALITY

Antigay sentiment is widespread among these youth, although there was a total confusion between sexual preference and gender behavior, which led to very low tolerance for gender nonconformity among boys. Usually we broached the topic of homosexuality toward the end of the interview and only with those students who seemed relatively mature or comfortable enough with the topic. Typically the researcher asked how the student would respond if a friend revealed to him/her that he or she was gay. They were also usually asked how their own life would change or how they would feel if they woke up one morning and found out they were gay.

In all, thirty-four students answered one or both of these questions (twenty-two girls and twelve boys). Most of these children expressed opposition to homosexuality in general, although white girls were more accepting of homosexuality than others. Most of the boys who discussed homosexuality in any way were clearly homophobic, although one boy seemed unsure and another indicated some acceptance of gays. Jason was adamant that "guys should go with girls and girls should go with guys." "It shouldn't be the same sex . . . that is eeww." Micah thought "it's nasty to be gay." When Dante was asked what would happen if he found out he were gay, he replied, "It would be extremely different and I would hate myself."

None of three nonwhite boys felt comfortable about homosexuality. The two African Americans, Marc and Tyrone, told interviewers that they thought being gay was wrong and "nasty." Lorenzo, a Latino American, did not condemn homosexuality, but neither did he indicate much tolerance for it.

In many instances, a feeling of disgust was cited as a rationale for judging gays, as in Jason's interview. This was especially common among boys, somewhat common among nonwhite girls, and the least common among white girls. Marc said, "I think they would be like, 'Stay away from me, I don't want you doing this and this,' and some people, when they go to the bathroom they would always be looking over their shoulder." Cynthia claimed that teachers might "pay close attention" to a gay student "just to make sure he doesn't do anything nasty around other kids and stuff."

Several of the respondents were horrified at the suggestion of being gay. Jason claimed he would shoot himself if he woke up gay, and Micah said, "I would be suicidal. I know that's wrong, but I would." Deirdre responded that if she were gay "I would like girls, which would be nasty." And Kay would be too embarrassed even to go to school. Prejudice by heterosexuals against gays appears to be very much internalized by most of the kids.

A substantial minority, however, expressed tolerant views. Katie felt that people should love who they want to love. When Jack, a seventh grader, was asked what life would be like if he were gay, he said nothing would really be different. He also claimed that he would remain friends with a gay boy, as long as the friend did not "like" him. But even the eleven tolerant youths expressed concern over the reactions of other people, especially peers, toward any indication of homosexuality. The fear of associating with gay peers was quite strong, even among the otherwise tolerant girls, who exhibited some sense of discomfort with the idea of a friend coming out as gay.

This confusion of sexuality and gender stereotypes feeds into the fear boys have about crossing gender boundaries. Responses to the hypothetical scenario about Marcus, the boy who wanted to be a cheerleader in high school, often raised doubts about his sexuality, even though there was absolutely no reference to sexuality in the scenario. All these responses were volunteered by the kids themselves.

Nearly all the children told the interviewers that Marcus would be teased. Forty-one percent of boys and 43 percent of girls suggested that other students would call Marcus gay, but more girls voiced support for the hypothetical Marcus. None of the respondents believed that Marcus must be gay if he wants to be a cheerleader. Rather, responses focused on the idea that he would be called gay and would have to prove his heterosexuality.

There was a widely held conviction that Marcus's peers would verbally abuse him. Jason admitted he would directly taunt Marcus: "I'd go up to his face and say, 'You are a little fruitcake, do you know that?'" But most students seemed to want to protect Marcus from taunts and bullying, especially from other boys. Ten girls and three boys who discussed Marcus getting teased mentioned boys as the primary teasers. Some students recommended that Marcus should "keep it hush-hush" or even reconsider his decision, because of the negative peer reaction it would invite. Jack said, "If I were him I would choose not to say anything about it or else everyone would make fun of me."

Most students acknowledged that if a boy wants to be a cheerleader in high school it does not necessarily mean he is gay, but 40 percent suggested their peers would operate on such an assumption. A few students thought that Marcus might not face much disapproval—that it would not be a big deal. But most kids told us that their peers severely tease male gender nonconformity. No one policed girls' sports behavior by insinuating girl athletes must be gay.

Homophobic Taunts and Enforcement of Masculinity

The Marcus scenario was not the only part of the interview that brought out the gender nonconformity = gay assumption for boys. When we asked students to give us a word to describe boys who are shy, quiet, maybe artistic or creative, and who like activities that girls usually do, four students asserted that such a boy is or would be called gay or some variant thereof. Jeffrey, for example, volunteered that there is no word for boys who act like girls, the way tomboy describes girls who act like boys, but he has heard such boys called "fruit." When we asked Marshall for a term to describe boys who like to do the kinds of activities girls usually do, he responded that "a lot of people call 'em gay." Similarly, without hesitation Deidre gave us the word *fag*. Other responses to this particular question indicated that such a boy would be teased in some way, even if he were not called gay.

Just as kids interpret boys' gender nonconformity as evidence of homosexuality, the flip side is that they also consistently associate homosexuality with gender nonconformity. Middle-school students assume that someone who is gay will violate gender norms. One male student told us that if he were gay, he would no longer like sports. In general, the kids assumed that gay males are more feminine than straight members of their sex. Jeffrey thought that if he were gay he "might like to hang around with girls a little more. Not like flirting, but acting like a girl or around girls."

Such presumptions lend legitimacy to the regulation of male gender nonconformity through antigay remarks. The stigmatizing of Marcus was in sharp contrast to responses to the hypothetical scenario about Jasmine, the girl who wanted to start a girls' football club. None of the students suggested that Jasmine's sexuality would be suspect, although a few suggested she might be teased or thought "weird" by other students. It seems that gender nonconformity is less policed among girls than boys and is much less likely to be presumed as a marker of sexuality for girls.

Kids fear being labeled gay by their peers, which makes this a powerful tool for policing gender. In general, when the kids were asked "what if you found out you were gay?" their first response was to discuss the reaction of their peers, rather than their parents or family members, providing further evidence that, for preadolescents, peers form a critical reference group. In fact, eighteen of twenty-one girls referred to peer disapproval when responding to hypothetical questions about being gay themselves or having a gay friend. Seven of nine boys did the same. Boys and girls consistently suggested that their peers would react negatively to them if they came out as gay. In several cases, respondents acknowledged that they might react negatively or would apply some type of sanction to a gay student.

Being called gay is evidently the worst insult and the most effective way to shame another student. When Cynthia spoke of a male friend of hers who is frequently bullied, she claimed that "most of the time he ignores it but if somebody ends up calling him 'gay' or something, he takes it really bad." Interestingly, Cynthia and others do not consider this friend to be particularly feminine, although they describe him as "scrawny" and "short." Rather, she believes that he is called gay because it is a dependable way for his attackers to insult him.

Branding nonconformists as gay in this middle-school context constitutes a primary form of regulation as well as harassment. When a boy is labeled as gay, it is not necessarily about his sexuality, but it is rather a surefire way to insult him. The gay stigma is not primarily used to tease someone as homosexual, but to deprive a boy of the status that comes with masculinity.[17]

Paradoxically, we have some very suggestive evidence that if a person actually does embrace a gay identity, he or she is freer to cross gender boundaries and to enjoy activities usually limited to the other sex. Mallory and several of the other children told us that a male gay student they knew was taunted by peers for a while, but the bullying leveled off substantially with time. Jamie told us that she has a gay female friend who had some problems with other students, "but people kind of just got over it, and said, 'hey, so what?'" Jamie claimed that other people were initially standoffish with her gay female friend, but they forgot about it by the next year.

In some cases, when discussing other students who are openly gay or lesbian, a student would claim that the teasing was not that bad. Cynthia said that her gay male friend is called names by "like two or three" of the girls in her class, but the boys do not really make fun of him. She thought that is because although he's told all the girls, he probably has not told the boys. When asked if the boys would make fun of him if they knew, she replied: "No, I think he has told them but they probably really don't consider it something big."

In response to the story about Marcus the cheerleader, Mallory described her gay friend, Jo, as an exception to the gender rules. She said,

> Now, I know for a fact that [Marcus would] be made fun of for that. Except Jo. Everybody knows Jo's going to do something like that, so nobody really cares if Jo did something like that. But if that boy is not Jo, he will probably get made fun of.

When asked why people do not make fun of Jo, Mallory explained that he's friends with half of the seventh grade, even though there are some people who "hate him." Jo, as openly gay, seems accepted by most of his peers. Mallory indicated that Jo enjoys some girl-type activities like dancing, but it is accepted because he is gay.

It is not possible to conclude from our data that openly gay students are not harassed precisely in ways similar to male gender nonconformists, but further research would do well to investigate the possibility. It is notable that all three examples of exempting gays and lesbians from sustained harassment in this study related to a specific person whom the respondent knew, whereas most of the respondents who thought a gay person would be subject to significant harassment were dealing with an imaginary scenario. Since stereotypes about gay people being gender nonconformist were common among our respondents, it makes sense that gay peers are not harassed for gender nonconformity in the same ways that heterosexuals are. Openly gay kids, having already acknowledged they are gay, face different challenges than their peers who are anxious to avoid the taunt of being a faggot or gay.

The data clearly show that most middle-school children in our sample still hold stereotypical views about gay people. For boys, no distinction is made between same-sex attraction and gender nonconformity. The children expect that boys who break gender norms will be teased and called gay. But the children in this study are quite diverse in their own opinions and many feel that although harassment would occur, it should not.

Discussion and Conclusion: Femininity on the Body, Masculinity as the Boy

Our findings confirm other studies about the narrow confines in which boys need to stay in order to avoid being teased by peers. What is perhaps more unexpected in our findings is that girls are now stigmatized for displaying some of the traditional markers of femininity. Girls look down on peers who are ultra-feminine, "wimpy," and afraid to get dirty or be competitive. The responses from girls in this study suggest that the way girls now "do gender" is restricted to "looks" and the body.

Girls have come to expect and take advantage of access to traditionally masculine arenas such as sports. They display heightened expectations of academic success in all subjects and are willing to compete with boys in those arenas. None of the girls discussed personally shying away from competition with boys, or worrying about their popularity if they did well in school, and no mention at all was made of fear of math and science. Girls in this study took for granted that they can be involved in different sports, and they rarely mentioned any constraints in their academic pursuits or their career plans.

The girls consistently expressed disdain for exaggerated notions of femininity and looked down on other girls who were seen as too passive, too prissy, or too vain. Girls who are good at sports and still exhibit a feminine bodily presentation are looked upon with favor. The traditional aspects of girlhood most related to subordination to boys are no longer revered or even accepted aspects of femininity. In a world where most mothers work for pay and all the girls expect to do so themselves, it makes sense that they've adopted the means to develop strong bodies and competitive minds.

In our view, the new concept "undoing gender" offered recently by Deutsch is the best framework for understanding contemporary girlhood.[18] These girls do not do gender the way generations before them did. They compete with other girls on the field and with boys in the classroom. They get dirty, and they expect to be taken seriously by teachers, parents, and boys.

While these girls have begun to "undo gender" as we knew it, they have not undone it completely. Their focus on femininity seems to have narrowed to concern and attention, even if sporadic, to their looks. For most girls, being feminine means wearing nice clothes, applying lip gloss, and paying attention to hairstyles. While girls are allowed, and perhaps even encouraged, to "undo gender" in how they behave, they still face pressures to be attractive, to be good-looking.

But the norms are contradictory. Most girls we questioned believe they should do gender with their body display. But if they concentrate too much on this aspect, they risk being looked down upon as overly feminine. They want to be seen as feminine, but not too much so.

On the other hand, boys gain no social approval by deviating from traditional definitions of masculinity. Any behavior remotely stereotyped as feminine is intensely policed by other boys and some girls. Being stigmatized as gay is the primary way masculinity is policed and enforced because it is a potent insult among young males. Being gay and being masculine are seen as contradictory, just as femininity and masculinity traditionally have been. The gay stigma among middle schoolers is really about deviating from gender expectations rather than about homosexuality, although it may draw upon insecurities about sexuality. It is a way of enforcing masculinity. When boys live up to those expectations, they not only establish themselves as masculine, but they also assert their superiority to girls. Boys who hesitate to participate in homophobic or gender-policing activities open themselves up to teasing.

Despite the great success in boosting acceptance of gender equality and women's rights, the peer culture of these tween-agers remains incredibly resistant to any changes in defining masculinity for boys. While middle-school girls now are free to sometimes act like boys, as long as they make an effort, at least occasionally, to look feminine, the fear of being called gay quite effectively polices boys' gender behavior. Boys' lives seem hardly influenced by any feminist transformation except that they must now compete with girls as well as with each other, at least in the classroom.

For both girls and boys, the truly feminine is looked down upon. For boys, this means that to be respected by other boys they must make continual efforts to act in masculine ways. Girls walk a different tightrope. They are strongly pressured to do gender with their bodies, although not so much so as to be seen as too girly. But they are free to cross gender borders in the other aspects of their lives.

Boys now have to compete with girls in nearly every realm of life. They can no longer take for granted that because they are boys, they are smarter or superior in any way to the girls they know. And yet their fear of teasing leaves boys more constrained by gender stereotypes than are girls. Perhaps the exaggerated gender difference is the last remnant of male privilege left to this generation of boys.

Boys need a "feminist revolution" of their own.

APPENDIX

Demographic Information for Middle Schoolers in the Study

Pseudonym	Sex	Race	Grade
Alison	Female	White	7
Audrey	Female	White	6
Brady	Male	White	6
Candace	Female	White	6
Cassie	Female	Black	6
Cynthia	Female	Biracial (black/white)	6
Dante	Male	White	6
Deb	Female	Asian-Indian	6
Deirdre	Female	Black	6
Eric	Male	White	6
Erica	Female	White	6
Eve	Female	White	6
Isabel	Female	Black	7
Jack	Male	White	7
Jackie	Female	Black	8
Jamie	Female	White	8
Jason	Male	White	7
Jeffrey	Male	White	7
Joleesa	Female	Black	6
Kamry	Female	White	8
Karlin	Female	White	8
Kay	Female	Black	7
Katie	Female	White	7
Kerri	Female	White	6
Kirsten	Female	White	8
Krista	Female	White	8
Lana	Female	Biracial (black/white)	6
Lola	Female	Biracial (black/white)	6
Lorenzo	Male	Latino	6
Mallory	Female	White	7
Marc	Male	Black	6

Marney	Female	White	6
Marshall	Male	White	8
Max*	Male	White	6
Micah	Male	White	6
Molly	Female	White	6
Mona	Female	White	6
Nathan	Male	White	6
Reese	Male	White	7
Samantha	Female	White	6
Samir	Male	Asian-Indian	6
Shawn	Male	White	7
Tyrone	Male	Black	6
Wayne*	Male	White	7

*Due to missing data, not included in this study.

NOTES

The authors' names are listed alphabetically. The authors thank other members of the research team for their collaboration with data collection. These colleagues include Rena Cornell, Carissa Froyum, Kris Macomber, Amy McClure, and Tricia McTague. We also thank Pallavi Banerjee, Stephanie Coontz, Carissa Froyum, Wilfrid Reissner, Kathleen Gerson, and Kelly Underman for their reviews of this manuscript.

1. Researchers have looked at how multicultural education works (Talbani, 2003) as well as how education and other cultural beliefs reinforce white privilege (Wellman, 1993).

2. Eder, Evans, and Parker (1995) examined the role of gender in the language and social-ization of a group of eighth graders.

3. "Doing gender" unlinks biological sex from gender by describing gender not as the traits of a person, but as the embedded social actions that a person takes to express socially accepted gender (West and Zimmerman, 1987).

4. Allison (1991), Cockburn and Clarke (2002), and Krane et al. (2004) discuss female athletes and the challenge of athletics to femininity, while Broad (2001) examines queer athletes. Malcom (2003), Adams, Schmitke, and Franklin (2005), and Enke (2005), on the other hand, discuss the remaking of femininity to include athletics. Adams et al. (2005) find that girls enjoy athleticism and take pride in being tough and competitive.

5. Adams and Bettis (2003), pp. 74–75.

6. *Ibid.*, p. 80.

7. This comes from Adams and Bettis's (2003) study on cheerleading.

8. Bettie (2003).

9. For more on peer groups and cliques, both Eder et al. (1995) and Adler and Adler (1998) explore adolescent culture. Cockburn and Clarke (2002), Adams and Bettis (2003), and

Adams et al. (2005) all examine these pressures to be attractive to boys in the context of female athletes. See also Lemish (1998) on modes of femininity and attractiveness.

10. Eder et al. (1995) map the gendered dynamics of teasing. Several researchers examine how this teasing functions to control boys through fear (Kehily and Nayak, 1997; Burn, 2000; Plummer, 2001; Phoenix, Frosh, and Pattman, 2003; Chambers, Tincknell, and Van Loon, 2004), including Pascoe's (2005) "Dude, You're a Fag." Thorne (1993) and Plummer (2001) describe this behavior in elementary school, and Eder et al. (1995), Adler and Adler (1998), and Phoenix et al. (2003) discuss it in middle school.

11. See Plummer (2001).

12. See Eder et al. (1995).

13. Pascoe (2003, 2007) and Phoenix et al. (2003) have written about masculinity and toughness, while Plummer (2001) and Pascoe (2005, 2007) write about teasing.

14. Froyum (2007).

15. Malcom (2003).

16. This gender-specific cheerleading is very region-specific. In some schools on the West Coast, cheerleading squads are either all-male or mixed sex. As cheerleading has become more athletically demanding, more boys are often included to lift and throw the girls.

17. For more on this, read Kehily and Nayak (1997), Plummer (2001), Pascoe (2003, 2005, 2007) and Phoenix et al. (2003).

18. See Deutsch (2007) for a description of the concept of "undoing gender." For an example of "undoing gender," in Gerson's (2002) article, she describes the process of young men and women choosing lives that are distinct from traditional gendered expectations.

35

Falling Back on Plan B

The Children of the Gender Revolution Face Uncharted Territory

Kathleen Gerson

Young adults today grew up with mothers who joined the workplace and parents whose relationships often departed from traditional marriage. Now facing their own choices, what do the women and men of this new generation hope and plan to do in their own lives? In contrast to popular images of twenty- and thirtysomethings returning to tradition, this chapter demonstrates that most young people want to create a lasting marriage (or a "marriage-like" relationship) and to find a personal balance between home and work. Most women and men are more alike than different in their aspirations, with both hoping to blend the traditional value of lifelong commitment with the modern value of flexible, egalitarian sharing. Yet, these children of the gender revolution are also developing strategies to prepare for "second-best" options. Fearful that they will not find the right partner to help them integrate work with family caretaking, most women see work as essential to their survival. Worried about time-greedy workplaces, most men hope to avoid the costs that equal sharing might exact on their careers. The differing fallback positions of "self-reliant" women and "neo-traditional" men may point to a growing gender divide, but they do not reflect this generation's highest aspirations.

Young adults today grew up with mothers who broke barriers in the workplace and parents who forged innovative alternatives to traditional marriage. These children of the gender revolution now face a world that is far different from that of their parents or grandparents. While massive changes in work and family arrangements have expanded their options, these changes also pose new challenges to crafting a marriage, rearing children, and building a career. Members of this new generation walk a fine line between their desire to achieve egalitarian, sharing relationships that can meld with satisfying work and succumbing to the realities of gender conflict, fragile relationships, and uncertain job prospects. The choices they make will shape work and family life for decades to come.

Social forecasters have reached starkly different conclusions about what these choices will be. Some proclaim that the recent upturn in "opt-out" mothers foreshadows a wider return to tradition among younger women.[1] Others believe the rising number of single adults foretells a deepening "decline of commitment" that is threatening family life and the social fabric.[2] While there is little doubt that tumultuous changes have shaped the lives of a new generation, there is great disagreement about how. Does the diversification of families into two-earner, single-parent, and cohabiting forms represent a waning of family life or the growth of more flexible relationships? Will this new generation integrate family and work in new ways, or will older patterns inexorably pull them back?

To find out how members of the first generation to grow up in these diversifying families look back on their childhoods and forward to their own futures, I conducted in-depth, life history interviews with a carefully selected group of young people between eighteen and thirty-two. These young women and men experienced the full range of changes that have taken place in family life, and most lived in some form of "nontraditional" arrangement at some point in their childhood.[3] My interviews reveal a generation that does not conform to prevailing media stereotypes, whether they depict declining families or a return to strict gender divisions in caretaking and breadwinning.

In contrast to popular images of twenty- and thirtysomethings who wish to return to tradition or reject family life altogether, the young women and men I interviewed are more focused on how well their parents met the challenges of providing economic and emotional support than on what form their families took. Now making their own way in early adulthood, women and men share a set of lofty aspirations. Despite their varied family experiences, most hope to blend the traditional value of a lifelong relationship with the modern value of flexibly sharing work, child care, and domestic chores. In the best of all possible worlds, the majority would like to create a lasting marriage (or a "marriage-like" relationship) that allows them to balance home and work in a flexible, egalitarian way.

Yet young people are also developing strategies to prepare for "second-best" options in a world where time-demanding workplaces, a lack of child care, and fragile relationships may place their ideals out of reach. Concerned about the difficulty of finding a reliable and egalitarian partner to help them integrate work with family caretaking, most women see work as essential to their own and their children's survival, whether or not they marry. Worried about time-greedy workplaces, most men feel they must place work first and will need to count on a partner at home. As they prepare for second-best options, the differing fallback positions of "self-reliant" women and "neo-traditional" men may point to a new gender divide. But this divide does not reflect a new generation's highest aspirations for blending lifelong commitment and flexible, egalitarian sharing in their relationships.

GROWING UP IN CHANGING FAMILIES

Even though theorists and social commentators continue to debate the merits of various family forms, my interviewees did not focus on their family's "structure."[4] Instead, I found large variation among children who grew up in apparently similar family types. Those who grew up in families with a homemaking mother and breadwinning father were divided in their assessments of this arrangement. While a little more than half thought this was the best arrangement, close to half reached a different conclusion. When being a homemaker and out of the workforce appeared to undermine a mother's satisfaction, disturb the household's harmony, or threaten its economic security, the children concluded that it would have been better if their mothers had pursued a sustained commitment to work.

Many of those who grew up in a single-parent home also expressed ambivalence about their parents' breakups. Slightly more than half wished their parents had stayed together, but close to half believed that a breakup, while not ideal, was better than continuing to live in a conflict-ridden or silently unhappy home.[5] The longer-term consequences of a breakup shaped the lessons children drew. If their parents got back on their feet and created better lives, children developed surprisingly positive outlooks on the decision to separate.

Those who grew up in a dual-earner home were the least ambivalent about their parents' arrangements. More than three-fourths believed that having two work-committed parents provided increased economic resources and also promoted marriages that seemed more egalitarian and satisfying.[6] If the pressures of working long hours or coping with blocked opportunities and family-unfriendly workplaces took their toll, however, some children concluded that having overburdened, time-stressed caretakers offset these advantages.

In short, growing up in this era of diverse families led children to focus more on how well—or poorly—parents (and other caretakers) were able to meet the twin challenges of providing economic and emotional support rather than on its form. Even more important, children experienced family life as a dynamic process that changed over time. Since family life is best seen as a film, not a snapshot, the key to understanding young people's views lies in charting the diverse paths their families took.

FAMILY PATHS AND GENDER FLEXIBILITY

Families can take different paths from seemingly common starting points, and similar types of families can travel toward different destinations. When young adults reflect on their families, they focus on how their homes either came to provide stability and support or failed to do so. About a third of my interviewees reported growing up in a stable home, while a quarter concluded that their families grew more supportive as time passed. In contrast, just under one in ten reported living in a chronically insecure home, while a bit more than a third felt that family support eroded as they grew up. Why, then, do some children look back on families that became more supportive and secure, while others experienced a decline in their family's support?

Parents' strategies for organizing breadwinning and caretaking hold the key to understanding a family's pathway.[7] Flexible strategies, which allowed mothers, fathers, and other caretakers to transcend rigid gender boundaries, helped families prevail in the face of unexpected economic and interpersonal crises. Inflexible responses, in contrast, left families ill equipped to cope with eroding supports for a strict division in mothers' and fathers' responsibilities.

RISING FAMILY FORTUNES

The sources of expanding support differed by family situation, but all reflected a flexible response to unexpected difficulties. Sometimes marriages became more equal as demoralized mothers went to work and pushed for change or helped overburdened fathers. Josh, for example, reported that his mother's decision to go to work gave her the courage to insist that his father tackle his drug addiction[8]:

> My parents fought almost constantly. Then my mom got a job. They separated for about five, six, seven months. Even though I was upset, I thought it was for the best. That's when (my dad) got into some kind of program and my mom took him back. That changed the whole family dynamic. We got extremely close. A whole new relationship developed with my father.

Chris recalled how his mother's job allowed his father to quit a dead-end job and train for a more satisfying career:

> Between 7th and 8th grade, my dad had a business which didn't work. It was a dead-end thing, and he came home frustrated, so my mom got him to go to school. It was hard financially, but it was good because he was actually enjoying what he was doing. He really flourished. A lot of people say, "Wow, your mom is the breadwinner, and that's strange." It's not. It is a very joint thing.

Parental breakups that relieved domestic conflict or led to the departure of an unstable parent also helped caretaking parents get back on their feet. Connie recounted how her mother was able to create a more secure home after separating from an alcoholic husband and finding a job that offered a steady income and a source of personal esteem:

> My father just sat in the corner and once in a while got angry at us, but [my mom] — I don't know if it was him or the money, but she didn't stand up for herself as much as I think she should. The tension with my dad never eased, and my mom had gotten sick with multiple bleeding ulcers. That was her real turning point. It was building inside of her to leave, 'cause she'd got a job and started to realize she had her own money. . . . [She] became a much happier person. And because she was better, I was better. I had a weight taken off of me.

More stable and egalitarian remarriages could also give children the economic and emotional support they had not previously received. Having never known her biological father, Shauna recalled how her stepfather became a devoted caretaker and the "real" father she always wanted:

> At first, I was feeling it was a bad change because I wanted my mom to myself. Then my mom said, "Why don't you call him daddy?" The next thing I was saying "Daddy!" I remember the look on his face and his saying "She called me daddy!" I was so happy. After that, he's always been my dad, and there's never been any question about it. . . . [He] would get home before my mom, so he would cook the dinner and clean. My dad spoiled me for any other man, because this is the model I had.

When Isabella's parents divorced, her grandfather became a treasured caretaker:

> It's not like I didn't have a father, because my grandfather was always there. He was there to take me to after-school clubs and pick me up. I was sheltered—he had to

take me to the library, wait till I finished all my work, take me home. I call him dad. Nobody could do better.

And when Antonio's single mother lost her job, his grandparents provided essential income that kept the family afloat:

> My mom and grandparents were the type of people that even if we didn't have [money], we was gonna get it. Their ideal is, "I want to give you all the things I couldn't have when I was young." My grandparents and my mother thought like that, so no matter how much in poverty we were living, I was getting everything I wanted.

Despite their obvious differences, the common ingredient in these narratives is the ability of parents and other caretakers to reorganize child rearing and breadwinning in a more flexible, less gender-divided way. Mothers going to work, fathers becoming more involved in child rearing, and others joining in the work of family life—all of these strategies helped families overcome unexpected difficulties and create more economically secure, emotionally stable homes. Growing flexibility in how parents met the challenges of earning needed income and caring for children nourished parental morale, increased a home's financial security, and provided inspiring models of adult resilience. While children acknowledged the costs, they valued these second chances and gleaned lessons from watching parents find ways to create a better life. Looking back, they could conclude that "all's well that ends well."

DECLINING FAMILY FORTUNES

For some children, home life followed a downward slope. Here, too, the key to their experiences lay in the work and caretaking strategies of those entrusted with their care, but here gender inflexibility in the face of domestic difficulties left children with less support than they had once taken for granted. Faced with a father's abandonment or a stay-at-home mother's growing frustration, children described how their parents' resistance to more flexible strategies for apportioning paid and domestic work left them struggling to meet children's economic and emotional needs. Over time, deteriorating marriages, declining parental morale, and financial insecurity shattered a once rosy picture of family stability and contentment.

When parents became stuck in a rigid division of labor, with unhappy mothers and fathers ill equipped to support the household, traditional marriages could deteriorate. Sarah explains how her mother became increasingly depressed and "over-involved" after relinquishing a promising career to devote all of her time to child rearing:

> When my sister was born, [my mom's] job had started up, career-wise, so she wasn't happy [but] she felt she had to be home. She had a lot of conflicts about work and home and opted to be really committed to family, but also resented it. . . . She was the supermom, but just seemed really depressed a lot of time. . . . [It came] with an edge to it—"in return, I want you to be devoted to me." If we did something separate from her, that was a major problem. So I was making distance because I felt I had to protect myself from this invasion. . . . She thought she was doing something good to sacrifice for us . . . but it would have been better if my mother was happier working.

Megan recalls her father's mounting frustration as his income stagnated and he endured the complaints of a wife who expected him to provide a "better lifestyle":

> My mother was always dissatisfied. She wanted my father to be more ambitious, and he wasn't an ambitious man. As long as he was supporting the family, it didn't matter if it was a bigger house or a bigger car. Forty years of being married to a woman saying, "Why don't we have more money?"—I think that does something to your self-esteem.

Unresolved power struggles in dual-earner marriages could also cause problems, as wives felt the weight of "doing it all" and fathers resisted egalitarian sharing. Juggling paid and domestic work left Justin's mother exhausted, while a high-pressured job running a restaurant left his father with no time to attend nightly dinners or even Little League games. Justin describes the strain his parents experienced and its effect on him:

> I was slightly disappointed that I could not see my father more—because I understood but also because it depends on the mood he's in. And it got worse as work [went] downhill. . . . [So] I can't model my relationship on my parents. My mother wasn't very happy. There was a lot of strain on her.

Harmful breakups, where fathers abandoned their children and mothers could not find new ways to support the family or create an identity beyond wife and mother, also eroded family support. Nina remembers how her father's disappearance, combined with her mother's reluctance to seek a job and create a more independent life, triggered the descent from a comfortable middle-class existence to one of abiding poverty:

> My mother ended up going on welfare. We went from a nice place to living in a really cruddy building. And she's still in the same apartment. To this day, my sister will not speak to my father because of what he's done to us.

Children (and their parents) sometimes lost the support of other caretakers. Shortly after Jasmine's father left to live with another woman and her mother fell into a deep depression, she suffered the loss of a "third parent" when her beloved grandmother died. Her grandmother's loss left her feeling especially bereft after her father's departure:

> It was so great when my parents were together and my grandmother was alive, so when she died, it was really hard. I lost [the money], and I lost her just being there. We were going through a real trauma in my whole family, so when [my father] left, it was like another death. I don't think it would have been any better if they'd stayed together, but my grandmother being alive would have been much more of a difference.

The events that propelled families on a downward track—including rising financial instability, declining parental involvement and morale, and a dearth of other supportive caretakers—share a common element. Whether parents faced marital impasses or difficult breakups, resistance to more flexible gender arrangements left them unable to sustain an emotionally or economically secure home. Their children concluded that all did not end well.

In sum, sustained parental support and economic security were more important to my informants than the form their families took. Since any family type holds potential pitfalls if parents do not or cannot prevail over the difficulties that arise, conventional categories that see families as static "forms" cannot account for the ways that families change as children grow to adulthood. Instead, young women and men from diverse family backgrounds recounted how parents and other family members who transcended gender boundaries and developed flexible strategies for breadwinning and caretaking were better able to cope with marital crises, economic insecurities, and other unanticipated challenges.

A range of social trends—including the erosion of single-earner paychecks, the fragility of modern marriages, and the expanding options and pressures for women to work—require varied and versatile ways of earning and caring. These institutional shifts make gender flexibility increasingly desirable and even essential. Flexible approaches to work and parenting help families adapt, while inflexible ones leave them ill prepared to cope with new economic and social realities.

CONVERGING IDEALS, DIVERGING FALLBACKS

How do young adults use the lessons of growing up in changing families to formulate their own plans for the future? Women and men from diverse family backgrounds share a set of lofty aspirations. Whether or not their parents stayed together, more than nine out of ten hope to rear children in the context of a satisfying lifelong bond. Far from rejecting the value of commitment, almost everyone wants to create a lasting marriage or "marriage-like" partnership. This does not, however, reflect a desire for a traditional relationship. Most also aspire to build a committed bond where both paid work and family caretaking are shared. Three-fourths of those who grew up in dual-earner homes want their spouse to share breadwinning and caretaking, but so do more than two-thirds of those from traditional homes, and close to nine-tenths of those with single parents. While four-fifths of women want an egalitarian relationship, so do two-thirds of men. In short, most share an ideal that stresses the value of a lasting, flexible, and egalitarian partnership with considerable room for personal autonomy. Amy, an Asian American with two working parents, thus explains that:

> I want a fifty-fifty relationship, where we both have the potential of doing everything—both of us working and dealing with kids. With regard to career, if neither has flexibility, then one of us will have to sacrifice for one period, and the other for another.

And Wayne, an African American raised by a single mother, expresses essentially the same hopes when he says that:

> I don't want the '50s type of marriage, where I come home and she's cooking. I want her to have a career of her own. I want to be able to set my goals, and she can do what she wants, too.

While most of my interviewees hope to strike a flexible breadwinning and caretaking balance with an egalitarian partner, they are also skeptical about their chances of achieving this ideal. Women and men both worry that work demands, a lack of child-rearing supports, and the fragility of modern relationships will undermine their aspirations to forge an enduring, egalitarian partnership. In the face of barriers to equality, most have concluded that they have little choice but to prepare for options that may fall substantially short of their ideals. Despite their shared aspirations, however, men and women face different institutional obstacles and cultural pressures, which are prompting divergent fallback strategies. If they cannot find a supportive partner, most women prefer self-reliance over economic dependence within a traditional marriage. Most men, if they cannot strike an equal balance between work and parenting, prefer a neo-traditional arrangement that allows them to put work first and rely on a partner for the lion's share of caregiving. In the event that Plan A proves unreachable, women and men are thus pursuing a different Plan B as insurance against their "worst case" fears. These divergent fallback strategies point toward the emergence of a new gender divide between young women, most of whom see a need for self-reliance, and young men, who are more inclined to retain a modified version of traditional expectations.

Women's Plan B

Torn between high hopes for combining work and family and worries about sustaining a lasting and satisfying partnership, young women are navigating uncertain waters. While some are falling back on domesticity, most prefer to find a more independent base than traditional marriage provides. In contrast to the media-driven message that young women are turning away from work and career in favor of domestic pursuits, the majority of my interviewees are determined to seek financial and emotional self-reliance, whether or not they also forge a committed relationship. Regardless of class, race, or ethnicity, most are reluctant to surrender their autonomy in a traditional marriage. When the bonds of marriage are so fragile, relying on a husband for economic security seems foolhardy. And if a relationship deteriorates, economic dependence on a man leaves few means of escape. Danisha, an African American who grew up in an inner-city, working-class neighborhood, and Jennifer, who was raised in a middle-class, predominantly white suburb, agree. Danisha proclaims:

> Let's say that my marriage doesn't work. Just in case, I want to establish myself, because I don't ever want to end up, like, "What am I going to do?" I want to be able to do what I have to do and still be okay.

Jennifer concurs:

> I will have to have a job and some kind of stability before considering marriage. Too many of my mother's friends went for that—"Let him provide everything"—and

they're stuck in a very unhappy relationship but can't leave because they can't provide for themselves or the children they now have. So it's either welfare or putting
up with somebody else's c– –p.

Hoping to avoid being trapped in an unhappy marriage or left by an unreliable
partner without a way to survive, almost three-fourths of women plan to build a
non-negotiable base of self-reliance and an independent identity in the world of
paid work.[9] But they do not view this strategy as incompatible with the search for
a life partner. Instead, it reflects their determination to set a high standard for a
worthy relationship. Economic self-reliance and personal independence make it
possible to resist "settling" for anything less than a satisfying, mutually supportive
bond.

Women from all backgrounds have concluded that work provides indispensable economic, social, and emotional resources. They have drawn lessons about
the rewards of self-reliance and the perils of domesticity from their mothers,
other women, and their own experiences growing up. They are thus seeking
alternatives to traditional marriage by establishing a firm tie to paid work, by
redesigning motherhood to better fit their work aspirations, and by looking to
kin and friends as a support network to enlarge and, if needed, substitute, for an
intimate relationship. These strategies do not preclude finding a life partner, but
they reflect a determination to set a high standard for choosing one. Maria, who
grew up in a two-parent home in a predominantly white, working-class suburb,
declares:

> I want to have this person to share [my] life with — [someone] that you're there for
> as much as they're there for you. But I can't settle.

And Rachel, whose Latino parents separated when she was young, shares this view:

> I'm not afraid of being alone, but I am afraid of being with somebody who's a jerk.
> I want to get married and have children, but it has to be under the right circum-
> stances, with the right person.

Maria and Rachel also agree that if a worthy relationship ultimately proves out
of reach, then remaining single need not mean social disconnection. Kin and
friends provide a support network that enlarges and, if needed, even substitutes
for an intimate relationship. Maria explains:

> If I don't find [a relationship], then I cannot live in sorrow. It's not the only thing
> that's ultimately important. If I didn't have my family, if I didn't have a career,

> if I didn't have friends, I would be equally unhappy. [A relationship] is just one slice of the pie.

And Rachel concurs:

> I can spend the rest of my life on my own, and as long as I have my sisters and my friends, I'm okay.

By blending support from friends and kin with financial self-sufficiency, these young women are pursuing a strategy of autonomy rather than placing their own fate or their children's fate in the hands of a traditional relationship. Whether or not this strategy ultimately leads to marriage, it appears to offer the safest and most responsible way to prepare for the uncertainties of relationships and the barriers to men's equal sharing.

Men's Plan B

Young men face a different dilemma: Torn between women's pressures for an egalitarian partnership and their own desire to succeed—or at least survive—in time-demanding workplaces, they are more inclined to fall back on a modified traditionalism that contrasts vividly with women's search for self-reliance. While they do not want or expect to return to a 1950s model of fathers as the only bread-winner, most men prefer a modified traditionalism that recognizes a mother's right (and need) to work, but puts his own career first. Although Andrew grew up in a consistently two-income home, he distinguished between a woman's "choice" to work and a man's "responsibility" to support his family:

> I would like to have it be equal—just from what I was exposed to and what attracts me—but I don't have a set definition for what that would be like. I would be fine if both of us were working, but if she thought, "At this point in my life, I don't want to work," then it would be fine.

Because equality may prove to be too costly to their careers, seven out of ten men are pursuing a strategy that positions them as the main breadwinner, even if it allows for two working spouses. When push comes to shove, and the demands of work collide with the needs of children, this approach allows men to resist equal caretaking, even in a two-earner context. Like women, men from a range of family, class, and ethnic backgrounds fall back on neo-traditionalism. They favor retaining a clear boundary between a breadwinning father and a caretaking mother, even when she holds a paid job. This neo-traditional strategy stresses women's primary status as mothers and defines equality as a woman's "choice" to add work onto mothering.

By making room for two earners, this strategy offers the financial cushion of a second income, acknowledges women's desire for a life beyond the home, and allows for more involved fatherhood. Yet, by claiming separate spheres of responsibility for women and men, it does not challenge a man's position as the primary earner or undermine the claim that his work prospects should come first. Although James's mother became too mentally ill to care for her children or herself, Josh plans to leave the lion's share of caretaking to his wife:

> All things being equal, it [caretaking] should be shared. It may sound sexist, but if somebody's going to be the breadwinner, it's going to be me. First of all, I make a better salary, and I feel the need to work, and I just think the child really needs the mother more than the father at a young age.

Men are thus more likely to favor a fallback arrangement that retains the gender boundary between breadwinning and caretaking, even when mothers hold paid jobs. From young men's perspective, this modified but still gendered household offers women the chance to earn income and establish an identity at the workplace without imposing the costs of equal parenting on men. Granting a mother's "choice" to work supports women's claims for independence, but it does not undermine men's claim that their work prospects should come first. Acknowledging men's responsibilities at home provides for more involved fatherhood, but it does not envision domestic equality. And making room for two earners provides a buffer against the difficulties of living on one income, but it does not challenge men's position as the primary earner. Modified traditionalism thus appears to be a good compromise when the career costs of equality remain so high.[10] New economic insecurities, coupled with women's growing desire for equality, are creating dilemmas for men, even if they take a different form than the ones confronting women. Ultimately, however, men's desire to protect work prerogatives collides with women's growing desire for equality and need for independence.

Across the Gender Divide

In contrast to the popular images of a generation that feels neglected by working mothers, unsettled by parental breakups, and wary of equality, these life stories show strong support for working mothers, a focus on the quality of a relationship, and a shared desire to create lasting, flexible, and egalitarian partnerships. The good news is that most young women and men had largely positive experiences with mothers who worked and parents who strove for flexibility and equality. Those who grew up with a caring support network and sufficient economic security, whether in a single- or a two-parent household, did well. Young women and men both recounted how gender flexibility in breadwinning and caretaking helped their parents (and other caretakers) overcome such increasingly prevalent family crises as the loss of a father's income or the decline of a mother's morale. By letting go of rigid patterns that once narrowly defined women's and men's "proper" places in the family and the wider world, all kinds of families were able to overcome unexpected challenges and create more financially stable and emotionally supportive homes. And most, even among those who grew up in less flexible families, hope to build on the struggles and gains of their parents' generation by seeking equality and flexibility in their own lives.

The bad news, however, is that most young adults remain skeptical about their chances of achieving their ideals. Amid their shared desire to transcend gender boundaries and achieve flexibility in their own lives, young women and men harbor strong concerns that their aspirations will prove impossible to reach. Faced with the many barriers to egalitarian relationships and fearful that they will not find the right partner to help them integrate work with family caretaking, they are also preparing for options that may fall substantially short of their ideals. Reversing the argument that women are returning to tradition, however, these divergent fallback strategies suggest that a new divide is emerging between "self-reliant" women, who see work, an independent income, and personal autonomy as essential to their survival, and "neo-traditional" men, who grant women's "choice" to work but also feel the need and pressure to be a primary breadwinner.

While women are developing more innovative strategies than are men, the underlying story is one of a resilient but realistic generation that has changed far more than the institutions it has inherited. Whether they grew up in a flexible home or one with more rigid definitions of women's and men's proper places, their hard-won lessons about the need for new, more egalitarian options for building relationships and caring for children are outpacing their ability to implement these goals.

Yet, young men and women still hope to reach across the divide that separates them. Aware that traditional job ladders and traditional marriages are both waning, they are seeking more flexible ways to build careers, care for families, and integrate the two.[11] Convinced that the traditional career, defined by orderly steps up an organizational chart, is a relic of the past, most hope to craft a "personal career" that is not bound by a single employer or work organization. Most men as well as women are trying to redefine the "ideal worker" to accommodate the ebb and flow of family life, even if that means sacrificing some income for a more balanced life.[12] They hope to create a shared "work-family" career that interweaves breadwinning and caretaking.

Growing up in changing families and facing uncertainty in their own lives has left this generation wary of rigid, narrowly framed "family values" that moralize about their personal choices or those of others. They are searching for a morality without moralism that balances an ethic of tolerance and inclusiveness with the core values of behaving responsibly and caring for others. The clash between self-reliant women and neo-traditional men may signal a new divide, but it stems from intensifying work-family dilemmas, not from a decline of laudable values.

Since new social realities are forcing young adults to seek new ways to combine love and work, the best hope for bridging gender divides lies in creating social policies that will allow twenty-first-century Americans to pursue the flexible, egalitarian strategies they want rather than forcing them to fall back on less desirable—and ultimately less workable—options. Whether the goal is equal opportunity or a healthy family landscape, the best family values can only be achieved by creating the social supports for gender flexibility in our communities, homes, and workplaces.

NOTES

1. Anecdotal but high-profile stories have touted an "opt-out revolution," to use Lisa Belkin's term (2003), although a number of analysts have shown that *revolution* is a highly misleading and exaggerated term to describe the recent slight downturn in young mothers' labor force participation (Boushey, 2008; Williams, 2007). Most well-educated women are not leaving the workforce, and even though the percentage of working mothers with infants has shown a small downturn from its 1995 peak, mothers with children over the age of one are still just as likely as other women to hold a paid job. Even mothers with children under age one show levels of employment that are much higher than the 1960s levels, which averaged 30 percent. Moreover, Williams (2007), Stone (2007), Bennetts (2007), and Hirshman (2006) also point out that the metaphor of opting out obscures the powerful ways that mothers are, in Williams's words, "pushed out."

2. Recent overviews of the rise of the number of unmarried adults can be found in studies by the Pew Research Center (2007a, 2007b) and by Roberts (2007). Prominent proponents of the "family decline" perspective include Blankenhorn (1995), Popenoe (1988, 1996), Popenoe, Elshtain, and Blankenhorn (1996), and Whitehead (1997). Waite and Gallagher (2000) focus on the personal and social advantages of marriage. For rebuttals to the "family decline" perspective, see Bengtston, Biblarz, and Roberts (2002), Coontz (2005), Moore et al. (2002), Skolnick and Rosencrantz (1994), and Stacey (1996).

3. Randomly chosen from a broad range of city and suburban neighborhoods dispersed throughout the New York metropolitan region, the group includes 120 respondents from diverse race and class backgrounds and from all parts of the country. In all, 54 percent identified as non-Hispanic white, 21 percent as African American, 18 percent as Latino, and 7 percent as Asian. About 43 percent grew up in middle- and upper-middle class homes, while 43 percent lived in homes that were solidly working class, and another

15 percent lived in or on the edge of poverty. With an average age of twenty-four, they are evenly divided between women and men, and about 5 percent identified as either lesbian or gay. As a group, they reflect the demographic contours of young adults throughout metropolitan America. See Gerson (2006, 2010) for a full description of my sample and methods.

4. Most research shows that diversity *within* family types, however defined, is as large as the differences *between* them. Acock and Demo (1994) argue that family type does not predict children's well-being. Parcel and Menaghan (1994) make the same case for different forms of parental employment.

5. In the case of one-parent versus two-parent homes, children living with both biological parents do appear on average to fare better, but most of the difference disappears after taking account of the family's financial resources and the degree of parental conflict before a breakup (Amato and Booth, 1997; Amato and Hohmann-Marriott, 2007; Booth and Amato, 2001; Furstenberg and Cherlin, 1991; Hetherington, 1999; McLanahan and Sandefur, 1994). In a recent study of the effects of divorce on children's behavior, Li (2007) shows that "while certain divorces harm children, others benefit them."

6. Decades of research have shown that children do not suffer when their mothers work outside the home. A mother's satisfaction with her situation, the quality of care a child receives, and the involvement of fathers and other caretakers are far more important factors (Galinsky, 1999; Harvey, 1999; Hoffman, 1987; Hoffman, Wladis, and Youngblade, 1999). Bianchi, Robinson, and Milkie (2006) report that parents are actually spending more time with their children. Recent research on the effects of day care have found only small, temporary differences. Barnett and Rivers (1996) demonstrate a range of advantages for two-income couples, and Springer (2007) reports significant health benefits for men whose wives work.

7. Hochschild (1989) refers to dual-earner couples' "gender strategies," although she focuses more on how these strategies reproduce gender divisions than on when, how, and why they might transcend gender distinctions. See Lorber (1994), Risman (1998), and West and Zimmerman (1987) for discussions of the social construction of gender. Zerubavel (1991) analyzes the social roots of mental flexibility.

8. All of the names have been changed to protect confidentiality, and some quotes have been shortened or lightly edited to remove extraneous phrases.

9. About a quarter of the women concluded that if work and family collide, they would rather make a more traditional compromise. These women worried about inflexible workplaces and the difficulty of finding an equal partner. Yet, they still hoped to fit work into their lives. This outlook, too, reflects the dilemmas facing young women who lack the supports to share work and caretaking equally. (See Gerson, *The Unfinished Revolution*, 2010, for a full analysis of the variation in women's fallback strategies.)

10. About three in ten men stress independence over traditional marriage, but autonomy has a different meaning for them than it does for women. Poor work prospects leave them determined to remain single unless they find a partner who does not expect financial support. Unlike self-reliant women, who hope to be able to support themselves and their children, autonomous men worry about their ability to earn enough to support a family. (See Gerson, 2010, for a full analysis of men's varied strategies.)

11. Moen and Roehling (2005).

12. Williams (2000).

CCF Facts

WOMEN'S EDUCATION AND THEIR LIKELIHOOD OF MARRIAGE: A HISTORIC REVERSAL

Jonathan Bearak and Paula England | April 2012

Historically, women who graduated from college were far more likely than any other group of women—whether high school dropouts, high school graduates, or women with some college—to remain single their entire lives. As late as 1950, a quarter of white female college graduates forty years of age had never married, compared to only 7 percent of their counterparts without a college degree. But what has happened since women have been completing college and obtaining advanced degrees at much higher rates, and since divorce has become easier to obtain?

On the one hand, highly educated men and women often postpone marriage until college or even graduate school is finished. Many choose to establish themselves in demanding careers before they even consider marriage. These factors suggest that marriage rates of the well-educated should be lower.

On the other hand, poorer and less educated men and women are most apt to have children outside marriage, while men lacking high school or college degrees are sometimes seen by themselves and their partners as less "marriageable" because stagnating wages have made them less reliable breadwinners (see discussion below). The latter suggests lower marriage rates for the less educated.

The key to resolving this puzzle is to realize that education affects not only the timing of marriage among those who eventually marry, but also whether people ever marry, and whether they divorce. As we'll see, these effects come into play at different ages for men and for women at different educational levels, and they also vary by race.

Our Analysis

To show how the education differences in marriage rates vary by age, we have graphed marriage rates separately by age for each of four education groups—those who ultimately finished less than high school, just high school, some college, and four years of college. We show the education-by-age graphs separately for blacks and whites, as well as for all races combined, and separately for men and women. Our data come from a national sample of people who were born between 1958 and 1965 and therefore turned twenty between 1978 and 1985, a period of rapid cultural and socioeconomic change. These individuals were followed for many years, allowing us to know their marital status at every age through forty-five. Most people who ever marry have done so by age forty-five, so, roughly speaking, we are able to see what percent of those in each group will ever marry.

Figures 1 and 2 show the percent of men or women who have ever married by each age, separately for each group by their ultimate education. In Figures 3 and 4, we look at the same thing except that we show what percent are "currently married" rather than what percent have "ever married." The difference between who is "currently" and "ever" married for any group is that those who have married but are now divorced or widowed but not remarried are included in the "ever married" but not the "currently married" figures.

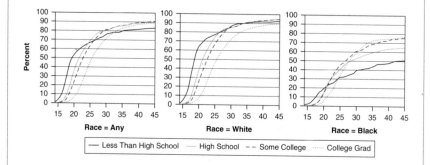

Figure 1 | Educational Differences in Percent of Women Who Have Ever Married by Each Age

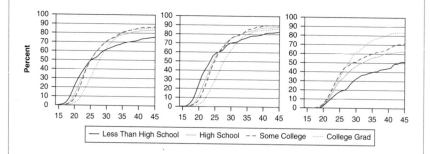

Figure 2 | Educational Differences in Percent of Men Who Have Ever Married by Each Age

Educational Differences in When or If Individuals Marry

Getting a lot of education delays marriage, but for women and men born after 1958, unlike for women born early in the twentieth century, the well educated are just as or more likely to ultimately marry as any other group. In Figures 1 and 2 we see that up into the twenties, the more education you have, the less likely you are to have married, with college graduates the least likely and those with less than a high school education the most likely. But somewhere between the mid-twenties and late thirties a catch-up of the more educated occurs. Although people who get more education typically wait till after they complete schooling to marry, making their marriages later, they are just as likely to ultimately marry by about age forty. In all education groups, roughly 75–90 percent will ever marry.

The patterns for whites look about the same as the patterns for the whole sample. But among black women, those with a college degree not only catch up to the marriage rates of the less educated, but far surpass them. Overall, black women have lower odds of ever marrying than white women. But getting a college education raises ultimate marriage rates by the thirties and forties much more substantially for blacks than whites. (The only group of women where a majority has not married by age forty-five is black women with no college education.)

The overall pattern for men is similar. Like women, men who complete fewer years of schooling are more apt to marry at young ages, but like women, higher-educated men catch up later. However, men's results differ from women's in three key ways. First, men typically marry a couple of years later than women, reflecting the convention that men in first marriages are slightly older than their wives. Second, higher-educated men catch up to lower-educated men sooner than higher-educated women catch up to lower-educated women. Finally, whereas black women with some college are as likely as black women who graduate from college to marry by forty-five, there is a notable difference between black men who do and do not finish college, with black college graduates much more likely to marry than black men with only some college.

Educational Differences in Who Is Currently Married: The Role of Divorce

On average, almost half of American marriages will end in divorce, but divorce rates are lowest for college graduates, and the education gap in divorce has increased in recent decades.[1] There are several reasons for this. Less educated individuals typically marry at an earlier age, which is associated with higher divorce rates. Additionally the lower incomes and greater economic insecurity of those with less education increase stress, affecting divorce.

In Figures 3 and 4, we look at the percentage of people who are currently married at each age, separately for each education group. These figures differ from the "ever married" percentages in Figures 1 and 2, in that those who have married but are divorced and have not remarried appear in Figures 1 and 2 as married but not in Figures 3 and 4 as currently married.[2] Thus, the "currently married" figures are influenced by educational differences not only in who marries, but also in who has divorced.

Looking first at women of all races, we see that after age thirty college graduates pull ahead in the percentage currently married. About 75 percent of college graduates are married at age forty, compared to about 70 percent of those who attained high school or some college and only about 60 percent of those who didn't

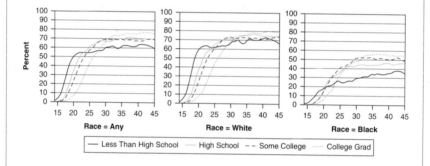

Figure 3 | Educational Differences in Percent of Women Currently Married at Each Age

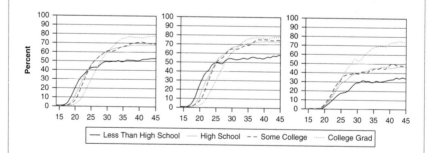

Figure 4 | Educational Differences in Percent of Men Currently Married at Each Age

complete high school. So even though female college graduates marry later, they are so much less likely to divorce that by age forty they are significantly ahead in the percentage currently married, while female high school dropouts fall even further behind. In yet another historical reversal, women with less than a high school education are the *least* likely to be currently married at all ages after thirty.

The figures for white women look quite similar to those described here for all women combined. But for black women, the percent currently married varies more dramatically by education than for whites. This is partly because, as we saw above, education differences are larger for blacks than whites in whether they ever marry by age forty. But there are also education differences in divorce for blacks, as for whites, so the higher divorce rates of less educated black women also contribute to the difference in how many are currently married.

Educational differences in the percent currently married are larger for men than women. Overall, as we saw for women, black men have much lower marriage rates than white men. The only exception is black male college graduates by age thirty-five. By age forty-five, about 75 percent of college-educated black men are married, whereas less than 55 percent of college-educated black women are married at the same age.

Men who attain less than a high school education are much less likely to be married than any other education group of men at most ages. Among white men, a similar percentage of all education groups except those who do not complete high school are married at age thirty, whereas among black men, college graduates have much higher percentages married, and high school dropouts much lower percentages married, compared to the middle education groups.

Summary of Education Differences in Marriage Patterns by Age

Early in the life cycle, those who ultimately get more education are less likely to have married than their less educated counterparts. This is because those staying in school longer also delay getting married longer. But by age forty, the well educated have caught up with the less educated and even surpassed them in the percentage that have married. Thus, ultimately the more educated are as likely or even more likely to marry as any other group. The education differences in whether people ever marry are small for whites, but quite large for blacks, owing partly to the very low marriage rates of the most disadvantaged blacks—those without high school or less.

If we look at who is *currently* married by age, educational differences get even more dramatic. Because the less educated divorce at higher rates, fewer of them are left still married as the decades go by. These differences are particularly pronounced for men.

In sum, if we focus on the early to mid-twenties, a higher percent of the less educated are married. The higher educated groups catch up and pull ahead in their late twenties and thirties, possibly because more of them have the economic resources that young people now consider a prerequisite to marriage. If we focus on the rest of life (represented in our data up to age forty-five), educational differences in those who are currently married are even larger once people move into their late thirties and forties because those at lower educational levels have higher divorce rates.

Why Do Less Educated Individuals Marry at Lower Rates?

One of the main reasons less educated individuals have lower rates of marriage is that rising expectations of marriage since the 1970s have been colliding with declining economic prospects for less educated workers. Interviews with impoverished individuals reveal that while they have high regard for marriage, they think that couples need to have stable jobs and be able to pay the bills for marriage to be appropriate, and those with the lowest education often can't meet this bar.

Data and Methods Used in This Fact Sheet

Our analysis makes use of the National Longitudinal Survey of Youth that began in 1979. This study employed a national probability sample of youth ages fourteen to twenty-two in 1979 (born in 1957 to 1964).[3] The cohort was interviewed every year or two; the study is ongoing, and we make use of the data through 2008 when the cohort was thirty-three to fifty years of age.

Notes

1. See McLanahan, Sara. 2004. "Diverging Destinies: How Children Fare Under the Second Demographic Transition." *Demography* 41(4): 607–627.

2. Those who are widowed are also counted as "ever married" but not currently married, unless they have remarried. However, in these data that only look at the life cycle to age forty-five, very few people have been widowed.

3. See http://www.bls.gov/nls/.

In the News

WOMEN SAY "I DO" TO EDUCATION, THEN MARRIAGE*

Study Highlights Historic Reversal: Women with Degrees More Likely to Wed than Less-Educated Counterparts

Chicago Tribune, May 2, 2012

Leslie Mann

Vicki Rautiokoski married at age 29 after earning bachelor's and master's degrees in engineering. Now, the 39-year-old Chicago resident represents a new demographic to sociologists—the educated woman who got married and stayed married.

For the first time, women with one or more college degrees are more likely to be married by age 40 than their lesser-educated counterparts, according to a long-term study by Paula England, professor of sociology at New York University. "Women's Education and Their Likelihood of Marriage: A Historic Reversal" is a national study that followed women born from 1958 to 1964.

"They marry later, but they catch up," said England. "By age 40, 75 percent of college-educated women are married, compared to 70 percent of those who attend high school or some college and 60 percent of those who did not complete high school."

This represents a gradual shift from previous generations, said England, when fewer female college graduates married.

"Before the 1950s, you still had the image of the college-educated spinster," said England. "Women chose between education and family. Many women went to college only to get their MRSs. Now, women choose to have both education and marriage."

"I got my education and established my career, while dating my husband long-distance. Then, I got married," said Rautiokoski, a materials scientist who lives with her husband, Timo, on the city's Northwest Side. "My mom, on the other hand, got married at age 18, then went to college while she had four kids at home."

Although most of the women in the study are white, the shift is more dramatic among the black participants.

"Overall, black women are less likely to marry than white women are," said England. "For black women, a college education means they are even more likely to marry."

Because the study group began in the 1970s, it does not include as many Hispanic and Asian women as a current sampling of American women would, said England.

The study reflects a change in expectations of the women and their husbands, said England. While many husbands of the 1950s women expected their wives to stay home, she said, their sons expected their wives to work.

"And, they saw the benefits—a higher family income, better lifestyle, ability to buy a house and the insurance of still having an income if one spouse lost a job," she said.

Meanwhile, the study also showed that lack of a college degree affected men's chances of marriage.

"They were seen as 'not marriageable' if they didn't have degrees," said England. "So they were less likely to marry if they didn't have a college education."

England said she sees a new reverence for marriage.

"You no longer need marriage for sex or to have kids," she said. "It's optional and revered. It's a choice and something women aspire to do when they and their partners can afford it."

"Now, marriage is an achievement women make after they are educated and start their careers," said Barbara Risman, professor of sociology at the University of Illinois at Chicago.

As a result, said Risman, college is no longer a "marriage partner market. College girls look at the men they are dating as Mr. Right Now, not Mr. Right. They know they can always find Mr. Right in the job market after college. Marriage is not necessarily what they do automatically after college."

While some of their grandmothers got fired for getting married, today's college graduate is not discriminated against in the workplace for being married, said Risman.

"She is still discriminated against for becoming a mother," said Risman. "But marriage doesn't necessarily equal motherhood. She may have no children, have fewer or delay having them."

In addition to marrying, educated women are more likely than their lesser-educated sisters to stay married, added England.

"There are several reasons," said England. "They marry later, have better incomes and are less likely to have had children before marrying."

Down the road, England will revisit marriage statistics to study the effects of the poor economy.

"The recession is preventing many people from achieving the middle-class things they want before they can marry, so many young women may delay marriage even more," she predicted. "Attitudes toward marriage will continue to evolve too. It's a combination of the two."

"To me, marriage is about security and commitment," said Rautiokoski. "Instead of being 'my boyfriend,' even if it is long-term, being 'my husband' means it's for real and forever. It means I have someone to come to. When I get home from work, there will be someone there to give me a kiss." ▰

36

Men's Changing Contribution to Family Work

Oriel Sullivan

While women still do most of the family work (including household tasks and child care), the balance of both quantitative and attitudinal evidence over the past forty years shows a slow but significant increase in men's contributions. In this chapter, I present some of this evidence and argue that it is the combination of these different kinds of evidence that provides the most convincing case for change. In order to continue to promote change, we must understand the processes involved both at the level of the couple (through analyzing women's efforts to negotiate change in the home) and at the institutional level (through an analysis of institutional obstacles to, and facilitations of, change).

For twenty years, research studies concluded that men's contribution to family work barely changed at a time when women were increasingly joining the workforce. The most common argument was that even though women were working longer hours on the job and cutting back on their own housework, men were not making up for women's lost hours of domestic work. But newer research has shown that men are doing significantly more, both domestic work and particularly child care. Using large-scale data and a longer perspective, it is possible to show a slow but significant change in the direction of a more equal division, with the result that more couples are sharing more tasks. While women still continue to do more family work than their male partners, convergence has been significant, with the result that the total amount of work contributed by men and women in two-parent dual-earner families—including paid work as well as unpaid family work—is now virtually identical.[1]

In addition, slow but significant changes have been observed in gender ideologies, as measured by attitudes to gender equality. For example, according to national opinion polls, Americans have become slightly more conservative about marriage and divorce than they were in the 1970s and 1980s, but the belief in gender equality within families continues to gain acceptance among both men and women. A 2007 national opinion poll conducted by the Pew Research Center provides recent evidence of the increasing importance of this gender equality ideal for Americans. Sixty-two percent of respondents ranked "sharing household tasks" as very important for a successful marriage, up from 47 percent in a similar poll from 1990. The Pew Center notes that sharing household tasks was the only item showing a sharp increase from 1990 to 2007, taking over the number three position from the item on the importance of children for a successful marriage.[2] And these trends are likely to continue: in 2010 a Pew poll showed that 72 percent of younger respondents aged between eighteen and twenty-nine agreed that the best marriage is one in which husband and wife both work and both take care of the house.[3]

In the light of these various kinds of evidence, I argue that the bulk of the past literature in this area has not taken a sufficiently long view of change. Where change has been acknowledged, it has often been accompanied by the claim that the amount of change has not been meaningful. But should we have expected to see a revolutionary change since the 1960s? The question is one of emphasis: Should we see the glass as half empty (by focusing on the fact that women still perform the bulk of domestic labor and child care) or half full (by focusing on the evidence for progressive change in men's contributions)? In contrast to the metaphor of the rapid, dramatic change implied by the word *revolution*, I think a different metaphor is more appropriate: a slow dripping of change, sometimes unnoticeable from year to year, but change that in the end is persistent enough to lead to the slow dissolution and reformation of previously existing structures in processes that stretch perhaps over generations.[4]

These changes *are* important, but we should not expect too much from them over a short period of time. Change can be slow and piecemeal, even at times appearing to have "stalled,"[5] but still in the end effect a radical transformation if we take the longer perspective. In this sense, I have a more optimistic view of slow, incrementally transformative change. It is true that, analyzed at any single point in time over the previous fifty to hundred years, the gender structure appears static and unequal (it still does). However, to emphasize current inequalities at the expense of processes of change is a missed opportunity, because without the will to recognize and analyze change we are stuck in endless contemplation of our half-empty glass while historical processes pass us by. Through an active recognition that change is occurring, albeit slowly and unevenly, we can begin to develop the theoretical frameworks and the empirical tools to recognize how it happens and how it can be promoted.

In the first part of this chapter, I present some of the diverse evidence for change, ranging from changes in attitudes toward gender equality to changes in actual gender practices in the domestic sphere. I address changes in images of masculinity, in particular in relation to fatherhood. Such changes are indicative of shifts both in gender ideologies and practices. While evidence for change in attitudes in itself does not necessarily mean that change is occurring in the performance of family work (that is, it is not sufficient evidence for such change), we might well consider it a necessary condition for meaningful change. I then turn to the quantitative empirical evidence for change in the performance of family work, as measured by the time spent by men and women on various kinds of unpaid family work over the period from the 1960s to the 2000s. My general argument is that the combination of these diverse kinds of evidence provides the most compelling argument in support of change.

EVIDENCE FOR CHANGE: THE CHANGING SOCIAL AND POLITICAL ENVIRONMENT

The association between attitudes to gender equality and the division of family work is by now well established from research based on large-scale data. In general, those men and women whose attitudes to gender equality are more positive ("liberal" or "progressive" in other formulations) tend to share domestic work more equally.[6] With respect to change in attitudes over time, the majority of research has observed movement toward a rejection of normatively defined "gender expectations" in the home. This has taken the form of greater acceptance of nonfamilial roles for women, particularly among younger women with higher levels of education, and rather less clear movement toward acceptance of more familial work for men.

Scott and her coauthors have provided cross-national comparisons of men's and women's attitudes from several countries in Europe on three types of gender-related beliefs and attitudes: the consequences of women working for pay, gender ideology, and the importance of paid work.[7] They found different patterns of change emerging across different countries, and they speculate as to how these differences may be related to (1) patterns of female employment, (2) the consciousness-raising effects of the women's movement, and (3) the relative emphasis on individual autonomy. Their overall conclusion is that despite intercountry and cross-time variations, "traditional gender roles" are increasingly rejected, although there is evidence that the pace of change slowed in the 1990s.[8] They also note that "women have been much more prepared than men to reject traditional gender role attitudes" but, significantly for the argument about change, they also report that within-cohort changes have been more rapid recently among men. This implies a faster process of change in which individuals of the same age group ("cohort") display changing attitudes over time, as opposed to changes occurring because younger cohorts have more egalitarian attitudes than older ones. An apparent slowdown in the pace of attitude change toward gender equality in the United States was recently reported by Cotter, Hermsen, and Vanneman.[9] However, any stagnation in their three indicators of attitudes about women, work, and motherhood—such as whether children suffer if their mother works outside the home—occurred only in the 1990s; the 2000s again showed a clear trend in the direction of more gender-egalitarian attitudes.

The significance of changes in attitudes among men toward gender equality is that this finding contradicts the argument that men are taking on more household responsibilities simply as a practical requirement as their partners take on paid jobs. Further evidence of men's changing attitudes comes from the recent growth of research on changing symbolic representations of masculinity.[10] Writers on masculinity have found changing images of masculinity and fatherhood and real changes in gender practice, particularly in relation to masculine caring behavior.[11] When images of men change in the media, we see the symbolic representation of the possibility of "the new father." This new, or "involved father," who bonds deeply with and cares for his children, according to Knijn, becomes part of male gender identification.[12] Hochschild argues for the existence of a wide diversity of choices of fathering styles, however, rather than one simplistic media image of the new father.[13] Smart and Neale take the point further when they refer to the image of the new father as being composed of different and often contradictory elements.[14] Nevertheless, a new normative image of involved fatherhood is increasingly reflected in public policy initiatives designed to promote gender equality by encouraging men to become more involved in the family, for example, through the extension of parental leave and the introduction of paternal leave.[15]

The question is: To what extent can the emergence of new, diverse, and shifting images and ideals of fatherhood and masculinity be linked to empirical changes in men's caring behavior? At the turn of the twenty-first century, there is considerable evidence for changes in paternal behavior—in particular, evidence for a substantial increase in paternal involvement in child care.[16] Moreover, there is now also more general agreement in support of Coltrane's claim that "the move is towards uncoupling gender from caring."[17] A growing body of research focuses on involved fathers or even "equal caretakers"—fathers who participate to greater degrees in caring for children, as opposed to only filling the traditional breadwinner role. At the extreme, involved fathers do not make a distinction between mothering and fathering in caring.[18]

A number of authors have directly addressed the theoretical reasons underlying such changes in the meaning and practice of fatherhood. Beck and Beck-Gernsheim argued that the social forces of late modernity generate increasing individualization, autonomy, and the weakening of family ties. The parent-child bond, however, is an enduring element in the family despite high rates of marital dissolution (Beck and Beck-Gernsheim 1995).[19] Other authors have placed more emphasis on issues of personal identity,[20] arguing that increases in involved fatherhood are "in line with the growing awareness of, or belief in, personal identity as a reflexive identity."[21] Men are now more likely to see themselves as choosing fatherhood, and how to do it, than simply following traditionally gendered life-course norms.

To summarize, the overall picture suggests shifts in attitudes and representations of masculinity occurring both within and between successive generations, and somewhat slower changes in practice, particularly in fathers' care of children. Such changes in attitudes and symbolic representations support the case for a change in the environment in which men and women make their choices. And, as I have already suggested, our strongest argument for change in the direction of gender equality is the *co-incidence* of changes in this wider context with the growing empirical evidence for changes in gender practices in the home. I now turn to the quantitative evidence for change in men and women's contributions to family work.

EVIDENCE FOR CHANGE: THE QUANTITATIVE DATA

The longitudinal multinational quantitative empirical evidence for change is based on nationally representative data sets, and stretches in time from the 1960s to the 2010s. The importance of the quantitative evidence is about consistency: consistent measures across time can actually measure change.

There are several sources of quantitative evidence for long-term changes over time in the allocation of family work, but time-use diary studies are by now perhaps the most widely used. In such diaries, people record their activities every ten or fifteen minutes throughout the day, which yields more accurate results than simply asking people how much time they spend in a particular activity per day. Researchers have analyzed time-use diaries and found growing evidence for change,[22] confirming that both within and across countries changes have taken place in the amount of time that men and women spend in housework and child care and that these changes are in the direction of greater equity.

At the start of the twenty-first century, the average full-time employed American married man with children has increased his contribution to child care by four hours a week since the 1970s, and his contribution to other family work by two hours a week. Overall, he now does six hours a week of child care and ten hours a week of other family work. By comparison, the average full- or part-time employed American married woman with children is employed for fewer hours per week on average than her male counterpart, but she does eleven hours of child care (an increase of seven hours from the 1970s) and nineteen hours of other family work (a decrease of three hours from the 1970s). So, over thirty years, she has increased her total time devoted to family work and child care by four hours (all of it in child care), while the average full-time employed married man has increased his total by six hours (four hours in child care and two hours in other family work).[23] The outcome of these changes is that the percentage of family work and child care done by men in families in which both partners are employed has increased from something over 20 percent in the 1970s to nearly a third at the start of the twenty-first century. Men's relative contributions are even greater in those families where both partners are employed full-time. Here the contribution of the man has increased from just under 30 percent in 1975 to 38 percent by the start of the twenty-first century.[24] A recent update by Bianchi and her co-authors (following up the data to the year 2010) confirms these trends for married mothers and fathers into the first decade of the twenty-first century.[25]

Similar trends are evident across other Western countries. Using data from a range of industrialized countries over the period from the 1960s, Hook showed an overall cross-country increase in men's contribution to family work (that is, including housework, child care, and shopping) from less than 20 percent to almost 35 percent.[26] This means that cross-nationally the share of all unpaid work done by women shows a striking downward trend (reflecting greater gender equality). Moreover, despite the negative view of the U.S. record expressed by many social observers and particularly well summarized by the family sociologist Stephanie Coontz in a 2013 *New York Times* article, American men in fact carry out a larger share of the unpaid work than do men in the other Anglophone countries (Canada, Australia, and the UK).[27] Moreover, the Anglophone countries as a group perform slightly better in terms of gender equity in unpaid work than the continental European states (France, Germany, and the Netherlands), and much better than the southern European countries (Spain and Italy), where men still do less than 30 percent of all unpaid work. Countries from Northern Europe (Denmark, Sweden, Norway, and Finland), however, seem to do somewhat better—Swedish men already did 41 percent of the total unpaid work by 2001.

Kan, Sullivan, and Gershuny showed how these trends toward greater gender equality varied according to the type of unpaid work for the countries of Western

Europe and North America.[28] The average time women in these countries spent in routine housework tasks (cleaning, cooking, and laundry) was very high in the 1960s (between 210 and 270 minutes per day). This dropped rapidly to between 120 and 190 minutes in the late 1980s (except in Italy, where the time spent in routine housework was significantly longer at 275 minutes per day). The average time men spent in cooking, cleaning, and laundry in the 1960s—around 20 minutes per day—was ten times less than the time that women spent in these tasks. However, this time increased gradually to an average of about 40 minutes per day in the 1980s in most countries. From the late 1980s to the early 2000s these converging trends continued, though on average at a slower rate than in the earlier period. Time spent caring for other family members (mainly children) showed a different pattern of change. In contrast to the decline in women's routine housework, the time women spent on care fluctuated and increased to some extent over the past four decades. Men spent relatively little time on care overall (an average of between 15 and 20 minutes a day in the early 2000s), although again with a slow increase since the 1960s. Shopping and domestic travel times showed a rising trend for both genders and are less unequally divided (though women still do the largest part of these activities, too).

To this point I have outlined some very broad-brush trends. However, an emphasis in the feminist literature has been the importance of looking at differences among and between subpopulations. Differences of this kind can inform us about the processes involved in change. One important area of difference is educational attainment, and this has been addressed in several recent papers.[29] I used U.S. and British time-use data sets to examine thirty-year changes in the division of domestic work and child care by educational attainment, comparing men and women parents in dual-earner couples. These more finely nuanced trends indicated that different processes of change were at work for different household and care tasks; for wives and husbands in different countries; and according to levels of educational attainment. In the case of child care, dual-earner parents from the highest level of educational attainment proportionately dramatically increased their time in child care over the period 1975–2003 in relation to those with lower levels of educational attainment. This process of social differentiation perhaps reflects both different parental investment in childhood activities likely to promote educational success and differential access to resources and benefits (such as paid leave or flex time) that make it possible for parents to spend more time with their children, and acts to reinforce patterns of differential human capital formation.

On the other hand, looking at changing differences in domestic work, a completely different picture emerges. In the case of dual-earner fathers, we observe a striking example of a reducing difference in which, for both the United States and Britain, fathers with lower levels of educational attainment increased their time in domestic tasks relatively more over the period, to equal the contribution of college-educated fathers. In earlier periods, college-educated dual-earner fathers spent more time on domestic tasks than did those with lower levels of educational attainment. But by the twenty-first century, education-based differences in fathers' domestic work had disappeared. In contrast, the proportionate decline in the domestic work time of dual-earner mothers with the highest levels of educational attainment is consistent with a simple opportunity-cost hypothesis in a situation where employment opportunities are growing for women.

To sum up, change is by now widely reported in different areas—but the question remains, are these changes meaningful in magnitude? It is true that the overall increase in men's contribution to core domestic work may not seem that impressive if we calculate the change over four decades (only 20 minutes more per day after more than thirty years). In addition, it is still reasonable to emphasize the ongoing discrepancy between the overall amount of time that women and men spend in domestic work tasks. But some authors continue to argue that the main effect involved in any change is that of women's reduction in hours spent doing housework. The upward trend for men as well as the downward trend for women in routine housework tasks is consistent in direction across different countries and statistically significant when controlling for other relevant variables. The fact that the trends for men and women move in opposite directions supports the change to greater gender equality in the performance of domestic tasks. And although statistical significance in itself does not translate directly to substantive importance, these trends are not only statistically robust but also consistent, both internally (that is, over time and space), and externally (in relation to other evidence for change).

How to Explain Change

Until now, I have focused on evidence for changes in men's contributions to family work. Understanding the processes that have been involved in such changes is crucial, both in attempting to understand circumstances that have enabled change and in continuing to promote it. The question is, then, how might we go about explaining change?

The model that I suggest emphasizes the importance of daily interaction between partners, for the couple relationship constitutes the arena for gender relations and practice within the domestic sphere. There is a message here for all of us, for through this focus on daily interaction it is possible to conceive of women's everyday struggles as a part of wider social processes of change. Individuals bring their own resources to this struggle. These resources involve their absolute and relative levels of income, their level of education, the status of their job, and their skills at negotiation or in the management of emotions.[30] In addition, all interaction necessarily occurs within a wider institutional and symbolic social context. Negotiation about household labor is embedded within wider structures of diminishing patriarchy and individualism within late modern capitalism, as well as within a local context of (changing) gender ideologies.

Within this context, individuals "do gender" in the domestic sphere. The "doing gender" perspective emphasizes processes of "situated behavior," in which gender is continuously being actively constructed in interaction.[31] According to this approach, for an individual woman or man the "accomplishment" of gender involves behaving in a way that is "accountable" to expectations of appropriate gender behavior. Thus, in general, men perform normatively masculine-defined tasks and women perform normatively feminine-defined tasks in order to be accepted as "proper" men and women. But since they are social constructions, the normative guidelines that regulate appropriate gender behavior are contingent on the situation, and they vary from time to time and from place to place. As such, the idea of doing gender in daily interaction clearly holds potential for the production of new gender relations and therefore for the possibility of change (referred to by Deutsch as "undoing gender"[32]).

One framework for conceptualizing such change is provided by the idea of gender consciousness. Gerson and Peiss describe *gender consciousness* as the extent of consciousness or awareness of gender issues.[33] This ranges from a generalized vague awareness of gender at one end of the continuum to a full consciousness of the rights that are associated with specific genders at the other. The development of this consciousness partly arises from the recognition of rights based on information from the wider society. The rise of feminism, for example, provided new conditions for the development of gender consciousness.

Critically for my argument, however, social interaction also influences the recognition of, and generation of, these rights. This means that the active bargaining and negotiation that women and men engage in daily can help to develop gender consciousness by acknowledging rights (and responsibilities) in social interaction. According to Thompson, gender consciousness thus constitutes a central component of women's attempts at change.[34] The key to understanding changes in the family roles of women and men is to integrate different levels of analysis—from changing gender attitudes, to images in the media, to couple's negotiations, to couple's division of domestic chores and child care.

The model I advance is an integrative approach, which treats gender as a structure that combines individual, interactional, and institutional dimensions.[35]

Thus, "actors shape the gender structure they inherit."[36] My argument is that, to better understand the processes of change that are occurring, we need to make connections between the wider social and political environment that affects both the public and the private spheres as well as the interactions and negotiations that individuals engage in daily, and to focus on gender relations and practices in the domestic sphere. It is critical to identify changes at the level of the ideologies and images that structure gendered interactions. In addition, we see how attitudes toward equality in the family have shifted across, and even within, generations. How these attitudes are shaped, and how they translate into (inter)action, is far less well researched. Empirical observations of changes in practice within the home, as measured by the time spent on different domestic tasks, are also by now well documented. But again, far less is known about the processes that have led to these changes. At this level, the key lies in the detailed analysis of processes of change as they occur in day-to-day intimate interaction. We must pay attention not just to observations of changes in practice but also to the resources, processes, negotiations, and struggles that have led to changes, as described by the actors themselves.

CONCLUSION

I have presented an argument that change has happened in the division of family work, and I argue that these changes in family life deserve our serious attention. I have shown that (slow) change is ongoing by reference to the large-scale empirical documentation of who does what at home, and with evidence from changes in attitudes and symbolic representations of masculinity. It is the combination of evidence that provides the convincing argument. Yet, we should not be complacent about these changes or their continuation. Several authors have recently described the existing institutional context as a significant barrier to further advances in gender equality.[37] The continuing gender segregation in domestic tasks in the home also presents a substantial barrier to further rapid gender convergence in domestic time use. Domestic tasks seem to remain divided as "masculine"-defined and "feminine"-defined, and these divisions do not appear particularly susceptible to change even in countries where gender ideologies are considered to be relatively nontraditional (the Scandinavian countries). This suggests that domestic gender equality will be most difficult to achieve in the feminine-defined areas of domestic work.

What is clear is that further changes in this direction will have been struggled for, fought over, and hard won, not only in the public and political arena but also during innumerable daily contestations and negotiations both in the home and outside of it. One goal of feminist research has been women's empowerment—and by focusing on it daily as a potentially transformative process, it is possible to conceive of women's everyday struggles with their male partners as part of social change. According to such a perspective, individual actors are also active agents of change, even if the process may not be a rapid or an easy one. Progressive change is not inevitable, and it may be subject to reverses. However, under the right conditions of changing gender ideologies and consciousness, we can see the possibility for effecting change. My argument is a return to the call of early second-wave feminism that "the personal is political." We should resist the fatalistic assertion that men and women come from different planets and are thus doomed to permanent miscommunication. Every small struggle to redefine boundaries, to open up the "marital conversation," to negotiate change in gender practices, can contribute in the long road to gender equality in the home and outside of it.

Notes

1. Bianchi, Robinson, and Milkie (2006); Gershuny, Robinson, and Sullivan (2014).
2. Pew Research Center (2007).
3. Pew Research Center (2010).
4. Sullivan (2006, 2011). The metaphor of the slow drip of change is cited in Ferree (2010).
5. England (2010).
6. See Goldscheider and Waite (1991).
7. Scott, Alwin, and Brown (1996).
8. *Ibid.*, p. 489.
9. Cotter, Hermsen, and Vanneman (2011).
10. Connell (2000).
11. See Coltrane (1998, 2004); Deutsch (1999); Marsiglio and Pleck (2004).
12. Knijn (1995).
13. Hochschild (1995).
14. Smart and Neale (1999).
15. O'Brien, Brandth, and Kvande (2007).
16. See Bianchi et al. (2006); Pleck and Masciadrelli (2003).
17. Coltrane (1998, p. 106).
18. Gerson (2001).
19. Beck and Beck-Gernsheim (1995).
20. See Giddens (1992); Knijn (1995).

21. Knijn (1995).
22. See Bianchi et al. (2006); Gershuny (2000); Robinson and Godbey (1999).
23. Numbers taken from Bianchi et al. (2006).
24. Fisher, Egerton, Gershuny, and Robinson (2007).
25. Bianchi, Sayer, Milkie, and Robinson (2012).
26. Hook (2006).
27. Gershuny et al. (2014).
28. Numbers taken from Kan, Sullivan, and Gershuny (2011), updated from Sullivan and Gershuny (2001).
29. Craig and Mullen (2012); England (2013); Sullivan (2010).
30. Benjamin and Sullivan (1999).
31. West and Zimmerman (1987); Ferree (1990).
32. Deutsch (2007).
33. Gerson and Peiss (1985).
34. Thompson (1993).
35. Connell (2000); Risman (2004).
36. Risman (1998).
37. England (2010); Ferree (2010).

In the News

IT'S NOT JUST US: WOMEN AROUND THE WORLD DO MORE HOUSEWORK AND HAVE LESS FREE TIME

ThinkProgress, March 14, 2014

Bryce Covert

In all of the 26 countries that make up the Organisation for Economic Co-operation and Development (OECD), women take on more than half of the unpaid work that needs to get done, such as caring for children or doing housework, according to OECD data reported by Shane Ferro at Reuters. That leaves them with less leisure time than men.

On average, women in these countries do 60 percent of the unpaid work, although it varies. In the U.S. it's just over 60 percent, while in Japan and Korea it's over 80 percent. Meanwhile, Norway gets the closest to equality at 54 percent, followed by Sweden and Denmark.

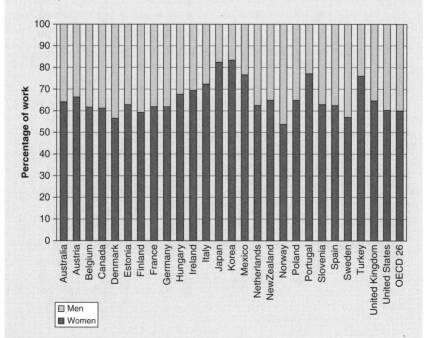

Figure 1 | Percentage of Unpaid Work Done by Gender

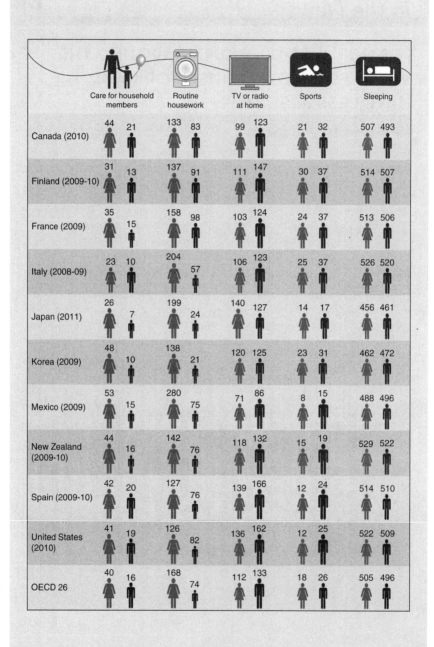

And while men spend more time in paid work—5.42 hours a day, on average across OECD countries, versus 4.55 hours for women—they get more leisure time, finding 5.33 hours a day, while women get just 4.7. In fact, among these countries, women spend 40 minutes per day caring for family members and 168 doing "routine housework," while men put in 16 and 74, respectively. Meanwhile, men get 21 more minutes for watching TV or listening to the radio and 8 more for playing sports. Here in the U.S., those disparities are also clear: Women put in 22 more minutes on care and 44 more on housework, while men get 26 extra minutes for TV and 13 for sports.

Past OECD data have shown that children are a big culprit for why women are spending so much of their time on paid or unpaid work: each additional child reduces a woman's discretionary time by 2.3 hours a week, but it only docks 1.7 hours out of a man's week. And when women are doing chores, they're more likely to be doing multiple tasks at once, spending 18 percent more time on "secondary" activities.

In the United States, there's also a disparity in the overall numbers of men and women performing these tasks. On a given day, half of American women will be found doing housework, while just 20 percent of men will do the same. Things have improved since the days of Ward Cleaver, as men do three times as much child care and more than double the housework they did in 1965. But given that women are still doing the vast majority of this work—while a record number of them are supplying most of their family's income—they are far more likely to be exhausted than men.

It's worth considering what's going on in the Nordic countries that are much closer to equality in these tasks. Norway, Sweden, and Denmark are some of the countries with the most generous paid family leave policies as well as publicly provided child care. That has given women's labor force participation a huge boost. And it is also likely part of why the genders are better about splitting unpaid work. In Sweden, fathers get up to 240 days of paid family leave, but they have to take at least two months in order for their families to get any time off. As a result, 85 percent take leave to be with their new children. The effects of men taking paid leave go beyond those initial months, as those who take longer leaves are more involved with their children's care later on.

Here in the U.S., just three states guarantee all workers paid family leave. The results from California's program show similar effects as Sweden's: before paid leave, 35 percent of dads took time off; now 76 percent do. But most dads don't get that luxury since the country only guarantees unpaid leave. Meanwhile, child care usually costs more than food or rent for the typical American family. ▪

37

Being "The Man" without Having a Job and/or
Providing Care Instead of "Bread"

Kristen Myers and Ilana Demantas

T his chapter looks at the ways that traditional "breadwinning" men felt about
themselves and their families when they became unemployed during the
recession of the early twenty-first century. During 2009–2011, a broad range of
jobs were eliminated. A lot of manual and seasonal labor, like construction jobs,
disappeared. But so did many high-paying positions, such as management. Typically, these jobs were held by men—so when these jobs went away, the men went
too. The media called this a "mancession" because men were hit so hard. And
men were hit hard personally as well as economically. Before the recession, the
forty men in our study thought that to be a "good man," they should be the chief
economic providers for their households. Once they lost their jobs, they could
no longer provide financially for their families. They had to find new ways to
be "the man." Interestingly, these men did not give up on manhood. Instead,
they creatively reworked manhood to fit their newfound circumstances, providing care to their families instead of providing for them financially. Ironically, they
redefined "women's work" as men's work in order to re-center themselves in their
households.

Beginning in 2007, workers in the United States began to feel the effects of what
would become a global economic crisis.[1] In October of 2009, the U.S. national
unemployment rate hit 10.1 percent. The United States had not experienced
unemployment on this level since 1983, in the era of "stagflation" when prices
went up but wages stayed the same. Economists have called the recent downturn the "Great Recession," the "Long Recession," and a "double-dip recession,"

because the economy dropped each time they forecasted recovery. As late as 2013, we were still seeing aftershocks from the initial decline six years earlier.

For many workers, unemployment was not a new phenomenon. For example, blue-collar workers in some industries, like steel, timber, and mining, have experienced chronic job loss for years.[2] In the case of timber, an entire community depended on that single industry. When it failed, the whole community broke down. Although devastating to those involved, these pockets of economic collapse were largely confined to narrow geographic areas and to populations of people who were connected to each other through community ties: their children went to the same schools, they shopped at the same stores, and they competed for the same jobs.

In contrast, the effects of the Great Recession were much broader. The U.S. Bureau of Labor Statistics shows that economic shocks from this recession affected many industries and job sectors, cutting across class lines and geographic boundaries. Semi-skilled workers were laid off as in past recessions, but so were highly educated workers. People lost all kinds of jobs: bankers, small business owners, managers, truck drivers, and construction workers were let go. This happened across the United States and also affected economies of countries across the globe. We were seeing something different.

As in past recessions, workers' sex affected whether they lost their jobs. According to the Bureau of Labor Statistics, 11.4 percent of adult men across the nation were unemployed in October 2009, as compared to 8.7 percent of adult women.[3] This trend differed from previous recessions, when more women than men lost jobs, if any sex disparity existed at all. This new pattern was labeled a "mancession" by the media,[4] who claimed that the economic downturn disproportionately affected men. As Meena Hartenstein wrote in 2010 in the *NY Daily News*, "Bad news fellas: as women's careers bounce back from the recession, statistics show the economic collapse has been so hard on men it should be called the 'Mancession.'" This headline-grabbing expression was both misleading and intriguing.

The term *mancession* was misleading because it implied that women fared better economically than men in the recession. On the surface, the fact that more men than women lost jobs *could* be interpreted as men doing worse than women, but that would be incorrect. Here's why: First, many women probably kept their jobs because they were paid less than men in similar occupations. To cut costs, employers may have found it more profitable to fire men than women.[5] Ironically, then, women's jobs may have been more secure in this recession precisely because their labor has been systematically devalued in society. Second, job sectors such as construction and other seasonal work were disproportionately hit by this recession. Those jobs were disproportionately held by men, not women, due to sex segregation in the workplace. Last, men seem to be recovering at a quicker rate than women. In July 2011, men's unemployment rate had improved to 9 percent, whereas women's was still 7.9 percent. In May 2013, the gap closed further: 7.1 percent of men were unemployed as compared to 6.7 percent of women. Therefore, the term *mancession* incorrectly pitted women's paid labor against men's.

Although misleading, the concept of a mancession is also sociologically intriguing. So many men across so many types of work lost jobs in markedly high numbers. In our society, being a "good man" has a complex connection to men's ability to provide for their families. Even in today's society, where almost as many women as men work for pay outside of the home, we are still influenced by the "breadwinner ideal." This is the notion that a man—as head of the household—should be able to earn what is called a "family wage,"[6] or enough money to provide for his entire family without any other income.[7] This logic presumes a paid worker (man), who works outside of the home and who lives with an unpaid worker (woman), who works at maintaining the household.[8] The archetypal man and woman are supposed to work symbiotically but separately to sustain a heterosexual family.[9]

Even though the family wage is uncommon and diminishing (it is simply not possible or even desirable for many families in the United States), the *ideal* of the breadwinner has flourished over the decades, fomenting gender inequality[10] in ways that shape the organization of our families and workplaces.[11] It also influences how we think about ourselves. Although there are many competing images of manhood today, Jiping Zuo calls breadwinning "one of the most salient masculine identities in American society"[12] and explains,

> Cultural norms about breadwinning compel individuals in the society to "do gender" to meet the expectations of others. . . . As a result, breadwinning serves as a powerful ideological device in forming individuals' self-identity, and in producing and reproducing gendered behavior and activities in everyday life.[13]

At its heart, breadwinning connects men's earnings to their negotiation of masculinity.[14] It affects—or frames—how people conceptualize themselves and others.[15]

Job loss disrupts not only economic security but also men's self-concepts. According to sociologist Raewyn Connell, men's job loss harms men and disrupts the gendered order, because "by virtue of a class situation and practice, these men have lost the institutional benefits of patriarchy."[16] Breadwinning is a core tenet of what she calls "hegemonic masculinity," the standard of manhood by which all men are measured, even if most men do not or cannot attain it.

In this chapter, we consider the conundrum of the mancession. We interviewed forty men who lost jobs in the current recession, and we asked them about their daily lives as unemployed workers. Interestingly, we did not ask them to talk about what it meant to be a man or what impact unemployment had on their status at home or in their communities. And yet almost every participant in our study talked about the ways that unemployment affected their manhood. In their interviews, participants were doing "identity work"[17] to save face as men who could no longer provide for their families—indeed, they provided no financial contributions to their households at all. Nevertheless, our participants found other ways to show that they were still men.

Talking to Men about Job Loss

This project started in early 2010. We had read a lot about the widespread effects of the recession, which supposedly ended in 2009, according to the Bureau of Labor Statistics. Despite optimistic reports from economists about impending recovery, families in our region continued to struggle. We decided to interview workers who had been downsized, or forced out of work, to learn how they were coping with job loss. We asked about their educational background, job training and skills, access to health care, and authority at work as well as their strategies for finding work in the future. We used semi-structured interview techniques, asking all of the men the same questions but allowing the men to tell their stories in their own ways. Interviews lasted from one to two hours, sometimes longer.

We did not intend to talk only to men, but nineteen out of twenty of our participants happened to be men. In answering our questions, these men talked about masculinity and their roles in their households. We did not expect that. We began to analyze their stories about the same time that the media started talking about the mancession. The men's stories resonated with the media accounts, and we decided to collect more data on men only. In summer 2012, we interviewed twenty-one more downsized men.

How Did We Find These Men?

In the first wave of interviews in 2010, we used a snowball convenience sample to locate people who had recently been laid off. Convenience sampling is common in qualitative research, especially for harder-to-reach populations.[18] Despite the high rate of unemployment in 2010, we considered these participants to be hard to reach because they were dispersed throughout a variety of occupations. Talking face-to-face with these men was hard. We occasionally found ourselves jettisoning tried-and-true interview techniques for establishing rapport, such as making eye contact and active listening, because we seemed to be exacerbating men's discomfort. Some men spoke haltingly, looked away, reddened, sweated, stood up and paced.[19] They may have had particular trouble talking about their experiences to female interviewers. Kristen is a middle-class white professor in her mid-forties and Ilana is a white first-generation immigrant in her late twenties. We found that, contrary to our training as interviewers, avoiding eye contact and maintaining physical distance between participant and interviewer seemed to relieve some of the men, allowing them to expound on their feelings.

After analyzing this first wave of interviews, we decided to conduct a second wave of interviews in 2012, at a time when the economy was presumably reviving. We focused exclusively on men, and we recruited them by placing an ad in two newspapers: *Backpage Chicago* and *Backpage Kansas City.* We picked Chicago and Kansas City as these are two large cities in the Midwest with high unemployment rates and with close proximity to our universities. Ilana had a small grant that allowed us to pay each participant $25 for his time.[20] We had more interested men than money to pay them, so we capped this wave at twenty-one participants. Ilana conducted all the interviews, using the telephone to interview all but three men. Phone interviews have the benefit of access to study participants, regardless of distance or location.[21] The phone also helped to create a social distance and greater sense of privacy that seemed to alleviate some of the anxieties we had observed in our face-to-face interviews of the first wave. In cases when men did get emotional, we could tell by the tone of their voice. Because some participants felt discomfort talking about these issues, we believe phone interviews actually produced more disclosure. All these interviews were at least as long as those in the first wave—several even longer.

Who Were These Men?

Our sample of forty men was diverse in terms of race, class, marital status, and length of unemployment. To the best of our knowledge, all men were heterosexual. They worked in a variety of occupations before job loss, including sales, truck driving, management, and construction. Most of their female partners worked in gendered jobs, including elementary school teachers, nurses, and retail associates. The average length of unemployment in this group was 10.1 months, which was about the national average. Seventeen men (43 percent) were married, and thirteen of those had at least one child. Sixteen (40 percent) were men living with their girlfriends, although nine of those were in long-term commitments with domestic partners. Six of these couples had at least one child together. Seven (17 percent) were single, although four of those relied on another female family member. Most of the participants were from the Chicago, Illinois, area (thirty-six); three were from Kansas City, Missouri, and one was from Raleigh, North Carolina. Our sample was racially diverse: 22 were white; 13 were black; 3 were Asian; and 2 were Latino.

Despite coming from different economic and racial backgrounds and communities, these men expressed similar ideas about men's role in the household. Here, we analyze these men's struggles to forge new identities in an economy that undermined their ability to be the primary breadwinner of their households.

WHAT MAKES A MAN?

When we talked to the men about job loss, we learned that losing work confronted their ideals about what it means to be a man. Most of the men in this study subscribed to traditional views of manhood, saying that men are supposed to provide for women and children. As Walter[22] (white, forty-nine, forklift driver) said, "A man is supposed to try to support a woman as much as possible." Similarly, Richard (white, sixty-one, journalist) said,

> From a very young age, we males are taught that we pay the bills. A woman doesn't pick up the check at dinner. It's just not the way things are.

Study participants said that men are supposed to be self-sufficient. Martin (African American, fifty-nine, truck driver) said, "A man is supposed to take care of themselves." Lionel (African American, thirty-seven, machine operator) said, "I was told as a kid that as a man I should be working, be responsible, be able to take care of your own self and not look for handouts." Lawrence (African American, forty-one, grocery store manager) said,

> The man is always the head of the household, even going back to my great, great-grandfather, when he was out of work from the railroad, okay? Just because my great-grandmother was a school teacher who was mainly making all the money, he was still the man. He still made the decisions. This reflects to this day. Nothing has changed. That hasn't changed.

Rex (African American, forty-two, real estate) said that men are supposed to be "the financial rock of the family." The men in this study were not pro-feminist progressives. They were traditional "men's men," as Lawrence and Martin referred to themselves: heads of households, providers. Job loss confronted their conceptualizations of manhood head-on.

When asked how they felt about losing their jobs, our participants talked about the ways that the economic crisis had altered their self-concepts *as men*. Joe (white, fifty-seven, banking) explained, "[Job loss] reduces your self-esteem considerably. I grew up always working and providing for my family and now I couldn't." Joe went on to say, "It is harder to keep up your dignity when you do not have a job. It makes you, or at least it did me, feel like less of a man." Similarly, Steve (white, twenty-eight, banking) said, "It's been tough because you know, you kind of feel almost worthless in a way because you know you are not producing anymore." Kenny (white, forty, restaurant owner) knew that the restaurant he owned with his parents was failing. He considered leaving town to find more secure work, but he didn't leave until the restaurant finally closed: "I didn't want to further burden my parents and be a piece of shit. I wasn't going to do that. I have a *little* bit of pride." These men talked about worth, dignity, and pride. These traditionally masculine self-concepts were fundamentally challenged as the men faced job loss.

Many men felt depressed after losing their jobs. Ben (white, fifty-eight, semi-skilled labor) said, "Ah, there are days, you know, when I don't even want to get up. I think I have depression but I don't want to get analyzed for that. But, yes, I'm depressed. I feel useless." Steve (white, twenty-eight, banker) described his sense of emptiness and loss:

> You know, for me, having a job and a career—that's what got you out of bed five days a week in the morning. And got you something to work at. And now you are just kind of sitting around and hop[ing] that somebody calls you and you can get back on that track. For now it's a lot more downtime. It's kind of depressing sometimes.

Several men described using alcohol and drugs to manage their depression. After he lost his job, for example, Alex (white, twenty-seven, construction management) said, "I drank for the first couple of days. Because, well, what else are you going to do." Carl (white, thirty, construction) said, "I am ashamed to say this but I've been drinking a lot lately because I am still heartbroken over being laid off." Similarly, Kenny said,

> I did a lot of drugs. Smoked a lot of pot. And I drank. I was in a state of depression. So it didn't matter to me. I didn't do much with my time. I kinda just existed.

These men's personal identities were upset profoundly by job loss and their inability to find more work. As Kenny said after his interview, "What I forgot to tell you about is the overwhelming sense of loss and failure that I felt for months and months."

In losing work, these men could not earn money, which would be problematic for anyone with bills to pay. But for these men, the problems associated with losing income were amplified by their belief in the breadwinner ideology. They argued that men are *supposed* to provide for their families. When they were unable to provide, their social identities faltered. As Adik (Malaysian, forty-three, teacher) said,

> Whether we like it or not, we are still living in a man's world. The assumption is that men are the breadwinners. So if you are not a breadwinner, you feel uncomfortable.

Joe said that job loss had added a lot more stress to his life: "[Losing your job] reduces your self-esteem considerably. I grew up always working and providing for my family, and now I couldn't do that." Pierre (white, fifty-five, chef) said,

> Well, in this culture, men are almost identified by what they do. It becomes a huge part of your self-esteem and your self-identity. It's tough, really tough when people ask where I'm working now.

Participants intertwined their conceptualizations of employment and manhood consistently throughout the interviews. They offered these gendered analyses in response to the question, "How did losing your job make you feel?" Their answers revealed the extent to which they bought into the breadwinner image, using it to measure their own worth as men.

MAKING ENDS MEET

To make ends meet, most of the men in this study became reliant on their female partners' income. John (white, sixty, sales account executive) said, "Since my wife has her position, you know, I'm not necessarily in dire straits." Similarly, Carl said,

> It's a lot harder to pay the bills, with me only working part-time making minimum wage. . . . It's a blessing that my wife works and makes good money. If I was living on my own, I would be in serious trouble.

Ben said,

> If she wasn't working, we'd be in a world of hurt. The utilities wouldn't get paid, food would not be [bought]. It's not that we eat anything extraordinary or extravagant, we are lucky with the food that we have, beef once a week, and pork, but if she wasn't working that would be a big deal.

James (African American, sixty, truck driver) said,

> My youngest two children are still in school. They don't have means of getting
> insurance and health care on their own, so I have to hustle and take care of them.
> I can't just leave them hanging. But my wife is still working, so it's evening out.

Despite the reversal of roles—men relying on women economically—these men
described their dependence matter-of-factly, without defensiveness. They framed
their wives' employment as fortuitous, "a blessing." Joe described his situation:

> For two days after being laid off I did small chores around the house. On the third
> day, I suffered a heart attack, and was in the hospital for a week before then recuper-
> ating at home. After getting through that period of time, I then went back to worry-
> ing about how we were going to be able to keep up with the bills that kept coming
> in. Now there were more, because of medical bills too. Luckily my wife has a really
> good insurance through the public school [where she works]. I can't even imagine
> the position we would have been if she hadn't been working there.

Rather than resenting his wife, he seemed truly grateful to her for getting him
through what he called his "worst-case scenario." Similarly, Pierre said this when
asked how he felt about his wife's employment:

> I'm grateful for it. She has a very good position and a lot of good benefits. We get
> medical insurance through her job. In three years she qualifies for a pension, and
> frankly if she didn't have that, we would be up the creek. The fact that her position
> basically enables us to keep our home and keep our vehicles and keep our insur-
> ance so medical bills are not eating us alive. Overall I'm grateful for it, there is no
> resentment at all, believe me.

Even though women's income could have signified a loss of traditional male
power in the household, our participants directed no acrimony toward their partners. Some were not wholly comfortable with the shift, however—like Ben, who
said this:

> I just feel bad I'm not contributing the way I used to, but I rely on her. I mean it's
> not that I shouldn't rely on her. It's the man in me, the protector-provider that you
> are supposed to be. I've fallen short, so.

But Ben internalized his discomfort rather than directing it toward his employed
wife.

BECOMING MR. MOM

As their households were restructured, housework was thrust upon these men. Our study participants did not consciously choose to prioritize their families over their careers, which has been a recent trend among some well-educated middle-class families.[23] The men in our study came to household labor reluctantly.

Some men used labels like "Mr. Mom" and "Mr. Housework" as they explained the new division of labor in their homes. They used feminized terms to describe what they did at home. When Ilana asked Rex (African American, forty-two, real estate) about housework, he said, "Whatever is dirty, needs to be cleaned, since I'm here, that pretty much falls on me." She asked, "And how do you feel about that?" He responded, "I've never been the at-home type. I'm not the Mr. Mom type. So if you are asking about whether I like it, no. I'd rather be earning some money on the job." But Rex did the work anyway because he was home, and his partner was at work.

Rather than shunning housework in response to job loss, which other researchers have found to be the case, many men in this study embraced what Jared (white, twenty-nine, manufacturing) called the "female role." Ben referred to himself as Mr. Housework:

> I make the bed every day. The bathroom needs to be wiped every day. A couple of times a week I'll vacuum because there is dog hair or stuff everywhere, depending on the weather, they [dogs] come with muddy paws. I'll take the steamer out, clean the spots. I'll clean kitchen floors. It just depends. I try to not let anything get out of hand where I'd have to spend a whole day cleaning the home. It's not like a routine. One day I mop downstairs, another day upstairs. Two times in between, I'll vacuum the carpet or dry out the floors, area rugs and hardwood floors, it's a combination of both. One day, I decide the kitchen floor is dirty, not clean enough that it needs to be scrubbed or mopped. I get like that randomly. I have no problem cleaning, you know. It all just depends on when it's messy enough that it bothers me. I get up, I take care of that.

Richard described his approach to housework:

> I won't even use a mop on a floor, just on my knees and stuff. I find it somewhat cathartic, believe it or not, but I roll the rugs up, the ones in the kitchen, shaking them outside, leaving them out. And then literally sweeping the closet, flipping the drawers, the refrigerator, the chairs, the table. And literally the basic hands and knees all Polish-lady-cleaning. I like to do that.

Ben and Richard did not take shortcuts like using a mop. They preferred a more labor-intensive approach to cleaning. Richard used gender and ethnicity—"Polish lady cleaning"—to underscore the authenticity of his attention to detail. He implied that "real men" clean like stereotypical immigrant women.

Lenny (white, forty-eight, construction) seemed to take real pleasure in the household tasks he had taken on after being laid off. He said, "I get up early and make coffee every day for Colleen (his wife) before she goes to work. I don't even drink coffee, but I make it for her. She gets to sleep a little longer then." Lenny took pride in finding deals at the grocery store: "Yesterday I found a good deal on coffee filters and I got Colleen some of that flavored creamer she likes." He seemed content in providing small treats for his wife. Tony (white, twenty-eight, construction) enjoyed his newfound time with his daughter:

> I've been playing Mr. Mom. I watch Christina [five-year-old daughter] when Stephanie goes to work. She has to work, make money so I'm there. I'm around. I keep the place tidy, clean; I do grocery shopping. I actually really love spending time with my daughter. It's kind of *priceless*.

Preston (white, twenty-six, graphic arts) saw unemployment as creating a space for him to be more active in the home:

> Oh, now that I'm unemployed, I am doing all that, clean the house, and I do a lot of cooking. There is just time now to do these things. This is the one thing that I probably enjoy about [unemployment]; I have a lot of time to do things that I didn't have before and so now it's kind of a responsibility that I obviously have taken on because I'm not making very much money from the state, so.

Similarly, James saw hidden opportunities in unemployment: "And I'm going to seriously consider going back to school, but for now, I'm just going to kick my feet up and enjoy being with my family. There is no rush."

Chuck explained his increased participation in the home as a rational exchange of services with his girlfriend, Sue, who supported him financially:

> I am fortunate that Sue is doing well. I live here with her. If I was on my own, I would be sleeping in my car. We have talked about things and she knows when the economy turns around I will be able to pick up the slack a little bit. But for now I pick up the slack around the house more because I feel like it is the only way to repay my duties that are lost.

Chuck saw his unpaid labor as a fair exchange for Sue's paid labor. He emphasized the importance of Sue's paid labor in keeping their family afloat:

> When Sue and I do things [for fun], it is because she has points on her credit card. She picks up those expenses. At the same time, she covers everything extracurricular. She is working every day. I am working a couple of hours every week. So I pick up the slack around the yard and house and she picks up everything financial. I am still a guy so my ego is hurt a little. But I know when I get a job again I will be able to make up for financial spending.

Chuck acknowledged his wounded ego—"I'm still a guy"—but he valued Sue for "picking up everything financial." Brian (African American, twenty-two, adolescent counselor) also struggled to reconcile his identity as a man with his new-found household duties:

> I thought I'd always be independent. I've always been the man, you know, not cleaning ever. But it's just the reverse right now. But I think everything is good, change is good for a reason, everything happens for a reason. I would prefer to be working but I just have to step up and be a man in a different kind of manner.

These men hoped that their housework would help make up for their lost wages and the increased burden on the women in their lives. They took pride in their new accomplishments. Like Jared said, "It took a lot of adapting to become the househusband and do all of these things that I've never done. . . . I'm a guy doing these things . . . and I'm proud to say that I'm a good househusband."

The men's acceptance of—and sometimes pleasure over—doing "women's work," as well as their appreciation for the women in their lives seemed to signify a small shift from their traditional gendered ideologies. Many seemed to feel it was their duty to do the unpaid work at home. Further, they defined household labor itself as evidence of their sustained manhood: it was hard work befitting men.

RE-WORKING MANHOOD

For the men in this study, job loss disrupted their lives and their identities as men. Men lost more than work: several were clearly depressed. To make ends meet, these men were forced into economic dependence on women. Women, not men, saved the day.

Being economically dependent on women flies in the face of the ways that men have been traditionally valued in the United States. They could not provide for their families economically. The media was implying that women were doing better than them. Yet these men did not express resentment toward the women in their lives, upon whom they depended, as previous research would suggest.

They adapted. This does not mean that the men had given up on masculinity. Instead, they found ways to decouple manhood from their financial contributions to the household. They used the work that they *were* able to do as evidence of their masculinity.

Providing Care, If Not Money

Many respondents found ways to redefine a core tenet of masculinity—providing—in ways that fit their new economic situations. Chuck, for example, said he would forgo paying his mortgage to make sure that he was able to purchase food and health care for his kids. He was still providing—just in ways that he could afford. Chuck salvaged his masculine identity by reconceptualizing "family man" as being child focused, not financially focused. Similarly, Kenny gave up everything—salary, home, food—to "provide" first for his restaurant's employees and then for his girlfriend's children. He salvaged his dignity by providing what he could. Brian said that doing housework allowed him to "be a man in a different manner." These men redefined and re-centered men's work as essential for the family, even if it was very different work.

Our respondents are not the first men to focus on care work in the home during dire economic times. In *The Modernization of Fatherhood*, Ralph LaRossa shows that fatherhood became important to many men during the Great Depression in the 1930s, when they could not find work. Similar to the unemployed men in our study, those men celebrated the work that they *could* do instead of dwelling on work they could not do. Although most men resumed their prioritization of paid work over care work after economic recovery, the "culture of fatherhood" that emerged in the 1930s remained, providing an alternative framework for men to draw on when performing masculinities. Our participants seemed to have tapped into the vestiges of "fathercraft" culture, using it to make sense of their situations during hard times.

Rational Exchange

Rational decision making is a core tenet of masculinity in our society. Throughout our interviews, the men described the rational decisions that they made about their role in the household. They looked for ways to divide the labor fairly and effectively, given their inability to work outside the home.

Many of the men in this study willingly took up household chores to correct what they saw as an imbalance. Just as they are not the first men to do care work, our participants are not the first men to do housework, either. In recent years, men have increased their low rate of household labor somewhat.[24] Some have even restructured their lives, taking pay cuts and status penalties to put home and family before career. The men in our study differ from these others in that they did not do much housework before they lost their jobs, nor was their nascent housework the result of feminist, egalitarian politics. Instead, they "picked up the slack" because they thought it was fair to do so: an exchange of unpaid work for paid work.

We do not know if men performed these duties as "mothers' helpers" or as true partners, and we do not know if their household labor eased the workload for their partners. We do know, however, that the men constructed their household labor as a sign of their manhood. And they stressed that they took up housework only to make up for their economic dependence. The men in our study did their duty in an attempt to repay women for their increased burdens.

Housework as Hard Labor

Richard, Ben, and Jared emphasized that housework was difficult labor, worthy of hard-working men. Richard said that he literally got on his hands and knees to clean the floors. Given the proliferation of mops that use hand-mounted levers for "effortless wringing," hands-and-knees scrubbing is not only rare, it's probably not even necessary to get the floor clean. Men like Richard not only did housework—they *over-did* housework as evidence of their strong work ethic. By stressing how intensely they embraced these chores, these men ironically redefined this "female role" as evidence of their masculinity. Concomitantly, they provided what LaRossa would call "masculine role models" for their children.

A TRUE SHIFT IN MANHOOD?

The Great Recession placed these men at a crossroads where traditional gender ideologies were changing shape. During that moment, when workers felt the impact of very high unemployment rates, men were presented with a unique space in which to renegotiate their social identities. As LaRossa said, "A poor economy can make new ideas more attractive."[25] Because men's identities are traditionally shaped by employment, analyzing their identity work during this recession provides insight into the endurance of the breadwinning ideology.

Although the breadwinner has been fundamentally tested, it remains an important part of these men's social identities and self-concepts as men. While talking with us, men simultaneously lamented their inability to be traditional providers and also tried to downplay the importance of breadwinning for the successful enactment of manhood. They redefined manhood to encompass "women's work," describing their housework and child care as valuable work worthy of real men.

These men had *not* embraced a feminist analysis of the tensions between paid and unpaid labor. Indeed, a lot of their rhetoric about masculinity could be seen as antifeminist. And yet, their valuing of housework could have feminist consequences in the long run. If "heads of households" and "men's men" see household labor as real work, this could elevate its worth in larger society. In their own ways, these men are undoing gender.[26]

Does this signify a lasting shift in men's conceptualizations of manhood and, relatedly, womanhood? Or is this a temporary shift, as LaRossa saw during the Great Depression? We need to know more before we can answer that. For example, do men value household labor in the same way when women do it? How do men talk about their household labor with men who are still employed? With their extended families? Do men continue their household labor once they go back to work outside of the home? We will be asking these questions and collecting more data as unemployment rates continue to level out in the future.

Previous research has shown that most unemployed men rigidly cling to traditional conceptions of manhood. Some of those men became more flexible, but only after prolonged unemployment and with a lot of familial support. In our study, we saw men beginning to shift within a shorter period of time and with little social and familial support. Thus we are cautiously optimistic that this unique recession will have different, more progressive social consequences. If so, the mancession may have a silver lining. Traditional, sexist frames seem to be yielding under all of this pressure. A new, more egalitarian gender frame may take root, eventually benefiting both men and women.

NOTES

1. The U.S. Department of Labor provides useful data and analysis of economic trends: www.bls.gov.

2. See Legerski and Cornwall (2010); Oberhouser (1995); Sherman (2009).

3. The unemployment rate is problematic because it excludes workers who are no longer searching for jobs and people who are underemployed (Kingdon and Knight, 2006). If the unemployment rate was calculated correctly, the economic situation would look much worse (Engel, 2010). As such, high unemployment rates indicate major economic problems.

4. See Hartenstein (2010); Mulligan (2009).

5. See Rivers and Barnett (2011).

6. Fraser (1994).

7. See Walby (1991).

8. Janssens (1998); Sainsbury (1996).

9. Ingraham (1994).

10. For more data on the waning saliency of "the family wage," see Coontz (2000); Meisenbach (2010); Raley, Mattingly, and Bianchi (2006).

11. For more on the ways that the breadwinner ideology contributes to household and workplace inequality, see Acker (2006); Arrighi and Maume (2000); Blair-Loy (2006); Craig and Mullen (2010); Daly and Rake (2003); England (2010); Hochschild (1989); Hook (2010); Lewis (2009); Risman (2009); Tichenor (2005); Williams, Muller, and Kilanski (2012).

12. Zuo (2004, p. 813).

13. *Ibid.*, p. 814.

14. For more on the connections between earning/providing and masculinity, see Connell (1987, 1991); Lane (2011); Nolan (2009); Warren (2007).

15. For more on gender frames and their effects on social interactions, see Cecelia Ridgeway's (2011) work.

16. Connell (1991, p. 165).

17. Identity work is the process through which people present their personal identities to others. For more on the concept of identity work, see Snow and Anderson (1987).

18. See Watters and Bernacki (1989).

19. For more on face-to-face interview guidelines, see Goffman (1981); Lofland et al. (2005); Warren and Karner (2009).

20. We did this because as much of the feminist scholarship posits, reimbursing subjects is a good way to reduce the power differences between the researcher and the researched that may shape the interview process (Sprague, 2005).

21. For more on the benefits of phone interviewing, see Hoppe et al. (2000).

22. As we refer to each man for the first time, we specify his race, age at the time of interview, and the job sector he was in before losing his job.

23. See, for example, Gerson's (1994) and Risman's (1999) work.

24. For more on men and household labor, see Lane (2011); Risman (1999); Risman and Johnson-Sumerford (1998).

25. LaRossa (1997, p. 13).

26. For more on undoing gender, see Butler (2004); Risman (2009).

CCF Symposium

EQUAL PAY SYMPOSIUM: 50 YEARS SINCE THE EQUAL PAY ACT OF 1963

Stephanie Coontz and Virginia E. Rutter | June 2013

Fifty years ago, on June 10, 1963, President John F. Kennedy signed the Equal Pay Act, amending the earlier Fair Labor Standards Act of 1938, to "prohibit discrimination on account of sex in the payment of wages by employers." So, how's that going? The Council on Contemporary Families has convened an online symposium representing the latest thinking from preeminent work-family scholars, top female executive Sheryl Sandberg, and advocates for low-wage workers and unions.

Gender Equality: Family Egalitarianism Follows Workplace Opportunity

UNSTICKING PROGRESS TOWARD GENDER EQUALITY IN THE LABOR MARKET— EXTENDING THE LEGACY OF THE EQUAL PAY ACT—WILL HELP MOVE FAMILIES FORWARD TOWARD MORE EGALITARIAN RELATIONSHIPS
Philip N. Cohen, University of Maryland

Gender inequality within families is reciprocally related to gender inequality in the paid workplace. That is why one of the legacies of the Equal Pay Act, which brought scrutiny and sanctions to bear on gender discrimination at work, has been growing egalitarianism within families as well. Research consistently shows the effect of workplace progress on equality within couples. Most recently, analysis of the American Time-Use Survey confirms that women's own earnings are associated with the amount of housework they perform. Each thousand dollars of earnings is associated with a 14-minute reduction in daily housework.

In 1962 fewer than one in seven nonfarm managers were women, according to Bureau of Labor Statistics data. Women earned less than 10 percent of degrees in law and medicine, and full-time employed women earned just 59 percent of what men made. Not surprisingly, at that time just 7 percent of wives ages 25–54 earned more than their husbands—and wives did almost six times as much housework as husbands. Their constrained workplace opportunity weakened their relative standing at home.

Today women hold about 40 percent of managerial jobs, receive almost half of law and medicine degrees (and the majority of BAs), and earn more than 75 percent of men's earnings. Wives outearn their husbands in 28 percent of couples—a historic high. These gains have led to an impressive reduction in the disparity between husbands' and wives' housework. Today wives only do 1.7 times as much housework as their husbands. Inequality at home and the workplace remain formidable, but labor market progress has made possible large steps toward parity within families.

Most of this progress, however, took place in the 1970s and 1980s. The stall in both arenas since then is unequivocal. As progress toward equal labor force participation and access to occupations and equal pay slowed, the division of labor within families got stuck as well. The ratio of wives' housework to men's housework, which fell below 2.0 in the early 1990s, hasn't moved appreciably since (see Figure 1).

Both workplaces and families are sites in which cultural expectations and attitudes play out. However, the paid workplace is more amenable to policy intervention, while families tend to be more tradition-bound. Unsticking progress toward gender equality in the labor market—extending the legacy of the Equal Pay Act—will help move families forward toward more egalitarian relationships.

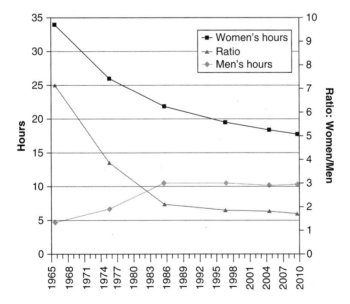

Figure 1 | Husbands' and Wives' Weekly Housework Hours, 1965–2010

Source: Bianchi, Suzanne M., Linda C. Sayer, Melissa A. Milkie, and John P. Robinson, "Housework: Who Did, Does, or Will Do It and How Much Does It Matter?" *Social Forces* 91, no. 1 (2012): 55–63.

Equal Pay? Not Yet for Mothers

It Is Time to Quit Viewing Motherhood as Incompatible with Employment
Shelley J. Correll, Professor of Sociology, Director of Clayman Institute for Gender Research, Stanford University

Hedge fund billionaire Paul Tudor Jones set off a controversy when he remarked that "you will never see as many great women investors or traders as men." In his experience, Jones claimed, a woman did fine until she had a child. But "as soon as that baby's lips touched that girl's [*sic*] bosom, forget it."

By virtually every measure, we are closer to gender equality today than we were fifty years ago—with one very big exception. As Joya Misra notes, the majority of the gender gap in wages is now the result of the lower earnings of mothers. This once led Denise Venable of the National Center for Policy Analysis to claim: "When women behave as men do [by not having children], the wage gap between them is small." But mothers not only earn less than childless women. They earn less than fathers. When women "behave as men do" and have children, the wage gap between fathers and mothers remains large.

Why is this? When we compare the earnings of mothers and childless women who work in the same types of jobs, have the same level of education, have the same amount of experience, and are equal on a host of other dimensions, mothers still earn 5 percent lower hourly wages *per child*. Mothers do work fewer hours per week, on aver-age, than other types of workers. However, working fewer hours does not explain why mothers earn lower wages *per hour* whether they are working full or part time.

Comments such as Jones's are the *cause*, not the objective description, of why mothers have less success in the workplace. Research demonstrates that many employers share Jones's belief that mothers are less committed to their jobs, so they are less willing to hire mothers into good jobs or to offer them high salaries.

In one study, fake resumes were sent to employers who advertised a high status job opening. When the resume indicated that the applicant was an officer in an elementary school parent-teacher association, thereby implying that she was a mother, employers were half as likely to call her back. A second study found out why. Compared with a childless woman with the same qualifications, the mother was rated as less com-mitted to her job, despite the absence of any evidence supporting this perception, and this substantially reduced her chances of getting the job.

It is time to quit viewing motherhood as incompatible with employment. According to the Bureau of Labor Statistics, 71 percent of mothers with children under the age of 18 are in the labor force today, up from 30 percent in 1960. Even with limited social support to help workers balance work and family, mothers are making important contributions at work, bringing home an increasing share of income for their families and helping make our nation be more productive. They deserve fair pay for their contributions.

The Gender Pay Gap by Race and Ethnicity

IS THERE MORE GENDER EQUALITY AMONG MINORITY MEN AND WOMEN THAN AMONG WHITES? NOT SO FAST

Jane Farrell, Research Assistant for Economic Policy, and Sarah Jane Glynn, Associate Director of Women's Economic Policy, Center for American Progress

On average, white women earn 81 percent of what white men make. At first glance it may appear that there is more gender equality among minority men and women than among whites. Hispanic or Latina women make 88 percent of what Latinos do and African American women make 90 percent of what their male counterparts make.

But when we add race to gender, these pay gaps become a veritable chasm. African American women earn 36 percent less than white men and Latinas a mere 45 percent. Interestingly, the gap between the earnings of Asian women and white men is smaller, just 12 percent, but that mounts up over a lifetime, and Asian American women earn just 73 percent of what Asian American men make.

Men lost jobs especially rapidly during the first phases of the Great Recession, but the ripple effects have led to layoffs of hundreds of thousands of state and local government workers, about 70 percent of whom were women and 20 percent of whom were African Americans.

And things are not likely to get better for women as the economy continues to pick up speed. While the majority of jobs lost in the recession were mid-range jobs, the majority of new jobs that have been created in the recovery are low-wage. Many of the occupations with the largest projected job growth are minority and female dominated, but they are jobs such as home health aides and personal care aides, with earnings of only about $20,000 per year.

Today, in spite of increasing educational gains, women of color are especially likely to work in minimum-wage jobs, where even a full-time, year-round worker will earn just $14,500 a year, scarcely enough to keep one person — let alone a family — afloat. In 2011, nearly 360,000 black and Latina women were paid hourly rates that were less than the minimum wage. Since Social Security benefits are based upon an individual's lifetime earnings, these low wages hurt women well into retirement, leaving many elderly women in poverty or on the brink.

Because gender, racial, and ethnic wage gaps are caused by multiple factors, multiple strategies are needed to ensure equity. Legislation like the Lilly Ledbetter Fair Pay Act was an important first step, but additional policies like the Paycheck Fairness Act, the Healthy Families Act, paid family and medical leave legislation, and raising the minimum wage would also go a long way in helping to combat the problem.

From the Folks Who Brought You the Weekend: What Unions Do for Women

HAD THE UNIONISTS GOTTEN THEIR WAY, THE GAINS FOR WOMEN WORKERS SINCE 1963 WOULD HAVE BEEN MORE EVENLY DISTRIBUTED ALONG CLASS LINES
Ruth Milkman, Professor of Sociology, CUNY Graduate Center; and Academic Director, Murphy Labor Institute

The Equal Pay Act is often presumed to be an accomplishment of the feminist movement of the 1960s. In fact, it was spearheaded by female trade unionists, who first introduced the bill in 1945 as an amendment to the 1938 Fair Labor Standards Act. The bill was defeated, largely because of staunch opposition from business interests, but a coalition of labor activists reintroduced it every year until it finally passed in 1963.

The bill originally required "equal wage rates for work of comparable character on jobs the performance of which requires comparable skills," wording that would have forced employers to pay women in traditionally sex-segregated jobs as much as men with comparable skills in traditionally male occupations. The 1963 act that finally passed was a compromise that instead required equal pay for "equal work." Given the pervasiveness of job segregation by gender, this weakened requirement for equity ensured that the law had a far more limited impact.

Had the unionists gotten their way, the gains for women workers since 1963 would have been more evenly distributed along class lines. Whereas for elite professionals and many other college-educated workers, job segregation by gender has been substantially reduced in the past half-century, the extent of segregation in working-class jobs is just as high as it was in 1963.

Most non-college-educated women remain trapped in the pink-collar ghetto, working as waitresses, child care and eldercare workers, or as clerical and retail sales workers. In such jobs women are typically paid at or near the minimum wage, often without even basic benefits like paid sick days, and with few opportunities for advancement. If the Equal Pay Act required equal pay for comparable work, child care workers, a traditionally female-dominated job, could not be paid less than zookeepers, for example.

Although female unionists led the campaign for the act, at the time they were woefully underrepresented in the organized labor movement. In 1960, 24 percent of U.S. workers were unionized, but women made up only 18.3 percent of union members. Half a century later, in 2012, women make up nearly half (48.3 percent) of the U.S. workforce and nearly as large a proportion (45.0 percent) of all union members. Yet at the same time, the power and reach of unions have declined dramatically. Today, only 11 percent of American workers are union members, and in the private sector, the figure is below 7 percent.

The simultaneous decline in union power and rise in female representation among unions reflects the massive expansion—starting in the 1960s and 1970s—of public-sector unionism, alongside the massive contraction of private-sector unionism over the same period. Women are overrepresented in public sector employment, making up a large majority of workers in fields like education, health care, and government administration—all now highly unionized sectors. In contrast, private-sector union membership is far more male-dominated, with strongholds in sectors like construction, utilities, transportation, and manufacturing.

Employers have successfully attacked private-sector unionism in the past few decades, and unionization rates have fallen apace. By contrast, until very recently public-sector unions remained largely intact. But starting in 2011, a wave of state-level legislation weakening collective bargaining rights for public sector workers has directly targeted teachers and other unionized female-dominated occupations. These attacks will roll back many of the gains women made since the 1960s. In 2012, the average hourly earnings of unionized women stood at $24.18, compared to $18.74 for nonunion women workers. Unionized workers also are much more likely than their nonunion counterparts to have access to benefits like employer-sponsored health insurance, paid sick days, and pensions. And union workers have more job security as well.

The labor movement has fought to improve women workers' situation throughout American history. And today, women have a bigger stake than ever before in the survival of unions—which now face unprecedented attacks and are virtually threatened with extinction. As we commemorate the 50th anniversary of the Equal Pay Act, we should not only recall the history of women in unions but also consider the potential impact of ongoing union decline on women working today.

Which Policies Promote Gender Pay Equality?

WHY DO WOMEN STILL EARN LESS THAN MEN? ONE CENTRAL FACTOR IS WOMEN'S CAREGIVING

Joya Misra, Professor of Sociology and Public Policy, University of Massachusetts, Amherst

Why do women earn less than men? Research points to a number of different explanations, but one of the central factors remains women's caregiving responsibilities. The wages of childless men and women have been converging steadily over the last three decades—but mothers continue to earn significantly less, while fathers earn a bit more. These motherhood and fatherhood effects have been stable over time while childless women's wages have been rising, even though mothers are increasingly likely to be employed.

If we want to promote gender pay equality, we need policies that will reduce wage differences between childless women and mothers. The motherhood penalty may be partly due to lost experience and seniority, particularly if mothers leave the labor force when children are young. But even after controlling for experience, survey research indicates that U.S. women suffer a wage penalty of about 4 percent per child. Both experimental and audit research in the United States also show that employers discriminate against women whose resumes indicate that they are mothers.

Motherhood penalties vary substantially cross-nationally, suggesting that social policies can reduce or exacerbate them. My research with Michelle Budig and Irene Boeckmann shows that public child care has tremendously powerful effects, boosting mothers' employment and wages. This is particularly true of public child care for children under three years of age. The per-child wage penalty is 9.5 percent in countries with minimal public child care for infants and toddlers, but shrinks to 4.3 percent in countries with more expansive public child care programs. Similarly, in countries with minimal public child care, the gap in employment probabilities between mothers and childless women is over 18 percentage points. This gap shrinks to less than 2 percentage points in countries with the highest observed child care enrollment rates.

Leaves also matter—though they need to be constructed in the right ways. Mothers' employment and wages suffer the most when there is no or very little paid leave. In these cases, mothers may be forced to leave employment to care for infants. Yet employment and wages also may suffer when mothers are offered very long, unpaid/poorly paid leaves, such as three-year "care leaves." Here mothers lose valuable job experience, and may find themselves in jobs with little prospect for career advancement. Indeed, research in Hungary shows that employers in countries with long leave policies discriminate against mothers, assuming they will leave employment for long periods. We find that motherhood wage penalties exceed 6 percent per child in countries with less than one year or more than three years of job-protected leave; the per child penalty is only slightly more than 1 percent per child in countries with around two years of job-protected leave.

Thus mothers' employment and wages are boosted when leaves are of moderate length and paid well, and also when some leave is reserved for fathers. Such leaves allow parents to care for infants at home, while maintaining their relationship with their workplaces. While relatively few countries have excellent paternity leave policies, we see very beneficial outcomes for mothers where these policies do exist. Sweden offers two weeks, Finland three weeks, and Israel six weeks of paid paternity leave. Mothers face lower wage penalties in these countries.

Our research further explores *when* policies are most effective. Policies do not operate in a vacuum but must be understood in relation to existing cultural norms. In countries where there is strong preference for maternal caregiving, policies that boost mothers' employment and wages have less of an impact. In countries where there is greater acceptance of maternal employment, these policies are more effective.

This is good news for the United States, where cultural attitudes favor maternal employment but policies are very meager in comparison to other wealthy countries. Recent research on California's paid leave shows positive outcomes for women's employment and wages. With focused investment on early child care and education, as well as moderate paid parental leaves for both fathers and mothers, the U.S. could narrow—and possibly eliminate—the motherhood penalty, and with it, the gender gap in wages.

Gender Bias and the Fight for Equal Pay

CAN WE HAVE AN OPEN CONVERSATION ABOUT BIASES THAT SUPPRESS WOMEN'S PAY?

Sheryl Sandberg, Chief Operating Officer, Facebook; and Founder, www.leanin.org

In 1947, Anita Summers, the mother of my longtime mentor Larry Summers, was hired as an economist by the Standard Oil Company. When she accepted the job, her new boss said to her, "I am so glad to have you. I figure I am getting the same brains for less money." Her reaction to this was not to get upset. Instead, she felt flattered. It was a huge compliment to be told that she had the same brains as a man. It would have been unthinkable for her to demand the same pay.

Fifty years after passage of the Equal Pay Act, much has changed. Yet the gender wage gap persists. In every industry and every country in the world, women continue to be paid less than men for the same work. Even in the United States, a recent study found that when faculty evaluated identical lab manager applications, the one with a man's name on it received a higher starting salary.[1]

There are many reasons why women receive lower pay, but gender stereotypes about competence and appropriate behavior are two factors that stand in women's way. Studies find that men are considered to be more competent than women, especially in domains traditionally seen as "masculine." We see these beliefs reflected in men and women's assessments of their own capabilities: Men tend to overestimate how they will perform and women tend to underestimate how they will perform.

This same social pattern influences salary expectations. A 2011 survey showed that long before they even hit the workforce, teenage girls expect lower starting pay than teenage boys.[2] And this trend continues throughout college, where a 2010 study revealed that women's expected peak-pay expectations were 33 percent lower than men's.[3]

Because we link salary with competence, not only do women often have lower salary expectations for themselves, but others expect to pay them less as well. A study found that having lower salary expectations resulted in a lower offer compared to similarly qualified candidates who had higher salary expectations.[4] Changing these lower salary expectations can reap real rewards.

Another stereotype that undermines fair pay for women is the expectation that women are communal—that they are warm, concerned with others (not money), and not focused on themselves. Some people put the fault on women for not negotiating more aggressively. But instead of blaming women, we need to recognize that women do not always advocate for fairer pay because it can backfire when they do. In fact, studies have found that when women negotiate on their own behalf they are often seen as aggressive and employers are less enthusiastic about working with them. That's a tough way to start a new job.

To close the gender wage gap, we need to have an open and honest conversation about the biases that suppress women's pay. The good news is that there are strategies that women can use (such as using communal language—*we* vs. *I*) that will increase the chances of negotiating successfully. People will still like them and want to work with them.

Leanin.org is dedicated to making men and women aware of workplace biases and offering strategies to help women navigate them. Our aim is to help women achieve their ambitions . . . and receive fair and equal pay while doing so. You can join us at www.leanin.org or www.facebook.com/leaninorg.

For more detailed information on negotiating strategies for women, check out Kim Keating's article "Thoughts on Achieving Equal Pay" at http://leanin.org/discussions/equal-pay-day/. Or watch Professor Margaret Neale from the Stanford Graduate School of Business share her wisdom in an instructional video at http://leanin.org/education/negotiation/.

NOTES

1. Corinne A. Moss-Racusin et al., "Science Faculty's Subtle Gender Biases Favor Male Students," *Proceedings of the National Academy of Sciences of the United States of America* vol. 109, no. 41 (2012): 16474–16479.

2. Charles Schwab, *2011 Teens & Money Survey Findings* (2011). Available from http://www.aboutschwab.com/images/press/teensmoneyfactsheet.pdf.

3. Mary Hogue, Cathy L. Z. DuBois, and Lee Fox-Cardamone, "Gender Differences in Pay Expectations: The Roles of Job Intention and Self-View," *Psychology of Women Quarterly* 34 (2010): 215–227.

4. Patrick Gavin O'Shea and David F. Bush, "Negotiation for Starting Salary: Antecedents and Outcomes among Recent College Graduates," *Journal of Business and Psychology* vol. 16, no. 3 (2002): 365–382.

Trends in Global Gender Equity

Progress and Disappointments from Countries around the World

Stephanie Seguino, Professor of Economics, University of Vermont

First the good news: Gender parity has already been reached in secondary educational enrollment rates in high-income countries and in Latin America and the Caribbean. From 1975 to 2010, the Arab region saw a remarkable rise in the ratio of female to male secondary enrollment rates, from 59 to 98 percent. In Asia and the Pacific region, there are 99 women in secondary education for every 100 men. Africa, too, has seen gains, with the ratio rising from 54 to 85 percent during this time period. And in 53 countries, ranging from Hong Kong to the Caribbean island of Dominica, women are now the majority of students enrolled in secondary schools.

There is also good news on the health front. Parity in life expectancy (taking into account men's and women's biological probabilities of long life) has been reached in all regions of the world. That means that in any region, on average, women's life expectancy relative to the biological goalpost is on par with men's, and in most regions, exceeds men's. One caution is that regional averages obscure some disturbing inequalities in individual countries. Women's relative life expectancy is less than 95 percent of men's in 26 countries, including Israel and Bahrain.

But these gains in education and health have not translated into economic parity—or at least, not enough to significantly narrow gender gaps. The widest gaps in labor force participation are in several Middle Eastern countries—Syria, Algeria, Iran, Jordan, Saudi Arabia, for example—where men are five times more likely to be in the labor force than women. Compare this to several African countries where parity has been achieved—Rwanda, Burundi, Mozambique, and Malawi. Even in otherwise egalitarian Scandinavia, gender gaps in labor force participation rates persist—with only 88 Norwegian women in the labor force for every 100 men, followed by 87 per 100 in Finland.

One reason gender gaps in labor force participation persist is women's greater responsibility for the care of children. (In African countries, where parity has been achieved, many women farm family land, making it easier to combine work with child care.) Without policies that support men's shared role in child care or that make it easier to combine paid work and family care, women are not in a position to spend as much time earning income as men.

Even among women and men who are in the labor force, women are more likely to experience unemployment than men. In the Caribbean, for instance, despite the fact that women comprise over 70 percent of students enrolled at the University of West Indies and, on average, have more education than men, they are twice as likely as men to be unable to find a job. The Great Recession that began in 2008 has been especially hard on women in the Euro area. In Greece, one of the worst-hit countries in that region, women's Depression-level unemployment rate is

31 percent, compared to 24 percent for men. And in the United States, where the crisis was labeled a "mancession" because men were the first to lose jobs, married mothers have had a harder time finding a job after being laid off than married dads and earn less once they do find work.

Nor have women's educational gains wiped out the gender pay gap, even in countries where women earn more degrees than men. In South Korea, for example, despite the virtual elimination of educational achievement differences between men and women, the median earnings of full-time female employees are still 40 percent lower than men's. Because of the wage gap in the United States, women have to work fifty-two years to earn the same income men earn in 40 years.

Strong gains in educational equality have also failed to translate into equal voice in political decision making. In only a handful of countries do women hold a share of parliamentary seats that comes close to representing their proportion of the population. The global average in 2010 was 19 percent, ranging from a low regional average of 8 percent in Arab countries to a high of 26 percent in rich countries. (Sweden stands out amongst rich countries at 45 percent, surpassed only by Rwanda at 56 percent.)

It is clear that attaining educational parity—or even superiority—does not ensure economic and political parity for women. And one worrying trend is that in fully 96 of the 135 countries where gender employment gaps have narrowed since 1991, this convergence is partly accounted for by declines in men's employment rates. In some countries, men's access to work has declined precipitously (by as much as 23 percentage points in Moldova, for example). Equalizing men's and women's employment rates or wages through the erosion of male well-being is hardly a viable basis on which to achieve the benefits of gender equity.

Men against Women, or the Top 20 Percent against the Bottom 80?

Leslie McCall, Professor of Sociology and Political Science, Faculty Fellow, Institute for Policy Research, Northwestern University

It used to be that the most economically successful women earned no more than the typical man, even when they had more education and held more highly skilled jobs. In 1970, the average woman in the top of the women's distribution (between the 85th and 95th percentiles) made less than the average man who fell in the middle of the men's distribution (between the 45th and 55th percentiles). The average female college graduate also earned less than the average male high school graduate.

But gender is no longer so predictive of earnings. Being at the top now outweighs being a woman. In 2010, high-earning women made more than 1.5 times as much as the typical man.

This shift reflects the rising importance of socioeconomic status in determining life's chances and complicates the struggle for gender equity. The equalizing effect of the Equal Pay Act and other measures that removed the most blatant forms of gender discrimination has been to some extent countered by the growing economic divide between the affluent and everyone else. As some women have made significant progress in breaking into the top tiers of their professions, they have pulled away from other women, and even from men, in the middle and at the bottom.

Recent attention to the extraordinary gains of the top 1 percent and to women's underrepresentation among these titans of industry can sometimes obscure the divergence in the economic and broader life experiences of women.

Although we do not yet have reliable information on the gender breakdown of the 1-percenters, we do know what's happening among the rest of Americans. Since 1970, when my analysis of the March Current Population Survey begins, women's earnings at the top grew faster than those of men at the top in every decade. For instance, in the decade from 2000 to 2010, these women's earnings grew 14 percent while men's grew 8.3 percent, among full-time workers. These elite women are making strong absolute gains, even as they face obstacles to keeping up with men of the same qualifications, who started their gains from a higher base.

By contrast, the median earnings of full-time women workers were flat over the last decade, just as they were for men. This marks a historical reversal of the healthy gains in earnings of nearly all women for the past several decades.

My analysis of a larger group of women in the middle (between the 45th and 55th percentiles of women's distribution) and at the bottom (between the 5th to the 15th percentiles) shows that the earnings of both groups lag considerably behind those of women at the top. As Figure 2 shows, inequality among women is steadily marching upwards. It closely tracks the more well-known rise in inequality among men.

In short, with most of the growth in women's earnings concentrated among top earners, the benefits of gender equality have been uneven. And the majority of women are now beginning to face some of the same kinds of economic challenges that have hampered the economic progress of men over the past quarter of a century.

The advantages of being a top earner are spilling over into advantages in family life as well, in two principal ways. First, as the marriage rates of most women declined, the average marriage rate of women with high pay increased—from 58 percent in 1980 to 64 percent in 2010. The most economically successful women are now more likely to be married than are other women, whereas the reverse was true in 1970.

Second, top-earning women often form dual-income households with top-earning men. So high-earning women and high-earning men double their earnings advantage when they marry, while the lower the earnings of a woman, the more likely she is, if she is married at all, to be with a low-earning man. The rise of income homogamy in marriage reinforces the widening gap in earnings.

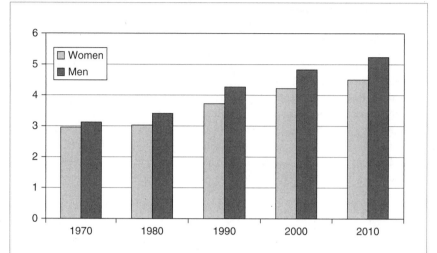

Figure 2 | Ratio of Top to Bottom Weekly Earnings among Full-Time Workers, 1970–2010

Source: Author analysis of the March Current Population Survey. Top earnings are the average earnings of workers in the 85th to 95th percentiles. Bottom earnings are the average earnings of workers in the 5th to 15th percentiles. Sample includes 25- to 54-year-olds who are not self-employed.

As Figure 2 shows, even in 1970, inequality among women was nearly as high as it was among men. But for those concerned about gender discrimination, this fact was overshadowed by the high degree of gender inequality. Today, we have a more complex mixture of trends toward gender equality and socioeconomic inequality. Women in the top echelons of society are improving both their economic and family status. But socioeconomic inequality is beginning to undercut the economic progress of large numbers of women.

The Wrong Route to Equality: Men's Declining Wages

THE IMPROVEMENT IN WOMEN'S WAGES RELATIVE TO MEN'S IS IN PART DUE TO MEN'S DECLINING WAGES

Heidi Shierholz, Labor Market Economist, Economic Policy Institute

In the late 1970s, after a long period of holding fairly steady, the gap in wages between men and women began improving. In 1979, the median hourly wage for women was 62.7 percent of the median hourly wage for men; by 2012, it was 82.8 percent. However, a big chunk of that improvement—more than a quarter of it—happened because of men's wage *losses*, rather than women's wage gains.

With the exception of the period of labor market strength in the late 1990s, the median male wage, after adjusting for inflation, has decreased over essentially the entire period since the late 1970s. Between 1979 and 1996, it dropped 11.5 percent, from $19.53 per hour to $17.27 per hour. With the strong labor market of the late 1990s, the median male wage partially rebounded to $18.93 by 2002. It then began declining again; at $18.03 per hour in 2012, the real wage of the median male was 4.7 percent below where it had been a decade earlier.

This cannot be blamed on economic stagnation. Between 1979 and 2012, productivity—the average amount of goods and services produced in an hour by workers in the U.S. economy—grew by 69.5 percent, but that did not translate into higher wages for most men. Over this period, the real wage of the median male *dropped* 7.6 percent. This is a new and troubling disconnect: in the decades prior to the 1970s, as productivity increased, the wages of the median worker increased right along with it.

Furthermore, looking at the median wage understates the losses many men have experienced since the 1970s. For men with a high school degree, real wages have fallen by more than 14 percent. It is not the case, however, that men's wages have fared poorly since the 1970s because men do not have the right education or skills. In the last ten years, even workers with a college degree have failed to see any real wage growth.

Nor are men's losses due to women's gains. The forces that were holding back male wage growth were also acting on women's wages, but the gains made by women over this period in educational attainment, labor force attachment, and occupational upgrading, along with greater legal protections against discriminatory pay, initially compensated for adverse forces. In the last decade, however, women's wages have also dropped.

Unlike the postwar period, when economic policy supported the expansion of good jobs, for the last thirty-five years, the focus has been on policies that were advertised as making everyone better off as *consumers* through lower prices: deregulation of industries, the Federal Reserve Board's prioritizing low inflation over full employment, weakening of labor standards including the minimum wage, a "stronger" dollar—which costs manufacturing jobs by making our goods relatively more expensive around the world and imports relatively cheaper to U.S. consumers—and the move toward fewer and weaker unions. The decline in unionization alone explains about a third of the rise in male wage inequality (and about a fifth of the increase in female wage inequality) over this period.

Together, these policies have eroded the individual and collective bargaining power of most workers, depleting access to good jobs. In other words, these policies have served to make the already affluent better off at the expense of the rest.

In the News

YES, I'VE FOLDED UP MY MASCULINE MYSTIQUE, HONEY

The Sunday Times of London, February 24, 2013

Stephanie Coontz

Males are in trouble at school and at work: not because women are on the rise but because they cling to a myth of manhood.

Fifty years ago last week, Betty Friedan published *The Feminine Mystique*, igniting an impassioned debate over her claim that millions of housewives were desperately unhappy, suffering from "the problem that has no name."

Women did seem to be floundering in the 1950s and early 1960s. Doctors puzzled over an epidemic of "housewife's fatigue" and numerous American women dropped out of university. *Newsweek* magazine reported that U.S. women were gripped with a malaise that was "deep, pervasive and impervious" to any known remedy—although many psychiatrists were sure that tranquillisers could help. In Europe, too, observers worried whether women could settle back into domesticity after the Second World War.

According to conventional wisdom, women were suffering because they were being "masculinised" by the pressures of the postwar world. Female students, as one prominent educator put it, were being forced to study a male curriculum rather than topics that would be of interest and use to them, such as "the theory and preparation of a Basque paella." An expanding economy was pulling women into the world of work and eroding their traditional feminine roles. The cure, most psychiatrists agreed, was for women to reject masculine activities and values and embrace their "feminine destiny."

Friedan had a different analysis. She argued that the problems facing women in the postwar world were caused by too much adherence to the norms of femininity and too little recognition that "women are people too." Women, Friedan claimed, had been ensnared by an insidious "feminine mystique" that promised them security, comfort and indulgence in return for accepting their "womanly" dependence and abandoning any aspirations beyond the home.

In Friedan's view, the feminine mystique offered short-term and superficial privileges at a high cost. In the long run it damaged women's health and wellbeing, prevented them from adapting to a changing world and ultimately made them less successful as wives and mothers. She urged women to develop an identity based on their individual talents and desires rather than on stereotypes about what it meant to be a "real" woman.

In the half century since publication of *The Feminine Mystique*, women have expanded tremendously the range of options and self-images available to them, successfully moving into new roles in public and private life. Today it is males who are floundering.

In America and Britain there is talk of a "boy crisis" in schools. Real wages have fallen more for men than for women. Traditional masculine occupations are erod- ing but men hesitate to enter many of the fastest-growing occupations in today's economy. Males are now less likely than females to apply to university and, if they enter, less likely to graduate.

Attempts to explain these contemporary problems are often the mirror image of 1960s claims about women. Many experts today blame men's troubles on the weakening of their traditional gender identity. Boys, they complain, are being forced to "act like girls" in school. Adult males have been stripped of their role as family providers and protectors. Society must find new ways to validate masculinity.

In fact, most of the problems men are experiencing today stem from the flip side of the 20th-century feminine mystique—a pervasive masculine mystique that pres- sures boys and men to conform to a gender stereotype and prevents them from exploring the full range of their individual capabilities.

The masculine mystique promises men success, power and admiration from oth- ers if they embrace their supposedly natural competitive drives and reject all forms of dependence. Just as the feminine mystique made women ashamed when they harboured feelings or desires that were supposedly "masculine," the masculine mystique makes men ashamed to admit to any feelings or desires that are thought to be "feminine."

Trying to live up to the precepts of the masculine mystique has always exacted a heavy price on males, especially in childhood. For girls, the feminine mystique was not rigorously enforced until puberty. A girl who enjoyed "boy things" such as sports and climbing trees was affectionately called a "tomboy." At the same time she was allowed to cry and was excused for failing ("that's way too hard for a little girl"; "I'll do it for you, honey").

Girls had such leeway precisely because they were never expected to compete for public success or to wield power over others.

By contrast, the masculine mystique demands an early and complete rejection of all activities and values traditionally associated with females. Boys who cross gen- der boundaries are derided as wusses, sissies, metrosexuals, called "wet" or written off as "mummy's boys." Training people to exercise power can be a brutal business, as many upper-class British men can testify from their own family and boarding school experiences.

Boys are held to higher standards of stoicism than girls and receive harsher treatment when they do not compete successfully. Throughout their lives men face constant pressure to demonstrate their masculinity to others.

Despite the personal costs exacted by adherence to the masculine mystique, for most of the 20th century "acting like a man" was a good recipe for success because it conferred what R. W. Connell, the sociologist, has called a "patriarchal dividend," giving males preference over females in almost every area.

Boys did not need to abide by "girlie" rules, such as obeying teachers and studying hard, because discriminatory wages ensured that the average male who got through school—or even those who dropped out—earned more than the average female university graduate working comparable hours.

Nor did men have much need for negotiating skills. In most countries husbands had the final say in household and financial decisions. The television series *Mad Men* depicts how men's bad behaviour towards wives, mistresses, secretaries and female co-workers carried few penalties and many rewards. Everyone assumed that women would put up with such behaviour.

Today, however, conforming to the masculine mystique bestows fewer rewards and more penalties. Sheryl Sandberg, chief operating officer at Facebook, notes in her forthcoming book, *Lean In: Women, Work and the Will to Lead*, that while the compliance and docility fostered by remnants of the feminine mystique still hold women back from top leadership positions in business and politics, those same traits do get rewarded in school. And in a world where educational achievement increasingly outweighs gender in the job market, that at least gets women in the door.

By contrast, adhering to the masculine mystique increasingly closes doors for boys and men. In a book to be published next month, the sociologists Thomas DiPrete and Claudia Buchmann demonstrate that most of the academic disadvantages of boys in education flow not from a "feminised" learning environment, as is often claimed, but from a masculinised peer culture that encourages disruptive behaviour and disengagement from school.

As Debbie Epstein, the British researcher, puts it, "real boys" are not supposed to study. "The work you do here is girls' work," one boy told an educational ethnographer. "It's not real work."

Reviewing studies from Europe and America, DiPrete and Buchmann report that trying to cater to the masculine mystique does not improve the academic performance of boys. In fact, the more the traditional gender distinctions are blurred, the better boys and girls do. Those boys who participate in music, art, drama and foreign languages have a higher attachment to school than the boys who reject such activities as "girlie."

The masculine mystique also contributes to the gender gap in university entry and completion rates. Just as the feminine mystique once encouraged women to neglect self-development in the hope that "some day my prince will come," the masculine mystique encourages men to pin their hopes on the return of that "patriarchal dividend."

One study of seven European countries, including Britain, found that although parents still favour sons in inheritance, they are more likely to fund education for daughters, largely, I suspect, because they reckon their sons will make it under their own steam.

Many of the short-term privileges that still exist for men come with serious long-term costs. A study of gender differences in American university drop-out rates, published this month in *Gender & Society*, found that one reason why men have higher drop-out rates than women is they are less willing to take on the high levels of debt that are increasingly needed to graduate.

In part this may be due to the pressure men feel to become breadwinners. But it is also partly because the average male university drop-out earns as much in his entry-level salary as the newly minted male graduate. By midlife, however, male university graduates can earn on average £13,100 more a year.

The costs that the masculine mystique imposes are not just monetary. Kristen Springer, a medical sociologist, found that the greater a man's investment in his male-provider image, the more his health and wellbeing are threatened if his wife earns more than he does. This is a serious health risk, given that today almost 38% of UK wives outearn their husbands.

While the masculine mystique may seem sexy in the movies, men who subscribe to it at home have less successful relationships than those who have moved beyond it. Wendy Sigle-Rushton, a researcher at the London School of Economics, examined 3,500 married couples in Britain and found that the higher a husband's participation in housework and childcare, the lower the incidence of divorce.

Research in America indicates that marriages where men and women are flexible in their gender roles tend to have the highest marital quality. Over the course of a marriage, husbands who become less invested in their masculine identity also report becoming happier.

As women did in the 1960s, men today are finding their traditional gender roles and values are becoming obstacles to their personal success and that they need to forge a new set of self-images and skills. It was not easy for women to defy the long-standing internal and external pressures demanding that we constantly prove our femininity. But our biggest gains came once we stopped feeling compelled to "act like a lady."

Now it is men's turn. They need to liberate themselves from the personal and societal pressure constantly to prove their masculinity. Men's lives will improve greatly when they assimilate the lesson that Friedan drove home to women half a century ago: act like a person, not a gender stereotype. ◼

In Other Words

STILL A MAN'S WORLD: THE MYTH OF WOMEN'S ASCENDANCE

Boston Review, January 10, 2013

Philip N. Cohen

The notion that women are outpacing men in economic achievement is becoming a post-feminist rallying cry. A legion of authors laments the man-children whom today's successful, focused career women are forced to date, coddle, and ultimately dump.

Two recent books, Hanna Rosin's *The End of Men* and Liza Mundy's *The Richer Sex*, collect the many strands of this tale of women ascendant. These authors are motivated by the same basic facts: women's attainment of college degrees has surpassed that of men; in early 2010 it briefly appeared that women would be the majority of the American labor force; the proportion of married couples in which the wife earns more than the husband has increased and now approaches 30 percent; unmarried, childless young women who work full time have high earnings relative to similarly situated men; and finally, a majority of workers in the fastest-growing occupations are women.

Together, these facts contribute to an important story that is well established among gender inequality researchers, but which remains a matter of confusion for some journalists and readers. Gender inequality in the economic realm has in fact narrowed dramatically since the mid-twentieth century, even as the overwhelming weight of evidence shows that men as a group maintain systematic advantages over women. However, the relative status of men and women is not built from singular data points, but rather from giant moving orbs of data with wide distributions around central tendencies. As the gender gap, then, has grown smaller overall—as the distributions have grown closer together—naturally there are circumstances in which women are doing better than men. The question is how to extrapolate from those circumstances.

Both Rosin and Mundy match selected statistics with compelling anecdotes to form narratives in which women not only are drawing even with men, but also are heading for inevitable economic dominance. But despite their assertions—and the progressive direction of change—there is no reason to expect their projections to come to pass in the foreseeable future. Their skillful writing and anecdotal reporting appear to provide convincing support for a narrative that is fundamentally untrue. And that is not a compliment to contemporary journalism.

That is not to say that Rosin and Mundy are simply replicating each other's mistakes. The two books diverge considerably despite their shared commitment to a similar overreaching economic forecast. Rosin's distortion, exaggeration, and carelessness are so ubiquitous as to undermine the reader's confidence in her reporting, which mostly reads as a series of shallow caricatures. Mundy's stories, on the other hand, which seem to draw from a larger pool of interviews, often are interesting descriptions of how modern women, men, and couples navigate the (relatively unusual) situation in which women have more financial clout than their potential or actual partners.

In this sense, Mundy is describing a possible future reality. The question is, will it come to pass on its own, as the inevitable product of economic rationality? Both books suggest an affirmative answer. But has the battle for equality been virtually won already? Or does equality still require concerted action?

For Rosin and Mundy, women's rise to the top of the economic heap begins with school. There is some justification for this view.

Women earn the majority of college degrees in the United States, and they are the majority of college students, having established better academic records in high school. To both authors this trend signals a major shift. But women surpassed men as the majority of BA earners in the early 1980s, and that advantage has only marginally increased since then, to 57 percent. Moreover, women continue to earn less at every level of education, and not merely as a function of time spent on family obligations and occupational choices. A recent study by the American Association of University Women, for example, found that even among full-time workers just one year after college graduation, women earn 82 percent of men's average earnings.

For college graduates, fields of study are a big part of the pay-gap story, and a reason not to focus exclusively on overall graduation rates. In the 1970s and 1980s, the segregation of men and women into different major fields decreased markedly, as women began majoring in psychology, biology, communications, and business in greater numbers. But health, education, and English are as predominately female as ever—and math and engineering remain stubbornly resistant to change.

In any event, when it comes to gender, proportional growth in educational programs is no guarantee of commensurate increase in labor market clout. In law and medical school, for example, women peaked at almost half of graduates in the last decade, but women are still less than 40 percent of doctors and lawyers in the 35- to 44-year-old age range, where they earn 72 percent and 81 percent of male counterparts' pay, respectively. The main reason for these gaps is that more women have dropped out of these professions, and more remain in specialties, such as pediatrics and family law, that pay less.

Women have improved their relative status in these high-value fields, but there is no sign of their dominance on the horizon.

In the face of such stubbornness on the part of the data, both Rosin and Mundy single out women's greater progress in the fields of pharmacy and veterinary medicine. These occupations are much smaller and less well paid than medicine, and neither is a steppingstone to physician jobs. Rather than seeing veterinarians and pharmacists as harbingers of future female dominance, then, it might be more accurate to describe them as inadequate safety valves for highly capable and well-educated women. The large number of women in those fields reflects not their upper hand, but rather frustrated opportunities for success in more lucrative and powerful fields.

So women are getting more education, with limited results in the labor market. How do we go from there to a new day in gender relations?

Here the transition to a postindustrial, service- and knowledge-based economy—in conjunction with declining gender discrimination driven by managerial rationalization—is important. It might seem to be leading inevitably to women's economic dominance. This deterministic story is intuitively appealing: the demands of the economy are shifting dramatically in women's favor, brains have superseded brawn, and social skills have become increasingly important, all of which favors women over men.

In support of this view, both authors use projections by the U.S. Bureau of Labor Statistics showing that the occupations with the largest expected growth in the next decade are dominated by women. But that description is superficial—misleading, even.

According to Mundy, nine out of ten occupations with the largest projected growth in the next decade—registered nurses, home health aides, customer service representatives, food preparation and service workers, personal care aides, retail personnel, office staff, accountants, nursing aides, and postsecondary teachers—are majority female. For Rosin it is twelve out of the top fifteen. This is impressive, except that there are hundreds of occupations overall, and with women almost half the labor force, many of those occupations are close to majority female. In fact, the employees of Mundy's top-ten occupations made up just 15 percent of the workforce in 2010, and are projected to make up only 17 percent by 2020. The top 15 are projected to increase from 22 percent to just 23 percent of the workforce. The growth in these jobs doesn't represent much of a change on an economy-wide scale. The bottom line is that women are projected to increase their share of the labor force by no more than 1 percent in the next decade.

This should not be that surprising. After the 1960s it was not change in the occupational structure that drove increases in women's employment, but rather the integration of existing occupations. However, integration has been stalled since the mid-1990s, and economic development since then barely favors women over men. Yes, there are more nurses and home health aides today than there were in the 1960s, but there are also fewer maids and domestic servants. And although blue-collar manufacturing jobs have declined, truck driving and construction have not. The decline of manufacturing is no longer shaping our gender story—the industry represents only 8.3 percent of workers. Ostensibly gender-neutral processes of economic transformation are not the sources of women's progress they once were.

So many people continue to be so attached to this narrative of women's rapid advance in the labor force that they haven't noticed there has been no advance in almost two decades: women occupied between 46 and 47 percent of the labor force every year from 1994 through 2011, the last year for which we have data. This stagnation undermines Rosin's and Mundy's accounts, in which continuous and fast-paced change is not just taking us toward equality but beyond it.

And that's the real danger in their exaggerated stories: creating the impression that women's progress is inevitable and unstoppable.

Mundy and Rosin assume that incomes favor young, single women and that this distribution holds up among married couples, too. Increasing numbers of married women are in fact out-earning their husbands—which is important—but both authors exaggerate the claim.

Women's higher rates of college completion are not turning into a landslide of female-breadwinner marriages. That is because the majority of couples marry on the same side of the college/non-college divide, on each side of which men's earnings are systematically higher. And after they marry, couples, with the cooperation of employers, tend to move very efficiently in the direction of male economic dominance. Childbearing, division of labor, and career-balancing practices all favor male breadwinning.

At present, a little more than a quarter of wives in their prime working years earn more than their husbands do, though the numbers are higher if you follow Mundy and Rosin, who restrict the pool to couples with working wives. Mundy calls the imagined impending majority of such families the "Big Flip," and devotes much of her book to how American men and women fail or succeed at adjusting to it. In this construction, any couple in which the wife earns more than her husband has already undergone the Big Flip, and the rest of the country is sliding rapidly down that path.

However, even when wives earn more, they almost always earn only a little more—which does not quite give them the authority to establish a "matriarchy" (Rosin's term) or qualitatively overturn gender relations, as implied by Mundy's flipping terminology. It's true that only 7 percent of wives outearned their husbands in 1970, so we have seen a real change in gender relations. If change continues at that pace, women really will be the majority earners in more than half of married couples by midcentury. Also, if world population growth keeps increasing at the rate it has in the past century, the earth will eventually become a ball of human flesh expanding at the speed of light. Neither of these outcomes is a sure bet; predicting the future is not as simple as extending the line on a graph.

Rapid change in the direction of equality has not produced equality. The biggest trend in the income distribution of married couples has been the decline of the zero-earning wife. In 1970, 44 percent of wives earned nothing. Today that figure is 21 percent. However, it is still almost three times more common for the husband than for the wife to be the only earner in the couple. As for the idea of female-dominant newlywed couples, this is rarer than the authors assume. Rosin, to create her illustrations, conducts an online survey looking specifically for such couples and, not surprisingly, finds some. Mundy focuses on Atlanta, writing, "Of all the major cities where young women outearn young men, Atlanta is number one."

But marriage markets aren't as simple as pairing eligible men and women together at random. Even in places where the average earnings are a little higher among unmarried women, a few simple sorting preferences produce (straight) couples that overwhelmingly lean male-dominant. The most important preferences are for race/ethnicity and education: most couples match up along these lines. Within racial/ethnic and education groups, men earn more at every level. On top of that, the male partner is usually a few years older. With those parameters set, men will earn more in most couples. If you add an additional preference for higher-earning men within a couple—which is still what most people appear to want, whether they say it explicitly or not—then the male-dominant skew in the resulting marriages is even stronger.

Take Atlanta. Among childless full-time workers there, unmarried young women earn more than unmarried young men, but Census data confirm that just-married men's incomes are higher than just-married women's. Three-quarters of Atlanta couples marry on the same side of the college/non-college divide, and in cases where both spouses have college degrees, women earn more in just one-third of couples. Overall, only 38 percent of newlywed Atlanta couples have a higher-earning wife. As these couples advance along their careers, that percentage is unlikely to rise.

The growing prevalence of breadwinning wives is an important phenomenon, but it is not the end of gender inequality as we know it, and that prevalence is not irreversibly increasing.

Mundy has argued that her critics, including me, are institutionally wedded to a glass-half-empty form of feminism, which is sliding toward irrelevance as women's progress gains steam. And we have indeed made much progress, as I've outlined above. But there is a lot of room for interpretation and speculation about what will—and should—happen next.

Mundy overreaches and oversells her interpretation. But at least enough of her facts are true that we can have a reasonable debate based on them. The same cannot be said of Rosin. In a blog post defending herself, she writes, "I hesitate to get drawn into data wars . . . . I've learned over the course of my research that data can support many different stories." But many of Rosin's errors are not matters of interpretation, the inevitable collateral damage from a data free-for-all in which we all focus on different bits of the larger story. Rather, they are factual claims that happen to be clearly and demonstrably untrue. Here are three examples:

1. The unsourced claim that "in Asia"—unqualified by any further detail, such as the name of a country or countries—"the average age of marriage for women is thirty-two." This is false not only for women across Asia as a whole, but also for every country in Asia, where women in the biggest countries mostly marry at or before age twenty (Indonesia, India); in their early twenties (China); or, at the high end, in their late twenties (Korea, Japan).

2. The description of sexual assault rates as "so low in parts of the country—for white women especially—that criminologists can't plot the numbers on a chart," which is nonsensical as well as untrue. Not only are U.S. rates of sexual assault plottable, they are not even low by the standards of wealthy countries.

3. "Women are now lead TV anchors, Ivy League College heads, bank presidents, corporate CEOs, movie directors, scatologically savvy comedians, presidential candidates—all unthinkable even twenty years ago." With one exception, each of those milestones not only was thinkable but had *already occurred* twenty years before she wrote, most of them long before. (The exception is a female Ivy League president, which wasn't recorded until nineteen years earlier, in 1993.)

Rosin also has an affinity for sweeping proclamations that do the work of facts without being testable. Thus, "Our vast and struggling middle class . . . is slowly turning into a matriarchy"; women are "taking over the middle class"; and Auburn, Alabama, of all places, has "turn[ed] itself into a town dominated by women."

And, for the careful reader, Rosin presents an exhausting parade of exaggerations, which are obvious if one consults her endnotes for verification. Some of these are simply aggravating stretches, such as referring to the health and education sectors as adding "about the same number" of jobs as were shed by the manufacturing sector in the 2000s, when the former number was 4.5 million and the latter was 5.7 million, a difference of 26 percent. Others are distorted to the point of falsehood. She wants us to believe that "young women" are earning more than "young men," but what she really has in mind is a much narrower group: single, childless, female full-time workers ages 22-30. That list of qualifications is indeed awkward, but without it, the fact is not a fact. Elsewhere Rosin reports, "Nearly a third of Brazilian women now make more money than their husbands," but her citation refers to only 28 percent, and then only among college-educated female full-time workers—a far cry from all Brazilian women. This is an abbreviated list.

Even if we do continue to advance toward gender equality, it might not accompany, or cause, fundamental transformation of gender patterns in those arenas that have been most resistant to change: male dominance of the highest echelons of political, economic, and institutional power; the cultural devaluation of work associated with women; the persistent difference-based gender socialization of the sexes from the earliest moments of childhood; the political domination of women's bodies by men; and the gendered division of labor, especially that which is unpaid.

Mundy and Rosin miss all this because they embrace mechanical and deterministic narratives of change. There is little apparent role for an active agenda promoting equality beyond the assumption that anti-discrimination laws and practices will advance continuously, driven, one supposes, by the inherent economic rationality of gender egalitarianism. And in these books there is no discussion of organized resistance on the part of men in positions of power and authority.

The economic, political, and cultural changes that motivate Rosin and Mundy are real. For example, there is a competitive price to pay for an old-fashioned attachment to sexism. Modern rationality exerts pressure in the direction of universalism, as the sociologist Robert Max Jackson argues in *Destined for Equality: The Inevitable Rise of Women's Status* (1998). But these changes also are old news. More pressing now is the question of how to unlock the door between the stalled present and further progress toward equality.

Feminist action on law and policy may now be as important as ever.

In the legal realm, gender discrimination suits are very hard to win unless a man and woman are being paid differently for doing exactly the same job for the same employer, as in the famous Lilly Ledbetter case.

In policy, the United States lags atrociously on vital matters of work-family integration. Specifically, paid family leave might reduce the career consequences of unpaid care-work obligations. Universal preschool education would smooth women's reentry into the labor force after childbirth while reducing the inequalities in childcare that help reproduce class inequality. And we might even stretch our imaginations to consider a shorter workweek, which besides reducing unemployment could help dislodge the hyper-present "ideal worker" image many hold dear, thereby shaking loose a more gender-balanced family life.

And in the mainstream culture, we need to challenge the crushing norm of intensive parenting and combat the resurgence of highly polarized gender socialization for children. The stalled progress that has become apparent since the mid-1990s arguably reflects a weakened feminist movement—its transformation into an inward-looking program of self-improvement under the mantra of empowerment and choice. Sitting back to watch the tide of women's dominance roll in will not help.

To these authors, feminism—rarely mentioned—is a cultural trend running as a bit player in the background, integrated into the stream of progress. (Mundy has described institutional feminist actors as a "fempire" of dour naysayers unwilling to accept a future of positive change.) Meanwhile, the men who would stand to lose their privileged positions thanks to feminism's success actually are resisting change. At the low end, many blue-collar men have blocked the entrance of women into their trades, passively or actively. At the high end, the board rooms and executive suites of corporate America are monuments to sexism's perseverance, with annual progress in women's representation measured in the fractions of a percent. Active gender discrimination—especially based on women's status as mothers—continues to plague working women.

We cannot assume a future of continuous, inexorable change in the direction of gender equality, the satiating lullaby of these tall tales. ▄

Conclusion

38

Families: A Great American Institution

Barbara J. Risman

Perhaps the greatest problem in American politics today is that so many people in Washington tend to think in two- and four-year cycles. We don't think long term, yet children are a long-term proposition.

—Howard Dean[1]

From the inside, no family ever seems typical.

—Sarah Palin[2]

I'll be a president that stands up for American families—all of them.

—President Barack Obama[3]

You don't ask for much. You never give up. You soldier on for your families and your communities.

—Hillary Clinton[4]

I think we all in America understand today that families have challenges and I know there's further challenges for my family, but I thank God every day for them.

—John McCain[5]

The American dream must never come at the expense of the American family. For decades we've had politicians in Washington who talk about family values, but we haven't had policies that value families.

—President Barack Obama[6]

From progressives to conservatives, American politicians universally proclaim "family" to be the cornerstone of American society. The diversity of families as they really are has some Americans worried that the increase in cohabitation, the frequency of divorce, and the proportion of children living outside of two-parent households means the family is being undermined, and failing us. Focus on the Family founder James Dobson, a minister, wrote in his group's newsletter, "The family as it has been known for more than five millennia will crumble, presaging the fall of Western civilization itself."[7] The government itself has acted as if it fears for the future of the American family. A key component of President Clinton's 1996 reform of welfare was an attempt to strengthen two-parent families. And President Bush's Healthy Marriage Initiative, run by the Department of Health and Human Services starting in 2003, spent $100 million annually, much of it to help couples learn relationship skills. Clearly, both clergy and the government sometimes worry that the family is breaking down.

Nearly all Americans seem to agree on the importance of a strong family. And yet, as we have seen, there is tremendous diversity in what people define as family and in what they see as the strengths and weaknesses of families. One reason that these debates matter is that, for all its diverse forms, a family is not just an individual choice. It is also a social institution. Sociologists identify twelve features that characterize a social institution, and I will conclude this book by showing how many of the chapters in this anthology illustrate those features. I believe that the analysis below provides clear evidence that the family is as strong an institution now as it has ever been.

1. Institutions are profoundly social. No social institution can exist unless it includes a group of people who interact with one another often and fulfill social roles that obligate them to behave in certain ways. Families are groups composed of people who take on social roles that come in sets, with obligations that are expected between people based on their positions as parents and children, husbands and wives, in-laws—or even as former partners. Although adults choose which families to join, once they are part of a family, they assume kin connections that take on an existence of their own. Even if a couple divorces after they marry, the former partners always remain "an ex" to each other, for better or for worse. We know that when divorced parents continue to argue or denigrate each other, children suffer. But divorced and blended families can also use their ties to construct new forms of social support, as when former in-laws or new stepparents provide resources or mentoring for children. Research on postmodern families suggests that the relationships between mothers and daughters-in law often survive even after a divorce, so that a previous mother-in-law might be a regular member of

Thanksgiving celebrations every fall.[8] Adult siblings often keep in contact, and help one another out, whether or not they like each other well enough to be friends beyond their family ties. The chapters by Robert-Jay Green and Karen Struening show us that one reason many same-sex partners want the chance to marry is that they desire to be part of a social institution that identifies their social role as spouse, creates public marital obligations to one another, and facilitates wider social bonds by bringing their families of origin into interaction as in-laws. Amy Brainer's chapter reveals the way that the social role of sibling creates a meaningful space for understanding of gay and straight lives.

2. Institutions endure across time and space. We can identify groups of people that have social role obligations to one another and are defined as family in every culture, and over history. The chapters by both Stephanie Coontz and Steven Mintz show that although families have changed over time, every society and subgroup within society has used its family ties to transmit values, behaviors, and obligations across generations and to maintain social ties across geographic boundaries. Joshua Coleman shows us that the norms around parenting continue long past children's coming of age.

3. Institutions entail distinct social practices that recur. Families throughout history have been a source of emotional support and intimacy. In some cultural systems, such support and intimacy are sought primarily from relatives of the same sex, such as sisters and mothers, or brothers and fathers. In the United States today, however, we expect the marital relationship to be the main source of support. But in the United States, married partners often have to rely exclusively on each other to manage life's challenges, as, for example, Shannon Davis and Brittany Owen explain in their chapter on couples and the Great Recession. Coontz argues that this over-reliance on spouses may end up being a burden too heavy for the institution of marriage to bear. Reproduction and the socialization of youth are also recurring social practices in families. Annette Lareau shows us how the distinctive parenting practices of people with different class and educational resources help reproduce class advantages and disadvantages over time.

4. Institutions both constrain and facilitate behavior by members. Families provide their members with a set of expectations for entering any family role. Such expectations provide people with guidelines for organizing daily life, so that they generally know what to do and what to expect in family interactions. They also set limits on people's freedom of action. Several chapters in this book show how the historical roles for wives and husbands facilitated a division of labor in the household that made it clear whose job was whose, but that also constrained women as they began to lobby for equality. Until

the 1970s, legal codes specifically defined which duties were assigned to husbands and wives. These legal codes have now been repealed, but the social norms associated with marriage are still strong, encouraging women to perform more housework when they marry than when they are single or cohabiting. The CCF symposium on equal pay details the legal and personal progress we've seen for working women.

5. Institutions have social positions characterized by expected norms and behaviors. In some historical periods, sexual pleasure has been dissociated from marriage, especially for men, who faced no sanctions for having mistresses or frequenting prostitutes. In contemporary American families, by contrast, the couple is presumed to be the major source both of emotional support and of sexual pleasure. One of the most widely expected norms for families today is that spouses will be active and mutual sexual partners. Yet, that norm often collides with older norms about women's sexual purity, as Pepper Schwartz points out. The discussion of divorce by Virginia Rutter and Philip Cohen builds from the taken-for-granted view that divorce is what happens when the norms for husbands and wives to love, honor, and be faithful to one another are contradicted or simply rejected.

6. Institutions are made, supported, and changed by real people. Donna Franklin presents interesting research to show us that African Americans pioneered modern marriage, in which husbands and wives are allowed to have serious careers as well as children. The chapters by Struening on family legal policy and by Amy Blackstone and Amy Greenleaf about childfree families show how men and women in the twenty-first century are redefining who is in a family and how you can be a family. With new technologies, there can be one family with three types of mothers—the genetically related egg donor, the surrogate birth mother, and the adopting social mother. Similarly, as same-sex couples demand to be in families, we have new legislation institutionalizing lovers into "domestic partnerships" with legal rights. Courts in states without same-sex marriage must now deal with the custodial battles of gay couples who married somewhere else and are now figuring out how to part without institutionalized guidelines. And families with no children are now gaining the recognition and self-understanding of themselves as family. Mignon Moore's chapter shows lesbians creating blended families and inventing their own norms around the household division of labor and couple power. These are real-life examples of the family as an institution being made anew in our own generation.

7. Institutions are important to their members, and their rules and expectations become internalized as important identities and parts of selves. Philip Cowan and Carolyn Cowan show us that what actually happens in families,

the processes of everyday life, are internalized in children's self-images or expressed in their behavior. The ability to lay claim to the identity of wife or husband clearly matters very much to many Americans. Green and Struening show how same-sex couples today want to be able to say "I do" and to call their loved one a wife or a husband.

8. Institutions have a legitimating ideology. The norms attached to the positions of people in families wield great ideological force. Despite the reality that those norms can and do change all the time, most people believe the social norms they follow are necessary and inevitable. We live in a society that presumes marriage is between one man and one woman, and even though many polygamous cultures exist, we take it for granted that a marriage involves two people and only two people. The result is that many people cannot even recognize the love and mutual support that exist in families that do not meet those conditions. Most people yearn for public recognition and validation. Kerry Ann Rockquemore and Loren Henderson show us that cross-racial couples who were forbidden to marry sued to make their love formally accepted within the institution of the family. Many same-sex couples also want the public recognition that comes with marriage, even if they can claim the same legal rights through a domestic partnership. Raine Dozier, writing about the experience of "guy moms," foregrounds how transgender parents, along with gay parents, seek to be legitimized in their family roles.

9. Institutions are inconsistent, contradictory, and rife with conflict. Families are always evolving, and that leads to contradictions between what used to be and what is. What was once so taken for granted as to be seen as inevitable, that marriage can only be between one man and one woman, has been successfully challenged in many states. Sometimes contradictions and change can create conflict between parents and children. Families may share many common interests, but different individuals within the family may have different interests in the distribution of resources, obligations, and authority, and they may openly contest or maneuver behind the scenes to further their individual interests. Kathleen Gerson's research suggests that young adults, both men and women, want egalitarian relationships. But if such relationships are out of reach, men and women have contradictory solutions: men want neo-traditional wives, and women prefer to go it alone rather than trade income for housekeeping services. If such men and women marry, their different Plan B's may indeed create conflict, producing outcomes that are different from those they both originally intended.

10. Institutions continuously change. Families as an institution are constantly in flux. Rockquemore and Henderson, Brian Powell and colleagues, Green,

Moore, Blackstone and Greenleaf, and Struening show clearly that those who even get to be defined as family has recently and is even at this very moment changing. Not only is a larger cast of characters now allowed into the institution, but the norms attached to gender relations inside marriage itself are shifting, as the chapters in the section on the gender revolution show clearly. Once it was assumed that marriage largely regulated a woman's entry into sexual activity. Chapters by Schwartz, by Adina Nack, and by Elizabeth Armstrong, Paula England, and Alison C. K. Fogarty show that Americans of both sexes become sexual actors long before they become wives and husbands, if they ever do. In their chapter, Pamela Smock and Wendy Manning show us how cohabitation has gone in a short period of time from being an alternative to marriage to a normal pathway into it.

11. Institutions are organized by and permeated by power. The most obvious way that families are permeated by power is between generations. Parents have traditionally had the right to impose their own norms, beliefs, and rules on their children. Many social institutions—from schools to child protective agencies—as well as norms now limit some aspects of parental power. But parents still exercise power over many of the circumstances of children's lives, consciously or unconsciously, as Georgiann Davis illustrates in the chapter on parents and their intersex children. When children are born with intersex traits, parents are thrust into a medical system that presumes sex can be only a binary, and they usually follow medical advice only to learn later that their children might grow up to view their bodies as simply part of the diversity that is humanity. Several authors in this book show that parents transmit their own social class privileges or disadvantages to their children. Schwartz argues that women's sexuality, even in marriage, is regulated by laws making sex toys used primarily by women illegal. Armstrong, England, and Fogarty show us that hooking up privileges men, at least when it comes to sexual pleasure.

12. Individuals must adapt to institutions, but they remake them at the same time. This final criterion for defining an institution is the theme of this anthology, recognizing "families as they really are." Nearly every child born into the world enters a family that is an institution constrained by the criteria explained in this chapter, and each child learns the norms attached to his or her familial social roles. Every adult who enters the institution of marriage has to cope with the norms and expectations that come with being a wife or a husband. So, too, when we become parents, we face the entire institutional weight of expectations about being good mothers or fathers. Even grandparents and aunts and uncles must adapt to institutional expectations about their relationships to new babies who enter into the extended kinship group.

Some people always do exactly what they believe the norms dictate, never questioning whether they're right or wrong for them or others. But other people bend, twist, and remake those rules so that they fit their own needs and desires. In this anthology, we've seen how American families have evolved over time, with more freedom for spouses to choose one another and to treat one another as equals. Similarly, we have seen how childhood is a social and cultural construct, redefined in every age and increasingly endowed with rights that in the past were not recognized. We have also seen how access to the institution of marriage itself has increased, as women and men who loved each other across race lines sued for the right to marry and to be recognized as family. Currently, gays and lesbians are using the same argument, making inroads into federal policy as well as in a growing number of states that provide same-sex marriage rights. None of these changes just happened. Rather, some people have always rebelled against the norms. And sometimes they have succeeded, especially when they are part of a larger social movement, in altering the institution to meet their own needs.

One reason that the family as an institution remains so strong, and so important to us, is that we have been able to change it. It is a sign of the family's strength, not its weakness, that Americans have been able to reject aspects of the institution, revise others, and invent new norms for relationships. Perhaps that is the secret of an enduring institution like the family: that it matters enough in people's lives for them to work on making it anew in every generation. Families "as they really are" are always works in progress.

On behalf of my colleagues at the Council on Contemporary Families, I hope that you can use the new research and clinical expertise presented in this volume not only to enhance your understanding of the social context and internal dynamics of your own families, and of those that differ from yours, but also to help you build the kind of family that can deliver the support and satisfaction you need in your intimate relationships. We hope that having accurate information will help you to preserve the family traditions that still work for you and to create the new family norms and relationships that you need, so that the family can remain a strong, thriving institution for the children of the next generation.

NOTES

1. Howard Dean on children, from his campaign website, DeanforAmerica.com, "On the Issues," November 30, 2002. Available at http://www.ontheissues.org/celeb/Howard _Dean_Families_+_Children.htm.

2. Sarah Palin in her 2008 National Republican Convention speech.

3. Barack Obama in a letter to Family Equality Council on August 1, 2008. Available at http://obama.3cdn.net/c97fcbdd343527466b_u5m6bt5hr.pdf.

4. Hillary Clinton during Presidential Election Season 2008, Obama Rally in Scranton, PA, October 12, 2008.

5. John McCain in interview with Charlie Gibson on September 3, 2008.

6. Barack Obama in a letter to Family Equality Council on August 1, 2008. Available at http://www.familyequality.org/blog/wp-content/family-equality-council-chrisler-08-01-08.pdf.

7. James Dobson in April 2004 edition of the *Focus on the Family Newsletter*.

8. See Judith Stacey's study of postmodern families in *Brave New Families: Stories of Domestic Upheaval in Late-Twentieth-Century America* (Berkeley: University of California Press, 1998).

Contributors

Etiony Aldarondo is Associate Dean for Research and Founding Director of the Dunspaugh-Dalton Community and Educational Well-Being Research Center in the School of Education and Human Development at the University of Miami. The recipient of various recognitions for academic excellence and community involvement, including the 2011 Social Justice Award from the American Psychological Association and the 2011 Elizabeth Beckman Award, his scholarship focuses on positive development of ethnic minority and immigrant youth, domestic violence, and social justice–oriented clinical practices. His publications include the books *Advancing Social Justice through Clinical Practice* (Routledge), *Programs for Men Who Batter: Intervention and Prevention Strategies in a Diverse Society* (Civic Research Institute with Fernando Mederos, Ed.D.), and *Neurosciences, Health and Community Well-Being* (San Luís, Nueva Editorial Universitaria with Dr. Enrique Saforcada and Mauro Muñoz). He is the Executive Director of the Council on Contemporary Families.

Edward Ameen is Assistant Director of the American Psychological Association of Graduate Students (APAGS) in Washington, DC. He earned his doctorate in counseling psychology from the University of Miami and previously attended Northwestern University and Boston College. After directing an outreach program for homeless youth in Miami, he continues to be active in research, advocacy, and community organizing related to disconnected youth, homelessness, immigration, and social justice. He also serves on the board of a local LGBT community organization and conducts pro bono asylum evaluations.

Elizabeth A. Armstrong is Professor of Sociology and Organizational Studies at the University of Michigan. Her research interests include sexuality, gender, social movements, sociology of culture, and higher education. With Laura T. Hamilton, she is author of *Paying for the Party: How College Maintains Inequality* (Harvard University Press, 2013). She was a fellow at the Radcliffe Institute for Advanced Study at Harvard University and a recipient of a National Academy of Education/Spencer Postdoctoral Fellowship.

Orit Avishai is Associate Professor of Sociology at Fordham University. She specializes in studies of gender, religion, and family, and her work has appeared in many peer-reviewed journals and edited volumes, including *Gender & Society*, *Qualitative Sociology*, *Journal of Contemporary Ethnography*, and *Contexts*. She is currently studying the marriage education movement.

Pallavi Banerjee is currently a postdoctoral fellow in the sociology department at Vanderbilt University. She received her PhD in sociology from the University of Illinois at Chicago in 2012. Her research interests are situated at the intersection of sociology of immigration, gender, transnational labor, minority families, globalization, and South Asia. She is currently working on a book manuscript titled *Dismantling Dependence: Gendered Migration of Indian Professional Families to the United States*. Banerjee has published in journals, including *Sociological Forum* and *Cities*, and she recently won the Davis P. Street Dissertation Prize for outstanding dissertation from the Sociology Department at the University of Illinois at Chicago.

Amy Blackstone is Associate Professor and Chair of Sociology and Director of the ADVANCE Rising Tide Center at the University of Maine. Her research includes studies of childfree adults and workplace satisfaction and harassment. Most recently, Blackstone's work has appeared in journals such as *Sociology Compass*, *American Sociological Review*, and *Society and Mental Health* and books, including *Employment and Older Adults* and *Disrupting the Culture of Silence*. She is the author of *Principles of Sociological Inquiry: Qualitative and Quantitative Methods* (Flat World Knowledge, 2012). Dr. Blackstone received her BA in sociology from Luther College and a PhD in sociology from the University of Minnesota.

Catherine Bolzendahl is Associate Professor of Sociology at the University of California, Irvine. Much of her research is comparative and examines the role of gender and family in various political arenas, including the impact of gender equality and family autonomy on social spending, gender differences in citizenship norms and participation, and sources of support for gender equality and family policy. She is a co-author of the ASA Rose Series book *Counted Out: Same Sex Relations and Americans' Definitions of Family*.

Amy Brainer is Assistant Professor of Women's and Gender Studies and Sociology at the University of Michigan–Dearborn. Her research examines family dynamics surrounding gender and sexuality with a focus on East Asia. She is currently working on a book manuscript based on her ethnographic fieldwork with three generational cohorts of gender and sexually nonconforming people and with their heterosexual siblings and parents throughout Taiwan. This research is supported by two grants from the Wenner–Gren Foundation. Dr. Brainer's previous research on young adults who have grown up with a lesbian, gay, or bisexual sibling has received awards from the National Council on Family Relations and the Society for the Study of Social Problems. She served as graduate assistant to the Council on Contemporary Families from 2008–2010.

Linda M. Burton is James B. Duke Professor of Sociology at Duke University. She currently serves on the Institute of Medicine's Committee on Child Maltreatment Research, Policy, and Practice for the Next Decade: Phase II, the Editorial Board of the *American Sociological Review*, and the *Journal of Marriage and Family*. In 2013 she was inducted into the Sociological Research Association (National Honor Society for Sociological Researchers), received the inaugural Alexis Walker Award for her scientific contributions to the study of families from the National Council on Family Relations, and is also a recipient of the Family Research Consortium IV Legacy Award and the American Family Therapy Academy Award for Innovative Contributions to Family Research. Dr. Burton directed the ethnographic component of *Welfare, Children, and Families: A Three-City Study* and is principal investigator of a multi-site team ethnographic study (*Family Life Project*) of poverty, family processes, and child development in six rural communities.

Natasha Cabrera received her PhD in educational psychology from the University of Denver (1994) and joined the University of Maryland faculty in 2002. Dr. Cabrera arrived at the University of Maryland with several years of experience as an expert in child development with the Demographic and Behavioral Sciences Branch (DBSB) of the National Institute of Child Health and Human Development (NICHD). Her current research topics include paternal and maternal involvement and its effect on children, theoretical frameworks related to father involvement, and children's developmental trajectories in low-income and minority families. She has published in peer-reviewed journals on policy, methodology, theory, and the implications of father involvement on child development. She is co-editor with Catherine Tamis-LeMonda of the *Handbook of Father Involvement: Multidisciplinary Perspectives* (Erlbaum, 2002).

Andrew J. Cherlin is Griswold Professor of Sociology and Public Policy at Johns Hopkins University. In 1999, he was president of the Population Association of America. In 2003 he received the Distinguished Career Award from the Family Section of the American Sociological Association. In 2005–2006, he was a Guggenheim Foundation Fellow. His research interests include the well-being of parents and children in low-income families and the changing nature of marriage and family life over the past century. His recent articles include "The Deinstitutionalization of American Marriage" in the *Journal of Marriage and Family* and "Family Instability and Child Well-Being" in the *American Sociological Review*. He is the author of *The Marriage-Go-Round: The State of Marriage and the Family in America Today* (Knopf, 2009) and *Labor's Love Lost: The Rise and Fall of the Working-Class Family in America* (Russell Sage Foundation, 2014).

Joshua Coleman is a psychologist in private practice in the San Francisco Bay Area specializing in couples and family issues. A frequent guest on the *Today* show and NPR, he has also appeared on *Sesame Street*, ABC's *20/20*, *Good Morning America*, the BBC, America Online Coaches, and numerous news programs for FOX, ABC, CNN, and NBC. He has served on the clinical faculties of the University of California, San Francisco, the Wright Institute Graduate School of Psychology, and the San Francisco Psychotherapy Research Group, and serves as co-chair for the Council on Contemporary Families. He is the author of four books, the most recent of which is *When Parents Hurt: Compassionate Strategies When You and Your Grown Child Don't Get Along* (HarperCollins, 2007).

Marilyn Coleman is Curators' Professor Emerita of Human Development and Family Studies at the University of Missouri–Columbia. She and her husband, Lawrence Ganong, have co-authored eight books and over two hundred journal articles, primarily focusing on postdivorce families. She is former editor of the *Journal of Marriage and Family* and serves on several editorial boards. She is a board member of the Council on Contemporary Families and the recent recipient of the National Council on Family Relations Felix Berardo Mentoring Award.

Stephanie Coontz teaches history and family studies at the Evergreen State College in Olympia, Washington, and serves as Director of Research and Public Education for the Council on Contemporary Families. Her books include *A Strange Stirring: The Feminine Mystique and American Women Since the Dawn of the 1960s* (Basic Books, 2011), *Marriage, A History: How Love Conquered Marriage* (Penguin, 2006), *American Families: A Multicultural Reader* (Routledge, 1998), and *The Way We Never Were: American Families and the Nostalgia Trap* (Basic Books, 2000). Professor Coontz is a frequent guest columnist for the *New York Times* and CNN.com and has appeared on the *Today* show, *The Colbert Report*, and MSNBC's *The Cycle*, along with many other national news outlets.

Carolyn Pape Cowan is Emerita Adjunct and Clinical Professor of Psychology at the University of California, Berkeley. She co-directs the Becoming a Family Project, the Schoolchildren and Their Families Project, and the Supporting Father Involvement Project—research and preventive intervention studies with couples who are parents of young children. The Cowans' couples group intervention model is currently being evaluated with low-income families in California, Connecticut, Canada, and the UK. Dr. Cowan has published widely in the literature on family research, family transitions, and father involvement. She co-edited *Fatherhood Today: Men's Changing Role in the Family* (Wiley, 1988) and *The Family Context of Parenting in Children's Adaptation to Elementary School* (Erlbaum, 2005) and is co-author with Philip Cowan of *When Partners Become Parents: The Big Life Change for Couples* (Erlbaum, 2000). Dr. Cowan consults widely on the development and evaluation of interventions for couples, and is a founding member of the Council on Contemporary Families.

Philip A. Cowan is Emeritus Professor of Psychology at the University of California, Berkeley, former Director of the Institute of Human Development and the Psychology Clinic. He co-directs the Becoming a Family Project, the Schoolchildren and Their Families Project, and the Supporting Father Involvement Project—research and preventive intervention studies with couples who are parents of young children. Dr. Cowan writes about the family context of child development and adaptation. His books include *Piaget: With Feeling* (Holt, 1978); co-author of *When Partners Become Parents: The Big Life Change for Couples* (Erlbaum, 2000); and co-editor of *Family Transitions* (Erlbaum, 1993) and *The Family Context of Parenting in Children's Adaptation to Elementary School* (Erlbaum, 2005). Dr. Cowan is a founding member of the Council on Contemporary Families.

Georgiann Davis is Assistant Professor of Sociology at the University of Nevada, Las Vegas. Her research is at the intersection of gender and the sociology of diagnosis theories. To date, she has published pieces in various outlets ranging from the *American Journal of Bioethics* to *Ms.* magazine. Her forthcoming book—*Contesting Intersex: The Dubious Diagnosis* (NYU Press)—focuses on intersex in contemporary U.S. society, specifically how it is experienced and contested by individuals with intersex traits, their parents, and medical experts since the formal introduction of "disorder of sex development" nomenclature in 2006. On January 1, 2014, she also took on a leadership role in the intersex community as President of AIS-DSD Support Group.

Shannon N. Davis is Associate Professor of Sociology at George Mason University. Her research examines the reproduction of gender inequality in social institutions, with particular focus on families and higher education. She is interested in how family members negotiate the intersection of paid and unpaid work in their daily lives and how gender inequality is reproduced in families, including the role of work-family gender ideologies in these processes. She has published articles in *Annual Review of Sociology, Journal of Marriage and Family*, and *Journal of Family Issues*, and was co-editor of a special issue of *Journal of Family Theory & Review* on "Why Study Housework?" and *Methods of Family Research* (3rd ed.) with Theodore N. Greenstein.

Ilana Demantas is a doctoral candidate in sociology at the University of Kansas. She specializes in the areas of gender, work, and immigration. Her dissertation explores how gender and immigration shape the strategies managers in the retail sectors use to exercise their authority. Her other work appears in the *Sociological Quarterly* and *Work, Employment and Society*. She has served as the graduate assistant at the Kansas University Center for Teaching Excellence and as the co-editor of *Social Thought and Research*.

Raine Dozier is Associate Professor in the Department of Human Services & Rehabilitation at Western Washington University. Dozier is a sociologist who studies both gender theory and social and economic inequality. Her article "Beards, Breasts, and Bodies: Doing Sex in a Gendered World" won the Distinguished Article in Sex and Gender Award from the American Sociological Association. Dozier's current research includes a qualitative study examining the work experiences of masculine females.

Paula England is Professor of Sociology at New York University. Her teaching and research focus on class differences in unplanned pregnancies, youth and young adult sexuality, and the sex gap in pay. She is author of numerous books and articles, including *Comparable Worth: Theories and Evidence* (Aldine, 1992) and *Unmarried Couples with Children* (Russell Sage, 2007; co-edited with Kathryn Edin). Dr. England is a former editor of the *American Sociological Review* and is the president of the American Sociological Association (2014–2015).

Alison C. K. Fogarty is a doctoral candidate in sociology at Stanford University. She specializes in sex, gender, and sexuality, and social psychology and her current research focuses on transgender discrimination in the workplace. She serves on the board of Friendfactor, a non-profit dedicated to helping people become visible and active LGBT allies.

Donna L. Franklin's first book, *Ensuring Inequality* (Oxford University Press, 1997), won two major awards: The American Sociological Association's William J. Goode Distinguished Book Award for "outstanding scholarship on the family" and *Choice Magazine*'s award for "outstanding academic book." She was the first African American author to win the ASA award. Her second book, *What's Love Got to Do with It? Understanding and Healing the Rift between Black Men and Women* (Simon & Schuster, 2000), is one of the first books to include a historical analysis of gender relations in the African American community. Professor Franklin has held academic appointments at the University of Chicago, Smith College, Howard University, and the University of Southern California. She was a member of the founding board of the Council on Contemporary Families and one of its National Chairs. She is currently working on a book about African Americans who have strong partnerships in marriage.

Frank F. Furstenberg Jr. is Zellerbach Family Professor of Sociology, Emeritus, and Research Associate in the Population Studies Center at the University of Pennsylvania. His recent books include *Behind the Academic Curtain: How to Find Success and Happiness with a Ph.D.* (2013), *Destinies of the Disadvantaged: The Politics of Teen Childbearing* (Russell Sage, 2007), *On the Frontier of Adulthood: Theory, Research, and Public Policy* (University of Chicago Press, 2005; co-edited with Richard A. Settersten Jr. and Ruben G. Rumbaut), and *Managing to Make It: Urban Families in High-Risk Neighborhoods* (University of Chicago Press, 1999; with Thomas Cook, Jacquelynne Eccles, Glen Elder, and Arnold Sameroff). His current research projects focus on cross-national research on the transition to adulthood and how intergenerational relationships may change in the context of aging societies. He is former Chair of the MacArthur Foundation Research Network on Transitions to Adulthood and has received numerous honors for his contributions to research on adolescence and public policy. Dr. Furstenberg is a member of the Board of Directors for the Council on Contemporary Families.

Lawrence Ganong, PhD, is Professor and Co-Chair of Human Development and Family Studies and a Professor in the Sinclair School of Nursing at the University of Missouri. He has co-authored over two hundred articles and book chapters as well as seven books, including *Stepfamily Relationships* (2004) and *Handbook of Contemporary Families* (2004) with Marilyn Coleman and *Family Life in 20th Century America* (2007) with Coleman and Kelly Warzinik. His primary research program has focused on postdivorce families, especially stepfamilies and what stepfamily members do to develop satisfying and effective relationships. He is a fellow in the MU Center for Excellence on Aging and the MU Center for Family Policy and Research.

Lorena Garcia is Associate Professor in the Department of Sociology and the Latin American and Latino Studies Program at the University of Illinois at Chicago (UIC). She is also an affiliated faculty member of the Gender and Women's Studies Program at UIC. Her research areas include gender, sexuality, race/ethnicity, and U.S. Latinas/os. She is the author of *Respect Yourself, Protect Yourself: Latina Girls and Sexual Identity* (New York University Press, 2012), as well as articles published in *Gender & Society*, *Latino Studies*, and *Identities: Global Studies in Power & Culture*. She has also co-edited a special issue of the *National Women's Studies Association Journal* (NWSA) [now *Feminist Formations*] on Latina sexualities.

Claudia Geist is Assistant Professor at the University of Utah, where she holds a joint appointment in Sociology and Gender Studies. Her research lies at the intersection of gender, families, and inequalities. She is a co-author of the award-winning book *Counted Out* (Russell Sage Foundation, 2010) and has published articles on topics such as the domestic division of labor in comparative perspective, the impact of family and gender on internal migration, and attitudes toward gender in *Demography*, *Journal of Marriage and Family*, and *Gender & Society*, among other places.

Kathleen Gerson is Collegiate Professor of Sociology at New York University and the 2015 Co-President of Sociologists for Women in Society. She is the author or co-author of numerous books and articles on the connections among gender, work, and family change, including *Hard Choices: How Women Decide about Work, Career, and Motherhood* (University of California Press, 1985); *No Man's Land: Men's Changing Commitments to Family and Work* (Basic Books, 1993); and *The Time Divide: Work, Family, and Gender Inequality* (with Jerry A. Jacobs, Harvard University Press, 2004). Her most recent book, *The Unfinished Revolution: Coming of Age in a New Era of Gender, Work, and Family* (Oxford University Press, 2011), examines young women's and men's experiences and responses to growing up in changing families and gender transformations. Her current research focuses on how the rise of the new economy is changing the contemporary landscape of work and care. Dr. Gerson is a past member of the Board of Directors for the Council on Contemporary Families.

Robert-Jay Green is Founder and Senior Research Fellow of the Rockway Institute, a national center for LGBT research, education, and public policy at the California School of Professional Psychology (CSPP), San Francisco. He also is Distinguished Professor Emeritus in CSPP's clinical psychology PhD program. He received several awards from the American Psychological Association and the American Family Therapy Academy for his work on LGBT couples and families. Among his over one hundred publications are the co-edited books *Family Therapy: Major Contributions* (International University Press, 1981) and *Lesbians and Gays in Couples and Families* (Jossey-Bass/Wiley, 1996). He is currently conducting a longitudinal study of the impact of marriage on same-sex couples and a study of psychological functioning of children conceived via gestational surrogacy and raised by gay male parents. Dr. Green is a founding member of the Council on Contemporary Families.

Amy Greenleaf is a student at Walden University's master's program in Marriage, Couples, and Family Therapy, and works as a behavioral health professional for KidsPeace of New England. She graduated from the University of Maine in 2012, where she earned BAs in both psychology and sociology. Her current research interests focus on the development of appropriate sex and relationship education.

Melanie Heath is an associate professor in the Department of Sociology at McMaster University in Ontario, Canada. Her research addresses the consequences of family, gender, and sexual politics on social inequality. She is author of *One Marriage Under God: The Campaign to Promote Marriage in America* (New York University Press, 2012). She has published in *Gender & Society, Qualitative Sociology, Contexts,* and the *Sociological Quarterly.* Her current research is a comparative study of competing rights and values in the government regulation of polygamy in the United States, Canada, France, and Mayotte.

Loren Henderson was a scholarship winner of the Ronald McNair Scholars Program in 2006–2007. She is the co-author of "Diversity in Illinois: Changing Meanings, Demographic Trends, and Policy Preferences" in the Illinois Report, 2008. She is the author of "Between the Two: Determinants of Bisexual Identity among African Americans" in the *Journal of African American Studies.*

Wendy D. Manning is Professor of Sociology at Bowling Green State University, Director of the Center for Family and Demographic Research, and Co-director of the National Center for Marriage Research. Her research focuses on adolescents' dating and sexual relationships, transitions from adolescence to early adulthood relationships, and adult relationship formation and maintenance. She is the author of numerous journal articles, including "The Changing Institution of Marriage: Adolescents' Expectations to Cohabit and to Marry" (*Journal of Marriage and Family*, 2007, co-authored with Monica Longmore and Peggy Giordano) and "Gender and the Meanings of Adolescent Romantic Relationships: A Focus on Boys" (*American Sociological Review*, 2006, co-authored with Monica Longmore and Peggy Giordano).

Steven Mintz is Professor of History at the University of Texas at Austin and Executive Director of the University of Texas System's Institute for Transformational Learning, which is charged with improving student learning outcomes and fostering innovation across the system's universities and health science centers. He is a former fellow at the Center for Advanced Study in the Behavioral Sciences and the author of *Huck's Raft: A History of American Childhood*, *Domestic Revolutions: A Social History of American Family Life*, and the forthcoming *The Prime of Life: A History of Modern Adulthood*. A pioneer in the application of new technologies to teaching and research, he created the Digital History website and served as president of H-Net: Humanities and Social Sciences Online. He is also past president of the Society for the History of Children and Youth and a past chair of the Council on Contemporary Families.

Mignon R. Moore is Associate Professor of Sociology and African American Studies at the University of California, Los Angeles. Her research interests are in the sociology of families, gender, race, sexuality, identity, and aging. Her book *Invisible Families: Gay Identities, Relationships and Motherhood among Black Women* (University of California Press, 2011) received the 2012 Distinguished Book Award from the Sex & Gender Section of the American Sociological Association and was a finalist for the 2012 C. Wright Mills Award from the Society for the Study of Social Problems. Dr. Moore is a member of the Board of Directors for the Council on Contemporary Families.

Kristen Myers is Director of Women's, Gender, and Sexuality Studies and Presidential Teaching Professor of Sociology at Northern Illinois University. Her research deals with intersections of race, class, gender, and sexuality. In addition to her work on unemployed men, she has studied job pressures among out gay and lesbian police officers, hyper-heterosexuality among elementary school girls, private race talk, and antifeminist messages in TV programming for kids.

Adina Nack is Professor of Sociology at California Lutheran University. Former Chair of the Sociology Department, she has also served as the Director of CLU's Center for Equality and Justice and CLU's Gender & Women's Studies Program. Nack is a medical sociologist whose research and publications have focused on sexual and reproductive health, social psychology, gender, and sexuality. An award-winning teacher and researcher, she has served as a reviewer for NSF, and authored the book *Damaged Goods? Women Living with Incurable*

STDs (Temple University Press). Most recently, Nack co-authored an article on abortion stigma, and she is currently collaborating on a study of physically traumatic childbirth experiences. Nack is a proponent of public sociology: she has written for *Ms.* magazine, she authors the "Bedside Manners" column for the feminist research blog *Girl w/ Pen*, and she is a board member of the Council on Contemporary Families.

Brittany Owen is pursuing an undergraduate degree in sociology, economics, and data analysis at George Mason University. Her honors thesis examines racial and ethnic humor among college students using a mixed methods approach. Her areas of interest include invisible work and underground economics, social inequality, public policy, and animals and society.

Becky Pettit is Professor of Sociology at the University of Texas–Austin. She is the author of two books and numerous articles that have appeared in the *American Sociological Review*, the *American Journal of Sociology*, *Demography*, *Social Problems*, *Social Forces*, and other journals. Her newest book, *Invisible Men: Mass Incarceration and the Myth of Black Progress*, investigates how decades of penal growth obscures even the most basic accounts of racial inequality. Her previous book, *Gendered Tradeoffs* (with Jennifer Hook), was named a noteworthy book in industrial relations and labor economics. Professor Pettit holds a PhD in sociology from Princeton University and a BA in sociology from the University of California, Berkeley.

Brian Powell is James H. Rudy Professor of Sociology at Indiana University. He is the author of numerous articles on how families confer advantages (or disadvantages) to their children and how structural and compositional features of families (e.g., parental age, family size, birth order, one- vs. two-parent households) influence children's well-being. His recent scholarship has focused on several increasingly visible groups of "atypical" family forms: families with older parents, bi/multiracial families, adoptive families, and gay/lesbian families. He is co-author — with Catherine Bolzendahl, Claudia Geist, and Lala Carr Steelman — of *Counted Out: Same-Sex Relations and Americans' Definitions of Family* (Russell Sage Foundation/American Sociological Association Rose Series, 2010). His research has been featured in the *Los Angeles Times*, *Washington Post*, *USA Today*, *ABC World News Tonight*, CPSAN, and National Public Radio, among others.

Pamela Anne Quiroz (PhD University of Chicago, 1993) is Professor of Sociology and Educational Policy Studies at the University of Illinois–Chicago. Author of *Adoption in a Color-Blind Society* (Rowman & Littlefield), Professor Quiroz focuses her research on adoption, children and youth, education and qualitative methods. She has published in the *Journal of Research on Adolescence*, *Journal of Family Studies*, *Sociology of Education*, *Childhood*, and the *Journal of Contemporary Ethnography*. She is currently board member and secretary on the Council on Contemporary Families, the North American editor for *Children's Geographies*, and co-editor of *Social Problems* (2014–2017), the journal of the Society for the Study of Social Problems. Her book *Marketing Diversity and the 'New' Politics of Desegregation: An Urban Education Ethnography* is scheduled for publication by Cambridge University Press in 2014. A second book is also scheduled for publication by McFarland Press: *Personal Advertising: Dating, Mating and Relating in Modern Society*.

Jennifer Randles is Assistant Professor in the Department of Sociology at California State University, Fresno. Through in-depth interviews and participant observation, her research explores how social and economic inequities affect American family life and how policies address intimate inequalities and family-formation trends. Her publications have appeared in *Gender & Society*, the *Journal of Policy Analysis and Management*, the *Journal of Contemporary Ethnography*, *Contexts*, and *Sociology Compass*. Her book *Learning and Legislating to Love: Marriage Politics, Education, and Inequality in America* is forthcoming from Columbia University Press. She received her PhD from the Department of Sociology at the University of California, Berkeley in 2011.

Barbara J. Risman is Professor and Head of the Department of Sociology at University of Illinois at Chicago. She was previously Distinguished Research Professor at North Carolina State University, and she has also taught at the University of Washington and the University of Pennsylvania. She is the author of *Gender Vertigo: American Families in Transition* (Yale University Press, 1998) and research articles about families and gender relations in a variety of scientific journals. The Southern Sociological Society has awarded her the Katherine Jocher–Belle Boone Beard Award for lifetime contributions to the study of gender. Sociologists for Women in Society has awarded her the Feminist Mentoring Award. She is currently President of the Board of Directors for the Council on Contemporary Families and is writing a book on gender structure theory. Professor Risman will serve as President of the Southern Sociological Society in 2016.

Kerry Ann Rockquemore, PhD, is President and CEO of the National Center for Faculty Development & Diversity. Her scholarship has focused on interracial families, biracial identity, and the politics of racial categorization. She is author of *Beyond Black* and *Raising Biracial Children*. After Dr. Rockquemore became a tenured professor, her focus shifted to improving conditions for pre-tenured faculty by creating supportive communities for writing productivity and work/life balance. Her award-winning work with underrepresented faculty led to the publication of her most recent book *The Black Academic's Guide to Winning Tenure — Without Losing Your Soul*. Dr. Rockquemore provides workshops for faculty at colleges across the United States, writes an advice column for *Inside Higher Ed*, and works with a select group of faculty each semester in the Faculty Success Program.

Kevin Roy is Associate Professor in the Department of Family Science at the University of Maryland School of Public Health. Through a mix of participant observation and life history interviews, he explores the intersection of policy systems, such as welfare reform and incarceration, with parents' caregiving and providing roles. His research focus is the life course of men on the margins of families and the workforce, and he has conducted research primarily in state correctional facilities and community-based fathering programs. He has received funding for his research from NICHD, the W. T. Grant Foundation, and the National Poverty Center. Dr. Roy has published articles in *Social Problems, American Journal of Community Psychology, Journal of Family Issues,* and *Family Relations,* and has co-edited a book titled *Situated Fathering: A Focus on Physical and Social Spaces* (Rowman & Littlefield, 2005). He received a PhD from the Human Development and Social Policy program at Northwestern University in 1999.

Virginia E. Rutter is Professor of Sociology at Framingham State University in Framingham, Massachusetts. Previously she was a health research scientist at the Battelle Centers for Public Health Research and Evaluation in Seattle and Arlington, Virginia, where she was a co-investigator in the NIH-funded National Couples Survey. She is co-author of two books, *The Gender of Sexuality* (Rowman & Littlefield, 2011) and *The Love Test* (Perigee, 1998), articles, book chapters, as well as pieces for general audiences. She pens the "Nice Work" column for *Girl w/ Pen!* on the Society Pages and is a board member of the Council on Contemporary Families. In 2012, she received the Distinguished Faculty for Excellence in Teaching Award at FSU.

Pepper Schwartz is Professor of Sociology at the University of Washington and a past Schrag Fellow. She is the past president of the Society for the Scientific Study of Sex and the Pacific Sociological Association and Chairperson of the Board of the Sexual Studies PhD program at the California Institute for Integral Studies. She is the author or co-author of more than fifty academic articles and twenty-two books, including *American Couples: Money, Work, Sex; Peer Marriage;* and most recently, *The Normal Bar: The Surprising Secrets of Happy Couples* and *50 Myths about Human Sexuality.* She is a board member of the Council on Contemporary Families and the winner of the American Sociological Association's award for Public Understanding of Sociology. Dr. Schwartz writes for the general public as a blogger for CNN .com and a columnist for AARP.org. (She also serves as AARP's Love and Relationship Ambassador.) She served for many years as the relationship expert for perfectmatch.com and created their matching system, Duet.

Elizabeth Seale is Assistant Professor of Sociology at the State University of New York College at Oneonta. She studies poverty and welfare, health and the human body, and social inequality, and teaches courses in research methods, gender and sexuality, and social policy. Her current work focuses on the reproductive and health autonomy of low-income women in the northeastern United States in addition to persuading undergraduate students to find research methods as exciting as she does.

Pamela J. Smock is Professor of Sociology at the University of Michigan–Ann Arbor. She is also Research Professor at the Population Studies Center. Professor Smock is a family demographer and sociologist. Her scholarship focuses on the causes and consequences of family patterns and change, engaging their intersections with economic, racial/ethnic, and gender inequalities. She has published on issues such as cohabitation, the economic consequences of divorce and marriage, nonresident fatherhood, child support, remarriage, and the motherhood wage penalty. Professor Smock has received funding from the Eunice Kennedy Shriver National

Institute of Child Health and Human Development (NICHD) to support her research on (1) nonresident fatherhood, (2) heterosexual cohabitation, and, (3) integrating and harmonizing fifty years of family and fertility surveys. Professor Smock has served as Chair of the Section on Family of the American Sociological Association, as member of the National Science Foundation Sociology Advisory Panel, as president of the Association of Population Centers, and is currently editor of the journal *Demography*.

Lala Carr Steelman is Professor of Sociology at the University of South Carolina. Her research focuses on the integral role that families assume in children's well-being. With Brian Powell, Catherine Bolzendahl, and Claudia Geist, she has been the recipient of multiple awards, including the American Sociological Association Family Section's William J. Goode Book Award, for *Counted Out: Same-Sex Relations and Americans' Definitions of Family* (Russell Sage Foundation/American Sociological Association Rose Series, 2010).

Karen Struening is Director of the Pre-Law Major and Pre-Law Advising at City College. She is an adjunct associate professor in the Department of Political Science and author of *New Family Values: Liberty, Equality, Diversity* (Rowman & Littlefield, 2002). She is currently completing research on prostitution loitering ordinances and their impact of the transgender community.

Oriel Sullivan is Professor of Sociology of Gender in the Department of Sociology, Oxford University, and Deputy Director of the ESRC-funded Centre for Time Use Research, home of the Multinational Time Use Study. Her research focuses on the comparative analysis of changing gender relations and inequalities. Key areas of research include changing gender relations within households and cross-national trends in housework and child care time. She is author of *Changing Gender Relations, Changing Families: Tracing the Pace of Change* (Gender Lens Series: Rowman & Littlefield, 2006), a theoretical and empirical investigation of the (slow) trend toward increasing gender equality in the domestic sphere.

Bryan L. Sykes is Assistant Professor of Criminology, Law and Society (and, by courtesy, Sociology and Public Health) at the University of California, Irvine, and a Research Affiliate in the Center for Demography and Ecology (CDE) at the University of Wisconsin–Madison, a faculty affiliate in the Center for Evidence-Based Corrections at UC Irvine, and a member of the Racial Democracy, Crime and Justice Network (RDCJN) at Ohio State University. He has been a National Science Foundation Minority Post-Doctoral Research Fellow at the University of Washington and a Visiting Scholar in the Institute for Research on Poverty (IRP) at UW–Madison. His research focuses on the intersection of demography and criminology with particular interests in fertility, health, mass imprisonment, and social inequality. His work has appeared in *The Lancet*, *The ANNALS of the American Academy of Political and Social Science*, and *Race & Justice*.

References

CHAPTER 2: One Thousand and Forty-Nine Reasons Why It's Hard to Know When a Fact Is a Fact
by Andrew J. Cherlin

Cherlin, Andrew J., Frank F. Furstenberg Jr., P. Lindsay Chase-Lansdale, Kathleen E. Kiernan, Philip K. Robins, Donna Ruane Morrison, and Julien O. Teitler. 1991. "Longitudinal Studies of Effects of Divorce on Children in Great Britain and the United States." *Science* 252: 1386–1389.

Cherlin, Andrew J., P. Lindsay Chase-Lansdale, and Christine McRae. 1998. "Effects of Parental Divorce on Mental Health throughout the Life Course." *American Sociological Review* 63: 239–249.

Glick, Paul C. 1941. "Types of Families: An Analysis of Census Data." *American Sociological Review* 6: 830–838.

Goodrich v. Department of Public Health. 2003. 440 Mass. 309.

Jencks, Christopher. 1994. *The Homeless.* Cambridge, MA: Harvard University Press.

Rosin, Hanna. 1999. "Same-Sex Couples Win Rights in Vermont; Gay Activists Say Ruling Is a Legal Breakthrough." *Washington Post,* December 21.

U.S. General Accounting Office. 1997. Letter to the Honorable Henry J. Hyde, Chairman, Committee on the Judiciary, from Barry R. Bedrick, Associate General Counsel. Reference: GAO/OGC-97-16 Defense of Marriage Act. January 31.

CHAPTER 3: When Is a Relationship between Facts a Causal One?
by Philip A. Cowan

Cherlin, Andrew J., P. Lindsay Chase-Lansdale, and Christine McRae. 1998. "Effects of Parental Divorce on Mental Health throughout the Life Course." *American Sociological Review* 63: 239–249.

Cowan, Philip A., and Carolyn Pape Cowan. 2002. "Interventions as Tests of Family Systems Theories: Marital and Family Relationships in Children's Development, and Psychopathology." *Development and Psychopathology, Special Issue on Interventions as Tests of Theories* 14: 731–760.

Cummings, E. Mark, and Patrick Davies. 1994. *Children and Marital Conflict: The Impact of Family Dispute and Resolution.* New York: Guilford Press.

Emery, Robert E. 1999. *Marriage, Divorce, and Children's Adjustment,* 2nd ed. Thousand Oaks, CA: Sage Publications.

Gottman, John M., and Clifford I. Notarius. 2002. "Marital Research in the 20th Century and a Research Agenda for the 21st Century." *Family Process* 41: 159–197.

Waite, Linda J., and Maggie Gallagher. 2000. *The Case for Marriage: Why Married People Are Happier, Healthier, and Better off Financially.* New York: Doubleday.

CCF Brief: The Trouble with Averages: The Impact of Major Life Events and Acute Stress May Not Be What You Think
by Anthony D. Mancini and George A. Bonanno

Belsky, J., and M. Pluess. 2009. "Beyond Diathesis Stress: Differential Susceptibility to Environmental Influences." *Psychological Bulletin* 135: 885–908. doi:10.1037/a0017376.

Bonanno, G. A., and A. D. Mancini. 2012. "Beyond Resilience and PTSD: Mapping the Heterogeneity of Responses to Potential Trauma." *Psychological Trauma: Theory, Research, Practice, and Policy* 4: 74–83. doi:10.1037/a0017829.

Bonanno, G. A., A. D. Mancini, J. L. Horton, T. M. Powell, C. A. LeardMann, E. J. Boyko, et al. 2012. "Trajectories of Trauma Symptoms and Resilience in Deployed US Military Service Members: Prospective Cohort Study." *British Journal of Psychiatry* 200: 317–323. doi:10.1192/bjp.bp.111.096552.

Currier, J. M., R. A. Neimeyer, and J. S. Berman. 2008. "The Effectiveness of Psychotherapeutic Interventions for Bereaved Persons: A Comprehensive Quantitative Review." *Psychological Bulletin* 134: 648–661.

Lilienfeld, S. O. 2007. "Psychological Treatments That Cause Harm." *Perspectives on Psychological Science* 2: 53–70. doi:10.1111/j.1745-6916.2007.00029.x.

Mancini, A. D., G. A. Bonanno, and A. E. Clark. 2011. "Stepping Off the Hedonic Treadmill: Individual Differences in Response to Major Life Events." *Journal of Individual Differences* 32: 144–152.

Mayou, R. A., A. Ehlers, and M. Hobbs. 2000. "Psychological Debriefing for Road Traffic Accident Victims: Three-Year Follow-Up of a Randomised Controlled Trial." *British Journal of Psychiatry* 176: 589–593.

CHAPTER 5: The Evolution of American Families
by Stephanie Coontz

Adams, David Wallace. 1988. *Education for Extinction: American Indians and the Boarding School Experience, 1875–1928.* Lawrence: University Press of Kansas.

Amott, Theresa L., and Julie M. Matthaei. 1991. *Race, Gender, and Work: A Multicultural Gender Economic History of Women in the United States.* Boston: South End Press.

Aswad, Barbara C., and Barbara Bilge. 1996. *Family and Gender among American Muslims: Issues Facing Middle-Eastern Immigrants and Their Descendants.* Philadelphia: Temple University Press.

Bailey, Beth L. 1989. *From Front Porch to Back Seat: Courtship in Twentieth-Century America.* Baltimore, MD: Johns Hopkins University Press.

Bianchi, Suzanne M., John P. Robinson, and Melissa A. Milkie. 2006. *Changing Rhythms of Family Life.* New York: Russell Sage Foundation.

Boydston, Jeanne. 1990. *Home and Work: Housework, Wages, and the Ideology of Labor in the Early Republic.* New York: Oxford University Press.

Burguiere, André, et al. 1996. *A History of the Family.* Cambridge, MA: Belknap Press.

Coontz, Stephanie. 1988. *The Social Origins of Private Life: A History of American Families.* New York: W. W. Norton & Company.

———. 2000. *The Way We Never Were: American Families and the Nostalgia Trap.* New York: Basic Books.

———. 2006. *Marriage, A History: How Love Conquered Marriage.* New York: Penguin Books.

Coontz, Stephanie, Maya Parson, and Gabrielle Raley. 2008. *American Families: A Multicultural Reader.* New York: Routledge.

Cott, Nancy. 2000. *Public Vows: A History of Marriage and the Nation.* Cambridge, MA: Harvard University Press.

D'Emilio, John, and Freedman, Estelle B. 1997. *Intimate Matters: A History of Sexuality in America,* 2nd ed. Chicago: University of Chicago Press.

Gabaccia, Danna, and Vicki L. Ruiz. 2006. *American Dreaming, Global Realities: Rethinking U.S. Immigration History.* Chicago: University of Chicago Press.

Gallup, George, and Evan Hill. 1962. "The American Woman." *The Saturday Evening Post,* December 22–29.

Gaspar, David Barry, and Darlene Clark Hine. 1996. *More than Chattel: Black Women and Slavery in the Americas.* Bloomington: University of Indiana Press.

Gottlieb, Beatrice. 1993. *The Family in the Western World from the Black Death to the Industrial Age.* New York: Oxford University Press.

Gullickson, Aaron. 2006. "Black/White Interracial Marriage Trends, 1850–2000." *Journal of Family History* 31(3): 1–24.

Hing, Bill Ong. 1993. *Making and Remaking Asian America through Immigration Policy, 1850–1990.* Stanford, CA: Stanford University Press.

Hirsch, Jennifer S. 2003. *A Courtship after Marriage: Sexuality and Love in Mexican Transnational Communities.* Berkeley: University of California Press.

Hua, Cai. 2001. *Society Without Fathers or Husbands: The Na of China.* Cambridge, MA: MIT Press.

Ingoldsby, Bron B., and Suzanna D. Smith. 2006. *Families in Global and Multicultural Perspective,* 2nd ed. Thousand Oaks, CA: Sage Publications.

Ishwaran, K. 1992. *Family and Marriage: Cross-Cultural Perspectives.* Toronto: Thompson Educational Publishing.

Katz, Michael J., Michael J. Doucet, and Mark J. Stern. 1982. *The Social Organization of Early Industrial Capitalism.* Cambridge, MA: Harvard University Press.

Kennedy, Cynthia. 2005. *Braided Relations, Entwined Lives: The Women of Charleston's Urban Slave Society.* Bloomington: Indiana University Press.

Lobo, Susan. 1998. *Native American Voices: A Reader.* New York: Longman.

Lott, Juanita Tamayo. 2006. *Common Destiny: Filipino American Generations.* Lanham, MD: Rowman & Littlefield.

Lyons, Clare A. 2006. *Sex among the Rabble: An Intimate History of Gender and Power in the Age of Revolution.* Chapel Hill: University of North Carolina Press.

May, Elaine Tyler. 1980. *Great Expectations: Marriage and Divorce in Post-Victorian America.* Chicago: University of Chicago Press.

———. 1988. *Homeward Bound: American Families in the Cold War Era.* New York: Basic Books.

McAdoo, Harriette Pipes. 2007. *Black Families,* 4th ed. Thousand Oaks, CA: Sage Publications.

McCurry, Stephanie. 1995. *Masters of Small Worlds: Yeoman Households, Gender Relations, and the Political Culture of the Antebellum South Carolina Low Country.* Athens: University of Georgia Press.

Maffi, Mario. 1995. *Gateway to the Promised Lands: Ethnic Cultures on New York's Lower East Side.* New York: New York University Press.

Miles, Tiya. 2005. *Ties That Bind: The Story of an Afro-Cherokee Family in Slavery and Freedom.* Berkeley: University of California Press.

Mintz, Steven, and Susan Kellogg. 1988. *Domestic Revolutions: A Social History of American Family Life*. New York: Free Press.

Moran, Rachel. 2001. *Interracial Intimacy: The Regulation of Race and Romance*. Chicago: University of Chicago Press.

Mullings, Leith. 1997. *On Our Own Terms: Race, Class, and Gender in the Lives of African-American Women*. New York: Routledge.

Ngai, Mae M. 2004. *Impossible Subjects: Illegal Aliens and the Making of Modern America*. Princeton: Princeton University Press.

O'Day, Rosemary. 1994. *The Family and Family Relationships, 1500–1900*. London: Palgrave Macmillan.

Peters, Virginia Bergman. 1995. *Women of the Earth Lodges: Tribal Life on the Plains*. New Haven, CT: Archon Books.

Rosen, Ruth. 2000. *The World Split Open: How the Women's Movement Changed America*. New York: Penguin Books.

Ritterhouse, Jennifer. 2006. *Growing Up Jim Crow: How Black and White Southern Children Learned Race*. Chapel Hill: University of North Carolina Press.

Rubin, Lillian B. 1994. *Families on the Fault Line*. New York: HarperCollins.

Ruiz, Vicki, and Ellen Dubois. 2000. *Unequal Sisters: A Multicultural Reader in U.S. Women's History*, 3rd ed. New York: Routledge.

Ryan, Mary P. 1983. *Cradle of the Middle Class: The Family in Oneida County, New York, 1790–1865*. New York: Cambridge University Press.

Seccombe, Wally. 1992. *A Millennium of Family Change*. London: Verso.

Skolnick, Arlene S., and Jerome H. Skolnick. 2003. *Family in Transition*, 12th ed. Boston: Allyn & Bacon.

Stacey, Judith. 1990. *Brave New Families: Stories of Domestic Upheaval in Late Twentieth-Century America*. New York: Basic Books.

Stavig, Ward. 1995. "'Living in Offense of Our Lord': Indigenous Sexual Values and Marital Life in the Colonial Crucible." *Hispanic American Historical Review* 75(4): 597–622.

Stevenson, Brenda E. 1996. *Life in Black and White: Family and Community in the Slave South*. New York: Oxford University Press.

Thorne, Barrie, and Marilyn Yalom. 1992. *Rethinking the Family: Some Feminist Questions*. Boston: Northeastern University Press.

Tung, Mae Paomay. 2000. *Chinese Americans and Their Immigrant Parents: Conflict, Identity, and Values*. Binghamton, NY: Haworth Press.

Vecchio, Diane C. 2006. *Merchants, Midwives, and Laboring Women: Italian Migrants in Urban America*. Champaign: University of Illinois Press.

Wallenstein, Peter. 2002. *Tell the Court I Love My Wife: Race, Marriage, and Law—An American History*. New York: Palgrave Macmillan.

Weiss, Jessica. 2000. *To Have and to Hold: Marriage, the Baby Boom, and Social Change*. Chicago: University of Chicago Press.

Wong, Bernard P. 2006. *The Chinese in Silicon Valley: Globalization, Social Networks, and Ethnic Identity*. Lanham, MD: Rowman & Littlefield.

Zinn, Maxime Baca, D. Stanley Eitzen, and Barbara Wells. 2008. *Diversity in Families*, 8th ed. Boston: Allyn & Bacon.

CHAPTER 6: American Childhood as a Social and Cultural Construct
by Steven Mintz

Axtell, James. 1974. *The School Upon a Hill: Education and Society in Colonial New England*. New Haven, CT: Yale University Press.

Belkin, Lisa. 2000. "The Making of an 8-Year-Old Woman." *New York Times*, December 24.

Chudacoff, Howard P. 1989. *How Old Are You? Age Consciousness in American Society*. Princeton: Princeton University Press.

Clement, Priscilla. 1997. *Growing Pains: Children in the Industrial Age, 1850–1890*. New York: Twayne.

Grant, Julia. 1998. *Raising Baby by the Book: The Education of American Mothers*. New Haven, CT: Yale University Press.

Heywood, Colin. 2001. *A History of Childhood: Children and Childhood in the West from Medieval to Modern Times*. Cambridge, UK: Polity Press.

Herman-Giddens, Marcia E., et al. 1997. "Secondary Sexual Characteristics and Menses in Young Girls Seen in Office Practice: A Study from the Pediatric Research in Office Settings Network." *Pediatrics* 99(4): 505–512.

Hulbert, Ann. 2003. *Raising America: Experts, Parents, and a Century of Advice about Children*. New York: Knopf.

Illick, Joseph. 2002. *American Childhoods*. Philadelphia: University of Pennsylvania Press.

Jones, Kathleen W. 1999. *Taming the Troublesome Child*. Cambridge, MA: Harvard University Press.

Kett, Joseph F. 1977. *Rites of Passage: Adolescence in America*. New York: Basic Books.

Kline, Daniel T. 1998. "Holding Therapy," March 7, History-Child-Family Listserv (history-child-family@mailbase.ac.uk).

Kolata, Gina. 2001. "Doubters Fault Theory Finding Earlier Puberty." *New York Times*, February 20.

———. 2001. "2 Endocrinology Groups Raise Doubt on Earlier Onset of Girls' Puberty." *New York Times*, March 3.

Lareau, Annette. 2003. *Unequal Childhoods: Class, Race, and Family Life*. Berkeley: University of California Press.

Macleod, David I. 1998. *The Age of the Child: Children in America, 1890–1912*. New York: Twayne.

Mintz, Steven, and Susan Kellogg. 1988. *Domestic Revolutions: A Social History of American Family Life*. New York: Free Press.

Nasaw, David. 1985. *Children in the City: At Work and at Play*. Garden City, NY: Anchor Press/Doubleday.

Robertson, Stephen. "The Disappearance of Childhood." Available from http://teaching.arts.usyd.edu.au/history/2044/

Schultz, James A. 1995. *The Knowledge of Childhood in the German Middle Ages, 1100–1350*. Philadelphia: University of Pennsylvania Press.

Scraton, Phil, ed. 1997. *"Childhood" in "Crisis"?* London: University College of London Press.

Stansell, Christine. 1986. *City of Women: Sex and Class in New York, 1789–1860*. New York: Knopf.

Weissbourd, Richard. 1996. *The Vulnerable Child: What Really Hurts America's Children and What We Can Do about It*. Reading, MA: Addison-Wesley.

CHAPTER 7: African Americans and the Birth of the Modern Marriage
by Donna L. Franklin

Bernard, Jessie. 1966. *Marriage and Family among Negroes*. Englewood Cliffs, NJ: Prentice-Hall.

Berlin, Ira, and Leslie S. Rowland, eds. 1998. *Families and Freedom: A Documentary History of African-American Kinship in the Civil War Era*. New York: New Press.

Bird, Carol. 1979. *The Two-Paycheck Family*. New York: Rawson, Wade.

Boris, Eileen. 1993. "The Power of Motherhood: Black and White Activist Women Redefine the Political." In *Mothers of a New World*, edited by Seth Koven and Sonya Michel. New York: Routledge.

Burbridge, Lynn C. 1995. "Policy Implications for a Decline in Marriage among African-Americans." In *The Decline in Marriage Among African Americans*, edited by M. Belinda Tucker and Claudia Mitchell-Kernan, 229–260. New York: Russell Sage Foundation.

Blumstein, Phillip, and Pepper Schwartz. 1983. *American Couples*. New York: Morrow.

Bowen, William C., and Derek Bok. 1998. *The Shape of the River: Long Term Consequences of Considering Race in College and University Admissions*. Princeton: Princeton University Press.

Butterfield, Fox. 2002. "Study Finds Big Increase in Black Men as Inmates Since 1980." *New York Times*, August 29.

Carby, Hazel V. 1987. *Reconstructing Womanhood: The Emergence of the Afro-American Woman Novelist*. New York: Oxford University Press.

Carlson, Shirley J. 1992. "Black Ideals of Womanhood in the Late Victorian Era." *Journal of Negro History* 77(2): 61–73.

Clinton, Catherine, and Nina Silber, eds. 1992. *Divided Houses: Gender and the Civil War*. New York: Oxford University Press.

Conrad, Cecelia A. 2008. "Black Women: An Unfinished Agenda." *The American Prospect* 19(10): A12–A15.

Coontz, Stephanie. 2006. *Marriage, A History: How Love Conquered Marriage*. New York: Penguin Books.

Cooper, Anna Julia. 1990. *A Voice of the South*, introduction by Mary Helen Washington. New York: Oxford University Press.

Cott, Nancy F. 2000. *Public Vows: A History of Marriage and the Nation*. Cambridge, MA: Harvard University Press.

Cuthbert, Marion. 1936. "Problems Facing Negro Young Women." *Opportunity* (February 2): 48.

Davis, Elizabeth Lindsay. 1933. *Lifting As They Climb: The National Association of Colored Women*. Washington, DC: National Association of Colored Women.

DuBois, W. E. B. 1924. *The Gift of Black Folk*. Boston: Stratford Press.

Epstein, Cynthia Fuchs. 1971. "Law Partners and Marital Partners: Strains and Solutions in the Dual-Career Family Enterprise." *Human Relations* 24(6): 549–563.

Faust, Drew Gilpin. 1996. *Mothers of Invention*. Chapel Hill, NC: University of North Carolina.

Foner, Eric. 1988. *Reconstruction: America's Unfinished Revolution. 1863–77*. New York: Harper and Row.

Franklin, Donna L. 1997. *Ensuring Inequality: The Structural Transformation of the African-American Family*. New York: Oxford University Press.

———. 2000. *What's Love Got to Do With It? Understanding and Healing the Rift Between Black Men and Women*. New York: Simon and Schuster.

Freeman, Elsie, Wynell Burroughs Schamel, and Jean West. 1992. "The Fight for Equal Rights: A Recruiting Poster for Black Soldiers in the Civil War." *Social Education* 56(2): 118–120.

Giddings, Paula. 1985. *When and Where I Enter: The Impact of Black Women on Race and Sex in America*. New York: Bantam Books.

———. 2008. *Ida: A Sword Among Lions: Ida B. Wells and the Campaign Against Lynching*. New York: Amistad.

Gordon, Linda. 1991. "Black and White Visions of Welfare: Women's Welfare Activism, 1890–1943." *Journal of American History* 78: 559–590.

Hacker, Andrew. 1992. *Two Nations: Black and White, Separate, Hostile, Unequal*. New York: Ballantine Books.

Hall, Francine S. 1979. *The Two Career Couple*. Reading, MA: Addison-Wesley.

Harley, Sharon. 1988. "Mary Church Terrell: Genteel Militant." In *Black Leaders of the Nineteenth Century*, edited by Leon F. Litwack and August Meier. Urbana: University of Illinois Press.

Harris, Barbara J. 1978. *Beyond Her Sphere: Women and the Professions in American History*. Westport, CT: Greenwood Press.

Higginbotham, Evelyn Brooks. 1993. *Righteous Discontent: The Women's Movement in the Baptist Church, 1880–1920*. Cambridge, MA: Harvard University Press.

Holmstrom, Lynda Lytle. 1972. *The Two Career Family*. Cambridge, MA: Schenkman.

Jones, Jacqueline. 1985. *Labor of Love: Black Women, Work, and the Family from Slavery to Present*. New York: Basic Books.

Kennedy, Susan Estabrook. 1979. *If All We Did Was to Weep at Home: A History of White Working Class Women in America*. Bloomington: Indiana University Press.

Kessler-Harris, Alice. 1982. *Out to Work: A History of Wage-Earning Women in the United States*. New York: Oxford University Press.

Landry, Bart. 2000. *Black Working Wives: Pioneers of the American Family Revolution*. Berkeley: University of California Press.

Lerner, Gerda. 1972. *Black Women in White America: A Documentary History*. New York: Vintage Books.

Litwack, Leon F. 1998. *Trouble in Mind: Black Southerners in the Age of Jim Crow*. New York: Knopf.

Loewenberg, Bert James, and Ruth Bogin, eds. 1976. *Black Women in the Nineteenth-Century American Life: Their Words, Their Thoughts, Their Feelings*. University Park: Pennsylvania State University Press.

Massey, Mary E. 1966. *Bonnet Brigades*. New York: Knopf.

Matthaei, Julie. 1982. *An Economic History of Women in America*. New York: Schocken Books.

McMurry, Linda O. 1998. *To Keep the Waters Troubled: The Life of Ida B. Wells*. New York: Oxford University Press.

Mills, C. Wright. 1959. *The Sociological Imagination*. New York: Oxford University Press.

Mintz, Steven, and Susan Kellogg. 1988. *Domestic Revolutions: A Social History of American Family Life*. New York: Free Press.

Moses, William Jeremiah. 1978. *The Golden Age of Black Nationalism*. New York: Oxford University Press.

Noble, Jeanne. 1956. "The Negro Woman's College Education." Ph.D. dissertation, Teachers College, Columbia University, New York.

Margaret M., and T. Neal Garland. 1971. "The Married Professional Woman: A Study in the Tolerance of Domestication." *Journal of Marriage and the Family* 33(3): 531–540.

Powdermaker, Hortense. 1939. *After Freedom: A Cultural Study in the Deep South*. New York: Viking Press.

Rapoport, Rhona, and Robert Rapoport. 1971. *Dual Career Families*. Middlesex, UK: Penguin Books.

Rouse, Jacqueline A. 1989. *Lugenia Hope Burns: Black Southerner Reformer*. Athens: University of Georgia Press.

Ruffin, Josephine St. Pierre. 1895. "Address to the First National Conference of Colored Women." Charles Street A. M. E. Church. Boston. July 29.

Satcher, David, et al. 2005. "What If We Were Equal? A Comparison of the Black-White Mortality Gap in 1960 and 2000?" *Health Affairs* 24(2): 459–464.

Scott, Ann Firor. 1970. *The Southern Lady from Pedestal to Politics: 1830–1930*. Chicago: University of Chicago Press.

Shaw, Stephanie J. 1996. *What a Woman Ought to Be and Do: Black Professional Women Workers during the Jim Crow Era*. Chicago: University of Chicago Press.

Smith-Rosenberg, Carol. 1985. *Disorderly Conduct: Visions of Gender in Victorian America*. New York: Knopf.

Vicinus, Martha. 1985. *Independent Women: Work and Community of Single Women, 1850–1920*. Chicago: University of Chicago Press.

Vinoskis, Maris A. 1989. "Have Social Historians Lost the Civil War? Some Preliminary Demographic Speculations." *Journal of American History* 76(1): 35–59.

Wells, Ida B. 1970. *Crusade for Justice: The Autobiography of Ida B. Wells*, edited by Alfreda M. Duster. Chicago: University of Chicago Press.

Wertheimer, Barbara M. 1977. *We Were There: The Story of Working Women in America*. New York: Pantheon Books.

Williams, Fannie Barrier. 1904. "The Women's Part in a Man's Business." *Voice* 1(11): 544.

Wilson, W. J., & Neckerman, K. M. 1987. "Poverty and family structure: The widening gap between evidence and public policy issues." In *The Truly Disadvantaged*, edited by W. J. Wilson, 232–259. Chicago: University of Chicago Press.

CHAPTER 8: Changing Counts, Counting Change: Americans' Movement toward a More Inclusive Definition of Family
by Brian Powell, Catherine Bolzendahl, Claudia Geist, and Lala Carr Steelman

Allport, Gordon W. 1954. *The Nature of Prejudice*. Reading, MA: Addison-Wesley.

McCutcheon, Allen L. 1987. *Latent Class Analysis*. Newbury Park, CA: Sage Publications.

Pettigrew, Thomas F., and Linda R. Tropp. 2006. "A Meta-Analytic Test of Intergroup Contact Theory." *Journal of Personality and Social Psychology* 90: 751–783.

Powell, Brian, Catherine Bolzendahl, Claudia Geist, and Lala Carr Steelman. 2010. *Counted Out: Same-Sex Relations and Americans' Definitions of Family*. New York: Russell Sage Foundation.

Smith, Dorothy E. 1993. "The Standard North American Family: SNAF as an Ideological Code." *Journal of Family Issues* 14: 50–65.

Weston, Kath. 1997. *Families We Choose: Lesbians, Gays, Kinship*, 2nd ed. New York: Columbia University Press.

CHAPTER 9: Interracial Families in Post–Civil Rights America
by Kerry Ann Rockquemore and Loren Henderson

Bonilla-Silva, E. 2001. *White Supremacy and Racism in the Post-Civil Rights Era*. Boulder, CO: Lynne Reinner.

———. 2003. *Racism Without Racists: Color-Blind Racism and the Persistence of Racial Inequality in the United States*. New York: Rowman & Littlefield.

Bratter, Jenifer, and Karl Eschbach. 2006. "What About the Couple? Interracial Marriage and Psychological Distress." *Social Science Research* 35: 1025–1047.

Childs, Erica. 2005a. "Looking Behind the Stereotypes of the 'Angry Black Woman': An Exploration of Black Women's Responses to Interracial Relationships." *Gender & Society* 19(4): 544–561.

———. 2005b. *Navigating Interracial Borders: Black-White Couples and Their Social Worlds*. New Brunswick, NJ: Rutgers University Press.

Collins, Patricia Hill. 2004. *Black Sexual Politics: African Americans, Gender, and the New Racism*. New York: Routledge.

Dalmage, Heather. 2000. *Tripping on the Color Line: Black-White Multiracial Families in a Racially Divided World*. New Brunswick, NJ: Rutgers University Press.

Davis, F. James. 1991. *Who Is Black? One Nation's Definition*. University Park: Pennsylvania State University Press.

Frankenberg, Ruth. 1993. *White Women, Race Matters*. Minneapolis: University of Minnesota Press.

Harris, David, and Jeremiah Sim. 2002. "Who Is Multiracial? Assessing the Complexity of Lived Race." *American Sociological Review* 67: 614–627.

Hitlin, Steven, J. Scott Brown, and Glen H. Elder, Jr. 2006. "Racial Self-Categorization in Adolescence: Multiracial Development and Social Pathways." *Child Development* 77(5): 1298–1308.

Kennedy, Randall. 2003. *Interracial Intimacies: Sex, Marriage, Identity and Adoption*. New York: Pantheon.

La Ferla, Ruth. 2003. "Generation E.A.: Ethnically Ambiguous." *New York Times*, December 28.

Lazarre, Jane. 1996. *Beyond the Whiteness of Whiteness: Memoirs of a White Mother of Black Sons*. Durham, NC: Duke University Press.

McNamara, Robert P., Maria Tempenis, and Beth Walton, 1999. *Crossing the Line: Interracial Couples in the South*. Westport, CT: Praeger.

Oliver, M., and T. Shapiro. 1997. *Black Wealth/White Wealth: A New Perspective on Racial Inequality*. New York: Routledge.

Omi, Michael, and Howard Winant. 1994. *Racial Formation in the United States: From the 1960s to the 1980s*, 2nd ed. New York: Routledge.

Qian, Zhenchou. 1997. "Breaking the Racial Barriers: Variations in Interracial Marriage between 1980 and 1990." *Demography* 34: 478–500.

Reddy, Maureen. 1994. *Crossing the Color Line: Race, Parenting and Culture*. New Brunswick, NJ: Rutgers University Press.

Renn, Kristen. 2004. *Mixed Race Students in College: The Ecology of Race, Identity, and Community on Campus*. Albany: State University of New York Press.

Rockquemore, Kerry Ann, and David Brunsma. 2001. *Beyond Black: Biracial Identity in America*. Thousand Oaks, CA: Sage Publications.

Root, Maria. 2001. *Love's Revolution: Interracial Marriage*. Philadelphia: Temple University Press.

Rosenblatt, Paul, Teri Karis, and Richard Powell. 1995. *Multiracial Couples: Black and White Voices*. Thousand Oaks, CA: Sage Publications.

Rosenfeld, Michael. 2007. *The Age of Independence: Interracial Unions, Same-Sex Unions, and the Changing American Family*. Cambridge, MA: Harvard University Press.

Russell, Kathy, Midge Wilson, and Ronald Hall, 1993. *The Color Complex: The Politics of Skin Color Among African Americans*. New York: Anchor Books.

Schuman, Howard, Charlotte Steeh, Lawrence Bobo, and Maria Kryson. 1997. *Racial Attitudes in America: Trends and Interpretations*, rev. ed. Cambridge, MA: Harvard University Press.

Simmons, Tavia, and Martin O'Connell. 2003. *Married-Couple and Unmarried-Partner Households: 2000*. Washington, DC: U.S. Census Bureau.

Steinbugler, Amy. 2005. "Visibility as Privilege and Danger: Heterosexual and Same-Sex Interracial Intimacy in the 21st Century," *Sexualities* 8(4): 425–443.

Todd, Judith, Jeanice McKinney, Raymond Harris, Ryan Chadderton, and Leslie Small. 1992. "Attitudes Toward Interracial Dating: Effects of Age, Sex, and Race." *Journal of Multicultural Counseling and Development* 21 (October): 202–208.

Twine, France Winddance, and Amy Steinbugler. 2006. "The Gap between Whites and Whiteness: Interracial Intimacy and Racial Literacy." *DuBois Review* 3(2): 341–363.

Wallace, Kendra. 2001. *Relative/Outsider: The Art and Politics of Identity Among Mixed Heritage Students*. Westport, CT: Ablex Publishing.

Zuberi, Tukufu. 2001. *Thicker Than Blood: When Racial Statistics Lie*. Minneapolis: University of Minnesota Press.

CHAPTER 10: Families "In Law" and Families "In Practice": Does the Law Recognize Families as They Really Are?
by Karen Struening

Administration for Children and Families, *Healthy Marriage Initiative*. Department of Health and Human Services, Washington, D.C. Retrieved on June 13, 2013, at http://acf.gov/programs/opre/index.html

Carbone, June. 2005. "The Legal Definition of Parenthood: Uncertainty at the Core of Family Identity." 65 *La. L. Rev.* 1295, 1306.

"Developments in the Law: IV. Changing Realities of Parenthood: The Law's Response to the Evolving American Family and Emerging Reproductive Technologies," 116 *Harv. L. Rev.* 2052 (May 2003).

Lambda Legal, *In Your State: Marriage and Relationships*, Washington, D.C. Retrieved on June 18, 2013 at http://www.lambdalegal.org/states-regions.

Liptak, Adam. 2013. "Two Major Rulings Bolster Gay Marriage," *New York Times*, June 26, 2013. Retrieved on June 26, 2013 at http://www.nytimes.com/2013/06/27/us/politics /supreme-court-gay-marriage.html.

Fineman, Martha. 2004. *The Autonomy Myth: A Theory of Dependency*. New York: The New Press.

Grossman, Joanna. 2012. "The New Illegitimacy: Tying Parentage to Marital Status for Lesbian Co-Parents." 20 *Am. U.J. Gender Soc. Pol'y & L.* 671.

Hinson, Diane S., and Maureen McBrien. 2013. *Surrogacy Across America*, CreativeFamily Connections.Com. Retrieved on June 17, 2013, from http://www.creativefamily connections.com/sites/default/files/FamilyAdvocateSurrogacyAcrossAmerica_0.pdf.

Hsueh, Joann, Desiree Principe Alderson, Erika Lunquist, Charles Michalopoulos, Daniel Gubits, David Fein, et al. 2011. *The Supporting Healthy Marriage Evaluation: Early Impacts on Low Income Families*, OPRE Report 2012-11. Washington, DC: Office of Planning, Research, and Evaluation, Administration for Children and Families, U.S. Department of Health and Human Services.

Liptak, Adam. 2013. "Two Major Rulings Bolster Gay Marriage." *New York Times*, June 26. Retrieved on June 26, 2013, from http://www.nytimes.com/2013/06/27/us/politics /supreme-court-gay-marriage.html.

McClain, Linda. 2006. *The Place of Families: Fostering Capacity, Equality, and Responsibility*. Cambridge, MA: Harvard University Press.

———. 2007. "Love, Marriage and the Baby Carriage: Revisiting the Channeling Function of Law." 28 *Cardozo L. Rev.* 2133 (April).

Meyer, David D. 2006. "Parenthood in a Time of Transition: Tensions between Legal, Biological, and Social Conceptions of Parenthood." 54 *Am. J. Comp. L.* 125 (Supplement, Fall): 139.

Movement Advancement Project, Family Equality Council and Center for American Progress. 2011. "All Children Matter: How Legal and Social Inequalities Hurt LGBT Families (Full Report)." 41 (October).

National Conference of State Legislatures. *State Law Limiting Marriage to Opposite Couples*, Washington, DC. Retrieved on June 12, 2012, from http://www.ncsl.org/issues-research /human services/state-doma-laws.aspx.

Office of Family Assistance, Agency for Children and Families. *About the Healthy Family Initiative*, Department of Health and Human Services, Washington, DC. Retrieved on June 12, 2013, from http://www.acf.hhs.gov/programs/ofa/programs/healthy-marriage /about.

Polikoff, Nancy. 1990. "This Child Does Have Two Mothers: Redefining Parenthood to Meet the Needs of Children in Lesbian Mother and Other Nontraditional Households." 78 *Geo L. R.* 459.

———. 2009. "A Mother Should Not Have to Adopt Her Own Child: Parentage Laws for Children of Lesbian Couples in the Twenty-First Century." 5 *Stanford Journal of Civil Rights and Civil Liberties* 201: 216.

Roberts, Dorothy E. 2001. "Kinship Care and the Price of State Care for Children." 76 *Chi-Kent. L. Rev.* 1619.

Russell, Christina. 2010. "Four Million Test-Tube Babies and Counting." *The Atlantic*, October 7. Retrieved on June 20, 2013, from http://www.theatlantic.com/technology /archive/2010/10/four-million-test-tube-babies-and-counting/64198.

Savage, David G. 2014. "Justices temper the rush on gay marriage; The Supreme Court halts weddings in Utah, buying more time to settle a major constitutional debate." *L.A. Times*. January 7. National Desk, Part A, p. 1.

Shanley, Mary Lyndon. 2001. *Making Babies, Making Families: What Matters Most in an Age of Reproductive Technologies, Surrogacy, Adoption, Same-Sex Marriage and Unwed Parents*. Boston: Beacon Press.

Silver, Nate. 2013. "How Opinion of Same-Sex Marriage Is Changing, What It Means." *New York Times Blog*, March 26.

Struening, Karen. 2002. *New Family Values: Liberty, Equality, Diversity*. Lanham, MD: Rowman & Littlefield.

———. 2007. "Do Government Sponsored Marriage Promotion Policies Place Undue Pressure on Individual Rights?" *Policy Sciences* 40(3): 241–259.

The Family Law Council. 2005. *The Future of Family Law: Law and the Marriage Crisis in North America* (New York: Institute for American Values), 12. Retrieved on January 16, 2013, from http://www.americanvalues.org/family/law.

Travernise, Sabrina. 2011. "Adoptions Rise by Same-Sex Couples, Despite Legal Barriers." *New York Times*, June 14, p. 11.

Uniform Law Commissioners, NCCUSL. 2002. *Summary of the Uniform Parentage Act* (Revised 2002). Retrieved on June 20, 2010, from http://www.nccusl.org/nccusl /uniformact_summaries/uniformacts-s-upa.asp.

Wadlington, Walter, and Raymond C. O'Brien. 2007. *Family Law in Perspective*, 2nd ed. New York: Foundation Press.

Zernike, Kate. 2012. "Court's Split Helps Provide Little Clarity on Surrogacy." *New York Times*, October 25, Section A, p. 22.

Legal Cases:

Alison D. v. Virginia M., 572 N.E. 2d 27 (N.Y. 1991).

Eisenstadt v. Baird, 405 U.S. 438 (1972).

Elisa B. v. Superior Court, 117 P. 3d 660 (Cal. 2005).

Griswold v. Connecticut, 381 U.S. 479 (1965).

Hernandez v. Robles, 855 N.E. 2d 1 (N.Y. 2000).

In re Adoption of Minor T., 17 Fam. L. Rptr. 1523 (D.C. Super. Ct. 1991).

In re Custody of H.S. H.-K., 533 N.W. 2d 419 (Wis. 1995).

In re Marriage of Buzzanca, 61 Cal. App. 4th 1410 (Cal. App. 1998).

In the Matter of Baby M, 537 A.2d 1227 (N.J. 1988).

Johnson v. Calvert 5 Cal. 4th 84 (1993).

Kristine H. v. Lisa R., 117 P.3d 690 (Cal. 2005).

Lawrence v. Texas, 539 U.S. 558 (2003).

Levy v. Louisiana, 391 U.S. 68 (1968).

Loving v. Virginia, 388 U.S. 1 (1967).

Meyer v. Nebraska, 262 U.S. 390 (1923).

Michael H. v. Gerald D., 491 U.S. 110 (1989).

Moore v. East Cleveland, 431 U.S. 494 (1977).

Nancy S. v. Michele G., 279 Cal. Rptr. 212 (Ct. App. 1991).

Pierce v. Society of Sisters, 268 U.S. 510 (1925).

Planned Parenthood v. Casey, 505 U.S. 833 (1992).

Prince v. Massachusetts, 321 U.S. 158 (1944).

Pub. L. 105-89 (1997).
Pub. L. 100-485 (1988).
Roe v. Wade, 410 U.S. 113 (1973).
Stanley v. Illinois, 405 U.S. 645 (1972).
Troxel v. Granville, 530 U.S. 57 (2000).
V.C. v. M.J.B., 748 A.2d 539, 550 (N.J. 2000).
Zablocki v. Redhail, 434 U.S. 374 (1978).

CHAPTER 11: Childfree Families
by Amy Blackstone and Amy Greenleaf

Angeles, Luis. 2010. "Children and Life Satisfaction." *Journal of Happiness Studies* 11: 523–538.

Blackstone, Amy. 2014. "Doing Family without Having Kids." *Sociology Compass* 8: 52–62.

Blackstone, Amy. 2013. "Setting the Record Straight on 6 Myths about Childless Adults." *Bangor Daily News*, September 17.

Bogenschneider, Karen. 2006. *Family Policy Matters: How Policy Making Affects Families and What Professionals Can Do*. Mahwah, NJ: Lawrence Erlbaum Associates.

Burman, Bonnie, and Diane de Anda. 1986. "Parenthood and Non-parenthood: A Comparison of Intentional Families." *Lifestyles* 8: 69–84.

DeOllos, Ione Y., and Carolyn A. Kapinus. 2002. "Aging Childless Individuals and Couples: Suggestions for New Directions in Research." *Sociological Inquiry* 72: 72–80.

Dye, Jane Lawler. 2008. "Fertility of American Women: 2006." Washington, DC: U.S. Census Bureau.

Gubrium, Jaber F., and James A. Holstein. 1990. *What Is Family?* Mountain View, CA: Mayfield.

Hansen, Thomas. 2012. "Parenthood and Happiness: A Review of Folk Theories versus Empirical Evidence." *Social Indicators Research* 108: 29–64.

Henslin, James M. 2010. *Sociology: A Down to Earth Approach, Core Concepts*, 4th ed. Boston: Pearson.

Horwitz, Steven. 2005. "The Functions of the Family in the Great Society." *Cambridge Journal of Economics* 29: 669–684.

Houseknecht, Sharon K. 1987. "Voluntary Childlessness." In *Handbook of Marriage and the Family*, edited by Marvin B. Sussman and Suzanne K. Steinmetz, 369–395. New York: Plenum Press.

Knox, David. 2011. *M&F*. Belmont, CA: Wadsworth, Cengage Learning.

Kramer, Laura. 2011. *The Sociology of Gender: A Brief Introduction*. New York: Oxford University Press.

Laslett, Barbara, and Johanna Brenner. 1989. "Gender and Social Reproduction: Historical Perspectives." *Annual Review of Sociology* 15: 381–404.

Osborne, Ruth S. 2003. *Percentage of Childless Women 40 to 44 Years Old Increases Since 1976, Census Bureau Reports*. U.S. Census Bureau Press Release.

Oswald, Ramona Faith, Libby Balter Blume, and Stephen R. Marks. 2005. "Decentering Heteronormativity: A Model for Family Studies." In *Sourcebook of Family Theory and Research*, edited by Vern L. Bengtson, Alan C. Acock, Katherine R. Allen, Peggy Dilworth-Anderson, and David M. Klein, 143–154. Thousand Oaks, CA: Sage Publications.

Oswald, Ramona Faith, and Elizabeth A. Sutter. 2004. "Heterosexist Inclusion and Exclusion during Ritual: A 'Straight versus Gay' Comparison." *Journal of Family Issues* 25: 881–899.

Somers, Marsha D. 1993. "A Comparison of Voluntarily Childfree Adults and Parents." *Journal of Marriage and the Family* 55: 643–650.

Tomczak, Lisa M. 2012. *Childfree or Voluntarily Childless? The Lived Experience of Women Choosing Non-Motherhood*. M.A. Thesis, Northern Arizona University. Ann Arbor: ProQuest.

Twenge, Jean M., W. Keith Campbell, and Craig A. Foster. 2003. "Parenthood and Marital Satisfaction: A Meta-Analytic Review." *Journal of Marriage and Family* 65: 574–583.

Veevers, Jean E. 1980. *Childless by Choice*. Toronto: Butterworths.

West, Candace and Donald Zimmerman. 1987. "Doing Gender." *Gender & Society* 1: 125–151.

Zagura, Michelle. 2012. *Parental Status, Spousal Behaviors and Marital Satisfaction*. M.A. Thesis, SUNY–Albany. Ann Arbor: ProQuest.

CHAPTER 12: New Couples, New Families: The Cohabitation Revolution in the United States
by Pamela J. Smock and Wendy D. Manning

Acs, Gregory, and Sandra Nelson. 2002. "The Kids Are Alright? Children's Well-Being and the Rise in Cohabitation." *New Federalism National Survey of America's Families*, B-48. Washington, DC: Urban Institute.

Brown, Susan. 2000. "Fertility Following Marital Dissolution: The Role of Cohabitation." *Journal of Family Issues* 21: 501–524.

Brown, Susan, and Alan Booth. 1996. "Cohabitation versus Marriage: A Comparison of Relationship Quality." *Journal of Marriage and Family* 58: 668–678.

Bumpass, Larry, and Hsien Lu. 2000. "Trends in Cohabitation and Implications for Children's Family Contexts." *Population Studies* 54: 9–41.

Bumpass, Larry, R. Kelly Raley, and James Sweet. 1995. "The Changing Character of Step-families: Implications of Cohabitation and Nonmarital Childbearing." *Demography* 32: 425–436.

Bumpass, Larry, and James Sweet. 1989. "National Estimates of Cohabitation." *Demography* 26: 615–625.

Casper, Lynne, and Suzanne Bianchi. 2002. *Continuity and Change in the American Family*. Thousand Oaks, CA: Sage Publications.

Clarkberg, Marin, Ross Stolzenberg, and Linda Waite. 1995. "Attitudes, Values, and Entrance into Cohabitational versus Marital Unions." *Social Forces* 74: 609–634.

Copen, Casey E., Kimberly Daniels, Jonathan Vespa, and William D. Mosher. 2012. "First Marriages in the United States: Data from the 2006–2010 National Survey of Family Growth." U.S. Department of Health and Human Services, *National Health Statistics Report* 49.

Fields, Jason, and Lynne Casper. 2001. *America's Families and Living Arrangements: Population Characteristics*. Current Population Reports, P20–537. Washington, DC: U.S. Census Bureau.

Gupta, Sanjiv. 1999. "The Effects of Transitions in Marital Status on Men's Housework Performance." *Journal of Marriage and Family* 61: 700–711.

Lisa and Christopher Jepsen. 2002. "An Empirical Analysis of the Matching Patterns of Same-Sex and Opposite-Sex Couples." *Demography* 29: 435–453.

Kennedy, Sheela, and Larry Bumpass. 2007. "Cohabitation and Children's Living Arrangements: New Estimates from the United States." *Center for Demography and Ecology Working Paper, 2007–20.* Madison: University of Wisconsin–Madison.

Lichter, Daniel T. 2012. "Childbearing among Cohabiting Women: Race, Pregnancy, and Union Transitions." In *Early Adulthood in a Family Context*, edited by Alan Booth, Susan L. Brown, Nancy S. Landale, Wendy D. Manning, and Susan M. McHale, 209–219. New York: Springer.

Lye, Diane, and Ingrid Waldron. 1997. "Attitudes Toward Cohabitation, Family, and Gender Roles: Relationships to Values and Political Ideology." *Sociological Perspectives* 40: 199–225.

Manlove, Jennifer, Suzanne Ryan, Elizabeth Wildsmith, and Kerry Franzetta. 2010. "The Relationship Context of Nonmarital Childbearing in the U.S." *Demographic Research* 23: 615–653.

Manning, Wendy. 2001. "Childbearing in Cohabiting Unions: Racial and Ethnic Differences." *Family Planning Perspectives* 33: 217–223.

——. 2010. Trends in Cohabitation: Twenty Years of Change, 1987–2008. FP-10-07, National Center for Family and Marriage Research. Available from http://ncfmr.bgsu .edu/pdf/family_profiles/file87411.pdf.

Manning, Wendy, and Susan Brown. 2006. "Children's Economic Well-Being in Married and Cohabiting Parent Families." *Journal of Marriage and Family* 68: 345–362.

Manning, Wendy, and Jessica A. Cohen. 2012. "Premarital Cohabitation and Marital Dissolution: An Examination of Recent Marriages." *Journal of Marriage and Family* 74: 377–387.

Manning, Wendy, Monica Longmore, and Peggy Giordano. 2007. "The Changing Institution of Marriage: Adolescents' Expectations to Cohabit and to Marry." *Journal of Marriage and Family* 69: 559–575.

Manning, Wendy, and Pamela Smock. 2002. "First Comes Cohabitation and Then Comes Marriage." *Journal of Family Issues* 23: 1065–1087.

——. 2005. "Measuring and Modeling Cohabitation: New Perspectives from Qualitative Data." *Journal of Marriage and Family* 67: 989–1002.

Musick, Kelly. 2002. "Planned and Unplanned Childbearing among Unmarried Women." *Journal of Marriage and Family* 64: 915–929.

Nock, Steven. 1995. "A Comparison of Marriages and Cohabiting Relationships." *Journal of Family Issues* 16: 53–76.

Smock, Pamela J. 2000. "Cohabitation in the United States: An Appraisal of Research Themes, Findings, and Implications." *Annual Review of Sociology* 26: 1–20.

Smock, Pamela, and Wendy Manning. 2004. "Living Together Unmarried in the United States: Demographic Perspectives and Implications for Family Policy." *Law and Policy* 26: 87–117.

Smock, Pamela, Wendy Manning, and Meredith Porter. 2005. "'Everything's There Except Money.' How Money Shapes Decisions to Marry Among Cohabitors." *Journal of Marriage and Family* 67: 680–696.

Smock, Pamela, and Mary Noonan. 2005. "Gender, Work, and Family Well-Being in the United States." In *Work, Family, Health and Well-Being*, edited by Suzanne Bianchi, Lynne Casper, and Rosalind Berkowitz King, 343–360. Mahwah, NJ: Lawrence Erlbaum Associates.

South, Scott, and Glenna Spitze. 1994. "Housework in Marital and Nonmarital Households." *American Sociological Review* 59: 327–347.

Stevens, Raymond. 1940. "Illegal Families Among the Clients of Family Agencies." *Social Forces* 19: 84–87.

Thornton, Arland, William Axinn, and Daniel Hill. 1992. "Reciprocal Effects of Religiosity, Cohabitation, and Marriage." *American Journal of. Sociology* 98: 628–651.

U.S. Census Bureau. 2012. *Married Couple Family Groups, by Presence of Own Children Under 18, and Age, Earnings, Education, and Race and Hispanic Origin of Both Spouses: 2012*. Table FG3. Retrieved on March 23, 2013, from http://www.census.gov/hhes/families/data/cps2012.html.

U.S. Census Bureau. 2012. *Opposite Sex Unmarried Couples by Presence of Biological Children Under 18, and Age, Earnings, Education, and Race and Hispanic Origin of Both Partners: 2012*. Table UC3. Retrieved on March 23, 2013, from http://www.census.gov/hhes/families/data/cps2012.html.

U.S. Department of Health and Human Services. 2005. *Fertility, Family Planning, and the Health of U.S. Women: Data from the 2002 National Survey of Family Growth*. Series 23–25. Hyattsville, MD: National Center for Health Statistics.

CHAPTER 13: Growing Up with a Lesbian, Gay, or Bisexual Sibling
by Amy Brainer

Balsam, Kimberly, Theodore Beauchaine, Ruth Mickey, and Esther Rothblum. 2005. "Mental Health of Lesbian, Gay, Bisexual, and Heterosexual Siblings: Effects of Gender, Sexual Orientation, and Family." *Journal of Abnormal Psychology* 114: 471–476.

Blanchard, Richard. 2004. "Quantitative and Theoretical Analyses of the Relation between Older Brothers and Homosexuality in Men." *Journal of Theoretical Biology* 230: 173–187.

Burke, Peter. 2004. *Brothers and Sisters of Disabled Children*. London: Jessica Kingsley Publishers.

———. 2010. "Brothers and Sisters of Disabled Children: The Experience of Disability by Association." *British Journal of Social Work* 40: 1681–1699.

Davis, Christine, and Kathleen Salkin. 2005. "Sisters and Friends: Dialogue and Multivocality in a Relational Model of Sibling Disability." *Journal of Contemporary Ethnography* 34: 206–234.

Emerson, Robert, Rachel Fretz, and Linda Shaw. 2011. *Writing Ethnographic Fieldnotes*, 2nd ed. Chicago: University of Chicago Press.

Erikson, Rebecca. 1993. "Reconceptualizing Family Work: The Effect of Emotion Work on Perceptions of Marital Quality." *Journal of Marriage and Family* 55: 888–900.

Filax, Gloria. 2006. *Queer Youth in the Province of the Severely Normal*. Vancouver: University of British Columbia Press.

Goffman, Erving. 1963. *Stigma: Notes on the Management of Spoiled Identity*. New York: Simon & Schuster.

Green, Sarah. 2003. "'What do you mean, what's wrong with her?' Stigma and the Lives of Families with Children with Disabilities." *Social Science & Medicine* 57: 1361–1374.

Hamer, Dean. 2011. *Science of Desire: The Gay Gene and the Biology of Behavior.* New York: Simon & Schuster.

Hilton, Angela, and Dawn Szymanski. 2011. "Family Dynamics and Changes in Sibling of Origin Relationship After Lesbian and Gay Sexual Orientation Disclosure." *Contemporary Family Theory* 33: 291–309.

Hochschild, Arlie. 1989. "Emotion Work, Feeling Rules, and Social Structure." *American Journal of Sociology* 85: 551–575.

Jenkins, David. 2008. "Changing Family Dynamics: A Sibling Comes Out." *Journal of GLBT Family Studies* 4: 1–16.

Rothblum, Esther. 2011. "Lesbian, Gay, Bisexual, and Transgender Siblings." In *Sibling Developments: Implications for Mental Health Practitioners*, edited by Jonathan Caspi, 123–146. New York: Springer.

Rothblum, Esther, Kimberly Balsam, and Ruth Mickey. 2004. "Brothers and Sisters of Lesbians, Gay Men, and Bisexuals as a Demographic Comparison Group." *Journal of Applied Behavioral Science* 40: 283–301.

Rothblum, Esther, Kimberly Balsam, Sandra Solomon, and Rhonda Factor. 2005. "Siblings and Sexual Orientation: Products of Alternative Families or the Ones Who Got Away?" *Journal of GLBT Family Studies* 1: 71–87.

———. 2007. "Lesbian, Gay Male, Bisexual, and Heterosexual Siblings: Discrepancies in Income and Education in Three US Samples." In *Sexual Orientation Discrimination: An International Perspective*, edited by M. V. Lee Badgett and Jefferson Frank, 62–75. New York: Routledge.

Sánchez, Francisco, Sven Bocklandt, and Eric Vilain. 2013. "The Relationship Between Help-Seeking Attitudes and Masculine Norms among Monozygotic Male Twins Discordant for Sexual Orientation." *Health Psychology* 23: 52–56.

Stalker, Kristen, and Clare Connors. 2004. "Children's Perceptions of Their Disabled Siblings: She's Different, but It's Normal for Us." *Children & Society* 18: 218–230.

CHAPTER 14: Life in a Dual-Earner Couple Before, During, and After the Great Recession
by Shannon N. Davis and Brittany Owen

Abraham, Martin, Katrin Auspurg, and Thomas Hinz. 2010. "Migration Decisions with Dual-Earner Partnerships: A Test of Bargaining Theory." *Journal of Marriage and Family* 24(7): 876–892.

Arrighi, Barbara A., and David J. Maume Jr. 2000. "Workplace Subordination and Men's Avoidance of Housework." *Journal of Family Issues* 21: 464–487.

Avellar, Sarah, and Pamela J. Smock. 2003. "Has the Price of Motherhood Declined Over Time? A Cross-Cohort Study Comparison of the Motherhood Wage Penalty." *Journal of Marriage and Family* 65(3): 597–607.

Barnett, Rosalind Chait. 2002. "Dual-Earner Couples: Good/Bad for Her and/or Him?" In *From Work-Family Balance to Work-Family Interaction: Changing the Metaphor*, edited by Diane F. Halpern and Susan Elaine Murphy, 151–171. Mahwah, NJ: Lawrence Erlbaum Associates.

Barnett, Rosalind Chait, Karen C. Gareis, and Robert T. Brennan. 2008. "Wives' Shift Work Schedules and Husbands' and Wives' Well-Being in Dual-Earner Couples With Children: A Within-Couple Analysis." *Journal of Family Issues* 29: 396–422.

Bartley, Sharon J., Priscilla W. Blanton, and Jennifer L. Gilliard. 2005. "Husbands and Wives in Dual-Earner Marriages: Decision-Making, Gender Role Attitudes, Division of Household Labor, and Equity." *Marriage & Family Review* 37: 69–94.

Becker, Gary S. 1981. *Treatise on the Family*. Cambridge, MA: Harvard University Press.

Becker, Gary S., Elisabeth M. Landes, and Robert T. Michael. 1977. "An Economic Analysis of Marital Instability." *Journal of Political Economy* 85: 1141–1187.

Becker, Penny Edgell, and Phyllis Moen. 1999. "Scaling Back: Dual Earner Couples' Work-Family Strategies." *Journal of the Marriage and Family* 61(4): 995–1007.

Berik, Günseli, and Ebru Konger. 2012. "Time Use of Mothers and Fathers in Hard Times: The US Recession of 2007–2009." Working Paper 726. Annandale-on-Hudson, NY: Levy Economics Institute of Bard College. Available from http://www.levyinstitute.org/files /download.php?file=wp_726.pdf&pubid=1547.

Bianchi, Suzanne M. 2000. "Maternal Employment and Time with Children: Dramatic Change or Surprising Continuity?" *Demography* 37: 401–414.

———. 2011. "Family Change and Time Allocation in American Families." *ANNALS of the American Academy of Political and Social Science* 638: 21–44.

Bianchi, Suzanne M., and Melissa A. Milkie. 2010. "Work and Family Research in the First Decade of the 21st Century." *Journal of Marriage and Family* 72: 705–725.

Bianchi, Suzanne M., John P. Robinson, and Melissa A. Milkie. 2006. *Changing Rhythms of American Family Life*. New York: Russell Sage.

Bianchi, Suzanne M., Liana C. Sayer, Melissa A. Milkie, and John P. Robinson. 2012. "Housework: Who Did, Does, or Will Do It and How Much Does It Matter?" *Social Forces* 91: 55–63.

Bielby, William T., and Denise D. Bielby. 1992. "I Will Follow Him: Family Ties, Gender-Role Beliefs, and Reluctance to Relocate for a Better Job." *American Journal of Sociology* 97(5): 1241–1267.

Booth, Alan, David R. Johnson, Lynn K. White, and John N. Edwards. 1986. "Divorce and Marital Instability over the Life Course." *Journal of Family Issues* 7: 421–442.

Boushey, Heather. 2008. "'Opting out?' The effect of children on women's employment in the United States." *Feminist Economics* 14(1): 1–36.

Boushey, Heather. 2011. *Not Working: Unemployment among Married Couples— Unemployment Continues to Plague Families in Today's Tough Job Market*. Washington, DC: Center for American Progress.

Boyle, Paul, Thomas J. Cooke, Keith Halfacree, and Darren Smith. 2001. "A Cross-National Comparison of the Impact of Family Migration on Women's Employment Status." *Demography* 38(2): 201–213.

Brayfield, April. 1995. "Juggling Jobs and Kids: The Impact of Work Schedules on Fathers' Caring for Children." *Journal of Marriage and Family* 57: 321–332.

Brewster, Karin L., and Ronald R. Rindfuss. 2000. "Fertility and Women's Employment in Industrialized Nations." *Annual Review of Sociology* 26: 271–296.

Brown, S. L., and A. Booth. 1996. "Cohabitation versus Marriage: A Comparison of Relationship Quality." *Journal of Marriage and the Family* 58: 668–678.

Budig, Michelle J., and Paula England. 2001. "The Wage Penalty for Motherhood." *American Sociological Review* 66: 204–225.

Bureau of Labor Statistics. 1997. *Employment Characteristics of Families: 1996.* Washington, DC: U.S. Department of Labor. Available from http://www.bls.gov/news.release/history /famee_061697.txt.

———. 2001. *Employment Characteristics of Families in 2000.* Washington, DC: U.S. Department of Labor. Available from http://www.bls.gov/news.release/history/famee_04192001 .txt.

———. 2006. *Employment Characteristics of Families in 2005.* Washington, DC: U.S. Department of Labor. Available from http://www.bls.gov/news.release/archives/famee _04272006.pdf.

———. 2013. Employment Characteristics of Families—2012. Washington, DC: U. S. Department of Labor. Available from http://www.bls.gov/news.release/famee.nr0.htm.

Cohen, Philip N. 2012. "Recession and Divorce in the United States: Economic Conditions and the Odds of Divorce, 2008–2010." Maryland Population Research Center Working Paper PWP-MPRC-2012-008. Available from http://papers.ccpr.ucla.edu/papers/PWP -MPRC-2012-008/PWP-MPRC-2012-008.pdf.

Coltrane, Scott. 1990. "Birth-Timing and the Division of Labor in Dual-Earner Families: Exploratory Findings and Suggestions for Future Research." *Journal of Family Issues* 11: 157–181.

———. 2000. Research on Household Labor: Modeling and Measuring the Social Embeddedness of Routine Family Work. *Journal of Marriage and Family* 62: 1208–1233.

Cooke, Lynne Prince, and Vanessa Gash. 2010. "Wives' Part-Time Employment and Marital Stability in Great Britain, West Germany, and the United States." *Sociology* 44: 1091–1108.

Coontz, Stephanie. 1992. *The Way We Never Were: American Families and the Nostalgia Trap.* New York: Basic Books.

Damaske, Sarah. 2011. *For the Family? How Class and Gender Shape Women's Work.* New York: Oxford University Press.

Davis, Shannon N. 2010. "Is Justice Contextual? Married Women's Perceptions of Fairness of the Division of Household Labor in 12 Nations." *Journal of Comparative Family Studies* 41: 19–39.

———. 2012. "Expected Career Prioritization in the Post-Recession United States: A Family Typology." Paper presented at the 75th Annual Meeting of the Southern Sociological Society, New Orleans, LA.

Davis, Shannon N., and Theodore N. Greenstein. 2004. "Interactive Effects of Gender Ideology and Age at First Marriage on Women's Marital Disruption." *Journal of Family Issues* 25: 658–682.

———. 2009. "Gender Ideology: Components, Predictors, and Consequences." *Annual Review of Sociology* 35: 88–105.

Davis, Shannon N., Shannon K. Jacobsen, and Julia Anderson. 2012. "From the Great Recession to Greater Gender Equality? Family Mobility and the Intersection of Race, Class, and Gender." *Marriage & Family Review* 48(7): 601–620.

Demaris, Alfred, and Monica A. Longmore. 1996. "Ideology, Power, and Equity: Testing Competing Explanations for the Perception of Fairness in Household Labor." *Social Forces* 74: 1043–1071.

Diamond, Lisa M., and Angela M. Hicks. 2012. "'It's the Economy, Honey!' Couples' Blame Attributions during the 2007–2009 Economic Crisis." *Personal Relationships* 19: 586–600.

Dillaway, Heather, and Clifford Broman. 2001. "Race, Class and Gender Differences in Marital Satisfaction among Dual-Earner Couples: A Case for Intersectional Analysis." *Journal of Family Issues* 22(3): 309–327.

Frisco, Michelle L., and Kristi Williams. 2003. "Perceived Equity, Marital Happiness, and Divorce in Dual-Earner Households." *Journal of Family Issues* 24: 51–73.

Gager, Constance T. 1998. "The Role of Valued Outcomes, Justifications, and Comparison Referents in Perceptions of Fairness among Dual-Earner Couples." *Journal of Family Issues* 19: 622–648.

Gager, Constance T., and Bryndl Hohmann-Marriott. 2006. "Distributive Justice in the Household: A Comparison of Alternative Theoretical Models." *Marriage & Family Review* 40: 5–42.

Galinsky, Ellen, Kerstin Aumann, and James T. Bond. 2011. *Times Are Changing: Gender and Generation at Work and at Home.* New York: Families and Work Institute. Available from http://familiesandwork.org/site/research/reports/Times_Are_Changing.pdf.

Garey, Anita Ilta. 1999. *Weaving Work and Motherhood.* Philadelphia, PA: Temple University Press.

Greenstein, Theodore N. 1990. "Marital Disruption and the Employment of Married Women." *Journal of Marriage and Family* 57: 31–42.

———. 1995. "Gender Ideology and Perceptions of the Fairness of the Division of Household Labor: Effects on Marital Quality." *Social Forces* 74: 1029–1042.

———. 1996. "Husbands' Participation in Domestic Labor: Interactive Effects of Wives' and Husbands' Gender Ideologies." *Journal of Marriage and Family* 58: 585–595.

Haddock, Shelley A., Toni Schindler Zimmerman, Scott J. Ziemba, and Kevin P. Lyness. 2006. "Practices of Dual Earner Couples Successfully Balancing Work and Family." *Journal of Family and Economic Issues* 27: 207–234.

Han, Wen-Jui . 2005. "Maternal Nonstandard Work Schedules and Child Cognitive Outcomes." *Child Development* 76(1): 137–154

Hardill, Irene, Anna E. Green, Anna C. Dudleston, and David W. Owen. 1997. "Who Decides What? Decision-Making in Dual Career Couples." *Work, Employment, & Society* 11: 313–326.

Hochschild, Arlie, and Anne Machung. 1989. *The Second Shift.* New York: Avon.

Hofferth, Sandra. 2001. "Women's Employment and Care of Children in the United States." In *Women's Employment in a Comparative Perspective,* edited by Tanja Van Der Lippe and Liset Van Dijk, 151–174. New York: Aldine de Gruyter.

Hostetler, Andrew J., Stephan Desrochers, Kimberly Kopko, and Phyllis Moen. 2012. "Marital and Family Satisfaction as a Function of Work-Family Demands and Community Resources: Individual- and Couple-Level Analyses." *Journal of Family Issues* 33: 316–340.

Jacobs, Jerry A., and Kathleen Gerson. 2004. *The Time Divide: Work, Family and Gender Inequality.* Cambridge, MA: Harvard University Press.

Kelly, Erin L., Phyllis Moen, and Eric Tranby. 2011. "Changing Workplaces to Reduce Work-Family Conflict: Schedule Control in a White-Collar Organization." *American Sociological Review* 76: 265–290.

Lachance-Grzela, Mylène, and Geneviève Bouchard. 2010. "Why Do Women Do the Lion's Share of Housework? A Decade of Research." *Sex Roles* 63: 767–780.

Landivar, Liana Christin. 2012. "The Impact of the Great Recession on Mothers' Employment." In *Contemporary Perspectives in Family Research, Volume 6: Economic Stress and the Family,* edited by Sampson Lee Blair, 163–185. Bingley, UK: Emerald Group.

Lareau, Annette. 2011. *Unequal Childhoods: Class, Race, and Family Life, 2nd Edition with an Update a Decade Later.* Berkeley: University of California Press.

Daniel T. 1980. "Household Migration and the Market Position of Married Women." *Social Science Research* 9: 83–97.

Liu, Siwei, and Kathryn Hynes. 2012. "Are Difficulties Balancing Work and Family Associated with Subsequent Fertility?" *Family Relations* 61: 16–30.

Livingston, Beth. 2011. "Bargaining Behind the Scenes: Spousal Negotiation, Labor, and Work-Family Burnout." *Journal of Management.* DOI: 10.1177/0149206311428355. Retrieved from http://jom.sagepub.com/content/early/2011/12/19/0149206311428355.

Lundberg, Shelly, and Elaina Rose. 2002. "The Effects of Sons and Daughters on Men's Labor Supply and Wages." *The Review of Economics and Statistics* 84(2): 251–268.

Magnuson, Sandy, and Ken Norum. 1999. "Challenges for Higher Education Couples in Commuter Marriages: Insights for Couples and Counselors Who Work with Them." *Family Journal* 7: 125–134.

Markham, William T., and Joseph H. Pleck. 1986. "Sex and Willingness to Move for Occupational Advancement: Some National Sample Results." *Sociological Quarterly* 27(1): 121–143.

Mason, Mary Ann, and Marc Goulden. 2002. "Do Babies Matter? The Effect of Family Formation on the Lifelong Careers of Academic Men and Women." *Academe* 88(6): 21–27.

Meteyer, Karen, and Maureen Perry-Jenkins. 2010. "Father Involvement among Working-Class, Dual-Earner Couples." *Fathering* 8: 379–403.

Jacob. 1978. "Family Migration Decisions." *Journal of Political Economy* 86: 749–775.

Morgan, S. Philip, Erin Cumberworth, and Christopher Wimer. 2011. "The Great Recession's Influence on Fertility, Marriage, Divorce, and Cohabitation." In *The Great Recession*, edited by David Grusky, Bruce Western, and Christopher Wimer, 220–245. New York: Russell Sage Foundation.

Noonan, Mary. 2013. "The Impact of Social Policy on the Gendered Division of Housework." *Journal of Family Theory & Review* 5: 124–134.

Payne, Krista K., and Larry Gibbs. 2013. *Economic Wellbeing and the Great Recession: Dual Earner Married Couples in the U.S., 2006 and 2011.* (FP-13-05). National Center for Family & Marriage Research. Available from http://ncfmr.bgsu.edu/pdf/family_profiles/file126564.pdf.

Pederson, Daphne E., and Krista Lynne Minnotte. 2012. "Dual Earner Husbands and Wives: Marital Satisfaction and the Workplace Culture of Each Spouse." *Journal of Family and Economic Issues* 33: 272–282.

Perry-Jenkins, Maureen, and Karen Folk. 1994. "Class, Couples and Conflict: Effects of the Division of Labor on Assessments of Marriage in Dual-Earner Families." *Journal of Marriage and Family* 56: 165–180.

Piña, Darlene L., and Vern L. Bengston. 1993. "The Division of Household Labor and Wives' Happiness: Ideology, Employment, and Perceptions of Support." *Journal of Marriage and Family* 55: 901–912.

Pixley, Joy E. 2008. "Life Course Patterns of Career-Prioritizing Decisions and Occupational Attainment in Dual-Earner Couples." *Work and Occupations* 35(2): 137–163.

Pixley, Joy E., and Phyllis Moen. 2003. "Prioritizing Careers." In *It's About Time: Couples and Careers*, edited by P. Moen, 183–200. Ithaca, NY: Cornell University Press.

Presser, Harriet B. 2003. *Working in a 24/7 Economy: Challenges for American Families.* New York: Russell Sage Foundation.

Raley, Sara B., Marybeth J. Mattingly, and Suzanne M. Bianchi. 2006. "How Dual Are Dual-Income Couples? Documenting Change from 1970 to 2001." *Journal of Marriage and Family* 68: 11–28.

Rosenbluth, Susan C., Janice M. Steil, and Juliet H. Whitcomb. 1998. "Marital Equality: What Does It Mean?" *Journal of Family Issues* 19: 227–244.

Sandberg, J. F., and Sandra L. Hofferth. 2001. "Changes in Children's Time with Parents: United States, 1981–1997." *Demography* 38: 423–436.

Sayer, Liana C. 2005. "Gender, Time and Inequality: Trends in Women's and Men's Paid Work, Unpaid Work and Free Time." *Social Forces* 84: 285–303.

Sayer, Liana C., and Suzanne M. Bianchi. 2000. "Women's Economic Independence and the Probability of Divorce." *Journal of Family Issues* 21: 906–943.

Scanzoni, John. 1978. *Sex Roles, Women's Work, and Marital Conflict*. Lexington, MA: Lexington Books.

Schneider, Barbara, and Linda J. Waite. 2005. "Couples Making It Happen: Marital Satisfaction and What Works for Highly Satisfied Couples." In *Being Together, Working Apart*, edited by B. Schneider and L. J. Waite, 196–216. New York: Cambridge University Press.

Schoen, Robert, Nan Marie Astone, Kentra Rothert, Nicola J. Standish, and Young J. Kim. 2002. "Women's Employment, Marital Happiness, and Divorce." *Social Forces* 81: 643–662.

Shreffler, Karina M., Amy E. Pirretti, and Robert Drago. 2010. "Work-Family Conflict and Fertility Intentions: Does Gender Matter?" *Journal of Family and Economic Issues* 31: 228–240.

Singley, Susan G., and Kathryn Hines. 2005. "Transitions to Parenthood: Work-Family Policies, Gender, and the Couple Context." *Gender and Society* 19(3): 376–397.

Sobotka, Tomas, Vegard Skirbekk, and Dimiter Philipov. 2011. "Economic Recession and Fertility in the Developed World." *Population and Development Review* 37: 267–306.

Soloway, Maxine N., and Rebecca M. Smith. 1987. "Antecedents of Late Birthtiming Decisions of Men and Women in Dual-Career Marriages." *Family Relations* 36(3): 258–262.

South, Scott J. 2001. "Time-Dependent Effects of Wives' Employment on Marital Dissolution." *American Sociological Review* 66: 226–245.

Spitze, Glenna, and Scott J. South. 1985. "Women's Employment, Time Expenditure, and Divorce." *Journal of Family Issues* 4: 105–126.

Stohs, Joann Hoven. 2000. "Multicultural Women's Experience of Household Labor, Conflicts, and Equity." *Sex Roles: A Journal of Research* 42: 339–361.

Suitor, Jill J. 1991. "Marital Quality and Satisfaction with the Division of Household Labor across the Family Life Cycle." *Journal of Marriage and Family* 53: 221–230.

Thompson, Linda. 1991. "Family Work: Women's Sense of Fairness." *Journal of Family Issues* 12: 181–196.

Tichenor, Veronica J. 2005. *Earning More and Getting Less: Why Successful Wives Can't Buy Equality*. New Brunswick, NJ: Rutgers University Press.

Torr, Berna Miller and Susan E. Short. 2004. "Second Births and the Second Shift: A Research Note on Gender Equity and Fertility. *Population and Development Review*, 30(1):109-130.

Voydanoff, Patricia, and Brenda W. Donnelly. 1999. "The Intersection of Time in Activities and Perceived Unfairness in Relation to Psychological Distress and Marital Quality." *Journal of Marriage and Family* 61: 739–751.

Winslow-Bowe, Sarah. 2006. "The Persistence of Wives' Income Advantage." *Journal of Marriage and Family* 68(4): 824–842.

CHAPTER 15: From Outlaws to In-Laws: Gay and Lesbian Couples in Contemporary Society
by Robert-Jay Green

Balsam, K. F., T. P. Beauchaine, E. D. Rothblum, and S. E. Solomon. 2008. "Three-Year Follow-Up of Same-Sex Couples Who Had Civil Unions in Vermont, Same-Sex Couples Not in Civil Unions, and Heterosexual Married Couples." *Developmental Psychology* 44: 102–116.

Bergman, K., R. Rubio, R.-J. Green, and E. Padron. 2010. "Gay Men Who Become Fathers via Surrogacy: The Transition to Parenthood." *Journal of GLBT Family Studies* 6: 111–141.

Biblarz, T. J., and E. Savci. 2010. "Lesbian, Gay, Bisexual, and Transgender Families." *Journal of Marriage & Family* 72: 480–497.

Bos, H., and N. Gartrell. 2010. "Adolescents of the U.S. National Longitudinal Lesbian Family Study: Can Family Characteristics Counteract the Negative Effects of Stigmatization?" *Family Process* 49: 559–572.

Brodzinsky, D. M., R.-J. Green, and K. Katuzny. 2012. "Adoption by Lesbians and Gay Men: What We Know, Need to Know, and Ought to Do." In *Adoption by Lesbians and Gay Men: Research and Practice Issues*, edited by D.M. Brodzinsky and A. Pertman, 233–253. New York: Oxford.

Castello, J. 2013. *Same-Sex Partners: Relationship Statuses, Commitment, Satisfaction, and Relational Ambiguity.* Paper presented at the American Psychological Association Convention, Honolulu, HI.

Clifford, D., F. Hertz, and E. Doskow. 2012. *A Legal Guide for Lesbian and Gay Couples,* 16th ed. Berkeley, CA: Nolo Press.

Craighill, P. M., and S. Clement. 2014. "Support for Same-Sex Marriage Hits New High; Half Say Constitution Guarantees Right." *Washington Post.* Retrieved on March 4, 2014, from http://www.washingtonpost.com/politics/support-for-same-sex-marriage-hits-new-high-half-say-constitution-guarantees-right/2014/03/04/f737e87e-a3e5-11e3-a5fa-55f0c77bf39c_story.html?hpid=z4.

Crowl, A. L., S. Ahn, and J. A. Baker. 2008. "A Meta-Analysis of Developmental Outcomes for Children of Same-Sex and Heterosexual Parents." *Journal of GLBT Family Studies* 4: 386–407.

D'Augelli, A. R., H. J. Rendina, K. O. Sinclair, and A. H. Grossman. 2006/2007. "Lesbian and Gay Youths' Aspirations for Marriage and Raising Children." *Journal of LGBT Issues in Counseling* 1: 77–98.

Dobson, J. 2006. "Two Mommies Is One Too Many." *TIME Magazine.* Retrieved on December 12, 2006, from http://www.time.com/time/magazine/article/0,9171,1568485,00.html.

Egan, P. J., M. S. Edelman, and K. Sherrill. 2008. *Findings from the Hunter College Poll of Lesbians, Gays, and Bisexuals: New Discoveries about Identity, Political Attitudes and Civic Engagement.* Retrieved on November 10, 2008, from http://www.nyu.edu/public.affairs/pdf/hunter_college_poll_report_complete.pdf.

Emilio, J. D. 1998. *Sexual Politics, Sexual Communities,* 2nd ed. Chicago: University of Chicago Press.

Faderman, L. 1991. *Odd Girls and Twilight Lovers.* New York: Columbia University Press.

Fingerhut, A. W., and L. A. Peplau. 2013. "Same-Sex Romantic Relationships." In *Handbook of Psychology and Sexual Orientation*, edited by C. J. Patterson and A. R. D'Augelli, 165–178. New York: Oxford.

Firestein, B., ed. 2007. *Becoming Visible: Counseling Bisexuals across the Lifespan*. New York: Columbia University Press.

Fox, R., ed. 2006. *Affirmative Psychotherapy with Bisexual Women and Bisexual Men*. Binghamton, NY: Haworth.

Gates, G. J. 2013. "The Real 'Modern Family' in America." Retrieved on March 25, 2013, from http://us.cnn.com/2013/03/24/opinion/gates-real-modern-family/index.html.

General Accounting Office. 2004. *Defense of Marriage Act: Update to Prior Report, GAO-04-353R*. Retrieved on October 23, 2004 from http://www.gao.gov/new.items/d04353r.pdf.

Gotta, G., R.-J. Green, E. Rothblum, S. Solomon, K. Balsam, and P. Schwartz. 2011. "Lesbian, Gay Male, and Heterosexual Relationships: A Comparison of Couples in 1975 and 2000." *Family Process* 50: 353–376.

Gottman, J. M., R. W. Levenson, J. Gross, B. L. Frederickson, K. McCoy, L. Rosenthal, A. Ruef, and D. Yoshimoto. 2003a. "Correlates of Gay and Lesbian Couples' Relationship Satisfaction and Relationship Dissolution." *Journal of Homosexuality* 45: 23–43.

Gottman, J. M., R. W. Levenson, C. Swanson, K. Swanson, R. Tyson, and D. Yoshimoto. 2003b. "Observing Gay, Lesbian, and Heterosexual Couples' Relationships: Mathematical Modeling of Conflict Interaction." *Journal of Homosexuality* 45: 65–91.

Green, R.-J., M. Bettinger, and E. Zacks. 1996. "Are Lesbian Couples Fused and Gay Male Couples Disengaged? Questioning Gender Straightjackets." In *Lesbians and Gays in Couples and Families*, edited by J. Laird and R.-J. Green, 185–230. San Francisco: Jossey-Bass.

Herdt, G., and R. Kertzner. 2006. "I Do, but I Can't: The Impact of Marriage Denial on the Mental Health and Sexual Citizenship of Lesbians and Gay Men in the United States." *Sexuality Research & Social Policy Journal of NSRC* 3: 33–39. Online ISSN 1553-6610.

Herek, G. M. 2006. "Legal Recognition of Same-Sex Relationships in the United States: A Social Science Perspective." *American Psychologist* 61: 607–621.

Herek, G. M., ed. 1998. *Stigma and Sexual Orientation: Understanding Prejudice against Lesbians, Gay Men, and Bisexuals*. Thousand Oaks, CA: Sage Publications.

Katz, J. N. 1992. *Gay American History: Lesbians and Gay Men in the U.S.A.*, revised sub ed.. New York: Plume.

Langer, G. 2013. *ABC/Washington Post Poll: Poll Finds Majority Acceptance of Gays from the B-Ball Court to the Boy Scouts*. Retrieved on May 9, 2013, from http://www.langerresearch.com/uploads/1144a19GayRights.pdf.

Lanutti, P. J. 2008. "Attractions and Obstacles While Considering Legally Recognized Same-Sex Marriage Relationships." *Journal of GLBT Family Studies* 4: 245–264.

Lewin, E. 2009. *Gay Fatherhood: Narratives of Family and Citizenship in America*. Chicago, IL: University of Chicago Press.

Lev, A. I. 2004. *Transgender Emergence: Therapeutic Guidelines for Working with Gender-Variant People and Their Families*. Binghamton, NY: Haworth Press.

Madsen, P. W. B., and R.-J. Green. 2012. "Gay Adolescent Males' Effective Coping with Discrimination: A Qualitative Study." *Journal of LGBT Issues in Counseling* 6: 139–155.

Meyer, I. H. 2003. "Prejudice, Social Stress, and Mental Health in Lesbian, Gay, and Bisexual Populations: Conceptual Issues and Research Evidence." *Psychological Bulletin* 129: 674–697.

Mitchell, V., and R.-J. Green. 2007. "Different Storks for Different Folks: Gay and Lesbian Parents' Experiences with Alternative Insemination and Surrogacy." *Journal of GLBT Family Studies* 3(2/3): 81–104.

Murray, M. 2013. *NBC/Wall Street Journal Poll: 53 Percent Support Gay Marriage.* Retrieved on April 12, 2013, from http://firstread.nbcnews.com/_news/2013/04/11/17708688 -nbcwsj-poll-53-percent-support-gay-marriage?chromedomain=nbcpolitics&lite.

Patterson, C. J. 2013. "Sexual Orientation and Family Lives." In *Handbook of Psychology and Sexual Orientation,* edited by C. J. Patterson and A. R. D'Augelli, 223–236. New York: Oxford.

Pew Research Center. 2013a. *A Survey of LGBT Americans: Attitudes, Experiences, and Values in Changing Times.* Retrieved on June 13, 2013, from http://www.pewsocialtrends.org /files/2013/06/SDT_LGBT-Americans_06-2013.pdf.

———. 2013b. *In Gay Marriage Debate, Both Supporters and Opponents See Legal Recognition as "Inevitable."* Retrieved on June 6, 2013, from http://www.people-press .org/2013/06/06/in-gay-marriage-debate-both-supporters-and-opponents-see-legal -recognition-as-inevitable/.

Ragins, B. R., R. Singh, and J. M. Cornwell. 2007. "Making the Invisible Visible: Fear and Disclosure of Sexual Orientation at Work." *Journal of Applied Psychology* 92: 1103–1118.

Rostosky, S. S., E. D. B. Riggle, S. G. Horne, and A. D. Miller. 2009. "Marriage Amendments and Psychological Distress in Lesbian, Gay, and Bisexual (LGB) Adults." *Journal of Counseling Psychology* 56: 56–66.

Ryan, C., D. Huebner, R. M. Diaz, and J. Sanchez. 2009. "Family Rejection as a Predictor of Negative Health Outcomes in White and Latino Lesbian, Gay, and Bisexual Young Adults." *Pediatrics* 123: 346–352.

Saad, L. 2013. *Gallup Poll: In U.S., 52% Back Law to Legalize Gay Marriage in 50 States.* Retrieved on July 29, 2013, from http://www.gallup.com/poll/163730/back-law-legalize -gay-marriage-states.aspx.

Sanchez, F. J., and E. Vilain. 2013. "Transgender Identities: Research and Controversies." In *Handbook of Psychology and Sexual Orientation,* edited by C. J. Patterson and A. R. D'Augelli, 42–54. New York: Oxford.

Schlatter, E. 2010. "18 Anti-Gay Groups and Their Propaganda." *Southern Poverty Law Center Intelligence Report, No. 140.* Retrieved on December 22, 2013, from http://www .splcenter.org/get-informed/intelligence-report/browse-all-issues/2010/winter /the-hard-liners.

Solomon, S. E., E. D. Rothblum, and K. F. Balsam. 2004. "Pioneers in Partnership: Lesbian and Gay Male Couples in Civil Unions Compared with Those Not in Civil Unions and Married Heterosexual Siblings." *Journal of Family Psychology* 18: 275–286.

U.S. Census Bureau. 2011. "Same-Sex Couple Households." *American Community Survey Briefs.* Retrieved on December 22, 2013, from http://www.census.gov/prod/2011pubs /acsbr10-03.pdf.

Weston, K. 1991. *Families We Choose: Lesbians, Gays, Kinship.* New York: Columbia University Press.

Wilson, B. D. M., and G. W. Harper. 2013. "Race and Ethnicity among Lesbian, Gay, and Bisexual Communities." In *Handbook of Psychology and Sexual Orientation,* edited by C. J. Patterson and A. R. D'Augelli, 87–101. New York: Oxford.

CHAPTER 16: Independent Women: Equality in African American Lesbian Relationships
by Mignon R. Moore

Abdulahad, Tania, Gwendolyn Rogers, Barbara Smith, and Jameelah Waheed. 1983. "Black Lesbian/Feminist Organizing: A Conversation." In *Home Girls: A Black Feminist Anthology*, edited by B. Smith, 293–319. New York: Kitchen Table Press.

Blumstein, Philip, and Pepper Schwartz. 1983. *American Couples: Money, Work, Sex*. New York: Morrow.

Bulcroft, Richard A., and Kris A. Bulcroft. 1993. "Race Differences in Attitudinal and Motivational Factors in the Decision to Marry." *Journal of Marriage and Family* 55(92): 338–355.

Carrington, Christopher. 1999. *No Place Like Home: Relationships and Family Life among Lesbians and Gay Men*. Chicago: University of Chicago Press.

Collins, Patricia Hill. 2004. *Black Sexual Politics: African Americans, Gender and the New Racism*. New York: Routledge.

Combahee River Collective. 1983. "A Black Feminist Statement." In *Words of Fire: An Anthology of African-American Feminist Thought*, edited by Beverly Guy-Sheftall, 232–240. New York: New Press.

Cornwell, Anita. 1983. *The Black Lesbian in White America*. Tallahassee, FL: Naiad Press.

Crenshaw, Kimberlé Williams. 1995. "Race, Reform, and Retrenchment: Transformation and Legitimation in Anti-Discrimination Law." In *Critical Race Theory: The Key Writings that Formed the Movement*, edited by Kimberlé Crenshaw, Neil Gotanda, Gary Peller, and Kendall Thomas, 103–122. New York: New Press.

Dang, Alain, and Somjen Frazer. 2004. "Black Same-Sex Households in the United States: A Report from the 2000 Census." New York: National Gay and Lesbian Task Force Policy Institute and the National Black Justice Coalition.

Dill, Bonnie Thornton. 1979. "The Dialectics of Black Womanhood." *Signs: Journal of Women in Culture and Society* 4: 543–555.

Esterberg, Kristin G. 1997. *Lesbian and Bisexual Identities: Constructing Communities, Constructing Selves*. Philadelphia: Temple University Press.

Ferree, Myra Marx. 1991. "The Gender Division of Labor in Two-Earner Marriages." *Journal of Family Issues* 12(2): 158–180.

Gartrell, Nanette, Amy Banks, Nancy Reed, Jean Hamilton, Carla Rodas, and Amalia Deck. 2000. "The National Lesbian Family Study: 3. Interviews with Mothers of Five-Year-Olds." *American Journal of Orthopsychiatry* 70(4): 542–548.

Gates, Gary. 2008. "Diversity among Same-Sex Couples and Their Children." In *American Families: A Multicultural Reader* (2nd ed.), edited by Stephanie Coontz, with Maya Parson and Gabrielle Raley, 394–399. New York: Routledge.

Hequembourg, Amy. 2007. *Lesbian Motherhood: Stories of Becoming*. New York: Harrington Park Press.

Hochschild, Arlie Russell. 1989. *The Second Shift: Working Parents and the Revolution at Home*. New York: Viking.

Hunter, Andrea G., and Sherrill L. Sellers. 1998. "Feminist Attitudes among African-American Women and Men." *Gender and Society* 12(1): 81–99.

Kamo, Yoshimore, and Ellen L. Cohen. 1998. "Division of Household Work between Partners: A Comparison of Black and White Couples." *Journal of Comparative Family Studies* 29(1): 131–145.

Kenney, Catherine T. 2006. "The Power of the Purse: Allocative Systems and Inequality in Couple Households." *Gender and Society* 20(3): 354–381.

Kessler-Harris, Alice. 2003. *Out to Work: A History of Wage-Earning Women in the United States*. New York: Oxford University Press.

King, Deborah. 1988. "Multiple Jeopardy, Multiple Consciousness: The Context of a Black Feminist Ideology." *Signs: Journal of Women in Culture and Society* 14(1): 42–72.

Kurdek, Lawrence A. 1993. "The Allocation of Household Labor in Gay, Lesbian, Heterosexual, and Married Couples." *Journal of Social Issues* 49(3): 127–139.

Landry, Bart. 2000. *Black Working Wives: Pioneers of the American Family Revolution*. Berkeley: University of California Press.

Mezey, Nancy J. 2008. *New Choices, New Families: How Lesbians Decide about Motherhood*. Baltimore, MD: Johns Hopkins University Press.

Moore, Mignon R. 2006. "Lipstick or Timberlands? Meanings of Gender Presentation in Black Lesbian Communities." *Signs: Journal of Women in Culture and Society* 31(1): 113–139.

———. 2008. "Gendered Power Relations among Women: A Study of Household Decision-Making in Black, Lesbian Stepfamilies." *American Sociological Review* 73: 335–356.

Nelson, Fiona. 1996. *Lesbian Motherhood: An Exploration of Canadian Lesbian Families*. Toronto: University of Toronto Press.

Patterson, Charlotte. 1995. "Families of the Lesbian Baby Boom: Parents' Division of Labor and Children's Adjustment." *Developmental Psychology* 31(1): 115–123.

Phelan, Shane. 1993. "(Be)Coming Out: Lesbian Identity and Politics." *Signs: Journal of Women in Culture and Society* 18(4): 765–790.

Ransford, H. Edward, and Jon Miller. 1983. "Race, Sex, and Feminist Outlooks." *American Sociological Review* 48(1): 46–59.

Schwartz, Pepper. 1994. *Peer Marriages: How Love Between Equals Really Works*. New York: Free Press.

Sullivan, Maureen. 2004. *The Family of Woman: Lesbian Mothers, Their Children, and the Undoing of Gender*. Berkeley: University of California Press.

Tichenor, Veronica Jaris. 2005. *Earning More and Getting Less: Why Successful Wives Can't Buy Equality*. New Brunswick, NJ: Rutgers University Press.

Walby, Sylvia. 1990. *Theorizing Patriarchy*. Oxford, UK, and Cambridge, MA: Oxford University Press.

Wolf, Deborah Goleman. 1979. *The Lesbian Community*. Berkeley: University of California Press.

CHAPTER 17: Why Is Everyone Afraid of Sex?
by Pepper Schwartz

Baumgardner, Jennifer. 2007. *Look Both Ways: Bisexual Politics*. New York: Farrar, Straus, and Giroux.

Bearman, Peter S., and Hannah Brückner. 2001. "Promising the Future: Virginity Pledges and the Transition to First Intercourse." *American Journal of Sociology* 106: 859–912.

Bogle, Kathleen A. 2008. *Hooking Up: Sex Dating and Relationships on Campus*. New York: New York University Press.

Boonstra, Heather D. 2009. "Advocates Call for a New Approach after the Era of 'Abstinence Only' Sex Education." *Guttmacher Policy Review* 12 (Winter).

Brandt, Allan. 1987. *No Magic Bullet: A Social History of Venereal Disease in the United States since 1880*. New York: Oxford University Press.

Brückner, Hannah, and Peter S. Bearman. 2005. "After the Promise: The STD Consequences of Adolescent Virginity Pledges." *Journal of Adolescent Health* 36: 271–278.

Campbell, D., and C. Robinson. 2007. "Religious Coalitions for and against Gay Marriage: The Culture War Rages On." In *Politics of Gay Marriage*, 131–154. Chicago: University of Chicago Press.

Carpenter, Laura M. 2005. *Virginity Lost*. New York: New York University Press.

D'Emilio, John, and Estelle B. Freedman. 1988. *Intimate Matters: A History of Sexuality in America*. New York: Harper and Row.

Jehl, Douglas. 1999. "For Shame: A Special Report; Arab Honor's Price: A Woman's Blood." *New York Times*, June 20.

Kamen, Paula. 2000. *Her Way: Young Women Remake the Sexual Revolution*. New York: New York University Press.

Kinsey, Alfred C., Wardell B. Pomeroy, and Clyde E. Martin. 1948. *Sexual Behavior in the Human Male*. Philadelphia: W. B. Saunders.

Klein, Marty, and Nadine Strossen. 2006. *America's War on Sex: The Attack on Law, Lust and Liberty*. Westport, CT: Praeger.

Lauman, Edward O., John H. Gagnon, Robert T. Michael, and Stuart Michaels. 1994. *The Social Organization of Sexuality: Sexual Practices in the United States*. Chicago: University of Chicago Press.

Laumann, Edward O., Jenna Mahay, and Yoosik Youm. 2007. "Sex, Intimacy, and Family Life in the United States." In *The Sexual Self*, edited by Michael S. Kimmel, 165–190. Nashville, TN: Vanderbilt University Press.

McWhirter, David P., Stephanie A. Sanders, and June M. Reinisch. 1990. *Homosexuality/Heterosexuality: Concepts of Sexual Orientation*. Kinsey Institute Series. New York: Oxford University Press.

Pascoe, C. J. 2007. *Dude, You're a Fag: Masculinity and Sexuality in High School*. Berkeley: University of California Press.

Reiss, I., and H. Reiss. 2002. "The Role of Religion in Our Sexual Lives." In *Sexual Lives: A Reader on the Theories and Realities of Human Sexualities*, edited by Robert Heasley and Betsy Crane. New York: McGraw-Hill.

Rom, M. C. 2007. "Introduction." In *The Politics of Same Sex Marriage*, edited by Craig Rimmerman and Clyde Wilcox, 1–38. Chicago: University of Chicago Press.

Schwartz, Pepper. 2007. "The Social Construction of Heterosexuality." In *The Sexual Self*, edited by Michael Kimmel, 80–92. Nashville, TN: Vanderbilt University Press.

Schwartz, Pepper, and Virginia Rutter. 2000. *The Gender of Sexuality*. Lanham, MD: Alta Mira Press.

Shilts, Randy. 1987. *And the Band Played On*. New York: St. Martin's Press.

Tannenbaum, Leora. 1999. *Slut! Growing Up Female with a Bad Reputation*. New York: Seven Stories Press.

Tiefer, Leonore. 1995. *Sex Is Not a Natural Act and Other Essays*. Boulder, CO: Colorado Westview Press.

Wilcox, Clyde, P. Brewer, S. Shames, and C. Lake. 2007. "If I Bend This Far I Will Break? Public Opinion about Gay Marriage." In *The Politics of Same Sex Marriage*, edited by Craig A. Rimmerman and Clyde Wilcox, 215–242. Chicago: University of Chicago Press.

CHAPTER 18: First Comes Love, then Comes Herpes: Sexual Health and Relationships
by Adina Nack

Adler, Patricia A., and Peter Adler. 2006. *Constructions of Deviance: Social Power, Context, and Interaction*, 5th ed. Belmont, CA: Thomson Wadsworth.

Albrechtsen, Susanne, Svein Rasmussen, Steinar Thoresen, Lorentz M. Irgens, and Ole Erik Iversen. 2008. "Pregnancy Outcome in Women Before and After Cervical Conisation: Population Based Cohort Study." *British Medical Journal* 337: a1343.

American Social Health Association (ASHA). 2013a. "STDs/STIs Statistics." Research Triangle Park, NC: American Social Health Association. Retrieved on June 8, 2013, from http://www.ashasexualhealth.org/std-sti/std-statistics.html.

———. 2013b. "STDs/STIs Pregnancy." Research Triangle Park, NC: American Social Health Association. Retrieved on June 8, 2013, from http://www.ashasexualhealth.org/std-sti/Herpes/pregnancy.html.

———. 2013c. "Treatment for Genital Herpes." Research Triangle Park, NC: American Social Health Association. Retrieved on June 8, 2013, from http://www.ashasexualhealth.org/std-sti/Herpes/treatment.html.

Bednarczyk, Robert A., Robert Davis, Kevin Ault, Walter Orenstein, and Saad B. Omer. 2012. "Sexual Activity–Related Outcomes after Human Papillomavirus Vaccination of 11- to 12-Year-Olds." *Pediatrics* 130(5): 2–9.

Centers for Disease Control and Prevention (CDC). 2013a. "CDC Fact Sheet: Incidence, Prevalence, and Cost of Sexually Transmitted Infections in the United States." Atlanta, GA: Centers for Disease Control and Prevention. Retrieved on June 8, 2013, from http://www.cdc.gov/std/stats/STI-Estimates-Fact-Sheet-Feb-2013.pdf.

———. 2013b. "Genital Herpes Screening: Frequently Asked Questions." Atlanta, GA: Centers for Disease Control and Prevention. Retrieved on June 8, 2013, from http://www.cdc.gov/std/herpes/screening.htm.

———. 2013c. "Teen Vaccination Coverage: 2011 National Immunization Survey (NIS)—Teen." Atlanta, GA: Centers for Disease Control and Prevention. Retrieved on June 8, 2013, from http://www.cdc.gov/vaccines/who/teens/vaccination-coverage.html.

D'Souza, Gypsyamber, Yuri Agrawal, Jane Halpern, Sacared Bodison, and Maura L. Gillison. 2009. "Oral Sexual Behaviors Associated with Prevalent Oral Human Papillomavirus Infection." *Journal of Infectious Diseases* 199: 1263–1269.

East, Leah, Debra Jackson, Kath Peters, and Louise O'Brien. 2010. "Disrupted Sense of Self: Young Women and Sexually Transmitted Infections." *Journal of Clinical Nursing* 19: 1995–2003.

Frank, Arthur W. 1991. *At the Will of the Body.* Boston: Houghton Mifflin Company.

Jakobsson, Maija, Mika Gissler, Jorma Paavonen, and Anna-Maija Tapper. 2009. "Loope Electrosurgical Excision Procedure and the Risk for Preterm Birth." *Obstetrics & Gynecology* 114(3): 504–510.

Kalliala I., A. Anttila, T. Dyba, T. Hakulinen, M. Halttunen, and P. Nieminen. 2011. "Pregnancy Incidence and Outcome among Patients with Cervical Intraepithelial Neoplasia: A Retrospective Cohort Study." *British Journal of Obstetrics and Gynaecology* 119: 227–235.

Kreimer, Aimée R. 2009. "Oral Sexual Behaviors and the Prevalence of Oral Human Papillomavirus Infection." *Journal of Infectious Diseases* 199: 1253–1254.

Kyrgiou, M., G. Koliopoulos, P. Martin-Hirsch, M. Arbyn, W. Prendiville, and E. Paraskev-aidas. 2006. "Obstetric Outcomes after Conservative Treatment for Intraepithelial or Early Invasive Cervical Lesions: Systematic Review and Meta-Analysis." *The Lancet* 367: 489–498.

Lichtenstein, Bronwen. 2003. "Stigma as a Barrier to Treatment of Sexually Transmitted Infection in the American Deep South: Issues of Race, Gender and Poverty." *Social Science & Medicine* 57(12): 2435–2445.

Melville, J. L., S. Sniffen, R. Crosby, L. Salazar, W. Whittington, D. Dithmer-Schreck, R. DiClemente, and A. Wald. 2003. "Psychosocial Impact of Serological Diagnosis of Herpes Simplex Virus Type 2: A Qualitative Assessment." *Sexually Transmitted Infections* 79: 280–285.

Nack, Adina. 2000. "Damaged Goods: Women Managing the Stigma of STDs." *Deviant Behavior* 21(2): 95–121.

———. 2002. "Bad Girls and Fallen Women: Chronic STD Diagnoses as Gateways to Tribal Stigma." *Symbolic Interaction* 25(4): 463–485.

———. 2008. *Damaged Goods? Women Living with Incurable Sexually Transmitted Diseases.* Philadelphia: Temple University Press.

National Cancer Institute (NCI). 2013. "HPV and Cancer." Bethesda, MD: National Cancer Institute at the National Institutes of Health, U.S. Department of Health and Human Services. Retrieved on June 8, 2013 from, http://www.cancer.gov/cancertopics/factsheet /Risk/HPV.

Rupp, R., Rosenthal, S., and L. Stanberry. 2005. "Pediatrics and Herpes Simplex Virus Vaccines." *Seminars in Pediatric Infectious Diseases* 16(1): 31–37.

Rutter, Virginia, and Pepper Schwartz. 2011. *The Gender of Sexuality: Exploring Sexual Possibilities.* Plymouth, UK: Rowman & Littlefield.

Schneider, Joseph W., and Peter Conrad. 1981. "In the Closet with Illness: Epilepsy, Stigma Potential and Information Control." *Social Problems* 28(1): 32–44.

Schwartz, Pepper. 2008. *Prime: Adventures and Advice on Sex, Love, and the Sensual Years.* New York: Collins.

Singhal, P., S. Naswa, and Y. S. Marfatia. 2009. "Pregnancy and Sexually Transmitted Viral Infections." *Indian Journal of Sexually Transmitted Diseases and AIDS* 30(2): 71–78.

Temte, Jonathan L. 2007. "HPV Vaccine: A Cornerstone of Female Health." *American Family Physician* 75(1): 28–30.

CHAPTER 19: Orgasm in College Hookups and Relationships
by Elizabeth A. Armstrong, Paula England, and Alison C. K. Fogarty

Anonymous, M. D. 2006. *Unprotected: A Campus Psychiatrist Reveals How Political Correctness in Her Profession Endangers Every Student.* New York: Sentinel HC.

Bailey, Beth L. 1989. *From Front Porch to Back Seat: Courtship in Twentieth-Century America.* Baltimore: Johns Hopkins University Press.

Bogle, Kathleen A. 2007. "The Shift from Dating to Hooking Up in College: What Scholars Have Missed." *Sociology Compass* 1/2: 775–788.

———. 2008. *Hooking Up: Sex, Dating, and Relationships on Campus.* New York: New York University Press.

Boswell, A. Ayers, and Joan Z. Spade. 1996. "Fraternities and Collegiate Rape Culture: Why Are Some Fraternities More Dangerous Places for Women?" *Gender & Society* 10: 133–147.

Braun, Virginia, Nicola Gavey, and Kathryn McPhillips. 2003. "The 'Fair Deal?' Unpacking Accounts of Reciprocity in Heterosex." *Sexualities* 6: 237–261.

Buss, David M. 1994. *The Evolution of Human Desire: Strategies of Human Mating.* New York: Basic Books.

Chodorow, Nancy. 1978. *The Reproduction of Mothering: Psychoanalysis and the Sociology of Gender.* Berkeley: University of California Press.

Crawford, Mary, and Danielle Popp. 2003. "Sexual Double Standards: A Review and Methodological Critique of Two Decades of Research." *Journal of Sex Research* 40: 13–27.

Darling, C. A., J. K. Davidson Sr., and D. A. Jennings. 1991. "The Female Sexual Response Revisited: Understanding the Multiorgasmic Experience in Women." *Archives of Sexual Behavior* 20: 527–540.

Denizet-Lewis, Benoit. 2004. "Friends, Friends with Benefits and the Benefits of the Local Mall." *New York Times*, May 30.

England, Paula, Emily Fitzgibbons Shafer, and Alison C. K. Fogarty. 2007. "Hooking Up and Forming Romantic Relationships on Today's College Campuses." In *The Gendered Society Reader*, 3rd ed., edited by Michael S. Kimmel and Amy Aronson. New York: Oxford University Press.

Fisher, Seymour. 1973. *The Female Orgasm.* New York: Basic Books.

Freitas, Donna. 2008. *Sex and the Soul: Juggling Sexuality, Spirituality, Romance and Religion on America's College Campuses.* New York: Oxford University Press.

Gagnon, John H., and William Simon. 1974. *Sexual Conduct: The Social Sources of Human Sexuality.* London: Aldine Transaction.

Gilmartin, Shannon K. 2005. "The Centrality and Costs of Heterosexual Romantic Love among First-Year College Women." *Journal of Higher Education* 76: 609–634.

Glenn, Norval, and Elizabeth Marquardt. 2001. *Hooking Up, Hanging Out, and Hoping for Mr. Right: College Women on Mating and Dating Today.* A report conducted by the Institute for American Values for the Independent Women's Forum, New York, NY.

González-López, Gloria. 2005. *Erotic Journeys: Mexican Immigrants and Their Sex Lives.* Berkeley: University of California Press.

Laura Hamilton and Elizabeth A. Armstrong. 2009. "Gendered Sexuality in Emerging Adulthood: Double Binds and Flawed Options" *Gender & Society* 23(5): 589–616.

Hite, Shere. 1976. *The Hite Report: A Nationwide Study of Female Sexuality.* New York: Seven Stories Press.

Holland, Dorothy C., and Margaret A. Eisenhart. 1990. *Educated in Romance: Women, Achievement and College Culture.* Chicago: University of Chicago Press.

Kasic, Allison. 2008. "Take Back the Date." Independent Women's Forum. Available at http://www.iwf.org/campus/show/20122.html.

Kass, Leon R. 1997. "The End of Courtship." *Public Interest* 126: 39–63.

Laumann, Edward O., John H. Gagnon, Robert T. Michael, and Stuart Michaels. 1994. *The Social Organization of Sexuality: Sexual Practices in the United States.* Chicago: University of Chicago Press.

Mah, Kenneth, and Yitzchak M. Binik. 2001. "The Nature of Human Orgasm: A Critical Review of Major Trends." *Clinical Psychology Review* 21: 823–856.

Martin, Karin. 1996. *Puberty, Sexuality, and the Self: Boys and Girls at Adolescence.* New York: Routledge.

Paul, Elizabeth L., Brian McManus, and Elizabeth Hayes. 2000. "'Hookups': Characteristics and Correlates of College Students' Spontaneous and Anonymous Sexual Experiences." *Journal of Sex Research* 37: 76–88.

Popenoe, David, and Barbara Defoe Whitehead. 2000. *The State of Our Unions, 2000: The Social Health of Marriage in America.* New Brunswick, NJ: National Marriage Project.

Richters, Juliet, Richard de Vissar, Chris Rissel, and Anthony Smith. 2006. "Sexual Practices at Last Heterosexual Encounter and Occurrence of Orgasm in a National Survey." *Journal of Sex Research* 43: 217–226.

Schalet, Amy. 2004. "Must We Fear Adolescent Sexuality?" *Medscape General Medicine* 6: 44.

——. Forthcoming. "Subjectivity, Intimacy, and the Empowerment Paradigm of Adolescent Sexuality." *Feminist Studies.*

Schwartz, Pepper, and Virginia Rutter. 2000. *The Gender of Sexuality.* Lanham, MD: AltaMira Press.

Sessions Stepp, Laura. 2007. *Unhooked: How Young Women Pursue Sex, Delay Love, and Lose at Both.* New York: Riverhead Books.

Stombler, Mindy. 1994. "'Buddies' or 'Slutties': The Collective Sexual Reputation of Fraternity Little Sisters." *Gender & Society* 8: 297–323.

Tanenbaum, Leora. 1999. *Slut! Growing Up Female with a Bad Reputation.* New York: Seven Stories Press.

Tolman, Deborah L. 2002. *Dilemmas of Desire: Teenage Girls Talk about Sexuality.* Cambridge, MA: Harvard University Press.

Townsend, J. M. 1995. "Sex without Emotional Involvement: An Evolutionary Interpretation of Sex Differences." *Archives of Sexual Behavior* 24: 173–206.

Waite, Linda J., and Maggie Gallagher. 2000. *The Case for Marriage: Why Married People Are Happier, Healthier, and Better Off Financially.* New York: Doubleday.

Waite, Linda J., and Kara Joyner. 2001. "Emotional Satisfaction and Physical Pleasure in Sexual Unions: Time Horizon, Sexual Behavior, and Sexual Exclusivity." *Journal of Marriage and Family* 63: 247–264.

White, Emily. 2001. *Fast Girls: Teenage Tribes and the Myth of the Slut.* New York: Simon & Schuster.

Yancey Martin, Patricia, and Robert A. Hummer. 1989. "Fraternities and Rape on Campus." *Gender & Society* 3: 457–473.

CHAPTER 20: The Marriage Movement
by Orit Avishai, Melanie Heath, and Jennifer Randles

Boo, Katherine. 2003. "The Marriage Cure," *The New Yorker*, August 18.

Brotherson, Sean E., and William C. Duncan. 2004. "Rebinding the Ties That Bind: Government Efforts to Preserve and Promote Marriage." *Family Relations* 53: 459–468.

Cherlin, Andrew J. 2009. *The Marriage-Go-Round: The State of Marriage and Family in America Today.* New York: Knopf.

Conger, Rand D., Katherine J. Conger, and Monica J. Martin. 2010. "Socioeconomic Status, Family Processes, and Individual Development." *Journal of Marriage and Family* 72: 685–704.

Coontz, Stephanie. 2005. *Marriage, a History: From Obedience to Intimacy, or How Love Conquered Marriage.* New York: Viking Press.

Edin, Kathryn, and Maria Kefalas. 2005. *Promises I Can Keep: Why Poor Women Put Mother-hood before Marriage*. Berkeley: University of California Press.

Hawkins, Alan. J., and Tamara A. Fackrell. 2010. "Does Relationship and Marriage Educa-tion for Lower-Income Couples Work? A Meta-Analytic Study of Emerging Research." *Journal of Couple & Relationship Therapy: Innovations in Clinical and Educational Interventions* 9: 181–191.

Heath, Melanie. 2012. *One Marriage under God: The Campaign to Promote Marriage in America*. New York: New York University Press.

Hymowitz, Kay S. 2007. *Marriage and Caste in America: Separate and Unequal Families in a Post-Marital Age*. New York: Rowman & Littlefield.

Pew Research Center. 2010a. Social & Demographic Trends Report, "The Decline of Mar-riage and Rise of New Families." November 18. Available from http://www.pewsocial trends.org/2010/11/18/the-decline-of-marriage-and-rise-of-new-families/.

———. 2010b. Social & Demographic Trends Report, "The Reversal of the College Marriage." October 7. Available from http://www.pewsocialtrends.org/2010/10/07/the-reversal -of-the-college-marriage-gap/.

Plummer, Ken. 2003. *Intimate Citizenship: Private Decisions and Public Dialogues*. Seattle: University of Washington Press.

Randles, Jennifer. 2014. "Partnering and Parenting in Poverty: A Qualitative Analysis of a Relationship Skills Program for Low-Income Unmarried Families." *Journal of Policy Analysis and Management* 33(2): 385–412.

———. Forthcoming. *Legislating Love: Marriage Education, Politics, and Inequality in America*. New York: Columbia University Press.

Sager, Rebecca. 2010. *Faith, Politics, and Power: The Politics of Faith-Based Initiatives*. New York: Oxford University Press.

Waters, Rob. 2004. "The Citizen Therapist: Making a Difference—5 Therapists Who Dared to Take on the Wider World." *Psychotherapy Networker*, Nov/Dec: Cover story.

Wilcox, Brad. 2010. *The State of Our Unions*. Available from http://www.stateofourunions.org/

Wood, Robert. G., Quinn Moore, Andrew Clarkwest, Alexandra Killewald, and Shannon Monahan. 2012. "The Long-Term Effects of Building Strong Families: A Relationship Skills Education Program for Unmarried Parents," Executive Summary. OPRE Report 2012-28B. Washington, DC: Mathematica Policy Research and the Office of Planning, Research, and Evaluation, Administration of Children and Families.

CHAPTER 21: The Case for Divorce
by Virginia E. Rutter

Amato, Paul R., and Juliana M. Sobolewski. 2001. "The Effects of Divorce and Marital Discord on Adult Children's Psychological Well-Being." *American Sociological Review* 66: 900–921.

Ananat, E., and G. Michaels. 2008. "The Effect of Marital Breakup on the Income Distribu-tion of Women and Children." *Journal of Human Resources* 43(3): 611–629.

Becker, Howard S. 1973. *Outsiders: Studies in the Sociology of Deviance*. New York: Free Press.

Campbell, Jacquelyn C., ed. 1998. *Empowering Survivors of Abuse: Health Care for Battered Women and Their Children*. Thousand Oaks, CA: Sage Publications.

Cherlin, Andrew J., Frank F. Furstenberg Jr., P. Lindsay Chase-Lansdale, Kathleen E. Kiernan., Philip K. Robins., Donna Ruane Morrison, and Julien O. Teitler. 1991. "Longitudinal Studies of Effects of Divorce on Children in Great Britain and the United States." *Science* 252: 1386–1389.

Cherlin, Andrew J., P. Lindsay Chase-Lansdale, and Christine McRae. 1998. "Effects of Parental Divorce on Mental Health through the Life Course." *American Sociological Review* 63: 239–249.

Coltrane, Scott, and Michele Adams. 2003. "The Social Construction of the Divorce 'Problem': Morality, Child Victims, and the Politics of Gender." *Family Relations* 52: 363–372.

Coontz, Stephanie, and Nancy Folbre. 2002 (April). "Marriage, Poverty, and Public Policy." A Briefing Paper from the Council on Contemporary Families. Retrieved on June 24, 2008, from http://www.contemporaryfamilies.org/public/briefing.html.

Cowen, Tyler. 2007. "Matrimony Has Its Benefits, and Divorce Has a Lot to Do with That." *New York Times*, April 19. Retrieved on June 20, 2008, from http://www.nytimes.com /2007/04/19/business/19scene.html?_r=0.

Fomby, Paula, and Andrew Cherlin. 2007. "Family Instability and Child Well-Being." *American Sociological Review* 72(2): 181–204.

Gottman, J. M. 1994. *What Predicts Divorce?* Hillsdale, NJ: Lawrence Erlbaum Associates.

Greenberg, P. E., L. E. Stiglin, S. N. Finkelstein, and E. R. Berndt. 1993a. "Depression: A Neglected Major Illness." *Journal of Clinical Psychiatry* 54: 419–424.

———. 1993b. "The Economic Burden of Depression in 1990." *Journal of Clinical Psychiatry* 54: 405–418.

Hawkins, Daniel N., and Alan Booth. 2005. "Unhappily Ever After: Effects of Long-Term, Low-Quality Marriages on Well-Being." *Social Forces* 84(1): 451–471.

Hetherington, E. Mavis. 1999. "Should We Stay Together for the Sake of the Children?" In *Coping with Divorce, Single Parenting, and Remarriage: A Risk and Resiliency Perspective*, edited by E. Mavis Hetherington, 93–116. Mahwah, NJ: Lawrence Erlbaum Associates.

Hetherington, E. Mavis, and John Kelly. 2002. *For Better or For Worse: Divorce Reconsidered.* New York: W. W. Norton & Company.

Hetherington, E. Mavis, and P. Stanley-Hagan. 1997. "Divorce and the Adjustment of Children: A risk and resiliency perspective." *Journal of Child Psychology & Psychiatry* 40: 129–140.

Heuveline, P. 2005. "The Tricky Business of Estimating Divorce Rates." A Briefing Paper from the Council on Contemporary Families. Last modified October 6, 2006. Retrieved on June 24, 2008, from http://www.contemporaryfamilies.org/public/briefing.html.

Kiecolt-Glaser, J. K., S. Kennedy, S. Malkoff, L. Fisher, C. E. Speicher, and R. Glaser. 1988. "Marital Discord and Immunity in Males." *Psychosomatic Medicine* 50: 213–299.

Li, Jui-Chung Allen. 2007. "The Kids Are OK: Divorce and Children's Behavior Problems." RAND Labor and Population Working Paper No. WR-489. Santa Monica, CA: RAND.

———. 2008. "New Findings on an Old Question: Does Divorce Cause Children's Behavior Problems?" A Briefing Paper from the Council on Contemporary Families. Retrieved on June 24, 2008, from https://contemporaryfamilies.org/wp-content/uploads/2013/11/2007 _Briefing_Allen-Li_The-impact-of-divorce-on-children-behavior.pdf.

Meadows, S. O., S. McLanahan, and J. Brooks-Gunn. 2008. "Stability and Change in Family Structure and Maternal Health Trajectories." *American Sociological Review* 73(2): 314–334.

Mintz, Steven. 2004. *Huck's Raft: A History of American Childhood*. Cambridge, MA: Harvard University Press.

Osborne, C., and S. McLanahan. 2007. "Partnership Instability and Child Well-Being." *Journal of Marriage and Family* 69(4): 1065–1083.

Robles, T. F., and J. K. Kiekolt-Glaser. 2003. "The Physiology of Marriage: Pathways to Health." *Physiology and Behavior* 79(3): 409–416.

Ruggles, Steven. 1997. "The Rise of Divorce and Separation in the United States 1880–1990." *Demography* 34(4): 455–466.

Rutter, V. E. 2004 (August). "The Case for Divorce: Under What Conditions Is Divorce Beneficial and for Whom?" Ph.D. dissertation, Department of Sociology, University of Washington.

Scafidi, B. 2008. *The Taxpayer Costs of Divorce: First-Ever Estimates for the Nation and All Fifty States*. New York: Institute for American Values.

Smock, Pamela J., Wendy D. Manning, and Sanjiv Gupta. 1999. "The Effect of Marriage and Divorce on Women's Economic Well-Being." *American Sociological Review* 64: 794–812.

Stevenson, B., and J. Wolfers. 2006. "Bargaining in the Shadow of Divorce Laws and Family Distress." *Quarterly Journal of Economics* 121(1): 267–288.

van Hemert, Dianne A., F. J. R. van de Vijver, and Ype H. Poortinga. 2002. "The Beck Depression Inventory as a Measure of Subjective Well-Being: A Cross-National Study." *Journal of Happiness Studies* 3(3): 257–286.

Veenhoven, Ruut. 2004. *World Database of Happiness: Continuous Register of Scientific Research on Subjective Appreciation of Life*. Rotterdam, The Netherlands: Erasmus University. Available from http://www.isqols2009.istitutodeglinnocenti.it/Content_en /Veenhoven_WDH-Prospectus_2009.pdf.

Waite, Linda J., Don Browning, William J. Doherty, Maggie Gallagher, Ye Luo, and Scott M. Stanley. 2002. *Does Divorce Make People Happy? Findings from a Study of Unhappy Marriages*. New York: Institute for American Values.

Wallerstein, J., and Sandra Blakeslee. 1988. *Second Chances: Men, Women, and Children a Decade after Divorce: Who Wins, Who Loses, and Why*. New York: Ticknor & Fields.

Weissman, M. M. 1987. "Advances in Psychiatric Epidemiology: Rates and Risks for Major Depression." *American Journal of Public Health* 77: 445–451.

Whisman, Mark A. 1999. "Marital Dissatisfaction and Psychiatric Disorders: Results from the National Comorbidity Survey." *Journal of Abnormal Psychology* 108: 701–706.

CHAPTER 22: Stepfamilies as They Really Are: Neither Cinderella nor the Brady Bunch
by Marilyn Coleman and Lawrence Ganong

Bohannon, P. 1984. "Stepparenthood: A New and Old Experience." In *Parenthood: A Psychodynamic Interpretation*, edited by R. S. Cohen, B. J. Cohler, and S. H. Weissman, 204–219. New York: Guilford Press.

Cherlin, A. 1978. "Remarriage as an Incomplete Institution." *American Journal of Sociology* 84: 634–650.

Daly, M., and M. Wilson. 1998. *The Truth about Cinderella: A Darwinian View of Parental Love*. New Haven, CT: Yale University Press.

Ganong, L., and M. Coleman. 2004. *Stepfamily Relationships: Development, Dynamics, and Intervention.* New York: Springer.

Ganong, L., M. Coleman, and T. Jamison. 2011. "Patterns of Stepchild-Stepparent Relationship Development." *Journal of Marriage and Family* 73: 396–413.

Papernow, P. 1987. "Thickening the Middle Ground: Dilemmas and Vulnerabilities of Remarried Couples." *Psychotherapy: Theory, Research, Practice, Training* 24: 630–639.

Pew Research Social and Demographic Trends. 2011. *A Portrait of Stepfamilies.* Available from http://www.pewsocialtrends.org/2011/01/13/a-portrait-of-stepfamilies/.

Stacey, J. 1998. *Brave New Families: Stories of Domestic Upheaval in Late-Twentieth-Century America.* Berkeley, CA: University of California Press.

CHAPTER 23: Beyond Family Structure: Family Process Studies Help to Reframe Debates about What's Good for Children
by Philip A. Cowan and Carolyn Pape Cowan

Ahrons, C. R. 2004. *We're Still Family: What Grown Children Have to Say about Their Parents' Divorce.* New York: HarperCollins.

Amato, P. R. 2000. "The Consequences of Divorce for Adults and Children." *Journal of Marriage and the Family* 62(4): 1269–1287.

———. 2001. "Children of Divorce in the 1990s: An Update of the Amato and Keith (1991) Meta-analysis." *Journal of Family Psychology* 15(3): 355–370.

Baumrind, D. 1980. "New Directions in Socialization Research." *American Psychologist* 35(7): 639–652.

Belsky, J., and N. Barends. 2002. *Personality and Parenting.* Mahwah, NJ: Lawrence Erlbaum Associates.

Blankenhorn, D. 1995. *Fatherless America: Confronting Our Most Urgent Social Problem.* New York: Basic Books.

Blankenhorn, D. G., S. Bayme, and J. B. Elshtain, eds. 1990. *Rebuilding the Nest: A New Commitment to the American Family.* Milwaukee, WI: Family Service America.

Brazelton, T. B., and J. D. Sparrow. 2001. *Touchpoints: Birth to Three.* Cambridge, MA: Perseus Books.

Bronfenbrenner, U., and S. J. Ceci. 1994. "Nature-Nurture in Developmental Perspective: A Bioecological Theory." *Psychological Review* 101: 568–586.

Caspi, A., and G. H. J. Elder. 1988. "Emergent Family Patterns: The Intergenerational Construction of Problem Behaviour and Relationships." In *Relationships within Families: Mutual Influences,* edited by R. A. Hinde and J. Stevenson-Hinde, 218–240. Oxford, UK: Clarendon Press.

Cherlin, A. J. 2005. "American Marriage in the Early Twenty-First Century." *The Future of Children* 15(2): 33–55.

Cicchetti, D., S. L. Toth, and A. Maughan. 2000. "An Ecological-Transactional Model of Child Maltreatment." In *Handbook of Developmental Psychopathology,* 2nd ed., edited by A. J. Sameroff, M. Lewis, and S. M. Miller, 689–722. New York: Kluwer Academic/ Plenum Publishers.

Conger, R. D., G. H. Elder Jr., F. O. Lorenz, R. L. Simons, and L. B. Whitbeck, eds. 1994. *Families in Troubled Times: Adapting to Change in Rural America.* New York: Aldine de Gruyter.

Cowan, C. P. and P. A. Cowan. 1995. "Interventions to Ease the Transition to Parenthood: Why They are Needed and What They Can Do." *Family Relations: Journal of Applied Family & Child Studies* 44(4): 412–423.

——Cowan, C. P., and P. A. Cowan. 2000. *When Partners Become Parents: The Big Life Change for Couples.* Mahwah, NJ: Lawrence Erlbaum Associates.

Cowan, C. P., P. A. Cowan, M. K. Pruett, and K. Pruett. 2007. "An Approach to Preventing Coparenting Conflict and Divorce in Low-Income Families: Strengthening Couple Relationships and Fostering Fathers' Involvement." *Family Process* 46(1): 109–121.

Cowan, P. A., and C. P. Cowan. 2002. "Interventions as Tests of Family Systems Theories: Marital and Family Relationships in Children's Development, and Psychopathology." *Development and Psychopathology*, Special Issue on Interventions as Tests of Theories, 14: 731–760.

——. 2006. "Developmental Psychopathology from a Family Systems and Family Risk Factors Perspective: Implications for Family Research, Practice, and Policy." In *Developmental Psychopathology*, edited by D. Cicchetti and D. J. Cohen, 530–587. Hoboken, NJ: John Wiley & Sons.

Cowan, P. A., C. P. Cowan, J. Ablow, V. K. Johnson, and J. Measelle, eds. 2005. *The Family Context of Parenting in Children's Adaptation to Elementary School.* Mahwah, NJ: Lawrence Erlbaum Associates.

Cowan, P. A., C. P. Cowan, N. Cohen, M. K. Pruett, and K. Pruett. 2008. "Supporting Fathers' Engagement with Their Kids." In *Raising Children: Emerging Needs, Modern Risks, and Social Responses*, edited by J. D. Berrick and N. Gilbert, 44–80. New York: Oxford University Press.

Cowan, P. A., C. P. Cowan, and G. Heming. 2005. "Five-Domain Models: Putting It All Together." In *The Family Context of Parenting in Children's Adaptation to Elementary School*, edited by P. A. Cowan, C. P. Cowan, J. Ablow, V. K. Johnson, and J. Measelle. Mahwah, NJ: Lawrence Erlbaum Associates.

Cowan, P. A., D. Powell, and C. P. Cowan. 1998. "Parenting Interventions: A Family Systems Perspective." In *Handbook of Child Psychology*, edited by W. Damon, 3–72. New York: John Wiley & Sons.

Cowan, P. A., C. P. Cowan, M. Pruett, K. Pruett, and P. Gillette. 2014. "Evaluating a Couples Group to Enhance Father Involvement in Low-Income Families Using a Benchmark Comparison." *Family Relations* 63(3): 356–370.

Cui, M., and R. Conger. 2008. "Parenting Behavior as Mediator and Moderator of the Association between Marital Problems and Adolescent Maladjustment." *Journal of Research on Adolescence* 18(2): 261–284.

Cummings, E. M., P. Davies, and S. B. Campbell. 2000. *Developmental Psychopathology and Family Process: Theory, Research, and Clinical Implications.* New York: Guilford Press.

Dadds, M. R., S. Schwartz, and M. R. Sanders. 1987. "Marital Discord and Treatment Outcome in Behavioral Treatment of Child Conduct Disorders." *Journal of Consulting & Clinical Psychology* 55(3): 396–403.

Davies, P. T., E. M. Cummings, and M. A. Winter. 2004. "Pathways between Profiles of Family Functioning, Child Security in the Interparental Subsystem, and Child Psychological Problems." *Development and Psychopathology* 16(3): 525–550.

M. R., S. A. Avellar, H. H. Zaveri, and A. M. Hershey. 2006. *Implementing Healthy Marriage Programs for Unmarried Couples with Children: Early Lessons from the Building Strong Families Project.* Washington, DC: Mathematica.

Durlak, J. A., and A. M. Wells. 1997. "Primary Prevention Mental Health Programs for Children and Adolescents: A Meta-analytic Review." *American Journal of Community Psychology* 25(2): 115–152.

Edin, K., and M. Kefalas. 2005. *Promises I Can Keep: Why Poor Women Put Motherhood before Marriage.* Berkeley: University of California Press.

Faber, A., and E. Mazlish. 1995. *How to Talk So Your Kids Will Listen.* New York: Simon & Schuster/Fireside Books.

Fagan, P. F., R. W. Patterson, and R. E. Rector. 2002. "Marriage and Welfare Reform: The Overwhelming Evidence that Marriage Education Works." Backgrounder #1606. Washington, DC: Heritage Foundation.

Harknett, K., L. Hardman, I. Garfinkel, and S. S. McLanahan. 2001. "The Fragile Families Study: Social Policies and Labor Markets in Seven Cities." *Children & Youth Services Review* 23(6–7): 537–555.

Haskins, R., and I. Sawhill. 2003. *Work and Marriage: The Way to End Poverty and Welfare.* Washington, DC: Brookings.

Hawkins, A. J., S. M. Stanley, P. A. Cowan, F. D. Fincham, S. R. H. Beach, C. P. Cowan, and A. P. Daire. 2013. "A More Optimistic Perspective on Government-Supported Marriage and Relationship Education Programs for Lower Income Couples." *American Psychologist* 68(2): 110–111.

Hetherington, E. M., and J. Kelly. 2002. *For Better or for Worse: Divorce Reconsidered.* New York: W. W. Norton & Company.

Johnson, M. D. 2012. "Healthy Marriage Initiatives: On the Need for Empiricism in Policy Implementation." *American Psychologist* 67(4): 296–308.

Lamb, M. E. 2000. "The History of Research on Father Involvement: An Overview." *Marriage & Family Review* 29(2–3): 23–42.

Luchetti, V. I. 1999. "Perceptions of Fatherhood in Parenting Manuals: A Rhetorical Analysis." Ph.D. dissertation, University of the Pacific, Stockton, CA.

Lundquist, E., J. Hsueh, A. Lowenstein, K. Faucetta, D. Gubits, C. Michalopoulos, and V. Knox. 2014. "A Family-Strengthening Program for Low-Income Families: Final Impacts from the Supporting Healthy Marriage Evaluation." *OPRE Report 2013-49A.* Washington, DC: Office of Planning, Research and Evaluation, Administration for Children and Families, U.S. Department of Health and Human Services.

Marquardt, E. 2005. *Between Two Worlds: The Inner Lives of Children of Divorce.* New York: Crown Publishers.

McLanahan, S. S., I. Garfinkel, J. Brooks-Gunn, H. Zhao, W. Johnson, L. Rich, et al. 1998. *Unwed Fathers and Fragile Families.* Princeton, NJ: Center for Research on Child Wellbeing.

McLoyd, V. C. 1990. "The Impact of Economic Hardship on Black Families and Children: Psychological Distress, Parenting, and Socioemotional Development." *Child Development* 61(2): 311–346.

Mincy, R. B., and A. T. Dupree. 2001. "Welfare, Child Support and Family Formation." *Children & Youth Services Review* 23(6–7): 577–601.

Mincy, R., and H. Pouncy. 2002. "The Responsible Fatherhood Field: Evolution and Goals." In *Handbook of Father Involvement: Multidisciplinary Perspectives,* edited by C. S. Tamis-LeMonda and N. J. Cabrera, 555–597. Mahwah, NJ: Lawrence Erlbaum Associates.

Mistry, R. S., E. A. Vandewater, A. C. Huston, and V. C. McLoyd. 2002. "Economic Well-Being and Children's Social Adjustment: The Role of Family Process in an Ethnically Diverse Low-Income Sample." *Child Development* 73(3): 935–951.

Moore, K. A., S. Jekielek, and C. Emig. 2002. *Marriage from a Child's Perspective: How Does Family Structure Affect Children, and What Can We Do about It?* Washington, DC: Child Trends.

Parke, R. D. 1996. *Fatherhood*. Cambridge, MA: Harvard University Press.

Plomin, R. 2003. *Behavioral Genetics in the Postgenomic Era*. Washington, DC: American Psychological Association.

Popenoe, D. 1996. *Life without Father: Compelling New Evidence that Fatherhood and Marriage Are Indispensable for the Good of Children and Society*. New York: Martin Kessler Books.

Powell, D. A. 2006. "Families and Early Childhood Interventions." In *Handbook of Child Psychology* (vol. 4, 6th ed.), edited by W. Damon, R. M. Lerner, K. Renninger and I. E. Sigel, 548–591. Hoboken, NJ: John Wiley & Sons.

Pruett, K. D. 2000. *Fatherneed: Why Father Care Is as Essential as Mother Care for Your Child*. New York: Free Press.

Pruett, M. K., and R. K. Barker. 2009. "Effectively Intervening with Divorcing Parents and Their Children: What Works and How It Works." In *Strengthening Couple Relationships for Optimal Child Development*, edited by M. S. Schulz, M. K. Pruett, P. K. Kerig, and R. D. Parke. Washington, DC: APA Books.

Rodgers, B., and J. Pryor. 1998. *The Development of Children from Separated Families: A Review of Research from the United Kingdom*. York, UK: Joseph Rowntree Foundation.

Seifer, R., and S. Dickstein. 2000. "Parental Mental Illness and Infant Development." In *Handbook of Infant Mental Health* (2nd ed.), edited by C. H. Zoanah Jr., 145–160. New York: Guilford Press.

Silverstein, L. B., and C. F. Auerbach. 1999. "Deconstructing the Essential Father." *American Psychologist* 54(6): 397–407.

Stacey, J., and T. J. Biblarz. 2001. "(How) Does the Sexual Orientation of Parents Matter?" *American Sociological Review* 66(2): 159–183.

Tamis-LeMonda, C. S., and N. Cabrera, eds.. 2002. *Handbook of Father Involvement: Multidisciplinary Perspectives*. Mahwah, NJ: Lawrence Erlbaum Associates.

Tully, L. A., L. Arseneault, A. Caspi, T. E. Moffitt, and J. Morgan. 2004. "Does Maternal Warmth Moderate the Effects of Birth Weight on Twins' Attention-Deficit/Hyperactivity Disorder (ADHD) Symptoms and Low IQ?" *Journal of Consulting & Clinical Psychology* 72(2): 218–226.

Twenge, J. M., W. K. Campbell, and C. A. Foster. 2003. "Parenthood and Marital Satisfaction: A Meta-Analytic Review." *Journal of Marriage and Family* 65(3): 574–583.

Waite, L. J., and M. Gallagher. 2000. *The Case for Marriage: Why Married People Are Happier, Healthier, and Better Off Financially*. New York: Doubleday.

Wallerstein, J. S., J. Lewis, and S. Blakeslee. 2000. *The Unexpected Legacy of Divorce: A 25 Year Landmark Study*. New York: Hyperion.

Wood, R. G., S. McConnell, M. Quinn, A. Clarkwest, and J. Hsueh. 2010. *Strengthening Unmarried Parents' Relationships: The Early Impacts of Building Strong Families*. Washington DC: Mathematic Policy Research, Inc.

CHAPTER 24: Parenting Adult Children in the Twenty-First Century
by Joshua Coleman

Ahrons, C. 2004. *We're Still Family*. New York: HarperCollins.

Ahrons, C., and J. L. Tanner. 2003. "Adult Children and Their Fathers: Relationship Changes 20 Years after Parental Divorce." *Family Relations* 52: 340–351.

Amato, Paul R., and Alan Booth. 1997. *A Generation at Risk*. Cambridge, MA: Harvard University Press.

Amato, Paul, and Julie Sobolewski. 2004. "The Effects of Divorce on Fathers and Children: Nonresidential Fathers and Stepfathers." In *The Role of the Father in Child Development* (4th ed.), edited by Michael Lamb, 341–367. New York: John Wiley & Sons.

Bateson, Gregory. 1980. *Steps to an Ecology of Mind*. New York: Ballantine.

Baum, N. 2006. "Postdivorce Paternal Disengagement." *Journal of Marriage and Family Therapy* 32: 245–254.

Bettelheim, Bruno. 1967. *The Empty Fortress: Infantile Autism and the Birth of the Self*. New York: Free Press.

Bianchi, Suzanne, John Robinson, and Melissa Milke. 2006. *Changing Rhythms of American Family Life*. New York: Russell Sage Foundation.

Coleman, Joshua. 2003. *The Lazy Husband: How to Get Men to Do More Parenting and Housework*. New York: St. Martin's Press.

———. 2007. *When Parents Hurt: Compassionate Strategies When You and Your Grown Child Don't Get Along*. New York: HarperCollins.

Coltrane, Scott. 1996. *Family Man: Fatherhood, Housework, and Gender Equity*. New York: Oxford University Press.

Coontz, Stephanie. 1997. *The Way We Really Are: Coming to Terms with America's Changing Families*. New York: Basic Books.

———. 2006. "How to Stay Married." *Times of London*, November 30.

———. 2008. *American Families: A Multicultural Reader*, 2nd ed. New York: Routledge.

Danziger, S., and P. Gottschalk. 2005. "Diverging Fortunes: Trends in Poverty and Inequality." In *The American People: Census 2000 Series*, edited by R. Farley. New York: Russell Sage Foundation and Population Reference Bureau.

Dunn, J., and R. Plomin. 1990. *Separate Lives: Why Siblings Are So Different*. New York: Basic Books.

Ehrensaft, Diane. 1997. *Spoiling Childhood: How Well-Meaning Parents Are Giving Children Too Much—But Not What They Need*. New York: Guilford Press.

Flanagan, Constance. 2006. "The Changing Social Contract at the Transition to Adulthood: Implications for Individuals and the Polity." In *Social and Political Change in Adolescent Development*, edited by R. Silbereisen. Invited paper symposium for the biennial meetings of the Society for Research on Adolescence, San Francisco, CA.

Freud, Sigmund. 1926. "Inhibitions, Symptoms, and Anxiety." In the *Standard Edition of the Complete Psychological Works*, vol. 20, 77–175. London: Hogarth Press.

Harris, Judith Rich. 1999. *The Nurture Assumption: Why Children Turn Out the Way They Do*. New York: Touchstone.

Hetherington, E. Mavis, and John Kelly. 2002. *For Better or Worse: Divorce Reconsidered*. New York: W. W. Norton & Company.

Knoester, Chris. 2003. "Transitions in Young Adulthood and the Relationships between Parent and Offspring Well-Being." *Social Forces* 81: 1431–1458.

Lacar, Marvi. 2006. "The Bank of Mom and Dad." *New York Times*, April 9.

Lareau, Annette, 2003. *Unequal Childhoods: Class, Race, and Family Life*. Berkeley: University of California Press.

Lin, I-Fen. 2008. "Consequences of Parental Divorce for Adult Children's Support of Their Frail Parents." *Journal of Marriage and Family* 70: 113–128.

Marano, H. E. 2004. "A Nation of Wimps." *Psychology Today*, November/December.

Mintz, Steven. 2004. *Huck's Raft: A History of American Childhood*. Cambridge, MA: Harvard University Press.

———. 2006. "How We All Became Jewish Mothers." *National Post*, February 17.

"Most Americans Falling for 'Get Rich Slowly Over a Lifetime of Hard Work' Schemes." 2005. *The Onion* 41(49), December 7.

Nielsen, L. 2004. *Embracing Your Father: How to Build the Relationship You've Always Wanted with Your Dad*. New York: McGraw-Hill.

Pew Research Center. 2006. *Adult Children and Parents Talking More Often*. February 23.

Putnam, Robert D. 2000. *Bowling Alone: The Collapse and Revival of American Community*. New York: Simon & Schuster.

Reiss, David, Jenae M. Neiderhiser, E. Mavis Hetherington, and Robert Plomin. 2000. *The Relationship Code: Deciphering Genetic and Social Influences on Adolescent Development*. Cambridge, MA: Harvard University Press.

Schwartz, Barry. 2004. *The Paradox of Choice: Why More Is Less*. New York: Harper Perennial.

Seligman, M. E. P. 1996. *The Optimistic Child: Proven Program to Safeguard Children from Depression and Build Lifelong Resilience*. New York: Houghton Mifflin.

Stearns, Peter N. 2003. *Anxious Parents: A History of Modern Childrearing in America*. New York: New York University Press.

Sullivan, Oriel, and Scott Coltrane. 2008. "Men's Changing Contribution to Housework and Child-Care." Discussion paper prepared for the Council on Contemporary Families, Chicago, IL.

Zelizer, Virgina, A. 1994. *Pricing the Priceless Child: The Changing Social Value of Children*. Princeton, NJ: Princeton University Press.

CHAPTER 25: "This Is Your Job Now": Latina Mothers and Daughters and Family Work
by Lorena Garcia

Ayala, Jennifer. 2006. "Confianza, Consejos, and Contradictions: Gender and Sexuality Lessons between Latina Adolescent Daughters and Mothers." In *Latina Girls: Voices of Adolescent Strength in the United States*, edited by Jill Denner and Bianca L. Guzmán, 29–43. New York and London: New York University Press.

Berridge, Clara W., and Jennifer L. Romich. 2010. "Raising Him to Pull His Own Weight." *Journal of Family Issues* 32: 157–180.

Cantú, Lionel. 2000. "Entre Hombres/Between Men: Latino Masculinities and Homosexualities." In *Gay Masculinities*, edited by Peter Nardi, 224–246. Thousand Oaks, CA: Sage Publications.

Carrillo, Héctor. 2002. *The Night Is Young: Sexuality in Mexico in the Time of AIDS*. Chicago: University of Chicago Press.

Carrington, Christopher. 1999. *No Place Like Home: Relationships and Family Life among Lesbians and Gay Men*. Chicago: University of Chicago Press.

Chafetz, Janet Saltzman. 1990. *Gender Equity: An Integrated Theory of Stability and Change.* Newbury Park, CA: Sage Publications.

Coltrane, S. 2000. "Research on Household Labor: Modeling and Measuring the Social Embeddedness of Routine Family Work." *Journal of Marriage and Family* 62: 1208–1233.

Collins. Patricia H. 1987. "The Meaning of Motherhood in Black Culture and Black Mother-Daughter Relationships." *Sage: A Scholarly Journal on Black Women* 4: 3–10.

Collins, Patricia Hill. 1994. "Shifting the Center: Race, Class, and Feminist Theorizing about Motherhood." In *Mothering: Ideology, Experience, and Agency,* edited by Evelyn Nakano Glenn, Grace Chang, and Linda Rennie Forcey, 45–66. New York: Routledge.

Deutsch, Francine. 2007. "Undoing Gender." *Gender & Society* 21(1): 106–127.

Dill, Bonnie Thornton. 1988. "Our Mother's Grief: Racial-Ethnic Women and the Maintenance of Families." *Journal of Family History* 13: 415–431.

Dreby, Joanne. 2010. *Divided by Borders: Mexican Migrants and their Children.* Berkeley: University of California Press.

Erickson, Rebecca J. 1993. "Reconceptualizing Family Work: The Effect of Emotion Work on Perceptions of Marital Quality." *Journal of Marriage and Family* 55(4): 888–900.

Erickson, Rebecca J. 2005. "Why Emotion Work Matters: Sex, Gender, and the Division of Household Labor." *Journal of Marriage and Family* 67(2): 337–351.

Fine, Michelle, Lois Weis, and Rosemary Roberts. 2000. "Refusing the Betrayal: Latinas Redefining Gender, Sexuality, Culture, and Resistance." *Education/Pedagogy/Cultural Studies* 22: 87–119.

Garcia, Lorena. 2012. *Respect Yourself, Protect Yourself: Latina Girls and Sexual Identity.* New York: New York University Press.

George, Sheba. 2005. *When Women Come First: Gender and Class in Transnational Migration.* Berkeley: University of California Press.

Gerson, Kathleen. 2010. *The Unfinished Revolution: How a Generation Is Reshaping Family, Work and Gender in America.* Oxford: Oxford University Press.

Glenn, Evelyn Nakano. 1994. "Social Constructions of Mothering: A Thematic Overview." In *Mothering: Ideology, Experience, and Agency,* edited by Evelyn Nakano Glenn, Grace Chang, and Linda Rennie Forcey, 1–32. New York: Routledge.

González-López, Gloria, and Salvador Vidal-Ortiz. 2008. "Latinas and Latinos, Sexuality, and Society: A Critical Sociological Perspective." In *Latinas/os in the United States: Changing the Face of America,* edited by Havidán Rodríguez, Rogelio Sáenz, and Cecilia Menjívar, 308–322. New York: Springer.

Hill, Shirley A. 1999. *African American Children: Socialization and Development in Families.* Thousand Oaks, CA: Sage Publications.

Hochschild, Arlie R. 1983. *The Managed Heart: Commercialization of Human Feeling.* Berkeley: University of California Press.

——. 1989. With Anne Machung. *The Second Shift: Working Parents and the Revolution at Home.* New York: Viking.

Hondagneu-Sotelo, Pierrette. 1994. *Gendered Transitions: Mexican Experiences of Immigration.* Berkeley: University of California Press.

——. 1997. "'I'm Here, But I'm There': The Meanings of Latina Transnational Motherhood." *Gender & Society* 11(5): 548–571.

Hurtado, Aida. 2003. *Voicing Chicana Feminisms: Young Women Speak Out on Sexuality and Identity*. New York: New York University Press.

Kane, Emily W. 2006. "'No Way My Boys Are Gonna Be Like That!' Parents' Responses of Children's Gender Nonconformity." *Gender & Society* 20(2): 149–176.

Lamont, Michèle. 2002. "Culture and Identity." In *Handbook of Sociological Theory*, edited by Jonathan H. Turner, 171–185. New York: Kluwer Academic/Plenum Publishers.

Lopez, Nancy. 2003. *Hopeful Girls, Troubled Boys: Race and Gender Disparity in Urban Education*. New York: Routledge.

Lorber, Judith. 2005. *Breaking the Bowls: Degendering and Feminist Change*. New York: W. W. Norton & Company.

Moore, Mignon. 2011. *Invisible Families: Gay Identities, Relationships and Motherhood among Black Women*. Berkeley: University of California Press.

Nelson, Fiona. 1996. *Lesbian Motherhood: An Exploration of Canadian Lesbian Families*. Toronto: University of Toronto Press.

Penha-Lopes, Vania. 2006. "'To Cook, Sew, to Be a Man': The Socialization for Competence and Black Men's Involvement in Housework." *Sex Roles* 54(3/4): 261–274.

Ridgeway, Cecilia. 2011. *Framed by Gender: How Gender Inequality Persists in the Modern World*. New York: Oxford University Press.

Risman, Barbara J. 1998. *Gender Vertigo: American Families in Transition*. New Haven, CT: Yale University Press.

Segura, Denise A. 1994. "Working at Motherhood: Chicana and Mexican Immigrant Mothers and Employment." In *Mothering: Ideology, Experience, and Agency*, edited by Evelyn Nakana Glenn, Grace Chang, and Linda Rennie Forcey, 211–233. New York: Routledge.

Segura, Denise A., and Jennifer Pierce. 1993. "Chicana/o Family Structure and Gender Personality: Chodorow, Familism, and Psychoanalytic Sociology Revisited." *Signs: Journal of Women in Culture and Society* 12(1): 62–91.

Shelton, B. A. 1992. *Women, Men and Time: Gender Differences in Paid Work, Housework, and Leisure*. Westport, CT: Greenwood.

Souza, Caridad. 2002. *Sexual Identities of Young Puerto Rican Mothers*. Dialogo 6 (Winter/Spring): 33–39.

Sullivan, Maureen. 2004. *The Family of Woman: Lesbian Mothers, Their Children, and the Undoing of Gender*. Berkeley: University of California Press.

Sullivan, O. 2006. *Gender Relations, Changing Families: Tracing the Pace of Change Over Time*. Lanham, MD: Rowman & Littlefield.

Swidler, Ann. 2001. *Talk of Love: How Culture Matters*. Chicago: University of Chicago Press.

Villeñas, Sofia, and Melissa Moreno. 2001. "To *valerse por si misma* between Race, Capitalism, and Patriarchy: Latina Mother-Daughter Pedagogies in North Carolina." *International Journal of Qualitative Studies in Education* 14: 671–687.

West, Candace, and Don H. Zimmerman. 1987. "Doing Gender." *Gender & Society* 1(2): 125–151.

Young, Alford A. Jr. 2004. *The Minds of Marginalized Black Men: Making Sense of Mobility, Opportunity, and Future Life Chances*. Princeton, NJ: Princeton University Press.

CHAPTER 26: Adoptive Parents Raising *Neoethnics*
by Pamela Anne Quiroz

Brian, Kristi. 2012. *Reframing Transracial Adoption: Adopted Koreans, White Parents, and the Politics of Kinship*. Philadelphia: Temple University Press.

Briggs, L. 2006. "Making 'American' Families: Transnational Adoption and U.S. Latin America Policy." In *Haunted by Empire: Geographies of Intimacy in North American History*, edited by Ann Laura Stoler, 606–644. Durham, NC: Duke University Press.

Cardello, Andrea. 2009. "The Movement of the Mother of the Courthouse Square: Legal Child Trafficking, Adoption and Poverty in Brazil." *Journal of Latin American and Caribbean Anthropology* 14(1): 140–161.

Dorow, Sarah. 2006. *Transnational Adoption: A Cultural Economy of Race, Gender and Kinship*. New York: New York University Press.

Fonseca, Claudia. 2002. "The Politics of Adoption: Child Rights in the Brazilian Setting." *Law & Policy* 24(3): 199–227.

———. 2006. "Traditional Influences in the Social Production of Adoptable Children: The Case of Brazil." *International Journal of Sociology and Social Policy* 26(3/4): 154–171.

Gailey, Christine. 2009. *Blue Ribbon Babies and Labors of Love: Race, Class, and Gender in U.S. Adoption Practice*. Austin: University of Texas Press.

Hearst, Alice. 2010. "Between Restavek and Relocation: Children and Communities in Transnational Adoption." *Journal of History of Childhood and Youth* 3(2): 273–292.

Hine, Christine. 2000. *Virtual Ethnography*. Thousand Oaks, CA: Sage Publications.

Hubinette, Tobias. 2012. "Post-racial Utopianism, White Color-blindness, and the Elephant in the Room: Racial Issues for Transnational Adoptees of Color." In *Intercountry Adoption: Policies, Practices, and Outcomes*, edited by Judith L. Gibbons and Karen Smith Rotabi, 221–229. Burlington, VT: Ashgate Publishing.

Jacobsen, Heather. 2008. *Culture Keeping*. Nashville, TN: Vanderbilt University Press.

Kim, Jodi. 2009. "An Orphan with Two Mothers: Transnational and Transracial Adoption, the Cold War, and Contemporary Asian American Cultural Politics." *American Quarterly* 61(4): 855–877.

Kim, Oh Myo, Reed Reichwald, and Richard Lee. 2013. "Cultural Socialization in Families with Adopted Korean Adolescents: A Mixed-Method, Multi-Informant Study." *Journal of Adolescent Research* 28(1): 69–95.

Kubo, Kazuyo. 2010. "Desirable Difference: The Shadow of Racial Stereotypes in Creating Transracial Families through Transnational Adoption." *Sociology Compass* 4(4): 263–282.

Lee, Richard M., A. Bora Yun, H. Choi Yoog, and K. Park Nelson. 2010. "Comparing the Ethnic Identity and Well-Being of Adopted Korean Americans with Immigrant/U.S.-born Korean Americans and Korean International Students." *Adoption Quarterly* 13(1): 2–17.

Leifson, Esben. 2008. "Child Trafficking and Formalization: The Case of International Adoption from Ecuador." *Children & Society* 22: 212–222.

McGinnis, H., S. Livingston Smith, S. D. Ryan, and J. A. Howard. 2009. *Beyond Culture Camp: Promoting Healthy Identity Formation in Adoption*. New York: Evan B. Donaldson Adoption Institute.

Meier, Patricia, and Xiaole Zhang. 2008. "Sold into Adoption: The Hunan Baby Trafficking Scandal Exposes Vulnerabilities in Chinese Adoptions to the United States." *Cumberland Law Review* 39(1): 87–130.

Ortiz, Ana Teresa, and Laura Briggs. 2003. "The Culture of Poverty, Crack Babies, and Welfare Cheats: The Making of the 'Healthy White Baby Crisis.'" *Social Text* 21(3): 39–57.

Palmer, John. 2011. *The Dance of Identities: Korean Adoptees and Their Journey toward Empowerment.* Honolulu: University of Hawaii Press.

Pew Internet and American Life Project. 2006. *Internet Evolution: Internet Penetration and Impact.* Report 202-419-4500 (April 26). Available from http://www.pewinternet.org.

———. 2008. *How Women and Men Use the Internet.* Report 202-419-4500 (April 11). Available from http://www.pewinternet.org.

Quiroz, Pamela Anne. 2012. "Cultural Tourism in Transnational Adoption: Staged Authenticity and Its Implications for Adopted Children." *Journal of Family Issues* 33(4): 527–555.

Race Forward: The Center for Racial Justice Innovation. 2011. "Shattered Families: The Perilous Intersection of Immigration Enforcement and the Child Welfare System. Available from https://www.raceforward.org/research/reports/shattered-families.

Rotabi, Karen S., Joan Pennell, Jini L. Roby, and Kelley McCreery Bunkers. 2012. "Family Group Conferencing as a Culturally Adaptable Intervention: Reforming Intercountry Adoption in Guatemala." *International Social Work* 55(3): 402–416.

Samuels, Gina. 2009. "Being Raised by White People: Navigating Racial Difference among Adopted Multiracial Adults." *Journal of Marriage and Family* 71: 80–94.

Selman, Peter. 2012. "The Rise and Fall of Intercountry Adoption in the 21st Century: Global Trends from 2001 to 2010." *International Social Work* 52(5): 575–594.

Shiao, J. L., Mia Tuan, and Elizabeth Rienzi. 2004. "Shifting the Spotlight: Exploring Race and Culture in Korean-White Adoptive Families." *Race and Society* 7: 1–16.

Simon, Rita, and Rhonda M. Roorda. 2007. *In Their Parents' Voices: Reflections on Raising Transracial Adoptees.* New York: Columbia University Press.

Smerdon, Usha R. 2008. "Crossing Bodies, Crossing Borders: International Surrogacy between the United States and India." *Cumberland Law Review* 39(1): 1–85.

Smolin, David. 2004. "Intercountry Adoption as Child Trafficking." *Valparaiso University Law Review* 39(2): 281–325.

———. 2005. "Child Laundering: How the Intercountry Adoption System Legitimizes and Incentivizes the Practices of Buying, Trafficking, Kidnapping, and Stealing Children." *Legal Repository.* Retrieved on December 5, 2006, from http://law.bepress.com/expresso/eps/749.

Sweeney, Kathryn A. 2013. "Race-Conscious Adoption Choices, Multiraciality, and Color-blind Racial Ideology." *Family Relations* 62: 42–57.

Trenka, Jane J., Julia C. Oparah, and Sun Yung Shin. 2006. *Outsiders Within: Writing on Transracial Adoption.* Cambridge, MA: South End Press.

Tuan, Mia, and Jiannbin Lee Shiao. 2011. *Choosing Ethnicity, Negotiating Race: Korean Adoptees in America.* New York: Russell Sage Foundation.

U.S. Census Bureau. 2003. *Adopted Children and Stepchildren: 2000. Census 2000 Special Reports.* Washington, DC: U.S. Department of Commerce: Economics and Statistics Administration.

Volkman, Toby Alice. 2005. *Cultures of Transnational Adoption.* Durham, NC: Duke University Press.

Waters, Mary. 1990. *Ethnic Options: Choosing Identity in America.* Berkeley: University of California Press.

CHAPTER 27: Parents as Pawns: Intersex, Medical Experts, and Questionable Consent
by Georgiann Davis

Chase, Cheryl. 1998. "Hermaphrodites with Attitude: Mapping the Emergence of Intersex Political Activism." *GLQ: A Journal of Gay and Lesbian Studies* 4(2): 189–211.

Committee on Genetics: Section on Endocrinology and Section on Urology. 2000. "Evaluation of the Newborn with Developmental Anomalies of the External." *Pediatrics* 106: 138–142.

Cools, M., S. L. Drop, K. P. Wolffenbuttel, J. W. Oosterhuis, and L. H. Looijenga. 2006. "Germ Cell Tumors in the Intersex Gonad: Old Paths, New Directions, Moving Frontiers." *Endocrine Reviews* 27(5): 468–484.

Davis, Georgiann. 2011. "'DSD is a Perfectly Fine Term': Reasserting Medical Authority Through a Shift in Intersex Terminology." In *Sociology of Diagnosis*, edited by P. J. McGann and David Hutson, 155–182. United Kingdom: Emerald.

Fausto-Sterling, Anne. 1993. "The Five Sexes: Why Male and Female Are Not Enough." *The Sciences* 33(2): 20–25.

Karkazis, Katrina. 2008. *Fixing Sex: Intersex, Medical Authority, and Lived Experience.* Durham, NC: Duke University Press.

Kessler, Suzanne J. 1990. "The Medical Construction of Gender: Case Management of Intersexed Infants." *Signs* 16(1): 3–26.

Lee, Peter A., Christopher P. Houk, S. Faisal Ahmed, and Ieuan A. Hughes. 2006. "Consensus Statement on Management of Intersex Disorders." *Pediatrics* 118(2): 488–500.

Pleskacova, J. R. Hersmuś, J.W. Oosterhuis, B. A. Setyawati, S. M. Faradz, M. Cools, K. P. Wolffenbuttel, J. Lebl, S. L. Drop, and L. H. Looijenga. 2010. "Tumor Risk in Disorders of Sex Development." *Sexual Development* 4: 259–269.

Preves, Sharon E. 2003. *Intersex and Identity: The Contested Self.* New Brunswick, NJ: Rutgers University Press.

———. 2004. "Out of the O.R. and Into the Streets: Exploring the Impact of Intersex Media Activism." *Research in Political Sociology* 13: 179–223.

CHAPTER 28: The Power of Queer: How "Guy Moms" Challenge Heteronormative Assumptions about Mothering and Family
by Raine Dozier

Bartley, Sharon J., Priscilla W. Blanton, and Jennifer L. Gilliard. 2005. "Husbands and Wives in Dual-Earner Marriages: Decision-Making, Gender Role Attitudes, Division of Household Labor, and Equity." *Marriage and Family Review* 37(4): 65–94.

Baxter, Janeen, Belinda Hewitt, and Michele Haynes. 2008. "Life Course Transitions and Housework: Marriage, Parenthood and Time on Housework." *Journal of Marriage and Family* 70(2): 259–272.

Bernard, Tara Siegel. 2011. "For Children of Same-Sex Couples, a Student Aid Maze." *New York Times*, October 15, p. B1.

Bianchi, Susan M., and Melissa A. Milkie. 2010. "Work and Family Research in the First Decade of the 21st Century." *Journal of Marriage and Family* 72(3): 705–725.

Biblarz, Timothy J., and Judith Stacey. 2010. "How Does the Gender of Parents Matter?" *Journal of Marriage and Family* 72(1): 3–22.

Bos, Henny M. W., Frank van Balen, and Dymphna van den Boom. 2007. "Child Adjustment and Parenting in Planned Lesbian-Parent Families." *American Journal of Orthopsychiatry* 77(1): 38–48.

Brinamen, Charles F. 2000. "On Becoming Fathers: Issues Facing Gay Men Choosing to Parent." *Dissertation Abstracts International* 61(5-B): 2794.

Chan, Raymond W., Risa S. Brooks, Barbara Raboy, and Charlotte J. Patterson. 1998. "Division of Labor among Lesbian and Heterosexual Parents: Associations with Children's Adjustment." *Journal of Family Psychology* 12(3): 402–419.

Chapman, Rose, Joan Wardrop, Phoenix Freeman, Tess Zappia, Rochelle Watkins, and Linda Shields. 2012. "A Descriptive Study of the Experiences of Lesbian, Gay and Transgender Parents Accessing Health Services for their Children." *Journal of Clinical Nursing* 21(7–8): 1128–1135.

Cohany, Sharon R., and Emy Sok. 2007. "Trends in Labor Force Participation of Married Mothers of Infants." *Monthly Labor Review.* 130(2): 9–16.

Cooper, Davina. 1995. *Power in Struggle: Feminism, Sexuality and the State.* New York: New York University Press.

Dempsey, Deborah. 2010. "Conceiving and Negotiating Reproductive Relationships: Lesbians and Gay Men Forming Families with Children." *Sociology* 44(6): 1145–1162.

Dozier, Raine. 2005. "Beards, Breasts, and Bodies: Doing Sex in a Gendered World." *Gender & Society* 19(3): 297–316.

Duggan, Lisa. 2002. "The New Homonormativity: The Sexual Politics of Neoliberalism." In *Materializing Democracy: Toward a Revitalized Cultural Politics*, edited by Russ Castronovo and Dana D. Nelson, 175–194. Durham, NC: Duke University Press.

Elizabeth, Vivienne, Nicola Gavey, and Julia Tolmie. 2012. "The Gendered Dynamics of Power in Disputes Over the Postseparation Care of Children." *Violence Against Women* 18(4): 459–481.

Gartrell, Nanette and Henny Bos. 2010. "U.S. National Longitudinal Lesbian Family Study: Psychological Adjustment of 17-Year-Old Adolescents." *Pediatrics* 126(1): 28–36.

Gartrell, Nanette K., Henny M. W. Bos, and Naomi G. Goldberg. 2011. "Adolescents of the U.S. National Longitudinal Lesbian Family Study: Sexual Orientation, Sexual Behavior, and Sexual Risk Exposure." *Archives of Sexual Behavior* 40(6): 1199–1209.

Giesler, Mark. 2012. "Gay Fathers' Negotiation of Gender Role Strain: A Qualitative Inquiry." *Fathering* 10(2): 119–139.

Goldberg, Abbie E. 2007. "(How) Does It Make a Difference? Perspectives of Adults with Lesbian, Gay, and Bisexual Parents." *American Journal of Orthopsychiatry* 77(4): 550–562.

——. 2009. "Lesbian and Heterosexual Preadoptive Couples' Openness to Transracial Adoption." *American Journal of Orthopsychiatry* 79(1): 103–117.

Goldberg, Abbie E., Deborah A. Kashy, and JuliAnna Z. Smith. 2012. "Gender-Typed Play Behavior in Early Childhood: Adopted Children with Lesbian, Gay, and Heterosexual Parents." *Sex Roles* 67(9–10): 503–515.

Goldberg, Abbie E., and Maureen Perry-Jenkins. 2007. "The Division of Labor and Perceptions of Parental Roles: Lesbian Couples across the Transition to Parenthood." *Journal of Social and Personal Relationships* 24(2): 297–318.

Goldberg, Abbie E., JuliAnna Z. Smith, and Maureen Perry-Jenkins. 2012. "The Division of Labor in Lesbian, Gay, and Heterosexual New Adoptive Parents." *Journal of Marriage and Family* 74(4): 812–828.

Golombok, Susan. 2007. "Research on Gay and Lesbian Parenting: An Historical Perspective across 30 Years." *Journal of GLBT Family Studies* 3(2–3): xxi–xxvii.

Grant, Jaime. 2009. "Sex and the Formerly Single Mom." In *Who's Your Daddy*, edited by Rachel Epstein, 328–334. Toronto: Sumach Press.

Gupta, Sanjiv. 2006. "The Consequences of Maternal Employment during Men's Childhood for Their Adult Housework Performance." *Gender & Society* 20(1): 60–86.

Halperin. 1995. *Saint Foucault: Towards a Gay Hagiography*. New York: Oxford University Press.

Heasley, Robert. 2005. "Queer Masculinities of Straight Men: A Typology." *Men and Masculinities* 7(3): 310–320.

Hochschild, Arlie, and Annie Machung. 2003. *The Second Shift*. New York: Penguin Books.

James, Susan Donaldson. 2009. "Lesbians Sue When Partners Die Alone." *ABC News*. Retrieved on May 19, 2013, from http://abcnews.go.com/Health/story?id= 7633058&page=1#.UZlC06LBOi4.

Johnson, Susanne. 2012. "Lesbian Mothers and Their Children: The Third Wave." *Journal of Lesbian Studies* 16(1): 45–53.

Johnson, Susanne, and Elizabeth O'Connor. 2002. *The Gay Baby Boom: The Psychology of Gay Parenthood*. New York: New York University Press.

Kane, Emily. 2006. "'No Way My Boys Are Going to be Like That!' Parents' Responses to Children's Gender Nonconformity." *Gender & Society* 20(2): 149–176.

Kitzinger, Celia. 2005. "Heteronormativity in Action: Reproducing the Heterosexual Nuclear Family in After-hours Medical Calls." *Social Problems* 52(4): 477–498.

Kluwer, Esther S., José A. M. Heesink, and Evert van de Vliert. 2002. "The Division of Labor across the Transition to Parenthood: A Justice Perspective." *Journal of Marriage and Family* 64(4): 930–943.

Lev, Arlene Istar. 2010. "How Queer! The Development of Gender Identity and Sexual Orientation in LGBTQ-Headed Families." *Family Process* 49(3): 260–290.

Lindsay, Jo, Amaryll Perlesz, Rhonda Brown, Ruth McNair, David de Vaus, and Marian Pitts. 2006. "Stigma or Respect: Lesbian-Parented Families Negotiating School Settings." *Sociology* 40(6): 1059–1077.

Lucal, Betsy. 1999. "What It Means to Be Gendered Me: Life on the Boundaries of a Dichotomous Gender System." *Gender & Society* 13(6): 781–797.

O'Neill, Kristal R., Helen P. Hamer, and Robyn Dixon. 2012. "A Lesbian Family in a Straight World: The Impact of the Transition to Parenthood on Couple Relationships in Planned Lesbian Families." *Women's Studies Journal* 26(2): 39–53.

Patterson, Charlotte J. 2006. "Children of Lesbian and Gay Parents." *Current Directions in Psychological Science* 15(5): 241–244.

Patterson, Charlotte J., Erin L. Sutfin, and Megan Fulcher. 2004. "Division of Labor among Lesbian and Heterosexual Parenting Couples: Correlates of Specialized versus Shared Patterns." *Journal of Adult Development* 3 (11): 179–189.

Reich, Vikki. 2013. "'My Daughter Is Not a Princess': An Essay from the 'Listen to Your Mother' Reading Series." Retrieved on May 13, 2013, from http://www.huffingtonpost.com/2013/04/23/listen-to-your-mother_n_3116946.html.

Ryan-Flood, Róisín. 2005. "Contested Heteronormativities: Discourses of Fatherhood among Lesbian Parents in Sweden and Ireland." *Sexualities* 8(2): 189–204.

Saffron, L. 1996. 'What about the Children?' Sons and Daughters of Lesbian and Gay Parents Talk about Their Lives. London: Cassell.

Schilt, Kristin. 2009. "Faeries, Bears, and Leathermen: Men in Community Queering Masculinity." Sex Roles: A Journal of Research 61(1–2): 144–145.

Schilt, Paige. 2012. "Passing (Or Not) at the Pool." Blog: Queer Rock Love . . . A Gay, Transgender, Rock-n-Roll Family Raising a Son in the Heart of the South. Retrieved on May 5, 2013, from http://queerrocklove.com/2012/01/20/passing-or-not-at-the-pool/.

———. 2009. "Genderqueer Mommy." Blog: Bilerico Project. Retrieved on May 5, 2013, from http://www.bilerico.com/2009/05/genderqueer_mommy.php.

Seidman, Stephen. 2002. Beyond the Closet: The Transformation of Gay and Lesbian Life. New York: Routledge.

Shotwell, Alexis, and Trevor Sangrey. 2009. "Resisting Definition: Gendering through Interaction and Relational Selfhood." Hypatia 24(3): 56–76.

Stacey, Judith, and Timothy J. Biblarz. 2001. "(How) Does the Sexual Orientation of Parents Matter?" American Sociological Review 66(2): 159–183.

Tasker, Fiona L., and Susan Golombok. 1997. Growing Up in a Lesbian Family: Effects on Child Development. London: Guilford Press.

U.S. Bureau of Labor Statistics. 2013. "Employment Characteristics of Families—2012." Table 6. Available from http://www.bls.gov/news.release/famee.t06.htm.

———. 2013. "Women in the Labor Force: A Databook." BLS Reports Report 1040: 1–104.

Valocchi, Stephen. 2005. "Not Yet Queer Enough: The Lessons of Queer Theory for the Sociology of Gender and Sexuality." Gender & Society 19(6): 750–770.

Vanfraussen, K., I. Ponjaert-Kristoffersen, and A. Brewaeys. 2002. "What Does It Mean for a Youngster to Grow Up in a Lesbian Family Created by Means of Donor Insemination?" Journal of Reproductive and Infant Psychology 20(4): 237–252.

Wainright, Jennifer L., and Charlotte J. Patterson. 2006. "Delinquency, Victimization, and Substance Use among Adolescents with Female Same-Sex Parents." Journal of Family Psychology 20(3): 526–530.

Wainright, Jennifer L., Stephen T. Russell, and Charlotte J. Patterson. 2004. "Psychosocial Adjustment, School Outcomes, and Romantic Relationships of Adolescents with Same-Sex Parents." Child Development 75(6): 1886–1898.

Wangsness, Lisa. 2011. "Archdiocese Issues No-Discrimination Admissions Policy." Boston Globe Retrieved on May 19, 2013, from http://www.boston.com/news/education/k_12/articles/2011/01/13/archdiocese_issues_no_discrimination_admissions_policy/.

West, Candace, and Don Zimmerman. 1987. "Doing Gender." Gender & Society 1(2): 125–151.

Weston, Kath. 1997. Families We Choose: Lesbians, Gays, Kinship. New York: Columbia University Press.

CHAPTER 29: The Immigration Kaleidoscope: Knowing the Immigrant Family Next Door
by Etiony Aldarondo and Edward Ameen

Allen, J. P. 2005. "How Successful Are Recent Immigrants to the United States and Their Children?" Presidential address at the annual meeting of the Association of Pacific Coast Geographers, Phoenix, AZ.

Berry, John. 2007. "Acculturation Strategies and Adaptation." In *Immigrant Families in Contemporary Society*, edited by Jennifer Lansford, Kirby Deater-Deckard, and Marc Bornstein, 69–82. New York: Guilford Press.

Briggs Jr., V. E. 2003. *Mass Immigration and the National Interest: Policy Directions for the New Century*, 3rd ed. Armonk, NY: M. E. Sharpe.

Camarota, S. A. 2007. "Immigrants in the United States, 2007: A Profile of America's Foreign-Born Population." Center for Immigration Studies Backgrounder. Retrieved May 1, 2008, from http://www.cis.org/articles/2007/back1007.pdf.

Capps, R., M. Fix, J. S. Passel, J. Ost, and D. Perez-Lopez. 2003. "A Profile of the Low-Wage Immigrant Workforce." Immigrant Families and Workers. Retrieved May 1, 2008, from http://www.urban.org/UploadedPDF/310880_lowwage_immig_wkfc.pdf.

Chang, H. F. 2003. "The Immigration Paradox: Poverty, Distributive Justice, and Liberal Egalitarianism." *DePaul Law Review* 52: 759–776.

Chapman, M. V., and K. M. Perreira. 2005. "The Well-Being of Immigrant Latino Youth: A Framework to Inform Practice." *Families in Society* 86: 104–111.

Chavez, L. R. 2001. *Covering Immigration: Popular Images and the Politics of the Nation*. Berkeley: University of California Press.

Chomsky, A. 2007. *"They Take Our Jobs!" and 20 Other Myths about Immigration*. Boston: Beacon Press.

Deaux, K. 2006. *To Be an Immigrant*. New York: Russell Sage Foundation.

DeSipio, L. 2008. "Do Home-Country Political Ties Limit Latino Immigrant Pursuit of U.S. Civic Engagement and Citizenship?" In *Immigration*, edited by I. Stavans, 69–89. Westport, CT: Greenwood Press.

Espenshade, T. J. 1997. "New Jersey in Comparative Perspective." In *Keys to Successful Immigration: Implications of the New Jersey Experience*, edited by T. J. Espenshade, 19–29. Washington, DC: Urban Institute Press.

Executive Office of the President. 2007. "Immigration's Economic Impact: June 20, 2007." Washington, DC: Author. Retrieved March 10, 2008, from http://www.whitehouse.gov/cea/cea_immigration_062007.pdf.

Falicov, C. J. 2002. "Immigrant Family Processes." In *Normal Family Processes*, 3rd ed., edited by F. Walsh, 280–300. New York: Guilford Press.

Farkas, S., A. Duffett, and J. Johnson. 2003. "Now That I'm Here: What Immigrants Have to Say about Life in the U.S. Today." New York: Public Agenda. Retrieved August 1, 2008, from http://www.publicagenda.org/files/pdf/now_that_im_here.pdf.

Fennelly, K. 2006. "Listening to the Experts: Provider Recommendations on the Health Needs of Immigrants and Refugees." *Journal of Cultural Diversity* 13: 190–201.

Fix, M., and R. Capps. 2004. "The Health and Well-Being of Young Children of Immigrants." Presentation at the meeting of the Brookings Institution's Policies for Children in Immigrant Families, Washington, DC.

Fuligni, A. J. 1998. "The Adjustment of Children from Immigrant Families." *Current Directions in Psychological Science* 7: 99–103.

Gallup/CNN/*USA Today* Poll. 2002 (September 2–4).

Gallup Poll. 2000 (September 11–13).

Gonzalez, E. T. 2006. "Regarding a Hearing on 'Contributions of Immigrants in the U.S. Military.'" Speech presented before the Senate Committee on Armed Services, Miami, FL, July 10.

Gonzalez, R. G. 2007. "Wasted Talent and Broken Dreams: The Lost Potential of Undocumented Students." *Immigration Policy in Focus* 5(13): 1–11. Retrieved March 12, 2008, from http://www.ilw.com/articles/2007,1121-gonzales.shtm.

Greico, E. 2002 (December). "Characteristics of the Foreign Born in the United States: Results from Census 2000." Retrieved May 1, 2008, from http://www.migrationinformation .org/USFocus/display.cfm?ID=71,

Guskin, J., and D. L. Wilson. 2007. *The Politics of Immigration: Questions and Answers.* New York: Monthly Review Press.

Hao, L., and R. W. Johnson. 2000. "Economic, Cultural, and Social Origins of Emotional well-being." *Research on Aging* 22: 599–629.

Harker, K. 2001. "Immigrant Generation, Assimilation, and Adolescent Psychological Well-Being." *Social Forces* 79: 969–1004.

Hernandez, D. J. 2004a. "A Demographic Portrait of Children in Immigrant Families." Presentation at the meeting of the Brookings Institution's Policies for Children in Immigrant Families, Washington, DC, December.

———. 2004b. "Demographic Change and the Life Circumstances of Immigrant Families." *Future of Children* 14: 17–47. Princeton, NJ: David and Lucile Packard Foundation.

Hernandez, M., and M. McGoldrick. 2005. "Migration and the Life Cycle." In *The Expanded Family Life Cycle: Individual, Family, and Social Perspectives*, 3rd ed., edited by B. Carter and M. McGoldrick, 169–184. New York: Pearson.

Hirschman, C. 2006. "The Impact of Immigration on American Society: Looking Backward to the Future." Social Science Research Council. Retrieved on March 20, 2008, from http://borderbattles.ssrc.org/Hirschman/.

Institute for the Future. 2007. Intuit Future of Small Business Report: First Installment, Demographic Trends and Small Business. Palo Alto, CA.

Koepke, L. A. 2007. "A Call to Action: Five Policy Proposals on Behalf of All Families. President's Address to the 2007 Groves Conference on Marriage and Family." *Journal of Feminist Family Therapy* 19: 1–12.

Leventhal, T., Y. Xue, and J. Brooks-Gunn. 2006. "Immigrant Difference in School-Age Children's Verbal Trajectories: A Look at Four Racial/Ethnic Groups." *Child Development* 77: 1359–1374.

Levitt, M. J., J. D. Lane, and J. Levitt. 2005. "Immigration Stress, Social Support, and Adjustment in the First Postmigration Year: An Intergenerational Analysis." *Research in Human Development* 24: 159–177.

Migration Policy Institute. 2004 (January). "What Kind of Work Do Immigrants Do? Occupation and Industry of Foreign-Born Workers in the United States." Immigration Facts. Retrieved May 1, 2008, from http://www.migrationpolicy.org/pubs/Foreign%20Born%20 Occup%20and%20Industry%20in%20the%20US.pdf.

Minuchin, S. 1984. *Family Kaleidoscope.* Cambridge, MA: Harvard University Press.

Mohanty, S. A., S. Woolhandler, D. U. Himmelstein, S. Pati, O. Carrasquillo, and D. Bor. 2005. "Health Care Expenditures of Immigrants in the United States: A Nationally Representative Analysis." *American Journal of Public Health* 95: 1431–1438.

Mutti, L. 2002. "Immigrants, Welfare and Work [Electronic version]." National Center for Policy Analysis, 400, 1–2.

New Democrat Network. 2007 (September 20). "Hispanics Rising: An Overview of the Emerging Politics of America's Hispanic Population." Retrieved May 1, 2008, from http://www.ndn.org/hispanic/hispanics-rising.pdf.

Passel, J. S. 2006. "Size and Characteristics of the Unauthorized Migrant Population in the U.S.: Estimates Based on the March 2005 Current Population Survey." Retrieved on May 1, 2008, from http://pewhispanic.org/files/reports/61.pdf.

Passel, J. S., R. Capps, and M. E. Fix. 2004. "Undocumented Immigrants: Facts and Figures." Urban Institute Fact Sheet. Retrieved May 1, 2008, from http://www.urban.org/url .cfm?ID=1000587.

Phinney, J. S., J. W. Berry, D. L. Sam, and P. Vedder. 2006. "Understanding Immigrant Youth: Conclusions and Implications." In *Immigrant Youth in Cultural Transition: Acculturation, Identity and Adaptation across National Contexts*, edited by J. W. Berry, J. S. Phinney, D. L. Sam, and P. Vedder, 211–234. Mahwah, NJ: Lawrence Erlbaum Associates.

Portes, A., and R. G. Rumbaut, eds. 2001. *Legacies: The Story of the Immigrant Second Generation*. Berkeley: University of California Press.

Pyke, K. D. 2000. "'The Normal American Family' as an Interpretive Structure of Family Life among Children of Korean and Vietnamese Immigrants." *Journal of Marriage and the Family* 62: 240–255.

Reardon-Anderson, J., R. Capps, and M. Fix. 2002. "The Health and Well-Being of Children in Immigrant Families." Policy Brief. New Federalism: National Survey of America's Families. Washington, DC: Urban Institute.

Rumbaut, R. G. 2002 (May). "Competing Futures: The Children of America's Newest Immigrants." Migration Information Source. Retrieved February 6, 2008, from http://www .migrationinformation.org/feature/display.cfm?ID=1.

Rumbaut, R. G., and W. A. Ewing. 2007 (Spring). "The Myth of Immigrant Criminality and the Paradox of Assimilation: Incarceration Rates among Native and Foreign-Born Men." Immigration Policy Center. Retrieved July 1, 2008, from http://www.immigrationpolicy .org/index.php?content=sr20070221.

Singh, G. K., and R. A. Hiatt. 2006. "Trends and Disparities in Socioeconomic and Behavioural Characteristics, Life Expectancy, and Cause-Specific Mortality of Native-Born and Foreign-Born Populations in the United States, 1979–2003." *International Journal of Epidemiology* 35: 903–919.

Sluzki, C. E. 1998. "Migration and the Disruption of the Social Network." In *Re-Visioning Family Therapy: Race, Culture, and Gender in Clinical Practice*, edited by M. McGoldrick. New York: Guilford Press.

Suárez-Orozco, C., and M. M. Suárez-Orozco. 2001. *Children of Immigration*. The Developing Child Series. Cambridge, MA: Harvard University Press.

Suárez-Orozco, C., M. M. Suárez-Orozco, and I. Todorova. 2008. *Learning a New Land: Immigrant Students in American Society*. Cambridge, MA: Belknap Press.

Trueba, H. T. 2002. "Multiple Ethnic, Racial and Cultural Identities in Action: From Marginality to a New Cultural Capital in Modern Society." *Journal of Latinos and Education* 1: 7–28.

CHAPTER 30: When Men Stay Home: Household Labor in Female-Led Indian Migrant Families
by Pallavi Banerjee

Aiken, L. H. 2007. "U.S. Nurse Labor Market Dynamics Are Key to Global Nurse Sufficiency." *Health Services Research* 42(3): 1299–1320.

Aiken, L. H., J. Buchan, J. Sochalski, B. Nichols, and M. Powell. 2004. "Trends in International Nurse Migration." *Health Affairs* 23(3): 369–377.

Brush, B. L., and A. M. Berger. 2002. "Sending for Nurses: Foreign Nurse Migration, 1965–2002." *Nursing and Health Policy Review* 1(2): 103–115.

Brush, B. L., J. Sochalski, and A. M. Berger. 2004. "Imported Care: Recruiting Foreign Nurses to U.S. Health Care Facilities." *Health Affairs* 23(3): 378–387.

Dicicco-Bloom, B. 2004. "The Racial and Gendered Experiences of Immigrant Nurses from Kerala, India." *Journal of Transcultural Nursing* 15(1): 26–33.

Espenshade, Thomas J. 2001. "High-end Immigrants and the Shortage of Skilled Labor." *Population Research and Policy Review* 20(2): 135–141.

George, S. M. 2005. *When Women Come First: Gender and Class in Transnational Migration.* Berkley: University of California Press.

Hochschild, A. R. 1989. *The Second Shift: Working Mothers and the Revolution at Home.* New York: Viking.

Khadria, B. 2007. "International Nurse Recruitment in India." *Health Services Research* 42(3): 1429–1436.

Kurien, P. 2002. *Kaleidoscopic Ethnicity: International Migration and the Reconstruction of Community Identities in India.* New Brunswick, NJ: Rutgers University Press.

Pittman, P. M., Folsom, A. J., and Bass, E. 2010. "U.S.-Based Recruitment of Foreign-Educated Nurses: Implications of an Emerging Industry." *American Journal of Nursing* 110(6): 38–48.

Polsky, D. S., J. Ross, B. L. Brush, and J. Sochalski. 2007. "Trends in Characteristics and Country of Origin among Foreign-Trained Nurses in the United States, 1990 and 2000." *American Journal of Public Health* 97(5): 895–899.

Rai, S. 2003. "Indian Nurses Sought to Staff U.S. Hospitals," *New York Times*, February 10.

Walton-Roberts, M. 2012. "Contextualizing the Global Nursing Care Chain: International Migration and the Status of Nursing in Kerala, India." *Global Networks* 12(2): 175–194.

Xiang, B. 2005. "Gender, Dowry and the Migration System of Indian Information Technology Professionals." *Indian Journal of Gender Studies* 12(2–3): 357–380.

CHAPTER 31: Diverging Development: The Not-So-Invisible Hand of Social Class in the United States
by Frank F. Furstenberg Jr.

Bendix, Reinhard, and Seymour Martin Lipset. 1966. *Class, Status, and Power.* New York: Free Press.

Bernstein, Basil. 1971. *Class, Codes and Control: Theoretical Studies towards a Sociology of Language,* vol. 1. London: Routledge & Kegan Paul.

Bernstein, Basil, and Dorothy Henderson. 1969. "Social Class Differences and the Relevance of Language to Socialization." *Sociology* 3(1): 1–20.

Blood, Robert O., and Donald M. Wolfe. 1960. *Husbands and Wives: The Dynamics of Married Living.* New York: Free Press.

Bourdieu, Pierre. 1973. "Cultural Reproduction and Social Reproduction." In *Knowledge, Education, and Cultural Change,* edited by Richard Brown. London: Tavistock.

———. 1986. "The Forms of Capital." In *Handbook of Theory and Research for the Sociology of Education,* edited by John G. Richardson. New York: Greenwood.

Bronfenbrenner, Urie. 1979. *The Ecology of Human Development: Experiments by Nature and Design*. Cambridge, MA: Harvard University Press.

Brown, Sarah S., and Leon Eisenberg, eds. 1995. *The Best Intentions: Unintended Pregnancy and the Well-Being of Children and Families*. Washington, DC: National Academy Press.

Buchmann, Marlis. 1989. *The Script of Life in Modern Society: Entry into Adulthood in a Changing World*. Chicago: University of Chicago Press.

Burton, Linda, and Carol Stack. 1993. "Conscripting Kin: Reflections on Family, Generation, and Culture." In *Family, Self, and Society: Toward a New Agenda for Family Research*, edited by Philip A. Cowan, Dorothy Field, Donald A. Hansen, Arlene Skolnick, and Guy E. Swanson. Hillsdale, NJ: Lawrence Erlbaum Associates.

Case, Anne, Angela Fertig, and Christine Paxton. 2005. "From Cradle to Grave? The Lasting Impact of Childhood Health and Circumstances." *Journal of Health Economics* 24: 265–389.

Chaudry, Ajay. 2004. *Putting Children First: How Low-Income Working Mothers Manage Child Care*. New York: Russell Sage Foundation.

Conley, Dalton, and Neil G. Bennett. 2000. "Is Biology Destiny? Birth Weight and Life Chances." *American Sociological Review* 65(3): 458–467.

Cook, Thomas D., Melissa R. Herman, Meredith Phillips, and Richard A. Settersten, Jr. 2002. "Some Ways in Which Neighborhoods, Nuclear Families, Friendship Groups, and Schools Jointly Affect Changes in Early Adolescent Development." *Child Development* 73(4): 1283–1309.

Cooley, Charles H. 1902. *Human Nature and the Social Order*. New York: Scribners.

Corsaro, William. 2005. *The Sociology of Childhood*, 2nd ed. Thousand Oaks, CA: Pine Forge Press.

Danziger, Sheldon H., and Peter Gottschalk. 1995. *America Unequal*. New York: Russell Sage Foundation.

Danziger, Sheldon H., and Jane Waldfogel. 2000. *Securing the Future: Investing in Children from Birth to College*. New York: Russell Sage Foundation.

Edin, Kathryn J., and Maria Kefalas. 2005. *Promises I Can Keep: Why Low-Income Women Put Motherhood Before Marriage*. Berkeley: University of California Press.

Elder, Glen H., Jr. 1974. *Children of the Great Depression: Social Change in Life Experience*. Chicago: University of Chicago Press (Reissued as 25th Anniversary Edition; Boulder, CO: Westview Press, 1999).

Ellwood, David T., and Christopher Jencks. 2001. "The Spread of Single-Parent Families in the United States since 1960." Cambridge, MA: John F. Kennedy School of Government, Harvard University, Working Paper RWP04-008.

Farkas, George, and Kurt Beron. 2004. "The Detailed Age Trajectory of Oral Vocabulary Knowledge: Differences by Class and Race." *Social Science Research* 33(3): 464–497.

Furstenberg, Frank F., Jr., Thomas D. Cook, Jacquelynne Eccles, Glen H. Edler Jr., and Arnold Sameroff. 1999. *Managing to Make It: Urban Families and Adolescent Outcomes*. The John D. and Catherine T. MacArthur Foundation Series on Mental Health and Development. Chicago: University of Chicago Press.

Furstenberg, Frank F., Sheela Kennedy, Vonnie McLoyd, Ruben G. Rumbaut, and Richard A. Settersten Jr. 2004. "Growing Up Is Harder to Do." *Contexts* 3(3): 42–47.

Gans, Herbert J. 1962. *The Urban Villagers*. New York: Free Press.

Garmezy, Norman. 1991. "Resilience and Vulnerability to Adverse Developmental Outcomes Associated with Poverty." *American Behavioral Scientist* 34(4): 416–430.

———. 1993. "Vulnerability and Resilience." In *Studying Lives through Time: Personality and Development*, edited by David C. Funder, Ross D. Parke, Carol Tomlinson-Keasey, and Keith Widaman. Washington, DC: American Psychological Association.

Goldstein, Joshua R., and Catherine T. Kenney. 2001. "Marriage Delayed or Marriage Forgone? New Cohort Forecasts of First Marriage for U.S. Women." *American Sociological Review* 66(4): 506–519.

Goldthorpe, John H., and Robert Erickson. 1993. *The Constant Flux: A Study of Class Mobility in Industrial Societies*. Oxford, UK: Oxford University Press.

Haggerty, Robert J., Lonnie R. Sherrod, Norman Garmezy, and Michael Rutter. 1994. *Stress, Risk, and Resilience in Children and Adolescents*. New York: Cambridge University Press.

Hart, Betty, and Todd R. Risley. 1995. *Meaningful Differences in the Everyday Experiences of Young American Children*. Baltimore: Paul H. Brookes Publishing.

Heinz, Walter R., and Victor W. Marshall, eds. 2003. *Social Dynamics of the Life Course: Transitions, Institutions and Interrelations*. Hawthorne, NY: Aldine de Gruyter.

Hertz, Tom. 2005. "Rags, Riches and Race: The Intergenerational Economic Mobility of Black and White Families in the United States." In *Unequal Chances: Family Background and Economic Success*, edited by Samuel Bowles, Herbert Gintis, and Melissa Osborne Groves. Princeton, NJ: Princeton University Press.

Hollingshead, A. de B. 1949. *Elmtown's Youth: The Impact of Social Classes on Adolescents*. New York: John Wiley & Sons.

Inkeles, Alex. 1968. "Society, Social Structure, and Child Socialization." In *Socialization and Society*, edited by John A. Clausen. Boston: Little, Brown.

Joyce, Theodore J., Robert Kaestner, and Sanders Korenman. 2000. "The Effect of Pregnancy Intention and Child Development." *Demography* 37(1): 83–94.

Kefalas, Maria. 2003. *Working Class Heroes: Protecting Home, Community and Nation in a Chicago Neighborhood*. Berkeley: University of California Press.

Kluckhohn, Clyde, and Alexander Murray, eds. 1948. "Personality." In *Nature, Society, and Culture*. New York: Knopf.

Komarovsky, Mira. 1987. *Blue-Collar Marriage*, 2nd ed. New Haven, CT: Yale University Press.

Lamont, Michele. 2000. *The Dignity of Working Men: Morality and the Boundaries of Race, Class and Immigration*. Cambridge, MA: Harvard University Press.

Lareau, Annette. 1989. *Home Advantage: Social Class and Parental Intervention in Elementary Education*. New York: Falmer Press.

———. 2003. *Unequal Childhoods: Race, Class and Family Life*. Berkeley: University of California Press.

Levy, Frank. 1999. *The New Dollars and Dreams*. New York: Russell Sage Foundation.

Lynd, Robert S., and Helen M. Lynd. 1929. *Middletown: A Study in Contemporary American Culture*. New York: Harcourt Brace & Company.

Magnuson, Katherine A., and Jane Waldfogel. 2005. "Early Childhood Care and Education: Effects on Ethnic and Racial Gaps in School Readiness." *Future of Children* 15(1): 169–196.

McLanahan, Sara. 2004. "Diverging Destinies: How Children Fare under the Second Demographic Transition." *Demography* 41(4): 607–627.

Mead, George Herbert. 1934. *Mind, Self, and Society: From the Standpoint of a Social Behaviorist*. Chicago: University of Chicago Press.

Mead, Margaret, and Martha Wolfenstein, eds. 1955. *Childhood in Contemporary Cultures*. Chicago: University of Chicago Press.

Medrich, Elliott, Judith Roizen, and Victor Rubin, with Stuart Buckley. 1982. *The Serious Business of Growing Up: A Study of Children's Lives Outside of School*. Berkeley: University of California Press.

Miller, Daniel R., and Guy E. Swanson. 1958. *The Changing American Parent*. New York: Wiley.

Mortimer, Jeylan, ed. 2008. "Social Class and Transitions to Adulthood." *New Directions for Child and Adolescent Development* 119 (Spring). San Francisco: Jossey-Bass.

Nelson, Charles A. 2000. "Neural Plasticity and Human Development: The Role of Early Experience in Sculpting Memory Systems." *Developmental Science* 3: 115–130.

Nelson, Charles A., Susan W. Parker, et al. 2005. "The Impact of Early Institutional Rearing on the Ability to Discriminate Facial Expressions of Emotion: An Event-Related Potential Study." *Child Development* 76(1): 54–72.

Newman, Katherine S. 1993. *Declining Fortunes: The Withering of the American Dream*. New York: Basic Books.

Noble, Kimberly G., M. Frank Norman, and Martha J. Farah. 2005. "Neurocognitive Correlates of Socioeconomic Status in Kindergarten Children." *Developmental Science* 8(1): 74–87.

Rhodes, Jean. 2002. *Stand by Me: The Risks and Rewards of Mentoring Today's Youth*. Cambridge, MA: Harvard University Press.

Rouse, Cecilia E. 2004. "Low Income Students and College Attendance: An Exploration of Income Expectations." *Social Science Quarterly* 85(5): 1299–1317.

Rutter, Michael. 1985. "Resilience in the Face of Adversity: Protective Factors and Resistance to Psychiatric Disorder." *British Journal of Psychiatry* 147: 598–611.

———. 2000. "Resilience Reconsidered: Conceptual Considerations, Empirical Findings and Policy Implications." In *Handbook of Early Childhood Intervention*, 2nd ed., edited by Jack P. Shonkoff and Samuel J. Meisels. New York: Cambridge University Press.

Settersten, Richard A., Jr, Frank F. Furstenberg, and Ruben G. Rumbaut, eds. 2005. *On the Frontier of Adulthood: Theory, Research, and Public Policy*. Chicago: University of Chicago Press.

Shonkoff, Jack P., and Deborah Phillips. 2000. *From Neurons to Neighborhoods: The Science of Early Childhood Development*. Washington, DC: National Academy Press.

Smyke, Anna. T., Sebastian F. Koga, et al. 2007. "The Caregiving Context in Institution-Reared and Family-Reared Infants and Toddlers in Romania." *Journal of Child Psychology and Psychiatry* 48(2): 210–218.

Tocqueville, Alexis de. 1835. *Democracy in America*. New York: Knopf.

U.S. Bureau of the Census. 2004. *Historical Income Tables*, Table F-1, Available from http://www.census.gov/hhes/www/income/data/historical/families/.

Wagmiller, Robert L., Jr., Mary Clare Lennon, Li Kuang, Philip M. Alberti, and J. Lawrence Aber. 2006. "The Dynamics of Economic Disadvantage and Children's Life Chances." *American Sociological Review* 71: 847–866.

Warner, William Lloyd. 1949. *Social Class in America*. Chicago: Science Research Associates.

Weber, Max. 1949. *The Methodology of the Social Sciences*. New York: Free Press.

Werner, Emmy. 1995. "Resilience in Development." *Current Directions in Psychological Science* 4(3): 81–85.

Whiting, Beatrice. 1963. *Six Cultures: Studies of Child Rearing*. New York: Wiley.

Wolff, Edward N. 2002. *Top Heavy: A Study of Increasing Inequality of Wealth in America.* New York: New Press.

———. 2004. "Changes in Household Wealth in the 1980s and 1990s in the U.S." Working Paper No. 407. Annandale-on-Hudson, NY: The Levy Economics Institute at Bard College.

Wu, Lawrence, and Barbara Wolfe, eds. 2001. *Out of Wedlock: Causes and Consequences of Nonmarital Fertility.* New York: Russell Sage Foundation.

CHAPTER 32: Not Just Provide and Reside: Engaged Fathers in Low-Income Families
by Kevin Roy and Natasha Cabrera

Allen, Sarah, and Alan Hawkins. 1999. "Maternal Gatekeeping: Mothers' Beliefs and Behaviors That Inhibit Greater Father Involvement in Family Work." *Journal of Marriage and Family* 61: 199–212.

Allen, W., and M. Conner. 1997. "An African American Perspective on Generative Fathering." In *Generative Fathering: Beyond Deficit Perspectives*, edited by A. J. Hawkins and D. C. Dollahite, 52–70. Newbury Park, CA: Sage Publications.

Black, Maureen, Howard Dubowitz, and Raymond Starr. 1999. "African American Fathers in Low-Income, Urban Families: Development, Behavior, and Home Environment of Their Three-Year-Olds." *Child Development* 70: 967–978.

Bronfenbrenner, Urie. 1979. *The Ecology of Human Development: Experiments by Nature and Design.* Cambridge, MA: Harvard University Press.

Cabrera, Natasha, Jeanne Brooks-Gunn, Kristin Moore, J. West, K. Boller, and C. S. Tamis-LeMonda. 2002. "Bridging Research and Policy: Including Fathers of Young Children in National Studies." In *Handbook of Father Involvement: Multidisciplinary Perspectives*, edited by Catherine Tamis-LeMonda and Natasha Cabrera, 489–524. Mahwah, NJ: Lawrence Erlbaum Associates.

Cabrera, Natasha, Hiram Fitzgerald, R. Bradley, and L. Roggman. 2007. "Modeling the Dynamics of Paternal Influence on Children over the Life Course." *Applied Developmental Science* 11(4): 185–190.

Cabrera, Natasha, and Cynthia Garcia Coll. 2004. "Latino Fathers: Uncharted Territory in Need of Much Exploration." In *The Role of the Father in Child Development*, 4th ed., edited by Michael Lamb, 98–120. New York: John Wiley & Sons.

Cabrera, Natasha, Rebecca Ryan, Jacqueline Shannon, Jeanne Brooks-Gunn, Cheri Vogel, Helen Raikes, Catherine Tamis-LeMonda, and Rachel Cohen. 2004. "Low-Income Fathers' Involvement in Their Toddlers' Lives: Biological Fathers from the Early Head Start Research and Evaluation Study." *Fathering: A Journal of Theory, Research, and Practice about Men as Fathers* 2: 5–30.

Cabrera, Natasha, Jacqueline Shannon, and Catherine Tamis-LeMonda. 2007. "Fathers' Influence on Their Children's Cognitive and Emotional Development: From Toddlers to Pre-K." *Applied Developmental Science* 11(4): 208–213.

Carlson, Marcia, and Frank Furstenberg. 2006. "The Prevalence and Correlates of Multipartnered Fertility among Urban U.S. Parents." *Journal of Marriage and Family* 68: 718–732.

Carlson, Marcia, and Sara McLanahan. 2002. "Fragile Families, Father Involvement and Public Policy." In *Handbook of Father Involvement: Multidisciplinary Perspectives*, edited by Catherine Tamis-LeMonda and Natasha Cabrera, 461–488. Mahwah, NJ: Lawrence Erlbaum Associates.

———. 2004. "Early Father Involvement in Fragile Families." In *Conceptualizing and Measuring Father Involvement*, edited by Randal Day and Michael Lamb, 241–271. Mahwah, NJ: Lawrence Erlbaum Associates.

Coley, Rebekah Levine. 2001. "(In)visible Men: Emerging Research on Low-Income, Unmarried, and Minority Fathers." *American Psychologist* 56: 743–753.

Doherty, William, Edward Kouneski, and Martha Erickson. 1998. "Responsible Fathering: An Overview and Conceptual Framework." *Journal of Marriage and Family* 60: 277–292.

Eggebeen, David. 2002a. "The Changing Course of Fatherhood: Men's Experiences with Children from a Demographic Perspective." *Journal of Family Issues* 23: 486–506.

———. 2002b. "Sociological Perspectives on Fatherhood: What Do We Know about Fathers from Social Surveys?" In *Handbook of Father Involvement: Multidisciplinary Perspectives*, edited by Catherine Tamis-LeMonda and Natasha Cabrera, 189–209. Mahwah, NJ: Lawrence Erlbaum Associates.

Eggebeen, David, and Peter Uhlenberg. 1985. "Changes in the Organization of Men's Lives: 1960–1980." *Family Relations* 34: 251–257.

Fagan, Jay, Rob Palkovitz, Kevin Roy, and Danielle Farrie. 2009. "Pathways to Paternal Engagement: Longitudinal Effects of Cumulative Risk and Resilience on Nonresident Fathers." *Developmental Psychology* 45: 1389–1405.

Hansen, Karen. 2005. *Not-So-Nuclear Families: Class, Gender, and Networks of Care*. New Brunswick, NJ: Rutgers University Press.

Hofferth, Sandra. 2003. "Race/Ethnic Differences in Father Involvement in Two-Parent Families: Culture, Context, or Economy." *Journal of Family Issues* 24: 185–216.

Hofferth, Sandra, Joseph Pleck, and Colleen Vesely. 2012. "The Transmission of Parenting from Fathers to Sons." *Parenting: Science and Practice* 12(4): 282–305.

Hogan, Dennis. 1981. *Transitions and Social Change: The Early Lives of American Men*. New York: Academic Press.

Jarrett, Robin, Kevin Roy, and Linda Burton. 2002. "Fathers in the 'Hood: Qualitative Research on African American Men." In *Handbook of Father Involvement: Multidisciplinary Perspectives*, edited by Catherine Tamis-LeMonda and Natasha Cabrera, 211–248. Mahwah, NJ: Lawrence Erlbaum Associates.

Kwon, Young In, and Kevin Roy. 2007. "Changing Social Expectations and Paternal Caregiving Experiences for Working Class and Middle Class Korean Fathers." *Journal of Comparative Family Studies* 38: 285–305.

Lamb, Michael. 1975. "Fathers: Forgotten Contributors to Children's Development." *Human Development* 18: 245–266.

———. 1997. "Fathers and Child Development: An Introductory Overview." In *The Role of the Father in Child Development*, 3rd ed., edited by Michael Lamb, 1–18. New York: John Wiley & Sons.

———. 2004. *The Role of the Father in Child Development*, 4th ed. Hoboken, NJ: John Wiley & Sons.

LaRossa, Ralph. 1997. *The Modernization of Fatherhood*. Chicago: University of Chicago Press.

Mott, Frank. 1990. "When Is a Father Really Gone? Paternal-Child Contact in Father-Absent Homes." *Demography* 27: 499–517.

Nelson, Margaret. 2005. *The Social Economy of Single Motherhood: Raising Children in Rural America*. New York: Routledge.

Palkovitz, Rob. 2002a. "Involved Fathering and Child Development: Advancing Our Understanding of Good Fathering." In *Handbook of Father Involvement: Multidisciplinary Perspectives*, edited by Catherine Tamis-LeMonda and Natasha Cabrera, 119–140. Mahwah, NJ: Lawrence Erlbaum Associates.

———. 2002b. *Involved Fathering and Men's Adult Development: Provisional Balances*. Mahwah, NJ: Lawrence Erlbaum Associates.

Pleck, Joseph, and Brian Masciadrelli. 2004. "Paternal Involvement by U.S. Residential Fathers: Levels, Sources, and Consequences." In *The Role of the Father in Child Development*, 4th ed., edited by Michael Lamb, 222–270. New York: John Wiley & Sons.

Roopnarine, Jaipaul. 2004. "African American and African Caribbean Fathers: Level, Quality, and Meaning of Involvement." In *The Role of the Father in Child Development*, 4th ed., edited by Michael Lamb, 58–97. New York: John Wiley & Sons.

Roy, Kevin. 2005. "Transitions on the Margins of Work and Family for Low-Income African American Fathers." *Journal of Family and Economic Issues* 26: 77–100.

———. 2006. "Father Stories: A Life Course Examination of Paternal Identity among Low-Income African American Men." *Journal of Family Issues* 27: 31–54.

Roy, Kevin, and Linda Burton. 2007. "Mothering through Recruitment: Kinscription of Non-Residential Fathers and Father Figures in Low-Income Families." *Family Relations* 56: 24–39.

Roy, Kevin, and Omari Dyson. 2005. "Gatekeeping in Context: Babymamadrama and the Involvement of Incarcerated Fathers." *Fathering: A Journal of Theory, Research, and Practice about Men as Fathers* 3: 289–310.

Roy, Kevin, Omari Dyson, and Ja-Nee Jackson. 2013. "Intergenerational Support and Reciprocity between Low-Income African American Fathers and Their Aging Mothers." In *Social Work with African American Males: Health, Mental Health, and Social Policy*, edited by Waldo Johnson. New York: Oxford University Press.

Roy, Kevin, Sarah Kaye, and Megan Fitzgerald. Under review. "Swap Reconsidered: Transitions in Paternal Involvement across Multiple Family Systems."

Roy, Kevin, Rob Palkovitz, and Jay Fagan. 2007. "Down but Not Out: Strategies for Stabilizing Involvement of Low-Income Fathers and Families." Paper presentation at National Poverty Center, Small Grants Program Conference, Ann Arbor, MI.

Shannon, Jacqueline, Catherine Tamis-LeMonda, and Natasha Cabrera. 2006. "Fathering in Infancy: Mutuality and Stability between 8 and 16 Months." *Parenting: Science and Practice* 6(2): 167–188.

Shannon, Jacqueline, Catherine Tamis-LeMonda, K. London, and Natasha Cabrera. 2002. "Beyond Rough and Tumble: Low-Income Fathers' Interactions and Children's Cognitive Development at 24 Months." *Parenting: Science and Practice* 2: 77–104.

Shwalb, D., J. Nakawaza, T. Yamamoto, and J. Hyun. 2004. "Fathering in Japanese, Chinese, and Korean Cultures: A Review of the Research Literature." In *The Role of the Father in Child Development*, 4th ed., edited by Michael Lamb, 146–181. New York: John Wiley & Sons.

Sobolewski, Julie, and Valarie King. 2005. "The Importance of the Coparental Relationship for Nonresident Fathers' Ties to Children." *Journal of Marriage and Family* 67: 1196–1212.

Tamis-LeMonda, Catherine, Jacqueline Shannon, Natasha Cabrera, and Michael Lamb. 2004. "Resident Fathers and Mothers at Play with Their 2- and 3-Year-Olds: Contributions to Language and Cognitive Development." *Child Development* 75: 1806–1820.

Toth, J., and X. Xu. 1999. "Ethnic and Cultural Diversity in Fathers' Involvement: A Racial/Ethnic Comparison of African American, Hispanic, and White Fathers." *Youth & Society* 31: 76–99.

Townsend, Nicholas. 2002. *The Package Deal: Marriage, Work and Fatherhood in Men's Lives.* Philadelphia: Temple University Press.

Waller, Maureen. 2002. *My Baby's Father: Unmarried Parents and Paternal Responsibility.* Ithaca, NY: Cornell University Press.

Waller, Maureen, and Sara McLanahan. 2005. "'His' and 'Her' Marriage Expectations: Determinants and Consequences." *Journal of Marriage and Family* 67: 53–67.

Walker, Alexis, and Lori McGraw. 2000. "Who Is Responsible for Responsible Fathering?" *Journal of Marriage and Family* 62: 563–569.

CHAPTER 33: Mass Incarceration and Family Life
by Bryan L. Sykes and Becky Pettit

Alexander, Michelle. 2010. *The New Jim Crow: Mass Incarceration in the Age of Colorblindness.* New York: The New Press.

Arditti, Joyce. 2012. *Parental Incarceration and the Family: Psychological and Social Effects of Imprisonment on Children, Parents, and Caregivers.* New York: New York University Press.

Arditti, Joyce, S. Smock, and T. Parkman. 2005. "It's Been Hard to be a Father: A Qualitative Exploration of Incarcerated Fatherhood." *Fathering* 3: 267–283.

Blumstein, Alfred, and Jacqueline Cohen. 1973. "A Theory of the Stability of Punishment." *Journal of Criminal Law and Criminology* 64: 198–206.

Braman, Donald. 2004. *Doing Time on the Outside: Incarceration and Family Life in Urban America.* Ann Arbor: University of Michigan Press.

Cho, Rosa Minhyo. 2010. "Maternal Incarceration and Children's Adolescent Outcomes: Timing and Dosage." *Social Service Review* 48(2): 257–282.

Clear, Todd. 2007. *Imprisoning Communities: How Mass Incarceration Makes Disadvantaged Neighborhoods Worse.* New York: Oxford University Press.

Comfort, Megan. 2008. *Doing Time Together: Love and Family in Shadow of the Prison.* Chicago: University of Chicago Press.

Cox, Robynn, and Sally Wallace. 2013. "The Impact of Incarceration on Food Insecurity among Households with Children." Fragile Families Working Paper 13-05-FF. Princeton, NJ: Princeton University.

Edin, Kathryn, and Maria Kefelas. 2005. *Promises I Can Keep: Why Poor Women Put Motherhood Before Marriage.* Berkeley: University of California Press.

Edin, Kathryn, Timothy Nelson, and Rechelle Paranal. 2003. "Fatherhood and Incarceration as Potential Turning Points in the Criminal Careers of Unskilled Men." In *Imprisoning America: The Social Effects of Mass Incarceration*, edited by Mary Patillo, David Weiman, and Bruce Western. New York: Russell Sage Foundation, 46–75.

Foster, Holly and John Hagan. 2007. "Incarceration and Intergenerational Social Exclusion." *Social Problems* 54(4): 399–433.

———. 2009. "The Mass Incarceration of Parents in America: Issues of Race/Ethnicity, Collateral Damage to Children, and Prisoner Reentry." *Annals of the American Academy of Political and Social Science* 623: 179–194.

Freudenberg, Nicholas. 2001. "Jails, Prisons, and the Health of Urban Populations: A Review of the Impact of the Correctional System on Community Health." *Journal of Urban Health: Bulletin of the New York Academy of Medicine*, 78(2): 214–235.

Garland, David. 2001. "The Meaning of Mass Imprisonment." In *Mass Imprisonment: Social Causes and Consequences*, edited by D. Garland, 1–3. London: Sage Publications.

Geller, Amanda, Carey E. Cooper, Irwin Garfinkel, Ofira Schwartz-Soicher, and Ronald B. Mincy. 2012. "Beyond Absenteeism: Father Incarceration and Child Development." *Demography* 49(1): 49–76.

Geller, Amanda, Irwin Garfinkel, Carey E. Cooper, and Ronald B. Mincy. 2009. "Parental Incarceration and Child Wellbeing: Implications for Urban Families." *Social Science Quarterly* 90(5): 1186–1202.

Geller, Amanda, Irwin Garfinkel, and Bruce Western. 2011. "Paternal Incarceration and Support for Children in Fragile Families." *Demography* 48(1): 25–47.

Glaze, Lauren. 2010. *Correctional Population in the United States, 2010*. Washington, DC: Bureau of Justice Statistics. Available from http://bjs.ojp.usdoj.gov/index.cfm?ty=pbdetail&iid=2237.

Guerino, P., Piege Harrison, and William Sabol. 2011. *Prisoners in 2010* (Revised). Washington, DC: Bureau of Justice Statistics. Available from http://bjs.ojp.usdoj.gov/index.cfm?ty=pbdetail&iid=2230.

Hagan, John, and Ronit Dinovitzer. 1999. "Collateral Consequences of Imprisonment for Children, Communities and Prisoners." *Crime and Justice: A Review of Research* 26: 121–162.

Hagan, John, and Holly Foster. 2012. "Intergenerational Educational Effects of Mass Imprisonment in America." *Sociology of Education* 85(3): 259–286.

Harding, David, Jeffery Morenoff, and Claire Herbert. 2013. "Home Is Hard to Find: Neighborhoods, Institutions, and the Residential Trajectories of Returning Prisoners." *Annals of the American Academy of Political and Social Science* 647: 214–236.

Johnson, Rucker, and Steven Raphael. 2009. "The Effects of Male Incarceration Dynamics on AIDS Infection Rates among African-American Women and Men." *Journal of Law & Economics* 52 (2): 251–294.

Lareau, Annette. 2003. *Unequal Childhoods: Class, Race, and Family Life*. Berkeley: University of California Press.

Lopoo, Leonard, and Bruce Western. 2005. "Incarceration and the Formation and Stability of Marital Unions." *Journal of Marriage and the Family* 67: 721–734.

Massoglia, Michael. 2008. "Incarceration, Health, and Racial Disparities in Health." *Law & Society Review* 42: 275–306.

Mauer, Mark. 2006. Race to Incarcerate. Washington, DC: The Sentencing Project.

Mumola, C. 2000. *Bureau of Justice Statistics Bulletin: Incarcerated Parents and Their Children*. Washington, DC: U.S. Department of Justice.

Nurse, Anne. 2004. "Returning to Strangers: Newly Paroled Young Fathers and Their Children." In *Imprisoning America: The Social Effects of Mass Incarceration*, edited by Mary Pattillo, David Weiman, and Bruce Western, 76–96. New York: Russell Sage Foundation.

Pager, Devah. 2003. "The Mark of a Criminal Record." *American Journal of Sociology* 108: 937–975.

Pettit, Becky. 2012. *Invisible Men: Mass Incarceration and the Myth of Black Progress.* New York: Russell Sage Foundation.

Pettit, Becky, Bryan Sykes, and Bruce Western. 2009. *Technical Report on Revised Population Estimates and NLSY 79 Analysis Tables for the Pew Public Safety and Mobility Project.* Cambridge, MA: Harvard University.

Pettit, Becky, and Bruce Western. 2004. "Mass Imprisonment and the Life Course: Race and Class Inequality in U.S. Incarceration." *American Sociological Review* 69: 151–169.

Pew Charitable Trusts. 2008. *One in 100: Behind Bars in America 2008.* Available from http://www.pewtrusts.org/en/research-and-analysis/reports/2008/02/28/one-in-100-behind-bars-in-america-2008.

Rosenfeld, Jake, Jennifer Laird, Bryan Sykes, and Becky Pettit. 2011. *Incarceration and Racial Inequality in Voter Turnout, 1980–2008.* Paper presented at the Population Association of American Annual Meetings, Washington, D.C., and the Annual Meetings of the American Political Science Association, Seattle, OR.

Springer, David, Courtney Lynch, and Allen Rubin. 2000. "Effects of a Solution-Focused Mutual Aid Group for Hispanic Children of Incarcerated Parents." *Child and Adolescent Social Work Journal* 17(6): 431–442.

Sykes, Bryan, and Alex Piquero. 2009. "Structuring and Recreating Inequality: Health Testing Policies, Race, and the Criminal Justice System." *Annals of the American Academy of Political and Social Science* 623: 214–227.

Tonry, Michael. 1995. *Malign Neglect-Race, Crime, and Punishment in America.* London: Oxford University Press.

Uggen, Christopher, and Jeff Manza. 2002. "Democratic Contraction? Political Consequences of Felon Disenfranchisement in the United States." *American Sociological Review* 67: 777–803.

Wakefield, Sara, and Christopher Uggen. 2010. "Incarceration and Stratification." *Annual Review of Sociology* 36: 387–406.

Wakefield, Sara, and Christopher Wildeman. 2011. Mass Imprisonment and Racial Disparities in Childhood Behavioral Problems." *Criminology and Public Policy* 10(3): 793–817.

Waller, Maureen. 2002. *My Baby's Father: Unmarried Parents and Paternal Responsibility.* Ithaca, NY: Cornell University Press.

Walmsley, Roy. 2011. *World Prison Population List* (9th Edition). Retrieved on September 6, 2012, from http://www.prisonstudies.org/research-publications?shs_term_node_tid_depth=27.

Western, Bruce. 2006. *Punishment and Inequality in America.* New York: Russell Sage Foundation.

Western, Bruce, Leonard Lopoo, and Sara McLanahan. 2004. "Incarceration and the Bond between Parents in Fragile Families." Chapter 2 in *Imprisoning America: The Social Effects of Mass Incarceration,* edited by Mary Pattillo, David Weiman, and Bruce Western. New York: Russell Sage Foundation.

Western, Bruce, and Becky Pettit. 2005. "Black-White Wage Inequality, Employment Rates, and Incarceration." *American Journal of Sociology* 111: 553–578.

Whitman, James. 2003. *Harsh Justice: Criminal Punishment and the Widening Divide between America and Europe.* London: Oxford University Press.

Wildeman, Christopher. 2009. "Parental Imprisonment and the Concentration of Childhood Disadvantage." *Demography* 46(2): 265–280.

———. 2010. "Paternal Incarceration and Children's Physically Aggressive Behaviors: Evidence from the Fragile Families and Child Wellbeing Study." *Social Forces* 89(1): 285–309.

———. 2014. "Parental Incarceration, Child Homelessness, and the Invisible Consequences of Mass Imprisonment." *Annals of the American Academy of Political and Social Science* 651(1): 74–96.

Wildeman, Christopher, and Bruce Western. 2010. "Incarceration in Fragile Families." *The Future of Children* 20(2): 157–77.

Wilson, William Julius. 1987. *The Truly Disadvantaged.* Chicago: University of Chicago Press.

CHAPTER 34: Betwixt and Be Tween: Gender Contradictions among Middle Schoolers
by Barbara J. Risman and Elizabeth Seale

Adams, Natalie, and Pamela Bettis. 2003. "Commanding the Room in Short Skirts: Cheering as the Embodiment of Ideal Girlhood." *Gender and Society* 17: 73–91.

Adams, Natalie, Alison Schmitke, and Amy Franklin. 2005. "Tomboys, Dykes, and Girly Girls: Interrogating the Subjectivities of Adolescent Female Athletes." *Women's Studies Quarterly* 33: 17–34.

Adler, Patricia A., and Peter Adler. 1995. "Dynamics of Inclusion and Exclusion in Preadolescent Cliques." *Social Psychology Quarterly* 58(3): 145–162.

———. 1998. *Peer Power: Preadolescent Culture and Identity.* New Brunswick, NJ: Rutgers University Press.

Allison, M. T. 1991. "Role Conflict and the Female Athlete: Preoccupations with Little Grounding." *Journal of Applied Sport Psychology* 3: 49–60.

Bettie, Julie. 2003. *Women without Class: Girls, Race, and Identity.* Berkeley: University of California Press.

Broad, K. L. 2001. "The Gendered Unapologetic: Queer Resistance in Women's Sport." *Sociology of Sport Journal* 18(2): 181–204.

Burn, Shawn Meghan. 2000. "Heterosexuals' Use of 'Fag' and 'Queer' to Deride One Another: A Contributor to Heterosexism and Stigma." *Journal of Homosexuality* 40: 1–11.

Canada, Geoffrey. 1998. *Reaching Up for Manhood: Transforming the Lives of Boys in America.* Boston: Beacon Press.

Chambers, Deborah, Estella Tincknell, and Joost Van Loon. 2004. "Peer Regulation of Teenage Sexual Identities." *Gender and Education* 16: 397–415.

Cockburn, Cynthia, and Gill Clarke. 2002. "'Everybody's Looking at You!': Girls Negotiating the 'Femininity Deficit' They Incur in Physical Education." *Women's Studies International Forum* 25: 651–665.

Connell, R. W. 1987. *Gender and Power: Society, the Person, and Sexual Politics.* Stanford, CA: Stanford University Press.

Deutsch, Francine M. 2007. "Undoing Gender." *Gender & Society* 21(1): 106–127.

Eder, Donna, Catherine Colleen Evans, and Stephen Parker. 1995. *School Talk: Gender and Adolescent Culture.* New Brunswick, NJ: Rutgers University Press.

Eitzen, D. S. 1990. *Fair and Foul: Beyond the Myths and Paradoxes of Sports.* Lanham, MD: Rowman & Littlefield.

Enke, Janet. 2005. "Athleticism and Femininity on a High School Basketball Team: An Interpretive Approach." *Sociological Studies of Children and Youth* 11: 115–152.

Fine, Gary Alan. 2004. "Adolescence as Cultural Toolkit: High School Debate and the Repertoires of Childhood and Adulthood." *Sociological Quarterly* 45(1): 1–20.

Froyum, Carissa. 2007. "At Least I'm Not Gay: Heterosexual Identity Making among Poor Black Teens." *Sexualities* 10(5): 605–624.

Gerson, Kathleen. 2002. "Moral Dilemmas, Moral Strategies, and the Transformation of Gender." *Gender & Society* 16(1): 8–28.

Hurrelmann, Klaus, and Stephen F. Hamilton. 1996. *Social Problems and Social Contexts in Adolescence*. New York: Aldine de Gruyter.

Kehily, Mary Jane, and Anoop Nayak. 1997. "'Lads and Laughter': Humour and the Production of Heterosexual Hierarchies." *Gender & Education* 9: 69–88.

Kling, Kristen C., Janet Shibley Hyde, Carolin J. Showers, and Brenda N. Buswell. 1999. "Gender Differences in Self-Esteem: A Meta-Analysis." *Psychological Bulletin* 125(4): 470–500.

Klomsten, Anne Torhild, Herb W. Marsh, and Einar M. Skaalvik. 2005. "Adolescents' Perceptions of Masculine and Feminine Values in Sport and Physical Education: A Study of Gender Differences." *Sex Roles: A Journal of Research* 52: 625–636.

Krane, Vikki. 2001. "We Can Be Athletic and Feminine, but Do We Want To? Challenging Hegemonic Femininity in Women's Sport." *Quest* 53: 115–133.

Krane, Vikki, Precilla Y. L. Choi, Shannon M. Baird, Christine M. Aimar, and Kerrie J. Kauer. 2004. "Living the Paradox: Female Athletes Negotiate Femininity and Muscularity." *Sex Roles: A Journal of Research* 50: 315–329.

Lemish, Dafna. 1998. "Spice Girls' Talk: A Case Study in the Development of Gendered Identity." In *Millennium Girls: Today's Girls around the World*, edited by Sherri A. Inness, 145–167. Lanham, MD: Rowman & Littlefield.

Mahaffy, Kimberly A. 2004. "Girls' Low Self-Esteem: How Is It Related to Later Socioeconomic Achievements?" *Gender & Society* 18(3): 309–327.

Malcom, Nancy L. 2003. "Constructing Female Athleticism: A Study of Girls' Recreational Softball." *American Behavioral Scientist* 46(10): 1387–1404.

Nayak, Anoop, and Mary Jane Kehily. 1996. "Playing It Straight: Masculinities, Homophobias and Schooling." *Journal of Gender Studies* 5: 211–231.

Pascoe, C. J. 2003. "Multiple Masculinities? Teenage Boys Talk about Jocks and Gender." *American Behavioral Scientist* 46: 1423–1438.

———. 2005. "'Dude, You're a Fag': Adolescent Masculinity and the Fag Discourse." *Sexualities* 8(3): 329–346.

———. 2007. *Dude, You're a Fag: Masculinity and Sexuality in High School*. Berkeley: University of California Press.

Peterson, Anne, Rainer K. Silbereisen, and Silvia Sorenson. 1996. "Adolescent Development: A Global Perspective." Chapter 1 in *Social Problems and Social Contexts in Adolescence*, edited by K. Hurrelmann and S. F. Hamilton. New York: Aldine de Gruyter.

Phoenix, Ann, Stephen Frosh, and Rob Pattman. 2003. "Producing Contradictory Masculine Subject Positions: Narratives of Threat, Homophobia and Bullying in 11–14 Year Old Boys." *Journal of Social Issues* 59(1): 179–195.

Plummer, David C. 2001. "The Quest for Modern Manhood: Masculine Stereotypes, Peer Cultures and the Social Significance of Homophobia." *Journal of Adolescence* 24: 15–23.

Sutton-Smith, Brian. 1982. "A Performance Theory of Peer Relations." In *The Social Life of Children in a Changing Society*, edited by K. Borman, 65–77. Hillsdale, NJ: Lawrence Erlbaum Associates.

Swidler, Ann. 1986. "Culture in Action: Symbols and Strategies." *American Sociological Review* 51(2): 273–286.

Talbani, Aziz. 2003. "Keeping Up Appearances: Multicultural Education in Postmodern Society." *Education and Society* 21(2): 5–18.

Thorne, Barrie. 1993. *Gender Play: Girls and Boys in School*. New Brunswick, NJ: Rutgers University Press.

Visser, Irene. 1996. "The Prototypicality of Gender: Contemporary Notions of Masculine and Feminine." *Women's Studies International Forum* 19(6): 589–600.

Wellman, David T. 1993. *Portraits of White Racism*, 2nd ed. New York: Cambridge University Press.

West, Candace, and Donald Zimmerman. 1987. "Doing Gender." *Gender & Society* 1: 125–151.

CHAPTER 35: Falling Back on Plan B: The Children of the Gender Revolution Face Uncharted Territory
by Kathleen Gerson

Acock, Alan C., and David H. Demo. 1994. *Family Diversity and Well-Being*. Thousand Oaks, CA: Sage Publications.

Amato, Paul R., and Alan Booth. 1997. *A Generation at Risk: Growing Up in an Era of Family Upheaval*. Cambridge, MA: Harvard University Press.

Amato, Paul R., and Bryndl Hohmann-Marriott. 2007. "A Comparison of High- and Low-Distress Marriages That End in Divorce." *Journal of Marriage and Family* 69(3): 621–638.

Barnett, Rosalind C., and Caryl Rivers. 1996. *She Works/He Works: How Two-Income Families Are Happier, Healthier, and Better-Off*. San Francisco: Harper.

Belkin, Lisa. 2003. "The Opt-Out Revolution." *New York Times Magazine*, October 26.

Bengtson, Vern L., Timothy J. Biblarz, and Robert E. L. Roberts. 2002. *How Families Still Matter: A Longitudinal Study of Youth in Two Generations*. New York: Cambridge University Press.

Bennetts, Leslie. 2007. *The Feminine Mistake: Are We Giving Up Too Much?* New York: Voice/Hyperion.

Bianchi, Suzanne M., John P. Robinson, and Melissa A. Milkie. 2006. *Changing Rhythms of American Family Life*. New York: Russell Sage Foundation.

Blankenhorn, David. 1995. *Fatherless America: Confronting Our Most Urgent Social Problem*. New York: Basic Books.

Booth, Alan, and Paul R. Amato. 2001. "Parental Predivorce Relations and Offspring Postdivorce Well-Being." *Journal of Marriage and Family* 63(1): 197–212.

Boushey, Heather. 2008. "'Opting Out?' The Effect of Children on Women's Employment in the United States." *Feminist Economics* 14(1): 1–36.

Coontz, Stephanie. 2005. *Marriage, a History: From Obedience to Intimacy, or How Love Conquered Marriage*. New York: Viking.

Furstenberg, Frank F., and Andrew J. Cherlin. 1991. *Divided Families: What Happens to Children When Parents Part*. Cambridge, MA: Harvard University Press.

Galinsky, Ellen. 1999. *Ask the Children: What America's Children Really Think about Working Parents*. New York: Morrow.

Gerson, Kathleen. 2006. "Families as Trajectories: Children's Views of Family Life in Contemporary America." In *Families between Flexibility and Dependability: Perspectives for a Life Cycle Family Policy*, edited by Hans Bertram, Helga Kruger, and Katarina Spiel. Farmington Hills, MI: Verlag Barbara Budrich.

———. 2010. *The Unfinished Revolution: How a New Generation Is Reshaping Family, Work, and Gender in America*. New York: Oxford University Press.

Harvey, Lisa. 1999. "Short-Term and Long-Term Effects of Early Parental Employment on Children of the National Longitudinal Study of Youth." *Developmental Psychology* 35(2): 445–459.

Hetherington, E. M. 1999. *Coping with Divorce, Single Parenting, and Remarriage: A Risk and Resiliency Perspective*. Mahwah, NJ: Lawrence Erlbaum Associates.

Hirshman, Linda. 2006. *Get to Work*. New York: Viking.

Hochschild, Arlie R. 1989. *The Second Shift: Working Parents and the Revolution at Home*. New York: Viking.

Hoffman, Lois. 1987. "The Effects on Children of Maternal and Paternal Employment." In *Families and Work*, edited by N. Gerstel and H. E. Gross, 362–395. Philadelphia: Temple University Press.

Hoffman, Lois, Norma Wladis, and Lise M. Youngblade. 1999. *Mothers at Work: Effects on Children's Well-Being*. New York: Cambridge University Press.

Li, Allen J. 2007. "The Kids are OK: Divorce and Children's Behavior Problems." Santa Monica, CA: Rand Working Paper WR 489.

Lorber, Judith. 1994. *Paradoxes of Gender*. New Haven, CT: Yale University Press.

McLanahan, Sara, and Gary D. Sandefur. 1994. *Growing Up with a Single Parent: What Hurts, What Helps*. Cambridge, MA: Harvard University Press.

Moen, Phyllis, and Patricia Roehling. 2005. *The Career Mystique: Cracks in the American Dream*. Lanham, MD: Rowman & Littlefield.

Moore, Kristin A., Rosemary Chalk, Juliet Scarpa, and Sharon Vandivere. 2002. *Family Strengths: Often Overlooked, But Real*. Washington, DC: Child Trends.

Parcel, Toby L., and Elizabeth G. Menaghan. 1994. *Parents' Jobs and Children's Lives*. New York: Aldine de Gruyter.

Pew Research Center. 2007a. "As Marriage and Parenthood Drift Apart, Public Is Concerned about Social Impact." Retrieved on June 19, 2008, from http://pewresearch.org/pubs/526/marriage-parenthood.

———. 2007b. "How Young People View Their Lives, Futures and Politics: A Portrait of the '"Generation Next.'" Retrieved on June 19, 2008, from http://www.people-press.org/2007/01/09/a-portrait-of-generation-next/.

Popenoe, David. 1988. *Disturbing the Nest: Family Change and Decline in Modern Societies*. New York: Aldine de Gruyter.

———. 1996. *Life without Father: Compelling New Evidence that Fatherhood and Marriage Are Indispensable for the Good of Children and Society*. New York: Martin Kessler Books.

Popenoe, David, Jean B. Elshtain, and David Blankenhorn. 1996. *Promises to Keep: Decline and Renewal of Marriage in America*. Lanham, MD: Rowman & Littlefield.

Risman, Barbara J. 1998. *Gender Vertigo: American Families in Transition*. New Haven, CT: Yale University Press.

Roberts, Sam. 2007. "Fifty-one Percent of Women Are Now Living without Spouse." *New York Times*, January 16.

Skolnick, Arlene, and Stacey Rosencrantz. 1994. "The New Crusade for the Old Family." *American Prospect*, 18(Summer): 59–65.

Springer, Kristen W. 2007. "Research or Rhetoric? A Response to Wilcox and Nock." *Sociological Forum* 22(1): 111–116.

Stacey, Judith. 1996. *In the Name of the Family: Rethinking Family Values in the Postmodern Age*. Boston: Beacon Press.

Stone, Pamela. 2007. *Opting Out? Why Women Really Quit Careers and Head Home*. Berkeley: University of California Press.

Waite, Linda J., and Maggie Gallagher. 2000. *The Case for Marriage: Why Married People Are Happier, Healthier, and Better Off Financially*. New York: Doubleday.

West, Candace, and Don H. Zimmerman. 1987. "Doing Gender." *Gender & Society* 1(2): 125–151.

Whitehead, Barbara D. 1997. *The Divorce Culture*. New York: Knopf.

Williams, Joan. 2000. *Unbending Gender: Why Family and Work Conflict and What to Do about It*. New York: Oxford University Press.

———. 2007. "The Opt-Out Revolution Revisited." *American Prospect* (March): A12–A15.

Zerubavel, Eviatar. 1991. *The Fine Line: Making Distinctions in Everyday Life*. Chicago: University of Chicago Press.

CHAPTER 36: Men's Changing Contribution to Family Work
by Oriel Sullivan

Beck, Ulrich, and E. Beck-Gernsheim. 1995. *The Normal Chaos of Love*. Cambridge, UK: Polity Press.

Benjamin, Orly, and Oriel Sullivan. 1999. "Relational Resources, Gender Consciousness and Possibilities of Change in Marital Relationships." *Sociological Review* 47: 794–820.

Bianchi, Suzanne M., John P. Robinson, and Melissa A. Milkie. 2006. *Changing Rhythms of American Family Life* (Rose Series in Sociology). New York: Russell Sage Foundation.

Bianchi, Suzanne M., Liana C. Sayer, Melissa A. Milkie, and John P. Robinson. 2012. "Housework: Who Did, Does or Will Do It, and How Much Does It Matter?" *Social Forces* 9: 55–63.

Connell, R. W. 2000. *The Men and the Boys*. Cambridge, UK: Polity Press.

Coltrane, Scott. 1998. *Gender and Families*. Thousand Oaks, CA: Pine Forge Press.

———. 2004. "Fathering: Paradoxes, Contradictions and Dilemmas." In *Handbook of Contemporary Families: Considering the Past, Contemplating the Future*, edited by Marilyn Coleman and Lawrence Ganong, 224–243. Thousand Oaks, CA: Sage Publications.

Cotter, David, Joan M. Hermsen, and Reeve Vanneman. 2011. "The End of the Gender Revolution? Gender Role Attitudes from 1977 to 2008." *American Journal of Sociology* 117: 259–289.

Craig, Lyn, and Killian Mullen. 2012. "How Mothers and Fathers Share Childcare: A Cross-National Time-Use Comparison." *American Sociological Review* 76: 834–861.

Deutsch, Francine M. 1999. *Halving It All: How Equally Shared Parenting Works*. Cambridge, MA: Harvard University Press.

Deutsch, Francine M. 2007. "Undoing Gender." *Gender & Society* 21: 106–127.

England, Paula. 2010. "The Gender Revolution: Uneven and Stalled." *Gender & Society* 24: 149–166.

———. (2013). "Educational Differences in U.S. Parents' Time spent in Child Care: The Role of Culture and Cross-Spouse Influence." *Social Sciences Research* 42(4): 971–988.

Ferree, Myra Marx. 1990. "Beyond Separate Spheres: Feminism and Family Research." *Journal of Marriage and Family* 52: 866–884.

———. 2010. "Filling the Glass: Gender Perspectives on Families." *Journal of Marriage and Family* 72: 420–439.

Fisher, Kimberley, Muriel Egerton, Jonathan I. Gershuny, and John P. Robinson. 2007. "Gender Convergence in the American Heritage Time Use Study (AHTUS)." *Social Indicators Research* 82: 1–33.

Gershuny, Jonathan. 2000. *Changing Times: Work and Leisure in Postindustrial Society.* Oxford, UK: Oxford University Press.

Gershuny, Jonathan, John P. Robinson, and Oriel Sullivan. 2014. "The Gender Revolution in Housework Has Not Stalled." Presented at Perspectives on Time Use in the U.S. Conference and Workshop. June 23–27, 2014, College Park, MD.

Gerson, J. M., and K. Peiss. 1985. "Boundaries, Negotiation, Consciousness: Reconceptualizing Gender Relations." *Social Problems* 32: 317–331.

Gerson, Kathleen. 2001. "Dilemmas of Involved Fatherhood." In *Shifting the Center: Understanding Contemporary Families*, edited by Susan J. Ferguson. Mountain View, CA: Mayfield Publishing.

Giddens, Anthony. 1992. *The Transformation of Intimacy.* Cambridge, UK: Polity Press.

Goldscheider, Frances K., and Linda J. Waite. 1991. *New Families, No Families? The Transformation of the American Home.* Berkeley: University of California Press.

Hochschild, Arlie Russell. 1995. "Understanding the Future of Fatherhood." In *Changing Fatherhood: An Interdisciplinary Perspective*, edited by M. C. P. van Dougen, G. A. Frinking, and M. J. Jacobs. Amsterdam: Thesis Publishers.

Hook, Jennifer L. 2006. "Care in Context: Men's Unpaid Work in 20 Countries, 1965–2003." *American Sociological Review* 71: 639–660.

Kan, Man Yee, Oriel Sullivan, and Jonathan Gershuny. 2011. "Gender Convergence in Domestic Work: Discerning the Effect of Interactional and Institutional Barriers from Large-scale Data." *Sociology* 45: 234–251.

Knijn, T. 1995. "Towards Post-Paternalism?" In *Changing Fatherhood: An Interdisciplinary Perspective*, edited by M. C. van Dougen, G. A. Frinking, and M. J. Jacobs. Amsterdam: Thesis Publishers.

Marsiglio, W., and J. Pleck. 2004. "Fatherhood and Masculinities." In *Handbook of Studies on Men and Masculinities*, edited by M. Kimmel, J. Hearn, and R. Connell, 249–69. Thousand Oaks, CA: Sage Publications.

O'Brien, Margaret, Berit Brandth, and Elin Kvande. 2007. "Fathers, Work and Family Life." *Community, Work and Family* 10: 375–86.

Pew Research Center. 2007. "As Marriage and Parenthood Drift Apart, Public Is Concerned about Social Impact: Generation Gap in Values, Behavior." Social and Demographic Trends Report. Available from http://pewresearch.org/pubs/526/marriage-parenthood.

———. 2010. "The Decline of Marriage and Rise of New Families." Social and Demographic Trends Report. Available from http://www.pewsocialtrends.org/2010/11/18/the-decline-of-marriage-and-rise-of-new-families.

Pleck, Joseph H., and Brian P. Masciadrelli. 2003. "Paternal Involvement: Levels, Sources, and Consequences." In *The Role of the Father in Child Development*, 4th ed., edited by Michael E. Lamb. New York: John Wiley & Sons.

Risman, Barbara. 1998. *Gender Vertigo*. New Haven, CT: Yale University Press.

———. 2004. "Gender as Social Structure: Theory Wrestling with Activism." *Gender & Society* 18: 429–450.

Robinson, John P., and Geoffrey Godbey. 1999. *Time for Life: The Surprising Ways Americans Use Their Time*, 2nd ed. University Park: Penn State University Press.

Scott, J., D. F. Alwin, and M. Brown. 1996. "Changing Sex-Role Attitudes." *Sociology* 30: 427–445, 489.

Smart, Carol, and Bren Neale. 1999. *Family Fragments?* Cambridge, UK: Polity Press.

Sullivan, Oriel. 2006. *Changing Gender Relations, Changing Families: Tracing the Pace of Change over Time* (Gender Lens Series). Lanham, MD: Rowman & Littlefield.

———. 2010. "Changing Differences by Educational Attainment in Fathers' Domestic Labour and Child Care." *Sociology* 44: 716–733.

———. 2011. "Gender Deviance Neutralization through Housework—Where Does It Fit in the Bigger Picture? Response to England, Kluwer and Risman." *Journal of Family Theory and Review* 3: 27–31.

Sullivan, Oriel, and Jonathan I. Gershuny. 2001. "Cross-National Changes in Time-Use: Some Sociological (Hi)stories Re-examined." *British Journal of Sociology* 52: 331–347.

Thompson, Linda. 1993. "Conceptualising Gender in Marriage: The Case of Marital Care." *Journal of Marriage and Family* 55: 557–569.

West, C., and D. H. Zimmerman. 1987. Doing Gender. *Gender & Society* 1: 125–151.

CHAPTER 37: Being "The Man" without Having a Job And/Or: Providing Care Instead of "Bread" *by Kristen Myers and Ilana Demantas*

Acker, Joan. 2006. *Class Questions, Feminist Answers*. Lanham, MD: Rowman & Littlefield.

Arrighi, Barbara, and David Maume Jr. 2000. "Workplace Subordination and Men's Avoidance of Housework." *Journal of Family Issues* 21: 464–487.

Blair-Loy, Mary. 2006. *Competing Devotions*. Cambridge, MA: Harvard University Press.

Butler, Judith. 2004. *Undoing Gender*. New York: Routledge.

Connell, R. W. 1987. *Gender and Power*. Sydney: Allen & Unwin.

———. 1991. "Live Fast and Die Young." *Australian and New Zealand Journal of Sociology* 27: 141–171.

———. 1995. *Masculinities: Knowledge, Power and Social Change*. Cambridge, UK: Polity Press.

———. 2000. *The Men and the Boys*. Sydney, Allen & Unwin; Cambridge, UK: Polity Press; Berkeley, CA: University of California Press.

Coontz, Stephanie. 2000. *The Way We Never Were*. New York: Basic Books.

Craig, Lyn, and Killian Mullen. 2010. "Parenthood, Gender, and Work-Family Time in the United States, Australia, Italy, France and Denmark." *Journal of Marriage and Family* 72: 1344–1361.

Daly, Mary, and Katherine Rake. 2003. *Gender and the Welfare State*. Malden, MA: Polity Press.

Engel, Mary. 2010. "The Real Unemployment Rate? 16.6%." *MSN Money*, June 4.

England, Paula. 2010. "Gender Revolution: Uneven and Stalled." *Gender & Society* 24: 149–166.

Fraser, Nancy. 1994. "After the Family Wage: Gender Equity and the Welfare State." *Political Theory* 22: 591–618.

Gerson, Kathleen. 1994. "A Few Good Men: Overcoming the Barriers to Involved Fatherhood." *The American Prospect* 16: 78–90.

Goffman, Erving. 1981. *Forms of Talk*. Philadelphia: University of Pennsylvania Press.

Hartenstein, Meena. 2010. "Men Hit Harder by Recession than Women, Lost More Jobs in Economic Meltdown Some Call 'Mancession.'" *New York Daily News*, June 6.

Hochschild, Arlie. 1989. *The Second Shift*. New York: Penguin Books.

Hook, Jennifer L. 2010. Gender inequality in the welfare state: Sex segregation in housework, 1965–2003. *American Journal of Sociology* 115(5): 1480–1523.

Hoppe, Marilyn J., Mary Rogers Gillmore, Danny L. Valadez, Diane Civic, Jane Hartway, and Diane M. Morrison. 2000. "Relative Costs and Benefits of Telephone Interviews versus Self-Administered Diaries for Daily Data." *Evaluation Review* 24: 102–116.

Ingraham, Chrys. 1994. "The Heterosexual Imaginary." *Sociological Theory* 12: 203–219.

Janssens, Angelique. 1998. "The Rise and Decline of the Male Breadwinner Family? An Overview of the Debate." In *The Rise and Decline of the Male Breadwinner Family?* edited by Angelique Janssens, 1–23. New York: Cambridge University Press.

Kingdon, Geeta, and John Knight. 2006. "The Measurement of Unemployment When Unemployment Is High." *Labor Economics* 13: 291–315.

Lane, Carrie M. 2011. *A Company of One*. New York: Cornell University Press.

LaRossa, Ralph. 1997. *The Modernization of Fatherhood*. Chicago: University of Chicago Press.

Legerski, Elizabeth Miklya, and Marie Cornwall. 2010. "Working-Class Job Loss, Gender, and the Negotiation of Household Labor." *Gender & Society* 24: 447–474.

Lewis, Jane. 2009. *Work–family Balance, Gender and Policy*. Cheltenham, UK: Edward Elgar.

Lofland, John, David Snow, Leon Anderson, and Lyn Lofland. 2005. *Analyzing Social Settings*. New York: Wadsworth.

Meisenbach, Rebecca. 2010. "The Female Breadwinner." *Sex Roles* 62: 2–19.

Mulligan, Casey. 2009. "What Explains the 'Mancession?'" *New York Times*, September 30. Available from http://www.economix.blogs.nytimes.com.

Nolan, Jane. 2009. "'Working to Live, Not Living to Work': An Exploratory Study of the Relationship between Men's Work Orientation and Job Insecurity in the UK." *Gender, Work & Organization* 16(2): 179–197.

Oberhauser, Ann. 1995. "Gender and Household Economic Strategies in Rural Appalachia." *Gender, Place and Culture* 2: 51–70.

Raley, Sara, Marybeth Mattingly, and Suzanne Bianchi. 2006. "How Dual Are Dual-income Couples? Documenting Change from 1970 to 2001." *Journal of Marriage and Family* 68: 11–28.

Ridgeway, Cecelia. 2011. *Framed by Gender*. New York: Oxford.

Risman, Barbara. 1999. *Gender Vertigo*. New Haven, CT: Yale University Press.

———. 2009. "From Doing to Undoing: Gender as We Know It." *Gender & Society* 23: 81–84.

Risman, Barbara, and Danette Johnson-Sumerford. 1998. "Doing It Fairly." *Journal of Marriage and Family* 60: 23–40.

Rivers, Caryl, and Roslind Barnett. 2011. "'Mancession' Focus Masks Women's Real Losses," May 4. Retrieved June 28, 2014, from http://www.womensenews.org/story/equal-payfair-wage/110503/mancession-focus-masks-womens-real-losses#.U68vgfldWgY.

Sainsbury, Diane. 1996. *Gender, Equality, and Welfare States*. Cambridge, UK: Cambridge University Press.

Sherman, Jennifer. 2009. "Bend to Avoid Breaking: Job Loss, Gender Norms, and Family Stability in Rural America." *Social Problems* 56: 599–620.

Snow, David, and Leon Anderson. 1987. "Identity Work among the Homeless: The Verbal Construction and Avowal of Personal Identities." *American Journal of Sociology* 92: 1336–71.

Sprague, Joey. 2005. *Feminist Methodologies for Critical Researchers*. New York: Rowman Altamira.

Tichenor, Veronica J., ed. 2010. "Gendered Bargain: Why Wives Cannot Trade Their Money For Housework" in *Shifting the Center: Understanding Contemporary Families*, 4th ed. New York: McGraw-Hill.

Walby, Sylvia. 1991. *Theorizing Patriarchy*. New York: Wiley-Blackwell.

Warren, Carol, and Tracy Karner. 2009. *Discovering Qualitative Methods*. New York: Oxford University Press.

Warren, Tracey. 2007. "Conceptualizing Breadwinning Work." *Work, Employment and Society* 21: 317–336.

Watters, J. K., and P. Biernacki. 1989. "Targeted Sampling: Options for the Study of Hidden Populations." *Social Problems* 36: 416–430.

Williams, Christine, Chandra Muller, and Kristine Kilanski. 2012. "Gendered Organizations in the New Economy." *Gender & Society* 26: 549–573.

Zuo, Jiping. 2004. "Shifting the Breadwinning Boundary: The Role of Men's Breadwinner Status and their Gender Ideologies." *Journal of Family Issues* 25: 811–832.

CHAPTER 38: Families: A Great American Institution
by Barbara J. Risman

Dean, Howard. 2002. "On the Issues," November 30. Available from http://www.ontheissues.org/celeb/Howard_Dean_Families_+_Children.htm.

Obama, Barack. 2008. Letter to Family Equality Council on August 1. Available from http://obama.3cdn.net/c97fcbdd343527466b_u5m6bt5hr.pdf.

Palin, Sarah. 2008. National Republican Convention speech. Available from http://elections.nytimes.com/2008/president/conventions/videos/transcripts/20080903_PALIN_SPEECH.html.

Stacey, Judith. 1998. *Brave New Families: Stories of Domestic Upheaval in Late-Twentieth Century America*. Berkeley: University of California Press.

Credits

Rachel Allison: "Hooking Up as a College Culture," *Gender & Society* (blog), February 25, 2014. Reprinted by permission of the author.

Pallavi Banerjee: "An Immigrant Wife's Place? In the Home, According to Visa Policy," *Ms.* (blog), June 19, 2013. Reprinted by permission of *Ms.* magazine, © 2013.

Crosby Burns: "FAFSA Form Will Now Recognize College Students' Same-Sex Parents," ThinkProgress.org, April 29, 2013. This material was created by the Center for American Progress (www.americanprogress.org).

Center for American Progress: Figures from "All Children Matter: How Legal and Social Inequalities Hurt LGBT Families," Movement Advancement Project, Family Equality Council and Center for American Progress, October 2011. This material was created by the Center for American Progress (www.americanprogress.org).

Andrew J. Cherlin: "The Picture-Perfect American Family? These Days, It Doesn't Exist," *The Washington Post*, September 7, 2008. Andrew J. Cherlin is Benjamin H. Griswold III Professor of Public Policy and Sociology at Johns Hopkins University. Reprinted by permission of the author.

Philip N. Cohen: "Silver linings divorce trend," *Family Inequality*, January 29, 2014. Reprinted with permission of the author.

"Still a Man's World: The Myth of Women's Ascendance," *Boston Review*, January 10, 2013. Reprinted with permission of the author.

Lois M. Collins: "Number of 'Older' Women Having Babies Continues to Grow," *Deseret News*, July 28, 2012. © Deseret News. Reprinted with permission.

Stephanie Coontz: "How to Stay Married," *The Times of London*, September 30, 2006. Reprinted with permission of the author.

"When Numbers Mislead." From *New York Times*, May 25, 2013, © 2013 The New York Times Company. All rights reserved. Used by permission and protected by the Copyright Laws of the United States. The printing, copying, redistribution, or retransmission of this Content without express written permission is prohibited.

"Yes, I've Folded Up My Masculine Mystique, Honey," *The Sunday Times of London*, February 24, 2013. Reprinted with permission of the author.

Bryce Covert: "No, Marriage Is Not a Good Way to Fight Poverty," ThinkProgress.org, January 9, 2014. This material was created by the Center for American Progress (www.americanprogress.org).

"It's Not Just Us: Women Around the World Do More Housework and Have Less Free Time," ThinkProgress.org, March 14, 2014. This material was created by the Center for American Progress (www.americanprogress.org).

Index